Public Policy

Sixth Edition

For
Sandy
and
Debbie, Kyle, and Darcy

Sara Miller McCune founded SAGE Publishing in 1965 to support the dissemination of usable knowledge and educate a global community. SAGE publishes more than 1000 journals and over 800 new books each year, spanning a wide range of subject areas. Our growing selection of library products includes archives, data, case studies and video. SAGE remains majority owned by our founder and after her lifetime will become owned by a charitable trust that secures the company's continued independence.

Los Angeles | London | New Delhi | Singapore | Washington DC | Melbourne

Public Policy

Politics, Analysis, and Alternatives

Sixth Edition

Michael E. Kraft
University of Wisconsin–Green Bay

Scott R. Furlong
University of Wisconsin–Green Bay

FOR INFORMATION:

CQ Press
An Imprint of SAGE Publications, Inc.
2455 Teller Road
Thousand Oaks, California 91320
E-mail: order@sagepub.com

SAGE Publications Ltd.
1 Oliver's Yard
55 City Road
London EC1Y 1SP
United Kingdom

SAGE Publications India Pvt. Ltd.
B 1/I 1 Mohan Cooperative Industrial Area
Mathura Road, New Delhi 110 044
India

SAGE Publications Asia-Pacific Pte. Ltd.
3 Church Street
#10-04 Samsung Hub
Singapore 049483

Acquisitions Editor: Carrie Brandon
Content Development Editors: Anna Villarruel,
John Scappini
Editorial Assistant: Duncan Marchbank
Production Editor: Tracy Buyan
Copy Editor: Melinda Masson
Typesetter: C&M Digitals (P) Ltd.
Proofreader: Ellen Howard
Indexer: Diggs Publication Services
Cover Designer: Michael Dubowe
Marketing Manager: Amy Whitaker

Printed in the United States of America

Library of Congress Cataloging-in-Publication Data

Names: Kraft, Michael E. | Furlong, Scott R., author.

Title: Public policy : politics, analysis, and alternatives / Michael E. Kraft, University of Wisconsin, Green Bay, Scott R. Furlong, University of Wisconsin, Green Bay.

Description: Sixth edition. | Thousand Oaks, California: CQ Press, [2018] | Includes index.

Identifiers: LCCN 2017000975 | ISBN 9781506358154 (pbk. : alk. paper)

Subjects: LCSH: Policy sciences—Evaluation. | Political planning—Citizen participation. | Political planning—United States—Evaluation. | Public administration—United States—Evaluation.

Classification: LCC H97.K73 2018 | DDC 320.60973—dc23
LC record available at https://lccn.loc.gov/2017000975

This book is printed on acid-free paper.

17 18 19 20 21 10 9 8 7 6 5 4 3 2 1

Brief Contents

Detailed Contents

PART I THE STUDY OF PUBLIC POLICY

nojustice

Mark Wilson/Getty Images

SAUL LOEB/AFP/Getty Images

PART II   ANALYZING PUBLIC POLICY

Spencer Platt/Getty Images

David McNew/Getty Images

5 Public Problems and Policy Alternatives 146

Daniel Acker/Bloomberg via Getty Images

6 Assessing Policy Alternatives 178

PART III   ISSUES AND CONTROVERSIES IN PUBLIC POLICY

Chip Somodevilla/Getty Images

AP Photo/Seth Wenig

AFP/FREDERIC J. BROWN

9 Welfare and Social Security Policy 316

PAUL J. RICHARDS/AFP/Getty Images

10 Education Policy 354

AP Photo/Max Becherer, File

11 Environmental and Energy Policy 396

Spencer Platt/Getty Images

12 Foreign Policy and Homeland Security 444

PART IV CONCLUSIONS

Sara D. Davis/Getty Images

Boxes, Figures, and Tables

Chapter 11

Chapter 12

Chapter 13

Preface

Forecasts about likely future conditions often are hard to make. But we can be sure of one thing. Health care costs are going to soar in the coming decades as the baby boom generation continues to age and demands an array of increasingly expensive medical services. From 2008 through 2013, U.S. health care spending grew by less than 4 percent annually, one of the lowest rates in more than fifty years, providing some modest relief from what had been an unrelenting upward spiral in costs. In 2014, the rate increased somewhat from these levels, rising to 5.3 percent, following a 2.9 percent rise in 2013, largely because of expanded coverage under the Affordable Care Act; and in 2015, the rate increased again, to 5.8 percent. Total health care spending rose to a record high of $3.2 trillion in 2015, or almost 18 percent of the nation's gross domestic product (GDP). The United States spent $9,900 per person for health care in 2015, a figure certain to grow substantially over the next decade. Indeed, the Centers for Medicare and Medicaid Services projects that per capita spending on health care by 2025 will be an astonishing $16,032 and that overall health care spending will rise to $5.6 trillion, or nearly 20.1 percent of GDP.

The new spending figures were released in late 2016, more than six years after President Barack Obama succeeded in gaining approval from Congress for his sweeping changes in health care policy, the Patient Protection and Affordable Care Act of 2010, also known as Obamacare. One purpose of the act was to slow the rate of increase in the nation's health care spending. Whatever effects the complex and far-reaching act may have, assuming that it survives continuing legal challenges and opposition by Republicans in Congress as well as the administration of President Donald Trump, we are still likely to see an ongoing rise in national health care costs. What is the best way to deal with these ballooning costs, particularly in light of other trends—for example, continuing high levels of obesity—that could drive up costs even further? How should we protect the solvency of the Medicare trust fund as demands from baby boomers threaten to bankrupt it and jeopardize benefits for future generations? Indeed, what forms of health care and Social Security will be available to the generation of citizens now in their teens and twenties? What are the alternatives from which we must choose, and on what basis should we decide?

Such public policy decisions touch nearly every aspect of daily life in the United States, although many people fail to recognize or fully understand their impacts. Social Security reform, for example, may not seem terribly urgent to most young people today, but it undoubtedly will shape the quality of their lives decades down the road. This is why citizens need to understand not only how governments make policy choices but also how to evaluate those choices in what is often a sea of conflicting and misleading information and arguments. We believe the reason to be politically aware is simple: policymakers are more responsive to the public's preferences and needs and, in some cases, are more effective when citizens take a greater interest in public affairs and play a more active role in the policymaking process. We hope this text stimulates readers' interest and concern while equipping them with the skills they need to think critically and creatively about policy problems.

The subtitle of this book—*Politics, Analysis, and Alternatives*—explicitly expresses what we are trying to accomplish, which differs from conventional books on public policy. This text integrates three aspects of public policy study: government institutions and the policymaking process, the concepts and methods of policy analysis, and the choices that we make collectively about substantive public policies at all levels of government. Throughout, we focus on the interrelationship of government institutions, the interests and motivations of policy actors both inside and outside of government, and the role of policy analysis in clarifying public problems and helping citizens and policymakers choose among policy alternatives. These central themes are reinforced by providing students with the tools they need—how to find key and reliable information, how to use specific evaluative criteria, how to apply policy analysis methods and critical thinking, and how to assess the role of politics in policymaking—to investigate issues and carry out policy analysis on their own. We believe that this hands-on approach is the best way to teach the skills of analysis and give students not only an understanding of the conduct of public policy but also a way *into* the process.

A Focus on Policy Analysis

By emphasizing the pervasiveness of public policy, we try to make its study a vital activity for students. They can better appreciate the power they wield to effect change in the system once they are armed with the tools of policy analysis. However, the logic of public policy and its study must be addressed before students encounter these powerful tools of the trade. In Part I, we demonstrate that public policy choices are not made in a vacuum. Social, economic, political, and cultural contexts matter, as do the distinguishing characteristics of the U.S. government and the rationales behind government intervention. An understanding of the structure of institutions, the motivation of policy actors (both formal and informal), and the unique nature of the U.S. political system will allow students to comprehend the complexity of government while discovering opportunities for engagement with the process. We present multiple perspectives on the policymaking process, from elite theory to rational choice theory, but concentrate on the policy process model—a portrayal of policymaking as a sequence of key activities from agenda setting to policy implementation—that is used in the rest of the book. We hope these chapters encourage students to ask how decisions are made as well as why they are made in one way and not another.

Part II gets to the heart of the book and explains the approaches and methods of policy analysis, laying a foundation for dissecting and understanding public problems and policy choices. With careful application of the tools and perspectives of policy analysis, students can interpret complex and conflicting data and arguments, evaluate alternative courses of action, and anticipate the consequences of policy choices. Specific cases—from tax cuts and cell phone use by drivers to immigration reform and energy policy—illustrate both the difficulty of policy analysis and its value in policymaking. Students learn how to find and interpret policy-relevant information and to acquire an understanding of the limitations to what government can do about public problems. The evaluative criteria at the book's core—a focus on effectiveness, efficiency, and equity—train students to think clearly about policy alternatives. Ethical considerations necessarily receive considerable attention as do the more common concerns over effectiveness and efficiency. Brief case studies, such as those involving organ donation, personal privacy in relation to homeland security goals, national energy policy and climate change, and the morality of contraceptive coverage under the Affordable Care Act, give students the opportunity to grapple with controversial issues for which no policymaker has *the* answer.

Part III consists of six substantive policy chapters designed to illustrate and apply the concepts and methods introduced in the first two sections of the book. The six core policy areas—economics and budgeting, health care, welfare and Social Security, education, energy and the environment, and foreign policy and homeland security—represent a substantial part of contemporary U.S. policymaking and also present a diversity of economic, political, and ethical issues for analysis. This part of the text offers a clear picture of the issues that beginning analysts would encounter in policymaking or in the evaluation of all areas of public policy. For readers who want to probe more deeply into those policy areas that we discuss peripherally—for instance, criminal justice and civil rights and liberties—we strongly recommend *Issues for Debate in American Public Policy* (2017), which offers selections from the *CQ Researcher* and abundant references to current policy debates.

Consistent with the text's emphasis on analysis, we begin each policy area chapter with a brief illustration of a policy scenario, such as the rising costs of health care and the gap between spending and results, the persistence of poverty in the United States, conflicts over energy policy and climate change, and the balance between domestic surveillance by the National Security Agency (NSA) and civil liberties, to spark student interest. A background section describes the public problems faced and the solutions chosen to date. We briefly summarize major policies and programs, discuss when and how they came into effect, review available policy evaluations, and suggest how students can investigate policy alternatives.

At the end of each chapter, we offer a focused discussion of policy reform in terms of several of the key evaluative criteria used throughout the text, particularly effectiveness, efficiency, equity, and ethics. These discussions link closely to the kinds of questions that can be asked about any proposal for policy change and how it might be addressed. In Part IV, a concluding chapter brings together the arguments of the text, evaluates opportunities for citizen involvement in policymaking, and looks to future challenges in public policy.

New to This Edition

We made a great many changes throughout the text while preparing this sixth edition. We updated material in every chapter, particularly those that focus on substantive policy topics, and streamlined content to present the most essential information. In all chapters, we incorporated new studies and interpretations and made use of new illustrations and case studies of policy controversies and actions. In addition, we sought throughout the text to improve the clarity of presentation and to update all references to websites and recommended readings. We continue to use *learning objectives* that begin each chapter; they help to guide students on key chapter content and takeaways. Graphics in Parts I and II of the book provide illustrations of processes and functions essential to policymaking, enlivening the text and providing more material for visual learners. Throughout, the content benefits from a *new interior layout* that we began in the last edition to refresh the book's look and bring a splash of color.

Special Features

To underscore the importance we place on active learning and critical engagement, we include two unique text boxes to guide students as they research policy problems: "Working with Sources" and "Steps to Analysis." The *Working with Sources* feature identifies important sources of information and how to utilize them, providing step-by-step suggestions on how to make good (and critical) use of the information found on Internet sites—among other resources—that offer important data sources and policy perspectives. The *Steps to Analysis* feature invites critical thinking about specific policy problems. It demonstrates how to ask the urgent questions that drive policy analysis, and then presents ways to narrow and refine these questions into feasible projects. To further direct students to the information they need, *discussion questions* at the end of each chapter get at, for instance, the "best" way to deal with health care concerns, environmental problems, education issues, or homeland security. These questions are followed by annotated *suggested readings*, *suggested websites*, a list of *major legislation* where appropriate, a list of *keywords*, and *chapter notes*. Students will find a list of *references* and a *glossary* at the end of the book as well. All have been updated for this edition of the text.

SAGE edge for CQ Press

This edition comes with a full range of high-quality, class-tested instructor and student ancillaries prepared by Chris Borick. Each ancillary is specifically tailored to *Public Policy*.

SAGE edge offers a robust online forum featuring an impressive array of tools and resources for review, study, and further exploration, keeping both instructors and students on the cutting edge of teaching and learning. SAGE edge content is open access and available on demand at http://edge.sagepub.com/kraft6e.

SAGE edge for students helps enhance learning and offers a personalized approach to coursework in an easy-to-use environment.

- Mobile-friendly eFlashcards strengthen understanding of key terms and concepts.
- Mobile-friendly practice quizzes allow for independent assessment by students of their mastery of course material.
- A customized online action plan includes tips and feedback on progress through the course and materials, which allows students to individualize their learning experience.
- Chapter summaries with learning objectives reinforce the most important material.
- Multimedia web links facilitate student use of Internet resources, further exploration of topics, and responses to critical thinking questions.

SAGE edge for instructors supports teaching by making it easy to integrate quality content and create a rich learning environment that helps students perform at a higher level. Go to http://edge.sagepub.com/kraft6e and click on "Instructor's Resources" to register and begin downloading resources.

- A comprehensive test bank provides multiple-choice, true/false, and short- and long-essay questions, as well as the opportunity to edit any question and/or insert personalized questions to effectively assess students' progress and understanding. The test bank is available in Word and fully loaded in ExamView, a flexible and easy-to-use test-generation software that allows instructors to build, customize, and even integrate exams into course management systems.
- Editable, chapter-specific PowerPoint slides offer complete flexibility for creating a multimedia presentation for the course.
- An instructor's manual features chapter overviews and objectives, lecture starters, ideas for class activities, assignments, and discussion questions.
- A set of all the graphics from the text, including all of the maps, tables, and figures, is available in PowerPoint, PDF, and JPEG formats for class presentations.

We have tried to make this text a distinctive and appealing introduction to the study of public policy while also maintaining a commitment to scholarly rigor. Our experience with students in many years of teaching tells us that they can handle demanding reading and exercises if these are linked firmly to concrete issues that affect society and students' personal lives.

Above all, the text emphasizes the urgency of making government more responsive to citizens' concerns and equips students with the skills they need to understand policy controversies. These skills are particularly important today, a time of significant political change in the nation and a renewed determination to alter the direction of public policy in many areas. Thus we hope the text inspires students to take a serious interest in government, politics, and public policy, and to participate enthusiastically in policy debates and decision making both today and throughout their lives.

Acknowledgments

Preparation of this text reflects contributions from many individuals and institutions. We are particularly grateful for support from the University of Wisconsin–Green Bay and our colleagues in the Department of Public and Environmental Affairs. Our students in Introduction to Public Policy, Public Policy Analysis, and other courses have taught us much over the years, especially about what they need to know to become informed citizens and effective policy professionals. We are also grateful to them for allowing us the liberty of asking them to read drafts of the chapters.

We appreciate as well the efforts of hundreds of creative public policy scholars whose work makes a book like this possible. Our citation of their publications is a modest way of acknowledging our dependence on their research and insights into policy analysis and policymaking. We are particularly indebted to the many scholars who reviewed the book's earlier editions and offered critical appraisals and perceptive, helpful suggestions. These include the following:

Susan Appe, State University of New York at Albany

Melissa Bass, University of Mississippi

Marci Berger, Rutgers University

Jessica Boscarino, Marist College

Donna Comrie, Florida International University

Valerie Cooley, Brown University

Jeronimo Cortina, University of Houston

Marc Eisner, Wesleyan University

Matthew Eshbaugh-Soha, University of North Texas

Jennifer Jackman, Salem State University

Aubrey Jewett, University of Central Florida

Joseph Karlesky, Franklin and Marshall College

Lael R. Keiser, University of Missouri

Paul Lewis, Arizona State University

Steven Maloney, University of St. Thomas

Marcus D. Mauldin, University of Tennessee–Chattanooga

Basilio Monteiro, St John's University

Bruce Nesmith, Coe College

Philip Nicholas, Bloomsburg University

Michael Rich, Emory University

Mordu Serry-Kamal, Winston-Salem State University

Deborah Stine, Carnegie Mellon University

Margaret Stout, West Virginia University

Linda Trautman, Ohio University

Shannon Vaughan, Western Kentucky University

Clayton Wukich, Sam Houston State University

Special thanks are also due to the skilled and conscientious staff at CQ Press and SAGE: Charisse Kiino, Carrie Brandon, Nancy Matuszak, Anna Villarruel, John Scappini, Duncan Marchbank, Tracy Buyan, and Melinda Masson. As always, any remaining errors and omissions rest on our shoulders. We hope readers will alert us to any such defects and suggest changes they would like to see in future editions. Contact us at kraftm@uwgb.edu or furlongs@uwgb.edu.

Michael E. Kraft
Scott R. Furlong

About the Authors

Michael E. Kraft is professor emeritus of political science and public affairs at the University of Wisconsin–Green Bay. He is the author of, among other works, *Environmental Policy and Politics,* 7th ed. (2018), and coauthor of *Coming Clean: Information Disclosure and Environmental Performance* (2011), with Mark Stephan and Troy D. Abel. In addition, he is the coeditor of *Environmental Policy: New Directions in the 21st Century,* 10th ed. (2018), with Norman J. Vig; *Toward Sustainable Communities: Transition and Transformations in Environmental Policy,* 2nd ed. (2009), with Daniel A. Mazmanian; and *Business and Environmental Policy: Corporate Interests in the American Political System* (2007) and *The Oxford Handbook of U.S. Environmental Policy* (2013), with Sheldon Kamieniecki. He has long taught courses in environmental policy and politics, American government, Congress, and public policy analysis.

Scott R. Furlong is Provost/Vice President for Academic Affairs at SUNY Oswego as of July 2017, after serving 10 years as dean of the College of Arts, Humanities and Social Services and professor of political science and public affairs at the University of Wisconsin–Green Bay. His areas of expertise are regulatory policy and interest group participation in the executive branch, and he has taught public policy for over twenty years. He is the author or coauthor of numerous book chapters and coauthor of *Rulemaking: How Government Agencies Write Laws and Make Policy,* 5th ed. (2017), with Cornelius M. Kerwin. His articles have appeared in such journals as *Public Administration Review, Journal of Public Administration Research and Theory, Administration and Society, American Review of Public Administration,* and *Policy Studies Journal.*

PART I

The Study of Public Policy

Chapter 1

Chapter Objectives

- Define and explain the nature of public policy.
- Identify key concepts associated with the study of public policy.
- Explain the different contexts in which public policy is made.
- Examine the reasons for governmental involvement in public policy.
- Explore why citizens should understand public policy.
- Describe the reasons for evaluating public policies today.

Ensuring public safety. Amusement parks are a big business in the United States, and millions of Americans visit them each year, particularly large facilities such as Walt Disney World and the Six Flags parks. Yet the occasional accident reminds us of the risk and possibly of the need for government intervention to provide adequate assurance of public safety. *(nojustice)*

Public Policy and Politics

Every year millions of people in the United States go to theme parks, state and county fairs, and other events that feature thrill rides. According to the International Association of Amusement Parks and Attractions, in recent years hundreds of millions of people attended the country's approximately four hundred parks, with revenues well into the billions of dollars.[1] This is clearly a large industry that includes not only amusement park giants such as Walt Disney World and Six Flags, but also a variety of smaller, permanently placed operations. In addition, many traveling operations set up temporary ride attractions at events such as state and county fairs.

While these parks and attractions provide safe entertainment and recreation for most visitors, periodic accidents—some fatal—are reported every year. In August 2016, three separate incidents occurred that called into question the safety of such rides. At Schlitterbahn water park in Kansas City, a ten-year-old boy died riding a water slide. A few days later, three people fell from a Ferris wheel when the car flipped at a county fair in Tennessee. Then a few days later, another child fell from a roller coaster at an amusement park in western Pennsylvania.[2] These are not onetime incidents. In October 2013, a number of people were trapped on Universal Orlando's Hollywood Rip Ride Rockit roller coaster for nearly three hours.[3] While there were no serious injuries as a result of this malfunction, it showed that things can go wrong with these sophisticated amusement rides. In some cases, accidents or deaths do happen, sometimes because malfunctions occur in the equipment and in some instances for no apparent reason other than the specific health of the visitor. Examples include a woman who fell from a roller coaster at a Six Flags park in Texas in July 2013 as well as a summer 2015 death that occurred at Walt Disney World's Magic Kingdom Space Mountain roller coaster, where a fifty-five-year-old woman lost consciousness upon exiting the ride and later died, likely due to her medical history.[4] When people go to these parks, they intend to have fun, and accidents in such venues can generate all sorts of media coverage. No one thinks they can get injured in Disney World, home of Mickey Mouse, Goofy, the Seven Dwarfs, and other beloved characters. So one might ask, what kinds of controls or regulations are in place to ensure individual safety in these amusement centers?

The answer in this case is a bit complicated. It spans different government levels and agencies and is a good illustration of the complexity of policymaking. The U.S. Consumer Product Safety Commission (CPSC) is a regulatory agency responsible for ensuring public safety for a wide range of consumer products. The commission currently regulates over fifteen thousand products, ranging from lawn mowers to baby cribs. It also, not surprisingly, has some authority over amusement park rides. Specifically, the CPSC monitors the safety of the "portable amusement rides" that travel from one location to another and are set up for particular events, such as county fairs. What about rides associated with permanent amusement parks such as Six Flags? Government regulation of these rides occurs at the state level, and in some cases states have no authority. Some states require government inspection of park rides, and others do not. Regulation may even vary within the state itself. Florida is a prime example. While some permanent parks are significantly regulated, those that hire more than one thousand employees are generally exempt from state regulations. (This includes places such as Universal Studios, Disney World, and Busch Gardens.) Why do you think these differences between and within states exist?[5]

Rep. Edward Markey, D-Mass., has long argued that there should be more systematic federal regulation of amusement park rides. For many years, he introduced legislation that would give greater authority to the CPSC to regulate the industry, including "big theme" players such as Disney and Universal.[6] He has not been successful getting this legislation passed, with opposition coming—not surprisingly—from the major theme parks, which claim that federal intervention is unnecessary, that these accidents occur rarely, and that the risks are minimal. They often also cite that many of the accidents are due to the fact that "patrons have risk-increasing, pre-existing medical conditions or fail to heed rules like those about staying seated or keeping their limbs inside the car."[7]

How risky are these rides? According to Markey, people die on roller coasters at a higher rate per mile traveled than those traveling by plane, bus, or train. Former representative Cliff Stearns, R-Fla., states, on the other hand, that amusement park rides cause fewer injuries than fishing.[8] So who is right? The answer may be that both are, and it illustrates how information and data can be handled to communicate preferred positions. Policy analysts often use risk analysis to examine the extent of a problem and how it can affect a population. In the case of amusement park rides, according to a study by the National Safety Council, in 2013 there were 1,356 reported ride injuries at fixed-site amusement parks—or about 4.65 injuries for every million attendees (or less than one injury for every million rides). The vast majority of these injuries are not considered to be serious; in fact, only about 7 percent of them required an overnight stay in a hospital.[9]

Once again, one might ask if this is a significant number. For comparison purposes, the CPSC estimated that in 2014 there were over 200,000 injuries from a category that included ATVs, mopeds, and minibikes, and over 395,000 injuries playing football. There are nearly 82,000 lawn mower accidents each year, and 244,000 accidents caused by toys.[10] Based on some of these comparisons, should we be concerned about the safety of amusement park rides?

Another question might be whether government needs to be involved at all in the regulation of amusement park rides. It is clear that such accidents do nothing to help the bottom line of the amusement park industry, and it has a powerful incentive to provide safe environments in order to continue attracting visitors. Might the self-regulation that currently occurs, particularly in the permanent parks, be sufficient to ensure safety? Or is this a case where government regulation is needed to protect the public's well-being? These are the kinds of questions to which elected and government officials must respond when making public policy.

While we are relatively certain that most people do not consider the role of government on their family vacation to Disney World, the examples above show that there are a variety of questions one might raise regarding government policy. The regulation of amusement park rides is an example of the constitutional issue of federalism (defined later in this chapter); how the perception of risk may affect decision making; and, ultimately, the role of government in a free-market or capitalist society. These kinds of questions are faced in nearly all areas of public policy, and they illustrate the diversity and the complexity of issues that arise. Ultimately, how these issues are resolved can have a profound impact on individual lives.

This account of amusement park ride safety and its regulation speaks to the importance of the process of public policymaking. That process involves many different institutions, people, and groups. The complex policy issues ideally are resolved only after long hours of research and debate that consider the underlying beliefs and assumptions as well as pertinent facts, including in this case the relative risk of accidents and injuries. Sometimes, however, the issues are not resolved, or they arise again in response to new concerns or data. In addition, a policy typically deals with a particular slice of American life, such as the family vacation, although it also may have important effects on the public's general well-being. Across the range of government activities today, it is no exaggeration to say that public policy deals with just about everything, affecting life in ways that are both obvious and sometimes difficult to recognize.

What Is Public Policy?

Public policy is what public officials within government, and by extension the citizens they represent, choose to do or not to do about public problems. Public problems refer to conditions the public widely perceives to be unacceptable and that therefore require intervention. Problems such as environmental degradation, *priv action → indiv. or corporations take resp.*

insufficient access to health care services, or as noted above consumer safety on amusement park rides can be addressed through government action; private action, where individuals or corporations take the responsibility; or a combination of the two. In any given case, the choice depends on how the public defines the problem and on prevailing societal attitudes about private action in relation to government's role.

For the amusement park ride example, governments at both the federal and state levels share responsibility in some cases, and in others responsibility for safety is left to private businesses or individuals. There are ongoing debates over whether or not having the industry regulate itself in these situations is sufficient, and when accidents do happen, those debates become much more public. When it comes to safety issues, government may decide to intervene, such as in regulation of medications, or allow for private industry to address the issue. For example, the U.S. Department of Agriculture (USDA) may order a recall of tainted meat that could be unfit for consumption. But there are other situations where the company or industry will make its own decision to recall the products, and the government may see no need to intervene to further protect the public's health or safety.

policy

The term *policy* refers in general to a purposive course of action that an individual or group consistently follows in dealing with a problem (J. Anderson 2015). In a more formal definition, a policy is a "standing decision characterized by behavioral consistency and repetitiveness on the part of both those who make it and those who abide by it" (Eulau and Prewitt 1973, 465). Whether in the public or private sector, policies also can be thought of as the instruments through which societies regulate themselves and attempt to channel human behavior in acceptable directions (Schneider and Ingram 1997).

The language used to discuss public policy can be confusing. Analysts, policymakers, and commentators sometimes speak without much clarity about intentions (the purposes of government action); goals (the stated ends to be achieved); plans or proposals (the means for achieving goals); programs (the authorized means for pursuing goals); and decisions or choices—that is, specific actions that are taken to set goals, develop plans, and implement programs (Jones 1984). These elements of public policy can be found in many different legal expressions such as laws, executive orders, regulations, and judicial rulings. They also can be seen in the way that policymakers, such as presidents, governors, or legislators, describe how they view public policy in any given area. Both the legal statements and the actions of policymakers can define what public policy is at any given time. We find it useful as well to distinguish between policy outputs (the formal actions that governments take to pursue their goals) and policy outcomes (the effects such actions actually have on society).

Policy outcomes → policy outputs

To pull some of these perspectives together, we offer this definition: Public policy is a course of government action or inaction in response to public problems. It is associated with formally approved policy goals and means, as well as the regulations and practices of agencies that implement programs. Looking at public

Pub pol = course of govt action or inaction in resp. to pub probs

policy this way emphasizes the actual behavior of implementing agencies and officials, not merely the formal statements of policy goals and means found in laws and other expressions of government policy. As we will stress throughout the book, this view means that students of public policy need to seek out the information that can tell them what policy actually is at any given time.

Any level of government, whether federal, state, or local, may be involved in a particular policy effort because social problems, and the public demand for action on them, manifest themselves from the local to the national level. At the local level, failing public schools, high crime rates, crowded highways, or air pollution might attract enough attention to spur the school board, mayor, or city council to find remedies. At the national level, concern about inequitable access to health care or how a country responds to a terrorist threat may galvanize policymakers and lead to policy development.

Whatever the level of government, proponents of policy actions seek a multitude of goals that also affect all members of society. For laws that govern personal conduct, such as speed limits, policies aim to restrict individual behavior as a way to protect lives or prevent injuries and property damage; that is, the goal is to promote the public's welfare or common good. After government enacts the laws, public policies also affect how the mandated services aimed at the **public good,** such as police protection, public education, maintenance of highways and bridges, or national defense, are provided. Direct government payments are another form of public policy, and they affect people's lives on the individual and societal level. Social Security payments for senior citizens, agricultural subsidies for farmers, and research grants to universities sustain long-term individual and collective well-being.

public good
- police prot.,
pub edu, etc.

Public policies reflect not only society's most important values but also conflicts among values. Policies represent which of many different values receive the highest priority in any given decision. David Easton (1965) captured this view in his often quoted observation that politics is "the authoritative allocation of values for a society." What Easton meant was that the actions of policymakers can determine definitively and with the force of law which of society's different and sometimes conflicting values will prevail. Examples can be found in nearly every walk of life: Should the federal government implement a carbon tax on industry to reduce emissions of greenhouse gases and address health and climate change concerns, even if doing so raises the cost of products? Or should such decisions be left to the marketplace and individual choice? Should the federal government uphold the mandate that citizens purchase health care insurance if they are not covered through their employers, as one way to ensure that all citizens have access to health care services? Should government continue to recognize a woman's right to choose to have an abortion, or should it restrict the choice and instead promote the rights of the fetus?

Because public policy often deals with tough questions like these, reflecting conflicts over fundamental human values, the resulting policies are going to affect people's lives. For these reasons, we designed this book with several goals in mind. The first is to help readers develop a fuller understanding of public policy and the ways governments make policy decisions. The second is to encourage readers to look ahead to the implications of policy choices. The third is to foster critical thinking about public policy and possible alternative courses of action. Because this last goal is so important, we introduce basic concepts related to policy analysis throughout the text. The aim is to equip readers with essential skills in analytical thinking that will enhance their understanding of policy issues and make possible more effective participation in the policy process.

Developing a critical, analytical approach to policy issues has many advantages over simply learning the details of policy history, understanding the present legal requirements in various programs, or gaining an overview of current policy debates. Such knowledge is important, but it is inherently limited, in part because public policies and debates over them continually change, making earlier accounts less useful. In contrast, those who learn the basic principles of policy-making and policy analysis will have a better grasp of why governments make their decisions and be better able to identify the strengths and weaknesses in present policies as well as in proposals to change them. Individuals can apply these skills to the wide range of problems everyone faces as citizens and in their personal lives and careers.

Defining Basic Concepts

It is useful at this point to clarify several additional concepts in the study of public policy. These include government, politics, and policy analysis. Although these terms are in common usage, no universal definition exists for any of them.

Government

Government refers to the institutions and political processes through which public policy choices are made. These institutions and processes represent the legal authority to govern or rule a group of people. In the United States, the federal Constitution describes the government's institutions, which include Congress, the president, the various agencies of the executive branch, and the federal court system. Each is granted specific but overlapping legal authority to act under a system of separation of powers, which we discuss in chapter 2. At state and local levels, parallel government institutions develop policy for citizens within their jurisdictions, guided by the authority granted in state constitutions and in state and local statutes and ordinances. The American system of governance adheres to the principle of **federalism**, also discussed in chapter 2; in a federal system, the national government shares authority with the states and local governments. Quite often national policies, such as those dealing with environmental protection, are implemented chiefly by the states through an elaborate system of intergovernmental relations in which the federal government grants legal authority to the states to carry out national policies. In other policy areas, such as education, crime control, and land-use regulation, state and local governments play the dominant role.

Politics

Politics concerns the exercise of power in society or in specific decisions over public policy. It has several different but complementary meanings. It is used to refer to the processes through which public policies are formulated and adopted, especially to the roles played by elected officials, organized interest groups, public opinion, and political parties. This is the politics of policymaking. Politics can also be thought of as how conflicts in society (such as those over rights to abortion services or gun control) are expressed and resolved in favor of one set of interests or social values or another. Politics in this case refers to the issue positions that different groups of people (gun owners, environmentalists, health insurance companies, automobile companies) adopt and the actions they take to promote their values. These collections of individuals with similar interests often become active in the policymaking process. So politics is about power and influence in society as well as in the processes of policymaking within government. It concerns who participates in and who influences the decisions that governments make and who gains and who loses as a result. Harold Lasswell ([1936] 1958) put it this way: Politics is about "who gets what, when, and how."

In the United States and most other democracies, politics is also related to the electoral processes by which citizens select the policymakers who represent them. In this sense, politics concerns political parties and their issue agendas and the political ideologies, philosophies, and beliefs held by candidates for office, their supporters, and their campaign contributors. The precise relationship of politics to public policy may not always be clear; defenders and critics of specific policy actions may offer arguments based in economics, history, ethics, philosophy, or any number of other disciplines we use to think about what is in the public interest. Still, no one doubts that electoral politics is a major component of the policymaking process.

Politics exerts this strong influence on policymaking, in part because elected officials necessarily must try to anticipate how their policy statements and actions might affect their chances for reelection. Policymakers are therefore sensitive to the views of the groups and individuals who helped them win office in the first place and whose support may be essential to keeping them in office. These political incentives motivate public officials to pay particular attention to the policy preferences of their core constituencies, especially the activists, while also trying to appeal to the general electorate. For Republicans, the core constituencies include business interests, political conservatives, farmers, and suburban and rural residents, among others. For Democrats, the core constituencies are labor interests, environmentalists, African Americans, political liberals, residents of urban areas, and others.

Politics is also one of the principal reasons public policy is so riddled with conflict and why it can be so difficult to analyze. Consider the debate over smoking and its health effects. For a number of years, the federal government has sought to discourage smoking out of concern for its adverse effects on public health (Derthick 2005; Fritschler and Rudder 2007). Yet while the Office of the Surgeon General and the Food and Drug Administration (FDA) take this position, the USDA has continued its longtime policy of subsidizing tobacco farmers. Clearly, tobacco policy today—whether higher cigarette taxes meant to curtail smoking (see chapter 6), public advertising campaigns to warn children and teenagers about the dangers of smoking, or actions to regulate tobacco as a drug—is both complex and controversial. Decisions are influenced by a public that is divided on the issue, by the actions of interest groups that represent the tobacco industry, and by public health studies that are used by other groups to press for further government action to reduce smoking. These various points of view and studies are parts of the contentious process of setting new policy directions.

It would be wrong to assume, however, that such conflicts merely reflect inconsistencies in government policies or, worse, that they demonstrate bad faith. In fact, the process of resolving conflicts helps to determine where the public interest lies. These conflicts illustrate the different public interests that U.S. policymakers attempt to meet. Promoting a health agenda through decreasing smoking will lead to a healthier society and a reduction in health care costs for both the individual and the nation. But the family farm is revered in the United States, and Congress has enacted many policies to protect it. The tobacco industry has been able to play upon this public interest of protecting farmers in its lobbying efforts, and yet policymakers have been shifting their emphasis away from protecting farmers and in favor of regulation. In 2009, for example, Congress approved broad new powers for the FDA to regulate cigarettes and other forms of tobacco for the first time.[11] Still, whether the subject is tobacco use, health care, or how to reform the tax code, such conflicts are a key element in policymaking.

Whether the debate is over tobacco support and public health, state support for colleges and universities, or expansion of background checks for purchase of guns, government officials, interest groups, and citizens promote their views about what to do, and they bring all kinds of information to bear on the decisions. Naturally, the different participants in the policy process can and do disagree vigorously about the kinds of public policies that are needed and the proper role of government in addressing the problems.

The policymaking process within government provides abundant, although not necessarily equal, opportunities for all of these participants, or policy actors, to discuss problems; to formulate and promote possible policy solutions to them; and to press for formal adoption by legislatures at the national, state, and local levels. Politics, as we defined it above, is evident throughout this process.

Ultimately, executive agencies and departments, such as the FDA, the Environmental Protection Agency (EPA), the Department of Defense, or a local police or public health department, are responsible for implementing what the legislators enact. Here too politics is often evident as an agency may reflect the political values and priorities of a president or governor, or try to respond to the views of other elected officials.

Policy Analysis

Analysis means deconstructing an object of study—that is, breaking it down into its basic elements to understand it better. Policy analysis is the examination of components of public policy, the policy process, or both. Put another way, it is the study of the causes and consequences of policy decisions. Duncan MacRae and James A. Wilde (1979, 4) have called policy analysis "the use of reason and evidence to choose the best policy among a number of alternatives." Policy analysis uses many different methods of inquiry and draws from various disciplines to obtain the information needed to assess a problem and think clearly about alternative ways to resolve it. The same information also shapes public debate and deliberation over what actions to take. At heart, policy analysis encourages deliberate critical thinking about the causes of public problems, the various ways governments and/or the private sector might act on them, and which policy choices make the most sense. Doing so requires not only knowledge of government and politics but also the ability to evaluate the policy actions. Chapter 6 discusses the major evaluative criteria used to make such judgments.

Why Study Public Policy?

As the discussion in this chapter will make clear, the study of public policy occurs in many different organizations and for diverse reasons. Policy analysts both in and outside of government have a professional concern for public policy. That is, they work on developing public policy solutions by studying public problems and various policy alternatives or choices that might be made. Scholars at universities and research institutions share some of the same interests as policy analysts, but they may also be concerned with building general knowledge and advancing theory, for example, of the policy process or the performance of government institutions. We will revisit these approaches to the study of public policy, especially policy analysis, in chapter 4.

For citizens who lack such professional reasons but who have strong personal interests in government and public policy, the U.S. political system affords numerous opportunities to become involved. Such interests alone are a good reason to study public policy, but it is not the only one. Studying public policy may help citizens sharpen their analytic skills, decide what political positions and policies to support, and determine how best to evaluate democratic governance. It may encourage students to consider careers in public policy, law, or government. Two additional reasons are presented here: to improve citizens' ability to participate in policy processes and their ability to influence policy decisions.

11

Working with Sources

Interest Groups on the Web

Interest group websites are treasure troves of policy information, but a word of warning is in order. Visitors to these sites need to be cautious about how they approach the materials and policy recommendations they find. Information on these sites is always selective; it may be limited in scope and biased in ways that a naive reader may not discern. Policy briefings and reports made available by such groups therefore merit careful and critical reading, and our goal here is to teach you how to be alert to the general political orientation of the group sponsoring the site. We start by asking about the credibility of the studies and reports you find there.

Visit the website for the Smoke-Free Alternatives Trade Association (SFATA) (www.sfata.org), the major trade association for the e-cigarette industry, and access reports and data regarding its positions on the health effects of e-cigarettes by selecting the link for Resources, and then Research. From there, you can read studies and clinical research on this issue. Note especially the language SFATA uses in its Statement of Principles (select the About SFATA link), such as "the science behind this new industry is not yet settled."

For a contrasting view, visit the website for the American Lung Association (ALA) (www.lung.org) and search for "e-cigarettes" in its search field. From here, you will see a number of links discussing the ALA's position on e-cigarettes and its concerns regarding potential health consequences.

- How credible is the information you found on the two websites? Which group do you think provides less biased information, and why do you think so?

- Does either supply references to authoritative sources for the information presented, such as government reports or studies published in scientific or scholarly journals?

- How else can you judge the facts and issue positions on these pages? By comparing the different positions and the language used to defend them, can you determine which group offers the most defensible stance on the health effects of e-cigarettes?

Note: Websites are changed and upgraded frequently. The sites provided throughout this text are meant to be current; however, design changes may require you to investigate a site more thoroughly than originally assigned.

Citizens' Ability to Participate and Make Choices

The United States is a representative democracy. Its citizens elect delegates to act for them, but that is not necessarily the end of citizen participation. Within democracies, citizens may speak out on policy development and government actions. Lack of knowledge about public problems, policies, government decisions, or politics does not normally keep people from acting in this way, but they can participate more effectively by improving their understanding of the issues. During political campaigns, candidates for public office state their positions on the issues through speeches and advertisements—and, increasingly, through social media sites such as Twitter and Facebook—in hopes of persuading voters to support them. Voters who study public policy are better equipped to understand the candidates' policy ideas and to evaluate them—that is, to determine what impacts they are likely to have and whether they are desirable. If elections are to turn on informed assessments of the issues rather than how good the candidate looks on camera, policy knowledge of this kind is essential.

Citizens can also join with others in an interest group to learn more about public policy. Scholars often observe that the **logic of collective action** suggests that a single individual would be irrational to join an interest group when almost no personal gain follows (Olson 1971). The enormous growth of citizen lobbies over the last several decades, however, clearly indicates that agreement with a group's goals persuades many people to sign up and participate (Berry 1997, 1999). Interest groups operate at all levels of government, and one of their roles is to educate policymakers and citizens about public policy issues. For example, many of them—from the National Rifle Association to the Sierra Club—commission policy studies and use them in the political process to advance their views (Cigler and Loomis 2015; Wolpe and Levine 1996). Nearly all of the major groups maintain websites that offer issue briefings and facilitate communication with public officials. The box "Working with Sources: Interest Groups on the Web" addresses the role of such groups in shaping public policy.

Working with Sources

The Public's Political Knowledge

As indicated throughout the text, the enormous amount of information available through websites makes citizen activism more feasible than ever before. After all, the potential for activism is facilitated by information as well as by individual motivation to get involved. Reliance on web sources, however, also presents a challenge: how to manage the huge amount of information.

The federal government's site, USA.gov (www.usa .gov), is an official portal to U.S. government websites. The mission of the site is to make government more accessible and seamless and to make it easier for citizens to find the services they seek and to complete transactions online. A new search engine developed specifically for accessing such material is capable of sifting through a vast number of pages of information from national, state, and local governments in a fraction of a second.

A simple exercise indicates how useful USA.gov can be. Let's assume you want to write to your senator and need to know his or her name and address. Go to the site, look under the Government Agencies and Elected Officials link, then select Contact Elected Officials. Click U.S. Senators, choose your state, and you have the names and contact information for your two senators.

A more challenging illustration of how to navigate through USA.gov involves finding information about a particular public policy issue or general information. Try entering "nutrition facts" into the search field. From here you can find information on how to use the Nutrition Facts Label.

Try to answer these questions:

- What is the Nutrition Facts Label, and why is it included on packaged food items?

- What is the Percent Daily Value?

- Where can you go to get information regarding food safety (use the search field)? What are the current recalls and alerts?

At state and local levels, citizens may have the opportunity to get more directly involved in policymaking through referendums, initiatives, or participation in public hearings and meetings (Cronin 1989), and perhaps have greater influence. A referendum is a law proposed by a state or locality for voters to approve or reject. An initiative is much the same, but a group of citizens organizes the effort to place it on the ballot. About half the states allow citizen-generated initiatives. Naturally, the voters can better determine whether to support or oppose a ballot measure if they understand the proposal and its possible effects. Obtaining that information and developing a sound position on the issues is often a challenge for the average voter; it is also one reason critics argue that many initiatives lead to bad public policy, especially when insufficient thought goes into the drafting of the proposals or the public acts emotionally, or in response to misleading media advertisements (Ellis 2002).

Public meetings afford perhaps the greatest opportunity to participate directly with other citizens and public officials to learn more about local problems and decide what to do about them. Notices of such meetings and hearings are posted in the local newspaper or on pertinent websites. The box "Working with Sources: The Public's Political Knowledge" is an introduction to a primary government source.

Citizens' Ability to Influence Policy Decisions

The ability of citizens to participate in decision-making activities can often lead to influence over the decisions that result. Policymakers and others involved in the policy process need information to understand the dynamics of a particular problem and develop options for action. As we show throughout this text, when examining policy alternatives, policymakers and other actors often make use of policy analysis. The more that citizens are aware of such studies and their implications, the better equipped they are to play an effective role in policymaking and help to shape the decisions that are made. One of the major objectives of this text is to help readers improve their capacity for reading and interpreting such policy studies.

We also want to build understanding of the policymaking process itself and alert readers to the many opportunities they have to make their views known. Most readers may recognize that Congress has chief responsibility for making public policy. However, they may not be as alert to the critical role that administrative agencies play in implementing the laws that Congress enacts. Whether the Centers for Medicare and Medicaid Services in the Department of Health and Human Services or the Office for Civil Rights in the U.S. Department of Education, such agencies have enormous influence over how programs are run and the services they deliver to citizens. Citizens may be particularly able to influence government decisions at the state and local levels where policymakers and administrators are easier to reach.

Whether at the national, state, or local level, citizens who wish to be effective need to be alert to the politics of any given situation. They need to know who the major policy actors are and the motives behind the positions they take.

We provide many examples in the chapters that follow. A simple one concerns reform of the Social Security system. Someone who wants to change it must recognize the interests of AARP, an interest group with millions of members over the age of fifty. AARP members have strong views on Social Security, can easily be mobilized to contact policymakers, and vote at a higher rate than other segments of the population. Not surprisingly, members of Congress and other policymakers tend to pay attention to AARP and take the group's positions on Social Security seriously.

The Contexts of Public Policy

Public policy is not made in a vacuum. It is affected by social and economic conditions, prevailing political values and the public mood at any given time, the structure of government, and national and local cultural norms, among other variables. Taken together, this environment determines which problems rise to prominence, which policy alternatives receive serious consideration, and which actions are viewed as economically and politically feasible. Some aspects of the policy environment, such as the U.S. system of separation of powers and the nation's free-market economy, are relatively stable. Others, such as which party controls the White House and Congress, the public mood or political climate, and media coverage of policy-related developments, can vary considerably over time. To underscore how these variables shape the policymaking process, we offer a brief description of the social, economic, political, governing, and cultural contexts of public policy.

Social Context

Social conditions such as demographics, or the composition of a population, affect policy decisions in myriad ways, as is evident in controversies over phenomena as diverse as early childhood education, child hunger, the rising costs of Medicare and Social Security, and immigration. Moreover, social conditions are dynamic, not static. The population changes because of immigration, growth in nontraditional households, and lower or higher birthrates. These social changes in turn alter how the public and policymakers view and act on problems ranging from crime to the rising cost of health care. Today, for example, senior citizens make up the fastest growing segment of the country's population. Their needs differ from those in other cohorts—or age groups—of the population, and they are more likely than younger citizens to demand that government pay attention to them. One critical concern is Social Security. As the elderly population increases, policymakers face difficult challenges, particularly how they can ensure the system's solvency as greater numbers of people begin to draw benefits and a smaller number pay into the system. Fifty years ago, Social Security was a government program that posed no special risk to budgetary resources. Now, however, public officials recognize that they must find politically and economically realistic ways to deal with an aging population and the retirement of the baby boom generation, those Americans born between 1946 and 1964.

How citizens relate to one another in their communities also influences public policymaking. City policymakers have been trying to reclaim their downtown areas and make them more vibrant and a destination place. These efforts have had some success as more people are seeking out these more urban living communities. Even so, do efforts of urban renewal and reclamation force out lower-income people who can no longer afford housing or rental prices? Do cities provide adequate services for these communities, or do folks need to drive out to the suburbs to purchase groceries? What is the appropriate balance between residential and commercial development, and should tax incentives be used to encourage businesses to locate in these areas? These perspectives can also affect public transportation and environmental policies as questions are asked about the need for mass transit (such as light rail systems that serve cities and their suburbs) or to build new highways or further expand existing ones.

Some of these trends have prompted public officials at all levels of government to think more about the "livability" of their communities over the next few decades. One solution is sustainable development—communities in which social, economic, and environmental concerns are approached in an integrated and comprehensive manner. The Partnership for Sustainable Communities, an interagency partnership, was created in 2009 "to help communities nationwide improve access to affordable housing, increase transportation options, and lower transportation costs while protecting the environment."[12] The federal government can support these efforts, but these initiatives often fall to public officials and local leaders in communities across the nation who search for innovative approaches to bring about sustainability. In the process, they are looking at public policies designed to affect urban growth, transportation, air and water quality, recreational opportunities, and the location of new industry and businesses, housing, and schools (Mazmanian and Kraft 2009; Paehlke 2013; K. Portney 2013).

Economic Context

The state of the economy also has a major impact on the policies governments adopt and implement. Economic policy deals with inflation and unemployment, but the economy itself affects the development of many other programs. For example, a strong economy often leads to lower unemployment, which in turn reduces the need for unemployment benefits, job training programs, and comparable assistance. Weaker economies often lead to different kinds of decisions. For example, in response to the continuing weak economy and limited revenues, state governments have made difficult decisions regarding their financial support for public higher education. The example illustrates how a change in economic conditions can affect the dynamics of public policymaking. As the United States shifts from a traditional industrial economy to one based on providing information and services, many similar impacts on public policy will become apparent.

Another way to appreciate the influence of the economic context is to consider budgetary politics. The United States often has a deficit, with the government spending more money than it collects in taxes and other revenues. Congress tried many ways to reduce the deficit, including the Balanced Budget and Emergency Deficit Control Act of 1985 and a proposed constitutional amendment mandating a balanced budget. Hypothetically, deficits are a concern because there would not be any money to pay for new policy initiatives. Nor could government continue to fund programs without increasing taxes, always a politically unattractive option.

While there were a few years of positive deficit news at the end of the Clinton administration, the deficit increased again due to policies of the George W. Bush administration. The president proposed and Congress approved a massive tax cut that greatly reduced government revenues. The tax cut—combined with a broad economic slowdown in 2001 and 2002; the economic toll of the September 11, 2001, attacks and the subsequent war on terrorism; and a large increase in defense spending—plunged the U.S. government back into deficit. These conditions, combined with the dramatically weaker economy and massive federal spending on economic recovery actions, led to astonishing projections by the Congressional Budget Office that in 2009, and possibly for years to come, the deficit would be over $1 trillion. The projections were correct; in 2009 the deficit rose to over $1.4 trillion, although by fiscal year 2015 it fell to $438 billion partially due to policies to reduce spending and raise revenue and also to the slow economic recovery. Many state governments also found themselves dealing with unexpected deficits as a result of the economic slowdown, although by

Social contexts influence policy development. Among the social contexts that influence public policy development is the diversity of the American population, which has been enriched by immigration over the years. Immigration became a key issue in the 2016 presidential campaign, with little agreement between the two parties. The photo shows Rutgers University students at a rally in opposition to Republican president-elect Donald J. Trump's proposed policy initiatives regarding immigration and the deportation of criminal undocumented immigrants. *(Albin Lohr-Jones/Pacific Press/ LightRocket via Getty Images)*

2014 quite a few were reporting budgetary surpluses as a result of the nation's economic recovery.[13] At the federal and state levels, policymakers struggled once more with tough decisions on spending priorities and budget cuts, a challenge that is certain to continue for years.

Political Context

It is impossible to understand public policy without considering politics, which affects public policy choices at every step, from the selection of policymakers in elections to shaping how conflicts among different groups are resolved. To appreciate the political context, one must be aware of the relative strength of the two major parties; the influence of minor parties; ideological differences among the public, especially the more attentive publics such as committed liberals and conservatives; and the ability of organized interest groups to exert pressure. It is equally important to consider how much interest the public takes in the political process, its expectations for what government ought to do, and the level of trust, confidence, and frustration it has in government. For example, both in the United States and in other industrialized nations there has been a notable erosion of public trust in government in recent decades (Dalton 2004), typically because of historical events such as the Vietnam War, the Watergate scandal, or government inaction that called government activities into question. Supporters of the Tea Party movement have questioned what they perceive to be the ever-increasing size and power of government, particularly in relation to federal efforts to address the struggling economy through new economic stimulus measures and approval in 2010 of the controversial Affordable Care Act. This trend affects not only the way people are likely to judge government programs and what public officials do, but also the way the press covers public policy debates and actions. It also leads to less traditional candidates attracting much public support in their campaigns for the presidency, such as Donald Trump and Bernie Sanders did in 2016, and in the case of Trump to being elected president.

In addition, it is more and more evident that Democrats and Republicans, liberals and conservatives, hold sharply different views about the legitimacy of government action and which policies are acceptable to them. During the 1990s, partisan differences widened, and on many policy issues, ideological polarization between the parties made government action difficult. This polarization and the seemingly endless bickering among politicians as they try to resolve their differences and find acceptable solutions to society's problems make the public even more critical of government and the political process (Hibbing and Larimer 2005). If anything, the polarization deepened in the 2000s and the 2010s as the two major parties frequently found themselves unable to agree on a wide range of policy actions, leading to further public disenchantment with government and politics and record low assessments of the U.S. Congress (Mann and Ornstein 2012; Persily 2015; Thurber and Yoshinaka 2015).[14] An example of this polarization and the inability to find common ground was the sixteen-day government shutdown in October 2013 that highlighted sharp differences between the parties, particularly in relation to the Affordable Care Act. Another was the unwillingness of the Republican-controlled Senate to hold hearings on President Obama's nomination of Judge Merrick Garland to replace Justice Antonin Scalia, who died in February 2016.

Ideological terms such as *liberal* and *conservative* are often used by the public to make sense of politics and also policy. The student of public policy needs to recognize, however, that these political labels are not always reliable guides to predicting specific policy positions. That is, it is simplistic to assume that conservatives always want smaller government and that liberals always prefer the opposite. Most conservatives argue for less government intrusion into the economy and decision making within business and industry, but they often favor a strong government role to achieve certain social goals, such as reducing crime or banning abortions and gay marriages. Liberals, on the other hand, rally against government threats to civil liberties and individual rights but are among the first to call for government regulation of business activity to protect consumers and workers, or to control air and water pollution.

Party labels themselves may be poor indicators of positions taken on policy issues. Although less common now, within the major political parties one can find ideological differences among members: some Democrats, particularly southerners, may be conservative, and some Republicans, particularly those from the Northeast or West Coast, may be much more moderate than most in their party. Yet today both parties, particularly in the U.S. Congress, tend to be much more ideologically cohesive than was the case several decades ago. The same is true within the minor or "third" party organizations such as the Green Party, the Libertarian Party, or the Constitution Party (also libertarian). Whether at the national or state level, it is entirely possible that voter disapproval of the two major parties might lead to the rise of such third-party movements. The Tea Party movement of the late 2000s, for example, reflected a strongly conservative stance, chiefly within the Republican Party, and it did very well in the 2010 elections. It continued to be influential in contests for the Republican nomination for the presidency in 2012, and in many state and congressional elections.

Because the United States has a weak party system, individual politicians not only run their own campaigns for office but also promote their own ideas. Many feel little obligation to support the official party position on policy issues, especially when electoral forces in their constituencies differ from those influencing the national party. In the same vein, the political context can vary greatly from one state to another, or even from one community in a state to another. Some states and cities tend to favor conservative policies, while others support liberal policies. Much depends on the alignment of party and ideological forces in the particular jurisdiction, in addition to the social and economic contexts.

Among the policy implications of the prevailing political context in the United States is the continual challenge of reconciling partisan and ideological differences. Policy actors who cannot agree on what action to take may decide to do nothing, allowing social problems to continue unchanged; or they might reach a temporary compromise that falls short of an ideal solution. It is not at all unusual in the U.S. political system to see enactment of such policy compromises, which may contain broad or vaguely worded components. The details, where the greatest conflicts often occur, are worked out later, typically by the rule makers and managers in the executive branch agencies.

Governing Context

The U.S. government is highly complex, and its structure has a major impact on public policymaking. The authority to act is widely dispersed among institutions and policy actors. As a result, the time needed to resolve differences can be lengthy. In addition, the inevitable compromises lead to policies that may be less focused or coherent than many would wish.

The separation of powers mandated by the Constitution requires that any policy developed at the national level be acceptable to a majority of Congress and to the president. Policymakers in both institutions must therefore find common ground. In recent decades, the search for consensus has been difficult because of divided government, with one political party in control of the White House and the other in control of one or both houses of Congress. Strong philosophical differences among policymakers over the role of government and the need to satisfy differing political constituencies often make them unwilling to compromise. Even with unified government, as the United States had in 2009 and 2010, it can be difficult to reach a compromise. Pundits often talk about the need for a filibuster-proof Senate, which would require a sixty-seat majority of the president's party. If policymakers dig in their heels and do nothing, outdated and ineffective policies will continue in force, and consideration of new and possibly more effective policies will not progress.

Under the U.S. political system, the federal government and the states share governing responsibilities. Prior to the New Deal, these institutions had defined areas of governance. The situation is less clear today; more often than not, state and federal government responsibilities overlap. For example, state governments traditionally were responsible for education policy, but since 1960 the federal government has become more involved in education. It provides billions of dollars in education grants to state and local governments and subsidizes student loan programs in higher education, but the funds can come with many strings attached. Newer legislation, such as No Child Left Behind and Race to the Top, increases federal involvement in education policy by pushing for evaluation of success in the nation's schools, including setting standards for what students should know and providing incentives to reform state educational systems. More recent efforts, such as adopting the Common Core State Standards, highlight concerns about standards being set centrally and for all states to follow.

In addition to overlapping responsibilities, the states and the federal government face other problems of divided authority that arise when federal and state agencies try to determine what they need to do to put a policy into effect. Sometimes, the federal government is willing to share governing responsibility, but not money. For example, the federal government has granted authority to the states to implement many environmental programs, such as those falling under the Clean Water Act, but the states say that the funds from Washington are insufficient to cover the costs of their new duties creating what many call unfunded mandates. It is clear that the states have a larger role today in the development and implementation of public policy. State and local governments have been forced to step in to fill the gap left by a shrinking or inattentive federal government. This devolution of authority to the states provides opportunities for innovation; however, it may also produce a "race to the bottom" as states compete with one another to save money. The evidence on the effects of such devolution is mixed to date (Donahue 1997; Rabe 2016).

Americans sometimes complain that "government can't get anything done." In light of the complexity of the U.S. governance structure, with its overlapping responsibilities and political disagreements, a more accurate statement might be that it is a minor miracle that policies get enacted and implemented at all.

Cultural Context

Political culture refers to widely held values, beliefs, and attitudes, such as trust and confidence in government and the political process, or the lack thereof. Political culture also includes commitment to individualism, property rights, freedom, pragmatism or practicality, equality, and similar values, some of which are distinctly American. These values are acquired through a process of political socialization that takes place in families, schools, and society in general, and that at times seems to reflect popular culture and television (Putnam 1995, 2000). Scholars have found that such political cultures vary not only from nation to nation but from state to state within the United States, and even from one community to another, as one might expect in a diverse society. These cultural differences help to explain the variation in state (and local) public policies across the nation (Elazar 1984; Lieske 1993) and also account for some of the differences in voting between "red" states (Republican) and "blue" states (Democrat). Differing political cultures, particularly in regard to rural areas, were one reason given for Donald Trump's presidential victory. You can see how political culture leads to different policies and perspectives in the area of gun control policy. Some states, such as Texas and Wyoming, have somewhat limited gun control policies compared to states such as New York. Another example includes policies regarding the recognition of same-sex marriages, where certain states have been supportive (Vermont, Maine, Minnesota, and New York) while others have not been (Alabama, Kansas, Wisconsin, and Utah).

At times, the policies under consideration are linked directly to cultural perspectives. For example, former secretary of education William Bennett and writer James Q. Wilson have connected what they see as a decline in public morality to crime, abortion, and lower achievements in education. Those who believe that the ideals of right and wrong have not been given sufficient weight in U.S. society tend to promote stricter punishments for convicted criminals. Those who believe in deterrence feel that education and opportunity can reduce crime. Recurring battles over family planning programs, immigration, abortion rights, and international population policy reflect cultural conflicts, especially over the role of women in society, that have yet to be resolved.

These kinds of value conflicts have translated into constraints on policymaking. While not a new issue, partisanship is more apparent than before at both the state and national levels. Members of Congress have observed that partisan rancor, ideological disputes, and decreased willingness to compromise on policy issues have made policymaking far more difficult than it was only a decade ago (Davidson, Oleszek, Lee, and Schickler 2016). As a result, government often finds itself deadlocked, completely unable to deal effectively with issues. The inability to solve public problems further erodes the public's trust in government and diminishes its willingness to get involved in the political process.[15]

The Reasons for Government Involvement

When the public and policymakers believe that government needs to intervene to correct a social problem, they create or alter policies. But this does not mean the matter is settled permanently. The rationales offered for government involvement in public policy were highly contested in the past, and they continue to be today. The arguments for and against government intervention in the economy and in people's lives draw from political philosophies and ideologies, specific beliefs about policy needs, and the positions that are advocated by political parties and interest groups. These arguments often are advanced during the processes of agenda setting (to discourage or encourage action), policy formulation (where the specific form of intervention is designed), or policy legitimation (where the rationale for intervention may be debated). The three leading, and somewhat overlapping, rationales for government intervention are political reasons, moral or ethical reasons, and economics and market failures. The last of these rationales warrants a longer discussion than the others because it is often thought to be more complex.

Political Reasons

The public and policymakers may decide that government should intervene to solve a problem for political reasons. The reasons vary, but often they reflect a notable shift in public opinion or the rise of a social movement pressing for action. After the 1954 Supreme Court decision on public school segregation in *Brown v. Board of Education of Topeka* and the rise of the civil rights movement, for example, the federal government began to act on civil rights. President Lyndon Johnson persuaded Congress to adopt new policies to prevent discrimination against minorities, including the Civil Rights Act of 1964. In the

1960s, the federal government began the Medicare program after more than twenty years of public debate in which critics argued that such actions were not legitimate for government and that they constituted a step toward "socialized medicine." During the 1960s and 1970s, the federal government also substantially increased its involvement in consumer protection, automobile safety, and environmental protection because of rising public concern about these issues. Sensing a shift in the political environment regarding concerns about same-sex marriage, a number of states (Washington, New York, and Vermont, among others) enacted legislation legalizing such marriages.

Moral or Ethical Reasons

In addition to the power of public opinion or a social movement, certain problems and circumstances may dictate that government should be involved for moral or ethical reasons. In other words, government action is seen as the right thing to do even without public pressure. Some portion of the population or members of an organized interest group may be unwilling to witness suffering from poverty, hunger, or human rights abuses, either at home or abroad, and want the government to do something about it. They may join groups to lobby policymakers or contact them directly to persuade them to take action.

There are many examples of government acting primarily for moral or ethical reasons. As we discuss in chapter 9, Social Security was adopted to ensure that the elderly, the disabled, and the minor children of deceased or disabled workers had sufficient income and would not suffer from the ravages of poverty. Debate over the future of the Social Security system continues this moral argument. Similar moral values lie behind the United States' long-standing support of family planning programs and economic assistance in developing nations. These operations have been defended as essential to promoting much-needed economic development that could rescue people from desperate poverty. The Bush administration offered many different reasons for its decision in 2003 to invade Iraq, but here too parallel moral arguments were advanced, including the need to remove dictator Saddam Hussein from power and to promote the growth of democracy and freedom in that nation. The moral imperative of ensuring health care for all was a primary reason offered by supporters of the Affordable Care Act, or Obamacare. Natural disasters often spark such an interest for government to step in to help people affected by floods, tornadoes, or other events, as was particularly evident following the devastation of Hurricane Sandy in 2012.

Economics and Market Failures

In a pure capitalist or market system, most economists would not consider the plight of family farmers who cannot compete with large agribusiness or the challenges that face many other small businesses a legitimate reason for government intervention. They would argue that government intrusion into the marketplace distorts the efficiency with which a competitive market economy can allocate society's resources. In such a market, voluntary and informed exchanges between buyers and sellers allow them to meet their needs efficiently, especially when large numbers of people are involved, so that the market operates fairly. In this world, competition sets the fair market value on houses, cars, and other goods.

Economists acknowledge, however, that a situation known as **market failure** warrants government intervention. A market failure occurs when the private market is not efficient. Market failures fall into four types: the existence of monopolies and oligopolies, externalities, information failure, and inability to provide for the public or **collective good**.

A monopoly or oligopoly exists when one or several persons or companies dominate the market and can control the price of a product or service. Examples abound. It is a rare community that has more than one cable television operator or electric power company. Monopolies of this kind are called "natural" or "technical" because they are essentially unavoidable. There would be little sense in having multiple cable TV operators or power companies in an average-sized city if greater efficiency can be achieved by having a single company invest in the necessary infrastructure. Governments usually accept this kind of monopoly but institute regulations to ensure that the public is treated fairly. Yet the balance between government regulation and economic freedom for the monopoly is the subject of ongoing debate.

Externalities are the decisions and actions of those involved in the market exchange that affect other parties, either negatively or positively. A **negative externality** occurs when two parties interact in a market and, as a result of that interaction, a third party is harmed and does not get compensation. Pollution is a negative externality. For example, consumers enter into an agreement with the utility to provide electricity. In the absence of government regulation, the utility may decide to use the least expensive fuel, most likely coal. When coal is burned, it sends pollutants into the atmosphere, which settle downwind and may cause health problems to a third party. The third party, not the two parties interacting in the electricity market, pays the costs of those health problems. Ideally, the health care costs associated with electricity production would be considered part of the cost of production, and government intervention may ensure that this happens. Through environmental regulation, the government requires utilities to install pollution-control technology on their plants to limit the amount of pollutants emitted.

A **positive externality** occurs the same way as a negative externality, but the third party gains something from the two-party interaction and does not have to pay for it. Higher education is a positive externality. Some policymakers argue that because society benefits from a well-educated population, it should be willing to provide financial support to encourage people to continue their education. Many state governments subsidize higher education tuition for their local institutions—admittedly at a significantly lower level now than in the past. For example, Georgia has a HOPE (Helping Outstanding Pupils Educationally) Scholarship program, which provides tuition for students who graduate from high school with a 3.0 average within a certain core curriculum and maintain that average in college.[16] In essence, this benefit increases students' incomes and enables them to afford more schooling.

Information failure is the third kind of market failure. According to the theories of market operation, to have perfect competition, willing buyers and sellers must have all of the information needed to enter into a transaction or exchange. When the information is not fully or easily available, a market failure may occur. At times, the consumers' lack of complete information about a product or service does not present a major problem: consumers can adjust their buying behavior if they believe there is something wrong with the goods or services they purchased. When the lack of information leads the consumer to suffer significant financial or personal loss, the government may step in. A clear example of such government intervention is its regulation of prescription and over-the-counter pharmaceuticals. Without government, consumers would find it impossible to figure out whether medical drugs are safe and effective. The federal Pure Food and Drug Act of 1906 established the modern FDA and authorized it to test proposed drugs to ensure their safety and efficacy. Another FDA example is the public warnings or recalls of particular food items that may cause sickness, such as alerts provided in early 2015 regarding ice cream linked with listeria and the frozen chicken recall due to concerns over salmonella. Chapter 8 discusses how well the FDA does its job.

A fourth kind of market failure occurs when markets cannot provide for the public good, also called the collective good. A public or collective good is defined by two criteria: the ability to exclude someone from getting the good and the ability to jointly consume the good. Exclusion within the U.S. economy typically occurs through pricing. If an individual can charge for a good or service, then he or she can exclude someone from getting it. Goods that can be jointly consumed are those in which one person's consumption does not prevent another from also consuming it. The two criteria can be displayed as a typology (see Figure 1-1) of private goods and public goods that clarifies the range of what analysts call collective goods.

A **pure private good**, as defined in the figure, refers to a good that is private and for which there is no market failure. It represents the normal, day-to-day interactions between the private sector and consumers. The other three kinds of goods refer to nonprivate or public goods, and they signal conditions that may require government intervention to alleviate the market failure.

Toll goods can be jointly consumed, and exclusion is feasible. An obvious example is a utility such as electricity or cable services. One person's use of cable services does not preclude another person's use, but a cable company's charges may exclude low-income individuals. Earlier, we identified such goods as natural monopolies. To keep essential services affordable, government intervenes by regulating prices. For years public utility commissions regulated prices that electric companies could charge their consumers. Experiments in electricity market deregulation have tried to create more competition and choices for consumers, but they have not always succeeded.

Figure 1-1 Private Goods and Public Goods

		NO JOINT CONSUMPTION	JOINT CONSUMPTION	
	Exclusion Is Feasible	**1** **Pure private goods** Examples: computers, automobiles, houses	**2** **Toll goods** Examples: cable TV services, electrical utilities	
	Exclusion Is Not Feasible	**3** **Common pool resources** Examples: air, water, grazing land, oceans, fisheries, wildlife	**4** **Pure public goods** Examples: national defense, public parks	

Common pool resources are goods that cannot be jointly consumed and for which exclusion is not feasible. For example, environmental scientists write about a "tragedy of the commons," which comes about from use of natural resources such as air, water, grazing land, fisheries, and the like. The tragedy is that each individual seeks to maximize his or her use of the common pool resources without regard to their degradation or depletion because no one owns them. Such individual behavior may lead to the loss of the resources for all, even when each person would benefit from their continued use. To ensure the preservation of these shared goods, government intervenes. It requires individuals to have a license to fish, which may preclude some from partaking in the good, but the funds raised through the licensing fee can be used to restock the fishery. Government may also set catch limits on different species to prevent overfishing, and it requires ranchers to pay a fee to allow their cattle to feed on public grazing land. For common pool resources, government's role is to develop policies to ensure their continuance or sustainability. Without government, the public would likely deplete these goods.

Finally, **pure public goods** can be jointly consumed, and exclusion is not feasible. They would not be provided at all without government intervention because the private sector has no incentive to provide them. National defense and public parks are examples. For these kinds of goods, government intervention is necessary to ensure the general public has them.

These three reasons for government intervention—political, moral and ethical, and economic or market failure—are not exhaustive. Other reasons may present themselves, and these three may not be mutually exclusive; that is, policymakers may favor government action for one or more reasons at the same time. The reasons also may change over time: policies are adopted and changed in a continuous cycle, which is part of society's response to public problems and efforts to find solutions. Government intervention is simply one of these options. When such intervention no longer works or no longer makes sense, policies may be changed in favor of private action or free markets once again. Much of the movement toward deregulation of financial markets in the 1980s and of energy markets in the late 1990s reflected such views. The adverse consequences of deregulation surrounding the financial markets prompted a new round of public debate in the late 2000s over what kind of government intervention best serves the public interest. Congress enacted the Dodd-Frank Wall Street Reform and Consumer Protection Act in 2010 as a result of diminished faith in the ability of Wall Street financial institutions to limit the kinds of risky investments that contributed heavily to the national and global economic turmoil of 2008 and 2009.

The Practice of Policy Analysis

There is one last topic we would like to introduce in this chapter. This is the value of policy analysis as a way of thinking about public policy. As we noted earlier, policy analysis is usually described as a systematic and organized way to evaluate public policy alternatives or existing government programs. Often it involves applying economic tools and other quantitative methods or measures (Bardach and Patashnik 2016). Policy analysis may therefore seem to some students of public policy to hold little relevance to anyone except policy specialists, but in reality everyone uses such analysis in many day-to-day activities. Buying a car, selecting a particular college course, or deciding on a restaurant for dinner all require thinking about the pros and cons associated with the available choices, including how to spend money.

Market failure and food safety. Once a rarity, the United States experienced an unusually high number of food contamination scares over the past two decades. The photo shows a sign at a Chipotle restaurant in Washington, D.C., on February 8, 2016. Chipotle closed its nearly 2,000 locations in the United States for several hours on that day for a video conference meeting with company executives on food security following outbreaks of E-coli, salmonella and norovirus in their restaurants in several states across the country. *(NICHOLAS KAMMI/AFP/ Getty Images)*

The Many Uses of Policy Analysis

Policy analysis can be used throughout the policy process, but it becomes especially important in the formulation of policies and evaluation of programs after they are implemented. In assessing a public problem, policy analysis may assist in describing its scope, such as the percentage of public schools that are failing. When developing alternatives and choosing a direction, a decision maker can use analysis to assess the feasibility of the choices based on economic, administrative, political, and ethical criteria. The same methods can be used to evaluate a program to determine its effectiveness or whether it has achieved its expected results.

In short, policy analysis represents an attempt to dissect problems and solutions in what is usually described as a rational manner. By this, practitioners mean that they bring information and systematic analysis to bear on policy issues and try to show how a given set of goals and objectives might be achieved most efficiently. Some analysts refer to this as "evidence-based policy."[17] Public policy goals and objectives are usually determined in a political process—for example, how much the government is willing to pay for health care services for the elderly—but analysis can help policymakers weigh competing ideas about how best to deliver such services.

Policy analysts argue that their systematic analyses should be given serious consideration as a counterweight to the tendency of public officials to make policy choices based on their partisan positions, ideology, or support from important constituencies and interest groups. They point to inconsistencies in public policy or to what some would describe as unwarranted or inefficient policy actions. For example, why does the federal government give subsidies to farmers growing tobacco while it also tries to reduce smoking? Why does Congress continue to subsidize mining and timber harvesting on public lands, which causes environmental damage and costs taxpayers more than the revenues these activities earn? Why do members of Congress vote to spend public money on particular projects they favor (such as a highway or bridge in their district, or defense installations) and at the same time complain about the government's wasteful spending? The answers lie mostly in interest group and constituency pressures that elected officials find difficult to resist, particularly when the general public fails to take an interest in such decisions.

Citizens' Use of Policy Analysis

Ordinary citizens and organizations also can benefit from policy analysis. Citizens with an interest in public policy or the political system may make decisions based on their general political views; for example, liberals usually favor government regulation to improve the environment. But most people would understand the benefit of a focused study of a particular program or proposal that put aside personal political views. Perhaps the liberal environmentalist will come to question whether regulation is the best way to achieve environmental goals. A conservative might be moved to reassess whether stringent laws that put first-time drug offenders in prison for years make sense given the very high cost of incarceration (see chapter 5).

It is not unusual for individuals or interest groups to use information developed through policy analysis to reinforce the arguments they make to government policymakers. An organization will often dangle its latest research or analysis to convince policymakers that the group is correct in its beliefs. For example, the following information was gathered from the website of the Environmental Defense Fund (EDF) (www.edf.org), discussing human responsibility for climate change.

The information on the website quoted the 2013 Intergovernmental Panel on Climate Change report:

- 95 percent—the scientific certainty that humans are to blame
- 3 feet—the amount sea levels could rise if climate change continues unabated
- 7.2 degrees Fahrenheit—the highest predicted surface temperature increase by 2100

By citing these presumably objective statistics, the EDF hopes to move the direction of climate change policy toward more direct action to reduce greenhouse gases.

The EDF's opponents in the business community will circulate information, sometimes from the same studies, that bolsters their arguments about the uncertainty of the climate change science and the high costs imposed on society if policies and regulations are overly restrictive. It is not unusual for groups opposed to climate change policy or other environmental issues to question the scientific basis of the studies, or raise the issues of costs to comply, and thus call into question the need for restrictive action.

Presented with conflicting assumptions and interpretations, students of public policy need to be aware of the sources of information and judge for themselves which argument is strongest. This book provides the tools and techniques to help students make informed judgments. In particular, chapters 4 through 6 cover the major approaches to policy analysis and some of the methods, such as cost-benefit analysis and risk assessment, that make clear what the studies say and how the findings relate to policy choice.

Steps to Analysis

How to Interpret Policy Studies

Policy analysis is pervasive and critically important for the policymaking process at all levels of government. To determine which studies are credible and which are not, and which might be used as a basis for making policy decisions, students of public policy need to hone their analytical skills. How to do this? One way is to ask questions such as the following:

- What is the purpose of the study, and who conducted it?

- Does it seek and present objective information on the nature of the problem and possible solutions?

- Does the information seem to be valid, and what standard should you use to determine that?

- Is the report's argument logical and convincing?

- Does the report omit important subject matter?

- Does the study lay out the policy implications clearly and persuasively?

We will address these kinds of questions throughout the book when summarizing particular studies.

For policymakers, policy analysis is an essential tool for the development of public policy and its evaluation. For citizens interested in public affairs, it provides a way to organize thoughts and information to be able to better understand the alternatives presented and the possible implications of these choices. Individuals do not have to know how to conduct complex economic analysis to recognize the importance of using a wide range of information when making decisions; they just need to be able to think about problems and solutions from different perspectives. The box "Steps to Analysis: How to Interpret Policy Studies" offers some suggestions for how to interpret the policy studies you encounter.

How to Decide Which Policy Is Best: Using Multiple Criteria

As the examples cited in this section suggest, much of the controversy over public policy, from international affairs to protection of public health, reflects conflicts over which values are most important. Does protection of national security warrant some infringement on individual rights? If so, to what extent? Should we continue or expand public programs (such as support of health services under Medicaid) even when they become very costly? Should we be more alert to the cost of military weapons systems, or should cost play no role in decisions to buy the weapons? When programs in any area (such as national defense, agricultural subsidies, environmental protection, or the war on terrorism) are not as effective as they should be, should we end them, or at least change them so they are likely to be more effective?

All of these questions suggest that citizens, analysts, and policymakers need to be aware of the multiple criteria that can be used to judge the merit or value of government policies and programs, and of proposed policy alternatives. We suggest that four criteria in particular deserve serious consideration: effectiveness, efficiency, equity, and political feasibility.

Effectiveness refers to whether a current policy or program or one that is being considered is likely to work. That is, how likely is it that the policy's goals or objectives will be achieved? In many policy areas, such as the environment, national defense, and energy, effectiveness may be affected by a proposal's technical or administrative feasibility. That is, it makes a difference whether a proposal is technically possible (for example, cheap, abundant, and clean energy sources) or whether an agency can adequately implement it.

Efficiency refers to what a policy or policy proposal costs in relation to its expected benefits to society. It also is sometimes described as a desire to realize the greatest possible benefit out of the dollars that government spends. Thus, considering a policy proposal's economic feasibility means asking whether it is "affordable" or will be considered a good use of public funds in an era when all programs compete for such funds. Many conservatives opposed the Affordable Care Act of 2010 because of its high costs, and many liberals challenged the continuation of tax cuts from the George W. Bush administration in part because of their high costs in lost federal revenue at a time when deficit reduction is important. More recently, there have been challenges even to federal support during times of natural disasters.

Equity refers to the consideration of what constitutes a fair or equitable policy choice. It may be a way to consider how a program's costs and benefits are distributed among citizens (that is, fairly or not). Think of who benefits or gains from decisions to raise or lower taxes, whether it would be fair to have taxpayers pick up the full bill for college tuition at public colleges and universities, or who would be most affected by a decision to reinstate a military draft. The criterion of equity is also a way to think about who is allowed to participate in policymaking processes, such as who gets to vote or who gets to speak at a public hearing. That is, it is about whether the process is open and fair to all concerned. During the 2016 presidential primary, there were complaints, raised primarily by Donald Trump and Bernie Sanders, that the delegate distribution process was unfair.

Political feasibility concerns how government officials and other policy actors appraise the acceptability of a proposal. Most often, references to political feasibility reflect a judgment about whether elected officials (for example, members of Congress or state legislators) are willing to support a policy proposal. In a democracy, policymakers must consider the preferences and potential reactions of the public, interest groups, and other government officials when developing policies.

These criteria are not meant to be exhaustive. Others, such as ethical acceptability or consistency with political values such as individual freedom or civil liberties, may also be relevant, depending on the issue at hand. In addition, these criteria may not have equal weight in the decision-making process. Public officials acting on national defense and foreign policy issues, for example, rarely consider economic costs as paramount in reaching decisions. Personal freedom might be the primary consideration for some when considering policies in areas such as abortion rights, gun control, crime, and the privacy of e-mail and cellular telephone communications. Chapters 4 through 6 more fully examine these criteria and the tools used to evaluate them.

Conclusions

The basic concepts of the study of public policy and policy analysis introduced in this chapter provide the foundation for understanding how and why public policy is made. Through these concepts, you will come to fully grasp both the actors involved in policymaking and the actions they take. Understanding the distinction between government and politics, for example, will help you to understand how these terms interact and interrelate. Public policy is not made in a vacuum. There are a myriad of variables that can affect how a problem is defined and the choices examined to solve it. Knowing, for instance, the political party makeup of

Congress or your state legislature will provide some information regarding what type of government activity may be deemed acceptable. Understanding changing demographics within your community can provide insight into what issues are likely to be brought forward for action.

There are many reasons why governments at any level decide to intercede. These reasons, such as the existence of a market failure or concerns about the ethics of a situation, allow us to better understand the rationale for government action. Ultimately, as citizens who are affected by multiple public policies every day of our lives, we should not only want to know more about the how and why of their development, but also be able to actively participate if we choose to do so. This chapter provided some of the basics to begin this journey.

The remainder of Part I continues an analysis of the big picture: the institutions involved and ways to approach public policy. Chapter 2 introduces the government institutions and actors involved in policymaking and how they interact. Chapter 3 explains the prevailing models and theories used to study public policy, focusing on the policy process.

Part II is a departure from other policy texts in its thorough coverage of policy analysis. In addition to an overview of policy analysis, chapter 4 presents the many different ways practitioners carry it out. Chapter 5 stresses problem analysis, or understanding the nature of public problems, their causes, and solutions. It also considers the various policy tools available to governments and how to think creatively about policy alternatives. Chapter 6 describes the leading methods of policy analysis and summarizes the most frequently used criteria to judge the acceptability of policy proposals.

The six chapters of Part III combine the material from the first two sections to delve into substantive policy topics. Each chapter follows the same format to illustrate how to think critically and constructively about public policy. These chapters highlight the nature of the problem, provide background on policy development, discuss different perspectives on policy change, and indicate how students might think about and assess the issues. Chapter 13 is a brief conclusion that emphasizes the role of citizen participation in policy choices.

The end of each chapter includes discussion questions to assist students in examining the implications of the material, short lists of suggested readings and useful websites, and keywords. Because of the transitory nature of the Internet, readers should expect that some web addresses will need to be updated. At the end of the book is a reference list for all of the works cited in the individual chapters.

DISCUSSION QUESTIONS

1. Have you ever joined an interest group? If so, why did you do so? What benefits did you expect to reap from joining? Do you agree with the "logic of collective action"? What do you think people get from participating in interest groups like the Sierra Club or the National Rifle Association?

2. How much government intrusion into daily life is acceptable? Is the reduction in personal freedom worth the benefits that the policy provides to society? What kinds of policies are acceptable and unacceptable in the United States? Is this the same in other nations? Consider these questions in relation to the security and terrorism issues or the Affordable Care Act of 2010 that mandates individual purchase of health care insurance.

3. Of the various evaluative criteria discussed in the chapter, effectiveness and efficiency are most often discussed. Why is equity not considered as often? For what types of policy issues should equity be a primary concern? Using these examples, how would you evaluate equity concerns?

4. State governments have generally reduced their support for public higher education. Discuss the economic, political, and moral reasons behind a state government's decision to do this.

KEYWORDS

collective good   24
common pool resources   26
effectiveness   30
efficiency   30
equity   31
federalism   8
information failure   25

logic of collective action   13
market failure   24
negative externality   24
policy outcomes   6
policy outputs   6
political culture   21
political feasibility   31

politics   9
positive externality   24
public good   7
public policy   5
pure private good   25
pure public goods   26
toll goods   25

SUGGESTED READINGS

James E. Anderson, *Public Policymaking: An Introduction*, 8th ed. (Stamford, Conn.: Cengage, 2015). A leading text on the policy process that describes multiple perspectives on politics and policymaking.

Thomas A. Birkland, *An Introduction to the Policy Process: Theories, Concepts, and Models of Public Policy Making*, 4th ed. (New York: Routledge, 2016). Another concise and readable text on the policy process, with concrete cases and illustrations.

Michael Moran, Martin Rein, and Robert E. Goodin, eds., *The Oxford Handbook of Public Policy*, paperback ed. (New York: Oxford University Press, 2008). Part of the ten-volume series *Handbooks of Political Science*, this volume comprehensively surveys the major approaches to public policy from the perspective of political science.

William Ker Muir Jr., *Freedom in America* (Washington, D.C.: CQ Press, 2012). A unique, perceptive, and well-written analysis of the concept of power and how it affects the ways American political institutions work.

Deborah Stone, *Policy Paradox: The Art of Political Decision Making*, 3rd ed. (New York: Norton, 2012). An original and provocative assessment of the role of policy analysis in the political process.

SUGGESTED WEBSITES

www.appam.org. Home page for the Association for Public Policy Analysis and Management, with useful links to the study of public policy and management, graduate education in the field, and public service careers.

www.apsanet.org. Home page for the American Political Science Association, with information on academic study of public policy and related fields in the discipline.

www.ipsonet.org. Policy Studies Organization home page.

www.policylibrary.com. Policy Library home page, with links to worldwide policy studies.

www.publicagenda.org. A guide to diverse policy issues and public opinion surveys.

www.usa.gov. The federal government's portal to government sites.

NOTES

1. International Association of Amusement Parks and Attractions, "Amusement Park Attendance and Revenue History," available at www.iaapa .org/resources/by-park-type/amusement-parks-and-attractions/attendance-revenue-history.

2. See "Boy Hurt on Pennsylvania Roller Coaster, Week's Third Amusement Park Injury," *Reuters,* August 11, 2016, available at www.reuters.com/ article/us-pennsylvania-rollercoaster-idUSKC N10M2FH.

3. See Desiree Stennett, "12 Rescued from Universal Rip Ride Rockit Roller Coaster," *Orlando Sentinel*, October 9, 2013, available at http:// articles.orlandosentinel.com/2013-10-09/news/ os-passengers-stuck-roller-coaster-universal-studi-20131009_1_roller-coaster-hollywood-rip-ride-rockit-tom-schroder.

4. See Sandra Pedicini, "Woman Died after Riding Space Mountain at Disney World, State Report Shows," *Orlando Sentinel*, October 23, 2015, available at www.orlandosentinel.com/business/ os-woman-died-space-mountain-20151023-post .html.

5. To explore these state differences some more, check out the Saferparks website: www.safer parks.org.

6. For more information, see "Bill Seeks Federal Oversight of Theme Park Attractions," *Orlando Business Journal*, December 3, 2007, available at www.bizjournals.com/orlando/stories/ 2007/12/03/story2.html.

7. See Ian Urbina, "When Thrill Rides Are Real Risks," *New York Times*, July 26, 2014.

8. "Theme Park Regulation Crippled," *Washington Post*, December 6, 2007.

9. National Safety Council, "Fixed-Site Amusement Ride Injury Survey, 2013 Update," January 2015, available at www.nsc.org/NSCDocuments_ Corporate/Fixed-site-amusement-ride-injury-survey-2013-update.pdf.

10. See U.S. Consumer Product Safety Commission, "NEISS Data Highlights—2015," available at www.cpsc.gov/s3fs-public/2015%20Neiss%20 data%20highlights.pdf.

11. See Duff Wilson, "Senate Approves Tight Regulation over Cigarettes," *New York Times*, June 11, 2009.

12. See Partnership for Sustainable Communities: www.sustainablecommunities.gov/mission/ about-us.

13. See Rick Lyman, "Battles Loom in Many States over What to Do with Budget Surpluses," *New York Times*, February 2, 2014.

14. On public disillusionment with government and politics, see "Public Trust in Government: 1958–2015," a Pew Research Center report released in November 2015, available at www .people-press.org/2015/11/23/public-trust-in-government-1958-2015/. The study found that in response to the question of whether people "trust the government in Washington to do what is right 'just about always' or 'most of the time,'"

only 3 percent chose the first answer and only 16 percent the second, for a total of 19 percent. In 1958, fully three-quarters of the public trusted the government in this way.

15. Morris Fiorina has argued that most Americans are moderate in their political views and not as polarized as the political activists and party leaders. See Fiorina (with Samuel J. Abrams and Jeremy C. Pope), *Culture War: The Myth of a Polarized America* (New York: Pearson Longman, 2004).

16. For more information, see www.gafutures.org.

17. See, for example, Nancy Cartwright and Jeremy Hardie, *Evidence-Based Policy: A Practical Guide to Doing It Better* (New York: Oxford University Press, 2012).

Chapter 2

Chapter Objectives

- Describe and explain the growth of government throughout U.S. history.

- Analyze the structure of the U.S. government and the implications for policymaking capacity.

- Explain the challenges of policymaking posed by the separation of powers.

- Describe and assess major governmental and nongovernmental actors most involved in the policy process.

- Examine ways to improve governmental policy capacity.

- Assess how citizen involvement can make a difference in policy development.

Stalemate over court nominations. Conflicts between the White House and Congress over both policy issues and nominations are not unusual. But they were especially sharp when the Republican Senate in 2016 refused to consider President Obama's nominee to the Supreme Court, Merrick Garland, to replace the late Antonin Scalia. The photo shows Sen. Dick Durbin (D-IL) calling for Senate Judiciary confirmation hearings for Garland during a news conference in front of the U.S. Supreme Court, September 7, 2016, in Washington, D.C. Sen. Durbin was joined by colleagues Sen. Cory Booker (D-NJ) (left), Sen. Richard Blumenthal (D-CT) (second from left), and Sen. Chris Coons (D-DE) (right). *(Mark Wilson/Getty Images)*

Government Institutions and Policy Actors

On February 13, 2016, Supreme Court Justice Antonin Scalia passed away unexpectedly while visiting Texas. Justice Scalia was appointed to the Court by Ronald Reagan in 1986 and during his tenure was considered one of its leading conservative voices. Justice Scalia was a strict interpreter of the Constitution, often arguing that judges should follow the actual language in the Constitution rather than applying modern interpretations. His death left the Court with eight justices until a new justice was seated, and set up a situation where there were strong possibilities of a deadlocked court on certain decisions. Whenever a Supreme Court justice needs to be added, there is a tremendous amount of political posturing and debate regarding potential nominees and their ideas regarding constitutional interpretation. This was particularly true in this case since Justice Scalia was such a strong judicial voice for the conservative movement.

The Constitution states that the president nominates justices to the Supreme Court—and, in fact, all federal judges—and the Senate provides "advice and consent" for those nominees. This process typically includes a number of hearings in front of the Senate Judiciary Committee and then a vote by that committee before heading to the full Senate for a vote. Within a day of Justice Scalia's death, some Republicans in the Senate, including the party's leadership, said they would not consider, or hold hearings on, any nominee from President Obama given that the country was in an election year, and that it was only right that the people have a voice in nominating the next Supreme Court justice through their election of the next president. In other words, they were suggesting that the country wait at least a year before the seating of the next Supreme Court justice. President Obama and Democrats within the Senate did not agree with the perspective of the Republicans. The president started his vetting process with every intention of following what he said was his constitutional responsibility to nominate someone to the Court. In mid-March, President Obama nominated Merrick B. Garland for the Supreme Court. Garland was the chief judge of the United States Court of Appeals for the District of Columbia Circuit, where he had served since 1997. His decisions on the court reflected a centrist judicial philosophy. As an appellate judge, he already had been through the Senate process and was confirmed on a 76–23 vote.[1]

No one questioned Judge Garland's qualifications for the Supreme Court, yet many Republicans within the Senate continued to state that they would not hold hearings on this candidate and in some cases would not even meet with him individually. Not surprisingly, Democrats cried foul and accused Republicans of not performing their constitutional duties and creating problems for the Supreme Court for the coming year. Republicans countered that the presidential election was so important to the direction of the country that the new president should be allowed to make the nomination, and this was about the voice of the people. Of course, just about everyone saw through the politics of the situation on both sides. Democrats and President Obama saw an opportunity to place on the Court a justice more to their liking than former justice Scalia. Republicans were hoping for, and received, a victory in November to ensure a more conservative leading nomination. The politics of the situation became even more apparent when some Republican senators said they would be open to considering Judge Garland after the November election, even suggesting that he may be a more acceptable candidate than one put forward by Democratic nominee Hillary Clinton.[2]

This situation regarding the seating of a new justice on the Supreme Court illustrates the continued conflict between the branches of government and the gridlock that can occur as a result of this conflict. It also testifies to the challenges of policymaking in the United States today, particularly when the proposed policies are hotly contested, and when both the parties and the citizens are deeply divided over the most appropriate action to take. Democrats and Republicans are frequently at odds over how best to deal with the nation's policies whether they are environmental issues, economic and tax policies, health care, or even something related to government operations such as the nomination and approval of a court justice. Sometimes the outcome is **policy gridlock** or stalemate. Nothing can be done because neither side in bitter disputes over job creation measures, health care reform, and reform of federal entitlement programs such as Social Security and Medicare is willing to compromise. As noted in chapter 1, one result has been record low levels of approval for governmental institutions and policymakers. The public understandably finds such policy stalemate in the face of serious national problems to be unacceptable (Persily 2015; Thurber and Yoshinaka 2015). Polls show a public that seeks resolution of the nation's problems and cooperation between the parties, and yet elected officials often are unable to reach any agreement in part because the core constituencies within each party adamantly hold firm.[3] Such stalemate also reminds us that the constitutional structure of the U.S. government does not make policymaking easy, as it requires agreement between Congress and the White House, and often the approval of the federal courts.

Most people see policy gridlock over health care reform, entitlement programs, and extending or ending various tax cuts and subsidies as a failure of government, and in many ways it is. But it is also true that U.S. political institutions were designed with the clear intention of making actions on public policy—and therefore the expansion of government authority—difficult. The chosen institutional structure reflected the prevailing political values and culture of late-eighteenth-century America. At that time, only about 4 million people lived in the United States, most of them in rural areas and small towns. By 2016, the population was nearing 325 million, with the overwhelming majority of people living in large metropolitan areas and their suburbs. At its founding, the nation faced relatively few public problems, and most people believed that it was more important to maintain their freedoms than to create a powerful government that could act swiftly in response to national problems. Many critics of the U.S. system wonder whether its political institutions are even capable of responding effectively to the highly complex and interdependent problems the United States faces at home and abroad today, from maintaining a strong economy to dealing with climate change or global terrorism (Chubb and Peterson 1989; Ophuls and Boyan 1992).

Understanding this system of government and how policy actors maneuver within it is essential for students of public policy. It enables us to assess the constraints on policy development and the many opportunities that nevertheless exist within the U.S political system for solving public problems through creative policy action. The complexity of many contemporary problems, such as urban sprawl, failing public school systems, or weaknesses in the nation's health care system, also hints at the crucial role that policy analysis plays, or can play, in designing effective, economically feasible, and fair solutions. The next chapter rounds out this introductory section of the text by offering a thorough description and analysis of the policymaking process, with particular attention paid to different theories used to explain why this process produces the results that it does, and the opportunities the process offers for public involvement and the use of policy analysis to clarify key issues.

Growth of Government

Most people recognize that government today is much larger than it was at the nation's founding, and that it is also much more likely to affect their lives, from regulation of broadcast media to provision of loans for college education. They may disagree, however, as liberals and conservatives often do, on whether such government involvement is a good thing or not. Most people value the services that government provides, but many also complain about government and the programs it creates, particularly their costs and effectiveness, and these complaints have grown louder in the past few years. Actions taken by the Obama administration and Congress, such as steps to revitalize the economy and dealing with the nation's health care needs, have increased the size of government or at least the government's presence even more, and as noted in chapter 1, we already have greatly increased federal spending and the deficit and national debt in recent years. So how did government come to be so big and, at least in some views, such an intrusive force in the lives of citizens?

The original U.S. government was quite small, as was the nation itself. The first Congress, representing thirteen states, had sixty-five representatives and twenty-six senators. The bureaucracy consisted of three cabinet-level departments (War, Treasury, and Foreign Affairs, to which one more, Justice, was added). In contrast, today there are fifteen departments, numerous bureaus and agencies, and about 2.7 million civilian federal employees, counting postal workers.[4] Despite widespread belief to the contrary, the federal government's size, measured by employees and not budgets, has been relatively stable since the 1970s. Indeed, it decreased during the 1990s, and has seen only a small increase since 2000. However, at the same time, the number of federal contractors and grant recipients has increased substantially since 1990, and particularly since the early 2000s. As Brookings Institution scholar Paul Light has argued, this group constitutes a kind of "hidden" federal workforce and disguises the true size of government today.[5] Much of the rest of the recent growth in government employees has been in the states. However, growth in government employment at the state level declined appreciably as states were forced to trim their budgets. Still, viewed in the broad sweep of history, it is important to understand why government has grown to its present size.

Obviously, part of the growth of government results from the expansion of the United States in physical area and population. As noted, the population has increased dramatically from the initial 4 million residents at the time of the first census in 1790. The population today is also heavily urban and well educated compared to that of 1790, and it occupies land from coast to coast as well as in Alaska and Hawaii. Demographics and geography, however, cannot fully explain the growth of government, which has more to do with the changing nature of public problems and citizen expectations for government services than it does with the nation's size.

One major reason for government's increasing size is that American society has become more complex, and faces more challenging problems. This added complexity, which comes in part from advances in science, technology, and business operations, has led to many kinds of government intervention, from regulation of television, radio, and satellite communications to airline and automobile safety; none was a reason for concern a hundred years ago.

Another reason for the growth of government is the public's acceptance of business regulation. Even though politicians still like to talk about the free-market economy, the United States has moved away from it to a regulated, or mixed, economy. Nowhere does the Constitution mention the power to prevent monopolies, provide for safe food and drugs, assure consumers of product safety, protect air and water quality, or require limits on child labor, but all of these policies are in effect, to varying degrees, today. They resulted not only from legislation but also from the Supreme Court's expansive interpretations of commerce and the necessary and proper clauses of the Constitution.

Viewed from a historical perspective, policy change on government regulation has been astonishing. Congress has enacted regulatory statutes that, prior to the Progressive Era of the late nineteenth and early twentieth centuries, would have been considered improper exercises of government authority. By then, however, social pressure for reform was strong enough that government had the backing to correct some of the excesses flowing from rapid industrialization in the 1800s. These included the prevalence of unsafe food and drugs and dangerous working conditions, and the domination of entire industries by monopolies. These social pressures also spurred major advances in business regulation during President Franklin Roosevelt's New Deal (Harris and Milkis 1996). At first resistant to New Deal legislation, the Supreme Court eventually ruled many of these acts constitutional. In doing so, the Court reflected society's endorsement of these new powers of government.

Attitudes have also changed about government's role in social welfare. Again, under the New Deal, the federal government signaled its responsibility to provide a minimal level of support for certain individuals, including the poor, farmers, and the elderly. By that time, many states had already developed such social programs for certain categories of individuals (Skocpol 1995). President Lyndon Johnson's Great Society agenda expanded those commitments in the 1960s. As government moved into the area of social welfare support, it also grew to administer these programs. For example, Social Security today is the single largest government program and requires a large organization to administer it.

America's role in the world has also contributed to government growth. After World War II (1941–1945), the United States emerged as a superpower and took a larger role in world affairs. The government had to grow to keep up with the new responsibilities in foreign affairs and national defense. This has meant an increase in the budget and personnel not only of the Departments of Defense and State, but also of agencies with peripheral connections to international affairs, such as the Environmental Protection Agency (EPA) and the Departments of Commerce and Agriculture.

In addition, the size, scope, and cost of certain projects mean that only the government can undertake them. They may come about because of a market failure, as discussed in chapter 1, or changes in public expectations of government. Some individuals and organized groups therefore argue that for social or economic progress to occur, government needs to become involved. No other entity, they say, can perform the functions of government, especially space exploration and other scientific research and development, including work in the areas of defense, energy, and health.

Finally, Americans must accept some responsibility for the growth of government. Citizen demands for government action continue to rise. Americans tend to be ideologically conservative but liberal in practice with respect to provision of government services, from police protection to health care for the elderly.

The rise of the Tea Party movement in recent years is partially in response to what its supporters see as a federal government that is overinvolved. One can see the evidence of an expanding role for government throughout the federal rulemaking process, which is a good indicator of the government's growth:

> The American people have long decried government in the abstract but rushed to its waiting arms with their problems or dreams. Throughout the 1980s, the 1990s, and into the 2000s, when skepticism and out-right hostility toward the federal government reached unprecedented levels, demands for specific public responses to private needs and desires continued unabated. (Kerwin and Furlong 2011, 89)

The Tenth Amendment to the Constitution declares: "The powers not del-egated to the United States by the Constitution, nor prohibited by it to the States, are reserved to the States respectively, or to the people." These powers are often called the reserve powers of the states and are the basis for their right to legislate in many areas. Despite the federal government's involvement in public policy issues that were formerly the states' exclusive domain, state and local govern-ments also have grown substantially over the past fifty years. Moreover, the trend toward devolution to the states (discussed later) has meant that many of these governments now are often at the leading edge of policy development.

The effects of government growth are many. First, government policies affect most of what people do every day. Second, government growth has led to an entire occupational sector. Not only are governments at all levels major employ-ers, but also their buying power has a substantial impact on numerous economic sectors that rely on government programs and spending. Third, the scope of government increases the likelihood of conflicting public policies and greater difficulty in addressing society's problems. Fourth, policymaking in a large, com-plex government organization takes more time and effort—to analyze problems, discuss alternatives, decide on solutions, and implement programs—than in a smaller entity. When such efforts do not succeed, the result is policy stalemate or gridlock, the phenomenon to which we referred at the chapter's opening. This is a major reason why we emphasize in this chapter how the government's **policy capacity**—its ability to identify, assess, and respond to public problems—might be improved.

Government Institutions and Policy Capacity

Many students are already familiar with the major U.S. government institutions. Even so, a brief review of their most notable features and the implications for public policymaking may be useful. The reason is that the way institutions are designed and structured is critical to how they function, as are the rules they adopt for decision making. Both affect their policy capacity.

The nation's founders created a system of checks and balances among the institutions of government, primarily to ensure that government could not tyrannize the population. That is, power would not be concentrated enough to pose such a threat. The formal structure of government they established well over two hundred years ago remains much the same today. The U.S. system is based on a tripartite division of authority among legislative, executive, and judicial institutions and a federal system in which the national government and the states have both separate and overlapping authority. Each branch of the federal government has distinct responsibilities under the Constitution but also shares authority with the other two. This system of separated institutions sharing power had the noble intention of limiting government authority over citizens and protecting their liberty, but the fragmentation of government power also has a significant impact on policymaking processes and the policies that result.

Fragmented power does not prevent policy action, as the routine administration of current national policies and programs and the development of new policies clearly indicate. Moreover, when conditions are right, U.S. policymaking institutions can act, sometimes quickly, to approve major policy advances. Often they do so with broad bipartisan support (Jones 1999; Mayhew 1991). Some examples include the enactments of the USA PATRIOT Act in 2001, the Energy Policy Act in 2005, and the Emergency Economic Stabilization Act in 2008. What conditions lead to such substantial policy changes in a system that generally poses significant barriers to such action? It is an intriguing question to ponder, and one that this chapter explores.

Despite policy successes, the fragmented U.S. political system generally makes it difficult for policymakers to respond to most public problems in a timely and coherent manner. The same can be said about the constitutional mandate for a federal system in which the states share power with the national government. The fifty states and about eighty thousand local governments chart their own policy courses within the limits set by the Constitution and national law. Stalemate at the national level usually increases during periods of divided government, when one political party controls the presidency and the other at least one house of Congress (Ripley and Franklin 1991; Thurber 1991; Thurber and Yoshinaka 2015). The reasons are clear: members of the same political party tend to have similar beliefs concerning the scope of government and the direction of policies, but the two major parties often hold strongly conflicting views on these matters. Although divided government makes agreement and cooperation difficult, policymaking can proceed even under these circumstances. In fact, David Mayhew (1991) argues that divided government has had only a limited impact on the enactment of major public policies at the national level. A good illustration is one of the most expansive laws ever written, the Clean Air Act Amendments of 1990, approved in a period of split-party control of the White House and Congress. Democrats took control of the presidency and both houses of Congress in 2009 with a popular president who wanted to bring the parties together to address problems. President Obama, by many measures, had very successful achievements during his first two years in office, including passing a massive economic stimulus package, addressing the financial industry crisis, passing major health care reform legislation, and making major changes to the college student loan program. These successes occurred primarily through support of the Democratic majority in Congress and were not a result of bipartisan efforts. Yet in the 2010 elections, voters backed Republicans at the national and state levels, and created a Republican majority in the House of Representatives beginning in 2011—and thus divided government once again. Results like these suggest that many Americans, and perhaps a majority, were not happy with at least some of the new policy directions.

While the above account makes it appear that there is a lot of variability in congressional elections, the truth is that there are very few House seats considered competitive in any given election. State legislatures set congressional district boundaries every ten years following a new national census, and they do so in a way to protect the party in power. As a result, many see this process as broken. According to some political analysts, such partisan decision making has resulted in congressional districts that produce more extreme or fringe candidates who believe they can safely ignore dissenting voices within their districts, particularly from the opposing party. In some states, the drawing of district lines also has affected control of the state legislature and congressional delegations—that is, where control in effect goes to the party that won a minority of the overall votes cast.[6] For these reasons, some states, most notably Iowa and California, have turned to a nonpartisan process for redistricting.[7]

Fragmented power can lead to other concerns. For example, states' policies, such as California's stringent air quality laws and Massachusetts's universal health care plan, sometimes result in significant advantages for their citizens that people living in other states do not enjoy. In addition, serious conflicts can develop between the federal government and the states. In the 1950s and 1960s, the federal government enacted legislation banning segregation in response to state Jim Crow laws that denied African Americans equal rights. But even passage of the federal Civil Rights Act of 1964, which ended legally sanctioned discrimination, did not resolve all of the conflicts (Williams 1987). A number of southern states refused to implement the federal statutes, resulting in continued civil rights abuses in those states.

It should be said, however, that the ways government institutions are structured and how they make decisions are not immutable. They can be changed, and occasionally they are, as citizens and policymakers seek to improve government performance or try new approaches to decision making. In fact, most of the time policymaking involves action that falls between gridlock and innovation. The norm in U.S. politics is **incremental policymaking**, especially for relatively noncontroversial policies. Incremental policy changes are small steps, often taken slowly. They are adjustments made at the margins of existing policies through minor amendments or the gradual extension of a program's mandate or the groups it serves. The Head Start preschool program is a good example of incremental change, made possible because it is seen as a success.

Presidents can play a role in pushing for change, and they sometimes favor dramatic shifts in policies or the structures of government. President Johnson pushed strongly in the early to mid 1960s for enactment of the new civil rights policies discussed above as well as the War on Poverty. In response to the September 11, 2001, attacks on the United States, President George W. Bush proposed creation of a new and large cabinet department, the Department of Homeland Security, to help prevent future terrorist attacks. And as noted, President Obama was instrumental in passing health care reform, which represented a major shift in policy in this arena. Figure 2-1 provides an overview of the U.S. political system, with a focus on its proactive elements—Congress, the president, and the rest of the executive branch. State governments are organized in a similar manner. The figure illustrates the different institutions and policy actors who play a role in public policy development and implementation. It can be read in two somewhat different ways. First, it serves as a reminder that the U.S. system imposes substantial barriers to a top-down, unilateral approach to making public policy. Second, it shows the many different points of access the system affords to policy advocates. State and local governments dominate in many policy areas, such as education and crime control. They also sometimes intervene when the federal government chooses not to act. For example, faced with federal inaction, many states have adopted climate change policies that try to reduce use of fossil fuels (Rabe 2004, 2016).

The next section discusses the major features of the U.S. government system, beginning with federalism and followed by the institutions of the federal government. The chapter continues with "informal" policy actors, those outside of government who shape public policy, including the general public and organized interest groups. The purpose of this review is twofold: first, to reacquaint readers with the basic components of government, and second, to encourage them to think about the choices that are represented in these arrangements. Why is government structured one way and not another? What difference does the structure of government make for public policymaking and the substance of public policy? What changes in government might be desirable in terms of improving performance, especially the effectiveness, efficiency, and equity of policies? Or in improving the responsiveness of government to the U.S. public?

Federalism

As noted earlier, the framers of the U.S. Constitution designed a system of government in which power is divided between the national government and the states (and, for some purposes, Native American tribes).[8] Both the national and state governments have the authority to enact laws or public policies. We focus here on the history of federalism, the federal-state relationship, the continuing controversies over the proper allocation of responsibility between the federal government and the states, and the variation among the states in their capacity for public policy innovation.

Figure 2-1   Federal, State, and Local Agents of Policymaking and Avenues of Policy Formation

The U.S. government is a highly complex system with multiple actors at all levels and multiple interactions among these different levels. But the system is also fragmented; public policy decisions can often be made within any of the units described. Because of this dispersal of power, the general public and interest groups alike have numerous points of access to decision-making organizations and thus may be able to influence policy decisions. This diagram illustrates these connections for the national level of government. It is also important to recognize that similar points of access occur at the state and local government levels. All state governments have a similar tripartite separation of powers with legislative committees and state-level agencies. Local governments also disperse power in a variety of ways that provide opportunities for groups and citizens to access policymakers.

CONGRESS

Congress acts on legislative proposals, appropriates money for all agencies, and oversees the operations of executive agencies.

EXECUTIVE

Executive agencies implement public policies in part by establishing rules and regulations under the discretion granted to them by Congress.

JUDICIARY

The judiciary affects public policy through established precedent. The courts interpret constitutional and legislative provisions and settle disputes that arise as a result of executive agency decisions.

Lobby legislators; testify to committees; provide information

Participate in rulemaking process; lobby for administrative appointments

Participates in rulemaking; has direct contact with agency personnel

Participates in voting and elections; has direct contact with members

Submit amicus briefs; bring court suits

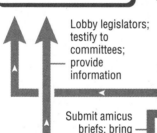

INTEREST GROUPS

There are tens of thousands of interest groups in the United States. Some focus on all levels of government, while others concentrate on one level only. Many participate in the electoral process through contribution, endorsements, and issue advocacy.

Joins interest groups

GENERAL PUBLIC

Approximately 235 million people in the United States can participate in the policy process in a variety of ways, including voting, joining interest groups, and contacting government officials directly. The public may have more opportunities to participate directly in policymaking at the state and local levels through such channels as referendums and initiatives.

The Evolution of Federal-State Relations

During the early history of the United States, disputes arose over how much power the national government should have and what should be left to the states. As the national government attempted to assert itself on issues such as the establishment of a national bank and the rules of interstate commerce, its authority was challenged. The Supreme Court, led by Chief Justice John Marshall, supported an expanded role of the national government. Yet, as disagreement over the spread of slavery to new states and the subsequent Civil War showed, major conflicts persisted over interpretation of the national government's powers.

The relationship between national and state governments in policymaking has evolved since the nation's founding. In the late eighteenth century, the functions or responsibilities of each level of government were quite distinct. State governments, for example, were responsible for education and transportation policies. The national government limited itself to larger issues such as national defense and international trade. Little integration of the two levels of government existed. This state of affairs is often referred to as **dual federalism**, and it persisted throughout the nineteenth century, in part because the federal government's activities remained fairly limited.

In the twentieth century, federal-state relations changed significantly, especially in response to the Great Depression of the 1930s. President Roosevelt's legislative program, known as the New Deal, was an expansive economic recovery program that began to break down the imaginary barriers between national and state policy. It was not unusual to see the national government become involved in what were traditionally considered state responsibilities. Thus dual federalism over time evolved into **cooperative federalism**, as collaboration on policymaking between the national and state governments increased. Many large-scale federal programs begun in the 1960s and 1970s, another period of government growth, relied on such a model. The federal clean air and clean water programs, for example, involved a mix of national and state responsibilities, with the national government setting environmental protection standards and the states carrying out most implementation actions.

Much of the cooperation that occurred between the national and state governments was a result of additional monies being provided to the states through **block grants** and **categorical grants**. Block grants are transfers of federal dollars to the states where the states have substantial discretion in how to spend the money to meet the needs of their citizens. Categorical grants also involve the transfer of federal dollars to the states, but in this case the funding must be used for specific purposes. During the 1970s and 1980s, critics of increasing federal power urged the states to retake some of their policymaking responsibilities. President Richard Nixon's "new federalism" initiatives in the early 1970s were designed to move away from categorical grants and toward block grants to give the states more discretion in how they used the funds. The devolution of policy to the states continued under President Ronald Reagan. His conservative philosophy and political rhetoric gave a significant boost to the trend already under way to restore greater authority to the states. Although many states welcomed this change, they also worried about the subsequent decrease in federal dollars coming into their treasuries. In addition, the national government had discovered a new way to enact popular policies without paying for them: it gave implementation responsibilities to the states. Federal policymakers received political credit for the new programs without spending federal tax dollars. These **unfunded mandates**—federal requirements placed upon the state governments without funds for implementation—added stress to the relationship between the national and state governments. That relationship continues to evolve. In 1995, Congress enacted the Unfunded Mandates Reform Act to limit future financial impacts on the states, but conflict over policymaking in a federal system did not vanish as a result. Congress continued to approve mandates with insufficient funding, at least according to state policymakers. The No Child Left Behind program is one example. Debate focused on the impact on the states of mandatory national standards for promoting primary and secondary school students to the next grade. Supporters of the standards wanted to ensure that students had the skills and knowledge to compete nationally and internationally. Few questioned the goal of improving the quality of the nation's schools, but many had doubts about imposing federal standards in a policy area that has traditionally been a state responsibility.

State Variation in Policy Capacity

Both of the major political parties seem interested in continuing the **decentralization** of power to the states—that is, the transfer of policy authority from the federal government to the states. The focus, however, has shifted to asking whether the states have the capacity to handle additional responsibilities. The issues that arise in this debate parallel the book's main evaluative criteria. For example, critics of decentralization are concerned about the implications for program effectiveness, efficiency, and equity because they recognize that the fifty states are quite different from one another both in their capacity to act on policy issues and in the kinds of policies they enact.

The states also differ in fundamental ways such as physical size, population, extent of industrialization, and affluence. Moreover, each state and region has a distinctive history and culture that shape policy actions (Elazar 1984; Lieske 1993). What may work well and be acceptable to residents of Wisconsin or Minnesota might not be appropriate or feasible in Texas or Mississippi. Some states have extensive state parks and other recreational facilities, while others have strict vehicle inspection programs to promote highway safety. Over thirty states do not permit smoking in restaurants, and California in 2008 became the first state to ban the use of trans fats in restaurants; New York City had adopted a similar restriction in 2006, and other cities followed suit.[9] There is nothing inherently negative about such policy variation among the states; indeed, throughout the nation's history, Americans have celebrated the rich diversity of state cultures and policy preferences. However, when a state's policies are so different from others that its residents may be deprived of essential human

Leading the way. In some instances, state and local governments are the first to take action, particularly when agreement at the national level is difficult to achieve. This has been the case with smoking in public places, climate change policy, and healthy eating. The photo shows employees advising clients on the more than twenty strands available at A Greener Today, a popular cannabis store in Seattle, Washington, on March 14, 2014. Because federal laws still prohibit the sale of legal cannabis, stores don't have access to the banking system and have to conduct all business in cash, which creates security issues as well as posing conflicts between states and the federal government over enforcement of conflicting laws. *(Gilles Mingasson/Getty Images)*

needs or federally protected rights, the federal government is likely to intervene. One might argue that this was the justification for No Child Left Behind: to ensure certain minimal expectations for students regardless of where they get their education. Similarly, many applauded a decision by the Food and Drug Administration (FDA) in November 2013 proposing a general ban on trans fats in food to protect public health.

Those who favor increasing state authority tend to believe that the states are capable of handling additional responsibilities and are better equipped than the federal government at defining their citizens' needs. Indeed, for some, the states are the "new heroes" of American federalism, with greater capacity for policy innovation and closer ties to citizens than a national government in which many have lost their faith. Studies show that over the past several decades state legislatures and bureaucracies have become more skilled than they were before at dealing with policy issues (Hedge 1998). Their new capacity comes from growth in their professional staffs and expertise, including the ability to appraise policy needs and evaluate programs with greater accuracy. Depending on its economic conditions, a state could also act on public problems because it may have sufficient funds to do so, from transfer of federal dollars and state taxation (Bowman and Kearney 2011). The best evidence supporting these arguments can be found in the many innovative and effective measures states have taken over the past several decades in various areas (Borins 1998; Rabe 2016; Teske 2004). For example, state and local governments are mainly responsible for highway safety, and states have been at the forefront in requiring seat belts and adopting speed limit laws. The box "Working with Sources: State Public Policies" indicates where readers can locate information about variation among the states in public policy.

Nevertheless, analysts have several reasons to remain skeptical of how much more decentralization of federal power to the states is desirable. For example:

- Policy performance varies from state to state, and citizens may suffer the consequences. For example, some states fail to fully test drinking water or to enforce clean air laws, even though they are violating federal environmental laws (Rabe 2016).
- States with more money and greater expertise than others can design better programs and offer more services to their citizens.
- Business and industry interest groups may exert more influence at the state than at the national level because of the states' eagerness to attract businesses and jobs. One example is the theme park industry in Florida.
- Decisions may be less open and less visible at the state level, despite the closer proximity of government to citizens.
- Many public problems, such as air and water pollution, cross state boundaries, suggesting that a higher level of government is needed to address them adequately.
- Only the federal government has sufficient resources to support policy activities such as scientific research for environmental protection and health care.

Working with Sources

State Public Policies

One way to become familiar with public policy variation among the fifty states is to explore what several of them have done in a particular policy area, such as education, health care, environmental protection, economic development, or criminal justice. The website for the National Conference of State Legislatures (NCSL) (www.ncsl.org) is a good place to go to see what differences there may be between states on a variety of issues. The NCSL site has extensive news reports on policy activities that affect the states, including policy innovation. Reading about different policy actions within the states is one of the best ways to become informed about state capacity for policy development and to see how the states differ from one another in this regard.

Visit the NCSL webpage, click on Research at the top of the page, and select Human Services and then Same Sex Marriage. Here you can learn more about what states will issue marriage licenses to same-sex couples or recognize such licenses from other states. You can also see other history and resources related to this issue. Note what states have adopted policies allowing for same-sex marriages.

You can do a Google search on how the federal government is addressing the issues related to same-sex marriage. Now that you have explored this policy from different states' perspectives, think about these questions:

- What states allow for same-sex marriage? Are there certain characteristics about these states that are similar and may explain their willingness to accept same-sex marriage?

- How does the federal government address this issue? What role does the federal government have in this area, if any?

- Why are certain decisions left to the states and others shared or left to the federal government?

It seems likely that public debate over the proper distribution of authority between the states and the federal government will continue. The question at the heart of the controversy is which level of government is best suited to address different kinds of public policies. That question has no automatic answer, however, and each person's position is likely to be influenced by his or her beliefs about the role of government in society, particularly the national government. As public policy students become acquainted with evaluative criteria and how they apply to public policy questions, the appropriate level of government to address them may become apparent.

Separation of Powers

One of the distinguishing characteristics of the U.S. Constitution is the separation of powers. Governing power is shared among the three branches of government: legislative, executive, and judicial. This arrangement reflected the founders' experience of living under what they saw as the tyranny of the British monarch. As we stated earlier, they feared that unrestrained government authority could abuse citizens' rights, and they believed that the checks and balances built into a system of separated powers would ensure that no one branch of government would have enough power to threaten liberty. In fact, under this system, the legislative and executive branches must cooperate to accomplish almost anything, and this is not always easy to achieve (Jones 1999). Most people would agree that the goal of preventing tyranny is a worthy one, but the separation of powers has added to the complexity and difficulty of policymaking, and to policy gridlock.

The number of policy actors within the U.S. government and their overlapping responsibilities contribute to the complexity, making it difficult to figure out who is responsible for any particular government action. Consider the recent debates surrounding immigration policy. Proposals vary widely both between our branches of government and even within the political parties. The lack of any statutory movement on the issue led to President Obama issuing an executive order halting the deportation of about five million undocumented immigrants. This issue and its response also showcases the continuing concerns of policy gridlock and the constant struggle for power between the executive and legislative branches of government.[10] Lack of clarity regarding responsibility is illustrated by the investigations of terrorist threats to the nation prior to September 11 and the seeming inability (or unwillingness) of the Federal Bureau of Investigation (FBI) and other intelligence agencies to share information and cooperate (Sanger 2002; Van Natta and Johnston 2002). And climate change, by its very nature a national and global problem, has been addressed more systematically by the states, not the national government, with over half of the states adopting some form of action on climate change by 2014, particularly measures requiring use of renewable energy sources. Indeed, the Bush administration tried repeatedly to block such state action when it considered some of those efforts to infringe on federal power (Rabe 2016; Rabe and Mundo 2007).

Difficulty in policymaking is a reflection of the government's capacity to respond to public problems in light of divided institutions and authority and the political conflicts that inevitably arise over how best to deal with those challenges. In other words, it is not easy to identify and define problems, develop suitable solutions, and approve the solutions in such a fragmented governing system. The following sections explore the branches of the national government, each branch's major characteristics, and the implications of these characteristics for policymaking. In general, all state governments have similar systems and must deal with comparable complexity and difficulty within their own policy processes.

Legislative Branch

The legislative branch of the United States is a **bicameral** (two-house) Congress, consisting of the House of Representatives and the Senate. The two chambers differ from each other in both their composition and operating style. The House, with members elected every two years from separate districts within each state, is the more representative or democratic chamber of the two. It has 435 voting members, each representing about 750,000 constituents.[11] Senators, of whom there are one hundred, serve six-year terms, giving them more independence than House members since they need not face voters as frequently. Moreover, with only one-third of its members up for reelection every two years, the Senate is also more insulated than the House from short-term political forces. Each state, regardless of its size, elects two senators so that the one hundred members serve quite different constituencies. California's senators, for example, represent about forty million people, while the senators from Wyoming represent fewer than six hundred thousand. The Senate also allows its members more freedom to debate issues than does the House. Senators have the right to **filibuster**, or to talk for an extended period of time in hope of delaying, modifying, or defeating a proposal. Threats of a filibuster can force policy compromises as members try to prevent having all other business grind to a halt. The box "Working with Sources: Congress" gives you the opportunity to see how the bicameral legislature often leads to different bills on the same general area and explore why this may be the case.

Article I of the Constitution spells out Congress's powers, but the most important today are its lawmaking and budgetary responsibilities. In addition to passing legislation, Congress each year must appropriate the funds necessary to run government programs. To accomplish these tasks, both chambers operate under a system that allows for division of labor and policy specialization. Policy development is concentrated within this elaborate system of committees and subcommittees, each of which is chaired by the party holding a majority of seats in Congress.

Each of the two hundred committees and subcommittees has specific jurisdiction over certain public policies and the executive agencies that administer them. Each has a substantial staff that can bring experience and expertise to bear on

Working with Sources

Congress

As stated in the chapter, policy gridlock sometimes occurs because of differences within our bicameral Congress. Members of the two houses, the Senate and House of Representatives, may differ significantly in how they view policy proposals even when the same party controls both. To illustrate this, go to Congress.gov, where you can access a wide range of information on Congress. On the site, you will see a section titled "Most-Viewed Bills." Click on one of the bills listed. From this point, you can get a variety of information about the bill, including the full text, a summary, committee assignment, and so on. You can also see the "related bills" associated with the selected bill. If you selected a House bill (designated with the letter *H*), select a related Senate (designated with an *S*) bill. Compare the two versions.

- What is the issue or problem that these bills address?

- What are some of the differences between the versions you are examining? What about similarities?

- Why do you think there are such discrepancies in these two versions? What is it about the two legislative bodies that may lead to such divergence?

lawmaking and on oversight and investigations of the executive agencies. Bills introduced into either chamber are referred to a committee for consideration. If the committee chooses to move ahead on the legislation, it typically conducts public hearings to acquire information on the advantages and disadvantages of the proposed law. Executive branch officials and experts from academia, think tanks, and interest groups may be invited to Capitol Hill to testify. It is easy to find verbatim accounts of testimony through services available at most college libraries, such as the LexisNexis congressional database. Eventually, the committees accept, modify, or reject the legislation. For bills that are to move forward, the committees submit reports on their findings and recommendations to the full chamber for consideration. To become law, a bill must pass both chambers in identical form and be signed by the president. Presidents may veto or reject a bill approved by Congress, and Congress in turn may override the president's veto with a two-thirds vote in both houses. Normally, Congress has a difficult time overriding a presidential veto.

The fragmentation of authority among the committees in Congress can pose an obstacle to policymaking, but there is an upside as well. The large number of committees and subcommittees creates multiple venues for highlighting public problems and considering policy proposals. In this way, almost any issue, from energy conservation to child care, can gain attention on Capitol Hill, and possibly by the media as well. During 2007, for example, Rep. James McGovern, D-Mass., and Sen. Daniel Akaka, D-Hawaii, got the House of Representatives to consider a bill that would impose civil and criminal penalties for fossil thefts from government lands. The law, in essence, gives fossils protections similar to those of cultural and archeological resources.[12] One has to wonder what effect the popular *Indiana Jones* films have on people's thinking about this kind of legislation.

Often the committees, or the full House and Senate, fail to agree on policy proposals, and policy gridlock results. It is tempting to fault members of Congress for inaction, but the causes of policy disagreement and stalemate are easy to understand. The parties are deeply divided ideologically, and on major issues—from health care policy to Social Security reform—members are lobbied intensely by organized interest groups as well as by political activists within their parties. Moreover, when Congress is divided on public policy, the nation often is as well. As a representative political institution, Congress reflects the larger society, for better or worse. In a sense, Congress struggles continuously with its dual roles of representation and lawmaking (Davidson, Oleszek, Lee, and Schickler 2016).

This tension is evident in the policy behavior of members of Congress. Incumbent members usually seek reelection and are overwhelmingly successful in retaining their seats. As David Mayhew (1974) has argued, because of their electoral incentive, members are strongly motivated to stay in the spotlight; take positions on the issues, even if they do nothing about them; and claim credit for public policy actions, particularly those that materially benefit the district or state. These pressures mean that members often introduce bills, make speeches, and distribute press releases on many issues, even when the legislation has no chance of moving forward. In many ways, Congress is a loosely connected assembly of 535 elected officials who, because of the electoral incentive, often go their own way. If they do not act as teammates, policy action that requires agreement may be stymied.

To rein in this natural tendency toward political individualism, Congress relies on the elected leadership within each house, which is organized by political parties. The majority party dominates the House and Senate agendas and decision-making processes to a substantial degree. Historically, the party leadership has been instrumental in overcoming ideological and regional divisions within Congress and forging consensus; it also negotiates with the president on potentially divisive policy issues (Jones 1999; Sinclair 2012). As parties have weakened and members have relied less on the support of their parties, however, the leadership role is less evident. There are numerous recent examples of the House and Senate leaders having a difficult time getting their rank and file to follow their lead. In addition, individual members of Congress rely on their substantial personal staffs to develop policy. Policy formulation of this kind is particularly likely in the Senate, where senators have larger staffs and attract greater media coverage than do House members.

In recent years, both the House and the Senate have been closely divided in party membership, which may force the two major parties to work together to fashion legislative compromises. Party control of each chamber remains highly important and is shown by the jockeying by the two parties as they attempt to capture the Senate, which has tended to be more subject to party control changes. As a result of the 2016 election, the Republicans held 52 seats in the Senate, and the Democrats 46 seats (there also were two Independents, both of whom caucused with the Democrats). The House of Representatives' distribution had a larger Republican majority at that time (241–194).

Executive Branch

The federal executive branch is responsible for carrying out the laws enacted by Congress. It is made up of the president, the vice president, the White House staff, and the federal bureaucracy. Although presidents do not make laws, they are actively involved in agenda setting, policy formulation and adoption, and implementation (J. Anderson 2015; Jones 1999). Other than the vice president, the president is the only federal official who is elected nationally. In effect, the president embodies the U.S. government, symbolizes U.S. culture and values, and speaks for the nation abroad. As such, he commands enormous public and media attention that gives him unequaled influence in agenda setting and policy leadership. For example, George W. Bush in 2001 was successful in focusing national attention on issues of homeland security. More recently, Barack Obama used his position as president to persuade Congress to approve major health care reform legislation.

In addition to the president, the entire White House staff and the **Executive Office of the President** (EOP) are intimately involved in policy development. The EOP consists of the White House offices and agencies that assist the president in the development and implementation of public policy. Among other offices, these include the Office of Management and Budget, the Council of Economic Advisers, the National Security Council, the Council on Environmental Quality, and the Office of Science and Technology Policy. Together, these offices constitute a "mini-bureaucracy" that provides the president and his staff with vital information and policy ideas in their respective areas. The EOP keeps the president informed about the plethora of policies being considered in Congress or implemented in the federal bureaucracy, giving him opportunities to influence policy direction. In most policy areas, the president's agenda and his positions, particularly on domestic issues, reflect his party affiliation and political ideology, as well as the constellation of constituencies most important to his party and—if he is in his first term—his reelection. Democratic and Republican presidents tend to adopt distinctive policy positions on most issues because of their differing philosophies of governance and the particular array of interests the parties represent. The federal bureaucracy constitutes the bulk of the executive branch. It includes all of the agencies and offices that fall under each of the cabinet departments and other offices and agencies whose mission is to develop and implement policy in specialized areas. The best known of these are the fifteen **cabinet-level departments**, each of which is managed by a secretary appointed by the president and confirmed by the Senate.

Each cabinet department includes subsidiary agencies, some of which may be better known than their home departments. For example, the Federal Aviation Administration (FAA), which has primary responsibility for aviation safety, is part of the Transportation Department; the FDA, responsible for ensuring the safety of food and medicine, is part of Health and Human Services; and the FBI, charged with protecting and defending the United States from foreign and domestic threats,

The president's cabinet choices.
A president appoints thousands of individuals to key positions in the executive branch, among the most important of them the heads of the fifteen cabinet departments. This file photo combination image created December 13, 2016, shows some of the cabinet nominees of U.S. president-elect Donald Trump. Top row (L–R): Secretary of State, Rex Tillerson; Secretary of Health and Human Services, Tom Price; and Energy Secretary, Rick Perry. Second row (L–R): Secretary of Education, Betsy DeVos; Secretary of Commerce, Wilber Ross; and Secretary of the Treasury, Steven Mnuchin. Third row (L-R): Secretary of Defense, James Mattis; Attorney General, Jeff Sessions; and Secretary of Housing and Urban Development, Ben Carson. Bottom row (L–R): Secretary of Labor, Andrew Puzder; Secretary of Labor, Elaine Chao; and Secretary of Homeland Security, John Kelly. Puzder withdrew from consideration for the Labor post in February 2017. *(STAFF/AFP/Getty Images)*

is the investigative arm of the Justice Department. The bureaucratic agencies issue reports and studies that enable the public to follow the agencies' activities in their special policy areas, much of which can be found on agency websites (see the box "Working with Sources: Executive Departments and Agencies").

Working with Sources

Executive Departments and Agencies

While often unknown by the general public, most public policy in the United States is actually made through various processes within government agencies. Environmental regulations to ensure clean drinking water, safety standards for various products, and crash standards for automobiles are all made within the federal government bureaucracy. You can get a sense of how agencies act on such problems by exploring their websites. Go to one of these sites by either typing its direct address or, if unknown, starting at the USA.gov site and selecting Government Agencies. From here, you can find any government agency. Agency sites differ quite a lot, so spend some time exploring your selection. Find a link that discusses policies, laws, regulations, or something similar and explore some of the issue areas in which the agency makes policy.

Consider the following questions:

- What is the main purpose of the agency (you may find something in a mission statement)?

- What policy did you select? What is its intent? What problem is it attempting to solve? How does it pursue these policies? In other words, what government tools, such as regulations and subsidies, does the agency use to meet its goals?

- Who or what group/business would be most interested in this policy? Why?

Each agency can be said to make policy within its specialized area through the interpretation of legislative language and development of regulations that are essential to policy implementation. Career federal officials in the agencies have considerable authority to shape public policy, even though ultimate responsibility for policymaking rests with the president's appointees at the top of each agency and department. The career officials work closely with the White House to ensure that agency and department policy decisions are consistent with the president's programs and priorities, at least where the decisions are not strictly limited by statutory specifications. As a result, the U.S. bureaucracy is more politicized than bureaucracies in many other developed nations, and its policies can change significantly from one administration to the next.

Presidential appointees tend to support the ideological perspective of the president, so the election of a new president often causes a shift in agency appointees as well. These appointments not only affect the managerial levels of an agency, but also can shape advisory committee selections. Many agencies, such as the FDA and the Centers for Disease Control and Prevention (CDC), use advisory committees to help inform government decisions in public health and other policy areas. The Department of Health and Human Services alone has more than 250 advisory committees of this kind. Because their interpretation of scientific evidence can push policy decisions one way or another, presidents and cabinet officials take a keen interest in who serves on these committees.[13]

Such a shift in political ideology also makes it difficult for the administration to fill important agency positions. A case in point occurred during the Obama administration, where its supporters argued that Senate Republicans were filibustering an unprecedented number of President Obama's nominees for federal positions. Data released in late 2013 by Senate Majority Leader Harry Reid, D-Nev., showed that by that time eighty-two of President Obama's nominees had been blocked compared to eighty-six total for all presidents who held office since 1949. As is often the case, each side had its own interpretations of the data.[14]

Conflicting ideological perspectives have also hindered the development of the Consumer Financial Protection Bureau, established by the Dodd-Frank financial regulatory act of 2010, approved in the 111th Congress in response to what Democrats in particular saw as weak regulation of Wall Street and financial markets, including mortgage lenders, credit reporting agencies, and payday loan businesses. One of the leaders in developing the consumer protection agency, former Harvard Law School professor and now senator Elizabeth Warren, was passed over as the first director because Congress would not have approved of her nomination. Republicans in particular were fiercely opposed because of what they considered to be her antibusiness attitudes.

Outside of the cabinet departments are the numerous independent executive and regulatory agencies. One of the best known is the EPA, an **independent executive agency** with an appointed administrator who has major policymaking and implementation responsibilities for environmental policy. Independent agencies differ from cabinet-level departments chiefly because they are responsible for a more focused policy area. Other examples include the National Aeronautics and Space Administration (NASA); the Central Intelligence Agency (CIA); and the Nuclear Regulatory Commission (NRC), which oversees the civilian use of nuclear energy.

The **independent regulatory commission** (IRC) is yet another breed of executive agency. Like cabinet secretaries, the commissioners are appointed by the president and confirmed by the Senate, but for fixed and staggered terms. These fixed terms are intended to insulate IRC decision making from political pressure from the president or Congress. In addition, most IRCs are responsible for the economic regulation of certain industries. For example, the Federal Communications Commission (FCC) regulates the broadcasting industry, and the Securities and Exchange Commission (SEC) regulates the financial markets. An IRC focuses on one industry, and therefore its scope of authority tends to be narrow.

Although each agency operates within its own area of expertise, what it does can be in conflict with another agency. For example, the EPA, intent on its mission to reduce pollution, for years wanted automobiles to have onboard pollution controls to cut emissions coming from engines. The National Highway Traffic Safety Administration (part of the Transportation Department), concerned with its mission of safe automobile travel, believed that such a mechanism would make cars more susceptible to explosion. Table 2-1 lists the fifteen federal cabinet departments and a selection of executive agencies.

TABLE 2-1 Federal Cabinet Departments and Major Agencies

Executive Departments	Selected Major Federal Agencies
Department of Agriculture	Central Intelligence Agency
Department of Commerce	Consumer Product Safety Commission
Department of Defense	Environmental Protection Agency
Department of Education	Equal Employment Opportunity Commission
Department of Energy	Export-Import Bank of the United States
Department of Health and Human Services	Federal Communications Commission
Department of Homeland Security	Federal Deposit Insurance Corporation
Department of Housing and Urban Development	Federal Reserve System
	Federal Trade Commission
Department of the Interior	National Aeronautics and Space Administration
Department of Justice	
Department of Labor	National Science Foundation
Department of State	Nuclear Regulatory Commission
Department of Transportation	Peace Corps
Department of the Treasury	Securities and Exchange Commission
Department of Veterans Affairs	United States Postal Service

Judicial Branch

The federal judiciary is made up of the nine-member Supreme Court, thirteen circuit courts of appeals, and ninety-four federal district courts, as well as special courts such as bankruptcy courts, a court of appeals for the armed services, and a court of federal claims. Although many would not think of them as policymakers, the courts play a vital role in the process by interpreting the policy decisions made by others; indeed, the courts often have the last word on policy—thus the intense political debate that occurs, particularly when filling a vacancy on the Supreme Court. The major distinction between the judiciary and the other two branches is that the courts' policymaking is *reactive* rather than *proactive*. Unlike Congress and the executive branch, which can initiate policy, the federal courts offer rulings and opinions only on cases brought before them. Yet these rulings may dictate policy far beyond the actual cases. Consider the Supreme Court's ruling in *Brown v. Board of Education of Topeka* (1954), which overruled the precedent of "separate but equal" public schools, thereby ending legally sanctioned segregation; or the Court's decision in *Roe v. Wade* (1973), which struck down state laws that made abortion a crime. Although each was an important case in its own right, the Court's ruling in each had greater policy implications than initially anticipated.

The federal courts' functions shape public policy in many ways. The courts serve as gatekeepers by deciding who has *standing to sue* (the legal term for the right to bring suit), the right to appeal to the federal courts, or whether a dispute is "ripe," or ready for review. The courts also set standards for review, including whether they will defer to the expert judgment of administrative agencies or review an agency's decisions more critically. Courts interpret the Constitution, statutory language, administrative rules, regulations, executive orders, treaties, and prior court decisions regarded as precedent—using prior court decisions to help make a current decision. The policy language in these various documents may be ambiguous or vague, or new situations may arise that the architects of the language failed to anticipate. The courts have the final say on what the law means, unless Congress revises the law to make its purpose clearer. Finally, courts also have some discretion in choosing a judicial remedy, such as imposition of fines, probation, or incarceration (O'Leary 2016).

The federal courts, therefore, are more constrained in their policymaking roles than Congress and the executive branch. In addition to having to wait for a suitable case, judges must anchor their rulings in law or precedent, not personal beliefs or interest group politics as elected officials are free to do. The legitimacy of the courts depends upon the public's willingness to abide by judicial rulings. If judges deviate too far from acceptable legal rationales for their decisions, they risk losing citizens' confidence. Still, judges clearly differ in their judicial philosophies, or the bases they use for decision making. Some are more conservative or liberal than others, and analysts tend to describe the federal courts, especially the Supreme Court, in terms of the justices' ideological or philosophical leanings.

Federal judges are nominated by the president and confirmed by the Senate, but their jobs are for life, if they choose to stay in them. For that reason, senators, along with interest groups and the public, scrutinize their views on public policy issues when they are nominated. Presidents usually get the judges they want appointed to office, but the Senate sometimes blocks nominees it finds unacceptable, often for ideological reasons. Given the typical lengthy service of a federal judge, a president's influence on public policy continues for decades after he leaves office. President George W. Bush's nomination in 2005 of John Roberts for the position of Chief Justice of the United States and, to a lesser extent, Samuel Alito, appointed in 2006, is a case in point. Roberts was easily confirmed by the Senate and assumed the position at age fifty, so he can be expected to serve on the Court for many years to come. Likewise, President Obama placed two justices on the Supreme Court (the Senate did not consider his third nominee Merrick Garland), Sonia Sotomayor and Elena Kagan, and in both cases the confirmations were relatively easy. A president's appointments to the federal courts have had a similar effect on the courts' shift to the right or left, depending on the ideological vision at the time, an effect that can last for years if the appointed justices are relatively young.[15] The box "Working with Sources: The Federal Judiciary" provides an opportunity to examine what types of Supreme Court decisions, and the justices who made them, have affected public policy.

Under the U.S. system of separated powers, it is essential that the three branches of government cooperate to ensure policy enactment and effective

Working with Sources

The Federal Judiciary

As mentioned in the text, federal jurists serve life terms and can leave lasting legacies for the presidents who appointed them. This is especially true at the U.S. Supreme Court, whose decisions and opinions guide the entire federal judiciary. To learn more, go to www.oyez.org and click on the Justices link. You can click on any of the justices to get biographical information, such as how long they served, which president appointed them, and other information. Note the length of time that these justices served on the Court. Another way to examine the Court's influence on public policy is to look at a series of cases dealing with a particular public policy issue—for example, abortion. From the front page of the site, under Cases, select Issue from the View by: menu and then Privacy. You will see a few choices, one of which is abortion and contraceptives. Some of the cases you may want to examine are *Roe v. Wade, Webster v. Reproductive Health Services,* and *Planned Parenthood of Southeastern Pennsylvania v. Casey.*

- How has the Court's position on this issue changed since 1973?
- Note that former chief justice William H. Rehnquist was involved in all three of these cases over this twenty-year period. Was he ever in the majority? Did his views change?
- What have been the issues in more recent cases addressing abortion, and how did the Court rule? How do these rulings affect abortion rights?

implementation. Indeed, policy results from the interaction of the branches rather than their separate actions. Constitutionally, the legislature may be the branch responsible for policymaking, but many other policy actors must also be involved. It is clear that each branch has a strong capacity to analyze public problems and devise solutions to them, but equally clear that building consensus among diverse policy actors with different political incentives and constituencies, although necessary, is rarely easy.

Informal Policy Actors and Policy Capacity

So far, this chapter has dealt with the formal government institutions involved in making public policy. It is easy for citizens to understand these institutions and the people who work in them. This next section discusses other players in the policymaking process, including the public itself (indirectly and directly) and organized interest groups. In addition, we discuss a theory of how the formal and informal actors work together in the development of policy.

Public Opinion and Policymaking

As one would expect in a democracy, public opinion is a major force in policymaking, even if it constitutes an indirect or passive form of action on the public's part. Public opinion influences what elected officials try to do, especially on issues that are highly salient, or of great importance to voters, or on those that elicit strong opinions, such as abortion rights or gun control. Although public opinion is rarely the determinative influence on policymaking, it sets boundaries for public policy actions. Policymakers cross those boundaries at their own risk. The broad direction of public policies therefore tends to reflect the concerns, fears, and preferences of the U.S. public (Manza, Cook, and Page 2002; Page 1992).

The common definition of **public opinion** is what the public thinks about a particular issue or set of issues at any point in time (O'Connor and Sabato 2006), but what is meant by "the public" is not always clear. The attentive public can be distinguished from the general public. The attentive public, typically less than 10 percent of the public, includes those who are apt to take an interest in a particular problem or policy. They are more likely than other people to become informed about the issues and to get involved in some way. Actions and communication from either of these groups may influence policy development, but the general public's opinions tend to shape only the overall direction of policy, while the views of the attentive public, especially of organized interests, tend to have a greater impact. This influence can be especially pronounced for policies with low salience for the general public.

Public opinion is usually expressed as the aggregate or sum of the individual attitudes and opinions of the adult population. Poll takers measure it through interviews, typically conducted over the telephone, with a random sample of the adult population. (In a random sample, each person in the population has an equal chance of being selected.) If standard opinion research methods are followed, a typical survey or poll of about a thousand to twelve hundred adults will be accurate to within about three percentage points, meaning that the result is only three percentage points higher or lower than it would be if the entire U.S. population had been interviewed. Before accepting a poll's results as accurate, however, the public policy student needs to ascertain whether the survey followed proper methods. For example, were the questions objective, or did they lead those responding to a particular position? Was a random sample used (Asher 2017)? Internet polls and other self-selected surveys almost always fail to meet these standards, as do many polls commissioned by interest groups, where the use of leading questions is common. The box "Steps to Analysis: Public Opinion" highlights some sources of public opinion data and shows how one might critically examine the questions and other methods used in surveys. Figure 2-2 illustrates what a well-conducted poll can reveal about the public's changing views over time, in this case about climate change from 1990 to 2016. The rising level of public concern in 2016 stimulated considerable debate over climate change in the 2016 presidential election campaign.

Americans have numerous ways and opportunities to voice their opinions, so policymakers at all levels of government need to be aware of the shifting beliefs of the population. Beyond answering polls or surveys, people can express their opinions through their political participation, which may include not just voting, but attending meetings, writing or speaking to government officials,

Steps to Analysis

Public Opinion

An enormous amount of contemporary poll data can be found on the Internet. Several specific examples illustrate the kind of material you can find and how you might evaluate it. If the particular poll data we discuss here are not available when you access the site, try to find comparable information in the newer polls that appear regularly.

One of the most popular public opinion polls is conducted by the Gallup organization. Go to its website at Gallup.com. Note along the top banner a Topics button.

Select one of these issues that is of interest to you (e.g., politics), and review the information and data provided within this topic.

- What conclusions would you draw from these data about public opinion on the issue?

- Is information provided that might allow you to determine how opinion has changed on this issue during the time of the polls? If so, what is this change?

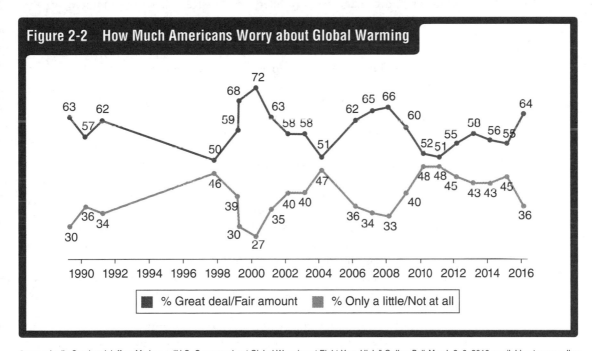

Figure 2-2   How Much Americans Worry about Global Warming

Legend: ■ % Great deal/Fair amount   ■ % Only a little/Not at all

Source: Lydia Saad and Jeffrey M. Jones, "U.S. Concern about Global Warming at Eight-Year High," *Gallup Poll*, March 2–6, 2016, available at www.gallup .com/poll/190010/concern-global-warming-eight-year-high.aspx?g_source=CATEGORY_CLIMATE_CHANGE&g_medium=topic&g_campaign=tiles.

joining interest groups, and backing referendums and initiatives placed on state or local ballots. These are forms of direct citizen involvement in policymaking, and many states permit their use. In 2012, for example, voters in Washington state approved by a margin of 54–46 percent a statewide ballot referendum that upheld a bill that would legalize same-sex marriage in the state. Votes on initiatives and referendums may also reflect public anger or frustration about an issue and not necessarily constitute good public policy. In another example from 2004, voters in Arizona approved Proposition 200, a ballot measure that was intended to slow the rate of illegal immigration into the state. Among other actions, it requires public employees to report illegal immigrants to federal authorities or face criminal charges. Not surprisingly, critics question the legitimacy and likely effectiveness of such laws.

It makes sense intuitively that public opinion should be important in a democracy, even if in a less direct way than a ballot initiative. The truth is, however, that most citizens pay relatively little attention to government, politics, and public policy. They are preoccupied with their families, jobs, homes, and other matters that are important to them on a day-to-day basis. As a result, they may not be well informed on policy issues, and they may have few strong opinions about them. Such opinions are often characterized as being low in both saliency and intensity. Saliency refers to how centrally important an issue is for an individual; intensity refers to the strength of the opinion, or how firmly it is held. Both qualities are important for predicting whether and how likely people are to act on their opinions.

Stability is another dimension of the opinions that people hold. It refers to the continuation of an opinion over time. Public opinion can be fleeting and change quickly, and it can be influenced by current events and the ways issues are presented in the media and by public officials. A good example is what public opinion analysts call the "rally 'round the flag" effect, which occurs among citizens when an international crisis stirs patriotic feelings and more than usual support for the president and other national leaders. President Bush clearly benefited from the effect following the September 11 attacks, as did President Obama after the finding and killing of Osama bin Laden; the evidence could be seen in their higher approval ratings. Mass shootings, such as the one at an Orlando bar in June 2016, can often change opinion regarding gun control policy or harden positions of those who strongly support or oppose more stringent gun regulations. As this discussion indicates, it is often difficult to figure out just what citizens want from government and what policy proposals they are prepared to endorse. Yet, the more stable public opinion is on an issue, the more likely policymakers are to pay attention and consider the public's views when making decisions.

Partly because so few Americans approach government and public policy with a clear, strong political ideology, they find it easy to hold inconsistent views on the role of government. Ideologically, a majority of Americans tend to be somewhat conservative; that is, they prefer limited government and, when offered the choice, less bureaucracy and regulation, at least in the abstract. This same majority, however, is likely to demand that government provide a great many services, from regulation of foods and drugs and environmental quality to provision of public education and police protection. The way people react to any given policy proposal depends greatly on *how* it is presented to them. When pollsters ask people about concrete policy programs, they generally find considerable public support for them. At the same time, politicians can elicit public sympathy if they attack government, bureaucracy, regulation, and taxation in a very general or abstract manner.

Despite the public's often weak grasp of many policy issues, there are reasons to believe that given the opportunity, citizens can take a keen interest in public affairs, inform themselves on the issues, voice their opinions, and influence public policies. Especially at the local level, citizens can and do get involved, and they can have a major voice in public policy (Berry, Portney, and Thomson 1993). Even in highly technical areas such as nuclear power and nuclear waste policy, studies suggest a substantial potential for citizen involvement and influence (Dunlap, Kraft, and Rosa 1993; Hill 1992). Moreover, governments have ways to encourage citizens to become more involved if they wish (Ingram and Smith 1993). Local communities that are trying to become more sustainable, for example, have created numerous opportunities for citizens to play a central role in the process (Mazmanian and Kraft 2009; K. Portney 2013).

Interest Groups, Nonprofits, and Public Policy

Organized interest groups are a major influence on public policy, and by most measures their numbers and activities have soared since the 1960s (Berry 1997; Cigler and Loomis 2015). The number of citizen groups, or so-called public interest groups, such as the Sierra Club, the National Rifle Association, the Christian Coalition of America, and Mothers Against Drunk Driving, has risen significantly during this period, but so has the number of what are usually termed *special interest groups*, those with a direct economic stake in public policy, such as organized labor, business groups, and professional associations. A good example is Google, a dominant Internet presence. In 2002, it spent almost nothing on lobbying, but by 2014, it spent nearly $17 million,[16] and its activities in Washington, D.C., go well beyond traditional lobbying. It works with Washington think tanks, nonprofit organizations, and many others on some issues of obvious importance to its business, such as copyright laws and temporary visas for foreign technical workers, but also on broad concerns related to the future of the Internet and new technologies.[17] Most groups are involved in direct lobbying of policymakers, indirect or grassroots lobbying aimed at mobilizing the public or the group's supporters, and public education campaigns. Some also engage in electioneering, such as endorsement and support for candidates for office, and in litigation, or challenging government action in the courts.

The term *nonprofit* typically refers to organizations that "provide goods or service but are neither private businesses nor government operated" (Vaughn and Arsneault 2013, 4). Many nonprofits can and do operate much like interest groups in that they attempt to influence or advocate for policy that is important to them. There are tax implications that affect the kinds of activities that these organizations can pursue. Many readers may have heard of 501(c)(3) tax-exempt organizations. To maintain this status, nonprofits need to be careful about their involvement in the policy process, but to be clear they are important players. According to Vaughn and Arsneault (2013), nonprofits and public policy interact in four primary ways: they make policy, they influence policy, they are affected by policy, and they are subject to policy governing operations.

Lobbying is probably the most visible group activity, but it is not what people often suspect—illegal pressure of some kind. Groups lobby legislators mainly by supplying information on their policy views or summaries of policy-related studies they or others have conducted. They may testify in legislative committee hearings, meet with individual members or their staffs, and urge their members and supporters to write or call legislators (Levine 2009). All of this activity generally is intended to support policy proposals the group favors, oppose those it does not, or keep certain issues or policy alternatives on or off the legislative agenda. Groups also lobby executive branch agencies by submitting studies and recommendations during formal public comment periods on proposed regulations, as well as through frequent and informal communication with agency officials.

In both the legislative and executive arenas, a great deal of interest group activity consists of trying to block proposals (Kingdon 1995). A good example is the intense efforts by lobbyists to seek financial help as part of the historic federal economic revitalization measures of 2008 and 2009, including the Big Three automakers. More recently, the health care sector and health insurance sector were very active during deliberations that ultimately led to the passing

Working with Sources

Interest Group Policy Strategies

Organized interest groups are pervasive in the policy process. Public interest groups tend to lobby for activities they believe will benefit the entire population. In contrast, special interest groups, particularly economic but also sometimes ideological, support actions that tend to benefit only members of their organization. To examine some of these differences more fully, go to the website of the National Rifle Association (nra.org), and under the Menu tab, select Politics & Legislation and then NRA-ILA. From here, you can click on the Menu and then Issues. Select one of these and read some of the information on this issue. Now go to any of a number of gun control organizations

such as Coalition to Stop Gun Violence (csgv.org) or Americans for Responsible Solutions (americansfor-responsiblesolutions.org) and read their perspective regarding gun control issues. Consider the following:

- Is it clear from the two organizations' mission statements whom the organizations represent?

- What do the groups state are their primary goals regarding the regulation of guns, the Second Amendment, or related issues? Do they mention recent accomplishments? If so, what are they, and how might such achievements affect their membership?

- What kinds of political tactics do these groups use to promote their ideals? Are there any differences between them?

of the Affordable Care Act. For example, insurance companies lobbied hard for the individual mandate under that act. The mandate helped to provide financial security to the industry as it faced changing practices and decision making on coverage. The box "Working with Sources: Interest Group Policy Strategies" explores the mission, activities, and achievements of two prominent organizations, one usually described as a public interest group and the other as a special interest group.

Many groups issue studies, reports, and news releases. They sometimes produce commercials that air on television and radio or appear in newspapers, on webpages, and on social media and are intended to educate the public. That is, groups provide information and perspectives on public policy issues and try to win the public to their side. Many interest groups participate actively in the electoral process. They openly endorse candidates for office, contribute money and other resources to their campaigns, and sponsor issue advocacy advertisements that are intended to affect voters' opinions on the issues and, the groups hope, their votes. These efforts are aimed at getting people who are sympathetic to the particular group's positions elected or reelected and defeating those who oppose its positions. Groups also use litigation as a policy tool. They may file a suit against an agency because of a ruling or regulation and try to get the courts to change the policy.

The lobbying directed at executive agencies is often intense; after all, the businesses and other groups have a great deal at stake. When administrative agencies implement policy, they write rules and regulations, including specific

Interested in policymaking. Organized interest groups play a major role in policymaking through lobbying of public officials. The photo shows Guy "Bud" Tribble, vice president of software technology at Apple Inc., testifying as Alan Davidson, director of public policy at Google Inc., center, and Jonathan Zuck, president of the Association for Competitive Technology, listen during a hearing of the Senate Judiciary Committee's Subcommittee on Privacy, Technology, and the Law in Washington, D.C. The subject of the hearing was customer rights to privacy as companies such as Apple and Google have made use of location data gathered from millions of smartphones. *(Brendan Smialowski/ Bloomberg via Getty Images)*

standards that affect business operations. These rules can have a major impact on business and industry, as well as on ordinary citizens. The federal Administrative Procedure Act of 1946 (APA) requires that the rulemaking process follow due process of law and be open and fair. Because of the importance of these administrative decisions, interest groups often discuss the issues informally with agency officials (Kerwin and Furlong 2011; Kraft and Kamieniecki 2007). For example, during 2015–2016, many industry representatives (and others) were keenly interested in a new Department of Labor regulation that increased overtime eligibility to millions of additional people. The proposed rule generated comments from 270,000 individuals and organizations.[18] Business, labor, and other interests act more formally through the rulemaking process as well, particularly when a proposed rule or regulation is open to public comment. The APA requires that agencies considering the issuance of regulations first propose them and allow for public comments before adopting and implementing them. The content of these comments varies widely, ranging from opinions on the rule's importance to extensive analysis of the rule's likely consequences, technical merits, costs, and benefits. Although anyone may provide comments to administrative agencies under these circumstances, the vast majority of comments come from interest groups that are directly affected by the agency's policy. Therefore, if the FAA proposes a rule to require that all children under the age of two be seated in a child safety seat on airplanes, one would expect the airlines, and perhaps groups representing consumers, to provide most of the public comments.

The role of interest groups in the U.S. system of government is important for understanding the policymaking process. It also raises questions that are fundamental to a democracy. For example, are ordinary citizens well represented in the activities of interest groups, or do certain groups and segments of the population, such as corporate interests and wealthy citizens, have privileged access at the expense of others? To what extent should the activities of interest groups be restricted in some way to promote policy developments that serve the public interest? There is little question that interest groups are omnipresent and highly influential in the policy process at all levels of government and within all branches. Yet analysts disagree on whether such restrictions would promote the public's interest or are consistent with constitutional guarantees of assembly and free speech (Berry 1997; Cigler and Loomis 2015).

Media

The First Amendment to the Constitution states that "Congress shall make no law . . . abridging the freedom of speech, or of the press," among other elements. In the United States, we value not only our freedom of speech but also the assurance that freedom of the press is protected. Democratic theorists would argue both are necessary for a well-functioning democracy. The media today play an interesting and evolving role in the policy process. At the most basic level, the media report information that helps to inform the citizenry about the politics of the day and the policies being debated and passed. This information helps shape public opinion regarding these policies. The media also can influence the policy agenda by the way they cover news stories and politics, perhaps picking up on a story and bringing it to the public's attention in such a way that raises its importance and sparks activity on the issue.

A full history of the evolution of the news media and their role in public policymaking is beyond the purposes of this section. It is important to realize, though, the significant change in the amount of media coverage, how we as citizens access this information, and the different media forums that transmit this information to us. For most of our history, news coverage occurred at set times of the day—the morning paper and the nightly news broadcast, which to some extent still exist today. But the media now constitute a twenty-four-hour, seven-day-a-week business with each media network trying to outscoop the other. Many citizens now receive their news from the web on their own time rather than waiting for the nightly newscast. The growth in the forms of media has also created outlets that tend to tailor their broadcasts to certain ideological audiences. For example, Fox News appeals to conservative viewers and MSNBC to liberals (Jamieson and Cappella 2008).

The changing nature of how we get our news showcases the importance of critically evaluating information and the sources from which it comes. Many organizations and businesses are funding their own "media" outlets to get certain kinds of information out as a way to sway public opinion. On the right, the Koch brothers have been one of the more active in this regard, and on the left, George Soros does the same. Of course, relying on just the one traditional source of news, as many did when they would watch Walter Cronkite present the evening news on CBS in the 1960s and 1970s, also can be problematic, as it might result in filtering or distortion of some news and a lack of informational depth. National newscasts only last about twenty-two minutes, and as a result, each story covered typically receives only a couple of minutes of coverage before the news anchors move on to the next story. For a different perspective and more in-depth coverage, readers may want to try watching *PBS NewsHour*.

One issue that came to the forefront during the 2016 election is the role of fake news. Stories from these sources often will "report" on some damaging characteristic or erroneous perspective. The hope by these sources is that it generates enough "buzz" and discussion so that many people believe the story is true. Even after being discredited by more legitimate sources, many people still believe the original, inaccurate or fake story. When these stories are picked up by social media sites such as Facebook, they potentially have a wide audience that may believe in the story because it appears to be from a legitimate source. This is why it is so important to know your sources and have a good understanding about the facts as you are evaluating policies and policymakers.

Media influence. As different forms of media have grown, so too have outlets tailored to audiences of a particular ideology. The photo shows television host Rachel Maddow on November 6, 2016, during election coverage. Maddow's news program on MSNBC attracts a loyal following of liberals, much as Fox News attracts a conservative audience. *(AP Photo/Chuck Burton, File)*

Policy Subgovernments and Issue Networks

Much policymaking occurs in less formal settings or venues and involves policy actors within particular issue areas, such as national defense, communications, agriculture, forestry, or energy. Political scientists refer to these informal arrangements as **subgovernments** or **issue networks** (Heclo 1978; Lowi 1979; McConnell 1966; McCool 1990). *Iron triangles* was another term often used to describe these arrangements because of the supposed power and autonomy of their three components: congressional subcommittees, an executive agency, and an outside economic interest group, such as cotton farmers or oil companies. These subgovernments usually operate under the radar of most citizens and are less likely than the more formal institutions to be influenced by citizen values or policy preferences.

The reality is that decision making about many programs and policies tends to be highly specialized. Because of the complexity of public problems and policies, and the often detailed knowledge required to understand them, specialization will no doubt continue to be the norm. One group of policy actors specializes in health care policy; another quite different group acts in defense policy, financial regulation, or environmental protection. Each develops its own distinctive channels of communication, even terminology, to discuss policy issues. The areas of specialization, and the people and institutions active in them, are known as issue networks, subgovernments, or subsystems to reflect the fact that decision making takes place below the level of the full system of government (J. Anderson 2015; J. Freeman 1965; Thurber 1996a). For example, defense procurement decision making (how much to spend on weapons systems and which ones to buy) involves the congressional armed services committees, the Department of Defense, and the private defense contractors who build the weapons. All tend to favor increased spending for defense, and they work together toward provision of defense systems, usually without much involvement, oversight, or criticism by those who are not part of the subgovernment or network.

Historically, the subgovernments have been exceptionally powerful in setting U.S. policy, particularly in areas of limited interest to the general public, such as agricultural subsidies, mining and forestry, weapons procurement, and highway and dam construction. Today, however, the subgovernments are less autonomous and generally operate with more visibility and "outside" participation. More policy actors are involved, sometimes hundreds of different institutions and individuals. Use of the term *issue network* rather than *subgovernment* reflects this evolution in U.S. policymaking (Heclo 1978). Nevertheless, these networks or subsystems are still important. To varying degrees, their participants remain preoccupied with narrow economic interests; they may afford limited participation beyond the core members; and they may be able to resist external influences (J. Anderson 2015). If nothing else, it is clear that much U.S. policymaking involves informal networks of communication in which prevailing policy ideas and the evaluation of new studies and information shape what is likely to be acceptable to the major policy actors (Kingdon 1995). Fortunately for students of public policy, it is much easier today to gain access to those networks and to see what the specialized policy communities are considering and where change may be possible.

Improving Policy Capacity

This chapter demonstrates that the design of U.S. government institutions and the conflicting demands of the nation's citizens make governing a difficult, though by no means impossible, task. The history of U.S. public policy development in many areas, as we will show in chapters 7 through 12, indicates a robust capacity for policy formulation, adoption, and implementation. The proof is in the extensive collection of public policies in operation today. Much the same can be said about the policy capacity of state and local governments. Although some are clearly more capable than others, considerable policy innovation and successful implementation are apparent at this level as well (Borins 1998; Hedge 1998).

Does policy capacity need to be improved? Almost certainly. By any measure, the challenges that governments at all levels will face in the future will require an even greater ability than they now possess to analyze complex problems and develop solutions. Whether the problems are worldwide terrorism, economic recessions, natural hazards such as hurricanes, or global climate change—or whether they are public needs for education, health care, and other social services—governments will have to do a better job of responding to these needs.

Consider one example. When a devastating hurricane struck New Orleans and other Gulf Coast areas in September 2005, critics described the responses by federal, state, and local governments as woefully inadequate. Hurricane Katrina killed over one thousand people and left a far larger number injured or homeless, many of them residents of poor and minority communities. The storm also destroyed countless businesses. Government agencies had to drain severely flooded neighborhoods, restore public services over a wide area, assist hundreds of thousands of residents displaced by the storm, and rebuild damaged levees and other structures across a wide stretch of the Gulf Coast. It was perhaps the worst natural disaster in U.S. history in terms of economic impact, costing between $100 billion and $150 billion, according to the Congressional Budget Office (CBO).[19] While governments cannot prevent hurricanes, they can do much to improve their capacities for emergency preparedness and disaster relief. One lesson from Katrina is that governments might have avoided the enormous human and economic toll had they made smarter decisions over the previous decade. The response to Hurricane Sandy in 2012 suggests that at least some lessons were learned, and the governmental response was much better. Similarly, after devastating floods in Louisiana in 2016, government agencies responded quickly to rescue stranded victims and provide aid in the rebuilding of homes and businesses.

What about the capacity of citizens to participate in public life? Here too there is much that can be done, and we will return to the subject in chapter 13. In brief, it is easy to argue that in a democracy, citizens should be given extensive opportunities to participate in policymaking. Yet some analysts worry that citizens have too little time and too little interest to inform themselves on the issues so that they can participate effectively. Others focus on what measures might be taken to assist citizens in learning more about the issues and encourage their participation. From either perspective, questions arise. For example, is it a good idea to create more state and local referendums to allow direct citizen participation in lawmaking? Many cities and states do that, and as we stated earlier, some highly innovative policies have been enacted through such direct citizen participation. But there is also a risk that such direct democracy can fuel public prejudice and allow special interest groups to have undue influence on the results (Cronin 1989; Ellis 2002).

So what is the best way to encourage citizen participation in government processes? It seems clear that additional citizen participation may enhance policy capacity at the state and local levels, but some programs designed to involve citizens are more effective than others. Most scholars today recognize the desirability of going beyond the conventional hearings and public meetings to offer more direct and meaningful citizen access to policymaking. Citizen advisory committees, citizen panels, and similar mechanisms foster more intense citizen engagement with the issues (Beierle and Cayford 2002). Governments at all levels continue to endorse collaborative decision making with local and regional stakeholders, especially on issues of urban planning and management, natural resource use, and the like.

Whatever the form of public involvement, its effectiveness needs to be considered. Increasing citizens' voices in policymaking can come at some cost in terms of the expediency of policy development and implementation. In other words, it can slow down the policy process and make it more difficult to resolve conflicts. Even with these qualifications, however, the successful involvement of the public in local and regional problem-solving processes, and in electoral processes, is encouraging for the future. Enhancing civic engagement in these ways might even help to reverse a long pattern of citizen withdrawal, not only from politics but also from communities (Bok 2001; Putnam 2000; Skocpol and Fiorina 1999). The enormous outpouring of support for Barack Obama in the 2008 presidential election, particularly by young voters, testifies to the potential of greater citizen involvement in the future, and also to the diversity of mechanisms for such involvement, from traditional organizational politics to web-based recruitment, fund-raising, and communication (Dalton 2009; McKenna and Han 2014).

Conclusions

This chapter covers a lot of ground, from the growth of government over time to the constitutional design for U.S. government to the way policy actors within the major institutions interact when dealing with public problems and policymaking. Government growth is a direct result of the increases in public policies that have been adopted in the United States throughout history. To fully understand the development of policy, we must pay attention to the various actors in our formal government systems and how they all have a role in making or obstructing policy. In addition, how people interact in this political and governmental process is a key factor in explaining if policy gets made at all and the policy choice that follows. In a democratic system of government, these actors outside the formal government structure, such as interest groups, the media, and citizens themselves, also influence the policy process. Understanding how these actors get involved in the policy process is important in explaining how and why policy gets made. It is also through both the formal and informal actors that individuals can get involved and help to move policy in a particular direction.

All of these factors help to explain why governing is so difficult, and why policy gridlock occurs so often. But the same factors also highlight the many strengths of the U.S. political system, particularly the opportunities it provides for citizens and organized groups to participate in the policy process and shape the decisions that are made. These strengths are found at all levels of government, but especially in the states' growing policy capacity and their efforts at policy innovation in recent years. Knowing how government is organized and makes decisions is the foundation for the study of public policy, but equally important is understanding the political incentives that motivate and influence how policy actors, both governmental and nongovernmental, relate to one another in the policy process. Armed with these tools, students of public policy can see why government sometimes works and sometimes does not, and what needs to be done to improve government's capacity for analyzing public problems and developing solutions to them. In the same vein, the chapter suggests that few changes would do more to enhance democracy than finding ways for U.S. citizens to become better informed about public policy and more engaged with government and the policy process.

Sharpen your skills with SAGE edge at http://edge.sagepub.com/ kraft6e. SAGE edge for students provides a personalized approach to help you accomplish your coursework goals in an easy-to-use learning environment.

DISCUSSION QUESTIONS

1. Do you think the U.S. government's system of checks and balances is a detriment to policymaking? Why or why not? Do the current partisan battles suggest that we may need to adjust our policymaking system? What might be done?

2. Under what conditions might states be better positioned to take the lead in making policy? Conversely, when should the federal government take the lead? Think about some current issues such as education standards, immigration, and gun control policy. Which level of government may be best positioned to address these issues?

3. Was the Obama administration effective during its tenure in policy development? Discuss some of

the major successes and failures and what factors contributed to the successes or failures.

4. Is the American public capable of playing a more active role in the policymaking process than it currently does? Or would greater public involvement in policymaking pose risks to the quality of decision making? Why do you think so?

5. What role does interest group information play in policymaking? What do you see as the potential positives and negatives of having groups provide this information to policymakers? What might policymakers want to take into account when receiving information and data from interest groups?

KEYWORDS

bicameral   52
block grants   47
cabinet-level departments   55

categorical grants   47
circuit courts of
    appeals   59

cooperative federalism   47
decentralization   48
dual federalism   47

SUGGESTED READINGS

Sandford Borins, *Innovating with Integrity: How Local Heroes Are Transforming American Government* (Washington, D.C.: Georgetown University Press, 1998). An analysis of the potential for state and local government policy innovation, with examples of successful action.

Ann O'M. Bowman and Richard C. Kearney, *State and Local Government*, 9th ed. (Florence, Ky.: Cengage, 2014). A leading text on government and politics in the American states.

Allan J. Cigler and Burdett A. Loomis, eds., *Interest Group Politics*, 9th ed. (Washington, D.C.: CQ Press, 2015). A leading volume on interest group activity in U.S. politics. Includes some of the best current work in the field.

Roger H. Davidson, Walter J. Oleszek, Frances E. Lee, and Eric Schickler, *Congress and Its Members*, 15th ed. (Washington, D.C.: CQ Press, 2016). The leading text on Congress and a treasure trove of information on the role of Congress in policymaking.

James A. Thurber, *Rivals for Power: Presidential-Congressional Relations*, 5th ed. (Lanham, Md.: Rowman and Littlefield, 2013).

SUGGESTED WEBSITES

www.ciser.cornell.edu/info/polls.shtml. Cornell University website that lists all major public opinion companies, with links to the Gallup organization, Roper Center for Public Opinion Research, *Washington Post*, Pew Research Center, and American National Election Studies at Stanford University and the University of Michigan. Includes the major state and regional polling organizations.

www.congress.gov. Official source for federal legislative information.

www.csg.org. Council of State Governments, with links to a wide range of data and policy issues affecting the states.

www.publicagenda.org. A nonpartisan opinion research organization website that includes reports from national firms on public policy issues such as race, health care, privacy, drug abuse, crime, the economy, poverty, welfare, the environment, immigration, and others. Includes a good collection of colorful graphs, tables, and advice on how to read public opinion polls.

www.usa.gov. Federal government web portal, with links to online services for citizens, businesses, and governments, and links to federal, state, local, and tribal government agencies. Includes links to all fifty state government home pages and national associations dealing with state and local issues.

www.uscourts.gov. Portal to the U.S. judiciary system.

www.whitehouse.gov. White House home page, with links to the president's stand on various policy issues, news, appointments, speeches, and more.

NOTES

1. See Michael D. Shear, Julie Hirschfeld Davis, and Gardiner Harris, "Obama Chooses Merrick Garland for Supreme Court," *New York Times*, March 16, 2016.

2. See Reuters, "Two GOP Senators Say They'll Consider Garland after Election," *Newsweek*, March 17, 2016, available at www.newsweek .com/orrin-hatch-jeff-flake-merrick-garland-election-438069.

3. For information regarding trust in government, see the Pew Research Center for the People and the Press's ongoing efforts to track public disenchantment at www.people-press.org/2015/11/23/beyond-distrust-how-americans-view-their-government/. Another measure relates to public approval of how Congress is handling its job. Only 18 percent approved in August 2016. For this information, see the Gallup poll data at www .gallup.com/poll/1600/congress-public.aspx.

4. For information on federal employment statistics, see U.S. Census Bureau, specifically the section available at www.census.gov/govs/apes/.

5. Measuring the size of government is not easy. Should it include only government employees or also count those in the private sector who produce goods and services for the government under contract? For an assessment of government size, see Paul C. Light, *The True Size of Government* (Washington, D.C.: Brookings Institution, 1999); and Christopher Lee, "Big Government Gets Bigger: Study Counts More Employees, Cites Increase in Contractors," *Washington Post,* October 6, 2006. See also Scott Shane, "In Washington, Contractors Take on Biggest Role Ever," *New York Times*, February 4, 2007. The *Times* article provides detailed estimates of the rise in contractor activities in the 2000s; the amounts spent on their contracts; and other actions by contractors, such as money they spent on lobbying and on campaign contributions.

6. See Chris Cillizza, "Did Republican Gerrymandering Cause the Government Shutdown?" *Washington Post*, October 9, 2013; Nate Silver, "As Swing Districts Dwindle, Can a Divided House Stand?" *New York Times*, December 2, 2012; Griff Palmer and Michael Cooper, "How Maps Helped Republicans Keep an Edge in the House," *New York Times*, December 12, 2012; and Sam Wang, "The Great Gerrymander of 2012," *New York Times*, February 3, 2013.

7. Redistricting decisions affect what happens with state legislative branches as well. In late 2016, a federal court ruled that the Wisconsin legislature's redrawing of state assembly districts to favor Republicans was an unconstitutional gerrymander. See Michael Wines, "Judges Find Wisconsin Redistricting Unfairly Favored Republicans," *New York Times*, November 21, 2016.

8. For many policy activities, Native American tribes constitute sovereign entities that deal directly with the federal government rather than with the states where tribal land is located.

9. In addition to state policies preventing smoking in restaurants and other public places, many localities have passed ordinances to do the same.

10. See "President Power," *CQ Researcher*, vol. 25, issue 10 (March 6, 2015).

11. In addition to the 435 members, the House of Representatives has four delegates and a resident commissioner, bringing the total to 440. These five positions were created by statute. Puerto Rico elects a commissioner, and Congress has approved nonvoting delegates for the District of Columbia, Guam, the Virgin Islands, and American Samoa. See Roger H. Davidson, Walter J. Oleszek, Frances E. Lee, and Eric Schickler, *Congress and Its Members*, 15th ed. (Washington, D.C.: CQ Press, 2016).

12. See Avery Palmer, "Protecting Dinosaur Fossils Takes Ages Too," *CQ Weekly* online edition, May 19, 2008, 1307–1317.

13. See Rick Weiss, "Political Science: HHS Panels Are Made Over in Bush's Image," *Washington Post National Weekly Edition*, September 23–29, 2002. See also Sheryl Gay Stolberg, "Bush's Science

Advisers Drawing Criticism," *New York Times*, October 10, 2002.

14. Senator Reid's graph implied that the eighty-six nominees prior to President Obama represented all presidents before Obama, but further analysis by PolitiFact found that cloture motions to end filibusters started in 1949. PolitiFact stated that Senator Reid's claim was "Mostly True." See Louis Jacobson, "Harry Reid Says 82 Presidential Nominees Have Been Blocked under President Barack Obama, 86 Blocked under All Other Presidents," *PolitiFact*, November 22, 2013, available at www.politifact.com/truth-o-meter/statements/2013/nov/22/harry-reid/harry-reid-says-82-presidential-nominees-have-been/.

15. See Charlie Savage, "Appeals Courts Pushed to Right by Bush Choices," *New York Times*, October 29, 2008.

16. For those interested in examining other information on lobbying data and campaign contributions, see the site sponsored by the Center for Responsive Politics (CRP) at www.opensecrets.org.

17. See Julie Kosterlitz, "Google on the Potomac," *National Journal,* June 21, 2008, 54–55; and Edward Wyatt, "Google's Washington Insider," *New York Times*, June 2, 2013.

18. See 29 C.F.R. Part 541.

19. The CBO estimate combines costs for Hurricane Katrina and Hurricane Rita, a less damaging storm that struck several weeks later. See "Statement of Douglas Holtz-Eakin, Director, Macroeconomic and Budgetary Effects of Hurricanes Katrina and Rita," testimony before the Committee on the Budget, U.S. House of Representatives, Congressional Budget Office, October 6, 2005.

Chapter 3

Chapter Objectives

- Describe different theories of public policy and how they help to explain the decisions made.

- Discuss the policy process model, from the steps associated with making public policy to the role of policy analysis in the design and formulation of policy actions and the evaluation of policies.

- Assess different types of public policy and how their characteristics affect their development and treatment in the policy process.

- Define the types of government functions and evaluate basic differences among policies and the political conditions that lead to them.

Making changes to policy. U.S. president Barack Obama and Vice President Joe Biden place flowers for the victims of the mass shooting at a gay nightclub at a memorial at the Dr. Phillips Center for the Performing Arts in Orlando, Florida, June 16, 2016. The Orlando shooting sparked new concern over both gay rights and how to limit gun violence in America. *(SAUL LOEB/AFP/Getty Images)*

Understanding Public Policymaking

On June 12, 2016, a gunman opened fire in a gay nightclub in Orlando, Florida. It was the worst mass shooting in the history of the United States, claiming forty-nine lives and injuring fifty-three more people. The gunman was armed with an assault weapon along with a handgun in what was described as a pure hate crime against the lesbian, gay, bisexual, transgender, and questioning (LGBTQ) community. This attack followed a number of high-profile mass shootings in the United States, including one in San Bernardino, California, that killed fourteen people in 2015 and the terrible assault at Sandy Hook Elementary School in Newtown, Connecticut, where twenty-six people were killed in 2012.[1] The Orlando gunman was apparently on the terror watch list, but was able to purchase the weapons legally.

President Obama, as he had for previous mass shootings, gave a heartfelt speech noting the tremendous loss to the families and community. He also continued to question the ease with which such a person might obtain a weapon: "This massacre is therefore a further reminder of how easy it is for someone to get their hands on a weapon that lets them shoot people in a school, or in a house of worship, or a movie theater, or in a nightclub. And we have to decide if that's the kind of country we want to be. And to actively do nothing is a decision as well."[2] As has happened often in response to such gun violence, many public officials began raising the issue of whether to adopt more stringent gun-control laws and regulations and questioning the general gun culture of the United States. Late-night television hosts John Oliver and Samantha Bee (and others) addressed these questions in a very direct way during broadcasts of their shows following the event. The National Rifle Association (NRA) also responded in a somewhat typical way by stating that "radical Islamic terrorists are not deterred by gun control laws. . . . The only way to defeat them is to destroy them—not destroy the right of law-abiding Americans to defend ourselves."[3]

Given that 2016 was an election year, both major party candidates had their perspective on this issue as well, and their comments generally followed what one might expect. Republican nominee Donald Trump basically took the same position as the NRA, and Democratic nominee Hillary Clinton discussed potential policies for additional control of guns. But the real interesting political activity occurred on the Senate and House floors of Congress. Senator Christopher Murphy, D-Conn., led a fifteen-hour filibuster on the Senate floor on gun violence. Senator Murphy and fellow Democrats held the floor to force a vote on gun control measures. A few days later, Democrats within the House of Representatives, led by civil rights leader John Lewis, D-Ga., staged a sit-in on the House floor, lasting over twenty-four hours, and demanded that the House leadership allow a vote on gun control. The political acrimony over the gun control issue was very clear.

What we are potentially seeing in the gun control debate represents some examples of how dramatic events, such as a highly visible public shooting, and changes to the political environment brought on by a presidential election or shifts within Congress can cause adjustments in policy proposals and actions. This occurs often within the policy context. Media coverage of a mass shooting, a natural disaster, or a terrorist attack reaches the public, key interest groups, and policymakers, and they begin to reconsider existing policies and programs. Our current homeland security and airline safety polices are a direct result of the terrorist attacks of September 11, 2001. Changes in food safety policy often follow major food recalls as attention is focused anew on food production and preparation practices that can make people ill. This process is not surprising in that problems such as food safety often are out of the public light and do not engender much attention until there is a real (or perceived) threat that may require more or different government action and people demand governmental action.

Of course, many other factors can influence the development of policies beyond the existence of a dramatic event such as a mass shooting, terrorist attack, or accident. The political process discussed in chapter 2 plays a large role in policy development, and so too does public opinion. For example, as it relates to gun control, the media as well as those supporting gun control measures often cited opinion polls stating that a strong majority of Americans favored stricter gun control policies, such as more thorough background checks before purchase of a weapon. Of course, those opposed to such policies argue that the right to gun ownership is protected by the Second Amendment to the Constitution and thus should not be affected by the majority's opinion. These kinds of developments and arguments showcase what can happen to the policy agenda when unexpected and striking events and perhaps shifts in opinion lead policymakers to address certain issues—in this case whether to change gun control policies. Policy and political analysts often study these kinds of developments to learn more about how and why decisions are made within the political and bureaucratic arenas.

A different but related kind of policy development occurred when Republican members of Congress sought repeatedly to roll back the 2010 Affordable Care Act, or Obamacare. The extraordinary level of news coverage of those efforts brought concerns over policy gridlock and decision making to the forefront of national debate. The new attention to these matters also raised intriguing questions about the process of policymaking: How do such conflicts and media coverage of them affect decisions about policies and budgets? What role do interest groups, such as those representing business interests that were actually pushing Republicans to ease back on their demands, play in these discussions and decisions? In the end, what most influenced members of Congress in making these decisions: their own political ideologies, constituency views, the stance of business and other interest groups, their sense of how their votes might affect their reelection chances, or the broader public opinion in the nation?

In short, what does this kind of experience tell us about the larger forces that shape policy decisions at any level of government, and about the capacity of both major political parties today to facilitate agreement on public policy to resolve such conflicts and demonstrate to citizens that government can indeed address their concerns in a constructive and bipartisan manner? We try to address these kinds of questions in this chapter as we turn to how we study the policymaking process. Knowing something about agenda setting, policy formulation, policy legitimization, and policy implementation can help in understanding why certain problems get addressed and others do not, and how politics in the broadest sense influences the decisions that are made.

Chapter 2 showed how the structure and rules of U.S. government institutions create certain political incentives that push policymakers toward the kinds of decisions they make as they focus on one policy problem or another and choose what to do about it. This chapter introduces several theories that further explain why policymakers reach decisions like these. After a brief consideration of five competing approaches, the chapter focuses on the policy process model or framework, which is widely used in the study of public policy. It is particularly helpful for clarifying the role of policy analysis in the design and formulation of the most appropriate policy actions government can take and for evaluating how well those policies work once they are implemented.

As we argued in chapter 2, policymaking in the U.S. political system is inherently difficult because of the institutional dispersal of power, the multiplicity of policy actors, and the sharp conflicts that often arise over what policy actions to take. Policy analysis can help to resolve the conflicts by clarifying the issues and bringing reliable information to bear on the decision-making process. It is especially useful when dealing with complex public problems—such as economic forecasts—that are not easy to understand and when policymakers need to make the best estimates they can about a proposal's likely effectiveness, costs, and fairness.

Theories of Politics and Public Policy

Social scientists use theories and models—abstract representations of the real world—to understand the way things work. They can create meaning out of what otherwise might seem to be a complicated and chaotic world in which nothing makes sense and all acts seemingly are random. Theories generally attempt to explain why certain things happen the way they do—in the case of policy theories, why certain policies are adopted. Models tend to be more descriptive in nature and are less concerned with explanation. The theories discussed here pertain to the world of government, politics, and public policy, and they provide the concepts and language that facilitate communication with others about these subjects. They also help to focus people's attention on the most important factors that affect government decision making. Political scientists use several different theories and models to explain and describe the nature of policymaking and the policies that result. Among the most common are elite theory, group theory, institutional theory, rational choice theory, political systems theory, and the policy process model (J. Anderson 2015; Birkland 2016; McCool 1995).

Each offers a different perspective on the principal determinants of decision making within government and, therefore, on what people might regard as the major forces that shape the direction and content of public policies. Social scientists use these theories to explain politics and policymaking, and students can use them to better understand how policies are made and why we get one policy rather than another. In other words, when asked why the United States has one kind of economic, agricultural, health care, or education policy and not another, the answer depends in part on which theory is used to offer insights into these choices.

Elite Theory

Elite theory emphasizes how the values and preferences of governing elites, which differ from those of the public at large, affect public policy development. The primary assumption of elite theory is that the values and preferences of the general public are less influential in shaping public policy than those of a smaller, unrepresentative group of people, or elites (Dye 2001; Schubert, Dye, and Zeigler 2014). These policy actors may be economic elites—foundations, wealthy people, corporate executives, oil companies, Wall Street investment bankers, and professionals such as physicians or attorneys—who some research has found have particular influence on public policy even when "majorities of the American public actually have little influence over the policies our government adopts" (Gilens and Page 2014, 577). They may be cultural elites, such as celebrated actors, filmmakers, recording artists, or other media stars. Elected officials constitute an elite as well, as do other influential policy actors, such as scientists and policy analysts. Elite theory, then, focuses on the role of leaders and leadership in the development of public policy.

We can see the application of elite theory by looking at those who dominate public policy decisions. A single power elite or establishment is seldom at the center of all policy decisions, because different elites tend to dominate in different policy areas. For example, one elite may be influential in foreign policy, another in defense policy, and others in areas as diverse as health care, agriculture, financial regulation, energy, and education. One elite may compete with another to win attention for its concerns or to secure a superior level of funding for the programs it favors. Still, by emphasizing the power of these groups, elite theory demonstrates that the U.S. policymaking process may not be as democratic as many believe it to be. For example, critics of President George W. Bush's energy and environmental policies were convinced that they were shaped with the interests of a corporate elite in mind, particularly one representing large manufacturers; oil and natural gas producers; electric power companies; and mining, timber, and similar interest groups (Kraft and Kamieniecki 2007). At the same time, conservatives often blame the liberal cultural elites of Hollywood and New York for what they see as lax moral standards in today's society. More recently, as the economic recovery in the United States failed to extend to middle- and working-class citizens, and public resentment over economic stagnation and high unemployment rates grew, we saw a twist on elite theory. The Occupy Wall Street movement and its variations around the nation highlighted the enormous inequities in income and wealth, symbolized by reference to the privileged "1 percent" of the population in comparison to the lives of the "99 percent." That perspective found its voice in Bernie Sanders's campaign for the Democratic Party nomination in 2016.

The role of different elites is particularly evident in the subgovernments or issue networks described in chapter 2 (Baumgartner and Jones 1993; Kingdon 1995; McCool 1990). This kind of elite dominance is in part a function of the low salience of policymaking within these subgovernments or issue networks. Most people outside of the narrow circles who are concerned about any given policy area, such as the Federal Communications Commission's regulation of the television and telecommunication industries, would have little reason to pay attention to the issues or to participate in policy decisions. In fact, most members of Congress also tend to defer to their colleagues who work regularly on these issues. Much the same can be said for the advice and influence that legislators seek from agribusiness on U.S. farm policy, the defense industry on weapons procurement policy, and pharmaceutical companies on health care policy. Parallels to these kinds of subgovernments, or narrow policy communities, also exist at state and local levels.

Group Theory

Group theory sees public policy as the product of a continuous struggle among organized interest groups (Baumgartner and Leech 1998; Cigler and Loomis 2015). In contrast to elite theory, supporters of group theory, particularly those who call themselves "pluralists," tend to believe that power in the U.S. political system is widely shared among interest groups, each of which seeks access to the policymaking process. That is, they say power is pluralistic rather than concentrated in only a few elites. In this view, some groups provide countervailing power to others—for example, labor unions versus manufacturing interests—as they lobby legislators and executive officials and appeal to the broader public through issue advocacy campaigns. This balance helps to ensure that no one group dominates the policy process. It is reasonable to assume, however, that the groups with greater financial resources, recognition, access to policymakers, and prestige are likely to have more influence than others. At the opposite end of the spectrum are those people—such as the poor and homeless—who are not well organized, lack significant political resources, and are inadequately represented in the policymaking process. When people speak of "special interests" influencing government decisions, they are using the concepts of group theory. Examples include what we discussed at the beginning of the chapter with efforts by the NRA to protect Second Amendment rights, and by the food industry to prevent government from requiring manufacturers to provide even more details about the ingredients in processed foods, an action long favored by consumer groups, particularly with rising concern over both adult and childhood obesity in the nation.[4]

A modern variant of interest group theory, the **advocacy coalition framework** (ACF), focuses on the "interactions of competing advocacy coalitions," particularly within a policy subsystem such as agriculture, telecommunications, energy, or environmental protection (Sabatier and Jenkins-Smith 1993). Each coalition consists of policy actors from different public and private institutions and different levels of government who share a particular set of beliefs about the policies that government should promote. In the clash between advocates for health care reform and health insurance companies, for example, each coalition tries to manipulate government processes to achieve its goals over time. Whether and to what degree the coalitions reach their objectives depends on forces in the rest of the political system and the larger society and economy that either provide opportunities or present obstacles. The ACF posits that policy change can occur over time, as each coalition uses its resources to change the views or policy beliefs of leading policy actors. Proving this concept, environmentalists to some extent have persuaded the business community to think about long-term goals of sustainable development. In turn, the business community has been able to persuade many actors in this policy arena that new policy approaches such as market incentives, collaboration, and information provision are more attractive than conventional regulation, which they view as burdensome and ineffective (Mazmanian and Kraft 2009; Vig and Kraft 2016).

Many students of public policy argue that group theory tends to exaggerate the role and influence of organized interest groups in policymaking and to underestimate the leadership of public officials and the considerable discretion they have in making policy choices. It is easy to believe that lurking behind every policy decision is a special interest group eager to have its way, but assigning too much power to organized groups oversimplifies a more complex dynamic in policymaking. Public officials also frequently use organized interest groups to promote their own political agendas and to build support for policy initiatives. The relationship between groups and policymakers is often a subtle, two-way exercise of influence (Kraft and Kamieniecki 2007).

When specific industries decide to lobby for or against a particular policy, they often become critical actors in the policymaking process. One example is support for the production of ethanol. As fuel prices increased in the 2000s, ethanol industries and many farmers' groups in states such as Iowa lobbied hard and successfully for legislation to encourage ethanol production through federal subsidies. But as food prices increased sharply in 2008 and subsequent years, organizations such as the Grocery Manufacturers Association were critical of these policies, which they argued were responsible for rising food prices.[5] Both of these perspectives have been important in the discussion of ethanol as an alternative fuel and the potential consequences associated with its production, particularly from food crops.

Institutional Theory

Institutional theory emphasizes the formal and legal aspects of government structure, which we discussed in chapter 2. Institutional models look at the ways governments are arranged, their legal powers, and their rules for decision making. These rules include basic characteristics such as the degree of access to decision making provided to the public, the availability of information from government agencies, and the sharing of authority between the national and state governments under federalism. A major tenet of institutionalism is that the structures and rules make a big difference in the kinds of policy process that occur and which policy actors are likely to be influential in them. Enactment of a very contentious farm bill in early 2014, for example—with its very generous agricultural subsidies—illustrates the power in the Senate of less populous agricultural states such as Iowa and South Dakota. Because the Constitution provides that each state has two senators, these small states have as much voting power in the Senate as the far more populous New York and California.

The term *institution* can have many meanings. It refers to "both the organizations and the rules used to structure patterns of interaction within and across organizations" (Ostrom 2007, 22). Therefore, in addition to a focus on organizations such as legislatures, courts, or bureaucracies, the term encompasses how people within organizations relate to one another and to those in other organizations— that is, the rules that govern their behavior. Many kinds of institutions can influence public policy: markets; individual firms or corporations; national, state, and local governments; voluntary associations such as political parties and interest groups; and foreign political regimes. Analysts use institutional theory to study how these different entities perform in the policymaking process as well as the rules, norms, and strategies used by individuals who operate within particular organizations, such as the U.S. Congress or the federal court system.

Although formal institutional analysis can become quite complex, institutional theory is a simple reminder that procedural rules and certain aspects of government structure can empower or obstruct political interests. A common axiom is that there is no such thing as a neutral rule. Rules have real consequences for the ways decisions are made, helping some and hurting others. They can make some groups more influential than others and some policy outcomes more likely than others. The Senate filibuster rule and its application discussed at the beginning of the chapter showed how a minority within that chamber had the ability to stop other Senate business, and forced the majority Republicans to schedule a gun control vote.

Rational Choice Theory

Rational choice theory, also called public choice and formal theory, draws heavily from economics, especially microeconomic theory, and often uses elaborate mathematical modeling. A highly developed and rigorous theory, rational choice has been widely applied to questions of public policy (Ostrom 1998, 2007; Schneider and Ingram 1997). Analysts have used it to explain actions as diverse as individual voter decisions and the calculations of public officials as they face national security threats. It assumes that in making decisions, individuals are rational actors; that is, they seek to maximize attainment of their preferences or further their self-interest. The theory suggests that analysts consider what individuals value, how they perceive a given situation, the information they have about it, various uncertainties that might affect the outcome, and how a particular context or the expectations of others—for example, rules and norms—might affect their actions. The goal is to deduce or predict how individuals will behave under a variety of conditions.

Rational choice theory tries to explain public policy in terms of the actions of self-interested individual policy actors, whether they are voters, corporate lobbyists, agency officials, or legislators. David Mayhew (1974) provided a simple illustration in his classic text, *Congress: The Electoral Connection.* Mayhew asked what kinds of behavior one might expect from members of Congress if their only incentive were reelection. He found that this simple assumption about individual motivation could reveal a great deal about the ways members behaved and even about what kinds of public policy actions such a Congress would be likely to produce. Mayhew found that the "electoral incentive" caused members to advertise themselves, claim credit, and take positions on the issues. This is not to imply that members of Congress and other politicians do not have many concerns other than getting reelected, including a genuine desire to promote the public welfare. However, Mayhew's example simply highlights the explanatory power of rational choice theory. It forces people to think about the core motivation of individual political actors and its consequences for the larger political system and for public policy.

The critics of rational choice theory argue that individuals are not always single-minded pursuers of their own self-interest. The critics also question the narrow and rigid assumptions that underlie the theory, such as the ability of individuals to behave rationally when they may lack pertinent information, or when decision makers have different and unequal information—a condition called information asymmetry (Green and Shapiro 1994; Shepsle and Bonchek 1997). Some say that the theory gives too little emphasis to the willingness of individuals to engage in collective action pursuits, such as joining public interest groups or participating in community organizations (Stone 2012).

Even so, rational choice theory provides insights into political behavior that can affect the design of public policies. It is especially useful to formulate predictions of how agency officials and the objects or targets of policy actions are likely to respond to policy initiatives (Schneider and Ingram 1997). For example, economists say that to persuade individuals to significantly reduce their fuel consumption would take a hike in the gasoline tax of fifty cents or more per gallon. Anything less would likely not alter the consumers' behavior because they would see the incentive as too small to make a difference in their personal welfare. Recent fluctuations in gasoline prices, although not tax related, seem to support this idea. As gas prices increased and passed four dollars per gallon in many places a few years ago, people turned more to mass transit, bicycles, car pools, and more efficient automobiles to get around. But when gasoline prices plummeted in 2015 and 2016 because of a global oil surplus, people not only returned to their cars; they began purchasing large and inefficient sport utility vehicles once again.

Legislating by the rules.
Senator Cory Booker (D-NJ) leaves in an elevator after assisting Senator Chris Murphy (D-CT) in waging an almost-15-hour filibuster on the Senate floor in order to force a vote on gun control on June 15, 2016, in Washington, D.C. Murphy wanted the Senate to vote on a measure banning anyone on the no-fly list from purchasing a weapon. *(Pete Marovich/Getty Images)*

Political Systems Theory

Political systems theory is more comprehensive, but also more general, than the other theories. It stresses the way the political system (the institutions and activities of government) responds to demands that arise from its environment, such as the public opinion and interest group pressures that we discussed in chapter 2 (Easton 1965). Systems theory emphasizes the larger social, economic, and cultural context in which political decisions and policy choices are made, such as a general preference for limited government or low taxes.

Systems theory is a formal way to think about the interrelationships of institutions and policy actors and the role of the larger environment. It also supplies some useful terms, such as *input, demands, support, policy outputs, policy outcomes,* and *feedback*. In systems theory, these terms operate in formal models. Input into the political system comes from demands and support. Demands are the claims individuals and groups seeking to further their interests and values make on the political system. For example, a union calls for safety regulations in the workplace. Support signifies the acceptance by individuals and groups of the actions of government as well as the actions' legitimacy. Support is evident when people obey the law and respect the system's rules and procedures and when they vote in elections and express trust and confidence in institutions and leaders. For example, there was support for the establishment of workplace safety regulations when the American Federation of Labor and the Congress of Industrial Organizations (AFL-CIO) made it a legislative priority and President Richard Nixon agreed to back legislation on the subject (Kelman 1980).

In this theory, the political system responds to demands and support in the process of policymaking and produces outputs (decisions, law, and policies) that over time may create real changes (called policy outcomes) in the situations that prompted the demands and support in the first place. Systems models incorporate yet another element—feedback from these kinds of outputs and outcomes—that can alter the environment and create new demands or support. An example is strong public support for additional policies to protect nonsmokers, such as bans on smoking in restaurants and bars, which followed other antismoking policies over the past four decades. In this example, an important policy outcome is that exposure of nonsmokers to dangerous secondhand smoke was reduced.

Systems theory is a simple way to portray how governments respond to society's demands on them. It proposes an almost biological model of politics suggesting that governments and public officials react to the political climate much as organisms respond to environmental stimuli. As the environment changes—for example, the economy deteriorates or the public becomes distressed with crime rates or corporate malfeasance—individuals and groups are moved to make demands on government to deal with the situation. Once government acts, the system readjusts in light of the particular decisions and their effects.

Each of these theories is helpful. Each offers a distinct conceptual lens through which to view politics and public policy, highlighting particular features of the political and institutional landscape. Yet none by itself is completely satisfactory.

Gasoline prices and transportation policy. Falling gasoline prices in 2015 and 2016 saved Americans almost $80 million a day but also raised new concerns about energy use and reliance on imported oil. New cars, SUVs, and trucks have much improved fuel economy thanks to federal standards and in cities served by mass transit systems, such as the Metro trains in Washington, D.C., many also have chosen to rely more on buses and light rail systems rather than driving, or to consider carpooling, walking, or bicycling. *(John McDonnell/The Washington Post via Getty Images)*

We believe another approach—the policy process model—is more useful than the others, in part because it can incorporate the most valuable elements of each of the others. It also has the advantage of portraying the activities of government and policymaking more clearly and using language that most people can understand intuitively. This chapter and the rest of the book make extensive use of the policy process model, also called the policy cycle model (J. Anderson 2015; Birkland 2016; Jones 1984).[6]

The Policy Process Model

The policy process model posits a logical sequence of activities affecting the development of public policies. It depicts the policymaking process and the broad relationships among policy actors within each stage of it. The model can also be helpful to understand the flow of events and decisions in different cultures and institutional settings; in other words, the concepts and language are general enough to fit any political system and its policy processes.

Table 3-1 presents the model as a set of six distinct, if not entirely separate, stages in policymaking, in keeping with the way the model is discussed in most textbooks. Sometimes the term **policy cycle** is used to make clear that the process is cyclical or continuous, rather than a onetime set of actions. Instead of a top-down listing of each stage, it could be presented as a series of stages linked in a circle, because no policy decision or solution is ever final. Changing conditions, new information, formal evaluations, and shifting opinions often stimulate

TABLE 3-1   The Policy Process Model

Stage of the Process	What It Means	Illustrations
Agenda setting	How problems are perceived and defined, command attention, and get onto the political agenda.	Health care reform rose sharply on the agenda during President Obama's first term and continued well into his second. Obamacare stayed high on the agenda as Republicans attempted repeatedly to overturn the law, and it remained a very visible issue as the program's rollout in late 2013 was plagued by faulty software, insufficient testing, and inadequate management.
Policy formulation	The design and drafting of policy goals and strategies for achieving them. Often involves the use of policy analysis.	The 2001 tax cut reflected conflicting economic assumptions and forecasts and differing estimates of future impacts on domestic programs.
Policy legitimation	The mobilization of political support and formal enactment of policies. Includes justification or rationales for the policy action.	The passage of health care reform in 2010 saw intense lobbying on the part of many of the affected interests. Ultimately, the bill was passed in the face of unanimous Republican opposition because Democrattic supporters argued that the reform plan would provide for better health coverage for most citizens.
Policy implementation	Provision of institutional resources for putting the programs into effect within a bureaucracy.	Implementation of the federal Endangered Species Act has lagged for years because of insufficient funding, which reduced its effectiveness.
Policy and program evaluation	Measurement and assessment of policy and program effects, including success or failure.	Efforts to measure the effectiveness of No Child Left Behind, an education policy that set national education standards to improve public education, have produced mixed results.
Policy change	Modification of policy goals and means in light of new information or shifting political environment.	New national security, airport security, and immigration reforms were adopted following the terrorist attacks of 2001, and subsequent changes were made in these areas such as the development of TSA Pre✓ to improve screening for low-risk travelers.

Sources: Drawn primarily from Charles O. Jones, *An Introduction to the Study of Public Policy,* 3rd ed. (Monterey, Calif.: Brooks/Cole, 1984); and Garry D. Brewer and Peter deLeon, *The Foundations of Policy Analysis* (Homewood, Ill.: Dorsey Press, 1983). The original policy process model can be traced to Harold Lasswell's early work on the policy sciences, "The Policy Orientation," in Daniel Lerner and Harold D. Lasswell, eds., *The Policy Sciences* (Stanford, Calif.: Stanford University Press, 1950).

reconsideration and revision of established policies. In addition, in the real world these stages can and do overlap or are sometimes skipped. In other words, policies might be formulated before they are high on the political agenda, or it may be impossible to differentiate policy formulation from legitimation.

Despite these complications, the policy process model captures important aspects of policymaking that correspond to political reality, as review of the six components—or stages—of the model makes clear. Moreover, policy analysis can potentially affect each of the stages; that is, methods of policy analysis can provide knowledge and insights that might influence every stage of policymaking, from how the agenda is set and policies are formulated to how existing programs are evaluated and changed. For example, economic and budgetary analysis had a powerful influence on the discussions and decisions regarding the Affordable Care Act. And this analysis continues through its implementation and could lead to changes and adjustments to the law in the future.

Problem Definition and Agenda Setting

Governments at all levels in the United States deal with many different public problems and policies each year. But how do the problems generate interest to begin with? That is, why do people pay attention to them, or why are they considered important enough to solve? And why do some problems, such as crime or the performance of public schools, command so much attention at times while others, such as population growth or energy use, tend to be ignored? If a problem does rise to a level of visibility, as immigration issues have in recent years, who determines that it is the government's responsibility to address it rather than leave it to individuals and the private sector? These questions are at the center of the problem-definition and agenda-setting stage of the policy process. In many ways, this step is the most critical of all. If a problem is not well defined, and if the public, the media, and policymakers cannot be persuaded to pay attention to it, it may go unresolved, even if society continues to suffer the ill effects.

Defining a Problem. It might seem relatively easy to identify a problem, to define it objectively, and to ensure that politics does not enter into the equation. If the issue is increases in violence and shootings, for example, who would not agree that these are serious problems and that society should do everything possible to prevent them? But are the causes of the problem equally clear? Perhaps they include easy access to firearms and the media's tendency to emphasize violence. Analysts may need to look for other causes as well. What about mental health concerns and who has the ability to access firearms, cited as an issue in the Sandy Hook Elementary School shootings? Or changing cultures that some may not be willing to accept, which underlie many concerns over immigration and its effects? Or, perhaps, what some Americans see as the moral decay in society?

As these examples illustrate, defining a problem and determining its causes are not always simple tasks, and the search for answers usually reflects a number of different perspectives. How one defines a problem also goes a long way toward shaping the solution offered. As John W. Kingdon (1995, 110) stated, "Problem definition and struggles over definition turn out to have important consequences." **Problem definition** may also come with some distinct biases. As Deborah Stone (2012, 160) put it:

> No language and no communication is free of symbols, and we couldn't have any discussion or do any analysis without them. Moreover, in the polis, symbolic devices do extra work. They function as weapons in the problem-definition arsenal (to use another metaphor). Political actors use them strategically to define problems in a way that will persuade doubters and attract support for their own side in a conflict.

In other words, "Where you stand depends on where you sit." A person's perspective and background determine how he or she defines a problem and relates to it. Personal ideology and values are likely to influence how the problem is defined or even if the individual considers a situation to be a problem at all. Internet pornography, for example, is thought of as an issue about protecting children or about protecting basic civil liberties, with very different implications. The financial rescue plan that Congress adopted in late 2008 was initially described as a Wall Street *bailout*, a distinctly less appealing definition from the perspective of those who favored it.

This is what political commentators mean when they refer to how issues may be "framed" or "spun." Those who favor one view of a problem or one kind of a solution use language that describes the problem or the policy action in a framework that reflects their perspective. Their opponents act similarly to convey a different perspective. Those who favor government support for family planning services, for example, frame the issue as a matter of individual rights or a health care service that government should provide. Opponents of family planning might frame the issue in moral terms and argue that government should not fund such services, especially for minors.[7] In a prominent example in 2005, President Bush initially spoke of creating innovative "private" Social Security accounts. But when Democrats successfully criticized the move as "privatization" of the system (which voters feared), the Bush administration switched to calling the accounts "personal" rather than private. In a similar display of the strategic use of language, in 2011 many conservatives voiced their opposition to "job-killing" regulations in an effort to portray government health, safety, and environmental regulations as detrimental to the public's welfare because they might dissuade businesses from creating new jobs or lead to loss of current jobs.[8]

Making comparisons is part of problem definition (Kingdon 1995; Stone 2012). Americans might think gasoline prices and taxes are too high and argue for relief. Yet if they compared the price of gasoline in the United States to that in Europe and Japan, where it is significantly higher because of government taxes, they might conclude that U.S. prices are in fact quite low (Parry 2002). In recent comparisons of test scores with students in other countries, American students lagged behind in mathematics.[9] This finding raised concerns about the quality of education in the United States. As these examples suggest, the way problems are defined and measured is not neutral; nor is it without important implications for whether and how public policies are formulated and implemented.

The different actors and institutions (formal and informal) reviewed in chapter 2 are almost always deeply involved in problem definition (Rochefort and Cobb 1994). Reports by executive agencies are crucial in supplying information on a problem and how it is changing over time, a good example being the highly respected reports on energy production and consumption from the Energy Information Administration of the Department of Energy. Congressional committees frequently hold hearings on public problems and invite testimony from various experts. Congressional advisory bodies, such as the Government Accountability Office (GAO) and the Congressional Budget Office (CBO), issue authoritative reports on nearly all public problems, from oil imports to health care. Even interest groups get involved. Most interest groups work hard not only to interpret the policy studies but also to supply other information that portrays a problem as they prefer to see it. For example, the Center for Responsive Politics, a research group concerned with money and its effects on elections and public policy, has for years provided data and reports highlighting this issue. Members of the private sector may also define public problems in areas of particular concern to them.

By supplying new, and often objective, information on the nature of a problem and its implications, policy analysts can help to steer political debate toward a rational assessment of the scope of the problem, its causes, and possible solutions. A study of urban sprawl, for example, might highlight the adverse impacts on highway congestion, land use, and water supplies, and suggest how better growth management could minimize those effects. The findings and recommendations of such a study would no doubt differ significantly from the arguments of real-estate developers and pro-growth public officials, as Atlanta, Georgia, and other high-growth metropolitan areas have learned in recent years (Jehl 2002; M. Murray 2002).

Setting the Agenda. Defining a problem is not enough; the public and policymakers must recognize it as a problem, and it must rise high enough on the agenda that action becomes likely. At that point, the search for solutions, or policy formulation, begins. Yet it is by no means easy for societal problems to reach agenda status, because at any given moment many issues are competing for social and political attention. Some make it onto the agenda, and some do not (Baumgartner and Jones 1993; Birkland 1997; R. Cobb and Elder 1983; Kingdon 1995).

Because of the competition for agenda space, many problems that government could potentially address never capture its attention and are neglected. Population growth is a prime example. The United States is growing as fast as or faster than any other industrialized nation in the world. Its growth rate (a little less than 1 percent a year) is five to ten times that of most European nations, partly because of its generous immigration policies. The Census Bureau projects that the U.S. population (about 325 million in 2016) is likely to rise to nearly 400 million by 2050, depending on the rate of immigration; this is a gain of 75 million people over its size in 2016, or the equivalent of adding about two states the size of California to the nation.[10] Except for a few cities and regions, however, population growth has never been an issue that commanded much attention from either the U.S. public or its elected officials.

The implications are plain. The mere existence of a problem is no guarantee that it will attract government attention or be addressed. Indeed, the term *nonissues* best distinguishes those problems that fail to gain attention from those that do. Some issues are intentionally kept off the agenda by those who oppose acting on them, as was true of civil rights in much of the South during the 1950s and 1960s. Others, such as population growth and energy use, often have been ignored by an indifferent public and policymakers. For the former, what some scholars call *agenda denial*, E. E. Schattschneider (1960, 71) explained the phenomenon:

> All forms of political organization have a bias in favor of the exploitation of some kinds of conflicts and the suppression of others because organization is the mobilization of bias. Some issues are organized into politics while others are organized out.[11]

When policymakers begin active discussions about a problem and potential solutions, the issue is said to be "on the agenda." Scholars distinguish between a **systemic agenda**, which the public is aware of and may be discussing, and an **institutional or government agenda**, to which policymakers give active and serious consideration (R. Cobb and Elder 1983). John W. Kingdon's (1995, 3) definition of the agenda captures the meaning of the institutional agenda. It is, he said, "the list of subjects or problems to which governmental officials, and people outside of government closely associated with those officials, are paying some serious attention at any given time." The term *agenda*, therefore, means the subjects that gain such attention and become possible objects of policy action. There is no official or formal listing of such an agenda; rather, it becomes evident in the subjects that elected officials choose to discuss, the media cover prominently, and interest groups and other policy actors work on at any given time.

Agenda setting is central to the policy process: if an issue does not attract the appropriate attention, chances are it will languish without government response. Therefore, the public policy student needs to understand what facilitates the movement of certain issues onto the agenda. Obviously, policymaking elites in government can define a problem and raise its visibility. Members of Congress or the president may highlight a particular concern or issue they want addressed, as President Lyndon Johnson did in the 1960s for civil rights, President Bush did in 2001 for education reform, and President Obama did in 2009 for health care reform, and Donald Trump did so in many issue areas upon taking office in 2017. Governors or mayors do the same at the state or local level, as illustrated by New Jersey governor Chris Christie's actions and statements on disaster relief following Hurricane Sandy. Government agencies that deal with a particular problem can also raise awareness and move related issues onto the agenda. The media, by deciding which issues to report on or not, also highlight public problems and may sway public opinion about them. Interest groups likewise emphasize those problems of greatest concern to them and try to define them according to their own political values and goals. The box "Steps to Analysis: What's on the Agenda?" is an exercise in determining what issues are currently attracting the government's attention.

Determinants of Agenda Setting. Some issues make it to the agenda automatically. They are mandated, or required, actions with which government must deal.

Steps to Analysis

What's on the Agenda?

Policymakers do not typically develop a list of ten items and say that these are what are on their agenda, but you can get a sense of what they feel are the important problems or issues based on what they are discussing in their press conferences or identifying on their websites. You can get some indication of what is on the agenda by using an array of web resources. First, go to the White House website at www.whitehouse.gov. From here, you can browse a number of links, such as Issues, to see the president's priorities. You can do the same for any state. Search for any state website using any search engine. For example, search for "Pennsylvania state government." From there, look for a link that discusses priorities or issues. Often there may be a number of ideas under a general category such as Education. You may be able to do something similar with local government sites. As you analyze these sites, keep these questions in mind:

- What appears to be the major issues for each level of government? Within the major issue, are there specific ones that appear to rise to the top?
- How are you making your judgment for your responses to the above? What evidence are you using?

- Are there any new programs being proposed? Are there suggestions to change or eliminate existing programs?

Next, sample one or more of the leading media sites to determine which issues their journalists believe merit the most coverage. Choose from ABC, CBS, NBC, Fox News, CNN, MSNBC, and other television networks, and from the *New York Times*, the *Washington Post*, and your city's newspaper. Here are the major links:

www.abcnews.go.com

www.cbsnews.com

www.nbc.com

www.foxnews.com

www.cnn.com

www.msnbc.com

www.newyorktimes.com

www.washingtonpost.com

- Do the government and media sites overlap, or do they cover different issues?
- Can you think of major problems—national, state, or local—that the media and elected officials are ignoring? What do you think are the reasons for this neglect?

Examples include passing the annual budget, legislating to reauthorize existing programs, and acting on a president's or governor's nominees for executive appointments. These issues alone probably take up most of the time that policymakers have available, leaving little to the discretionary issues. So what determines which of the optional issues receive attention and possibly policy action? In one of the best attempts to answer that question, Kingdon (1995) points to the intersection of three largely independent sets of activities in what he calls the problem, policy, and political "streams" that flow through society. When the streams converge, they create opportunities to consider certain issues. Whether they successfully move to the political agenda and are acted on is sometimes in the hands of influential policy entrepreneurs, or leaders who invest much of their time and resources in the issue.

The **problem stream** refers to the various bits of information available on the problem, whom it affects, and in what ways. Government reports and other studies are a valuable resource. They are released frequently and can assess the magnitude of the problem, in terms of both how serious it is and how widespread. Some issues, such as airline security or the safety of nuclear power plants, warrant attention because of their potential harm to large numbers of people. Information about a problem or a possible solution works both ways: it may either help an issue make it to the agenda or prevent it. Acid rain and climate change, for example, did not become agenda items until a sufficient amount of information had been collected to document the problems. Policymakers may not, however, spend time on a problem if the technology is not available for a solution. Sometimes the failure or inability of the private sector to address an issue will get it on the agenda. For example, the private sector cannot deal to any great extent with poverty in the United States or provide Social Security for the elderly. The scope of the problems makes them candidates for the national policy agenda. Finally, government programs may have spillover effects that spur concern about another area.

A focusing event, such as a crisis, usually improves an issue's chance of getting on the agenda, in part because of the exceptional media coverage it receives. The terrorist attacks of September 11, 2001, clearly altered the agenda status of airport and airline security in extraordinary ways. Likewise, natural disasters such as Hurricanes Katrina in 2005 and Sandy in 2012 or wildfires in the West in 2015 and 2016 can focus attention on the risk to the public well-being caused by hurricanes, floods, earthquakes, and fires; Katrina clearly did so for hurricanes, and it stimulated a government response. Similarly, the massive BP Deepwater Horizon oil spill in the Gulf of Mexico in 2010 highlighted the weaknesses of federal oversight of offshore oil drilling and the limitations of self-regulation by the industry. These focusing events are sometimes linked to powerful national priorities, such as defense, public safety, and public health, which may spur government action.

The **policy stream** refers to what might be done about the problem—that is, the possible alternative policies. Legislators and their staffs, executive agency officials, interest groups, academics, and policy analysts all may develop policy proposals. Often, the ideas are floated as trial balloons—potential solutions—to see how they are received. Some become the subjects of speeches, press releases, legislative proposals, hearings, and study reports. The policy ideas tend to circulate within the specialist communities, or issue networks, of those most concerned about the problem, and with the public through books, magazines, the broadcast media, and the Internet. Kingdon (1995) compares this process to evolution because only the fittest ideas survive. Policy alternatives that are inconsistent with the current political climate, the "unfit," may be dropped from consideration temporarily and incubated until the climate improves. Those that fit better with the political climate may receive serious attention from policymakers and other policy actors. What Kingdon calls the "criteria for survival" are what this text refers to as evaluative criteria, such as economic feasibility and political acceptability. Chapter 6 addresses these criteria.

The **political stream** refers to this political climate or public mood. It is evident in public opinion surveys, the results of elections, and the activity and strength of interest groups. For example, Ronald Reagan's election in 1980 abruptly changed the political climate by greatly increasing the acceptability of conservative policy ideas. George W. Bush's election in 2000 did much the same thing, and there was a dramatic shift with Barack Obama's election in 2008 that was altered somewhat after Republicans retook the House of Representatives after the 2010 election. Although it is never easy to decipher the political mood of the nation—and it can change quickly—elected officials have a well-developed ability to detect a shift in public attitudes, especially in their own constituencies.

When these three streams converge, policy entrepreneurs have their best chances to move problems and policy ideas onto the agenda and step closer to approval. Moreover, policy entrepreneurs may help to bring about such a convergence. They may be inside government or outside; they may be official policymakers or one of the legions of unofficial policy actors, such as interest group leaders. The president holds a unique position as a powerful agenda setter, in part because of the enormous media attention the office receives. At the state or local level, the parallel would be a governor or mayor.

As chapter 2 noted, however, one of the intriguing characteristics of the U.S. political system is the dispersal of power, meaning that policy leadership can come from many sources. At the national level, congressional committees and subcommittees are often hotbeds of innovative policy ideas precisely because members and their staffs are continually seeking ways not only to improve public policy but also to enhance their own visibility and compete with the other major party. Policy think tanks and interest groups are rich sources of policy proposals. Indeed, as the next three chapters explain, one of the major purposes of policy analysis is to conduct studies that evaluate the potential of new policy ideas. When the politically astute activist think tanks and interest groups put their weight behind these studies, influential policymakers and their staffs are likely to read them and take note of the results. Colleges and universities, professional associations, state and regional think tanks, citizens' groups, and the business community are also sources of policy ideas.

Another way to think about why one issue may gain agenda status while another does not is to look to the particular issue's characteristics, especially its salience and potential for conflict (Walker 1977). Salience refers to the issue's relative importance to the general public, and conflict refers to the level of disagreement over it. The logic here is that policymakers would rather deal with a problem the public believes is important than deal with one it is ignoring. In addition, policymakers prefer to avoid conflict and so will tend to shy away from contentious issues. Therefore, one would expect that the issue with the best chance of getting on the agenda would be one that is highly salient but low in conflict, and the one with the worst chance would have low salience and high conflict.

Policy Formulation

Policy formulation is the development of proposed courses of action to help resolve a public problem. As noted, policy alternatives are continually being studied and advocated as part of the policy stream and constantly being evaluated against the prevailing standards for policy acceptance. Among the standards for policy acceptance are economic cost, social and political acceptability, and likely effectiveness in addressing the problem. Policy analysis is abundant at this stage of the policy process, as the leading policy actors (formal and informal) look for information and ideas that will allow them to pursue their goals. The next three chapters deal with policy analysis in depth, but here it is sufficient to note that formulation is a technical as well as a political process. Policies that are carelessly formulated—for example, by using inadequate data, questionable projections, or unreasonable assumptions—may fail. A case of failure was the rollout of the Affordable Care Act website in late 2013 when it became apparent that the site could not handle the enormous amount of traffic and the technical demands associated with the program. In addition, perhaps too much weight was placed on meeting a specific deadline. Another widely cited example is the decision to launch the war in Iraq in 2003. Toward the end of his term of office, even President Bush conceded that it was based on faulty intelligence that suggested Saddam Hussein's government posed a serious risk to the security of the United States because it apparently had weapons of mass destruction. No such weapons were ever found (see chapter 12).

Who is involved in policy formulation? Chapter 2 discussed the formal policy actors in government, such as legislators, chief executives, and agency officials, who are especially influential at this stage. In most policy areas, the appointed and career officials in a bureaucracy are among the most experienced and knowledgeable policy actors. They have the technical information needed to develop policy and the political knowledge that comes from working in the policy arena. Their expertise can cut both ways, however. On the one hand, it can be valuable in formulating new policy approaches. On the other hand, current officials who are strongly wedded to traditional policy approaches may be concerned about the implications of new policies for their offices, resources, and careers. In short, agency officials may be conservative about policy proposals and favor only incremental changes, while those outside the agency are willing to experiment with innovative policy designs.

In addition to agency expertise, legislators and executive branch officials have access to many other sources of information and advice as they formulate public policy proposals. The president, for example, draws not only from his White House staff but also from the Executive Office of the President, which includes specialized agencies such as the National Security Council, the Council of Economic Advisers, the Council on Environmental Quality, and the Office of Management and Budget. The last agency serves as a well-staffed, centralized policy clearinghouse for the White House. Legislators, particularly at the national level, also have sources of expertise and advice. Working for Congress are the GAO (a diversified program evaluation office), the CBO (for budgetary and economic analysis), and the Congressional Research Service (for policy research). These offices are supplemented by extensive staffs that serve the several hundred committees and subcommittees where policy formulation is concentrated; some estimates, for example by C-SPAN, put the congressional staff totals at about twenty thousand people. Executives and legislators at state and local levels have far fewer resources for policy formulation, but the larger states and cities may nevertheless be well equipped to address the kinds of questions that arise during formulation.

Interest groups are active contributors to policy formulation. Like the bureaucracy, interest groups have a great deal of information at their disposal to provide

Steps to Analysis

Appraising Policy Formulation

What steps would you take to determine whether a policy proposal was properly formulated in any area of concern, such as health care, education, national security, or the economy? One issue that was in the news following the 2016 election had to do with concerns surrounding non-U.S. students and undocumented students and their ability to continue to study. Some college and university presidents suggested that they create "sanctuary campuses" to protect these students. The discussion quickly turned into claims that these presidents were advocating such a policy. Do some simple research on the issue of sanctuary campuses. You may also want to do an Internet search on "sanctuary campus" to get additional information. Use the following to help guide your thinking on policy formulation:

1. Start by examining the assessments of the problem to determine whether they were based on appropriate data and analysis.

2. Next, try to find out who was involved in the formulation process, who dominated it, and whether any serious conflicts of interest existed. You could also review the main assumptions made and any analysis that was used to determine whether they were valid.

3. In your judgment, was this potential campus policy examined sufficiently and evaluated fairly?

background or specific solutions to problems. This information ranges from technical details about the problem to judgments about whether a proposal is likely to have political support. But interest groups also attempt to shape policy to serve their own economic or political needs. One example has been the response from Wall Street to the Dodd-Frank financial reform legislation and the subsequent regulations associated with it. Wall Street banking interests lobbied intensely to undermine the law as well as to weaken the regulations adopted to implement it.[12] The box "Steps to Analysis: Appraising Policy Formulation" suggests some questions that might be asked about the reliability and fairness of the process of formulation as it applies to any area of public policy.

Policy Legitimation

Policy legitimation is defined as giving legal force to decisions, or authorizing or justifying policy action. It may come from a majority vote in a legislature or a formal executive, bureaucratic, or judicial decision (Jones 1984). From some perspectives, the process of legitimation includes the legitimacy of the action taken—that is, whether it is thought to be a proper exercise of government authority and its broad acceptability to the public and/or other policy actors.

Legitimation as a step in the policy process is at once both simple and complex. It is simple when it merely means that a recognized authority considered and approved a policy proposal. A bill becomes a law at the national level if both houses of Congress approve it and the president signs it, but does that process necessarily imply that the measure was legitimated? This question may be especially pertinent for the large number of policy measures that are part of omnibus legislative packages, or the government's growing tendency to adopt budget riders, which are policy actions attached to mandatory appropriations bills. These riders often are buried deep within budget bills precisely to avoid legislative scrutiny and public criticism (Davidson et al. 2016). Yet another barrier to policy legitimation is the public's very low appraisal of Congress. As discussed previously, polls have regularly found record low approval ratings of the institution, with some rating the honesty of members of Congress below that of telemarketers, lobbyists, and car salespeople. If the American people do not trust the members and their behavior, they might well doubt that Congress is acting in their interests.[13]

The complex view is that legitimation requires more than a majority vote or legal sanction by a recognized authority. Policy legitimacy or acceptability in this sense flows from several interrelated conditions: the action is consistent with the Constitution or existing law, it is compatible with U.S. political culture and values, and it has demonstrable popular support. Legitimation also may follow from a process of political interaction and debate that involves all major interests and a full and open airing of the issues and controversies (Lindblom and Woodhouse 1993). A careful assessment of any policy analyses or other technical studies might be part of this process of discussion and debate. So too might public participation through public meetings, hearings, and citizen advisory bodies, or endorsement by respected community or national leaders. Sometimes lawmakers call on cultural elites, athletes, and other celebrities to convince the public of the worthiness of the issue under consideration. Congressional committees have heard testimony on various issues from actors Michael J. Fox, Dennis Quaid, and Julia Roberts; model Christie Brinkley; singer Kevin Richardson of the Backstreet Boys; and former heavyweight boxing champion Muhammad Ali. Even comedian Stephen Colbert provided "testimony" regarding immigration reform although

Steps to Analysis

Judging Policy Legitimation

It is never easy to judge whether a policy proposal had been fully legitimated as it was considered for approval. Among other evidence, analysts would look for information that indicated public support for the action, that the views of major interest groups were considered, that policymakers took enough time to think carefully about their decisions and the consequences, and that appropriate information was used in making decisions.

On January 18, 2017, the National Oceanic and Atmospheric Administration (NOAA) and the National Aeronautics and Space Administration (NASA) reported that in 2016 the earth reached the highest temperatures on record. The new readings broke a record set in 2015, which in turn broke a record set in 2014. Scientists at NOAA and NASA, along with their colleagues in other scientific organizations, attributed most of the recent warming to human activity, most notably the burning of fossil fuels—coal, oil, and natural gas—and a small part of the change in 2015 and 2016 to the weather pattern called El Niño, where the Pacific Ocean releases energy and water vapor to the atmosphere.[a]

You can find the most recent assessments of climate change in 2016 at websites for both NOAA and NASA at www.noaa.gov/stories/2016-marks-three-consecutive-years-of-record-warmth-for-globe and www.giss.nasa.gov/research/news/20170118/.

These reports appeared two days before the Donald Trump administration was to take office. Trump, many of his cabinet appointees, and many Republican members of Congress had long questioned the reality of climate change advanced by the vast majority of climate scientists. They also promised to roll back most of President Barack Obama's initiatives to combat it. They argued that the science was unsettled, that the economic costs of climate change actions were too high, and that maintaining the Obama policies would harm U.S. industries and consumers, and in particular the fossil fuel industry.

Consider this case and try to determine whether efforts to pull back from climate change action meet expectations noted in the text for policy legitimation.

- If a president, members of Congress, or other policymakers reject scientific findings on climate change as reflected in the NOAA and NASA reports, is this necessarily in conflict with norms of policy legitimation?

- How important is it in this case to consider the interests of the fossil fuel industry, which might be adversely affected by climate change policies?

- How important is it to consider public preferences in making these decisions? By late 2016, public concern about climate change was at an eight-year high, and the public favored the climate change policies of the Obama presidency. Recent polls on the subject can be found at the Gallup website: www.gallup.com/poll/190010/concern-global-warming-eight-year-high.aspx.

a. Justin Gillis, "Earth Sets a Temperature Record for the Third Straight Year," New York Times, January 18, 2017.

it caused some controversy when it was conducted in character, while others questioned his expertise to be speaking on the issue.[14]

Policies that are adopted without such legitimation face serious hurdles. They may well fail to command public support, affected interest groups may oppose them or even challenge them in court, and their implementation could be adversely affected. Such was the case with President Obama's executive order on immigration that he signed in 2014. The president issued the executive order in response to inaction by the Congress on the issue. The executive order provided for temporary legal status to millions of illegal immigrants. Much of the controversy surrounding the policy had to do with the perceived illegitimacy of the president's unitary actions and thus bypassing of the legislative process.[15] The legitimacy was questioned to such an extent that a number of states sued, and ultimately the case went to the Supreme Court, which failed to support the executive order. Policy formulation has both technical and political elements, but the process of policy legitimation is mostly political. Nevertheless, policy analysis is still applicable at this stage; assessment of a policy's political feasibility and social acceptability remains relevant. Analysis of public opinion on the policy is also useful, as is measuring interest group support and opposition. Ethical analysis is both appropriate and helpful to determine what is fair and equitable in a policy decision or how it affects individual freedom or liberty. These kinds of questions arise frequently in public debates over welfare reform, access to higher education, patients' rights, family planning and abortion, fetal stem-cell research, and many other issues. The box "Steps to Analysis: Judging Policy Legitimation" poses some questions that might be asked about the process of legitimation in any political venue.

Policy Implementation

For many, the passing of a law by the U.S. Congress, a state legislature, or a city council signals the end of the policy process. In reality, it is just the beginning of government activity that ultimately will affect citizens and businesses more than they may realize. When Congress enacted the Clean Air Act Amendments of 1990, did industry automatically comply and stop polluting the air? When Congress or state legislatures increase the highway speed limit, are drivers immediately allowed to legally drive seventy miles per hour? The obvious answer to both of these questions is "no." Once a policy is formulated and adopted, it must be implemented.

According to Charles Jones (1984), implementation is the "set of activities directed toward putting a program into effect." Three activities—organization, interpretation, and application—are particularly important to successful implementation. Organization is the establishment of resources, offices, and methods for administering a program. Interpretation means translating the program's language—the plans, directives, and regulatory requirements—typically found in a law or regulation into language that those affected can understand. Application is the "routine provision of services, payments, or other agreed upon program objectives or instruments" (Jones 1984, 166). In other words, **policy implementation** depends on the development of the program's details to ensure that policy goals and objectives will be attained. One of the primary mechanisms agencies use to implement the laws is regulation. A regulation, which has the force of law, is simply the rule that governs the operation of a particular government program.

Policy implementation is a crucial stage of the policy process because it is where one sees actual government intervention and real consequences for society (Goggin et al. 1990; Mazmanian and Sabatier 1983). For example, the Occupational Safety and Health (OSH) Act is a relatively short law that governs workplace health and safety in the United States. The law itself provides few details on how the Occupational Safety and Health Administration (OSHA) is to go about the business of protecting workers. It has been the implementation of the OSH Act, rather than its adoption, that has most directly affected workplace health and safety conditions. Critics of OSHA often have blamed it for weak implementation decisions. For example, a review of the agency's actions from 1982 to 2002 concluded that it frequently declined to seek prosecution of industries responsible for workplace deaths even when employers were found to have willfully violated safety standards. Later assessments drew much the same conclusion about OSHA's implementation of the law throughout the George W. Bush administration.[16] Another example concerns the landmark Food Safety Modernization Act that Congress approved in early 2011 to reduce the occurrence and severity of food safety problems. The Food and Drug Administration (FDA) acknowledged soon after its passage that implementing the law would be "an enormous undertaking," particularly with severe budgetary constraints. Moreover, even though the food industry supported the policy as in its own interests, some members of Congress nonetheless sought to eliminate all funding for the new program. In 2013, the FDA finally adopted its rules to implement the act.[17]

Executive branch agencies implement most public policies within the United States. The traditional view was that they and their personnel were nonpolitical administrators who simply carried out the will of the legislature by following the established guidelines, with no say in the policy beyond its execution. This viewpoint, however, is unrealistic and fails to take into consideration the influence agencies and their administrators have in formulating policy and the discretion they have in its implementation.

Because of this degree of discretion, agency decisions often reflect the political philosophy and preferences of the chief executive who appointed the agency's administrators. Chief executives try to place in the top agency jobs people who agree with them on matters such as interpreting the law, deciding on agency priorities and budget allocations, and choosing which policy tools to use. In addition, debates that occur during policy formulation often continue during implementation. A good example was the conflict between the Bush White House and the intelligence agencies over conduct of the war in Iraq.[18] These conflicts continued long after the president decided to invade Iraq in March 2003. At times, the executive's enthusiasm for the law, or lack thereof, becomes apparent when it comes time to write the rules. When the Federal Election Commission began to set standards for implementing the controversial campaign finance reform law of 2002, the law's sponsors in Congress complained that the rules "would severely undermine the new law" (Mitchell 2002).

All government agencies and programs depend on a continuing supply of money to operate and carry out the various activities of policy implementation. The federal government uses an annual budget process that begins with the president's budget recommendations to Congress and ends with Congress passing appropriations bills, without which, according to the Constitution, no money can be spent. In between these two steps, Congress decides whether to accept or modify the president's budget and in what ways. Some of those decisions depend on performance assessments, judgments about how well the agencies are implementing their programs. The programs that have proved successful probably have an easier time securing the same or larger budgets; those seen as less so may have to get along with less money. State governments often use a biennial budget process rather than an annual one and usually make adjustments in the second year. The overall process is similar to what occurs at the national level. Ultimately, agency budgets reflect a compromise between what the chief executive wants and what the legislature is willing to give.

Policy Evaluation

The last two stages of the policy process are evaluation and change. **Policy evaluation**, or program evaluation, is an assessment of whether policies and programs are working well. In particular, analysts look for evidence that a program is achieving its stated goals and objectives. For example, did the Affordable Care Act increase the number of people with health insurance? Or did the No Child Left Behind law increase student test scores? Do the programs have unanticipated consequences, particularly any that are viewed as harmful? For example, in the rush to house victims of Hurricane Katrina in 2005, the Federal Emergency Management Agency (FEMA) ordered nearly $3 billion worth of trailers and mobile homes, only to discover later that many of those temporary housing units had excessive levels of formaldehyde, a dangerous chemical. That outcome was attributed to FEMA's weak contracting with the manufacturers, inconsistent regulation, and use of low-quality plywood imports from China. Evaluation involves judging a program's success in terms not only of the program's policy outcomes but also of its legitimacy or need, regardless of how well it is working, especially for controversial programs such as family planning or affirmative action.

Of the many reasons governments engage in policy and program evaluation, costs may be among the most important. Government programs are usually expensive, and policymakers, who must be accountable to the voters, want to know if the results are worth the money—a question that lies at the heart of policy analysis. In addition to costs versus benefits, analysts have many other

methods for evaluating policies and programs, but as with policy formulation, legitimation, and implementation, evaluation is not merely about technical studies of program results. It also involves political judgments about a program's worth, decisions that are likely to be of great interest to all policy actors involved with the program. In this sense, programs are continually, if often informally, evaluated by members of Congress, interest groups, think tanks, and others.

Policy Change

Should government expand a program or reduce its scope? Should the administrators try a different policy approach? Questions like these may follow the evaluations and lead to **policy change**, which refers to the modification of policy goals, the means used to achieve them, or both; the change could be minor, moderate, or extensive. Termination of a policy or program is one of many kinds of changes that might be considered, although it is rare. Most often a policy or program undergoes incremental change in an attempt to make it more effective or to meet the objectives of its main constituencies and other policy actors. A clear illustration relates to improving K–12 education. During the George W. Bush administration, Congress passed and the president signed the No Child Left Behind legislation in 2001. The general purpose of the law was to increase standards and improve childhood education. This was to be done through a mechanism of testing and accountability to ensure all students were meeting minimum standards. Many saw the law as overly prescriptive and found that it was nearly impossible to meet the act's goals. Changes began to roll out incrementally with the

Department of Education issuing waivers to certain areas that were not meeting the original standards set by the law. By 2015, Congress passed and the president signed the Every Student Succeeds Act (ESSA), which provided more flexibility into the achievement of standards and returned authority to the states.

Yet sometimes policy change is more than incremental; it represents a major departure from previous efforts. The Affordable Care Act is a case in point. Democrats had tried for years to adopt some form of national health care policy that would provide insurance and therefore health care services for the millions of Americans who are not covered by employer-provided or other forms of health insurance. Virtually every other developed nation in the world has such a policy. A major effort early in the Clinton administration failed to secure congressional support in part because the Clinton White House did not consult sufficiently with members of Congress (Hacker 1997). But in 2009 and 2010, the Obama White House and backers of that policy change on Capitol Hill garnered enough votes to succeed. Since its passage, the Affordable Care Act has survived Supreme Court review and numerous attempts by Republicans to roll it back. Its passage demonstrates that major public policy change is possible today under the right circumstances.

Passage of the Affordable Care Act reflects what Baumgartner and Jones (1993, 2002) call a **punctuated equilibrium model** of policy change. Rather than emerging gradually and enacted in small steps as in the classic incrementalism view of the policy process, the punctuated equilibrium model suggests that we can get dramatic policy change when the conditions are right. Thus we may have long periods in which policy stability is the norm, in part because those who dominate the policy process are "privileged groups of elites" who are largely satisfied with the status quo. But this seemingly stable condition can be undermined when new ideas make it onto the policy agenda, receive enhanced media and public attention, and are sufficiently endorsed by new policy actors to force change. Hence we have long-term stability or equilibrium that is on occasion punctuated by short-term and sometimes volatile policy change. In this way, newly emergent challenges, such as those evident in health care, the environment, energy, immigration, and many other areas, lead to sometimes abrupt policy advances.

The education act and the health care reform act demonstrate that the policy process never really ends. What is thought to be a resolution of a problem through policy adoption at one point is later evaluated and judged to be unacceptable. Interested parties then advocate changes. Another round of the policy cycle begins as the newly recognized needs reach the political agenda and a different policy is formulated and adopted. There is nothing wrong with this process. Indeed, all public policies can be considered to be experiments in which government and the public learn what works well and what does not. Even major policy reforms in welfare, education, immigration, and taxation, among other areas, have not always produced the changes the reformers had in mind, and further assessment and policy change often is needed (Patashnik 2008; Sabatier and Jenkins-Smith 1993).

Instruments of Public Policy

We have reviewed the various stages of the policy process model in the sections above. A related topic concerns the options that government policymakers have available at any point in this process, whether it is formulation, legitimation, or implementation. This is the role that government might play in addressing public problems, and especially the policy alternatives among which policymakers can choose. (See Figure 3-1.) We put this discussion at the end of the chapter because it serves as a transition to what we go on to consider in chapters 4 through 6 on the perspectives and insights of policy analysis.

As we indicated earlier, one of the first decisions to be made is whether government should intervene at all to deal with a problem or simply leave its resolution to individual action or the marketplace. For example, governments chose for years not to regulate smoking in public places, and then chose to do so in

Figure 3-1 Instruments of Public Policy

INSTRUMENT	ACTION	EXAMPLES
Regulation	Government decrees that require or prevent individuals, corporations, and other units of government from doing something	• Laws enacted by the legislature • Rules adopted by the bureaucracy
Government management	Implementation of services or management of resources directly to citizens	• Education and defense • Municipal services like police and fire protection
Education, information, and persuasion	Education of citizens in an attempt to persuade them to behave in a certain way	• Appeal to support relief efforts after a disaster • Nutrition labeling to encourage healthy eating
Taxing and spending	The collection or expense of money to achieve policy goals	• Social Security to support the elderly in retirement • Cigarette tax to discourage smoking and raise revenue for other programs
Market mechanisms	Use of the market to provide the public with incentives to make choices or correct problems	• Revenue-neutral carbon tax to discourage the use of fossil fuel • Publication of the energy efficiency of appliances

an escalating series of actions as scientists learned more about the health consequences of exposure to secondhand smoke, so that now many states even prohibit smoking in bars and nightclubs. Similarly, most cities and states chose to do nothing about rising levels of childhood obesity because they determined this was largely a matter of private or family choice. By 2011, however, cities and states across the nation were intervening in varying ways, from prohibiting certain kinds of foods in school vending machines and cafeterias, to mandating physical exercise for students, to attempts to outlaw the selling of extra-large servings of soft drinks.[19] The Los Angeles Unified School District has even banned flavored milk and made other changes to its school lunch program to promote healthier eating.[20] Chapter 1 described the most common rationales for such intervention, which include political reasons, moral reasons, and market failures. Complicating the decision about government action is that liberals and conservatives often disagree—sometimes heatedly—about what course to take, and especially about whether government or private action is most appropriate.

Should citizens and policymakers decide that government intervention is indeed necessary, they can choose from a diverse menu of possibilities. We have provided a number of examples in the chapter. Policymakers consider many questions when deciding which **policy instrument** to use to address a particular issue or problem. The most obvious is whether the instrument will be effective in addressing the problem, but others include its political acceptability, technical feasibility, economic impact, and long-term effects. Chapter 5 examines policy alternatives in some detail. The following sections explain the most common policy tools that governments use.

Managing public problems. Among the many options that policymakers can consider as they respond to various public problems is government management, in which government directly delivers services to the public or manages the resources at issue. Examples include the operation of public schools, national defense, national parks, and most local government services such as police and fire protection. The photo shows a park ranger greeting visitors near the ocean entry, a point where active flowing lava meets the Pacific Ocean, on December 12, 2016, at Volcanoes National Park, Hawaii. *(George Rose/Getty Images)*

Regulation

One of the best-known policy instruments, regulation, encompasses several different kinds of government actions, including the laws that legislatures enact and the rules that bureaucracies adopt. Regulations are government decrees that either require citizens to do something or prevent them from doing so. Particular requirements ensure compliance by individuals, corporations, and other units of government. Typically, the regulations impose sanctions, such as fines or imprisonment, for failure to comply. For the most part, citizens and corporations adhere to these legal requirements voluntarily, but the means are available to enforce the regulations when necessary.

Government Management

Governments use the direct services or direct management of resources as instruments of public policy. Education, defense, public parks, and most municipal services, such as police and fire protection, are examples of policies that governments implement by providing the service directly to citizens. Governments offer most of these services because they need to be provided in a specific way, such as making national parklands available to all for a modest fee. Today, it is not unusual for governments, especially at the local level, to contract out a wide variety of services and pay private companies to provide them.

The questions of which government services might be handled by private businesses and whether doing so is a good idea are the subjects of ongoing public policy debate. According to James E. Anderson (2011, 17), "privatization supports transferring many government assets or programs to the private sector and contracting with private companies to handle many public services, whether the collection of garbage or the operation of prisons." Policymakers evaluate the options by using criteria such as effectiveness, cost, and accountability to the public, and the public sector remains responsible for ensuring the quality of the work, even though the private sector is providing the services. To date, many services and programs that were once part of the public sector have been privatized or contracted out, including solid waste collection, jail and prison management, firefighting, highway construction and maintenance, and much more (Savas 2000). But even before the privatization movement, the government relied on the market to provide services. A clear example is that the government has always contracted with private companies in the defense industry to build aircraft, tanks, ships, and missiles.

Taxing and Spending

Governments also use their ability to tax and spend to achieve policy goals and objectives. One form of spending policy is the direct payment of money to citizens. Social Security is an obvious example: the federal government transfers money from people who are working to retirees or others who are covered by the system's rules. Governments also provide monetary payments as a way of promoting certain activities. For example, under welfare reform, the federal government provides money to the states to distribute as they see fit to those needing assistance, but the states must show that they have reduced the welfare rolls or risk losing some of this federal funding.

Governments also use tax policy to promote or discourage certain activities. For example, the federal government promotes home buying by allowing homeowners to deduct their mortgage interest from their taxable income. Many state governments have increased the tax on cigarettes not only to discourage smoking but also to raise revenue for other programs. These taxes vary quite widely from state to state, from a low of 17 cents per pack in Missouri to a high of $4.35 per pack in New York (see chapter 6).[21]

Market Mechanisms

Governments can take advantage of market mechanisms as a form of public policy. Using the market may be an explicit decision by the government not to intervene in any way but instead to allow the laws of supply and demand to work. For the most part, the government has chosen not to regulate electronic commerce on the Internet, or even to impose taxes on Internet purchases, much to the dismay of local merchants who have found themselves losing market share to Amazon.com and other companies.[22]

Governments also actively use market incentives rather than other approaches to achieve policy goals. For example, when Congress passed the 1990 Clean Air Act Amendments, it required a certain amount of reductions in sulfur dioxide and nitrogen oxides, which are precursors to acid rain. In the past, Congress may have used regulation as the tool to achieve these reductions, but under the 1990 act, the government used marketable permits to get the reductions. The permits, which are emission allowances, are provided to companies based on their previous emissions levels, but with the target of lower emissions over time. Companies then decide how to use these permits; they can buy, sell, trade, or bank the permits, using whatever strategy allows them to meet the emissions targets at the least cost. If companies can emit less pollution than they have allowances for, they can sell their additional permits to companies for which emissions reductions are more difficult and more costly (A. Freeman 2006). This market mechanism, also called "cap and trade," has been suggested as one way to address the release of greenhouse gases that lead to global climate change, and a number of cap-and-trade bills have been introduced in Congress in recent years. California adopted its own state cap-and-trade program rather than wait for Congress to act; it took effect in 2012.

Education, Information, and Persuasion

Another policy instrument available to the government is educating citizens while attempting to persuade them to behave in a certain way. Following a natural disaster in the United States, the president usually makes a personal appeal to Americans to support relief efforts. This kind of message is called exhortation, or a hortatory appeal (Schneider and Ingram 1997), and the bully pulpit can be an effective instrument of public policy under certain circumstances.

Public opinion polls, however, have shown that trust in government and its leaders has decreased over the past forty years (Nye, Zelikow, and King 1997), although the pattern was reversed temporarily following the September 11 terrorist attacks (Mackenzie and Labiner 2002). As trust decreases, so too does the effectiveness of persuasion as a public policy instrument. People may not comply with a request of a public official if they question the official's justification in making it or the government's overall legitimacy.

Providing information to the public can be a powerful policy instrument. Anne L. Schneider and Helen Ingram (1997) call it a "capacity-building" tool with the potential to inform, enlighten, and empower people through training, education, technical assistance, and other ways of making information available. Use of this instrument has increased in recent years and is common in the areas of health, safety, and environmental protection (Graham 2002). For example, the FDA requires nutritional labeling as a way of informing consumers about the substances in their food and allowing them to make decisions on healthy eating. The Environmental Protection Agency each year collects and makes available on its website information about emissions of toxic chemicals from industries around the nation. In creating this policy in 1986, Congress hoped, with some success, that publicizing toxic emissions would give businesses an incentive to correct their pollution problems (Graham and Miller 2001; Kraft, Stephan, and Abel 2011). We also rely heavily on information disclosure to inform people on the sources of election campaign funds, the energy efficiency of appliances, the fuel economy of cars and trucks, and the financial activities of corporations, among other policy concerns.

Policy Typologies

Policymakers are likely to think about policy options in terms of the tools at their disposal. For example, what will be more effective in reducing toxic chemical emissions, regulation or information provision approaches? Which instrument will work better to cut fuel consumption, regulation (raising vehicle fuel efficiency standards) or a market incentive (imposing a larger gasoline tax)? Public policy scholars think about the different kinds of policies that governments adopt and why they do so for a slightly different reason (McCool 1995). The goal is to understand the basic differences among policies and the political conditions that lead to one kind of policy rather than another. To that end, this chapter concludes with a review of the best-known and most frequently cited typology, developed by Theodore Lowi (1964).

According to Lowi, all government functions can be classified into three types: distributive, redistributive, and regulatory. Individual programs or grants that a government provides without regard to limited resources or zero-sum situations (where one group's gain is another's loss) are characterized as **distributive policies**. Examples include college research grants, weapons procurement, agricultural subsidies, highways and bridges, and other public construction projects.

Many people label these kinds of programs *pork barrel*, the term used to describe the attempts of elected officials, such as members of Congress, to provide government programs and services that directly benefit their constituencies. Such politicians are said to excel at "bringing home the bacon." These kinds of policies are often noncontroversial because they tend to be visible only to those directly involved, and members usually do not seriously question each other's pet projects because to do so may jeopardize their own. One might expect such policies to be particularly attractive when spending limits and budget deficits are viewed as unimportant, because the potential exists for most members of Congress to get something out of this kind of spending. But even in fiscally difficult times, elected officials may continue to support costly distributive policies. One particular project sarcastically labeled as the "bridge to nowhere" received a lot of media attention with the selection of Alaska governor Sarah Palin as the Republican vice presidential nominee in 2008. The bridge was proposed to link a small island in Alaska to the mainland at a cost of $223 million.[23] The direct electoral rewards of providing such benefits to their states and districts appear to override politicians' concerns about the budget.

Conflict is what makes **redistributive policies** different from distributive policies. For every redistributive policy, winners and losers are associated with its approval, which makes such policies controversial and difficult to adopt. Because redistributive policies provide benefits to one category of individuals at the expense of another, they often reflect ideological or class conflict. Some examples include welfare, Social Security, affirmative action, and tax policy. A proposed tax cut may benefit chiefly upper-income taxpayers while eroding services that assist lower-income citizens because of reduced government revenue. If a company adopts an affirmative action policy in hiring women or racial minorities, these groups may benefit at the expense of others.

Lowi's final policy type is **regulatory policy**. According to Kenneth Meier (1993, 82), a leading scholar of regulation, "Regulatory policy is government restriction of individual choice to keep conduct from transcending acceptable bounds." This definition covers a wide range of government activities, from protecting consumers to ensuring environmental quality. The range is so broad that some scholars divide regulatory policies into two subcategories. The first, **competitive regulation**, is mostly associated with regulating specific industries and their practices, such as computer software and communications companies. The second, **protective or social regulation**, protects the general public from activities that occur in the private sector (Eisner, Worsham, and Ringquist 2007; Ripley and Franklin 1991).

Competitive regulatory policy includes the licensing of radio and television broadcasting, antitrust actions, and policies associated with net neutrality, which is intended to keep Internet access free and open, that is, without blocking or discriminating against any particular applications or content on a network. Protective regulatory policy includes consumer protection and workplace health and safety rules, such as those administered by the Consumer Product Safety Commission and OSHA. These kinds of policies are controversial because they require the government to intervene in the activities of private businesses, often leading to increased operating costs or restrictions on corporate behavior.

Lowi's policy typology provides a simple but helpful way to classify different kinds of government programs and policies. The characteristics associated with each type allow the student of public policy to understand the debate surrounding the issue, why policies may or may not gain approval, how they might be implemented, and the public's acceptance of them.

Conclusions

This chapter describes the leading theories used to explain the politics of policymaking. Students of public policy use these theories to help explain why decisions are made the way they are. One could use these theories to help understand why, for example, President Obama and Congress pursued health care reform through adoption of the Affordable Care Act rather than choosing another option, such as a single-payer plan or expanding Medicare to cover the entire population. The answer likely lies in the need to respond to the various interest groups active on health care reform as well as to secure the votes of members who could not support a more radical departure from the status quo. We choose to focus primarily on the policy process model and explore each of its stages, noting the roles of different policy actors and the potential for policy analysis in each. We believe this model enables the public policy student to formulate effective questions about the policy process. It also aids in evaluating the information and arguments used to advance certain policy proposals or to criticize existing programs. The models and theories introduced here are the tools for figuring out what policy actors are doing at any given time and why they are doing it, and why policy actors might prefer one of the different types of policy action discussed in the chapter to another.

The next three chapters explore in more detail some of the themes touched on so far. They cover the nature of policy analysis and its growth over time, particularly through the rise of independent think tanks and the expansion in interest group analysis and policy promotion. They introduce concepts and methods for measuring and analyzing public problems and thinking creatively about possible policy alternatives for dealing with them. They elaborate on the leading criteria for evaluating policy proposals and the range of policy analysis methods that can provide information about the likely effects of those proposals.

for CQ Press

Sharpen your skills with SAGE edge at **http://edge.sagepub.com/ kraft6e. SAGE edge for students** provides a personalized approach to help you accomplish your coursework goals in an easy-to-use learning environment.

DISCUSSION QUESTIONS

1. With a current public policy example, such as immigration reform or various proposals to cut or raise federal taxes and modify entitlement programs such as Social Security and Medicare, use the theories of policy (e.g., elite, group, or rational choice) to help explain why a particular policy choice was selected. How do the assumptions associated with these theories help to explain the outcome?

2. There has been a lot of discussion surrounding special interests and their ability to influence policy. How large a concern is this? Are there examples you can think of where such interest group activity may be a benefit to policy development?

3. What steps within the policy process does the general public hear about most often? Why do you think that is? Why might it be a good idea for the public to know about and pay attention to the other steps?

4. What helps to explain why some issues make it onto government agendas and receive much discussion and media coverage and others do not? Do you think that most issues on local, state, and national agendas are propelled there because of the political and economic interests of legislators (e.g., pork-barrel projects), because of the power of interest groups, or in response to the needs of the public? Why do you think so?

5. Consider a current issue or problem being discussed. How might different policy instruments (e.g., regulation, market incentives, or public education) address the problem? What are the pros and cons of using the different instruments?

KEYWORDS

SUGGESTED READINGS

Frank R. Baumgartner and Bryan D. Jones, *Agendas and Instability in American Politics* (Chicago: University of Chicago Press, 1993). A classic analysis of agenda setting and policy change, with change often attributed to punctuated equilibrium rather than incrementalism.

Frank R. Baumgartner and Bryan D. Jones, eds., *Policy Dynamics* (Chicago: University of Chicago Press, 2002). A first-rate edited collection that illustrates policy change through processes of punctuated equilibrium.

Thomas A. Birkland, *An Introduction to the Policy Process: Theories, Concepts, and Models of Public Policy Making*, 4th ed. (New York: Routledge, 2016). An accessible and insightful text that describes the U.S. policymaking process.

John W. Kingdon, *Agendas, Alternatives, and Public Policies*, 2nd ed. (New York: Pearson, 2011). A classic analysis of agenda setting in U.S. politics, with exceptional insight into the policy process, particularly agenda setting. This updated version includes an epilogue examining health care reform efforts from Presidents Clinton to Obama.

Eric M. Patashnik, *Reforms at Risk: What Happens after Major Policy Changes Are Enacted?* (Princeton, N.J.: Princeton University Press, 2008). One of the best contemporary analyses of what happens after major policy reforms are adopted and why some efforts at policy change are more effective than others.

SUGGESTED WEBSITES

The websites listed at the end of chapter 1, especially those of major government institutions and public opinion surveys, are also useful here. Sites for the leading policy think tanks are listed at the end of chapter 4. In addition, see the following for the study of public policy and policymaking:

www.comparativeagendas.net. The website for the Comparative Agendas Project, with an extensive database; permits users to "investigate trends in policy-making across time and between countries." Sponsored by a number of universities from around the world including the University of Texas at Austin.

www.ipsonet.org. The Policy Studies Organization's home page.

www.napawash.org. The National Academy of Public Administration's home page, with links to events and academy publications on government and public policy.

www.usa.gov. The citizen portal for USA.gov, with links to news, government studies and reports, consumer action, and government e-services.

NOTES

1. See Liam Stack, "Orlando Shooting: What We Know and Don't Know," *New York Times*, June 12, 2016.
2. See "Remarks by the President on Mass Shooting in Orlando," *White House Office of the Press Secretary*, June 12, 2016.
3. Chris W. Cox, "Gun Laws Don't Deter Terrorists: Opposing View," *USA Today*, June 14, 2016.
4. See Cindy Skrzycki, "U.S. Sees No Percentage in Food Content Labeling," *Washington Post*, June 14, 2005.
5. For more information, see Shawn Zeller, "Grassley and Food Manufacturers Go Toe-to-Toe on Ethanol," *CQ Weekly*, June 2, 2008, 1456–1456.
6. The policy process model is not without its critics. Some argue that it should be replaced by a more accurate and genuinely causal model of policy activities that lends itself to empirical testing and the incorporation of a broader variety of policy actors and behavior. See Paul A. Sabatier and Hank C. Jenkins-Smith, eds., *Policy Change and Learning: An Advocacy Coalition Approach* (Boulder, Colo.: Westview, 1993); and Paul A. Sabatier and Christopher M. Weible, eds., *Theories of the Policy Process*, 3rd ed. (Boulder, Colo.: Westview, 2014). We disagree with the critique. The policy cycle model can be useful for describing the diversified players in the policy game and for alerting observers to pertinent actions that contribute to understanding public policy and politics. One should not, however, treat the stages in the model as anything more than helpful constructs.
7. For a review of how the two major parties used such strategies in past election contests,

see Matt Bai, "The Framing Wars," *New York Times Magazine*, July 17, 2005, 38–45, 66–71.

8. See, for example, Joe Nocera, "Killing Jobs and Making Us Sick," *New York Times*, September 16, 2011.

9. See the data provided by the U.S. Department of Education, Institute for Education Sciences, National Center for Education Statistics, "Program for International Student Assessment (PISA)," available at http://nces.ed.gov/surveys/pisa/.

10. See the Population Reference Bureau's *2016 World Population Data Sheet*, available at www.prb.org.

11. On the subject of nonissues and decisions to keep issues off the agenda, see Peter Bachrach and Morton S. Baratz, *Power and Poverty: Theory and Practice* (New York: Oxford University Press, 1970). We think the agenda-setting theories of John Kingdon (1995) and Frank Baumgartner and Bryan Jones (1993) offer equally, if not more, useful insights on the process.

12. See Jonathan Weisman and Eric Lipton, "In New Congress, Wall Street Pushes to Undermine Dodd-Frank Reform," *New York Times*, January 13, 2015.

13. See the results of any recent Gallup poll on the subject at the poll's website: www.gallup.com.

14. See Dan Zak, "Stephen Colbert, in GOP Pundit Character, Testifies on Immigration in D.C.," *Washington Post*, September 25, 2010. To see a video of Colbert's testimony, see HuffPost Politics, September 24, 2010, available at www.huffington post.com/2010/09/24/stephen-colbert-hearing-v_n_737813.html.

15. For additional information regarding this policy see Max Ehrenfreund, "Your Complete Guide to Obama's Immigration Executive Action," *Washington Post*, November 20, 2014, available at www.washingtonpost.com/news/wonk/wp/2014/11/19/your-complete-guide-to-obamas-immigration-order/.

16. See David Barstow, "U.S. Rarely Seeks Charges for Deaths in Workplace," *New York Times*, December 22, 2003; Stephen Labaton, "OSHA Leaves Worker Safety Largely in Hands of Industry," *New York Times*, April 25, 2007; and R. Jeffrey Smith, "Asleep on the Job: OSHA Career Officials Say Bush Appointees Ignored Danger and Favored Employers," *Washington Post National Weekly Edition*, January 5–11, 2009.

17. See William Neuman, "On Food Safety, a Long List but Little Money," *New York Times*, August 22, 2011; and Stephanie Strom, "F.D.A. Offers Sweeping Rules to Stop Food Contamination," *New York Times*, January 4, 2013.

18. For an example, see Douglas Jehl, "Report Says White House Ignored C.I.A. on Iraq Chaos," *New York Times*, October 13, 2005.

19. See Patricia Leigh Brown, "Bake Sales Fall Victim to Push for Healthier Foods," *New York Times*, November 10, 2008.

20. See Mary MacVean, "L.A. Unified Removes Flavored Milk from Menus," *Los Angeles Times*, June 15, 2011.

21. These rates are as of August 1, 2016, and are from the Campaign for Tobacco-Free Kids website: www.tobaccofreekids.org/research/factsheets/pdf/0097.pdf.

22. Yet pressure is building to impose an online sales tax. See Jonathan Weisman, "Push to Require Online Sales Tax Divides the G.O.P.," *New York Times*, April 28, 2013.

23. For additional examples of what many might consider "pork," see Scott Bittle and Jean Johnson, *Where Does the Money Go?* (New York: HarperCollins, 2008); and the Heritage Foundation's "Top 10 Examples of Government Waste," available at www.heritage.org/research/budget/bg1840.cfm.

PART II

Analyzing Public Policy

Chapter 4

A driver uses a phone while behind the wheel of a car on April 30, 2016, in New York City. As the text indicates, accidents involving drivers using phones for texting or other purposes are rising. New York lawmakers are considering new measures to curb the practice, including a test called the Textalyzer, which would allow police to examine phone records of drivers involved in accidents to determine if the phone was used while driving. *(Spencer Platt/Getty Images)*

Policy Analysis

An Introduction

In 2013, a twenty-one-year-old East Texas driver checking her iPhone for messages crashed into an SUV, killing both the driver and a passenger and severely injuring a child. She was found guilty in a jury trial of criminally negligent homicide, and in a twist in what has become an increasingly common form of accidents linked to distracted driving, families of the victims filed a product liability lawsuit against Apple. They said that the company should have known that its phones would be used for texting under dangerous conditions and yet chose not to incorporate technology that could make texting while driving impossible. The argument is that Apple should have been aware that public education and laws on texting and driving have had little impact to date, suggesting the necessity of a technological solution to cell phone use by drivers.[1] Accidents of this kind have led the states to adopt varied laws on use of cell phones while driving. By 2016, forty-six states and Washington, D.C., had banned text messaging for all drivers, and nearly all of them provide for primary enforcement; that is, one can be cited for this traffic violation alone. However, only fourteen states and the District of Columbia prohibit all drivers from using handheld cell phones while they are driving, and thirty-seven states and the District of Columbia ban all cell phone use by novice or teen drivers. Twenty states prohibit school bus drivers from any cell phone use while driving.

Are such laws changing driver behavior? Not very much, it seems. Recent surveys tell us that more than half of drivers ages twenty-one to twenty-four say they text behind the wheel, and about two-thirds of all drivers report they have used a cell phone while driving. About three-quarters of young drivers say that they are very or somewhat confident they can safely text while driving, despite evidence to the contrary.[2]

In light of these findings, is there a case to be made for going beyond current restrictions on cell phone use while driving? For example, should *any* use of hand-held cell phones, talking or texting, while driving be prohibited for all drivers? What about use of hands-free cell phones in cars, particularly smartphones with Bluetooth connectivity or a wired connection that can convert a cell phone to a hands-free device? This may be a distinction without a difference since studies suggest the real driver distraction is associated not with holding the phone but rather with talking on it. Studies have measured that risk as equal to driving with a blood alcohol level at the legal maximum, and the risk rises substantially if one is texting while driving.[3] For that matter, the infotainment systems built into many new cars, often allowing access to the Internet and social networks, provide even more opportunity for taking one's eyes off of the road while driving.[4]

The implications of all this new technology are not lost on federal and state officials concerned with transportation safety. In December 2011, the National Transportation Safety Board (NTSB), an independent federal agency, called for a total ban on cell phone use while driving (no calling, texting, or updating), citing the risks of distracted driving; it said that drivers should use cell phones only in an emergency. Its call was similar to one issued by the National Safety Council in 2009, but the decision to ban cell phones was up to the states.[5] Also in 2011, the Obama administration's secretary of transportation, Ray LaHood, continued to press for additional restrictions on texting and cell phone use, and other forms of distracted driving. His department set up a special federal webpage on the subject to offer the public key facts and arguments (www.distraction.gov), and President Obama used his executive authority to forbid federal employees from texting while driving. In the following year, 2012, the NTSB sent a letter to the wireless industry trade association that urged the companies to prevent all drivers from using their cell phones while driving.[6]

Given these developments, would you favor the NTSB's recommendation to ban all cell phone use while driving? Should something also be done about other distractions in the car? Washington, D.C., approved a cell phone restriction in 2005 that also bans driving while "reading, writing, performing personal grooming, interacting with pets or unsecured cargo or while playing video games."[7] Is that going too far? Would a public education campaign be preferable to such restrictions, and would it work? As drivers and citizens, everyone should ask how policymakers can ultimately reach decisions like these that are effective, fair, and reasonable. This chapter demonstrates that policy analysis may be able to help answer these kinds of questions.

Chapter 3 elaborated on the policy process model, which is useful for understanding how policy analysis contributes to government decision making. Whether in testimony before legislative committees, studies and reports on the Internet, or articles and reports, policy analysis is usually performed at the policy formulation stage. Here, policymakers search for the proposals they believe hold promise for addressing public problems. But policy analysis is also used throughout the policymaking process, starting with defining the nature of the problem right through implementing and evaluating policies within administrative agencies.

This chapter examines the nature and purposes of policy analysis, including basic steps in the policy analysis process. It also surveys the diverse ways in which analysts and research organizations engage in their work. The next two chapters go into greater detail on how we study public problems and seek solutions to them, using different methods and criteria to evaluate what might be done. No one expects these chapters to make students instant analysts; rather, their purpose is to convey the challenge of understanding and solving public problems and the need for clear, critical thinking about public policy, whether the issue is how to reduce texting while driving, how to lower student loan debt, or how to combat terrorism. Readers should learn what policy analysis is all about, how to question the assumptions that analysts make about their work, and how analysis of all kinds is used in support of political arguments and policy actions. We also try to direct readers to a variety of information sources about public policy and provide some guidelines for using them.

The Nature of Policy Analysis

As discussed in chapter 1, the term *policy analysis* covers many different activities. It may mean examining the components of the policymaking process, such as policy formulation and implementation, or studying substantive public policy issues, such as ensuring access to health care services, or both. Policy analysis usually involves collecting and interpreting information that clarifies the causes and effects of public problems and the likely consequences of using one policy option or another to address them. Because public problems can be understood only through the insights of many disciplines, policy analysis draws from the ideas and methods of economics, political science, sociology, psychology, philosophy, and other scientific and technical fields (J. Anderson 2015; Weimer and Vining 2016).

Most often, policy analysis refers to the assessment of policy alternatives. According to one scholar, it is "the systematic investigation of alternative policy options and the assembly and integration of the evidence for and against each option" (Jacob Ukeles, quoted in Patton, Sawicki, and Clark 2016, 22). Policy analysis is intended not to determine policy decisions but rather to inform the process of public deliberation and debate about those decisions. As in the case of cell phone use by drivers, analysis can provide useful information and comparisons to answer the kinds of questions people raise about what might be done about the problem. Ultimately, however, the public and its elected officials must decide what course of action to take.

Policy analysis, then, is part science and part political judgment. Doing analysis often means bringing scientific knowledge to the political process, or "speaking truth to power" (Wildavsky 1979). To put it in a slightly different way, policy analysis involves descriptive or empirical study, which tries to determine the facts of a given situation, as well as a normative or value-based assessment of the options. Policy analysis can never be reduced to a formula for solving public problems, but as we will show, it can bring valuable information to both policymakers and the public. In those cases where public involvement in decisions is important, analysis also may enhance the democratic process (Ingram and Smith 1993).

The study of public policy and the conduct of policy analysis are rarely simple matters. Public problems are usually complex and multifaceted, and people are bound to disagree over how serious they are, what might be done about them, and the role of government in relation to the private sector. Some problems, such as global climate change or the challenge of terrorism, are monumental. Others, such as how best to provide for a high-quality public school system or limit urban sprawl, may be a bit easier to grasp. But they still are not simple. If they were, the course of action would be clear and not very controversial—removing snow from urban streets and collecting household trash, for example. Unfortunately, dealing with most public problems is not so straightforward.

So what exactly does policy analysis do? One of its primary functions is to satisfy the need for pertinent information and thoughtful, impartial assessments in the policymaking process. This is particularly true when decisions must be made quickly because of impending deadlines or when the issues are politically controversial. Essentially, policy analysis involves looking ahead to anticipate the consequences of decisions and thinking seriously and critically about them. It is an alternative to "shooting from the hip" or making snap decisions based on ideology, personal experience, or limited or biased assessment of what should be done.[8] Even though such policy analysis is an intellectual activity, it takes place within a political setting (Dunn 2016). The way the analysis is done and its effects on decision making reflect that basic political reality.

Policy alternatives for urban services. Cities and states can choose among many policy alternatives as they try to meet recurring needs such as removing snow from city streets and collecting household waste. The photo shows heavy equipment clearing the street of snow on the Upper West Side of New York City on January 24, 2016. The city was hit with more than two feet of snow at that time. *(Astrid Riecken/ Getty Images)*

The role of politics is readily apparent in policy areas such as guaranteeing—or limiting—a woman's right to choose an abortion, controlling illegal immigration, or ensuring that biological evolution is included in public school science curricula. All were subjects of great controversy in Kansas, Pennsylvania, and other states in the 2000s. These issues touch on fundamental questions of values, and people may hold intense views on them. It is no surprise, then, that politics sometimes trumps policy analysis when decisions are made on such issues. Yet the political nature of policymaking is also evident in nearly every policy area, from setting foreign policy objectives to reforming the nation's health care system. Policy choices usually reflect some combination of political preferences and various assessments of the problem and possible solutions to it. Policy analysis can help to clarify the problem, the policy choices available, and how each choice stands up against the different standards of judgment that might be used, such as those we emphasized in chapter 1: effectiveness, efficiency, and equity. Ultimately, however, policymakers and the public choose what kinds of policies they prefer to have.

Steps in the Policy Analysis Process

The most common approach to policy analysis is to picture it as a series of analytical steps or stages, which are the elements in rational problem solving (Bardach and Patashnik 2016; MacRae and Whittington 1997). According to models of **rational decision making,** one defines a problem, indicates the goals and objectives to be sought, considers a range of alternative solutions, evaluates each of the alternatives to clarify their consequences, and then recommends or chooses the alternative with the greatest potential for solving the problem. This process is similar to the way most of us make everyday decisions, although we do it much more casually.

Often, the so-called **rational-comprehensive approach** to analysis and decision making is not possible, and the less demanding **incremental decision making** is substituted. Still, essentially the same steps are involved. The only difference is that incremental decision making is more limited than the rational-comprehensive approach in the extent of analysis required; often it means making modest changes in policy or making them gradually. In political settings, incremental decision making is a more realistic approach, given ideological and partisan constraints and the ever-present pressure from interest groups and other constituencies. All can restrict the range of policy options to be taken seriously and the kinds of questions that are asked about them (J. Anderson 2015; Lindblom and Woodhouse 1993).

Figure 4-1 summarizes the major steps in policy analysis and the kinds of questions analysts typically pose. It also illustrates how each stage of analysis might apply to a particular policy problem. Each step is considered briefly here as a summary description of what policy analysis aspires to do. Chapters 5 and 6 examine each of these steps in greater detail. Note as well how these steps in

Figure 4-1 Steps in the Policy Analysis Process

STEPS	TYPE OF QUESTIONS	ILLUSTRATIONS
Define and analyze the problem	• What is the problem faced? • Where does it exist? • Who or what is affected? • How did it develop? • What are the major causes? • How might the causes be affected by policy action?	• How is cell phone use, including texting, related to automobile accidents? • What is the potential to reduce accident rates through policy action? • How does talking on a cell phone or texting compare to other distractions while driving, such as use of navigation systems, drinking coffee, or talking to passengers?
Construct policy alternatives	• What policy options might be considered for dealing with the problem?	• To reduce drivers' cell phone use, should state governments institute sanctions such as fines? • Should states try to educate drivers on cell phone use? • Should cell phones be disabled in a moving car if effective technology to do so becomes available?
Choose evaluative criteria	• What criteria are most suitable for the problem and the alternatives? • What are the costs of action? • What will the costs be if no action is taken? • What is the likely effectiveness, social and political feasibility, or equity of alternatives?	• What criteria are most important for regulation of cell phones? • Will people find these options acceptable? • Is it ethical to restrict individual behavior to achieve a social goal? • What options are the most effective in discouraging drivers from talking on their cell phones or texting?
Assess the alternatives	• Which alternatives are better than others? • What kind of analysis might help to distinguish better and worse policy alternatives? • Is the evidence available? If not, how can it be produced?	• Which policy options are most likely to reduce drivers' use of cell phones and texting: public education or economic sanctions such as fines? • How successful are the efforts of states and localities to regulate cell phone use and texting? • What kinds of evidence are needed to answer these questions?
Draw conclusions	• Which policy option is the most desirable given the circumstances and the evaluative criteria? • What other factors should be considered?	• Should state governments impose stiff fines on use of cell phones or texting while driving? • Would such fines be accepted as a legitimate governmental action? • If they work, how might such actions be made more acceptable to the public?

the analysis process relate to the stages of the policymaking process discussed in chapter 3. Defining and analyzing problems is usually part of the agenda-setting stage of policymaking, and sometimes so is the construction of policy alternatives, especially if some potential alternatives are not considered seriously at all. Usually, however, the formal construction of alternatives is part of policy design and hence fits into the policy formulation stage of policymaking. Development of evaluative criteria also can be part of policy formulation, but it mainly falls into the stage of policy legitimation or approval. Assessing alternatives similarly can take place during both the formulation and legitimation stages of policymaking as policy actors consider which solutions they prefer and which may succeed politically. The same is true of the last stage of analysis, drawing conclusions. Analysts and policymakers may draw conclusions about preferred policy alternatives as policy is formulated, debated, and adopted. Since the policymaking process is continuous, these analytic steps also can be found in the implementation, evaluation, and policy-change stages of policymaking as current policies are assessed critically and alternatives considered.

Define and Analyze the Problem

The first step in any policy analysis is to define and analyze the problem. Everyone knows what the word **problem** means, but for policy analysts the term specifically refers to the existence of an unsatisfactory set of conditions for which relief is sought, either through private means or from the government. Analysts therefore need to describe that set of conditions, usually through the collection of facts or data on its magnitude or extent. For example, who is affected by the problem, and how seriously? How long has the situation existed, and how might it change over the next several years or decades? How amenable is it to intervention through one means or another? The goals and objectives of such intervention, whether private or governmental, may not be clear to all concerned.

It may also be necessary to clarify what is meant by the set of conditions, to define it clearly, and to develop accurate measures of it. If the problem is homelessness in the United States, for example, an analyst will need to be clear about what is meant by homelessness, how to determine the extent of it, and which segments of the population are affected by it.

Beyond gathering basic information about the problem, analysts want to identify its causes, which is not always an easy task. Without a good idea of how and why the problem came about, however, it is difficult to think usefully about possible solutions to it. This kind of diagnosis of the problem is akin to what a physician does when a patient is ill or what a mechanic does when a car is not running properly. The importance of the diagnosis is clear if one looks at how policymakers are trying to cope with an issue as imposing as global terrorism. Without an understanding of the causes of terrorism—and they may be both numerous and difficult to deal with—policy actions are unlikely to be effective. To use a more concrete example, one has first to diagnose the reasons for failing

International economic assistance. The United States and other developed nations have long provided economic assistance to help developing countries deal with their poverty and also with the effects of severe storms or other natural disasters with which they are poorly equipped to cope. The photo shows Filipinos carrying boxes with aid from the U.S. relief organization USAID after an Osprey aircraft of the U.S. Navy landed in the Eastern Samar town of Balangiga City on November 16, 2013. This was seven days after one of the most powerful typhoons ever recorded struck the area, killing nearly four thousand people and leaving others in dire circumstances. *(MARK RALSTON/AFP/Getty Image)*

public schools before a solution can be sought. Otherwise, there is little reason to believe that some of the proposed solutions (for example, formation of charter schools, use of school vouchers, or changing the nature of teacher evaluations) will improve the quality of education.

A long-standing dispute over international development assistance speaks to the importance of careful measures and analysis of public problems. Economic assistance to developing countries from twenty-eight donor nations, including the United States, totaled $131 billion in 2015, or about 0.3 percent of the donor nations' combined gross national income. The United States contributed about $31 billion of that total.[9] But what impact does spending this money have on developing nations? Critics say the impact is far less than it should be. Yet looking only at the overall statistical portrait misses the real success stories in economic assistance. Experience suggests that economic aid is most likely to work when it comes in relatively small, well-targeted, and tightly controlled investments rather than in large sums delivered to a government that may waste it.[10]

Construct Policy Alternatives

Once analysts believe they understand the problem, they begin to think about alternative ways of dealing with it. The policy typologies introduced in chapter 3 suggest several different approaches, such as regulation, subsidies, taxing and spending, market incentives, and public education or information provision. The point is that government has a finite number of actions from which to choose. Based on the available inventory of possibilities, analysts could construct a set of policy options for further study and consideration, such as the relative advantages of regulation and information disclosure for ensuring that financial markets operate properly and limit the risk of another economic collapse like the one that occurred in 2008 and 2009. Chapter 5 introduces some useful ways to lay out a range of policy alternatives.

Constructing policy alternatives is perhaps the most important stage in the policy analysis process. If analysts and policymakers cannot think of creative ways of solving problems, conventional approaches that may no longer be appropriate will continue to be used. Early in the process, therefore, analysts are called upon to think imaginatively and critically about how the problem might be addressed, both within government and outside it. One approach that has gained increasing acceptance is privatization, the transfer of public services from government to the private sector. Such private sector solutions, recommended by many policy analysts and organizations, and sometimes endorsed by the government, are said to be more appealing, and perhaps more effective, than reliance on a government agency, although the evidence on that is mixed. Chapter 5 suggests some fruitful ways for students of public policy to think creatively about generating policy options of this kind.

Choose Evaluative Criteria

When the policy alternatives have been identified, the analysis shifts to assessing their potential. This task calls for deciding on suitable evaluation criteria. As chapter 1 discussed, this text focuses on effectiveness or the likely success of proposals in solving the problem at hand, the economic costs and efficiency of proposals, and the implications for social equity. There are, however, many other appropriate criteria, such as political, administrative, and technical feasibility; environmental impacts; ethical considerations; and any number of political values, such as personal freedom, against which to assess policy proposals. These are further explored in chapter 6 and summarized in Figure 6-1, on page 183.

No matter how long a list of potential evaluative criteria analysts might develop, some criteria will be more appropriate for a given problem than others. For example, for years the United States has been considering and funding the development of a missile defense system for protection against a ballistic missile attack from a so-called rogue nation like North Korea or Iran. On what basis should analysts evaluate the proposal, particularly in relation to other national security needs? One criterion would have to be technical feasibility. Can the missile defense system, which is based on highly complex computer software and state-of-the-art technology, do what it is supposed to do? Another would be the costs. The Pentagon spent more than $100 billion over four decades, with relatively few positive results.[11] Moreover, the cost of a fully deployed system depends on how extensive a shield the government decides to construct, and some estimates put the total cost by the year 2025 at well over $200 billion. Is this outlay of taxpayer money reasonable in light of the gains to the nation's defense and the risk that the technology might not work as planned? Do new concerns over the nation's deficits and rising debt make a difference in how we appraise the value of such a program? How would an analyst go about determining the answer?[12]

Plenty of information is available about the missile defense system, but a good deal of it is contradictory, and analysts disagree heatedly about the core issues, such as technical feasibility. Any assessment of the desirability of creating and funding a system as technically complex as missile defense would be a demanding undertaking. Nevertheless, policymakers and analysts need to ask the questions and try to find answers.

For some policy actions—for example, whether and how to regulate or control gun ownership, or whether to permit concealed weapons to be carried in public places—the evaluative criteria would likely include political values. Personal rights will be weighed against other needs, such as protecting the public's safety and well-being. As this example indicates, conflicts may arise among criteria. The war on terrorism that began after the September 11 attacks raises similar questions: On what basis should policy analysts, citizens, and policymakers judge the suitability of policy options, such as military action against terrorist bases, economic development assistance to poor countries, or expanding offshore oil and gas drilling? Or the short-term national security implications

Public policies on guns. Among policy alternatives considered by states in recent years has been the expansion of citizen rights to own and carry weapons. The photo shows open-carry gun activists participating in a march on November 16, 2015, in Ferguson, Missouri. About a dozen supporters of gun rights gathered in Ferguson on that day for what the organizers hoped would be a racially integrated open-carry march to demonstrate that Second Amendment rights are for everyone. *(Michael B. Thomas/AFP/ Getty Images)*

of destroying terrorist operations versus the longer-term need to deal with the root causes of terrorism? In many policy disputes, much of the battle between proponents and opponents of government action is over which criteria to use as well as which conclusions to draw. Policymakers, analysts, and lobbyists of one stripe or another are likely to bring their ideological biases to these debates, such as a conviction by conservatives and many businesses that government regulation should be minimal and that economic growth is the primary national goal to be sought. Those beliefs tend to frame their selection of evaluative criteria and therefore their assessment of the problem and the solutions they are willing to consider.

Assess the Alternatives

With evaluative criteria at hand and a collection of possible courses of action to take, analysis turns to **assessing alternatives**. That is, the analysts ask which of the several alternatives that might be considered seriously is most likely to produce the outcome sought—whether it is to reduce the crime rate, improve the plight of the homeless, raise educational quality, reform the health care system, or rebuild the nation's infrastructure of highways and bridges. This exercise involves making judgments about how well each policy option fits in relation to the most relevant criteria. The analysts might rank the options in terms of overall desirability or consider them in terms of each criterion, such as effectiveness, economic cost, and equity.

Some authors refer to this stage of the process as projecting the outcomes or assessing impacts (Patton, Sawicki, and Clark 2016; Starling 1988). A number of different methods or tools are used to do this, and they are discussed at length in chapter 6. They range from cost-benefit analysis to ethical analysis. Given their frequent use in policy studies and debates today, it is important even for the beginning student of public policy to understand these methods and their strengths and limitations.

Analysts have many ways to present the alternatives so that policymakers and other interested parties can understand the analysis and the choices they face. For example, if three policy options are offered for consideration, the analyst might present each in terms of its likely effectiveness, economic efficiency, and equity. Trade-offs are inevitable in this kind of decision making. Only rarely does a given policy option rank highest on all of the evaluative criteria. Analysts therefore attach weight to each criterion. Should governments focus on providing access to health care for those without insurance, as President Obama and Congress tried to do with the Affordable Care Act of 2010? Or should the sharply rising costs of health care be more of a concern? What about the mandate in the 2010 law that forces individuals to buy health care insurance? Is that reasonable, and is it essential to achieve the other objectives of the health care reform law? As analysts consider more than a few conflicting bases for assessing policy options, the necessity for weighting criteria increases.

Draw Conclusions

Most studies draw conclusions about what kind of policy action is desirable, and some strongly advocate a particular position on the issues. Many studies do not recommend a single policy action. Rather, the analysts summarize their findings and draw conclusions about the relative merits of competing policy proposals but leave the choice of policy action to policymakers and the public.

Whichever approach is taken, all analysis is of necessity partial and limited. That is, analysis cannot ever be complete in the sense of covering every conceivable question that might be raised. It also cannot be free of limitations, because every method or tool that might be used is subject to some constraints. Policy analysts need to develop a robust ability to deal with uncertainty, which comes with the territory.

The later chapters consider these challenges and how to deal with them. Students will become familiar with the range of methods employed in the practice of public policy and how to use the different approaches, and therefore will be better prepared to cope with the challenges. For example, the amount of information available might be so overwhelming that finding the desirable course of action seems impossible; or there may be so little that no one can draw firm conclusions. Analysts may be faced with conflicting studies and interpretations that start with varying definitions of the problem and evaluative criteria that render their conclusions and recommendations difficult to compare and judge.

At this stage, we urge students to learn to ask critical questions about the information they collect, especially regarding its validity. Where did the information come from, and how reliable is the source? Is there any way to double-check the facts and their interpretation? Do the information and analysis seem on their face to be believable? Are there any signs of bias that might affect the conclusions that the study offers? If two or more studies contradict one another, why is that the case? Is it because of conflicting political ideologies, differences in the preferred policy actions, or disagreement in the way the problem is defined? Are the authors too selective in deciding what information should be presented and what can be left out? By gathering information from multiple sources and comparing different interpretations, students might find it easier to determine which of the studies is the most credible. Chapter 1 touched briefly on the need to develop these critical skills in appraising public policy information and studies, and the point is stressed throughout the book.

The best policy studies are those that are also sensitive to political reality. Their authors have made a special effort to understand the information needs of decision makers and the public, whether at the local, state, or national level. A common complaint within policy studies is that much analysis goes unread and unused either because it does not address the questions that decision makers think are important or because it is not communicated effectively to them so they can consider it. Analysis that is designed from the start to address these kinds of questions is far more likely to have an impact on the policy process (Bardach and Patashnik 2016; Lindblom and Cohen 1979; C. Weiss 1978).

Types of Policy Analysis

No matter what kind of public problem needs a solution, from airline safety and urban transportation to persistent poverty, there is usually no shortage of policy studies that might apply. Some come from government offices themselves, such as the Government Accountability Office and the Congressional Research Service, or from executive agencies and departments such as the Food and Drug Administration, the Department of Transportation, and the Department of Defense. Policy analysis is becoming common at the state level (Hird 2005) and globally, both within government agencies and in the private and nonprofit sectors. A great number of studies, however, come from interest groups and independent policy research institutes or think tanks, many of which advocate specific political agendas (Rich 2004).

The abundance of policy studies reflects not only the dramatic rise in the number of think tanks since the 1970s but also the even more striking increase in the number of interest groups that seek to shape public opinion on the issues and affect the policy process. This shift in the political environment is most evident at the national level, where policy researchers and interest groups pay rapt attention to the debates in Congress and the activities of administrative agencies. Even at state and local levels of government, particularly in the larger states and cities, policy studies and advocacy are common, especially as national groups such as the conservative American Legislative Exchange Council (ALEC) seek to influence policymaking in the states.

Scholars have noted the rise and influence of think tanks in particular, given their visibility in contemporary policymaking (McGann and Sabatini 2011; Rich 2004). Carol Weiss's study of these organizations attributes their dramatic growth and popularity within the United States to several trends and needs. First, government policymakers and the public increasingly need to understand and cope with complex problems. Second, policymakers find it useful in a time of political cynicism to demonstrate the reasonableness and rationality of their positions and actions, and policy analysis symbolizes an acceptable, or proper, procedure for decision making. Third, policy officials value independent research and analysis as supplements to the knowledge and skills within government and see the analyses as helping to persuade skeptical politicians and citizens. Fourth, certain interests who believe they are underrepresented in government circles seek to make their views known and promote their causes (C. Weiss 1992).

The leading think tanks, such as the Brookings Institution, American Enterprise Institute for Public Policy Research, Urban Institute, Center for Strategic and International Studies, and Heritage Foundation, are well endowed financially and can afford large professional staffs. Many receive significant and continuing support from foundations and industry or from government agencies for whom they conduct research under contract.[13] These research institutes are therefore generally well equipped to distribute their analyses throughout government, the Washington policy community, academia, and major media outlets nationwide (Ricci 1993; C. Weiss 1992). At the end of the chapter is a list of websites for think tanks and for other sources of policy studies. See the box

"Steps to Analysis: Think Tank Positions on Policy Issues" for a comparison of the findings of two prominent think tanks, the conservative Heritage Foundation and the liberal Center for American Progress, on gun control.

One way to compare think tanks is to understand the kinds of policy studies or policy analyses available today, a matter addressed briefly in chapter 1. Policy analyses fall into three broad categories: scientific, professional, and political. All serve valid purposes, but they have varying goals and objectives and use different methods. Figure 4-2 summarizes the distinctions among the three perspectives.

Figure 4-2   Orientations to Policy Analysis

TYPE OF ANALYSIS	OBJECTIVES	APPROACHES	LIMITATIONS	EXAMPLES
Scientific	Search for "truth" and build theory about policy actions and effects	• Use the scientific method to test hypotheses and theories • Aim for objective and rigorous analysis • Attribute less importance to policy relevance than to advancing knowledge	• May be too theoretical and not adequately address information needs of decision makers	Academic social scientists and natural scientists, National Academy of Sciences, Intergovernmental Panel on Climate Change
Professional	Analyze policy alternatives for solving public problems	• Synthesize research and theory to understand consequences of policy alternatives • Evaluate current programs and their effects • Aim for objectivity, but with goal of practical value in policy debate	• Research and analysis may be too narrow due to time and resource constraints • May neglect fundamental causes of public problems	Brookings Institution, Urban Institute, American Enterprise Institute, Government Accountability Office
Political	Advocate and support preferred policies	• Use legal, economic, and political arguments consistent with value positions • Aim to influence policy debate to realize organizational goals and values	• Often ideological or partisan and may not be credible • May lack analytic depth • Level of objectivity and rigor varies	Sierra Club, AFL-CIO, Chamber of Commerce, National Rifle Association, Heritage Foundation, American Legislative Exchange Council

Sources: Drawn in part from Peter House, *The Art of Public Policy Analysis* (Beverly Hills, Calif.: SAGE Publications, 1982); and David L. Weimer and Aidan R. Vining, *Policy Analysis: Concepts and Practice*, 6th ed. (New York: Routledge, 2016).

Steps to Analysis

Think Tank Positions on Policy Issues

All think tanks conduct analysis and advocate positions on public policy issues, but some of these groups are committed to political or ideological standpoints that affect their analyses and recommendations. Gun control is one issue that think tanks of varying political persuasions have studied over the past several decades. The shooting at Sandy Hook Elementary School in Newtown, Connecticut, in December 2012 and shootings at many other locations, such as a nightclub in Orlando, Florida, since then raise a number of issues related to use of firearms. These include the possible expansion of background checks required for those seeking to purchase a firearm, a limit on size of the ammunition clips available, a ban on assault-style weapons, and additional restrictions on gun purchases by those with diagnosed mental illness.

President Obama proposed a number of changes to federal gun control laws after the Sandy Hook shooting, but Congress ultimately enacted no changes in the laws. That decision reflected in part the opposing positions taken by Washington interest groups and think tanks, as well as a somewhat divided public. The following summaries come from two think tanks that represent distinctive positions on the ideological spectrum: the conservative Heritage Foundation and the liberal Center for American Progress.

What Did the Heritage Foundation Say about Gun Control?

All Americans, from whatever walks of life and of whatever political or philosophical convictions, abhor the death of innocent human beings and had a visceral reaction of shock and pain to the killing of 20 schoolchildren and six staff members in Newtown, Connecticut, in December 2012. In responding to this attack, Americans must consider with great reflection and care how best to proceed, in a manner consistent with our laws and our traditions, to protect innocent lives.

First, we must identify the specific problems to be addressed involving school safety, mental illness, the cultural climate, and the misuse of firearms.

Second, we must analyze potential solutions to the specific problems identified, examining the facts and taking into account the costs and benefits of the potential solutions to ensure that sound judgment governs the emotions inescapably attached to the subject.

Finally, Americans must implement appropriate solutions in a manner that is consistent with the Constitution, including the Second Amendment guarantee of the right to keep and bear arms, the traditional role of the states in our federal system, and the central significance of family.

Source: John Malcolm and Jennifer A. Marshall, "The Newtown Tragedy: Complex Causes Require Thoughtful Analysis and Responses," January 17, 2013, available at www.heritage.org/research/reports/2013/01/the-newtown-tragedy-complex-causes-require-thoughtful-analysis-and-responses.

What Did the Center for American Progress Say about Gun Control?

The tragedy at Sandy Hook Elementary School in Newtown, Connecticut, on December 14, 2012, reignited the debate on whether to strengthen federal and state gun laws. . . . Under current federal law, vendors in the business of selling guns must get a license, conduct background checks, and keep records. But unlicensed "private" sellers—persons who maintain they sell only occasionally at gun shows, online, or anywhere else—are able to sell guns with no questions asked. . . .

(Continued)

(Continued)

As a policy matter, most research suggests that making it more difficult for dangerous people to acquire guns will have a significant impact in reducing the more than 30,000 gun deaths that happen every year in America. As a political matter, polling conducted before and after Newtown show[s] that 80 percent to 90 percent of Americans support expanding background checks, including most gun owners. . . .

All potentially dangerous individuals need to be identified as such and prohibited from gun ownership. Many such people are already covered by the federal law—including felons, fugitives, some domestic abusers, and the dangerously mentally ill—but there are additional categories of people who should also be barred from possessing guns, such as violent misdemeanants, convicted misdemeanant stalkers, and certain domestic abusers who are not covered by the current law.

Source: Arkadi Gerney and Chelsea Parsons, "The Gun Debate 1 Year after Newtown: Assessing Six Key Claims about Gun Background Checks," December 13, 2013, available at www .americanprogress.org/issues/guns-crime/report/2013/ 12/13/80795/the-gun-debate-1-year-after-newtown/.

- What conclusions can you draw about how these two policy research organizations evaluate gun control?

- What are the similarities and differences in their positions?

Scientific Approaches

Some individuals, especially academics, study public policy for scientific purposes—that is, to build understanding of public problems and the policymaking process. They seek "truth" through scientific methods, regardless of whether the knowledge is relevant or useful in some immediate way. For example, social science studies in the scientific category typically are not intended to influence public policy directly. Their purpose is, as one author put it, "to deepen, broaden, and extend the policy-maker's capacity for judgment—not to provide him with answers" (Millikan 1959, 167). On a substantive issue such as climate change, natural and social scientists may be interested mainly in clarifying what we know about climate change, its causes, and its probable effects on the environment, the economy, and people's well-being, not necessarily in recommending policy action.

Professional Approaches

As we have seen in this chapter, others study public policy for professional reasons, such as conducting policy analyses for government agencies, think tanks, or interest groups. Many policy analysts, both in and out of government, are committed to producing the best analysis possible, and they adhere to strong professional norms for economic analysis, modeling of complex situations, forecasting future trends, and program evaluation. The comparison of the Brookings Institution and the American Enterprise Institute (AEI) in the box "Working with

Sources: Comparing Think Tanks" nicely illustrates the kinds of topics addressed by such analysts and how they express their purpose. Even though Brookings and AEI are usually described as left and right of center, respectively, both can be categorized as engaging in professional analysis.[14]

Working with Sources

Comparing Think Tanks

Policy research institutes, or think tanks, differ in many ways. Some are large and cover many policy issues, while others are small and highly specialized. Some aim for professional analysis of the issues, and others promote a policy or ideological agenda. Here, we highlight two prominent Washington think tanks that are well regarded for their analyses of policy issues. They also reflect different political philosophies: the Brookings Institution is usually characterized as slightly left of center, and the American Enterprise Institute as right of center.

As you read the think tanks' descriptions below, pay attention to specific language in their mission statements that points to their political philosophy and to possible bias in their analyses.

- Reviewing the topics that each covers, and the way those topics are summarized, can you detect differences between the two organizations in what they think is important, and the kinds of policies they will likely favor?

The Brookings Institution

Website: www.brookings.edu

Founded: 1922

Orientation and mission: Aims to "conduct high-quality, independent research" that leads to "pragmatic and innovative ideas on how to solve problems facing society." Its "300 leading experts in government and academia from all over the world . . . provide the highest quality research, policy recommendations, and analysis on a full range of public policy issues."

Sources of funding: Financed largely by an endowment and through support of philanthropic foundations, corporations, and private individuals.

Research programs fall into the following categories: Cities and Regions, Global Development, International Affairs, U.S. Economy, U.S. Government and Politics, Business and Industry, Defense and Security, Education, Health Care Policy, and Social Issues.

The American Enterprise Institute

Website: www.aei.org

Founded: 1938

Orientation and mission: Says that AEI is "committed to making the intellectual, moral, and practical case for expanding personal freedom, increasing individual opportunity, and promoting free enterprise in America and around the world. Our work explores ideas that can further these goals." Notes also that "AEI scholars take part in this pursuit with academic freedom," that AEI "operates independently of any political party and has no institutional positions," and that "scholars' conclusions are driven by rigorous, data-driven research and broad-ranging evidence."

Sources of funding: Supported primarily by grants and contributions from foundations, corporations, and individuals.

Research programs include work in the following areas: Economics, Foreign and Defense Policy, Health Care, Education, Politics and Public Opinion, Poverty Studies, and Society and Culture.

Sources: Taken from the websites for Brookings and AEI. The statements are summaries of what each presents as its mission and current areas of research.

Political Approaches

Some analysts may be as rigorous in the methods they use as the professionals, but they are also committed to specific policy values and goals and sometimes to ideological and partisan agendas. As one would expect, they try to emphasize the studies and findings that help to advance those values and goals. This kind of policy study can be described as political, rather than professional or scientific. Analysts who work for interest groups or activist organizations, such as the National Organization for Women, Planned Parenthood, ALEC noted earlier, or the National Rifle Association, are especially likely to have this orientation. So too are those who work for political parties and ideological groups, such as Americans for Democratic Action, the American Civil Liberties Union, or the American Conservative Union. The two think tanks compared in the previous "Steps to Analysis" box (pp. 133–134), the Heritage Foundation and the Center for American Progress, fit into this category of political policy analysis because of their strong commitments to conservative and liberal policies, respectively.

What Kind of Analysis Is Needed?

No matter what policy area is involved, there is never a single correct way to conduct a policy study or one set of methods or tools to use. The next two chapters have more to say about appropriate methods and tools, but here it is worth emphasizing that regardless of whether the policy research falls into the scientific, professional, or political category, analysts face important choices about the kind of assessment needed for a given study and what approaches to use.

Deal with Root Causes or Make Pragmatic Adjustments?

One of the basic questions that all analysts must answer is whether they should focus on the **root causes** of public problems or examine policy actions that might ameliorate a pressing problem but do nothing about its underlying causes. Political scientist James Q. Wilson argued for the latter view in his influential book *Thinking about Crime* (1977, 55–59). The "ultimate causes cannot be the object of policy efforts," he said, because they cannot be changed. As he explained, criminologists, for example, know that men commit more crimes than women, and younger men more than older ones. It is a scientifically correct observation, Wilson said, but not very useful for policymakers concerned about reducing the crime rate. Why not? The answer is that society can do nothing to change the facts. So rather than address the root causes of crime, he suggested that policymakers concentrate on what governments can do to reduce the crime rate, or deal with what some call the **proximate causes**, or immediate causes, of the problem:

> What is the condition one wants to bring into being, what measure do we have that will tell us when that condition exists, and what policy tools does a government (in our case, a democratic and libertarian government) possess that might, when applied, produce at reasonable cost a desired alteration in the present condition or progress toward the desired condition? (59)

In contrast, the distinguished scholar Charles E. Lindblom (1972, 1) wrote that the kind of policy analysis illustrated by Wilson's statement can become a "conservative and superficial kind of social science" that fails to ask fundamental questions about the social and economic structures of society. It considers, according to Lindblom, "only those ways of dealing with policy that are close cousins of existing practices," and therefore reinforces a prevailing tendency to maintain current policies and practices even when they may be unsuccessful in addressing the problem.

Analysts who favor Lindblom's perspective would examine the fundamental or root causes as well as the proximate causes of public problems. These analysts would not dismiss as fruitless idealism the possibility of taking action on the root causes of problems in some circumstances. For example, the George W. Bush White House announced in July 2005 that the president's energy bill, then nearing approval in Congress, would help to address "the root causes of high energy prices," chiefly by expanding domestic production of energy.[15] Critics of the controversial energy bill were just as quick to suggest that the root cause most in need of attention was the nation's increasing appetite for energy, and that intensive programs fostering energy conservation and efficient energy use were needed more than an increase in supply. Both sides were correct in emphasizing the need to address not just the high price of energy in 2005 but the underlying causes of the problem.

Even an incremental adjustment in policy that does not look seriously at root causes can make a big difference. Consider the imposition of a national minimum drinking age of twenty-one that was intended to combat the high percentage of automobile accidents attributable to alcohol, especially among younger drivers. In 1984, the federal government decided to deny a percentage of federal highway funds to states that refused to comply with the minimum drinking age requirement. An assessment of the policy's results in Wisconsin showed that it had "immediate and conclusive effects on the number of teenagers involved in alcohol-related crashes." Accident rates declined by 26 percent for eighteen-year-olds and 19 percent for nineteen- and twenty-year-olds (Figlio 1995, 563).

High-profile measures. Among the public policy alternatives that received much attention in recent years were a variety of economic stimulus measures intended to stabilize or jump-start the U.S. economy and create jobs. This January 2013 photo shows contractors at work on the East Side Access project beneath midtown Manhattan in New York. East Side Access is one of three major projects under New York that by 2019 will expand what is already the nation's largest mass-transit system. *(AP Photo/ Mary Altaffer)*

Comprehensive Analysis or Short-Term Policy Relevance?

Should analysts use the most comprehensive and rigorous approaches available to ensure the credibility of their results, even though doing so may take longer and cost more? Or should they aim for a less comprehensive and less rigorous study that might provide pertinent results faster and cheaper, even at some risk of the credibility of the results? The answer depends on the nature of the problem under consideration. The most complex, controversial, and costly policy choices might require the most comprehensive analysis, while more limited studies might suffice in other situations.

Academic scientists (social and natural) tend to favor rigorous, comprehensive studies. They place a high value on methodological precision because they believe that only demanding scientific investigations produce knowledge that inspires confidence. Sometimes, however, a study can take so long to complete that it has less impact on policy decisions than it might have had if the results were known earlier. For example, in the 1980s, the federal government sponsored a decade-long study of the causes and consequences of acid rain, at a cost of $500 million. Although widely viewed as first-rate scientific research, the study also was faulted for failing to address some critical topics in time to influence decision makers. By most accounts, it had less influence than it should have had on the adoption of the Clean Air Act Amendments of 1990, the first national effort to deal seriously with acid rain (Russell 1993).

Professional policy analysts are often distinguished from social science researchers in part because of the analysts' interest in applied policy research.

The professionals are far more likely to aim their research at policymakers and other policy actors as evident in the brief descriptions of Brookings and AEI provided in the "Working with Sources" box on page 135.

Analysts associated with advocacy organizations in the "political" category shown in Figure 4-2 are the most likely to emphasize short-term policy relevance. They also typically bring a strong commitment to the values embodied in the organization. It is not surprising that the studies by the Natural Resources Defense Council and the Sierra Club are unabashedly pro-environment, while those by the National Rifle Association and the Nuclear Energy Institute support gun ownership and nuclear power, respectively. Such policy advocacy does not necessarily mean that the studies are invalid; many are just as well done and valuable as those released by ostensibly more objective research institutes. One recent assessment of the liberal Center on Budget and Policy Priorities, for example, described its analyses as "academically rigorous" yet clearly "intended to influence lawmakers, aides, lobbyists, and journalists." The center had become, the author noted, "a powerful source of knowledge that helps out-of-power Democrats counter White House experts at the Office of Management and Budget."[16] Because of these kinds of political commitments, however, reports from advocacy organizations warrant a critical reading to detect any possible bias (Rich 2004).

Consensual or Contentious Analysis?

Should analysts adhere closely to consensual norms and mainstream public values, or should they challenge them and propose new values or new ways of thinking about the problem under consideration? Political theorist Martin Rein (1976) argued for what he called a value-critical approach to policy research, urging analysts to be skeptical of and distrust orthodoxy. He advocated approaches to policy study that made the analyst a "moral critic" who questions the value and belief assumptions behind policy research. He suggested three ways to engage in such research, with increasing degrees of critical inquiry: using consensual or mainstream approaches, using contentious or value-critical approaches, and—the most radical—using paradigm-challenging approaches.

Most contemporary policy analyses fall into the first category, a much smaller number into the second, and a negligible number into the third. Yet one could argue that many public policies today are very much in need of bold new thinking and radical challenges, much as Rein suggested in the mid 1970s. Consider the case of health care policy, the subject of chapter 8. With sharply rising costs and widespread dissatisfaction with access to and delivery of health care services today, some analysts and policymakers are beginning to suggest the need for radical change that goes beyond the Affordable Care Act of 2010. Much the same is true as analysts and decision makers around the country confront the various federal and state entitlement programs—from Social Security and Medicare to Medicaid and public employee pension systems—and seek innovative and sometimes radical solutions to deal with dire forecasts of rising costs.

Reliance on Rational Analysis or Democratic Politics?

Policy analysts are trained to engage in the rational assessment of public problems and their solutions, and they often use economic analysis and other quantitative methods to find the most logical, efficient, and (they hope) effective ways to deal with public problems. But should analysts also try to foster **democratic political processes**, such as citizen involvement (deLeon 1997; Gormley 1987; Jenkins-Smith 1990)? As noted, some advocates of policy analysis believe that public problems and policy choices are so complex that technical scientific analysis is essential to reach a defensible decision. These views sometimes conflict with the expectation that the public and elected officials are ultimately responsible for choosing the policy direction for the nation. In short, as citizens, we value rigorous analysis, but we also expect democracy to prevail unless there is some good reason (for example, national security) to limit public involvement.

Consider the case of nuclear waste disposal in terms of this dilemma. Federal government analysts and most of those working for the nuclear industry and technical consulting companies have relied on complex risk assessment, a form of policy analysis dealing with threats to health and the environment. Nearly all of the studies concluded that risks from the radioactive waste to be housed in a disposal facility are minor and manageable, even over the thousands of years that the proposed repository at Yucca Mountain, Nevada, was to contain the waste without significant leakage. Critics of the government's position, however, including the state of Nevada, countered that the scientific questions were far from settled and that the public's concerns about nuclear waste have not been satisfactorily addressed. They called for a decision-making process that allowed for greater citizen involvement and consultation, no matter how long it would take to build public trust (Dunlap, Kraft, and Rosa 1993; Kraft 2013; Wald 2002). Proponents of the waste site in turn assert that the critics merely reflect the common NIMBY (Not-in-My-Backyard) syndrome; they argue that local opposition to such waste repositories and other unwanted facilities is inevitable and cannot be the sole basis for a policy decision.

How can this kind of tension between reliance on technical analysis and democracy be resolved? Does the best solution lie in more analysis of these various risks and better management by the federal government and the states? Or should more weight be given to the public's fears and concerns, and should policymakers turn to a more open and democratic political process for making the necessary choices?

Other Aspects of Policy Analysis

The differences among the fundamental types of policy research are evident in the great variety of academic journals and other professional outlets, many of which are available on the Internet. Some publications, for example the *Journal of Policy Analysis and Management*, emphasize the economic aspects of public policy, while others, such as the *Policy Studies Journal* and the *Review of Policy Research*, stress institutional and political factors. A few journals, such as *Philosophy and Public Affairs*, examine the ethical aspects of public policy, and nearly every law journal discusses the legal considerations of public policy. We urge students to browse the websites as well as the journals in their campus libraries to see what information is available on different topics. Most think tanks and advocacy organizations (and most government agencies) publish their studies, either in full or summarized, on their webpages as well as in journals, books, and reports.

The primary focus of this text is substantive policy analysis, which aims at answering questions such as what effects school voucher programs have on the quality of education, or whether regulation of cell phone use in cars reduces accident rates. But a great deal of work in the public policy field, especially by political scientists, focuses instead on describing how government and policymakers actually behave. Such work tries to address questions such as how Congress makes decisions on defense policy or agricultural subsidies, and how the White House influences agency regulatory decision making (J. Anderson 2015).

The perspectives and approaches of policy analysis apply to institutional issues as well as to substantive policy questions (Gormley 1987). This kind of analysis is especially helpful for examining proposals for institutional change. For example, institutional policy analysis might address a question such as what consequences could result if environmental protection policy were to be decentralized to the states (Rabe 2010, 2016). Or, in light of controversies over the 2000 presidential election, what kinds of ballots are most likely to minimize voter error and be counted accurately? Or what would be the likely consequences for the new state "voter ID" laws that went into effect in many states in recent years (see chapter 13)?

Ethical issues in the conduct and use of policy studies deal with honesty and scruples. For example, what ethical obligations do analysts have to design and conduct their studies in a certain manner? To what extent are they influenced by the source of funding, particularly when the funds come from interest groups with a stake in the outcome, such as the tobacco companies that want to learn about the impact of antismoking initiatives? Does the analyst work primarily for the client who pays for the study, or does the analyst have a duty to represent the larger public interest (Weimer and Vining 2016)? At a minimum, most analysts would agree that they are obliged to be open and transparent about their values and policy preferences, their funding sources, the methods they use, the data they collect, and any critical assumptions they make in the analysis of the data and the conclusions they reach (J. Bowman and Elliston 1988; Tong 1986). Chapter 6 goes further into the criteria, including ethical standards, that can be used to evaluate policy alternatives.

Conclusions

The example at the beginning of the chapter on cell phone use and driving shows the challenge of making policy decisions when so many questions can be raised about the problem and the implications of taking action. Yet most students and practitioners of public policy are convinced that analysis can advance solutions by clarifying the problem, collecting information, and suggesting ways to make decisions. For that reason, this chapter surveys the practice of policy analysis and shows how it relates to the policymaking process and to politics in general. The chapter also emphasizes that there are many different types of analysis, and that the one that is used in a given case should reflect the particular challenges that are faced.

Today, analysis is ubiquitous, and it enters policy debate everywhere it occurs. Analysis is conducted in formal think tanks, interest groups, executive agencies, and legislative committees at all levels of government. Its thoroughness, objectivity, and purpose vary markedly, as one might expect. Students of public policy therefore need to be alert to the strengths and weaknesses of particular policy studies and prepared to question everything: the assumptions, the methods, and the conclusions. At the same time, however, students need to explore the many available sources of policy information and to think creatively about how to become engaged with contemporary policy problems.

for CQ Press

Sharpen your skills with SAGE edge at **http://edge.sagepub.com/ kraft6e. SAGE edge for students** provides a personalized approach to help you accomplish your coursework goals in an easy-to-use learning environment.

DISCUSSION QUESTIONS

1. Consider the case of using cell phones while driving a car, whether for talking or texting. Given the information provided in the chapter, would you favor restricting drivers' use of handheld cell phones? What about hands-free cell phones? What about restrictions on texting? How would you defend this policy choice?

2. Much of the policy analysis that is used in public debates today comes from interest groups that are strongly committed to one side of the issue or another, or from think tanks that espouse a particular ideology, on the left or the right. Do you think these policy commitments make the quality of the analysis suspect? Why or why not?

3. Review the two contrasting think tank positions on gun control presented in the "Steps to Analysis" box on pages 133–134. Which do you think is more persuasive? Why is that?

4. Should policy analysts try to deal with the fundamental causes of social problems, such as crime, poverty, and homelessness, or aim instead for a more pragmatic and limited approach that may be more realistic and more politically acceptable? Why do you think so?

KEYWORDS

SUGGESTED READINGS

James E. Anderson, *Public Policymaking*, 8th ed. (Stamford, Conn.: Cengage Learning, 2015). One of the best general treatments of the U.S. policy-making process.

Eugene Bardach and Eric M. Patashnik, *A Practical Guide for Policy Analysis: The Eightfold Path to More Effective Problem Solving*, 5th ed. (Washington, D.C.: CQ Press, 2016). A short but readable guide to the essentials of policy analysis, particularly for practitioners.

Carl V. Patton, David S. Sawicki, and Jennifer J. Clark, *Basic Methods of Policy Analysis and Planning*, 3rd ed. (New York: Routledge, 2016). One of the leading texts in policy analysis, with a focus on methods for basic or quick analysis.

Deborah Stone, *Policy Paradox: The Art of Political Decision Making*, 3rd ed. (New York: Norton, 2012). An imaginative critique of conventional policy-making and policy analysis, with an emphasis on the role of politics and values in policymaking.

David L. Weimer and Aidan R. Vining, *Policy Analysis: Concepts and Practice*, 6th ed. (New York: Routledge, 2016). A widely used text in policy analysis that draws heavily from economics.

SUGGESTED WEBSITES

www.aei.org. American Enterprise Institute for Public Policy Research, a major policy research institute that tends to favor conservative positions.

www.alec.org. American Legislative Exchange Council, a national conservative research institute that assists state legislators in advancing the principles of limited government and free markets.

www.brookings.edu. Brookings Institution, a major policy research organization that is usually described as somewhat left of center or liberal.

www.cato.org. Cato Institute, a libertarian think tank.

www.cbpp.org. Center on Budget and Policy Priorities, a liberal policy research organization that focuses on fiscal policy and its effects on low- and moderate-income families and individuals.

www.cei.org. Competitive Enterprise Institute, a conservative think tank and advocacy organization.

www.csis.org. Center for Strategic and International Studies, a think tank that focuses on global challenges and foreign and defense policy issues.

www.heartland.org. Heartland Institute, a conservative think tank.

www.heritage.org. Heritage Foundation, a conservative think tank.

www.hudson.org. Hudson Institute, a conservative think tank.

www.publicagenda.org. Nonpartisan briefings on policy and polling; news, legislation, and studies; and research sources.

www.rand.org. RAND Corporation, the first organization to be called a think tank.

www.rff.org. Resources for the Future, a think tank specializing in economic analysis of environmental and natural resource issues.

www.urban.org. Urban Institute, a leading policy research center that deals with diverse urban issues such as housing, poverty, employment, health, crime, and the economy.

LEADING GENERAL JOURNALS OF PUBLIC POLICY

Journal of Policy Analysis and Management
Journal of Policy History
Journal of Public Policy

Policy Sciences
Policy Studies Journal
Review of Policy Research

MAJOR PROFESSIONAL NEWSWEEKLIES WITH POLICY COVERAGE

CQ Magazine

National Journal

NOTES

1. Matt Richtel, "Phone Makers Could Cut Off Drivers. Why Don't They?" *New York Times*, September 25, 2016.
2. Statistics on distracted driving and driver use of cell phones can be found at www.textingand drivingsafety.com and www.distraction.gov.
3. See Matt Richtel, "In Study, Texting Lifts Crash Risk by Large Margin," *New York Times*, July 28, 2009; and Tara Parker-Pope, "A Problem of the Brain, Not the Hands: Group Urges Phone Ban for Drivers," *New York Times*, January 13, 2009.
4. See Bill Vlasic, "Designing Dashboards with Fewer Distractions," *New York Times*, July 5, 2013.
5. See Matt Richtel, "Federal Panel Urges Cell Phone Ban for Drivers," *New York Times*, December 13, 2011; and Joan Lowy, "Safety Council: Ban Cell Phones while Driving," Associated Press release, January 12, 2009. Data on state and local action on use of cell phones while driving can be found at the website for the safety council: www.nsc.org.
6. Richtel, "Phone Makers Could Cut Off Drivers."
7. See Damien Cave, "Note to Drivers: Lose the Phone (and Lipstick)," *New York Times*, October 1, 2005; and Katie Hafner and Jason George, "For Drivers, a Traffic Jam of Distractions," *New York Times*, March 3, 2005.
8. Practical policy analysis is also sometimes referred to as "quick analysis" or "quickly applied basic methods," but the intention is to offer an analytical and objective assessment of the issues, even when policymakers must make decisions quickly. See Behn and Vaupel (1982) and Patton, Sawicki, and Clark (2016).
9. The data are taken from the Organisation for Economic Co-operation and Development report "Statistics on Resource Flows to Developing Countries," updated through December 2016, available at www.oecd.org/dac/stats/statisticson resourceflowstodevelopingcountries.htm.
10. Michael M. Weinstein, "The Aid Debate: Helping Hand, or Hardly Helping?" *New York Times*, May 26, 2002.
11. For a recent review of the missile system's challenges, see Eliot Marshall, "Missing the Mark," *Science* 342 (November 22, 2013): 926–929.
12. See Steven Pifer, "The Limits of U.S. Missile Defense," Brookings Institution, March 30, 2015. Current data on the nation's missile defense system can be found at the website for the Defense Department's Missile Defense Agency: https://www.mda.mil/.
13. For example, many organizations and think tanks on the right side of the political spectrum have received substantial funding from foundations supporting conservative causes and publications. Among the most notable are the John M. Olin Foundation, Scaife Family Foundation, Koch Family Foundations and Philanthropy, Lynde and

Harry Bradley Foundation, and Adolph Coors Foundation. For an objective overview of the role of conservative foundations, see Shawn Zeller, "Conservative Crusaders," *National Journal*, April 26, 2003, 1286–1291.

14. Critics of both think tanks have noted that many of their scholars also write op-ed articles and engage in various forms of advocacy, such as testifying before congressional committees and sometimes sitting on corporate boards. See, for example, Eric Lipton, Nicholas Confessore, and Brooke Williams, "Think Tank Scholar or Corporate Consultant? It Depends on the Day," *New York Times*, August 8, 2016.

15. The statement was made by White House spokesperson Scott McClellan and is reported in Carl Hulse, "As Energy and Highway Bills Near Completion, Congress Gives Itself a Hand," *New York Times*, July 29, 2005.

16. See Andrew Taylor, "Democrats' Go-To Guy Gets the Facts Straight," *CQ Weekly*, March 7, 2005, 552–553.

Chapter 5

Policy for public problems. Immigration continues to be one of the most intractable public policy issues that the United States faces, and it will continue to be debated in legislatures and on the campaign trail. The photo shows a woman carrying a piñata based on Republican presidential candidate Donald Trump during one of several May Day marches on May 1, 2016, in Los Angeles, California. *(David McNew/Getty Images)*

Public Problems and Policy Alternatives

On September 29, 2011, the state of Alabama's new policy on immigration went into effect, but complaints about it quickly followed both within the state and nationwide. The law resembled the effort the previous year in Arizona, which approved a stringent and much-criticized anti-immigration law that sought to identify, prosecute, and then deport illegal immigrants. Like Arizona, Alabama wanted to impose tough new restrictions on illegal immigrants in the face of what it saw as federal inaction to address the problem of illegal immigration, a perennially controversial subject and one of the key issues in Donald Trump's 2016 presidential campaign.[1] The Alabama law required proof of immigration status (such as citizenship or legal residency) for "any transaction between a person and the state or a political subdivision of the state." This included renewal of a driver's license, a business license, or a vehicle registration, but also, depending on who was interpreting the law, the provision of utilities such as electricity, water, and natural gas to undocumented immigrants.

Some Alabama residents soon found themselves unable to cope with the new requirements because they could not locate a birth certificate or easily acquire other acceptable evidence of citizenship. Others had the necessary paperwork, but found that they had to spend hours in line to prove their citizenship for routine government services. Public officials who did not carry out the law's requirements fully could find themselves liable for civil or criminal penalties. Even observing a violation of the law and not reporting it to authorities was a crime, and a government employee who violated the law could be convicted of a felony offense, surely enough to encourage most to stick to the letter of the law.

By November, an increasing number of state lawmakers were calling for changes in the sweeping measure because of these kinds of effects, as well as concern in the business community that the law was harming the state's economy. As one lawmaker put it, "The longer the bill has been out, the more unintended consequences we have found." He concluded that "all of us realize we need to change it." Yet most of the Alabama public seemed to like the new law, making any fundamental changes in it politically difficult.[2] Even so, about seven months after the law was adopted, the state legislature revised it, weakening requirements to show proof of citizenship or legal status for routine governmental services. In addition, the federal Justice Department and civil rights groups, among others, filed lawsuits to block parts of the law from being implemented.[3]

Beyond the obstacles that state residents faced because of the new law and the predictable legal challenges to it, Alabama farmers learned that they might suffer substantial economic losses; they could no longer count on having sufficient numbers of workers, and the law went into effect just as their crops needed to be harvested. The workers they hired previously were hesitant to remain in the state for fear of arrest and deportation. In addition, many businesses that the state had aggressively recruited in recent years to strengthen its economy, including Mercedes-Benz, Hyundai, and Honda, had expressed reluctance to expand their presence in the state, and those companies still being recruited began to lose interest because of the new immigration law. Undocumented immigrants constitute only about 4 percent of Alabama's workforce, or about a hundred thousand people. Yet there was little evidence that Alabamians were eager to fill the sudden vacancies left by farm laborers, restaurant workers, retail service personnel, and others who accepted such low-wage jobs. The same is true nationwide. Of the eleven million undocumented immigrants estimated to reside in the United States, some seven million are in the workforce, but often in jobs that few Americans seem to want even in times of high unemployment.[4] Indeed, a comprehensive study of the overall societal costs and benefits of illegal immigration at the time concluded that the difference was "close enough to zero to be essentially a wash." That is, undocumented immigrants were not found to be dragging down the U.S. economy, as is often assumed to be the case, even if some states and some industries are significantly affected.[5]

The growing national debate over immigration has been emerging for well over a decade, and it reflects the widespread belief that previous immigration control laws failed to deal effectively with the problem. More fundamentally, there was little agreement on what the problem of illegal immigration really was about. To some, it had been captured by periodic reports that the number of undocumented immigrants in the United States had increased, particularly in the West and South, although recent studies have found no net increase in migration in recent years, and in fact document a significant decline.[6] Among other concerns, critics have focused on the cost to the states of providing education and medical care for undocumented workers and their families. Some worried that a high rate of illegal immigration suggested that U.S. borders lacked the security that is essential to prevent entry by potential terrorists. Still others, particularly business owners, were inclined to minimize the problem, saying that the health of the U.S. economy depended on immigrant workers and would suffer without their contribution, as many businesses in Alabama discovered. Some also cited the economic benefits to the immigrants' home countries of their employment here, as well as benefits to the U.S. economy.[7]

What should the United States do today about illegal immigration? To some extent, the problem diminished significantly during the recession that began in 2008, when immigrants found it difficult to secure work and returned to their home countries. Nonetheless, the long-term concerns remained. So should the nation provide for a selective guest worker program to fill jobs for which there are no U.S. workers available, an idea favored by business and labor groups? Should it strengthen the borders, especially the 1,933-mile boundary with Mexico, and add physical barriers such as the 700 miles of fence that Congress authorized in 2006, or an electronic virtual fence that the government tried and then canceled in early 2011? During his 2016 campaign, Donald Trump famously called for building a "wall," and promised that Mexico would pay for it. Should the government increase the number of Border Patrol agents to control illegal entry?[8] Should it provide some kind of path to legal residency or citizenship for at least some undocumented immigrants already in the nation if they meet specific requirements? There are few simple answers to any of these questions, in part because policy actors hold sharply divergent views on immigration, emotions on the subject often run high, and both Democrats and Republicans are acutely aware of the political risks of staking out a position on the issue. Congress struggled with immigration reform in 2013 and 2014, but could not resolve sharp differences between the Senate and House in an election year. After that time, the issue became so heavily politicized that few held out hopes of a workable, bipartisan solution to immigration.

As we argued in earlier chapters, policy analysis is no panacea for a political system vulnerable to emotional and shortsighted decision making, all too evident in the history of immigration policy. Yet it can, under the right conditions, help to counteract such tendencies and push the policy process toward more thoughtful and effective actions. This chapter focuses on two elements in policy analysis: how to define and analyze public problems and how to think about possible solutions. It also suggests some strategies for studying public problems and for finding useful information.

Problem Analysis

The beginning of any policy study involves a description of a problem. Sometimes the problem—and perhaps even its causes—is obvious. For example, if the problem is teenage smoking and how to curtail it, one can find abundant information about the number of teenage smokers, why they choose to smoke, and the implications for lifelong smoking habits and the associated health problems that accompany them. Some states, most notably California, have used that information to adopt educational programs aimed at prevention and other policies that have successfully reduced the rate of teenage smoking.

The example of teenage smoking shows how simple some kinds of **problem analysis** can be. The problems may be relatively straightforward, and the information needed to make a policy choice is at hand, thanks to national or state reports or surveys that collect it. Although few public problems are entirely without controversy, there are also many, such as this one, about which reasonable people from all political ideologies can agree on what actions to take. Such agreement is made easier when the facts about the problem are readily available and easily understood.

The Nature of the Problem

Most public problems are not so simple; nor is the path to policy action as clear as trying to reduce teenage smoking. Nevertheless, the first step in policymaking is the same whether the problem is straightforward or complicated: define and analyze the problem. Problem analysis involves trying to answer the basic questions about the nature of the problem, its extent or magnitude, how it came about, its major causes, and why it is important to consider as a matter of public policy. At heart, addressing these kinds of questions requires students of public policy to think critically and creatively about the problem. What does it entail? What do we already know about it? What are the possible solutions? It also requires us to begin gathering the necessary information. We discuss the logic of information searches and useful strategies for them later in the chapter.

Public problems are often difficult to understand. The challenge is even more daunting given that we are bombarded daily with limited, biased, and conflicting messages in numerous electronic and print formats. Whether the sources are talk radio, partisan television news shows, Internet blogs, position statements issued by candidates or political parties, reports by interest groups, or serious policy studies by think tanks, one of the most vexing issues is how to interpret information that comes to us without a meaningful context. The "contextual data," or background information, to which the cartoon refers are essential to make sense of a problem, to see how it compares to other concerns in our personal lives or in society, and to estimate what effects a proposal or action might have.

Definitions and Measures. An essential step in the policy process is to define the problem. The definitions enable those seeking a solution to communicate with one another with a degree of precision that otherwise might not be possible. For example, if analysts are studying the plight of the poor in the United States, they need to define what poverty means. Is being poor only a matter of having insufficient money or income, or does it include other characteristics, such as the lack of certain skills or abilities? Should poverty be defined in relative terms (poorer than others) or in absolute terms (unable to meet essential human needs)? For 2015, the U.S. government reported that 43.1 million Americans were poor,

or about 13.5 percent of the population; this was down from 14.8 percent in 2014, meaning that 3.5 million fewer people were living in poverty. For comparison, the rate was 19 percent when President Lyndon Johnson declared the War on Poverty in 1964.[9] In 2016, the federal government placed the poverty line for a family of four in the forty-eight contiguous states at $24,300 (it is higher in Hawaii and Alaska), and the number is important. It determines who is eligible for federal aid programs such as the Head Start preschool program, supplemental nutrition assistance, and children's health insurance, among others. Real consequences result from this particular definition, which many students of poverty have long criticized as unrealistic.[10] Sometimes a quick literature search, discussed later in the chapter, will reveal both the usual definition of the concept and the debate that surrounds it.

Public policy arguments also turn on **operational measures**, or quantitative indicators, of problems. As the previous example indicates, rather than refer to poverty in the abstract, analysts want to know how many people live in poverty, how the rate has changed over time, and how poverty affects different segments of the population, such as the elderly or minorities. If discussing educational quality in the public schools, analysts want to see test scores and other student evaluations to determine what kind of problems exist in the schools and how the schools in one community compare to those in another, or how U.S. schools compare to those in other nations.

In recent years, Congress considered establishing an independent, web-based, and comprehensive national indicator system that would bring together high-quality data on the economy, society and culture, and the environment. Led by the National Academies, a consortium of two hundred institutions and individuals worked on a "State of the USA" document of this kind (U.S. Government Accountability Office 2004). The plan became a reality in 2008, with the establishment of the nonprofit and privately funded institution State of the USA, Inc., whose website was launched in 2009 (http://stateoftheusa.org). The organization promises a comprehensive collection of "the best quality measures and data on the most important issues facing the country." Of course, such data already exist in many different locations, particularly government agencies.

Quantitative measures are abundant for most contemporary public problems, from energy use and population growth to economic growth, unemployment, and public health, and using them can be enormously helpful for understanding the nature of a given problem (Lewis and Burd-Sharps 2010; Miringoff and Miringoff 1999). How much statistical information needs to be provided is a matter of judgment, but at a minimum, most issue papers or problem analyses would include some basic descriptive statistics. One is the frequency count, such as the percentage of the population at different income levels or the number of people in a survey who favor or do not favor a particular issue position. Another type is the mean, or average, measure of a group or category, such as the average score on an examination. An alternative is the median of a variable, or the point where half of the group lies above and half below. One such example is the median price of homes sold in different regions of the nation, a commonly used statistic on the state of the nation's housing market. Some idea of the range of variation (the standard deviation) or the correlation or relationship between two variables, such as race and income, may be useful as well.

Statistical information can be displayed in many ways in a report, as we will indicate throughout the text. These include tables that show frequency counts or percentages of what is being studied, such as the percentage of different age groups in the population who smoke. Information can be superimposed on maps to show geographic variations such as rates of urban growth or the income levels for adjacent urban and suburban areas. Graphic figures—pie charts or bar charts—are common, as are line figures that show how the magnitude of a problem changes over time, such as the number of people without health care insurance from 1970 to 2016 (Ammons 2009; Berman and Wang 2017). As one example, Figure 5-1 shows the nation's health care expenditures for calendar year 2015 using two pie charts that clearly distinguish revenues and expenditures in a visually striking manner. Figures like this can help readers not only to understand the total costs of health care, which have been rising rapidly, but to see where the money comes from and where it goes.

There is an art to choosing how best to display quantitative information. At a minimum, reports should aim for clarity. But some visual displays are also more likely to capture the reader's attention than others. Computer-generated color graphics allow for using a range of different formats, both in written form and in PowerPoint or similar presentations. The best advice we can give is to keep the audience and its needs firmly in mind when choosing the format, the information to be included, and the kind of tables, figures, or other graphics that best convey the conclusions.

Figure 5-1   National Health Expenditure and Revenue by Category, 2015

The Nation's Health Dollar ($3.2 Trillion), Calendar Year 2015: Where It Went

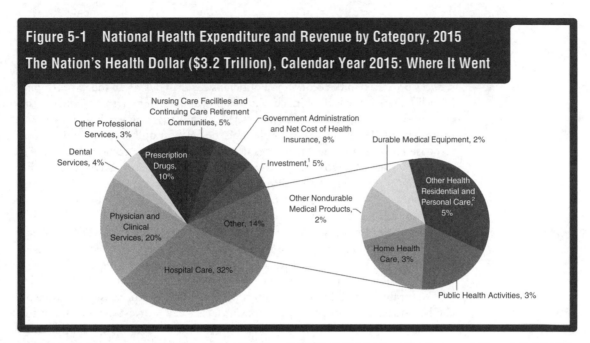

Source: Centers for Medicare and Medicaid Services, Office of the Actuary, National Health Statistics Group. https://www.cms.gov/Research-Statistics-Data-and-Systems/Statistics-Trends-and-Reports/NationalHealthExpendData/Downloads/PieChartSourcesExpenditures2015.pdf.

Notes: Sum of pieces may not equal 100 percent due to rounding.

[1]Includes Noncommercial Research (2%) and Structures and Equipment (3%).

[2]Includes expenditures for residential care facilities, ambulance providers, medical care delivered in nontraditional settings (e.g., community centers, senior citizens' centers, schools, and military field stations), and home and community-based waiver programs under Medicaid.

The Nation's Health Dollar ($3.2 Trillion), Calendar Year 2015: Where It Came From

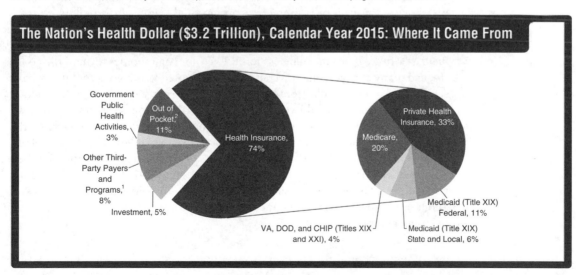

Source: Centers for Medicare & Medicaid Services, Office of the Actuary, National Health Statistics Group. https://www.cms.gov/Research-Statistics-Data-and-Systems/Statistics-Trends-and-Reports/NationalHealthExpendData/Downloads/PieChartSourcesExpenditures2015.pdf.

Notes: Sum of pieces may not equal 100 percent due to rounding.

[1]Includes work-site health care, other private revenues, Indian Health Service, workers' compensation, general assistance, maternal and child health, vocational rehabilitation, Substance Abuse and Mental Health Services Administration, school health, and other federal and state local programs.

[2]Includes co-payments, deductibles, and any amounts not covered by health insurance.

The use of quantitative data also carries some risks. Analysts need to be alert to the possibility of inaccurate or misleading data in a report or an invalid measurement that does not truly capture the problem (Eberstadt 1995). For example, we use the gross domestic product (GDP) to measure the sum total of goods and services produced in the economy. Politicians see the GDP as an indicator of public well-being, or the lack of it. They invariably applaud a rising GDP and express concern over a sagging GDP, but many critics argue that it is seriously flawed as a measurement. The GDP, for example, does not place a dollar value on work that a spouse may do at home, but it does if someone is hired to come to the home to do exactly the same work (e.g., to cook or clean the house). Environmentalists have long argued that the GDP does not account for the use or loss of natural resources, such as forests. Cutting down forests for timber production, for instance, adds positively to the GDP. But economists do not subtract the loss of value when forest ecosystems are lost or harmed by timber production. Some economists have proposed developing a new method called the genuine progress indicator (GPI) to substitute the GDP and more accurately reflect human well-being (C. Cobb, Halstead, and Rowe 1995; www.rprogress.org).

Naturally, not all human concerns, such as happiness or sense of well-being, can be reduced to quantitative measures. Analysts can, however, make use of surveys that ask people whether they are happy, enjoy living in their communities, believe their children's schools are doing a good job, think the local environment is healthy or not, and so forth.[11] Where public problems cannot be measured directly, this kind of survey data may be a useful substitute. Economists also say that people can be asked to estimate the dollar value of many activities for which no market value exists. Their responses can help to calculate whether certain actions, such as preserving open space or planting trees, are justifiable uses of tax dollars.

An illustration of how to develop quantitative indicators is found in the effort of communities to become sustainable. Critics have derided *sustainable development* as a fuzzy if not meaningless term. Even so, communities around the country, and many colleges and universities, have adopted it as a goal, and many have selected quantitative indicators of sustainability to see whether they are making progress toward that goal over time (www.sustainablemeasures.com). The residents and policymakers are clear enough about what *sustainability* means—the integration of economic, social, and environmental goals—that they are able to engage the public and work cooperatively in thinking about the future of their communities (Mazmanian and Kraft 2009; K. Portney 2013). The box "Working with Sources: Sustainable Development Indicators" provides further information about sustainable communities and sources of information for various indicators of sustainability.

The Politics of Problem Definition. Defining and measuring problems is not merely an exercise in analysis. People often disagree about a problem and what should be done about it. As Deborah Stone (2012) says, there are "no fixed goals" in the policy process; instead, policy actors fight over "competing conceptions of abstract goals." Moreover, she says, "problem definition is never simply

Working with Sources

Sustainable Development Indicators

Analysts and activists have developed a collection of indicators that allow a community, region, or nation (or a college or university) to measure its progress toward sustainability. These indicators typically involve some commonsense measurements, such as the number of people and automobiles in the geographic area of concern, energy and water consumption, greenhouse gas emissions, and the like. Some less obvious but equally useful social and economic indicators include the percentage of households that can afford to buy an average-priced house, high school graduation rates, and extent of citizens' community involvement (Mazmanian and Kraft 2009). The availability of these kinds of statistics has allowed communities across the nation to convert the abstract concept of sustainable development into something that citizens and policymakers can easily understand. By developing quantitative measures, communities are able to compile a kind of sustainability status report and to track progress over time toward shared community goals. The following websites compile sustainability statistics:

www.aashe.org. Association for the Advancement of Sustainability in Higher Education (AASHE), an association of colleges and universities in the United States and Canada working to promote sustainability in all sectors of higher education.

www.communityindicators.net. The Community Indicators Consortium (CIC) shares information and indicators for the "advancement of people, the quality of community life and the sustainability of our shared environment."

www.rprogress.org. Redefining Progress, an organization devoted to the use of new measurements of progress and environmental, social, and economic sustainability.

www.sustainablemeasures.com. Sustainable Measures, a unique and comprehensive collection of sustainability indicators, with clear explanations of why some are more useful than others. Includes a database of indicators and extensive links to work on sustainability.

The best way to understand the kind of information collected at these sites is to visit one and look for particular indicators. For example, go to the Sustainable Measures site and select the link to Sustainability Indicators 101, and then Indicators of Sustainability, to see a description of the qualities of indicators the site's analysts think are important. Read their description of a "sustainable community indicator checklist" under the heading A Checklist for Evaluating Indicators for a point-by-point review of what is important in selecting indicators to use for this purpose. Or visit the AASHE site to see what colleges and universities are doing to become more sustainable, such as becoming more energy efficient and trying to reduce greenhouse gas emissions. As you visit these sites, you might ask why some focus on some issues more than others. For example:

- Why does Redefining Progress emphasize the necessity to rethink conventional views of economic growth?

- Why does AASHE think that colleges and universities should try to become much more sustainable?

- How useful do you think the kinds of measures promoted by the CIC or Sustainable Measures sites will be to communities trying to develop a sustainability plan?

a matter of defining goals and measuring our distance from them. It is rather the strategic representation of situations." By this, she means a description of any given situation will vary, depending on a policy actor's perspective. The process becomes strategic, or political, because "groups, individuals, and government

Climate change and energy sources. Energy use and climate change have emerged as major issues in recent years, and the federal government has strongly encouraged renewable energy sources such as wind and solar power. The photo shows the GE-Alstom Block Island Wind Farm off of Rhode Island in September 2016. The large wind turbines are the first marine-based wind farm in the United States. *(Scott Eisen/Getty Images)*

agencies deliberately and consciously fashion portrayals so as to promote their favored course of action."[12]

One example of what Stone means concerns the irradiation of meat intended for human consumption, a process the federal government approved in 2000. The largest U.S. irradiator of ground beef lobbied members of Congress to define irradiated meat as "pasteurized." A farm-state senator inserted the provision into a major agricultural bill at the last minute. Obviously, the meat processor believed that the word *pasteurized* would be more acceptable to the public than *irradiated*. At the time the legislative language was proposed, the U.S. Department of Agriculture and the Food and Drug Administration had yet to agree that meat that is irradiated qualifies as pasteurized.[13] Similar political, or strategic, actions occur in nearly every major policy area, from Social Security and health care reform to energy policy.

Some analysts might challenge Stone's view of the inherently political nature of problem analysis, but students of politics would probably agree with her. The evidence supports the observation that policymakers and interest groups will do whatever they can to set the policy agenda in their favor by defining problems their way. Political scientists refer to this practice as **issue framing**, and they see it as a key part of the process of agenda setting that is discussed in some detail in chapter 3. It is also pervasive in contemporary politics and policymaking as each side in a debate carefully selects language that puts its argument in the most favorable light. Hence we see opposition to certain regulations that are described as "job killing," which will likely attract more support from voters than would a stance against health and safety requirements. And we see health care reform described by its opponents as a "government takeover" of personal health care decisions even when that reform leaves in place a largely private health care marketplace and individual choice within it (see chapter 8).

Political scientists have thoroughly studied such issue framing and agenda setting (Baumgartner and Jones 1993; Guber and Bosso 2013b; Kingdon 1995; Rochefort and Cobb 1994). Still, most analysts would likely argue that meaningful resolution of a public problem—homelessness, crime, poor-quality schools, urban sprawl, energy needs, access to health care services—depends at least in part on the ability to clarify the nature of the problem, collect the most pertinent data, and foster a public debate over what might be done about it.

Anticipating the Future. One other aspect of defining and measuring problems deserves mention. Any consideration of the present state of affairs must be grounded in an assessment of how it is likely to change over time. What will the problem look like in several years or decades? Forecasts, or projections, usually involve an extrapolation of current trends, but that is only one method for looking ahead.

Examples of forecasting include economic projections (how large will the nation's deficit be in five, ten, or twenty years?), population estimates (how large will the U.S. population be by 2025 or 2050, or how many senior citizens will need to be covered by Social Security or Medicare in twenty or thirty years?), and future energy needs (how much will we need in thirty years, and on what sources are we likely to rely?). Such projections are especially helpful if they reveal how that change will likely unfold with or without policy intervention. For example, if the nation adopted significant tax cuts or spent more to stimulate the economy, what would be the impact on job creation and economic growth?

Such forecasting has become an integral part of the public debate over the anticipated rise in Medicare and Social Security benefits as the baby boom generation ages; economic policy, such as the assumptions made about government spending and taxation over time; and health care reform in light of projections of the rising costs of health care services. As with other forms of policy analysis, it is always necessary to look at the assumptions that lie behind the forecasts to judge their validity. Circumstances also change, and a forecast made one year may not be as useful in subsequent years.

Thinking about Causes and Solutions

Any assessment of a public problem requires thinking about its **causes**, how the problem came about, and why it continues. The answers make a big difference in whether and how public policy might help to resolve it. For example, consider the dramatic rise in prison populations in the United States over the past four decades, when they more than quadrupled to over two million inmates.

The United States imprisons a larger proportion of its citizens than any other country in the world.[14] But why was there an increase of this magnitude in the prison population, especially at a time when crime rates generally were on the decline, and how might the trend be reversed?

Part of the answer on the causes of rising inmate populations is that states passed tougher sentencing laws and the public was willing to continue building prisons—often at the expense of funding for higher education. In many states, the growth in the prison population can be traced specifically to new laws that put even nonviolent drug offenders in jail and to the adoption of "three-strikes-and-you're-out" laws. These laws mandated long sentences, even life sentences, on conviction for a third-felony offense, even for a relatively innocuous crime.[15] In one case, a California shoplifter charged with stealing $153 worth of video-tapes was sentenced to fifty years in prison because of his prior convictions. In a similar case in 2016, a shoplifter in New Orleans walked out of a store with $31 of candy in his pockets, and faced a twenty-year to life sentence under state guidelines for habitual offenders. He had been arrested some twenty-four times and convicted of eight felonies. Eventually, however, he was sentenced to only two years.

Many also are questioning the wisdom of sentencing drug offenders to prison, in terms of both the justification for the harsh penalties and the cost of keeping them in prison. For example, former Republican governor Mike Huckabee of Arkansas noted that the long mandatory sentences were "good politics but bad public policy," adding that the system is locking up "people we are mad at but not afraid of."[16] Nearly half a million drug offenders were in prison in the early 2000s, many on a first conviction for possession; that represented a tenfold increase since 1980.[17]

How might this trend be reversed? One way is to change the laws that led to the growth of the prison population in the first place. In 2000 in California, where one in three prisoners was incarcerated for a drug-related crime, the voters did just that. They approved a state referendum requiring that first- and second-time nonviolent drug offenders be put into treatment centers instead of prison, a move that was expected to reduce the prison population significantly but which yielded somewhat mixed results. In 2012, the state's voters approved yet another referendum that abolished life sentences for nonviolent offenders. Early results of the new policy were promising, with only a small percentage of the former prisoners returning to prison for newly committed crimes.[18] By 2016, such successes had attracted attention in Congress, where a growing consensus was emerging for criminal justice reforms that sought to reduce mandatory prison sentences for nonviolent crimes.[19]

As discussed in chapter 4, most policy studies focus on what can be called proximate, or immediate, causes of public problems, such as the reasons for rising prison populations. The greater challenge is to deal with the root causes of problems. Taking policy action might be more difficult than it was in California because of long-standing **public attitudes and habits** that are resistant to change. For example, consider urban traffic congestion. Why does it exist? The obvious answer is that large numbers of people are driving their cars on a limited number of roads at any given time. In addition, Americans are driving more miles per year—to go to work or school, to shop, and for other purposes. Is the solution to build more highways? Or is it to think about ways to reduce the use of automobiles in urban areas, where congestion is greatest? Some urban designers and environmentalists offer a more radical solution, at least for new communities: build cities with adequate mass transit and where people can live closer to where they work. Many states and communities are adopting "smart growth" policies with similar ambitions for managing anticipated growth over the next several decades. Use of such systems seems to depend on people's calculations of relative cost. When gasoline prices spiked to well over four dollars per gallon in 2008, mass-transit systems saw a substantial increase in ridership. People's preferences for housing also seem to have shifted from large homes in distant or fringe suburbs to smaller homes in inner suburbs and central cities, particularly in pedestrian-friendly neighborhoods that allow residents to rely more on walking and mass transit.[20]

Most public problems have multiple causes, not a single cause, and people often disagree over which is the most important and which ought to be the object of public policy. Liberals and conservatives may disagree about the causes of poor school performance, crime, environmental degradation, or anemic economic growth, and what might be done about them. Smart students of public policy learn how to deal with the politics and often overheated rhetoric that can sometimes cloud an objective review of the evidence.

Problem analysis can begin with making an explicit list of the goals and objectives of various policy actors and a determination of what might be done to reach them (Patton, Sawicki, and Clark 2016). The objectives may include a specific measure of what is to be achieved, such as improving access to health care services, reducing the rate of teenage smoking, curbing drunk driving, or reducing cell phone use while driving. When analysts think of potential **solutions** to public problems, they try to identify the opportunities for policy intervention. They attempt to imagine how a change in public policy might affect the problem; for example, would raising the price of cigarettes reduce the rate of teenage smoking? Would a hike in the gasoline tax persuade people to use their cars less and therefore reduce the nation's reliance on imported oil?

Finally, sometimes analysts want to describe the benefits and costs of trying to solve the problem. They look at how the consequences of policy action, positive or negative, are distributed across population subgroups, such as those in certain regions, occupations, or social groups—in other words, who gains and who loses if the problem is resolved. Politicians and other major policy actors are sometimes very clever about addressing these kinds of distributive concerns. They are almost always interested in knowing about them. They may speak about solving public problems as though the entire nation will benefit equally, but the reality is that some segments of the population are more likely than others to enjoy the benefits of acting on a problem, and some are more likely than others to pay the costs. For example, members of Congress from states with a large number of defense contractors naturally would be concerned about how a decrease in defense spending would affect the economy and employment in their state or district, and they may seek ways to block such spending cuts. So students of public policy would be wise to think about how to present such information in any studies they complete. The box "Steps to Analysis: Major Components of Problem Analysis" summarizes basic elements in problem analysis. The list can also be a guide to what questions might be addressed in preparing a problem analysis or issue paper.

Steps to Analysis

Major Components of Problem Analysis

Define the problem. If the problem is educational quality, what does that mean? In other words, what is the nature of the education problem under study? Has quality declined? Is it lower than many people believe it ought to be? Is it lower in the United States than in other developed nations?

Measure the problem. Find a way to measure the problem that is consistent with the way it is defined. This step is sometimes called "developing an operational definition." What kinds of quantitative indicators are available from reliable sources? What is the best measurement to use for educational quality: Student scores on standard examinations? Other measures of student learning? Indicators of the quality of a school's faculty?

Determine the extent or magnitude of the problem. Using available indicators, try to determine who is affected by the problem and by how much. Try to answer these kinds of questions: What groups in the population suffer from the problem being studied, how long have they been affected by it, and to what extent are they affected? For example, how does educational quality vary from one school district or state to another? From urban districts to suburban districts? From schools in less affluent neighborhoods to those in more affluent areas?

Think about the problem's causes. How did the problem come about, and why does it continue? What are the leading causes of the problem, and what other causes should be considered? Knowing the causes of a problem is critical to developing solutions to it. How has educational quality changed over the past several decades, and why? If students today are less well prepared for higher education or the workplace than in earlier periods, why is that so?

Set goals or objectives. What should be done about the problem, and why? Are certain goals and objectives of paramount importance, widely agreed upon, and economically or socially feasible? Over what period of time should the goals and objectives be sought? For educational quality, what goals or objectives are most appropriate? If quality is to be improved, how much progress should be expected for a given period of time?

Determine what can be done. What actions might work to solve the problem or to reach the specified goals and objectives? What policy efforts might be directed at the causes of the problem? What variables can be affected by such efforts? If the goal is improving educational quality to a certain extent, what needs to be done? Improving teacher quality? Reducing class sizes? Changing the curriculum? Increasing the school budget? Fostering competition through charter schools or voucher programs?

Sources: Patton, Sawicki, and Clark (2016) and authors. Patton, Sawicki, and Clark devote a full chapter to steps in defining a problem. For other treatments of problem diagnosis, see Starling (1988) and Bardach and Patashnik (2016).

How to Find Information

To perform problem analysis and the other activities related to it, students of public policy need to collect reliable information. Indeed, good information is critical to successful analysis, but where does one find it? This chapter provides some guidelines. The websites listed at the end of each chapter and mentioned within the chapters are sources of extensive data on specific problems, as are articles in academic journals, books on the subject, and the better newspapers and professional newsweeklies. Because the substantive policy chapters in the book provide many particular examples about using the data in policy studies and arguments, the information here is intended to be fairly general.

Most university libraries have a variety of online databases that contain full-text articles and can be searched by subject matter, title, or author, as can the library's own holdings. One of the best search tools, however, is available to anyone. This is Google (www.google.com), which can return many useful links for specific public policy inquiries. The federal government offers a general portal for searches of government documents that is similar to the now-defunct Google Uncle Sam; it can be found at www.usa.gov.

Consider the example of cell phones and texting discussed in chapter 4. To identify articles or reports on the frequency of use of cell phones by drivers or other aspects of distracted driving, use any search engine and type in the keywords *cell phone*, *texting*, and *driving* to find a suitable list of studies and public opinion surveys. To vary the search—for example, to find material on whether younger drivers face greater challenges than older drivers or to examine other aspects of distracted driving—add or substitute keywords such as *young people*, *teenagers*, or *distracted driving*.

A good way to begin preparing issue papers and problem analyses is with an overview of a subject from sources such as the *New York Times*, *Washington Post*, *Wall Street Journal*, *CQ Magazine*, or *National Journal*. These and similar newspapers and newsweeklies provide valuable information about current policy debates, particularly on a national level, and some background on the nature of the problem. For a broader historical perspective on public policy actions to address the problem, CQ Press's annual *Almanac* and its quadrennial volume *Congress and the Nation* are invaluable. Similar sources can be consulted for information at the state and local levels, and most can be found in college and university libraries.

The main concern at this point of a search is to find enough information to understand the basics about a given policy problem. How much information is enough? If the initial search yields three or four high-quality articles that provide an idea of the history of the problem, describe the policy efforts and recent controversies, and cover the different points of view about desirable policy actions, that may be sufficient to proceed. At this point, the researcher should be able to determine what else he or she needs to know to complete the assessment and then seek more detailed sources of information. An intense literature search could be profitable at this stage because the researcher knows what to look for and can focus on the best sources.

Most college and university libraries have access to online sources, such as LexisNexis Academic, that include indexing and abstracting services. One of the most useful for public policy research is the congressional database ProQuest Congressional. It includes an index to, and abstracts of, nearly all congressional documents, from testimony at committee hearings to committee reports on proposed policies. Those documents are excellent sources for the most current analyses of public problems and policy actions. For example, the records of testimony by policy experts at committee hearings may also offer excerpts from their latest research findings before they are available elsewhere. LexisNexis Academic also covers documents that include statistical data, but this database is by no means restricted to statistical analysis. Rather, it covers any description of a problem that includes numbers, such as population trends, crime rates, or the success of welfare reform. LexisNexis also includes extensive databases for legal research. Major university and college libraries are also government depository libraries and have many documents on paper if they are not available online.

Another way to locate pertinent information is to visit the website for the government agency most directly related to the issue. For example, the Department of Defense is the first place to look for information about U.S. defense strategies, the Department of State for U.S. foreign policy, and the Environmental Protection Agency for most major environmental issues. For health and welfare issues, see the Department of Health and Human Services, and for national security issues at home, such as airport screening procedures, see the Transportation Security Administration in the Department of Homeland Security. At the state and local levels, the same logic applies: visit the websites of the local or state government agencies that deal with the subject matter. In addition, the websites for the major interest groups active in the policy area often have extensive reports and commentaries, as do the sites for policy think tanks. Many of those websites also incorporate search engines that allow you to quickly locate important documents. Comprehensive websites such as www.publicagenda.org and others listed at the end of chapter 4 offer a portal to many of the most useful public policy sites.

In addition to LexisNexis, other indexing and abstracting services are available to help locate articles, government reports, and other major documents. Which are most useful depends on the subject being studied. For most of these sites, users need to gain access through a library with a subscription to the service. Among the most helpful for public policy in general are Academic Search Complete (EBSCO*host*'s database of more than seven thousand full-text periodicals and abstracts from eleven thousand periodicals), OmniFile Full Text Mega (a multidisciplinary database providing the full content from six of the Wilson company's full-text databases, and now part of EBSCO), Worldwide Political Science Abstracts, JSTOR (a database of major scholarly journals), and ProQuest Newsstand or Newspaper Source Plus (each of which covers over a thousand state and local newspapers). Some similar services are available without a subscription, such as the Catalog of U.S. Government Publications and the Government Publishing Office access to online services (www.gpo.gov) and the congressional Internet services site, which offers extensive links to both governmental and nongovernmental sites, particularly those dealing with congressional activities (www.congress.gov). Most libraries have research guides that outline these services and discuss how best to use them.

If possible, students should arrange visits to government and other offices to obtain information and interview policy actors. At the local level especially, policymakers and other actors often welcome a visit by someone who is interested in what they are doing because they only rarely hear from the press and are often eager to discuss their work. Advance preparation is essential for this strategy. Students should know what information they are seeking and who is most likely to be able to provide it. Reading local newspaper coverage of the issue is a good place to begin.[21]

Beyond conducting a search and locating the documents, one of the most challenging aspects of a literature review is the interpretation of the information gathered. As the text has emphasized throughout, policy analyses vary greatly in quality and are often prepared as ammunition in policy debates, with selective and sometimes highly misleading summaries and commentaries. Just because a statement appears in print or on the web is no guarantee that it is true. It is always essential to find out the source of the information, the reliability of the author or organization, any critical assumptions that are made in a study or report (such as what is included or omitted), and any interpretations that might not be justified. At a minimum, the student researcher will want to determine whether the facts are current and accurate.

This description of how to find pertinent policy information is intended to be a general introduction to policy research. The real excitement in policy studies comes from having a strong interest in a particular policy area and learning where to find the information about it. For example, the student who is passionate about equal pay for women in the workforce will find the search for appropriate data and studies exhilarating. For the researcher worried about the rising costs of college education and students' burden of debt upon graduation, the hunt for information about the costs of attending specific colleges and the availability of student loans will be easy and a real learning experience.

Constructing Alternatives

After problem analysis has yielded a good sense of what the problem is, how extensive it is, why it occurs, and what the goals are for resolving it, the next step is to think about courses of action. Chapter 6 introduces a range of relevant criteria for evaluating policy options and some of the tools of analysis that can provide the requisite information to evaluate the policy alternatives. This section focuses on how to develop the list of alternatives that merit such further consideration. It emphasizes learning how to think creatively about public policy, particularly when ineffective policies and programs need to be replaced.

What Governments Can Do

So how do analysts know which alternatives to consider? As we discussed in chapter 3, the starting point is to see what governments are doing or can do. Among their options, governments can regulate, subsidize, ration, tax and spend, contract out, use market incentives, privatize, charge fees for service, educate, create public trusts, and conduct or commission research (J. Anderson 2015; Patton, Sawicki, and Clark 2016). Figure 5-2 summarizes these activities and illustrates them with examples.

If current policies are not working well enough and a change is needed, analysts might suggest modifying the present policies or trying a different policy approach or strategy. Present policies could be strengthened; for example, the federal government could raise standards and penalties for clean air or water policies or toughen regulation of Wall Street banks. Or policymakers could fund programs at a higher level, which might permit improved research, better enforcement, and better public information campaigns. Analysts and policymakers also consider alternatives to conventional regulatory policies, as was done for many environmental policies during the 1980s and 1990s (Mazmanian and Kraft 2009; Vig and Kraft 2016). These might include a combination of market-based incentives, public information campaigns, and various forms of what the Bill Clinton administration called "regulatory reinvention," which are more flexible and efficient policy reforms.

For some policies and agencies, policymakers might try different institutional approaches, such as a new way to organize the bureaucracy in charge. Reorganization was proposed in 2002 for the much-maligned Immigration and Naturalization Service (INS), widely considered to be one of the least effective federal agencies. The George W. Bush administration endorsed a plan to replace the INS with three new agencies, one for customs and border protection, one for immigration services, and one for immigration and customs enforcement. All three agencies were incorporated into the new Department of Homeland Security. Along with agency reorganization, the present federal-state relationship, some form of which pervades most policy areas, can also be changed. For example, many policies during the 1980s and 1990s were further decentralized, giving the states greater authority to make decisions and allocate funds.

Many state and local governments are trying another interesting institutional reform option. They make routine government services available online, from providing tourist information to supplying government forms that can be filled out and filed online. The federal government is also moving in this direction and has instituted an Internet portal for all federal information at USA.gov (www.usa.gov).

For many policy areas, actions are rooted in one of two views of the problem being confronted, what might be called **supply and demand perspectives.**

Figure 5-2 What Governments Can Do

ACTION	ILLUSTRATIONS
Regulate	Licensing, inspection, enforcement of standards, application of sanctions **Specific examples:** environmental, health, and workplace safety regulations; corporate financial regulations
Subsidize	Loans, direct payments or benefits, tax credits, price supports **Specific examples:** student loans; subsidies to farmers or oil companies; dairy price supports; low-interest loans for disaster recovery
Ration	Limit access to scarce resources **Specific examples:** permits for backpacking in national parks; the Oregon Health Plan's limitations on coverage of health care services
Tax and spend	Tax an activity at a level that encourages or discourages it **Specific examples:** allowing home mortgage deductions to encourage home ownership; imposing cigarette taxes to discourage smoking Spend money on preferred program **Specific examples:** defense weapons, prisons, AmeriCorps, public higher education
Contract out	Contract for government services from the private sector or buy products for government agencies **Specific examples:** contracts for defense weapons procurement and for economic rebuilding efforts after wars; purchase of computers and fleet vehicles for federal or state governments or public schools
Use market incentives	A special category of taxation or imposition of fees that creates incentives to change behavior and achieve goals and objectives **Specific examples:** raising gasoline taxes to encourage conservation of fuel and reduce carbon dioxide emissions; tax rebates for purchasing hybrid vehicles or installing solar or wind power sources
Privatize	Transferring public services from government to the private sector **Specific examples:** turning over management of public schools or correctional institutions to private companies
Charge fees	Fees for select services **Specific examples:** hunting and fishing licenses; requiring students to pay to ride the school bus; college tuition
Educate	Provide information to the public through formal programs or other actions **Specific examples:** formal public meetings; public education services; food safety labels; information on toxic chemical releases; automobile fuel efficiency labels
Create public trusts	Holding public property in trust for citizens indefinitely **Specific examples:** local land conservation trusts; state and national parks and recreation areas
Conduct research	Conduct or support research and development **Specific examples:** National Science Foundation support for academic studies; defense and environmental research; medical science research funded through the National Institutes of Health

If analysts believe a problem such as energy scarcity results from an insufficient supply of energy, they will likely recommend the policy alternative of increasing supply. They will consider actions to boost supplies of energy, whether from fossil fuels (oil, natural gas, and coal), nuclear energy, or alternative energy such as wind or solar power. The actions may include changes in rules that control exploration on public lands, various tax credits and incentives, and support for research that could speed up the introduction of new energy sources. The Bush administration took this position in its national energy policy proposal of 2001, much of which was approved by Congress in 2005. But what if the problem is too much demand for energy rather than too little supply? Policymakers may consider energy conservation and efficiency measures, such as increasing fuel economy standards for cars or providing tax credits for high-mileage hybrid or electric vehicles. The most likely scenario will be a combination of the supply and demand perspectives.

In addition to considering which policy options will work best or be more efficient or fair, policymakers have to think about the philosophical and ideological aspects. Conservatives and liberals, and Republicans and Democrats, differ significantly in the kinds of policy solutions they favor. For example, Republicans in Congress were unanimous in opposing the Obama health care reform proposals that were approved in 2010 because they opposed such a far-reaching extension of the federal government's authority and in particular its mandate for individuals to purchase health care insurance. Many states under Republican control sued the federal government in an effort to have the act declared unconstitutional or at least substantially modified. Democrats generally favored the act.

Policy Typologies as Analytic Tools

Chapter 3 introduced a typology that analysts can use to consider whether another kind of policy approach might be appropriate if a previously adopted policy proves to be unsuitable. For example, if a regulatory policy is not working or is no longer politically feasible, the policymaker could consider self-regulation, market incentives, or information provision as alternatives or supplements to regulation.

In a related effort, Anne Schneider and Helen Ingram (1997) developed an intriguing typology as part of their work on **policy design**. The term refers to the careful consideration, during the policy formulation stage, of the role of government "agents" and the "target population"—those who receive benefits or who are the objects of government regulation. Schneider and Ingram argue that, for public policies to stand a chance of working, they must be thoroughly grounded in an understanding of the attitudes and motivations of the policy actors who will decide how the policies are implemented and whether they have the desired effects. Underlying this view of policymaking is a variation of rational choice theory that we discussed in chapter 3: if policy actors are rational beings who respond to the incentives and disincentives incorporated into a given policy, then the policymakers should be able to design policies that encourage people to behave in the way that is sought.

Viewed from this perspective, policy tools, according to Schneider and Ingram (1997, 93), are "the elements in policy design that cause agents or targets to do something they would not otherwise do with the intention of modifying behavior to solve public problems or attain policy goals." The choice of such tools, they say, reflects different views of how people behave and what might lead them to change their behavior. They distinguish five such policy tools, which are summarized in the box "Steps to Analysis: Policy Design Tools." Governments can invoke their authority and ask for compliance, provide incentives or

Steps to Analysis

Policy Design Tools

Policy design is the consideration of a variety of possible approaches, instruments, or tools that may be appropriate for a given policy problem. The tools described here derive from anticipating how different policy actors are likely to respond to what governments attempt to do. They are similar to the list we provide in Figure 5-2 for what governments might do to address any public problem. This typology, however, seeks to categorize different policy tools in a way that highlights key differences among them.

Authority tools. Governments use their authority to urge or require people to behave in a certain way. The use of such tools, not always effective or democratic, depends on the perceived legitimacy of government. These tools may be particularly suitable during times of crisis, when favorable responses by the public are more likely.

Inducements and sanctions. Governments provide incentives or penalties to appeal to individuals' rational pursuit of their self-interest. Inducements encourage people to act in a certain way because they will gain from doing so. Sanctions are negative incentives or penalties that are thought to discourage behavior that is inconsistent with policy goals.

Capacity-building tools. Governments make available training, education, information, and technical assistance, and they can aim to inform or enlighten and thus empower people, either those in the target population or policy agents.

Hortatory tools. Governments invoke images and values through speeches, proclamations, and other communication to exhort people to behave in a certain way.

Learning tools. Governments can encourage policy agents and target populations to participate and learn, for example, through citizen advisory panels and collaborative processes.

- How might government use these different tools? Which seem to be the most useful?

- Consider a specific problem, such as the use of cell phones or texting by drivers, discussed in chapter 4. Which of these tools might be the most effective in reducing cell phone use or texting by drivers?

- How about the use of seat belts in cars? Which of these tools is most likely to encourage drivers and passengers to "buckle up" and thus reduce their risk of injury or death in the event of an accident? Why do you think so?

- Or consider the case of immigration reform discussed at the beginning of this chapter: which of these tools can help to reduce the rate of illegal immigration or to address another component of the problem?

Source: Adapted from Anne Larason Schneider and Helen Ingram, *Policy Design for Democracy* (Lawrence: University Press of Kansas, 1997).

inducements to elicit compliance, apply sanctions or penalties for noncompliance, try to inform and enlighten the public and promote learning, and exhort people to change their behavior. The choice of which tools to use and how depends on the analysis of a given case and the process of political deliberation and debate that usually occurs at the stage of policy formulation and adoption.

Although it may seem an abstract exercise, this policy design approach offers many insights into human behavior that can help analysts and policymakers figure out what kinds of policy action will likely succeed. Consider a situation that was unfortunate for California in 2001. Electricity prices in the state rose dramatically in 2000 and 2001 as a consequence of a poorly conceived state energy deregulation policy and a short-term shortage of electricity, which was brought about in part by the power companies' manipulation of the energy supply. As one solution, state policymakers adopted the nation's largest energy conservation program, with a strong focus on incentives for individuals to conserve energy. In this example, these individuals are the "target population." Those who cut their previous electricity use by 20 percent or more would earn a special rebate of 20 percent on their 2001 energy bills in addition to the direct savings they enjoyed from using less electricity. The state called this a "pay-to-conserve" program.

State policymakers were counting on individual incentives to alter the behavior of this target population; it had been difficult to change in prior attempts. California's policy is a good example of what Schneider and Ingram mean by offering inducements that persuade individuals to adjust their behavior because they realize they will be better off by doing so. In this particular case, hortatory tools— the governor and news media urging people to conserve energy—probably also made a difference, as Californians were determined to break out of their energy crisis. The policymakers had calculated that 10 percent of the public would take advantage of the pay-to-conserve program, but by November 2001, more than one-third had done so. The financial inducement worked in part because rising energy prices provided a powerful financial incentive for individuals to save energy.[22]

Many other public policies are equally dependent on assumptions about how those affected by policy rules will behave. Traffic laws, for example, depend on drivers' willingness to stop at red lights and to abide by the posted speed limit. When people do not respond as expected, additional sanctions may be necessary. Jurisdictions impose substantial fines and other penalties for driving under the influence of alcohol as a way of discouraging this behavior. Some states maintain the death penalty for severe crimes in hope that it will deter criminals. Here too the assumption is that a person contemplating a criminal act would adjust his or her behavior with the understanding of the possible punishment.

These examples show that policy typologies, such as that proposed by Schneider and Ingram, can be useful when thinking about a government's possible courses of action. In conjunction with other analytic techniques, typologies like these can help analysts focus on the condition they are trying to bring about and what changes in human behavior may be necessary. Then they can consider various policy actions that may provide the necessary incentives.

Creative policy action. In recent years, hundreds of public schools across the nation have tried to discourage students from eating junk food and encourage the eating of healthy food as one way to deal with rising levels of childhood obesity and the health care needs that come with it. In this photo, a Naugatuck (Connecticut) High School student displays his lunch under the new federal guidelines, which say students must take one cup of fruit or vegetables, a cup of milk, two ounces of whole grains, and two ounces of meat or other protein. *(AP Photo/Laraine Weschler/Republican American)*

Thinking Creatively about Policy Action

Beyond considering policy typologies or variations on existing policies, students of public policy can try other techniques to expand the list of alternatives. Patton, Sawicki, and Clark (2016) offer a pertinent discussion of how to apply **creative thinking** to policy action. Among other strategies, they suggest the following: no-action analysis, quick surveys, literature reviews, comparison to real-world situations, passive collection and classification, use of analogies and metaphors, brainstorming, and comparison with an ideal.

No-action analysis begins with the status quo, or present policy, as a kind of baseline. It suggests not that governments do nothing about a given problem, but that keeping present policies or programs, or defending them, may be a viable option. Many will favor this strategy during times of budget constraints, when programs are vulnerable to cutbacks or elimination. A clear example is the idea of keeping Amtrak, the national railroad passenger corporation, alive by continuing its government subsidies because the passenger train system is an alternative to travel by car or airplane. The no-action option may also be a useful point of departure for considering other alternatives. One advantage of such choices is they are *not* the status quo, which may be unacceptable to critics of the current program. The greater the dissatisfaction with the status quo option, the more likely policymakers and the public are to favor a search for alternatives and give them serious consideration.

A **quick survey** involves talking with people in a particular policy network or searching through hearing transcripts, minutes of meetings, newspaper accounts, and the like for pertinent information about a problem and policy alternatives.

The idea here is that people familiar with the issues have probably raised many alternatives, and interviewing them, distributing questionnaires to them, or reviewing what they have written or said on the issues should produce a shortlist of possible policy alternatives. This technique could be particularly useful at the local level, where gaining access to principal policy actors is a real possibility.

A literature review is an examination of books, journal articles, Internet sites, and other sources. The purpose here is to look for policy alternatives that have been proposed or considered previously. This kind of search could extend to a survey of the options that policymakers have considered or adopted in other policy areas as well. Consider an intriguing law that Congress enacted in 1986, the False Claims Amendments Act, which encourages whistle-blowers to air their concerns about improper actions such as fraudulent contracts with the government. The law provides that those who blow the whistle, or come forward with such accusations, may receive up to a quarter of the money that the government recovers. After more than three decades, the act—which imposes triple damages on companies that commit fraud—produced over $48 billion for the federal treasury; in 2015 alone it produced over $3.5 billion. It also has provided over $1 billion for hundreds of whistle-blowers who reported the abuses. One individual, a former Swiss banker, was awarded $104 million for helping the Internal Revenue Service (IRS) locate overseas tax cheats. A Justice Department spokesperson has said the law has been "highly effective in ferreting out individuals and companies that commit fraud."[23]

Rather than think only about abstract ideas, analysts might ask what has worked well in specific or real-world situations, and therefore what might be considered an effective alternative to the present policy. Analysts would also want to know which alternatives have been tried elsewhere and found wanting. This kind of information is likely to be available because one of the great virtues of the U.S. federal system is that the fifty states and their approximately eighty thousand local governments often demonstrate great creativity in addressing public problems. As Supreme Court Justice Louis D. Brandeis observed long ago, "A single courageous State may, if its citizens choose, serve as a laboratory; and try novel social and economic experiments without risk to the rest of the count."[24] Today, states frequently engage in innovative public policy actions. If several states have experimented with welfare reform, then other states or the federal government might look to them for ideas about what to consider. Indeed, the federal welfare reform measure of 1996 was based largely on what Wisconsin and a few other states were already doing.

Similar to the quick survey approach, passive collection means finding out what others have suggested in a given policy area. Analysts might speak with a program's clients or administrators, advocates of various positions, and organizations that have taken a position on the issue. Do they offer creative ways of dealing with the problem that depart from present practices? Do those closely associated with a given policy area believe that some policy alternatives are politically infeasible because they have been raised and rejected earlier? Finding out these answers now can save analysts time and effort later.

Another approach is to look at a **parallel situation** in other policy areas for ideas about what might be done. What seems to be a new problem may present many of the same issues as an earlier one. Analysts need to be alert to possible analogies. By listing and thinking about the attributes of the present problem, they may see its relationship to other problems. For example, measures to deal with the rights of persons with disabilities have borrowed concepts and language from analogous civil rights legislation from the 1960s. Another approach to using analogies is to imagine oneself in the position of a client served by a given program. As a client, how do you respond to present policies? What would you like changed?

A popular technique to encourage creative thinking in public policy or in organizational change is **brainstorming**, which usually takes place in an informal meeting of people who share an interest in finding solutions to a given problem. In the brainstorming session, the participants bounce ideas around with the goal of producing a list of possibilities. Ideas are offered and recorded as they are made, with no attempt to criticize or evaluate them. The freewheeling discussion of the issues should produce creative thinking and numerous suggestions. In the second phase of the meeting, the participants pare down the suggestions to come up with a shorter list of alternatives worthy of further consideration. Brainstorming can also take the form of written suggestions rather than verbal responses in open meetings. Some variations on the brainstorming theme suggest that creativity is enhanced when some structure is introduced into the discussions (Goldenberg, Mazursky, and Solomon 1999).

Sometimes analysts compare policy alternatives with an **ideal situation**. For example, as part of smart growth planning or sustainability efforts, many communities hold "visioning" meetings in which residents are encouraged to think about the community they want for the future: What kind of residential neighborhoods would it have? What kind of downtown? What kind of recreational opportunities? The goal is to envision an ideal future and use that vision to generate ideas for moving in the desired direction. Too often in public policy debates, the participants assume that an ideal situation is unattainable and therefore not worthy of serious consideration, but excluding the ideal guarantees that it will never come about. By encouraging the expression of an ideal, analysts can ensure that at least the more pragmatic ideas that do receive consideration are evaluated in terms of how close they come to the ideal.

Any one of these strategies for generating a list of policy alternatives should help an analyst to think clearly about how to solve a problem. At this point in the process, neither the cost nor the political feasibility of a particular option is the primary concern; rather, it is to think critically about the problem and try to imagine the various ways to address it. Chapter 6 suggests methods for evaluating the various policy options. In this chapter, however, the emphasis is on fostering the most creative thinking possible, especially if conventional policy action is thought not to be working well and alternatives are needed.

Consider this example. Studies have shown that the rate of obesity among children and teenagers has risen substantially over the past two decades, as have rates of early-onset heart disease and type 2 diabetes. Chapter 8 discusses the serious health consequences for individuals and the significant costs to society if these conditions persist. So what might be done beyond encouraging people to eat healthier diets? Some states have thought about what public schools can do to reduce the availability of foods that contribute to the problem. They proposed restrictions on fast-food franchises in public schools and the imposition of a tax of several cents per can on soft drinks, which are loaded with sugar and calories. Predictably, soft drink makers oppose such initiatives, and they often point instead to a sedentary lifestyle as the culprit. Other schools, especially in states like California where state law demands it, began trying to eliminate junk food from the school premises, a move applauded by public health officials. But are these kinds of responses the right way to act, and will they be effective? Would you favor such a move? If not this kind of action, what else do you think might reduce the high levels of obesity among children and teenagers?

Conclusions

John Gardner, the founder of the nonprofit organization Common Cause and a longtime political reformer, once said, "What we have before us are some breathtaking opportunities disguised as insoluble problems."[25] That is a fitting thought for this chapter on problem analysis and the creation of policy alternatives. It conveys a sense of optimism about how to face any public problem, from inadequate performance of public schools to an inability of local governments to deal with urban sprawl. Rather than complain, analysts, policymakers, and citizens could try to figure out just what the problem is and why it exists, gather some basic information about it, and think about what might be done. As challenging as many public problems are, they are also opportunities to consider the role of government—and the private sector—in fresh ways and to imagine possibilities for changing unsatisfactory circumstances.

This chapter provides an overview of problem analysis. It explains how to describe and measure public problems, and how you go about finding the information you need to do that. It also discusses how to think about the various causes of public problems and possible solutions to them, and it reviews the various policy tools that governments might use to address public problems. Finally, it offers a number of strategies for thinking creatively about which policy alternatives or tools are likely to work best in solving a particular problem. The chapter also makes clear that an analysis of public problems takes place within a political context that often leads to a proliferation of competing diagnoses and recommendations and sometimes to outright misleading and inaccurate portrayals of the problems faced. The skillful analysts learn to deal with the situation. They know how to conduct a critical review and appraisal of whatever studies and reports they find on a subject. Developing a healthy sense of skepticism, however, need not mean a loss of idealism or the willingness to think creatively about public policy change.

Sharpen your skills with SAGE edge at **http://edge.sagepub.com/ kraft6e. SAGE edge for students** provides a personalized approach to help you accomplish your coursework goals in an easy-to-use learning environment.

DISCUSSION QUESTIONS

1. Consider the case of illegal immigration presented at the beginning of the chapter. What is the nature of the immigration problem? What kinds of evidence would you want to see to decide how best to deal with the problem? Where would you go to get that evidence?

2. Think about the example of seat belt use, which varies greatly from state to state as well as among groups in the population. Young drivers tend not to use seat belts as frequently as older drivers do. What actions would you recommend to increase seat belt use, especially by young drivers? Why do you think those actions would be successful? Can

you think of any creative solutions that have not been tried so far?

3. How would you determine whether a particular source of information on policy issues is reliable or not? What would you look for that could distinguish a solid, professional analysis of an issue from one that is weaker or biased?

4. What kinds of measures do you think would be the most accurate in determining whether public high schools are performing well or not? The SAT or ACT scores of graduating seniors? National achievement test scores in a variety of subject areas? State test scores? Something else?

KEYWORDS

SUGGESTED READINGS

Eugene Bardach and **Eric M. Patashnik,** *A Practical Guide for Policy Analysis: The Eightfold Path to More Effective Problem Solving,* 5th ed. (Thousand Oaks, Calif.: CQ Press, 2016). A short and useful introduction to how to do policy analysis.

Frank R. Baumgartner and **Bryan D. Jones,** *Agendas and Instability in American Politics* (Chicago:

University of Chicago Press, 1993). A major work on agenda setting, with many insights into the policymaking process and policy change.

Evan Berman and **XiaoHu Wang,** *Essential Statistics for Public Managers and Policy Analysts,* 3rd ed. (Thousand Oaks, Calif.: CQ Press, 2012). A useful overview of basic statistics that can be applied in policy analysis.

Anne L. Schneider and Helen Ingram, "Policy Design: Elements, Premises, and Strategies," in *Policy Theory and Policy Evaluation*, ed. Stuart Nagel (Westport, Conn.: Greenwood, 1990). A shorter version of Schneider and Ingram's argument in *Policy Design for Democracy*. Not easy reading, but well worth the effort.

————, *Policy Design for Democracy* (Lawrence: University Press of Kansas, 1997). One of the best treatments of policy design, with particular attention to incentives that policies provide to government officials and target populations to achieve policy success.

SUGGESTED WEBSITES

www.congress.gov. One of the most comprehensive public sites for legislative searches.

https://fedstats.sites.usa.gov/. A site that provides easy access to a vast amount of federal data on policy problems, organized by agency as well as substantive policy area.

www.gao.gov. U.S. Government Accountability Office, a treasure trove of reports on government agencies and programs, especially evaluation studies.

www.gpo.gov. Access to the U.S. Government Publishing Office site for location of government documents.

www.publicagenda.org. Nonpartisan briefings on policy and polling; a digest of news, legislation, and studies; and research sources.

www.usa.gov. Portal for federal government websites.

NOTES

1. For a description of the Arizona law, see Randal C. Archibold, "Arizona Enacts Stringent Law on Immigration," *New York Times*, April 23, 2010.

2. Campbell Robertson, "In Alabama, Calls for Revamping Immigration Law," *New York Times*, November 16, 2011.

3. See Benjy Sarlin, "How America's Harshest Immigration Law Failed," MSNBC, December 16, 2013, updated on March 9, 2014.

4. Ibid. See also the editorials "The Price of Intolerance," *New York Times*, November 27, 2011; and "How Alabama's Immigration Law Is Crippling Its Farms," *Washington Post*, November 3, 2011. The estimates of undocumented immigrants come from the Pew Research Center Hispanic Trends Project: www.pewhispanic.org.

5. See a summary of the study in Bill Keller, "The Good Newt," *New York Times*, December 11, 2011. The study was conducted in December 2009 by Gordon Hanson, an economist at the University of California, San Diego, and is available at http://gps.ucsd.edu/_files/faculty/hanson/hanson_publication_immigration_econ.pdf.

6. See Jens Manuel Krogstad, Jeffrey S. Passel, and D'Vera Cohn, "5 Facts about Illegal Immigration in the U.S.," Pew Research Center, November 3, 2016, available at www.pewrescarch.org/fact-tank/2016/11/03/5-facts-about-illegal-immigration-in-the-u-s/.

7. For a summary of a 2016 study by the National Academy of Sciences, *The Economic and Fiscal Consequences of Immigration*, see Thomas Edsall, "What Does Immigration Actually Cost Us?" *New York Times*, September 29, 2016. The academy found the net benefits of immigration to be integral to economic growth in the United States, and a plus for the nation's "capacity for innovation, entrepreneurship, and technological change."

8. The construction of the border fence drew considerable criticism. See Randal C. Archibold and

Julia Preston, "Despite Growing Opposition, Homeland Security Stands by Its Fence," *New York Times*, May 21, 2008, 1. The wall that Trump proposed in the 2016 campaign was far more controversial.

9. Bernadette D. Proctor, Jessica L. Semega, and Melissa A. Kollar, "Income and Poverty in the United States: 2015," U.S. Census Bureau, Report Number: P60-256, September 13, 2016, available at www.census.gov. A newspaper account with useful graphics can be found in Patricia Cohen, "Millions in U.S. Climb out of Poverty, at Long Last," *New York Times*, September 25, 2016.

10. The federal government's guidelines for who qualifies as poor can be found at https://aspe.hhs.gov/computations-2016-poverty-guidelines. One of many critical views of the official poverty level measures can be seen in Jillian Berman, "Federal Poverty Line Doesn't Adequately Reflect Cost of Living in America, Analysis Finds," *Huffington Post*, July 3, 2013.

11. For one example of such a study, see Lora L. Warner, David Wegge, and Ashley Heath, *Brown County LIFE Study* (October 2011), available at www.lifestudy.info. The study of Brown County, Wisconsin, is part of a larger study of the Fox River Region completed in 2011. An updated study was under way in 2017.

12. The quotation comes from the 2002 edition of Stone's *Policy Paradox: The Art of Political Decision Making*, p. 133. We cite the new third edition elsewhere in the text.

13. Elizabeth Becker, "Bill Defines Irradiated Meat as 'Pasteurized,'" *New York Times*, March 5, 2002.

14. Michelle Ye Hee Lee, "Yes, U.S. Locks People Up at a Higher Rate Than Any Other Country," *Washington Post*, July 7, 2015.

15. "Nation's Inmate Population Increased 2.3 Percent Last Year," *New York Times*, April 25, 2005, Associated Press release. The U.S. Bureau of Justice Statistics estimated that the nation's jails and prisons held 2.2 million people in 2014, mostly in state and local facilities. Despite a falling crime rate, the prison population remains high, in part because of the tough policies enacted in the 1980s and 1990s.

16. *The Diane Rehm Show*, National Public Radio, February 18, 2003.

17. Ironically, the longer sentences and increase in the prison population were not deterring people from committing crimes. The recidivism rate rose in part because, to save money, state governments cut back on rehabilitation programs such as drug treatment, vocational education, and classes that help prepare convicted criminals to return to society. See Fox Butterfield, "Study Shows Building Prisons Did Not Prevent Repeat Crimes," *New York Times*, June 3, 2002.

18. Evelyn Nieves, "California Gets Set to Shift on Sentencing Drug Users," *New York Times*, November 10, 2000; and Linda Greenhouse, "Winds of Change," *New York Times*, September 18, 2013. The effects of the 2012 policy shift are summarized in Erik Eckholm, "California Convicts Are Out of Prison after Third Strike, and Staying Out," *New York Times*, February 26, 2015.

19. Timothy Williams, "One Robber's 3 Life Sentences: '90s Legacy Fills Prisons Today," *New York Times*, July 4, 2016.

20. Clifford Krauss, "Gas Prices Send Surge of Riders to Mass Transit," *New York Times*, May 10, 2008; and Christopher B. Leinberger, "The Death of the Fringe Suburb," *New York Times*, November 25, 2011. When gas prices fell in 2015 and 2016 to about $2.20 per gallon, some of these incentives diminished.

21. For an overview of methods that can be used to obtain policy information, see Patton, Sawicki, and Clark (2016), chapter 3; and Janet Buttolph Johnson, H. T. Reynolds, and Jason D. Mycoff, *Political Science Research Methods*, 7th ed. (Thousand Oaks, Calif.: CQ Press, 2012). Patton, Sawicki, and Clark offer a helpful guide for arranging and conducting interviews with policymakers. Any recent social science methods text will discuss how to construct and use questionnaires as well as how to conduct interviews. See,

for example, Earl Babbie, *The Practice of Social Research*, 13th ed. (Belmont, CA: Wadsworth, Cengage, 2013).

22. See Timothy Egan, "Once Braced for a Power Shortage, California Now Finds Itself with a Surplus," *New York Times*, November 4, 2001.

23. See Associated Press, "For Some Whistle-Blowers, Big Risk Pays Off," *New York Times*, November 29, 2004; and Associated Press, "Whistle-Blower Awarded $104 Million by I.R.S.," *New York Times*, September 11, 2012; and U.S. Department of Justice, "Justice Department Recovers over $3.5 Billion from False Claims Act Cases in Fiscal Year 2015," press release, December 3, 2015. A nonprofit organization called the Taxpayers Against Fraud Education Fund maintains an extensive website on the False Claims Act at www.taf.org.

24. *New State Ice Co. v. Liebmann*, 285 U.S. 262, 311 (1932).

25. Quoted in a *Science* magazine editorial by Donald Kennedy, March 22, 2002, 2177.

Chapter 6

Chapter Objectives

- Describe evaluative criteria for judging the value of policy proposals or alternatives.

- Explain how to apply the methods of policy analysis.

- Identify three key economic approaches to policy analysis.

- Distinguish between the different types of decision making and impact analyses.

- Compare the ethical approach of policy analysis against other methods.

Looking for alternatives. The sharp drop in gas prices in recent years no doubt pleased most consumers, but it also led to a surge in purchase of large SUVs, which undercut vehicle fuel efficiency goals that were designed to reduce reliance on oil and limit greenhouse gas emissions. The photo shows gas prices on a sign outside a fueling station in Chillicothe, Illinois, on December 11, 2015. By early 2017, prices had risen to about $2.30 a gallon, still historically low. *(Daniel Acker/Bloomberg via Getty Images)*

Assessing Policy Alternatives

When gasoline prices surged in 2011 and 2012, automobile makers responded by heavily promoting a new generation of more efficient vehicles, touting their highway fuel economy of more than 40 miles per gallon. Nearly all of them also invested heavily in development of new hybrid or electric models to meet rising public demand for efficient cars, trucks, and SUVs. The same forces led the Obama administration to strike a new deal with U.S. auto companies that took effect in 2012 and will raise fuel efficiency standards to a fleet average of 54.5 miles per gallon by 2025. It was a move that was sure to have important impacts not only on energy use but on national security, jobs and the economy, climate change, and the health of the U.S. population.[1] Beyond all of these developments, as we noted in chapter 3, the United States in 2010 had the worst offshore oil spill in its history with the BP Deepwater Horizon accident in the Gulf of Mexico, sparking a reorganization of the federal agency charged with regulating offshore oil drilling.

The political debates over what to do about gasoline prices and other energy issues were similar to those just four years earlier when a sharp increase in the cost of gasoline affected nearly everyone in the United States. The price of oil in 2008 soared to $147 a barrel on the international market and to more than $4 a gallon in the United States, resulting in short-term, widespread economic pain. The cost of goods increased as a result of shipping costs, people began buying more fuel-efficient cars, and demand for mass transit rose so much that many cities doubted they could cope.[2] The candidates in the 2008 presidential election debated how best to respond to the problem, including competing proposals to lower the federal gasoline tax to ease the burden on consumers; increase fuel efficiency requirements (which had just been raised in late 2007); and promote energy conservation, efficiency, and the use of alternative or renewable fuels through boosts in federal research and tax credits.[3]

The year 2015, however, brought a major reversal in many of these trends as a global glut of oil from high levels of production and diminishing demand sent gasoline prices plummeting to less than $2 a gallon. Even by late 2016, the price for a gallon of regular gas was about $2.16. What impact did the falling prices have? Among other changes, vehicle manufacturers stopped touting the fuel economy of their new cars and trucks and reverted to emphasizing power and performance characteristics in the ever-abundant television and online advertisements.

These fascinating twists and turns in energy use and debate over it during the last decade included nearly every criterion and method that policy analysts typically use to assess public policy proposals. Commentators and policymakers at all levels of government raised questions about access to energy sources and their costs; national security implications of U.S. dependence on imported oil; environmental, health, and safety risks of energy exploration, development, and use; the role of government and regulation (e.g., in setting fuel efficiency standards and in supervision of offshore drilling); and the importance of economic incentives for energy development, including renewable sources such as wind and solar power, because of rising concern for climate change. There were also questions about whether to continue generous oil company subsidies, the technical feasibility of offshore drilling in certain areas, and the likely effectiveness of such drilling: if and when it would produce substantial quantities of oil and how much such efforts would affect the price of gasoline and the nation's dependence on foreign oil. Each side in these debates pointed to arguments that bolstered its position, and each challenged the other's assumptions and portrayals of the situation.

It was a fairly typical policy debate. It illustrated well the tendency of policymakers and their staffs to engage in intensive issue framing and to use policy studies to reinforce and advocate their positions and as ammunition against opponents. It showed as well the importance of asking which proposals, such as subsidies for purchase of electric vehicles, increases in the gasoline tax, development of a new carbon tax, or continued support for fossil fuel development, would be most likely to meet competing national needs, and which would be technically feasible, economically acceptable, fair, and socially and politically acceptable. In this context, consider one particular study that did get some attention during the 2008 debate, even if it changed few minds. The Department of Energy (DOE) reported in 2007 that new drilling in the offshore areas would not have a significant effect on oil production before 2030, and that the ultimate effect on prices would be "insignificant" because oil is traded globally and the amounts would be too little to affect worldwide prices.[4]

Whether policymakers use them well or not, policy analyses like the one by the DOE are integral to the modern policymaking process precisely because the issues often are complicated and involve highly technical questions well beyond the expertise of elected officials, not to mention the ability of the public to sort out facts from campaign rhetoric and other political stances. At the core of such analyses is a clear delineation of the criteria developed for judging policy alternatives and the application of available tools and methods to provide information essential to decision making. Yet as the case of energy policy shows well, even the best studies may persuade few elected officials and their supporters in the heat of political competition.

This chapter reviews the leading evaluative criteria used today as well as the methods of policy analysis most commonly employed. These methods range from cost-benefit analysis that addresses economic criteria to political and institutional assessments that estimate political or administrative feasibility. The combination of clear evaluative criteria and careful analysis should make it easier to determine whether one policy alternative is better than another. Policy analysts and those involved in making policy choices want to know whether one alternative is more likely than another to be more effective, or whether one will be cheaper. They want to ask as well about differences in equity or fairness, such as how these alternative policy options will distribute their costs or benefits across the population. That is, will some groups (such as wealthy or retired citizens) gain more than others, and will some (such as the middle class or those in the workforce) pay more than others for that policy? It is the purpose of policy analysis to provide that kind of information, and it is up to policymakers and the public to decide what to do with it.

Evaluative Criteria for Judging Policy Proposals

Evaluative criteria are the specific dimensions of policy objectives (what policy proposals seek to achieve) that can be used to weigh policy options or judge the merits of existing policies or programs. Evaluative criteria can also be regarded as justifications or rationales for a policy or government action. The use of explicit evaluative criteria establishes relatively clear standards that can keep policy analysis objective and focused on the issues of greatest concern to the analyst, the intended audience, or the client. Such standards also allow users to rank alternatives in order of their preferences. It makes sense to choose the criteria that fit a given policy area and set of circumstances. Obviously, some criteria make more sense for judging access to health care services than they would for determining whether Congress should cut or increase agricultural subsidies. In addition, as Brian W. Hogwood and Lewis A. Gunn (1984) argued, policy analysis for the real world is always contingent on the political and institutional context of policy debate and is influenced by available resources and time.

The dimensions of policy objectives that are most often the target of inquiry and political argument include effectiveness, efficiency (costs in relation to benefits), risks, uncertainty, ethics, political feasibility, administrative feasibility, equity or fairness, liberty or freedom, legality, and (sometimes) constitutionality. This is quite a long list, and analysts seldom address all of these elements in any single study. Chapter 1 suggested the usefulness of focusing on four of these criteria: effectiveness, efficiency, equity, and political feasibility. Concern about effectiveness, or how well a policy is working, is nearly universal. Because most public policies, from defense to education, spend public money, analysts consider efficiency—what clients get for their money—to be just as important. Many also argue that equity, which concerns the fairness of government programs in relation to the needs of different groups in the population, should always be a concern; it comes up regularly in discussions of tax reform, for example, over whether proposed tax cuts benefit primarily the wealthy or the middle class. Of all the criteria discussed in the text, effectiveness, efficiency, and equity capture the most politically important standards used to judge policy proposals today.

It should be said that policymakers, interest groups, and analysts often favor use of one criterion over another without being very clear about why they do so. In the case of the energy policy debate summarized above, for example, advocates of offshore drilling emphasized the need to expand domestic oil supplies, a component of effectiveness. They said little about the relative efficiency of that strategy in relation to other policy options or even how likely it was that increased drilling would lower the price of gasoline, which was arguably the public's greatest concern at the time. On the other side of this debate, environmentalists challenged the likely effectiveness of a drilling strategy in relation to other policy options, such as increased fuel efficiency standards, but many emphasized even more what they viewed as the unacceptable risks of oil spills, made concrete by the BP Deepwater Horizon spill. Neither side made equity considerations a prominent part of its argument, although some opponents of drilling did note that U.S. consumption of oil was disproportionate to its population size (and hence unfair in a global context), which reinforced arguments for decreasing reliance on oil, whether produced domestically or imported. In the practical world of politics, policy actors use the arguments they think will best make their case without necessarily trying to address every consideration or every criterion.

Figure 6-1 lists these criteria along with four others often used in policy analysis and policy debate. The figure gives the meaning of each criterion and the limitations in using it as a standard of judgment. It also indicates the type of public policies for which it is most apt. Critics such as Deborah Stone (2012) underscore the inherent ambiguities and problems of interpretation associated with such criteria. These qualities need not prevent their use in practical policy analysis, but they do suggest the need to be alert to such limitations in how they are applied.

Typically, when these criteria are used, they must be expressed in terms of operational measurements or indicators, such as those discussed in chapter 5. For example, analysts usually speak of efficiency in terms of dollar cost in relation to the value of benefits expected to be realized from governmental action, such as improved workplace safety that might follow adoption of federal ergonomics standards, or the number of lives that would be saved through improvements in vehicle safety or actions against distracted driving. Effectiveness can be measured in terms of the likelihood of reaching a specific policy objective, such as reducing automobile accident rates by 20 percent over a five-year period or keeping the costs of health care from rising by more than the level of inflation.

Figure 6-1 Selected Criteria for Evaluating Public Policy Proposals

CRITERION	DEFINITION	LIMITS TO USE	WHERE MOST LIKELY USED
Effectiveness	The likelihood of achieving policy goals and objectives or demonstrated achievement of them.	Estimates involve uncertain projection of future events.	Virtually all policy proposals where concern exists over how well government programs work.
Efficiency	The achievement of program goals or benefits in relationship to the costs. Least cost for a given benefit or the largest benefit for a given cost.	Measuring all costs and benefits is not always possible. Policy decision making reflects political choices as much as efficiency.	Regulatory policies, such as consumer product protection, food safety, workplace safety, and environmental protection; consideration of market-based approaches.
Equity	Fairness or justice in the distribution of the policy's costs, benefits, and risks across population subgroups.	Difficulty in finding techniques to measure equity; disagreement over whether equity means a fair process or equal outcomes.	Civil rights, disability rights, tax cuts for the well off and/or middle class, access to health services and higher education.
Liberty/freedom	The extent to which public policy extends or restricts privacy and individual rights and choices.	Assessment of impacts on freedom is often clouded by ideological beliefs about the role of government.	Proposed national identification cards, restrictions on Internet use, property rights, abortion rights, regulatory actions that constrain choices of corporations and individuals.
Political feasibility	The extent to which elected officials accept and support a policy proposal.	Difficult to determine. Depends on perceptions of the issues and changing economic and political conditions.	Any controversial policy, such as gun control, immigration, raising the gasoline tax, tax cuts for the wealthy, or subsidies for oil and gas drilling.
Social acceptability	The extent to which the public will accept and support a policy proposal.	Difficult to determine even when public support can be measured. Depends on saliency of the issues and level of public awareness.	Any controversial policy, such as crime control or abortion rights, and from 2010 to 2013, health care reform.
Administrative feasibility	The likelihood that a department or agency can implement the policy well.	Involves projection of available resources and agency behavior that can be difficult to estimate.	Expansion of agency duties, use of new policy approaches or new technologies, policies with complicated institutional structures.
Technical feasibility	The availability and reliability of technology needed for policy implementation.	Often difficult to anticipate technological change that would alter feasibility.	Science and technology policy, environmental and energy policies, automobile safety regulations, telecommunications, defense policies.

For most of these criteria, multiple indicators are available, and analysts normally use several to compensate for the limitations of any one of them. Some criteria, however, involve making qualitative judgments rather than using such indicators, for example, when questions of equity arise or when the debate turns on the loss of personal liberty for the benefit of the larger public welfare. The personal liberty issues arise in controversies as diverse as gun control, freedom of religious practice, restrictions on private property rights, and actions to constrain possible terrorist activity. Indeed, they are a frequent subject of debate in nearly all areas in which government authority may impinge on individual rights. Recent proposals to reform the federal tax code involve questions of equity or fairness even if that criterion is not always made clear or the proposals are framed in terms of how they will affect economic growth or job creation.

Most policy debates resemble the battles over energy policy and gasoline prices; they involve multiple and competing criteria. Policymakers and analysts want policy action to be effective, but they also want to minimize costs, or to promote the most equitable solution, or to maintain individual rights against expansion of governmental authority. It is a rare policy action that can maximize each of these criteria simultaneously. Those concerned with public policy must therefore figure out which criteria are most important and use those preferences to rank policy alternatives from best to worst. In a more formal exercise, policy analysts might assign weights to each of the various criteria to reflect their relative importance. Then multiple criteria can be used at the same time to assess the attractiveness of different policy options. A brief discussion of the three most frequently used criteria should clarify their meanings and suggest how they might be used in policy analysis. The fourth major criterion, political feasibility, is addressed separately at the end of the chapter as part of a review of methods of policy analysis.

Effectiveness

The need for the effectiveness criterion is evident in the all-too-frequent complaints about the failure of government programs. Analysts and policymakers speak informally of what does and does not work, about policy success and the lack of it. In a narrow sense, effectiveness refers to reaching a policy or program's stated goals and objectives. For a program already in existence, evaluation of its effectiveness usually turns on whether it has achieved the expected results or policy outcomes. For example, does a city's use of school vouchers or charter schools raise the overall quality of education? (See chapter 10.) Or do federally funded abstinence-only programs to prevent teenage pregnancy—which have been enthusiastically backed by conservatives—actually produce lower rates of pregnancy? Nonpartisan analyses suggest they do not, and as a result, some states have chosen to turn down federal funds offered for such initiatives. In 2009, the Obama administration sought to curtail federal funding for the programs on the grounds that they were ineffective in reducing teen pregnancy; instead, it favored comprehensive sex education, as did many state legislatures.[5]

Assessments like these generally require that analysts develop suitable indicators or measurements for the specified outcomes. For a proposed policy rather than an existing program, they try to estimate the likelihood that such goals and objectives would be attained if the proposal were adopted. For example, in 2011, Google was quietly lobbying policymakers in Nevada to approve legislation that would make the state the first to permit self-driving cars to be used on public roads, which had been illegal in all fifty states. The proposal also would permit the car's occupants to send text messages even if sitting in the driver's seat. As was evident by 2016, professional transportation analysts consider self-driving cars a serious option for the future, and some vehicles, such as Tesla cars with Autopilot, already have much of this capability. Analysts anticipate ever-increasing congestion on public roads and thus the need eventually for smart roads and computer-driven or autonomous vehicles that will be able to move at high speeds with greatly reduced risk of accidents. Nevada approved Google's request, and in August 2016, Pittsburgh, Pennsylvania, allowed Uber to begin using experimental self-driving vehicles in the city, albeit with human supervisors in the driver's seat. If these experiments go well, we can anticipate self-driving delivery vans and big-rig trucks, all of which are expected to reduce the cost of transporting people and goods. Many also hope that such vehicles will spark other innovations in the application of artificial intelligence technology and be a critical element in future economic growth. These are among the reasons why the federal government in September 2016 announced its support for automated car technology by issuing formal guidelines for the new industry.[6]

The view of effectiveness we summarize here is a little narrow, however, because programs usually have multiple goals and objectives and may succeed at some and fall short on others. Moreover, some objectives may be attainable only over a long period of time, making assessment of short-term outcomes problematic. Another limitation is that estimating the probability that a proposal will be effective, or more effective than the present policy, requires a forecast of future conditions and events, an uncertain activity at best. In addition, analysts must learn to deal with a political environment in which politicians often exaggerate the weaknesses of current programs and tout the strengths of alternatives based more on ideological beliefs than any assessment of empirical evidence of program effectiveness.

On the plus side, the federal Government Performance and Results Act of 1993 requires regular evaluations of all existing programs and demonstrations of their performance or achievements. The act encourages agencies to focus on results, service quality, and public satisfaction, and it mandates annual performance plans and reports. The current political mood in Washington, D.C., and across the nation creates a strong expectation that new policy proposals will be able to meet the same standards of effectiveness as policies already in place or improve upon them. The economic recession that began in 2008 and subsequent soaring budgetary deficits reinforce these expectations at both the federal and state levels. With scarce budgetary dollars, policymakers are likely to be highly attentive to program effectiveness and eager to cut or terminate programs that cannot prove their worth. Analysts who evaluate policy proposals in terms of likely effectiveness or who try to measure the achievements of existing programs therefore find a ready audience for their assessments.

Efficiency

If policy effectiveness is nearly universally expected in contemporary policymaking, so too is an interest in keeping the cost of government programs within reason. Whether efficiency is a specific measurement of costs in relation to benefits or gaining the most benefits for a fixed cost, the criterion amounts to the same thing. It strongly encourages analysts to think about the overall costs and benefits of existing programs and the various proposals to change them or replace them with something different.

Essentially, efficiency is a way of justifying government action on the basis of economic concepts. Sometimes efficiency is expressed in terms of the relative virtues of government intervention and the operation of a free market in promoting social welfare. As we discussed in chapter 1, government involvement may be called for when the market economy cannot adequately protect the public's well-being, for example, from crime, threats to national security, or urban air pollution. Efficiency is highly prized in the United States, and it is much praised by policy analysts (Stone 2012). Its role reflects the high value Americans place on a smoothly functioning market economy and the promotion of economic well-being.

The logic of efficiency in the allocation of scarce government resources is compelling. From an economist's perspective, fiscal resources must be used to best meet human needs—in other words, to increase the well-being of members of society. When the costs of programs are greater than the benefits, the possible alternative uses of the labor, capital, and materials are foregone, depriving society of their value (Patton, Sawicki, and Clark 2016; Weimer and Vining 2016). Thus if the government spends more on one activity—for example, prescription drug expenses under Medicare—than is needed to gain the benefits of the action—better health for senior citizens—it will have fewer resources for other services, such as public education and national defense. Similarly, policymakers may choose to reduce an agency's spending because it is politically popular to do so even when that action saves no money. For example, in recent years, Congress has cut the Internal Revenue Service (IRS) budget in a way that cost the government billions of dollars annually because the agency lacked the staff to collect taxes that are owed but not paid. A 2014 report on the IRS noted that for each additional dollar in its enforcement budget, the agency collects six more dollars in revenue, seemingly a very good deal unless one intensely dislikes the IRS and is inclined to cut its budget despite the lost revenue.[7]

A striking illustration of inefficiency came to light in late 2005 in a *New York Times* exposé of the New York State Medicaid program. The state's Medicaid spending on prescription drugs had doubled within five years, rising to $3.8 billion in 2005, in part because the state was unwilling to constrain the soaring costs of prescription drugs. As reporter Michael Luo put it, "New York lacks even the most basic controls that dozens of other states and private health insurers have used."[8] Among other examples of wasteful spending, the state was paying millions of dollars for prescription drugs for which far cheaper over-the-counter equivalents were available. It was also paying for some expensive drugs that experts said were largely ineffective and rarely approved for use in other states.

As the Medicaid spending example illustrates, application of the principle of promoting efficiency can be difficult, yet it is by no means impossible. Consider another example. The federal Centers for Disease Control and Prevention (CDC) reports that tobacco use in the United States is responsible for one out of five deaths annually, or 480,000 a year, 42,000 of which are attributed to second-hand smoke exposure; this amounts to 1,300 deaths every day. In addition, 16 million people suffer from at least one serious illness related to tobacco use, such as emphysema. What does smoking cost the country? The CDC says it amounts to more than $300 billion a year. Some $156 billion of that amount is attributed to lost economic productivity and $170 billion to direct health care expenditures.[9] Should government do more to restrict smoking to reduce these costs, particularly to lower the rate of smoking among young people? The CDC reports that each day about 3,200 people younger than eighteen years old smoke their first cigarette, and 2,100 youths or young adults who have been occasional smokers begin smoking on a daily basis. Or should all smokers, young and old, be left alone to make their own choices? Over the past decade, many states raised cigarette taxes, in part to discourage smoking and in part to raise revenue. The national average cost for a pack of cigarettes, counting all taxes, rose to more than $6 in 2016, but the price varies widely by state and even by locality. In New York City, new taxes drove the price higher than $14 a pack on average.

Calculating these kinds of social benefits and costs is not always easy, particularly when they must be expressed in dollar terms, although economists have developed a number of methods for doing so, as we will see later in the chapter. One could ask, for example, how analysts might estimate the economic and social advantages of illegal immigration as well as the costs that such immigration imposes on the United States and on the nations from which immigrants come. Can it be done? Should it be done? We can appreciate that putting a dollar value on costs and benefits in this case can be a challenge intellectually and politically. But what about a qualitative consideration? Either way, making the costs and benefits of policy action more explicit and more understandable should contribute to making smarter choices simply because the public and policymakers can be better informed.

Critics of the use of efficiency as a criterion argue that one important constraint is the fact that benefits and costs are not equally distributed among the population. Often, the benefits of policies such as agricultural subsidies or subsidized tuition for college students go to particular groups in the population, but all taxpayers bear the costs. For regulatory policies, such as controls on polluting power plants or regulation of Wall Street financial institutions, the larger society receives the benefits, but the corporate owners of the plant or banks—and the

Getting around a problem.
Even with recently low gasoline prices, many urban residents rely increasingly on bicycles to get around town. The photo shows the new bicycles that are part of LA Metro's Bike Share program, where up to 1,000 bicycles and up to 65 bike share stations were made available throughout the downtown area for the first time, in Los Angeles, California, on July 7, 2016. *(Marcus Yam/Los Angeles Times via Getty Images)*

stockholders—bear the costs. The implication of this critique is that analysts need to inquire into the distribution of benefits and costs as part of any attempt to examine economic efficiency and its acceptability. This is a subject addressed in the next section, about equity.

In fact, no matter what reservations are expressed about using the efficiency criterion in policy analysis and decision making, political reality dictates that it be addressed in some form. The smart analyst can find ways to do so that are reasonable and fair. Moreover, the great weight placed on policy costs today opens the door for creative ways to get policymakers and the public to think about the consequences of proposals under consideration. Actions that seem justifiable on some grounds might appear far less desirable once the costs of action are taken into account.

Equity

The term *equity* has at least two different meanings in contemporary policy debates: process equity and outcomes (end-result) equity. The first refers to the decision-making process that is used. Is it voluntary, open, and fair to all participants? If so, analysts and citizens might judge the results to be equitable even if some people ultimately fare better than others by gaining benefits such as higher education, better jobs, greater income, nicer houses, and so forth. This view is often associated with the political philosopher Robert Nozick and his book *Anarchy, State, and Utopia* (1974). Those who hold these views tend to believe strongly in the rights of individuals and the freedom to use and dispose of their resources as they see fit. They resist government efforts to promote equality beyond ensuring equal opportunity to participate in society's decisions. As this description suggests, political conservatives identify strongly with the concept of process equity.

John Rawls promoted quite a different conception of equity, particularly in his book *A Theory of Justice* (1971). Rawls argued that equity or fairness refers to just outcomes or the fair distribution of societal goods such as wealth, income, and political power. His reasoning is that political institutions and social structures, such as racism and other forms of discrimination, affect the achievement of such goods. In other words, the acquisition of societal goods is not solely a function of the individual qualities of ambition, talent, and a strong work ethic. People who hold this view are more likely than others to favor government intervention to promote the equitable distribution of society's resources. Political liberals tend to identify with the concept of outcomes equity.

Equity criteria are likely to be central to any consideration of redistributive policies, such as tax reform, welfare reform, efforts to enhance access to education or health services, and assistance to the poor. They may also crop up in other policy areas where the debate and decisions turn on who gains and who loses as a consequence of policy action. The policy analyst might want to ask who receives the benefits of policy action, who does not, and who pays for the costs of the program. *Who* in this context means not individuals, but different groups or categories of people. They can be wealthy, middle class, or poor; city dwellers or suburbanites; ordinary people or huge corporations. Equity issues are pervasive in policy disputes, from tax reform proposals to actions that might restrict access to higher education—such as raising tuition levels.

Concern for economic inequality rose sharply in 2011 and continues to be an issue, as evidence mounted that both wealth and income in the United States had become increasingly unequal, and as the nation's policymakers continued to debate the merits of tax cuts and other economic policy as part of the larger deficit reduction goals. Across the country, the Occupy Wall Street movement addressed what participants viewed as an unacceptable level of inequality and opportunity for economic advancement between the top 1 percent of the population and the remaining 99 percent. In late 2011 in a widely reported speech in Kansas, President Obama focused on data showing that in the last three decades the average income of the top 1 percent in the nation had gone up by more than 250 percent, to $1.2 million a year. In contrast, for most taxpayers in the same period, income hardly rose at all over the level of inflation.[10] Presidential candidate Bernie Sanders focused heavily on this kind of economic inequality in his campaign for the Democratic Party nomination in 2016. Consistent with the president's argument, the Organisation for Economic Co-operation and Development (OECD) announced late in 2011 that income inequality in the United States was at its highest in over thirty years; was continuing to rise; and was greater than in all developed countries other than Chile, Mexico, and Turkey.[11]

This kind of concern over economic inequality has long been a fixture of economic policy, particularly fiscal policy (see chapter 7), and it is likely to continue as policymakers at both federal and state levels debate how to deal with deficit spending. Tax reform measures are certain to be part of that discussion, as they have been over the past decade. For example, one of the most striking debates during the 2000s was what to do about the federal estate tax, a tax on property that is imposed when the owner dies, and which is paid by the heirs to the estate, typically other family members. Using the kind of issue framing we discussed in chapter 3, conservative critics have called the estate tax a "death tax," and have argued that it is unfair to family members and owners of small businesses. They would prefer to have the tax fully repealed even though doing so would be very costly for federal revenues. Not surprisingly, liberals have argued that repealing or weakening the estate tax is also inequitable because most of the benefits would go to the very wealthy.

Should the estate tax be kept and applied to most families out of concern for social equity and sound fiscal policy? Should it be repealed so that even the richest families can leave most of their wealth to their children? Or should the tax be imposed only on estates above a particular monetary level so that most families and small businesses are exempt, and if so, what level would be fair to taxpayers? In 2013, Congress increased the size of an estate that is exempt to $5 million for individuals and $10 million for couples, levels that it also chose to peg to inflation so they will rise over time; for 2016, the level for couples to pay no estate tax had risen to $10.9 million. As a result, 99.8 percent of families will face no estate tax at all.[12] Was this an acceptable compromise? Was it too generous to wealthy families at the expense of others?

Ethical influences on public policy. Some public policy alternatives historically have been evaluated using ethical criteria rather than economic efficiency, political feasibility, or other standards. Women's health care and reproductive rights are examples. The photo shows pro-choice and pro-life activists demonstrating on the steps of the U.S. Supreme Court on June 27, 2016, in Washington, D.C. In a 5–3 decision, the U.S. Supreme Court struck down one of the nation's toughest restrictions on abortion, a Texas law that women's groups said would have forced more than three-quarters of the state's clinics to close. *(Pete Marovich/Getty Images)*

Ethics and Political Values

In a classic essay on the role of principles in policy analysis, political theorist Charles W. Anderson (1979, 713) argued that there are "certain fundamental considerations that must be accounted for in any policy evaluation." This "repertoire of basic concepts" includes "authority, the public interest, rights, justice, equality, and efficiency." They are, Anderson said, not simply an analyst's preferences but "*obligatory* criteria of political judgment."

In the practical world of policy analysis, some of Anderson's requisite criteria or standards of policy judgment are likely to be ignored. Indeed, some political scientists argue that it is unnecessary or even improper for policy analysts to include ethical or normative dimensions in their work. They say this in part because they think ethics and normative values, such as liberty and equality, are beyond the bounds of rational analysis. Or it may be that they believe analysts are incapable of objective analysis because they inevitably inject their personal biases into any such assessment. Some also argue that analysis of normative values is unnecessary because the political process exists to address and resolve ethical and value disputes (Amy 1984). An easy rejoinder to the last argument is that explicit analysis of ethics and values could greatly enhance the quality of argument and debate in policymaking bodies. No doubt, it is easier for analysts to stress criteria such as effectiveness and efficiency, where an assessment can be based on hard data such as measurable costs and benefits. Normative issues, however, deserve serious consideration. As Anderson (1979) argues, analysis that ignores basic issues such as the role of government authority, individual rights, or the public interest is incomplete and inadequate.

Policy debates over personal privacy (for example, cell phone records), property rights, copyright laws, research on human stem cells derived from embryos, and many other contemporary issues clearly require an assessment in terms of normative and legal criteria, not just economics. Even for a seemingly technical subject such as nuclear waste disposal, it is both possible and necessary to analyze ethical issues such as the effects on future generations, whether it is fair for governments to offer monetary compensation to communities if they agree to host a waste repository, and how much public involvement in decision making should be required (Kraft 2000; Shrader-Frechette 1993; E. Weiss 1990).

As this review of evaluative criteria indicates, there are many different bases on which to analyze policy. Students of public policy should be aware of the range of standards that are applied and alert to their strengths and limits and the trade-offs between them. Sometimes, promoting the public's welfare—for example, through food safety, consumer safety, or environmental protection policies—imposes a cost on individuals and corporations. Restrictions on their freedom or liberty may be justified by the public's gains. Conversely, at times the protection of individual rights and liberties is so important that society is willing to tolerate activity that many people find abhorrent. Thus Internet pornography is protected because of the First Amendment's free-speech guarantees, and the

Constitution extends elaborate protections to those accused of criminal behavior, even for horrific crimes such as serial murder or terrorism.

A recent decision in election law illustrates the importance of how these competing criteria, particularly the right to free speech and the broader public welfare, are used and assessed. The Supreme Court decided in early 2010 in the case of *Citizens United v. Federal Election Commission* that spending money on election campaigns is a form of protected free speech under the First Amendment. Therefore the government cannot prevent corporations or unions from spending their money to support or criticize candidates. The corporations and unions cannot give the money directly to candidates (which is prohibited by campaign finance laws), but they can spend as much as they desire on television and other ads intended to influence voters. The controversial ruling led many to complain that the Court's decision protects the free-speech rights of corporations (and unions) over the broader citizen interests in having competitive and fair election campaigns. Then in a related ruling in 2014, *McCutcheon v. Federal Election Commission*, the Court struck down long-established limits on what one person could donate to federal candidates and political parties in each election cycle. The result was a surge in contributions by, and presumably political influence of, wealthy individuals and families.[13]

The use of diverse evaluative criteria can help in another way. Too often policymakers, analysts, and commentators make statements that reflect their strong ideological beliefs when they discuss pending policy choices. Liberals know what they like and dislike and apply those philosophical standards to the full range of contemporary policies, and conservatives do the same, although both sides would have much to gain from dispassionate assessments of current government programs and proposed policies. An objective analysis of this kind could be grounded in one or more of the evaluative criteria described in this chapter. Doing so does not mean that citizens and policymakers need to abandon their convictions about what government should or should not be doing. Rather, it means that they ought to be sure they have the facts about a given issue, be it school vouchers, gun control, or health care alternatives, and think about a range of considerations in addition to their personal values and policy beliefs. They will have an easier time defending the position they take, and the policy positions they endorse will stand a better chance of success.

Using the Methods of Policy Analysis

This section of the chapter surveys the most frequently used methods of policy analysis and highlights their strengths and most significant weaknesses or limitations. The suggested reading list at the end of the chapter provides substantial coverage of analytic methods. Those wishing to read further will find this list a good place to start. The leading methods of policy analysis draw heavily from economics and focus on the evaluative criterion of efficiency, particularly for cost-benefit and cost-effectiveness analyses (Dunn 2016; Weimer and Vining 2016). The ideas found in these and related methods are useful even for nontechnical analysis. The methods are tools for critical thinking about public policy that anyone can use.

By now, however, it should be clear that public policy evaluation is about more than economics. It is also about effectiveness, equity, liberty, and, fundamentally, politics. As stated earlier, analytic methods can be used to clarify problems and policy choices, but decisions about which policies to adopt or maintain are up to policymakers and, ultimately, up to the public that elects them.

The overview of analytic methods that follows groups them into four categories. One is economic approaches that include cost-benefit analysis, cost-effectiveness analysis, and risk assessment methods. Another is decision making and impacts, which includes forecasting and impact assessment. A third is political and institutional analysis, which includes assessment of political feasibility as well as policy implementation and program evaluation. The last category is ethical analysis, where the concern is consideration of the ethics of policy action.

Economic Approaches

As discussed earlier in the chapter, economic analysis pervades the study of public policy, and for good reason (Weimer and Vining 2016). Public policies can be expensive, and in ways that are sometimes not so obvious to the public and policymakers. Use of economic approaches can help us understand the real costs of government programs and the trade-offs involved in choosing one policy alternative over another. As we have seen, however, economic analysis also has its critics, who worry that emphasis can be placed too much on the dollar value of government action and too little on what they see as the necessity of addressing some public needs regardless of cost. A review of the most frequently used economic approaches is helpful for appreciating both the strengths and limitations of such methods.

Cost-Benefit Analysis

Most readers are already familiar with cost-benefit analysis, also called benefit-cost analysis, and they use the techniques even if they do not use the terms. When a high school senior decides which college to attend, he or she probably makes a list of the advantages and disadvantages of each important option. One college offers a stronger program in the student's area of interest, but it is expensive. Another is affordable but falls a little short on the number of courses in the anticipated major. In addition, the student considers the differences in the range of campus activities, housing, sports facilities, and other qualities of college life. How to make this decision? The student, probably with the help of a counselor and parents, weighs the advantages and disadvantages of each, perhaps writing them down in several columns to compare the choices. Cost-benefit analysis is simply a more systematic method for doing the same thing.

One economist described cost-benefit analysis as follows:

> It seeks to determine if the aggregate of the gains that accrue to those
> made better off is greater than the aggregate of losses to those made
> worse off by the policy choice. The gains and losses are both measured
> in dollars, and are defined as the sums of each individual's willingness
> to pay to receive the gains or to prevent the policy-imposed losses. If the
> gains exceed the losses, the policy should be accepted according to the
> logic of benefit-cost analysis. (A. Freeman 2000, 192)

He added that in some respects cost-benefit analysis is "nothing more than organized common sense," even if the term usually refers to a more narrowly defined and technical calculation.

The usefulness of thinking in terms of what public policies and programs cost and what society gets from them should be clear enough. Consider the enormous costs inflicted by Hurricane Katrina in 2005. Over 1,300 people lost their lives, and many thousands lost their homes and businesses, suffered pain or trauma, or had their lives otherwise uprooted. The economic impact on both New Orleans and the nation was substantial, and it continued for years. In addition, highways, utilities, schools, and other public structures in New Orleans and other cities had to be rebuilt at considerable expense, easily over $100 billion in repairs and reconstruction costs. What would it have taken to provide greater protection for the New Orleans area by building stronger flood levees and improving the city's emergency preparedness capacity? Surely a great deal less than $100 billion. Most estimates were in the range of a few billion dollars. Indeed, following Katrina, one expert on cost-benefit analysis, Harvard economist W. Kip Viscusi, said the comparison of costs and benefits "was not a close call." Instead, it was "a no-brainer that you do this," meaning to invest in a much larger flood-prevention effort.[14]

Short of Category Five (the most severe) hurricanes, there are plenty of examples of routine policy decisions that are equally instructive on the value of thinking about costs and benefits. Consider the costs of protecting the U.S. border. In one case, the government spent nearly $1 billion on a new virtual border fence project that proved to be ineffective and was abandoned.[15] Should the initial cost estimates have ruled this out? What about the Obama administration's ambitious efforts to foster the development of a high-speed rail system in the United States to rival those that have operated for years in China, France, Japan, Spain, and elsewhere?[16] Was the initial federal investment of $8 billion for fiscal 2012 a wise decision? What about the anticipated total of $53 billion over six years? Would the long-term societal benefits be far greater than the costs? How would we go about determining that? House Republicans voted in November 2011 to kill the program, unconvinced that it served the national interest, and Republican governors in some states, such as Wisconsin, rejected the federal funds to develop high-speed rail, convinced that in the long run such an initiative was not justifiable.[17]

Or consider the cost of the Iraq war and the broader war on terrorism. Should we place a dollar value on protecting the nation from terrorists? What about launching and continuing a war in another country such as Iraq? At the beginning of the Iraq war in 2003, President George W. Bush assured Congress and the nation that under the "worst case" assumptions the war would cost no more than $200 billion, reflecting confidence at that time that it would be relatively short and successful. Yet by the tenth anniversary of the terrorist attacks in New York, Pennsylvania, and Washington, D.C., the *New York Times* and a number of independent economists concluded that costs of the war on terrorism, including the cost of fighting in Iraq and Afghanistan, had reached $3.3 trillion.[18] Other estimates were even higher, depending on what was counted. For example, the U.S. government has tended not to count long-term costs such as care for returning veterans, many of whom will require lifelong medical treatment. Should costs like this be a factor in the decision to go to war, or in decisions to continue a war for a long period of time?

Conducting a cost-benefit analysis is relatively straightforward in theory. The analyst (1) identifies all the important long-term and short-term costs and benefits; (2) measures the tangible costs and benefits in monetary terms; (3) uses a discount rate, which adjusts for changes in value over time, to ensure that all are expressed in commensurable terms; (4) estimates the intangible or qualitative considerations; and (5) aggregates, or totals, the costs and benefits.

This total is expressed in one of two ways: as the net benefit (benefits minus costs) or as the ratio of benefits to costs (the benefits divided by the costs). The box "Steps to Analysis: Conducting a Cost-Benefit Analysis" indicates how it is done, and policy analysis texts provide many other examples (e.g., Boardman et al. 2011; Gupta 2011). Public policy students might try to apply these methods to a particular problem—perhaps a current campus issue such as whether to expand parking lots or to provide incentives to students, faculty, and staff to use other means of transportation to reach the campus. In this particular case, thorough analysis suggests the virtue of trying to discourage automobile use on economic as well as environmental grounds (Toor and Havlick 2004).

Some of the limitations of cost-benefit analysis are evident even in the brief summary provided here and in the fuel-tax example used in the box. Determination of what costs and benefits are important enough to be included is in part a judgment call. Measuring them in monetary terms is easier for some costs and benefits than others. The analyst may emphasize costs because they are more identifiable and measurable. What the benefits turn out to be is less certain and may be realized only after a period of time. Economists often try to estimate **opportunity costs**, which refer to the value of opportunities that are forgone when time or resources are spent on a given activity. For example, being stuck in traffic imposes an opportunity cost on drivers because they could be doing something more productive with their time. Federal regulations that require companies to spend more than necessary on safety or environmental regulations impose an opportunity cost because this money might have been invested in additional research, plant modernization, enhanced employee benefits, and so forth.

Steps to Analysis

Conducting a Cost-Benefit Analysis

Conducting a cost-benefit analysis can be a fairly simple or quite complicated process, depending on the issue. In general, an analyst completes the following procedure:

1. Identify all of the important costs and benefits.

2. Measure those costs and benefits that can be expressed in dollar terms and either estimate or acknowledge those that cannot be measured easily.

3. Adjust the measurements for changes in value over time.

4. Sum up and compare all the costs and benefits and conclude whether the costs outweigh the benefits or vice versa.

Let us apply these steps to a policy example.

1. **Identify all of the important costs and benefits.** Consider the U.S. federal gasoline tax, which is the lowest among the world's industrialized nations. Those who support raising it contend that doing so would yield many tangible benefits, among them lowering the country's dependence on imported oil. It would reduce urban air pollution and improve public health; reduce carbon dioxide emissions and the risk of climate change; cut back on traffic congestion and drive time; and lessen traffic accidents, thereby saving lives and preventing injuries. A higher gas tax could yield all of these benefits and substantially increase government tax revenues by internalizing the social costs of driving and providing an incentive to people to drive fewer miles or seek alternative forms of transportation. Raising the gas tax, however, imposes direct costs on drivers and on a variety of services that depend on transportation, and it can have a particularly adverse impact on low- and moderate-income citizens who have few alternatives to using automobiles, and on those who live in sparsely populated areas where they need to drive and who also may travel long distances.

2. **Measure those costs and benefits that can be expressed in dollar terms and either estimate or acknowledge those that cannot be measured easily.** Because a complete cost-benefit analysis of raising the gasoline tax can become exceedingly complicated, we consider a study that took on only part of the challenge. In a paper prepared for Resources for the Future (RFF), Ian Parry and Kenneth Small examined many of these costs in an effort to determine the "optimal" level for a gasoline tax in the United States. Although economists cannot easily measure all of the benefits noted, they have estimated that the pollution damages amount to about 40 cents a gallon, the carbon dioxide emissions 6 cents a gallon (estimates vary widely here), traffic congestion about 70 cents a gallon on average, and traffic accidents 60 cents a gallon, for a total of $1.76 a gallon. To take into account that gasoline taxes actually tax the fuel purchased as opposed to the distance that is traveled and some of the negative economic effects of raising fuel taxes, the analysts lowered this amount to about a dollar per gallon (Parry 2002).

3. **Adjust the measurements for changes in value over time.** In this example, no such adjustment is made. All costs and benefits are assumed to apply to the present. Conceivably, however, one could make such adjustments for those benefits expected to come only in the future, such as the value of reducing expected climate change from buildup of carbon dioxide emissions. The adjacent text discusses how such "discounting" of future benefits is done.

4. **Sum up and compare all the costs and benefits and conclude whether the costs outweigh the benefits or vice versa.** The study reached its conclusion about an optimal level of taxation

without considering the economic costs of dependence on foreign oil, which another study estimated to be around 12 cents a gallon; the military costs of defending access to Middle Eastern oil fields; or the damage caused by the production, transportation, and use of gasoline—such as oil spills and leaking storage tanks. Some environmental groups have tried to estimate all of those effects and, not surprisingly, came out with a much higher total. Still, according to the RFF analysis, the dollar-per-gallon optimal tax that would internalize the major social costs is more than twice the average combined federal and state taxes on gasoline in the United States, which in 2016 totaled about 48 cents per gallon.

- Would you change any of the major social costs considered in this analysis?

- Are there other costs and benefits that should be considered if the gasoline tax is to be raised?

- Do you think that economists can fairly estimate the dollar value of things like improved public health because of reduced air pollution or the value of time lost by those stuck in traffic?

- Does the conclusion of the study present a cogent argument for raising gasoline taxes?

Source: Ian W. H. Parry, "Is Gasoline Undertaxed in the United States?" *Resources* 148 (summer 2002): 28–33.

Using a **discount rate** allows analysts to determine the value of future benefits today, but the choice of the rate, essentially an estimate of inflation over time, clearly can have a profound impact on the results. For example, consider the present value of $100 earned a hundred years from now, with varying assumptions of a discount rate. At a 1 percent discount rate, that $100 is worth $36.97; at 2 percent, $13.80; at 3 percent, $5.20; and at 5 percent, only $0.76. As these calculations illustrate, distant benefits may be of minimal value in current dollars, and a cost-benefit analysis can therefore yield wildly different results depending on the rate selected.

Because the choice of a discount rate can have a great effect on how one appraises policy options, that choice underlies innumerable conflicts over government policy decisions, from protection against hurricanes like Katrina or efforts to reduce the risk of future climate change. The benefits of preventing damage from hurricanes or of slowing or halting global climate change are real and often substantial, but they may occur so far in the future that discounting the benefits to today's values tends to minimize them in a cost-benefit calculation. In contrast, the costs of hurricane damage mitigation or dealing with climate change can be quite large, and they will be paid for in today's dollars. These complications lead economic analysts to suggest other methods for discounting in a responsible way that consider long-term costs and benefits.[19] Yet, as noted above, at least one calculation in the aftermath of Katrina did employ such discounting and nonetheless concluded that the benefits of a massive investment in disaster prevention could easily have been justified on economic grounds.[20] Many public officials in New York drew similar conclusions about the logic of spending now on infrastructure improvements that could help to minimize the economic costs in the future should a storm like 2012's Hurricane Sandy strike the area again; that storm caused an estimated $70 billion in damages to New York and New Jersey.[21]

Another vulnerable part of the process of cost-benefit analysis is the estimate of intangible human costs and benefits, such as well-being, aesthetic preferences, or even the value of a life or of human suffering. Some analysts choose not to include them at all in a cost-benefit analysis and instead highlight that omission in reporting the results. Others prefer to use available economic methods to estimate intangible or nonmarket values and then include them in the cost-benefit analysis. For example, economists use techniques known as **contingent valuation methods**, which are essentially questionnaires or interviews with individuals, designed to allow an estimate of the dollar value of the time spent stuck in traffic or the preservation of lakes or forests. If done well, such methods can provide a useful estimate of the value people attach to certain intangibles. The use of **sensitivity analysis** can minimize to some extent the weaknesses inherent in cost-benefit analysis. When the calculations are "sensitive" to a basic assumption such as the chosen discount rate, the analyst can report on several different rates, and the reader can choose the assumptions that seem most reasonable.

Even with its obvious limitations, cost-benefit analysis is a powerful tool that is widely used in government decision making. It forces analysts and policymakers to define what they expect government action to do (produce benefits) and to consider the costs associated with that action. If done properly, cost-benefit analysis can help justify public policy that might otherwise be ignored or challenged. Consider the case of lead in gasoline and its effect on public health. During the 1980s, the Environmental Protection Agency (EPA) asked for a reduction in the amount of lead allowed in gasoline from 1.1 grams per gallon to 0.1 grams; lead was used to boost the octane level of gasoline. The benefits of controlling lead in this way included a reduction in adverse health and cognitive problems in children, a lowered level of high blood pressure and cardiovascular disease in adults, and reduced automobile maintenance costs. Not all of those benefits could be measured, but counting those that could produced a benefit-cost ratio of 10 to 1 (A. Freeman 2000, 194). That calculation helped gain approval for eliminating lead in gasoline despite opposition from automobile companies and oil refineries and the Ronald Reagan administration's concerns about the action. Lead was completely eliminated from U.S. gasoline by 1996, and it also has been phased out of gasoline nearly all over the world, often with dramatic effects on children's health.[22]

Critics of cost-benefit analysis claim that the method can be abused if only some costs and benefits are considered and inappropriate measures are used to estimate their value (Stone 2012; Tong 1986). Their concerns are genuine, even though in the real world of policy debate, it is likely that analysts on both sides of the policy question will carefully scrutinize any cost-benefit analysis. Moreover, the Office of Management and Budget (OMB) has set out elaborate guidelines that federal government agencies are expected to follow for the conduct of such studies.

OMB's Office of Information and Regulatory Affairs (OIRA) has been in charge of this process since President Reagan's 1981 executive order mandating that economic analysis be used to justify proposed regulations. Each successive president has established a similar review process, albeit with differing guidelines and expectations, and the agencies have improved their ability to conduct them. Under legislation approved in 2000, the Data Quality Act, OIRA is also charged with establishing guidelines for how agencies ensure the accuracy of the data on which regulations are based.[23] Despite these expectations and procedures, the public policy student should always ask about the underlying assumptions in a cost-benefit analysis and how the costs and benefits were estimated. As noted in several other examples, estimates of a new government regulation's future costs often reveal very wide ranges, indicating that the analysts used quite different assumptions and calculations.

Cost-benefit analysis is used less in areas of public policy where such measurements are not readily available. Even in these areas, however, one could carry out a kind of qualitative cost-benefit analysis in which the important benefits and costs are listed and considered, but without an attempt to place a dollar value on them. Such an exercise might allow citizens, analysts, and policymakers to think comprehensively about the pros and cons of government policies for which they have either no dollar estimates of costs or only partial information.

Cost-Effectiveness Analysis

Sometimes the concerns about the ability to measure the benefits of a policy action are so significant that cost-benefit analysis is not useful. For example, many policies, such as health regulations, highway safety, and medical research, may prevent disease or devastating injury, and may save lives. But how do analysts place a dollar value on human life and health? Government agency officials and analysts, along with insurance companies, have methods for estimating how much a life is worth, even though many critics object in principle to making such calculations (Tong 1986). The advantage of **cost-effectiveness analysis** is that it requires no measurements of the value of intangible benefits such as human lives; it simply compares different policy alternatives that can produce these benefits in terms of their relative costs. That is, analysts are asking which actions can save the most human lives given a fixed dollar cost, or which dollar investments produce the greatest benefits.

For example, in the early 1990s, Oregon created a prioritized list as part of the Oregon Health Plan, which chiefly serves the state's Medicaid beneficiaries. The plan ranked 709 medical procedures "according to their benefit to the entire population being served." Coverage was to be provided for all conditions that fell above a threshold on the list, and the state legislature was to determine the cutoff points each year on the basis of estimates for health care services and budget constraints. The state used a cost-benefit methodology to establish the list, consulting fifty physician panels and surveying the Oregon public. The choices were based on factors such as the likelihood that treatment would reduce suffering or prevent death, the cost of care, and the duration of benefits. In effect, the state was trying to determine how to get the greatest benefit to society from the limited resources available for health care. As might be expected, the state's innovative approach was highly controversial, and the federal government initially rejected it, but it later approved a modified form.[24] Oregon modified the plan in 2012, and transferred the prioritization of health services to a Health Evidence Review Commission, whose members are appointed by the governor and confirmed by the state senate. The plan also was expanded to cover a larger number of individuals and families under the state's Medicaid program as part of its response to the Affordable Care Act of 2010. Is such a cost-effective approach to state health care benefits a good idea? What are its strengths and weaknesses?

Similar comparisons are also common in safety and environmental regulation, where the cost of the regulations in terms of lives that would be saved is often ten, one hundred, or even one thousand times greater than other actions that could be taken. In these circumstances, critics of regulation cite the wide disparities in costs to argue against the adoption of measures aimed at, for example, improving workplace safety or eliminating toxic chemicals from the environment. Or they suggest that the same benefits might be achieved by taking other, sometimes far cheaper, action (Huber 1999). One recent example concerns directives from the Federal Emergency Management Agency (FEMA) in 2004 that pressed cities and states in earthquake-prone areas, including Memphis and other communities close to the New Madrid Seismic Zone (located near parts of Arkansas, Illinois, Indiana, Kentucky, Mississippi, Missouri, and Tennessee), to set building construction standards comparable to those required in California. Yet according to critics, FEMA proposed the plan "with almost no consideration of costs and benefits," even though the risk of a major earthquake in this area was only one-tenth to one-third that of California's. The critics suggest that the same money invested in such health and safety measures as highway upgrades, flu shots, and heart defibrillators could save many more lives.[25]

Risk Assessment

Risk assessment is a close relative of cost-benefit analysis. Its purpose is to identify, estimate, and evaluate the magnitude of the risk to citizens from exposure to various situations such as terrorism, natural hazards such as hurricanes and flooding, radiation from nuclear power plants, or threats from the kind of financial risks that Wall Street investment banks took in the mid 2000s at the height of the housing bubble. Reducing risks conveys a benefit to the public, and this benefit can be part of the calculation in a cost-benefit analysis. But societal risks vary widely in their magnitude, and that is the reason to try to identify and measure them; the more significant risks presumably should receive a higher priority for government action. Risks are associated with many activities in daily life, such as driving a car, flying in an airplane, consuming certain foods, smoking cigarettes, drinking alcohol, and skiing down a mountain, among others. Most of life's risks are fairly minor and not especially alarming, although people may worry a great deal about the ones they understand least well and fear, such as hazardous waste, toxic chemicals, and radiation.

Consider this example of risk assessment. In late 2002, the Federal Aviation Administration (FAA) proposed a new regulation that would require airlines to build safer seats to reduce the risk of severe injury or death in the event of an accident. Under the proposal, the airlines would have fourteen years to develop and install the new seats, at an estimated cost of $519 million. The seats would have better belts, improved headrests, and stronger anchors to hold them to the aircraft floor under the stress of an accident. The FAA's risk assessment indicated that the new seats would prevent an estimated 114 deaths and 133 serious injuries in the twenty years after the regulation took effect.[26] Was the FAA's risk assessment reasonable? Is it possible to project accident rates, injuries, and deaths over twenty years when the technology of aircraft design and other elements in aviation safety, not just the seat design, is likely to change?

Other examples of risk analysis are intriguing, even in the early stages of development. For example, over the past decade, the National Highway Traffic Safety Administration (NHTSA) has been studying the feasibility of requiring automobiles to have vehicle-to-vehicle communication technology (called V2V). Doing so, the agency says, could dramatically reduce the risk of accidents and therefore save lives and prevent injuries. Agency research shows that the vast majority of accidents can be prevented through use of such technology, in which vehicle sensors and onboard computers either alert drivers to an impending accident or move the vehicle out of the way to avoid an accident, much like automatic braking and lane departure warning systems already do in vehicles equipped with those technologies. Potentially such a change could save thousands of lives each year in the United States, and prevent hundreds of thousands of injuries, not to mention lowering the costs of vehicle repairs. Over thirty-three thousand people a year die in automobile accidents today, and over two million are injured, many severely. Ultimately, the adoption of new safety requirements will have to be justified through some form of risk-cost-benefit analysis.[27]

Risk assessments of this kind are widely used today in part because of public fears of certain technological risks and the adoption of public policies to control or reduce these risks (Kraft 2017). Workplace safety and food safety are two examples. Risk assessments are also prepared to estimate and respond to national security risks, such as terrorist attacks or other threats to the United States. Throughout the Cold War period, from the late 1940s to about 1990, defense and security analysts regularly made assessments of the risk of nuclear war and other security threats. They continue to conduct similar studies today.

Risk is usually defined as the magnitude of adverse consequences of an event or exposure. As noted, the event may be an earthquake, flood, car accident, nuclear power plant accident, or terrorist attack, and an exposure could come through contaminated food, water, or air, or from being in or near a building or another structure under attack (Andrews 2006b; Perrow 2007). The public's concern about risk has deepened in recent years as the media have increased their coverage of these situations. Books on this topic seem to sell well, another indicator of public concern.[28]

Professionals view risk as a product of the probability that the event or exposure will occur and the consequences that follow if it does. It can be expressed in the equation $R = P \times C$. The higher the probability of the event or exposure (P), or the higher the consequences (C), the higher the risk (R). Some risks, such as an airplane crash, have a low probability of occurring but high consequences if they do. Others, such as a broken leg from a skiing accident, have a higher probability but lower consequences. People tend to fear high-consequence events even if their probability is very low, because they focus on what *might* happen more than on its likelihood. Partly for this reason, there is often a substantial difference between experts and the lay public in their perception of risks. Public fear of nuclear power and nuclear waste (which experts tend to think are small risks) is a good example (Slovic 1987).

People also underestimate much more significant risks, including climate change, natural disasters, and medical calamities such as pandemics. In the case of the latter, in 2011 experts were so concerned about the risk that they warned scientific journals not to publish details about biomedical experiments that could be exploited by terrorists.[29] Even experts sometimes seriously misjudge risks, as the National Aeronautics and Space Administration (NASA) did in managing the space shuttle program. After two catastrophic accidents, in 2005 NASA recalculated the risk of a major failure during a space shuttle mission using probabilistic risk assessment that combined actual flight experience, computer simulations, and expert judgment. It put the risk at a very high 1 in 100.[30]

The tendency of people to misjudge the probability of various events is evident in the purchase of lottery tickets. When the Powerball lottery jackpot rose to an astonishing $1.6 billion in early 2016, people turned out in droves to buy tickets, even though they were far more likely to die from falling out of bed than to win even a portion of the lottery jackpot. The odds of winning the full amount that year were less than 1 in 292 million, whereas lottery officials calculated that the odds of being hit by an asteroid or comet were 1,000 times better.[31]

People also greatly underestimate risks associated with the U.S. food supply. The CDC reported in 2016 that about one in six Americans, or about 53 million people, get sick; about 128,000 are hospitalized; and about 3,000 die each year in the United States from food poisoning.[32] Yet except for the occasional scare over peanut butter, chicken, ground beef, eggs, or various vegetables that could be contaminated, the American public does not seem to be overly concerned about food safety. Nonetheless, in late 2010, Congress approved the Food Safety Modernization Act to ensure that the U.S. food supply is safe. The act was designed to shift the emphasis to prevention of contamination from response to it. Among other provisions, the act requires the Food and Drug Administration (FDA) to establish "science-based standards for the safe production and harvesting of fruits and vegetables to minimize the risk of serious illnesses or death."[33]

If risk assessment is the use of different methods to identify risks and estimate their probability and severity of harm, **risk evaluation** is a determination of the acceptability of the risks or a decision about what level of safety is desired. Typically, higher levels of safety, or lower risk, cost more to achieve. **Risk management** describes what governments or other organizations do to deal with risks, such as adopting public policies to regulate them (Presidential/Congressional Commission on Risk Assessment and Risk Management 1997).

Analysts use many different methods to conduct risk assessments, ranging from estimating the likelihood of industrial accidents to calculating how much radioactivity is likely to leak from a nuclear waste repository over thousands of years. For some assessments, such as the risk of automobile accidents or the likely injury to children from deployment of airbags during an accident, the task is relatively easy because plenty of data exist on the actual experience of drivers, vehicles, and airbag deployment. As a result, insurance companies can figure out how much to charge for car insurance once they know the age of the driver, what kind of car is in use, and where and how far it is driven each day. For other estimates, the lack of experience means that analysts must depend on mathematical modeling and computer projections, for example, to project the risk of climate change and the consequences for society if average temperatures rise, rainfall patterns shift, or severe storms occur more frequently.[34]

As with cost-benefit analysis, conservatives and business interests have long favored the use of risk assessment methods for domestic policy conflicts. They believe that many risks that government regulates are exaggerated and that further study will show they are not worth the often considerable cost to society (Huber 1999; Wildavsky 1988). It is equally likely, however, that risk assessments will identify genuine and serious risks to public health and welfare that merit public policy action.

The great loss of life and severe property damage inflicted by Hurricane Katrina in New Orleans and other Gulf Coast areas in late August 2005; similar damage from a severe tornado outbreak in the spring of 2011, which killed over three hundred people in six states; and comparable storms in 2016 also illustrate the policy challenges of risk assessment and risk management. How much more should state and local governments do to try to anticipate the risks of natural hazards such as hurricanes, tornadoes, earthquakes, and heavy rainstorms and the floods they create? If emergency preparedness officials and others are able to forecast such events, and thus provide some basis for judging the severity of possible risks, what obligations do the various levels of government have to protect their citizens? In retrospect, many state and local officials in the Gulf states in 2005, and many in the federal government as well, either did not pay sufficient attention to the risk of major hurricanes in the area or failed to implement adequate disaster preparedness measures. Even when the levees in New Orleans collapsed after Katrina struck the city, responsible officials in Louisiana and in Washington, D.C., did not act quickly enough. Warnings about floodwaters entering the city were misunderstood or ignored. The consequences in the case of Katrina and a later storm, Rita, were tragic because most of the loss of life and damage could have been prevented with better planning and a more timely response to the flooding. That need still exists because climate change forecasts suggest that the intensity of the 2005 hurricanes may be repeated in future years.

The decision-making process.
During 2014, the failure of General Motors (GM) to issue timely recalls on cars with significant safety issues was frequently in the news, and also attracted much attention on Capitol Hill. Senate Consumer Protection Subcommittee Chair Sen. Claire McCaskill, D-Mo., holds up a document as she questions GM CEO Mary Barra in Washington on April 2, 2014, during a hearing on GM. McCaskill said the new GM, which emerged from bankruptcy in 2009, had ample time to recall cars equipped with a faulty ignition switch that was linked to at least thirteen deaths. GM began recalling the cars only in February 2014, more than a decade after it learned of the ignition switch problem. *(AP Photo/Pablo Martinez Monsivais)*

Decision Making and Impacts

Throughout the text, we have emphasized the centrality of decision making in the study of public policy. The methods discussed in this section focus on formal ways to model the choices that policymakers face as well as techniques to consider how information about possible future events can be brought into the decision-making process. By introducing new perspectives and information in this way, the hope is that policymakers and the public can better determine which policy alternatives hold the most promise.

Forecasting

In chapter 5, we discussed the logic of forecasting in terms of understanding how present problems, such as public demand for Social Security and Medicare benefits, might change over time as the number of senior citizens increases. We also referred to it just above in our discussion of the risk of hurricanes striking the Gulf Coast states. Forecasting can be defined as "a procedure for producing factual information about future states of society on the basis of prior information about policy problems."[35] That is, forecasting methods allow analysts to anticipate what the future is likely to hold based on their understanding of current conditions and how they expect them to change over time. This information can be exceptionally valuable because public problems are dynamic, not static. In other words, when policymakers aim at public problems, they face a moving target.

In the cases of Social Security and Medicare, each program produces annual reports that include updated estimates of future demand for these services as well as estimates of the economic gap between the cost of providing the services and the expected revenues to cover those costs. Agency officials and other experts say both programs face enormous shortfalls in the future. They also argue that making long-term forecasts that look ahead seventy-five years, even with some degree of uncertainty, is essential to provide critical information for policymakers.[36]

For example, the population of the United States was about 325 million in 2016, but what will it be in twenty-five or fifty years? The U.S. Census Bureau (www.census.gov) has a population clock that reports continuously on the changing U.S. and global populations. It also offers several different projections of the nation's future population. All of these projections depend on a series of assumptions about the average number of children each woman is likely to have, the rate of immigration, and other factors. The bureau offers four different scenarios, with alternate assumptions. The medium projection is most widely cited, and it indicates that the United States has been growing by about 0.7 percent a year. At that rate, the bureau has estimated a U.S. population of about 360 million in 2030 and 396 million in 2050.[37] Cities and states that are growing more rapidly—or more slowly—than the nation as a whole find their specific forecasts helpful in determining how to cope with the anticipated demand for public services.

Projections of what is usually called geometric or exponential growth, such as population growth, are fairly easy once one knows the rate of growth. It is the same equation used to determine compound interest: $A_n = P(1 + i)^n$, where A is the amount being projected, n is the number of years, P is the initial amount, and i is the rate of growth. The formula is quite handy for determining how much a given amount will grow in one, five, or ten years. A savings account deposit of $100 ($P$) that grows at 3 percent a year will be worth $103 after one year, $116 at the end of five years, and $134 after ten years. As this example illustrates, even a small rate of annual increase can produce sizeable changes over time.[38]

Most forecasting is more complex than the examples provided here, but the principles are the same. Forecasting can include a variety of quantitative methods, such as econometric models for estimating future economic growth and job creation. Qualitative, or intuitive, methods are also widely used. These include brainstorming, the so-called Delphi method of asking experts to estimate future conditions, scenario development, and even simple monitoring of trends that looks for signs of change (Patton, Sawicki, and Clark 2016; Starling 1988).

As one might guess, whether quantitative or qualitative, forecasting methods are necessarily limited by available data, the validity of the basic assumptions made in projecting the future from present conditions, and how far out the projection goes. A look backward to earlier forecasts is sobering.[39] Quite often the futurists have been dead wrong in their projections, sometimes spectacularly so. For example, during the 1970s, electric power companies believed that energy demand would grow indefinitely at 6 percent to 7 percent a year. They planned for and built power plants that turned out not to be needed, and in some cases drove the power companies into bankruptcy.

Lest we think that forecasts about technological change are inevitably better today, it is worth noting that even as late as 1990, few analysts anticipated the explosive demand for home personal computers, not to mention the proliferation of smartphones and inexpensive laptop and tablet computers that spread computing and communication far from the office and home. Development of the Internet throughout the 1990s was a major reason for that rapid growth, as were falling computer prices and the development of easy-to-use web browsers. Even in the business community, where the ability to make accurate forecasts is essential for a company's success, hundreds of major firms and thousands of start-up companies greatly overestimated the demand for Internet business services, and many did not survive the dot-com implosion of the late 1990s. To compensate for these kinds of egregious forecasting errors, most analysts recommend using a number of forecasting methods, in the hope that a few of them will come up with comparable findings and increase confidence in the results. Even with the qualifications that should always accompany forecasting studies, being able to anticipate societal changes and prepare for them is a far better strategy than being surprised when problems develop.

Impact Assessment

During the highly contentious debate in 2002 over oil and gas drilling in the Arctic National Wildlife Refuge (ANWR), proponents of drilling repeatedly cited a 1990 economic study suggesting that opening the refuge for commercial oil production would create some 735,000 jobs. Independent economists said that number was suspect because the assumptions on which it was based were probably no longer valid. Indeed, a separate study prepared for the DOE in 1992 indicated that approximately 222,000 jobs would result, but only when ANWR reached peak production; the jobs would be chiefly in construction and manufacturing. Environmentalists argued that the correct number was lower still, perhaps 50,000 jobs. The wide variation in estimates of job creation may seem to indicate that analysts are unable to forecast economic impacts very well, but the real lesson is probably that studies of this kind may be seriously flawed because of the fanciful assumptions they make. Policy advocates often are more interested in scoring political points in a highly contentious debate than in arriving at a sound estimate of these jobs.

Given the concern in recent years over persistently high unemployment, estimates of new job creation become even more central in policy debates. Conservatives have criticized government regulations as "job killers" and tout tax cuts and deregulation for their potential to create jobs. In 2011, for example, many Republicans argued that Congress should not impose additional taxes on "job creators"—that is, on wealthy individuals and corporations. Yet citation of studies on how much impact regulations or taxes actually have on job creation was rare.[40] This kind of job impact analysis should be relatively straightforward for economists who work with models of the U.S. economy. Such an analysis merely asks what difference a given action, such as cutting specific regulations or reducing certain taxes, would have on the economy, and job creation in particular.

Job impact studies like this are one kind of **impact assessment**. Others include technology impact analysis, environmental impact analysis, and social impact analysis. They are similar in that analysts share an interest in trying to project or predict the consequences of adopting a policy proposal or taking some other form of action. Robert Bartlett (1989, 1) describes the approach this way: "Impact assessment constitutes a general strategy of policymaking and administration—a strategy of influencing decisions and actions by a priori analysis of predictable impacts. A simple, even simplistic, notion when stated briefly, making policy through impact assessment is in fact an approach of great power, complexity, and subtlety."

Much like forecasting, the purpose of an impact assessment is to see if analysts can systematically examine the effects that may occur from taking a certain action. That action may be introducing or expanding the use of new Internet technologies or deploying a national missile defense system. No matter the subject, the analyst tries to identify possible impacts and the likelihood they will occur.

Impact assessments are not new. Federal law has required environmental impact analyses since the National Environmental Policy Act (NEPA) was passed in 1969. The logic was simple and powerful. Before governments undertake major projects that are likely to have significant effects on the environment, policymakers ought to identify and measure those impacts, and they also ought to consider alternatives that may avoid the undesirable effects. The law's strength is in its requirement that the impact assessments be made public, which creates an opportunity for environmental groups and others to influence agency decision making. The agency, in turn, is forced to deal with a concerned public and to respond to the information produced by the impact assessment. The hope was that the combination of information and political forces would "make bureaucracies think" and dissuade them from making poor decisions that could harm the environment. Evaluations of NEPA indicate that it has been quite successful on the whole (Caldwell 1998).

Political and Institutional Approaches

At this point in the chapter, the reader may be wondering whether policy analysis ever considers more than economic and technical estimates. The answer is clearly yes. Political scientists in particular are likely to use political and institutional approaches to understanding proposed policy alternatives and to evaluating existing programs. Such studies are often more qualitative than the methods discussed so far, but they may also be just as rigorous and just as valuable for understanding public policy.

Political Feasibility Analysis

Political feasibility, a criterion for evaluating suggested policy changes, as discussed earlier in the chapter, is the extent to which elected officials and other policy actors support the change. No formula is available for estimating political feasibility. Even experienced and thoughtful observers of politics acknowledge how difficult it is to determine the level of support that might be forthcoming for a proposal in local or state government, or at the national level. It may be easier to recognize the actions that are unlikely to fly politically, particularly in a time of intense political polarization in the nation that often makes it extremely difficult to build support for controversial actions (Mann and Ornstein 2012; Persily 2015; Thurber and Yoshinaka 2015). Examples are plentiful. The Affordable Care Act passed Congress with not a single Republican vote in favor, and a Republican House voted over sixty times to repeal the act. Comprehensive immigration reform, which the Senate managed to pass in 2013, was blocked by concerted Republican opposition in the House. This kind of polarization and gridlock lies behind the sharp rise in public frustration with government today, as noted earlier in the text.

Aside from partisan differences, interest group influence can make even broadly supported public policy actions unlikely to be successful. Gun control measures are a classic example of that pattern. The vast majority of Americans and even members of the National Rifle Association (NRA) support many gun control measures, such as enhanced background checks and barring people on terrorist watch lists from purchasing guns. Yet proposals of this kind have failed to gain traction because they are opposed by the NRA and elected officials fear the group's electoral wrath. This is why, despite many cases of mass shootings, Congress has been unwilling to approve additional gun control measures, and why it also has banned federal funding for research on gun violence.[41]

One of the most notable cases occurred after the shootings at Sandy Hook Elementary School in Connecticut in late 2012. President Obama mounted a campaign to improve gun safety laws, with emphasis on criminal background checks for all gun sales, reinstatement of a ban on assault weapons, and limiting ammunition magazines to ten rounds; however, he was unable to secure congressional approval. Additional mass shootings since that time, such as the attack on a nightclub in Orlando, Florida, in June 2016 that killed forty-nine people and injured more than fifty others, have not altered the political calculation as the NRA continues to maintain its opposition to these kinds of measures.

At the margins of policy debate, however, it may be possible to anticipate how slight changes in proposed legislation or regulations, or an alteration in the political or economic environment, can create a majority in favor of action. Sometimes a shift on the part of a few legislators or a marginal change in policymaker perceptions of what the public will support make the difference in the success or failure of a policy proposal.

Some simple determinations can provide a good idea of political feasibility. Analysts could begin by identifying the policy actors who will likely play a significant role in the decision. These actors may be members of a city council or a state legislature, or they may be members of Congress. To the formal policy-makers, analysts would add other players, such as representatives of major interest groups and administrative officials—for example, the mayor, the governor, and top officials in a pertinent bureaucracy. For each of the major policy actors, analysts could determine their positions on the issues, perhaps by investigating their previous stances, such as the NRA's opposition to gun control measures or business groups' reluctance to endorse action on climate change. Sometimes it is possible to estimate their positions based on their party affiliation, general political attitudes, and where they stand on comparable issues. Finally, an estimate can be made of their level of interest in the particular decision (how salient it is to them), and the intensity of their views or their motivation to get involved in the decision. These factors are likely to be shaped by the level of interest and preferences of the constituencies they represent, which in turn are influenced by how much the media cover the controversy and how the issues are presented. All of this information can be pulled together to estimate political feasibility.

We need to bear in mind that not all policy actors are equal in influencing feasibility. Relatively small groups with intensely held views on a subject are often capable of defeating proposals that have the broad support of the U.S. public. As noted, gun control is a policy area where this has long been the case, but there are many other examples. For a great many public policy disputes, especially those that do not rise to the highest levels of visibility, political feasibility is likely to depend on the views of a small number of people and organizations.

Implementation Analysis and Program Evaluation

The discussion of **implementation analysis** and the related program evaluation is relatively brief here because these methods are covered in the substantive policy chapters that follow. As is the case with assessment of political feasibility, these methods draw far more from the disciplines of political science and public administration than is true for most of the others reviewed here.

Policy implementation is one of the most important steps in the policy cycle, and one that often gets insufficient attention by analysts and policymakers. Enactment of any public policy is only one part of policymaking, as we discussed in chapter 3. Policies must be put into action by administrative agencies, and this involves judgment about what the policy calls for; adoption of pertinent rules, regulations, and guidelines; and the use of resources (staff and money) to carry out the critical components of the policy. Sometimes the process goes smoothly and sometimes not, and thus policy success depends on how well implementation goes (Patashnik 2008).

Consider the initial implementation of the Affordable Care Act (or Obamacare) in late 2013, which did not go at all well. The federal government had rushed to set up its webpage for enrollment in the program (www.healthcare.gov), relied too much on outside consulting companies for its development, did not test the site sufficiently before it went live, and failed to establish clear lines of oversight for its operation. As a result, the site was technically flawed in many respects, and it proved to be unable to handle the large volume of applications. Implementation of the act was further compromised when many states chose not to establish their own insurance exchanges under the law, throwing many more people onto the problematic federal exchange, and some states actively sought to undermine the act because of political disagreement with it.[42] After an urgent and massive effort by the Obama White House and the Department of Health and Human Services to repair the site, enrollment under the health care law went much more smoothly late in 2013 and early in 2014, and ultimately it did manage to meet the government's initial projections. Nonetheless, the law's longtime critics were quick to remind voters of these many failures, and they continued to call for the law's repeal. Students of public policy were handed a prime example of why implementation analysis is essential for program success.

As this case illustrates, policies are almost never self-implementing, and many circumstances can affect their success: the difficulty of the problem being addressed, the soundness of the initial policy design, the suitability of the statute's objectives and legal mandates, and multiple political, economic, and institutional factors. These include an agency's resources and technical capabilities, the commitment and skills of its leadership, the degree of public and political support, and influence from affected constituencies (Goggin et al. 1990; Mazmanian and Sabatier 1983).

Implementation analysis is based on the assumption that it is possible to identify some of the likely challenges either in advance of a policy's adoption or after implementation begins. In the first case, the analysis can help in the design of the policy to ensure that it can be implemented well. In the second, the analysis can document how well implementation has gone and the aspects of the policy or the parts of the implementing agency that are responsible for any success or failure. Policies can then be modified as needed. Initial policy failures can be reversed if policymakers understand the reasons and are prepared to take corrective action. It is not unusual that major policies need to be evaluated over time, and this kind of revision undertaken (Mazmanian and Sabatier 1983). The Affordable Care Act may well be one example, as its initial years of implementation did not fully yield the results hoped for, whether the problems were chiefly in the initial policy design or in the extensive and often relentless criticism directed at the act, and even efforts by opponents to block its success (see chapter 8).

Program evaluation focuses more on policy results or outcomes than on the process of implementation, but as noted, the two go together. Evaluation of any program may be an essential part of long-term implementation success, and there are many different ways to evaluate a program.

Most evaluations rely on a diversity of methods to identify a program's goals and objectives, measure them, gather data on what the program is doing, and reach some conclusions about the extent of its success (Rossi, Lipsey, and Freeman 2004; C. Weiss 1997). For example, we can ask how well immigration policies are doing in terms of limiting illegal immigration to the United States or their success in providing for high-demand employment in technical areas where the number of qualified U.S. citizens is insufficient. In both cases, we would gather information on the outcomes we expect to see, such as reduced immigration rates, or whether high-demand employees are indeed being recruited in sufficient numbers. Or we can ask about the extent to which health care policies are working in terms of meeting specific outcome measures such as the number of people previously without health insurance who became covered, a key object of the Affordable Care Act of 2010 (see chapter 8). For environmental and energy policies, we would want to determine if they are meeting specific goals, such as improvement in air quality or drinking water quality, or development of wind and solar power or expansion of nuclear power (see chapter 11). For education policies, we would seek data on educational outcomes to judge whether certain reforms, such as creation of charter schools, make a difference (see chapter 10).

As with other policy analyses, the intention is to complete those tasks in a systematic way that fosters confidence in the accuracy of the results (Rossi, Lipsey, and Freeman 2004). Done well, the studies sometimes make a real difference. Despite the many criticisms of the Affordable Care Act, for example, it did succeed in insuring many people who previously had no health care coverage, and thus in improving their access to health care services. The Department of Health and Human Services touted these kinds of achievements, as well as others, in its reports on the act's impacts.[43] For other policies, evaluation studies sometimes point to their ineffectiveness, suggesting that new approaches need to be tried, a question that we emphasize throughout the rest of the text. For example, analysis revealed that, after years of increased funding, the nation's most popular program to discourage drug use among schoolchildren was ineffective. As a result, the U.S. Department of Education announced that its funds could no longer be used on the Drug Abuse Resistance Education, or DARE, program, which had paid for police officers to visit schools to convey antidrug messages.[44]

Ethical Analysis

As noted in this chapter, many policy analysts view **ethical analysis**, or the systematic examination of ethical or normative issues in public policy, as problematic. Because they are not quite sure how to do it and sometimes fear that entering the quagmire of ethics compromises the objectivity of their analysis, they often leave ethical issues to the policy advocacy community. Ethical issues most definitely are raised as part of policy debate, but they may not receive the kind of careful analysis that we have come to expect for economic issues or even for political and institutional issues (Tong 1986).

Two brief examples, however, illustrate the need for ethical analysis. The first involves family planning programs. The George W. Bush administration, much like other Republican administrations since the mid 1980s, was under pressure from antiabortion groups to curtail U.S. contributions to the United Nations Population Fund. The fund supports family planning programs around the world, but some people accuse it of condoning abortions. It has repeatedly denied those charges and has assured the U.S. government that none of the nation's funds will be used in support of abortion, which U.S. law forbids. Responding to political pressure from the antiabortion lobby, in 2002 Bush withheld $34 million from the UN program, which amounted to 13 percent of the agency's total budget. According to an agency spokesperson, the effect of a $34 million cut "could mean 2 million unwanted pregnancies, 800,000 induced abortions, 4,700 maternal deaths, and 77,000 infant and child deaths."[45] Note the qualification of "could mean" in this statement. It is difficult to project the consequences of the budget cut because other groups might make up some of the difference of the funds withheld. For example, the Population Fund and other organizations concerned about family planning services could ask their members for increased donations for this purpose. Even so, one could ask how likely the Bush administration's action was to achieve its goal of reducing abortions. If the consequences were even close to what the UN official indicated, was the administration's action largely symbolic and political, but one with detrimental consequences for public health? Can the decision be justified in terms of moral or ethical criteria?

The second example concerns the dramatically altered circumstances of airline travel in the aftermath of the September 11, 2001, terrorist attacks. Federal law required random searches of individuals and carry-on luggage at the initial security checkpoint. Federal officials were concerned that if they adopted a system of passenger profiling based on demographic characteristics—that is, groups of people who might require special screening, such as young Arab men—they would violate principles of civil liberties. Civil libertarians argued that racial or ethnic profiling should be unacceptable in a free society that values diversity, and many found that view persuasive.

The federal government opted for a system of random checks without profiling, but many experts said that while such a system has little chance of preventing hijacking, it imposes high costs and inconvenience on travelers. What is the most acceptable way to promote airline security? Does profiling travelers violate their civil liberties? Even if it did, is this practice a justifiable use of government authority to protect the country? In 2014, the Obama administration announced new restrictions on racial profiling by federal officials, but also said that some officers and Department of Homeland Security agents would be allowed to continue to use some forms of profiling, particularly when screening airline passengers and guarding the southwestern border.[46] Was this the decision justifiable on ethical grounds?

Other contemporary policy issues, from human cloning and embryonic stem-cell research to how to deal with illegal immigration, raise comparable ethical and value concerns. By 2016, many states had adopted laws to govern research on embryos and fetuses, and some of them chose to ban any experiments involving human embryos.[47] Was this position reasonable? Opponents of these laws argued that they could seriously impede important medical research.[48] Indeed, in 2002, California enacted legislation to explicitly allow research on stem cells that are obtained from fetal and embryonic tissue, a direct repudiation of federal limits on such research imposed by the Bush administration in 2001 (though lifted by President Obama in early 2009). Antiabortion groups and the Roman Catholic Church opposed California's action.[49]

Steps to Analysis

Ethical Analysis: The Case of Organ Donation

A recent assessment of human organ donation to save lives contained some striking data and offered a creative solution, but one with ethical implications. Every day in the United States, more than seventy-nine people receive an organ transplant, but about eighteen die because there are not enough donor organs to meet the demand. In 2016, more than 119,000 people in the United States were waiting for an organ transplant, and one more is added every ten minutes. People's dire medical conditions do not allow them to wait indefinitely. Indeed, since 1995, more than forty-five thousand Americans have died while waiting for a suitable donor organ to become available; currently about twenty-two people in this situation die each day.

The shortage is not because people are opposed to organ donation in principle. In fact, the overwhelming majority of Americans (about 95 percent of adults) approve of organ donation. But only about 45 percent sign up to donate their organs (such as hearts, kidneys, lungs, and livers) upon death, a number that varies widely by state; only about 13 percent of New York State residents have signed up as donors whereas 80 percent of Alaskans have. Unfortunately, the number of transplant operations has remained flat for years while the number of people needing organ transplants has risen significantly.[a]

So how might the number of available organs be increased? Current U.S. policy requires an affirmative step of signing an organ donation card or registering online for donation (and generally notifying family members of one's intention). But what if the policy were flipped so that the default position is that organs are suitable for donation unless an individual opted out by indicating that he or she did *not* want to be an organ donor, for example, because of strong religious beliefs? What difference would that make?

Experience in Europe provides some answers. Two quite different approaches are used for what could be termed a "no-action default" policy, where an individual's failure to make a decision results in a given condition. In one recent assessment, twenty-four European countries (including Austria, Belgium, France, Spain, and Sweden) were found to rely on "presumed consent," where people are deemed organ donors unless they have registered not to be. Others follow the U.S. approach, where "explicit consent" is required; that is, no one is assumed to be an organ donor unless he or she has registered to be one. In Europe, the effective percentage of organ donors in the first case is between 86 and 100 percent, but in the second case it ranges from 4 to 27 percent. The implication is that a change in approach within the United States could result in thousands of additional organ donations a year, and thus in thousands of lives that would be saved, although there is much debate about all of the consequences of such a change.

Should the United States change its policy to one of presumed consent? Issues of individual freedom and social equity or justice are central to how one answers that question. What arguments, particularly those grounded in ethical concerns, would you make in support of that change? Should the United States continue to rely on the explicit consent model? What arguments would you make in support of this position?

- What does this exercise tell you about the possibility or desirability of analyzing ethical issues in public policy?

- Should analysts try to address ethical issues like this?

- Can that be done as professionally as conducting cost-benefit analysis or assessing political feasibility?

Sources: Eric J. Johnson and Daniel Goldstein, "Do Defaults Save Lives?" *Science* 302 (November 21, 2003): 1338–1339; Tiffanie Wen, "Why Don't More People Want to Donate Their Organs?" *The Atlantic*, November 10, 2014; www.organdonor.gov (official U.S. government website for organ and tissue donation and transplantation); and www.unos.org (United Network for Organ Sharing). For a broader discussion of organ transplantation in the United States in relation to the broader concern over health care services, see David L. Weimer, *Medical Governance: Values, Expertise, and Interests in Organ Transplantation* (Washington, D.C.: Georgetown University Press, 2010).

a. See the U.S. government's website on organ donation: www.organdonor.gov. One reason for the low number of transplant operations despite the need is that only about three in one thousand people die in a way that permits organ transplants.

The "Steps to Analysis" box "Ethical Analysis: The Case of Organ Donation" offers an intriguing policy question for which ethical analysis would be appropriate.

Conclusions

This chapter describes the leading evaluative criteria in the study of public policy, with special emphasis on effectiveness, efficiency, political feasibility, and equity concerns. All policy analysis relies on such evaluative criteria to judge policy proposals, even if they are not always made explicit, and these are among the most important of the criteria commonly used. The chapter also briefly reviews the major kinds of policy analysis and their strengths, weaknesses, and potential contributions to the policymaking process. Students of public policy should understand that analysts select from these criteria and methods, with significant implications for the breadth and utility of their findings. They should also be alert to the assumptions and choices made in such studies and ask how they affect the validity of the conclusions reached.

The chapter emphasizes that policy analysis is both a craft and an art. The craft comes in knowing the methods of policy analysis and how to apply them in specific situations. For example, when would you use one of the economic approaches, such as cost-benefit analysis or risk analysis? When would you use analysis dealing with decision making or the impacts of policy, such as forecasting? When instead would you rely on political feasibility analysis or ethical analysis?

The art of policy analysis lies in selecting suitable criteria for policy assessments, in recognizing the limitations of the available methods, and in drawing and reporting on appropriate conclusions. An artful policy analyst recognizes and is sensitive to the public mood and the political and institutional context in which the analysis is conducted and reported. He or she may also find ways to use policy analysis to empower citizens and motivate them to participate in the democratic process (deLeon 1997; Ingram and Smith 1993).

Some critics of policy analysis complain that analysts tend to view politics—that is, public opinion, interest group activity, and the actions of policymakers—as an obstacle to adopting the fruits of their labors, which they believe represent a rational, and therefore superior, assessment of the situation (Stone 2012). It is possible, however, to view the relationship of policy analysis and politics in a different light. Analysis and politics are not incompatible as long as it is understood that analysis by itself does not and should not determine public policy. Rather, its purpose is to inform the public and policymakers so that they can make better decisions. A democratic political process offers the best way to ensure that policy decisions further the public interest (Lindblom and Woodhouse 1993).

DISCUSSION QUESTIONS

1. Which of the many evaluative criteria do you think are the most important? Economic costs or efficiency? Policy effectiveness? Equity? Why do you think so? Are some criteria more important for certain kinds of policy questions than for others?

2. Discuss how you would go about applying cost-benefit analysis to one of the following issues: (1) instituting a campus program for recycling paper, aluminum cans, and similar items; (2) getting a city to build bicycle lanes on selected streets to promote safety for cyclists; or (3) increasing the number of crossing guards at roadway intersections close to elementary schools. What steps would you go through, and what kinds of data would you need to conduct such an analysis?

3. Choose one of the following examples relating to the use of ethical analysis: budgets for family planning programs, restrictions on using embryonic stem cells for medical research, profiling in airport security screening, or an opting-in system for organ donation. How would you apply ethical analysis to clarify the policy choices involved in that case?

4. If you had to forecast changing student demand for programs of study at a college or university for the next ten to twenty years, how would you go about doing that?

5. What are the most important factors to consider in conducting a political feasibility analysis? Answer this with respect to a specific example, such as instituting a tax on carbon-based fuels as one response to climate change, cutting mandatory prison sentences to lower the cost of keeping nonviolent offenders in custody, or providing tuition free education at public colleges and universities.

KEYWORDS

contingent valuation methods   198
cost-benefit analysis   193
cost-effectiveness analysis   199
discount rate   197

ethical analysis   211
impact assessment   207
implementation analysis   209
opportunity costs   195
program evaluation   210

risk assessment   200
risk evaluation   202
risk management   203
sensitivity analysis   198

SUGGESTED READINGS

Eugene Bardach and Eric M. Patashnik, *A Practical Guide for Policy Analysis: The Eightfold Path to More Effective Problem Solving*, 5th ed. (Thousand Oaks, Calif.: CQ Press, 2016). A concise and helpful handbook on the basics of conducting and presenting policy analysis in the real world.

Dipak K. Gupta, *Analyzing Public Policy: Concepts, Tools, and Techniques*, 2nd ed. Thousand Oaks, Calif.: CQ Press, 2011). A comprehensive and readable text that introduces the methods of policy analysis, including a discussion of basic statistics, forecasting, decision theory, game theory, and cost-benefit analysis.

Carl V. Patton, David S. Sawicki, and Jennifer J. Clark, *Basic Methods of Policy Analysis and Planning*, 3rd ed. (New York: Routledge, 2016).

David L. Weimer and Aidan R. Vining, *Policy Analysis: Concepts and Practice*, 6th ed. (New York: Routledge, 2016). One of the leading policy analysis texts, drawing heavily from economics.

SUGGESTED WEBSITES

www.aei.org. American Enterprise Institute, one of the most visible and influential conservative research organizations in Washington, D.C.

www.americanprogress.org. Center for American Progress, a progressive, nonpartisan policy research institute in Washington, D.C.

www.appam.org. Association for Public Policy Analysis and Management, which offers guides to careers and education in public policy.

www.brookings.edu. Brookings Institution, one of the most widely cited public policy organizations in Washington, D.C., that engages in a wide range of research, from economic analysis to work on U.S. government and politics.

www.cato.org. Cato Institute, a prominent libertarian and conservative think tank in Washington, D.C.

www.opm.gov/qualifications/standards/Specialty-stds/gs-policy.asp. The U.S. Office of Personnel Management webpage, offering a description of policy analysis positions in government.

www.rff.org/Research_Topics/Pages/SubTopics.aspx?SubTopic=Benefit-Cost%20Analysis. Selected cost-benefit analyses done at Resources for the Future.

NOTES

1. On the effects of the new fuel economy standards, see Thomas L. Friedman, "This Is a Big Deal," *New York Times*, December 4, 2011.

2. Lena H. Sun, "On the Mass Transportation Bandwagon: Record Ridership Shows Continued Popularity of Leaving the Driving to Someone Else," *Washington Post National Weekly Edition*, December 15–21, 2008; and Peter S. Goodman, "Fuel Prices Shift Math for Life in Far Suburbs," *New York Times*, June 25, 2008.

3. On the gas tax holiday debate, see John Maggs, "Tax-Holiday Blues," *National Journal*, May 10, 2008, 64–65. Few economists favored the proposal; in fact, both conservative and liberal economists joined in opposing the gas tax suspension. Polls at the time also showed that a majority of Americans opposed lowering the gas tax.

4. Energy Information Administration, "Impacts of Increased Access to Oil and Natural Gas Resources in the Lower 48 Federal Outer Continental Shelf" (Washington, D.C.: Department of Energy, 2007), available at www.eia.doe.gov/oiaf/aeo/otheranalysis/ongr.html.

5. See Rob Stein, "Not That Kind of Sex Ed," *Washington Post National Weekly Edition*, December 24, 2007–January 6, 2008; and Sabrina Tavernise, "Colorado's Effort against Teenage Pregnancies Is a Startling Success," *New York Times*, July 5, 2015. See also Sharon Jayson, "Obama Budget Cuts Funds for Abstinence-Only Sex Education," *USA Today*, May 11, 2009. The National Conference of State Legislatures reports regularly on state policies regarding sex education in schools at www.ncsl.org/research/health/

state-policies-on-sex-education-in-schools.aspx. You can find the latest studies and state policies summarized at that site.

6. See John Markoff, "Google Lobbies Nevada to Allow Self-Driving Cars," *New York Times*, May 10, 2011; and Mike Isaac, "What It Feels Like to Ride in a Self-Driving Uber," *New York Times*, September 14, 2016; and Cecilia Kang, "U.S. Signals Backing for Self-Driving Cars," *New York Times*, September 19, 2016.

7. In recent years, the IRS faced an expanding workload and reduced congressional funding. See Jackie Calmes, "I.R.S. Fights Back against House Republicans' Attacks," *New York Times*, April 21, 2016; and Chuck Marr and Joel Friedman, "Cuts in IRS Budget Have Compromised Taxpayer Service and Weakened Enforcement" (Washington, D.C.: Center on Budget and Policy Priorities, June 25, 2014).

8. Michael Luo, "Under New York Medicaid, Drug Costs Run Free," *New York Times*, November 23, 2005.

9. Centers for Disease Control and Prevention, "Smoking and Tobacco Use: Fast Facts," available at www.cdc.gov/tobacco/data_statistics/fact_sheets/fast_facts/.

10. The Congressional Budget Office reported in 2011 that since 1979 the after-tax income of the top 1 percent of taxpayers more than quadrupled, increasing by 275 percent, but that for middle-income taxpayers, after-tax income rose by only 40 percent, and for those at the lowest end of the economic scale, income rose only 18 percent. See the summary by Andrew Taylor, "Top 1 Percent Has Nearly Quadrupled Income Since 1979," *Christian Science Monitor*, October 28, 2011. A fairly complete and continuously updated compilation of "fiscal facts" on taxpayer income in various percentiles can be found at the Tax Foundation, which uses data from the IRS: www.taxfoundation.org/.

11. Michael A. Fletcher, "OECD Report Cites Rising Income Inequality," *Washington Post*, December 5, 2011. See the OECD's own data and reports at www.oecd.org/social/inequality.htm.

12. See Paul Sullivan, "The End of a Decade of Uncertainty over Gift and Estate Taxes," *New York Times*, January 4, 2013.

13. Adam Liptak, "Justices, 5–4, Reject Corporate Spending Limit," *New York Times*, January 21, 2010; and Liptak, "Supreme Court Strikes Down Overall Political Donation Cap," *New York Times*, April 2, 2014.

14. See Jonathan Rauch, "The Loss of New Orleans Wasn't Just a Tragedy. It Was a Plan," *National Journal*, September 17, 2005, 2801–2802.

15. Associated Press, "Adding Up the Costs of Protecting the Border," *New York Times*, June 26, 2011.

16. Lisa Caruso, "Is Obama on the Right Track?" *National Journal*, May 15, 2010, 30–34.

17. Joan Lowy, "Congress about to Kill High-Speed Train Program," Associated Press, November 17, 2011.

18. Shan Carter and Amanda Cox, "One 9/11 Tally: $3.3 Trillion," *New York Times*, September 8, 2011. See also Joseph E. Stiglitz and Linda J. Bilmes, *The Three Trillion Dollar Conflict: The True Cost of the Iraq Conflict* (New York: Norton, 2008).

19. See Paul R. Portney, "Time and Money: Discounting's Problematic Allure," *Resources* 136 (Summer 1999): 8–9. See also Paul R. Portney and John P. Weyant, eds., *Discounting and Intergenerational Equity* (Washington, D.C.: Resources for the Future, 1999).

20. Rauch, "The Loss of New Orleans."

21. "Hurricane Sandy's Rising Costs," *New York Times*, November 27, 2012.

22. See the EPA fact sheet on lead in the environment; the actions taken to ban or reduce its presence; and its effects, particularly on children: www.epa.gov/haps/health-effects-notebook-hazardous-air-pollutants. See also the Global Lead Network for information on global action to remove lead from the environment: http://globalleadnet.com/36/about-the-network.

23. The new guidelines for agency scientific data were pushed through Congress as a rider attached to a fiscal 2001 appropriations bill in late 2000,

largely at the request of business and industry groups, and signed by President Bill Clinton. Business groups have long maintained that many government regulations are based on faulty data, and the law will make it easier for them to challenge regulations they view as burdensome. See Rebecca Adams, "OIRA Directs Guidelines on Data Quality," *CQ Weekly*, March 23, 2002, 827. For a review of the kinds of government regulation that OIRA studies and how it calculates costs and benefits, see the OMB website for OIRA (available at www.whitehouse.gov/omb) and the dedicated site for regulatory review (www.reginfo.gov/public/). Note that both sites may change in the Trump administration.

24. See Richard Conviser, "A Brief History of the Oregon Health Plan and Its Features" (Salem: Office of Oregon Health Policy and Research, 1995). The Oregon experience is examined in detail in Peter J. Neumann, *Using Cost-Effectiveness Analysis to Improve Health Care: Opportunities and Barriers* (New York: Oxford University Press, 2004). See also a recent review of the Oregon experiment that argues it has met the "test of time" and is something of a model for new efforts for the kinds of comparative effectiveness studies called for under the Affordable Care Act of 2010: Somnath Saha, Darren D. Coffman, and Ariel K. Smits, "Giving Teeth to Comparative-Effectiveness Research: The Oregon Experience," *New England Journal of Medicine* 362 (February 18, 2010).

25. See Seth Stein and Joseph Tomasello, "When Safety Costs Too Much," *New York Times*, January 10, 2004, A31.

26. The proposal can be found at the FAA website: www.faa.gov.

27. See "U.S. Department of Transportation Announces Decision to Move Forward with Vehicle-to-Vehicle Communication Technology for Light Vehicles," available at the NHTSA website: www.nhtsa.gov.

28. For example, a book published a year after the September 11 terrorist attacks discusses public anxiety over unfamiliar and highly publicized risks and attempts to assess the true risk: David Ropeik and George Gray, *Risk: A Practical Guide for Deciding What's Really Safe and What's Really Dangerous in the World around You* (Boston: Houghton Mifflin, 2002). The book sold briskly at Amazon.com and Barnes and Noble's online site.

29. For a comparative review of the major risks facing the U.S. population, see Bruce Nussbaum, "The Next Big One," *Businessweek*, September 19, 2005, 35–45. For the case of keeping details of biomedical experiments out of scientific journals, see Denise Grady and William J. Broad, "Seeing Terror Risk, U.S. Asks Journals to Cut Flu Study Facts," *New York Times*, December 20, 2011.

30. See William J. Broad, "NASA Puts Shuttle Mission's Risk at 1 in 100," *New York Times*, July 26, 2005, A16.

31. The odds are taken from Larry Laudan, *The Book of Risks: Fascinating Facts about the Chances We Take Every Day* (New York: Wiley, 1994), as cited in a May 20, 1998, CNN story, when an earlier Powerball lottery jackpot reached $175 million. See also Lizette Alvarez, "The Biggest Powerball Jackpot Ever: The Odds and Where the Money Goes," *New York Times*, January 12, 2016.

32. The CDC's summary statistics can be found at www.cdc.gov/foodsafety/foodborne-germs.html.

33. The quotation comes from the FDA publication "Food Safety Legislation Key Facts," available at www.fda.gov/Food/GuidanceRegulation/FSMA/ucm237934.htm.

34. To see how climate change modeling estimates such risk, see the website for the Intergovernmental Panel on Climate Change: www.ipcc.ch.

35. The quotation is from William J. Dunn, *Public Policy Analysis: An Introduction*, 3rd ed. (New York: Longman, 2004), 130.

36. Edmund L. Andrews and Robert Pear, "Entitlement Costs Are Expected to Soar," *New York Times*, March 19, 2004.

37. The Census Bureau webpage has these kinds of forecasts, for example, in its National Population Projections. An easier way to see the estimates for the United States and to compare them to other nations is to view the annual World Population

Data Sheet published by the Population Reference Bureau and available on its website: www.prb.org.

38. A compound interest calculator is available on the web at https://illuminations.nctm.org/Activity.aspx?id=3568. To use it, enter a principal amount of money, a contribution amount, an interest rate, and the number of years the money will be invested, and immediately see how much the initial amount changes over this time period—in both tabular and graphic formats.

39. Burt Solomon, "False Prophets," *National Journal*, December 11, 1999.

40. See David Brooks, "The Wonky Liberal," *New York Times*, December 5, 2011; and Robb Mandelbaum, "Do Small Business Owners Feel Overtaxed and Overregulated? A Survey Says No," *New York Times*, November 21, 2011.

41. Michael S. Rosenwald, "Most Gun Owners Support Restrictions. Why Aren't Their Voices Heard?" *Washington Post*, October 9, 2015; and New York Times Editorial Board, "The Republican Fear of Facts on Guns," *New York Times*, December 24, 2015.

42. For an overview of the many problems in implementing the act, see Ezekiel J. Emanuel, "How to Fix the Glitches," *New York Times*, October 22, 2013. On the state efforts to obstruct the new law, see "Blocking Health Care Reform in Florida," *New York Times*, September 19, 2013; and Lizette Alvarez, "In Florida, Opposition by the State and Snags in Signing Up on the Web," *New York Times*, October 10, 2013. President Obama's remarks about the weak rollout of the act can be found in "Transcript: President Obama's Oct. 21 Remarks on Problems with the Obamacare Rollout," *Washington Post*, October 21, 2013.

43. See various reports on the department's website: www.hhs.gov/healthcare/facts-and-features/fact-sheets/aca-is-working/index.html.

44. Kate Zernike, "Antidrug Program Says It Will Adopt a New Strategy," *New York Times*, February 15, 2001. Several years later, a panel convened by the National Institutes of Health reviewed evidence on the causes of youth violence and also concluded that "scare tactics" such as those used in the DARE program do not work. However, the panel did find that a number of other intervention programs offer promise. See Associated Press, "'Get Tough' Youth Programs Are Ineffective, Panel Says," *New York Times*, October 17, 2005.

45. See Barbara Crossette, "U.N. Agency on Population Blames U.S. for Cutbacks," *New York Times*, April 7, 2002. Similar calculations are made regularly by the Guttmacher Institute, the policy analysis arm of Planned Parenthood. Its studies are available at www.guttmacher.org.

46. Sari Horwitz and Jerry Markon, "Racial Profiling Will Still Be Allowed at Airports, along Border Despite New Policy," *Washington Post*, December 5, 2014.

47. For a review of state policies on embryonic and fetal research, see a National Conference of State Legislatures report at www.ncsl.org/research/health/embryonic-and-fetal-research-laws.aspx.

48. Sheryl Gay Stolberg, "Washington Not Alone in Cell Debate," *New York Times*, July 23, 2001.

49. Associated Press, "California Law Permits Stem Cell Research," *New York Times*, September 23, 2002.

PART III

Issues and Controversies in Public Policy

Chapter 7

Chapter Objectives

- Describe the role of federal economic policymaking and its challenges.

- Explain the major goals associated with economic policy.

- Describe the tools used by the Federal Reserve Board and the government to achieve positive outcomes.

- Identify the major steps of the federal budgetary process.

- Discuss two notable economic policies and their consequences.

- Explain some of the critical economic issues of the day.

- Discuss how to address the federal deficit and the ways in which to evaluate it.

A difference in policy objectives. Left to right, Sen. Patty Murray (D-WA), Sen. Richard Durbin (D-IL), Sen. Harry Reid (D-NV), and Sen. Charles Schumer (D-NY) participate in a news conference to call on Republicans to pass legislation to fund efforts to deal with the Zika virus, at the U.S. Capitol in Washington, D.C., April 27, 2016. *(Chip Somodevilla/Getty Images)*

Economic and Budgetary Policy

Politics and the art of political spin are alive and well in the federal government's budget processes, emergency fund requests, and discussions of them. Chapter 2 highlighted the issue of political gridlock as it related to the Senate failing to hold hearings in 2016 on President Obama's Supreme Court nominee. Over the years, and particularly in recent history, such gridlock and partisanship have been increasingly common in federal budgetary decisions, and they led to government shutdowns and the use of continuing resolutions and omnibus legislation to fund government operations at existing levels without much debate within Congress.

During 2016, the Zika virus threat became a major issue in the news. The virus is transmitted by mosquitos, and is particularly a danger to the fetus of pregnant women; the virus "can inflict serious damage to many parts of the fetal brain beyond microcephaly."[1] The virus was prevalent in South and Central America, but soon migrated to Florida, where it became a significant health concern. In February, President Obama requested from Congress $1.9 billion in emergency funds to address the outbreak, and only in late September of the year did Congress approve a far smaller amount ($1.1 billion); it was clear that politics was entering into the discussion yet again. Some in Congress, concerned about increased federal spending, argued that dollars to address Zika should come through cuts in other areas (offsets). Others, primarily Republicans, proposed that any spending bill also place limits on funding Planned Parenthood and exclude the organization from receiving "new funding for contraception to combat the spread of the virus."[2]

An assessment released by the Brookings Institution argues that the dysfunction that occurs through the general federal budget process leads to situations where it is harder for Congress to respond to such emergency actions as well. Molly E. Reynolds argues that because some of these larger political and policy discussions are limited through our normal budget process, there are no choices for members of Congress but to raise the issues during consideration of such emergency measures. As she stated, "When members have fewer other outlets for both policy and political conflicts, we may see them transfer the debates that would otherwise be hashed out on the individual appropriations bills to the emergency measures."[3]

This breakdown in political dialogue has two major effects. First, thorough debates and discussions do not happen as they should for the year-to-year budget. Work doesn't get done, time runs out, and Congress and the president have to turn to omnibus legislation, often following threats of, or actual, federal government shutdowns. Second, the lack of an opportunity to discuss general budget issues carries over to emergency requests and can prevent or delay the necessary dollars to address the concerns. We have seen this a number of times over the past few years in regard to emergency requests to address natural disasters such as Hurricanes Irene and Sandy, and in the present case of funding to combat the Zika outbreak. It does not help, as this report notes, that the definition of an emergency has been stretched quite far, and in some cases includes questionable items.

Equally important in these emergency expenditure requests are the political benefits gained by those politicians whose constituents will benefit from the programs. Being part of the solutions and responding to the pain and suffering generate significant political goodwill. Yet, supporting programs that try to prevent the emergency from happening in the first place may not, even if the prevention of the problem is less expensive than responding to it after the fact.[4]

These concerns highlight the ongoing discussions regarding the size of government and government spending that often are brought up in the context of the federal deficit and national debt. Deficits occur when the amount expended by the government is greater than the revenue raised through taxes and other avenues. Almost everyone understands government spending on programs and projects. These expenditures can take many forms and may include items such as dollars to build infrastructure such as roads and bridges, military weapons contracts, or Pell Grants for low-income students attending college. In the Zika case discussed above, often these emergency expenditures are passed "off budget," and this concerns deficit hawks wanting to reduce expenditures and the deficit itself. In deficit policy, one way to reduce the deficit is by decreasing such spending on government programs. On the other hand, government can address deficits by turning to the revenue side of the equation. For example, an increase in tax revenue or implementation of a user fee for entry into a national park might be such a choice. From a deficit reduction perspective, both reducing government spending and increasing revenue are economically neutral. In the former case, there is less expenditure, and in the other, the government generates more revenue. Both are perfectly acceptable economic tools for deficit reduction. Yet, politically, these choices are quite distinct. Conservatives have traditionally been much more interested in cutting spending than raising revenue. This is clear when you consider almost any debate regarding the potential to raise taxes. The next election is never too far off, and the major parties are always reluctant to anger their base supporters. A sitting president never wants to see a suffering economy going into an election season. Presidents are often held accountable for economic hardships of the nation, yet they rarely receive any credit during economic boom times. The reality is that the economy is extremely complex, and presidential policies can only have a limited effect on it. Nevertheless, politicians will try to claim credit or avoid blame. As noted in the case above, politicians also use or do not use certain words (political spin or issue framing) in describing the economy. For example, the term *recession* is avoided like the plague and is sometimes referred to as the "*R* word" because of the potential implications that such an admission may carry.

The U.S. economy has been slowly recovering since President Obama's election by almost any of the traditional measures used. Yet, listening to the Republican candidates for president during 2016, you would think the nation was in the midst of a depression. The recovery has been slow and uneven in its effect on the nation. This uncertainty caused considerable anxiety and anger within much of the American public, which likely led to the success of the Donald Trump and, to a lesser extent, Bernie Sanders campaigns. It is clear that the economy will continue to be a major issue in upcoming elections.

These debates will likely focus on a number of issues. The weak economy and the ability of everyone to be positively affected by an improving economy will be one. The appropriate role of government in these situations will be another. Perhaps more substantive are the longer term issues associated with an increasing deficit and federal debt. Deficit spending rose rapidly, starting in 2008 and continuing through 2011. Deficits have decreased since then, with the 2016 estimated deficit coming in at $590 billion according to the Congressional Budget Office (CBO). This is still a significant amount, and CBO estimates show further reductions in the next few years. Entitlement spending continues to eat up an increasing portion of the entire budget, and certain programs such as Medicare and Social Security in particular face dire financial straits in the future attributable to increasing demands by the very large baby boom generation that has begun to retire and collect benefits.[5] Infrastructure funding is insufficient for the needs of the nation; emergency spending continues to be necessary, as the natural disasters associated with storms, flooding, and tornadoes over the past few years showed convincingly; and billions continue to be spent. It appears that the nation will be "in the red" for a long time to come. The result is that both parties are at least giving lip service to the federal deficit again and raising concerns about a nation living beyond its means. Not surprisingly, the parties remain quite far apart in terms of how to address the deficit.

The economic health of the nation and more specific concerns such as the federal deficit are highly dynamic, and they can change dramatically in a short period of time. For example, deficit projections can easily change because they are based on a series of assumptions that may not hold over time. Moreover, the projected deficits become less reliable as one begins to extend the forecasts out two, five, or even ten years. The CBO does provide such projections, however.

According to these estimates, the United States saw a nearly $590 billion deficit in 2016, and can expect continued deficits in the coming years.[6] Yet these budget projections are not necessarily reliable. As we discussed in chapter 6, long-term forecasting of this kind can be accurate only to the extent that the initial assumptions continue to be reasonable. What might change to make them unreasonable? For one thing, economic growth may be less than projected, which would lead to less revenue coming into the Treasury. For another, new laws could be enacted that would require more government spending, a decrease in taxes, or both. Or natural disasters such as a major hurricane might require the federal government to spend a great deal more money to assist victims and reconstruct damaged areas. Or a prolonged recession and a change in political leadership may dictate particular economic policies. Any one of these scenarios could throw off future deficit (or surplus) projections.

Another issue to consider is how policymakers think about these economic projections. In particular, do they consider them to be serious enough to require strong action? Until recently, the answer seemed to be no. Former vice president Dick Cheney commented to the secretary of the Treasury that "Reagan proved the deficits don't matter." The recent deficits have occurred during times of both Republican and Democratic administrations and, for the most part, a Republican Congress. Traditionally, Republicans tout their fiscal conservatism and budget austerity when campaigning for office and administering government, but the policies during the Bush administration did not follow this perspective. When President Obama took office in 2009, deficits were seen as secondary compared with policies to attempt to address the economic downturn. Yet elections of more conservative Republicans have brought new emphasis to fiscal austerity and a preference for ensuring that any new expenditures be accompanied by comparable decreased spending in other areas. Also evident in these disputes is that parties are quick to claim credit when there is good news on the economy, but equally quick to point fingers when the news is less than inspiring. It is fair to say, however, that until now neither party showed much restraint in government spending; so is it any wonder, then, that budget deficits have grown sharply in recent years?

This chapter explores how economic policy attempts to address such issues as the deficit and other goals of economic policy. It assesses economic policy in the United States through a broad review of the powers of government to influence the economy, including the role of the budget. The chapter concentrates on the major goals that policymakers attempt to promote while coping with the inevitable value conflicts and policy choices. The tools and approaches of policy analysis are as appropriate to assessing economic policy as they are to the other policy areas covered in the chapters that follow.

Background

Managing national deficits and debt is only one of the economic and budgetary tasks to which the federal government must attend on a continuous basis.

For much of the latter part of the twentieth century, the federal deficit dominated discussions regarding economic policy, and it clearly had major impacts on the nation's capacity to support other policy actions. Indeed, massive tax cuts at the beginning of President Ronald Reagan's administration in 1981 and the subsequent decline in government revenues greatly constrained spending by the U.S. Congress across a range of public programs. In addition, the U.S. national debt soared during the 1980s, and continues to do so.

Economic policy is critical to all other government functions, but most people probably do not recognize it as readily as they do other substantive policy areas such as the environment, education, health care, or welfare. One reason is that the general public does not connect actions such as tax cuts with attempts to influence economic growth or unemployment. In addition, so much attention is given to the Federal Reserve Board's monetary policy and its impact on the economy that the public tends to forget that the government's fiscal policies—its taxing and spending decisions—also have major impacts on the economy. A cut in tax rates or a decision to spend more money on highway construction—both forms of fiscal policy—can have significant effects on the nation's economy. It is generally only during extremely difficult economic times that the population pays much attention to government activities as they relate to economic policy. For example, in 2008, as the nation's economy continued in a recession, interest in tax rebates, the role of the government in the home mortgage crisis, and other economic policy issues became more salient. Continued disagreements regarding the Affordable Care Act led to an impasse in the federal budget process, which ultimately led to a government shutdown in 2013. And in 2009, as Congress debated a huge economic stimulus package, these discussions and proposals became front-page news. Discussions regarding the raising of the debt ceiling and the unwillingness of certain members of Congress to do so led to a government shutdown. Economic policymaking is crucial to almost everything the government does. In a narrow sense, economic policy is the development of particular programs and policies that are intended to affect economic conditions in the nation, such as reducing unemployment or increasing economic growth. Public policy students should be aware, however, that the development and implementation of other public policies also have substantial effects on the economy and subsequently on the economic policies that the government pursues. For example, conservatives argue that too much government regulation to protect the environment retards economic growth. Because one of government's major economic goals is to encourage such growth, conflict between the two policy goals is likely. For this reason, as well as others, environmentalists emphasize the idea of sustainable development, which they believe can help reconcile economic and environmental goals that may be at odds (Mazmanian and Kraft 2009; K. Portney 2013).

Since the 1980s, the United States has generally been burdened by large federal deficits. As noted above, the CBO projected a deficit of nearly $600 billion for 2016, meaning that the government spent $600 billion more than it brought into the Treasury during the 2016 fiscal year. Economists often debate the potential impacts of deficits, and sometimes politicians will make choices knowing that little money is available. In the early 1990s, budget austerity constrained proposals of any grand ideas about what the government should be doing, such as reforming the health care system. Until 2009, such austerity had not occurred in the twenty-first century, with government continuing to expend funds on a range of activities—both foreign and domestic—without regard for their fiscal implications. Perhaps this is because things can change quickly in the world of economic policy. During the 1990s, an unprecedented eight years of strong, sustained economic growth replaced budget deficits with projections of budget surpluses. In 2001, the nation struggled with an economic recession, and in 2002, growth slowly returned. While the economy showed improvement by most traditional measures during the Obama administration, there continues to be a sense of unease regarding the recovery and its impact, particularly for those on the lower rungs of the economic ladder.

To achieve these and other goals, the government uses fiscal policy—the sum of all taxation and spending policies—as well as the monetary policy tools of the Federal Reserve Board (the Fed, as it is called) to influence the U.S. economy. It does so with varying degrees of success. In addition, government regulation of business has become prevalent since the Depression. Business regulation also increased in the 1960s and 1970s, as citizens demanded more government assurances that health, safety, and the environment would be protected. These regulations have major effects on the budget and economic goals of the United States. The looming deficits in the late twentieth century worried public officials and introduced another major goal for them to consider as they developed economic policy.

When the traditional indicators of economic growth suggested a healthy economy during the 1990s, policymakers were eager to find ways to maintain that strength. With the economic downturn since 2007 and the slow recovery, policymakers were just as concerned with making policy choices that could return the nation to economic good times, particularly with the consideration of tax cuts and government spending to stimulate economic growth. Both options have a significant impact on the size of the projected deficit over the next several years and the extent to which this deficit is reduced or increased.

Goals of Economic Policy

Policymakers try to promote various goals and objectives in relation to economic policy. Government officials in Congress, the White House, and the Treasury Department, and those who sit on the independent Federal Reserve Board, have a number of tools to use in pursuing these goals. What is taking place at the federal level is paralleled in states and localities, as their public officials attempt to promote certain economic goals, such as the growth of local and regional businesses. State and local governments also regulate business practices related to health, safety, the environment, and consumer protection, much as the federal government does. Recent concerns regarding listeria contamination of frozen vegetables remind us of the role that government plays in ensuring safety for certain products, including medications. Yet such regulation may impose costs on businesses, influence economic competition, and affect a range of other economic values. Yet the major economic goals that government attempts to promote are nonetheless fairly constant. They are economic growth, low levels of unemployment, low levels of inflation, a positive balance of trade, and management of deficits and debt.

Economic Growth

Economic growth means an increase in the production of goods and services each year, and it is expressed in terms of a rising gross domestic product (GDP). Such growth usually means that, on average, people's incomes increase from year to year. Many benefits flow from economic growth. First, a strong economy is likely to add to the government's tax revenues. As mentioned, one of the major contributing causes of the budget surpluses of the late 1990s was strong economic growth and the tax revenues it generated. A low rate of economic growth can be a sign of an impending recession, which is generally defined as negative growth over two or more consecutive quarters. Like the federal government, many state governments benefited from economic growth for years and enjoyed budget surpluses. We subsequently saw between 2007 and 2011 economic slowdowns in the states and declining tax revenues, prompting budget cuts in many programs, including higher education.

Second, economic growth may make redistributive programs palatable because people are more likely to accept policies that redirect some of their money to others if they have experienced an increase in their own wealth. Economic growth also allows more people to receive benefits or increases in existing benefits from government programs. For a simple explanation, imagine the government is dealing with four areas of expenditures in a given year. If in the following year the economy grows, the budget pie becomes larger. From a budgeting perspective, this means that each of the four areas also can become larger. But if there is little or no economic growth, in order for one program to gain, it must take from one or more of the other three programs, which will likely cause political conflict.

Percent changes in the GDP over the past twenty years have ranged from a low of –2.0 (2009) to a high of 6.7 (2005). The rate of growth remained somewhat consistent during the Obama years at 3.5 to 4.0 percent.[7] Vigorous economic growth and the resulting tax revenues, while obviously welcome news, also send up warning flags. If the economy grows too fast, it could lead to damaging levels of inflation, which the government seeks to avoid. Theoretically, high levels of growth cause wages to go up; and, if people have more money, they can spend more on houses, cars, and other goods. Higher prices usually follow strong consumer demand, particularly for products or services in scarce supply. A high level of economic growth may lead to a budget surplus, at which point government needs to make decisions regarding how to deal with it. Should spending be increased? Should taxes be cut? Should surplus funds be used instead to reduce the federal debt? Or perhaps we need some combination of such policy decisions.

In the market for a job. The severe economic crisis brought on by the recession that began in 2009 cost millions of people their jobs as factories, retail stores, and many other businesses laid off employees to cope with a shrinking demand for products and services. By early 2017, the economy was much stronger and the unemployment rate stood at about 4.7 percent. In this photo, an Aflac Inc. representative, right, shakes hands with a job seeker at a county career fair in Santa Ana, California, in October 2016. *(Troy Harvey/Bloomberg via Getty Images)*

On the other hand, low levels of growth can contribute to a budget deficit, which raises different questions on how to address the budget shortfall. We turn to these policy challenges in the focused discussion at the end of the chapter.

Low Levels of Unemployment

Low unemployment, or **full employment**, has obvious benefits to the economy as well as to individuals. In the United States, jobs and people's ability to help themselves are regarded as better alternatives to government social programs to assist the poor. Americans are generally more comfortable than citizens of many other nations in helping individuals find jobs and use their abilities to improve their standard of living than they are providing public assistance; therefore, Americans have chosen low levels of unemployment as a policy goal.

Unemployment not only harms the people without jobs but also has two deleterious effects on the economy and the government's budget. First, the higher the number of people who are unemployed, the lower the number of people who are paying income or Social Security taxes, and that means less revenue is coming into the Treasury to pay for government programs. Second, the unemployed may be eligible for a number of government programs geared toward people with low incomes, such as Medicaid, food stamps, or welfare payments. So the government needs to pay out more money when unemployment levels rise. Most of these programs are entitlements, meaning that the government is required to pay all those who are eligible. If this number is higher than expected, budget estimates will be thrown off.

For most of our recent history, the United States has succeeded in keeping unemployment levels at a reasonable rate. Unemployment in the United States stayed between 4 and 6 percent between 1997 and 2008, but it increased to over 9 percent in 2009 and continued at these higher rates for a few years before showing a continuous decline since 2011.[8] These rates, of course, can vary greatly from state to state and city to city. When unemployment rates are very low, businesses may find it difficult to hire qualified employees. For a recent college graduate, that is good news; jobs are plentiful, and opportunities abound. But low unemployment levels can be problematic for local or state economies because businesses cannot expand without an available labor supply, and that constrains economic development. Businesses may be forced to offer generous incentives to attract and keep their most valued employees. In turn, the businesses may demand that local and state policymakers reduce their tax burdens or provide some other financial benefits. It is probably safe to say, though, that policymakers very much prefer a situation of unemployment being too low compared to being too high.

Although the overall unemployment rate has been low in recent years, the rate is not distributed evenly across the population. There are often geographic, ethnic, and age differentiations in this unemployment data. For example, African Americans men continue to have much higher rates of unemployment than white men, with a rate almost twice as high in 2015. The Bureau of Labor Statistics compiles these kinds of data for the Labor Department. See the box "Steps to Analysis: Employment and Unemployment Statistics," where you can explore variations in unemployment statistics by demographics and geographic location, particularly differences among the states.

Another aspect of employment that influences public policy is the changing character of jobs in the U.S. economy and in other advanced, industrialized nations. During most of the twentieth century, many of the best jobs for those without a college education were in manufacturing, but a shift from this traditional sector to the service economy has occurred, and, in general, jobs in the

Steps to Analysis

Employment and Unemployment Statistics

The Labor Department's Bureau of Labor Statistics is the primary agency responsible for collecting data on employment and unemployment. You already know that the rates vary by geography and demographics. To see these distinctions, go to the following website: www.bls.gov/CPS. The opening page provides current statistics regarding employment and unemployment. What is the current unemployment rate in the United States?

Now look at some of the more detailed state statistics and see what differences you can find. You can access state-level unemployment data at the Local Area Unemployment Statistics site: www.bls.gov/LAU. Select two or three states from different regions of the country (such as Alabama, New York, and Washington) and see what differences exist by state. What is the trend for each state regarding unemployment? Are there regional differences? Why do you suppose these differences exist?

service sector do not pay as much as factory jobs. Workers at fast-food restaurants or sales personnel in retail stores may earn the minimum wage or just a little more. Many workers who had jobs that paid quite well, often supported by unions, now see fewer positions of this kind, as competition from abroad and greater efficiencies in production have reduced the need for skilled labor. Some of these workers have been forced to move to the service sector to find employment.

The past several decades have witnessed a significant increase in the two-income family even in the face of higher divorce rates and the increasing number of single-parent families. Several reasons can be cited for this change. First, many families need the income that two wage earners bring home to maintain their lifestyle, to pay for their children's education, or to provide other benefits to their families. Second, more women are entering the workforce than in the past. This is because they want careers and have greater job opportunities than before. Even with the large influx of women into the workforce over the past thirty to forty years, the number of jobs available continues to grow for people with the right qualifications. The expanding labor force and job opportunities result from a healthy economy.

Low Levels of Inflation

A simple definition of inflation is an increase in the costs of goods and services. Inflation is an inevitable part of the U.S. economy, but policymakers try to keep it under control—that is, no more than about 3 percent a year. If wages are increasing at the same rate, the rising prices of goods and services carry little significance to most people. They would be of greater concern, understandably, for those on fixed incomes. If inflation continues and grows worse, however, it eventually affects all citizens, which is probably why government policymakers often seem more concerned with inflation than unemployment. To demonstrate this tendency, one has only to check the various government responses and political rhetoric that have occurred as gasoline prices rise. In some cases, state policymakers proposed suspending their state gasoline taxes, and even members of Congress suggested that the federal government partially suspend its excise taxes. These actions were in direct response to the public outcry about the rising price and the potential political fallout of not doing anything about it.

In the recent past, the United States had a good record on inflation. During the past ten years, inflation, as measured by the **Consumer Price Index (CPI)**, was between –0.4 percent and 3.2 percent, although in 2009 the CPI actually was a negative number, suggesting deflation in the economy. A CPI between 1 and 4 percent is one that most government policymakers can accept as tolerable. What is interesting is that many believe that even this small number may overstate the actual level of inflation because of the way the CPI is calculated. A commission headed by Michael Boskin, who served as President George H. W. Bush's chief economic adviser, found that the CPI overstates inflation by about 1.1 percent.[9] Why should this seemingly small discrepancy matter? Many government programs such as Social Security are tied directly to the CPI as the official measure of inflation. Increases in Social Security benefits are based on the calculated CPI.

Working with Sources

The Consumer Price Index

The Consumer Price Index (CPI), the statistic most frequently used to measure inflation in the United States, represents the average change in price over time of a market basket of consumer goods and services. The Bureau of Labor Statistics makes this calculation by collecting data on goods and services from across the country. They can be consolidated into eight major categories, shown here.

It should be noted that some economists have argued that the CPI overestimates the actual inflation rate. This may be true, for example, if the CPI does not take into consideration the fact that consumers may substitute similar goods when prices increase. There are other inflation measures used as well. One is the GDP deflator, which measures the cost of goods purchased by consumers, government, and industry. This measure is not based on a fixed basket of goods but is allowed to vary based on changing consumption patterns. Which of these do you think is the most useful measure? To learn more about inflation and its indicators, visit the Bureau of Labor Statistics site at www.bls.gov/bls/inflation.htm.

Source: "Consumer Price Indexes: Frequently Asked Questions," Department of Labor, Bureau of Labor Statistics, at www.bls.gov/cpi/cpifaq.htm.

Category of Goods	Examples
Food and beverages Housing Apparel Transportation Medical care	breakfast cereal, milk, coffee, chicken, wine, full-service meals and snacks
	rent of primary residence, owners' equivalent rent, fuel oil, bedroom furniture
	men's shirts and sweaters, women's dresses, jewelry
	new vehicles, airline fares, gasoline, motor vehicle insurance
	prescription drugs and medical supplies, physicians' services, eyeglasses and eye care, hospital services
Recreation	televisions, cable television, pets and pet products, sports equipment, admission fees to national parks
Education and communication	college tuition, postage, telephone services, computer software and accessories
Other goods and services	tobacco and smoking products, haircuts and other personal services, funeral expenses

If these inflation estimates were reduced by 1 percent, it would save the government a substantial amount of money in cost-of-living adjustments over a sustained period. The box "Working with Sources: The Consumer Price Index" explains how the CPI is calculated.

Positive Balance of Trade

A positive **balance of trade** is an economic goal related to the role of the United States in an international economy. Many argue that the goal should be for the nation to export more than it imports, which would be a positive balance of trade. Another way of stating this is the United States would prefer to sell more goods to other nations than it is purchasing from them (in terms of the total dollars). For a number of decades, the nation has failed to meet this goal; in fact, it has had a large negative balance of trade. Among the many reasons for this state of affairs are the large amounts of oil imported into the United States (although this has been on the decrease in recent years), the desire of consumers to purchase foreign products such as Japanese or German electronics, and the relative weakness in other countries' economies that translates into their inability to purchase U.S. goods. In addition, labor is cheaper in many parts of the world than it is in the United States, which has led to what critics maintain is an export of jobs to nations that produce the clothing, toys, and many other consumer goods that Americans buy at home. This situation would seem to be problematic, but others question that conclusion, asking whether it matters that the United States has a negative balance of trade. These issues also relate to the increasing globalization of the world economy. One of the biggest reasons for the rise in gasoline prices, discussed earlier, has much to do with the greater demand for oil from nations such as China as they begin to further develop their economies.

Those concerned about negative trade balances, often referred to as "protectionists," answer with a number of reasons why the United States should attempt to rectify the situation. First, they see the negative balance as evidence that U.S. goods are not as competitive as foreign goods. If this assertion is correct, a number of U.S. industries and jobs may be at risk. Second, certain industries are crucial to the nation's security and economic well-being. For example, steel manufacturing may be seen as critical for national security because steel is essential to support the military. Third are the equity considerations with regard to trade. Some countries place prohibitive tariffs or quotas on U.S. goods that prevent American companies from competing on an equal footing. Protectionists say that in fairness to domestic industries, the United States should impose similar trade restrictions. On the political side, policymakers need to support industries (and unions) where jobs may be threatened by trade imbalances.

Some analysts argue, however, that negative balances are not necessarily a problem for the United States. They believe that if it makes economic sense for a country to import more than it exports, the government should not intervene; after all, if the countries involved in the trade relationships do not see mutual benefits, they will not make the trades. Economists often use the theory of comparative advantage versus comparative disadvantage when analyzing international trade issues. Countries that produce a good particularly well and have the comparative advantage should overproduce that good and export the excess to a country that does not produce the same good very well. By the same token, a country should import goods that it does not produce as well (comparative disadvantage). For example, the United States is a prime producer of wheat and should therefore take advantage of this capacity by overproducing and selling the excess to countries, such as Saudi Arabia, that do not produce wheat very well or at all. This argument is just one that free traders cite to promote their point of view.

Managing Deficits and Debt

The United States saw budget surpluses in the late 1990s, but it still had a large **national debt** to pay off, and that debt has increased as the nation has returned to deficit spending. The national debt, which is the accumulation of all of the deficits the nation has run, was nearly $20 trillion in December 2016. Like any other borrower, the United States must pay interest on its debt. In 2015, this interest amounted to over $402 billion and constituted one of the government's largest single expenditures.[10] This expenditure was interest only; no principal was repaid. The problem for the nation is the same as a credit card holder paying only the minimum amount billed every month: when the interest due is added, the payment the following month will be very close to the original amount. During the years of budget surpluses, most policymakers believed the federal government should have used at least part of the surplus to begin paying the national debt, even if they disagreed over how much of a commitment to make to this goal.

Limiting the occurrences of federal deficits and the amount of the national debt are serious goals for the United States because they show fiscal responsibility. In other words, they demonstrate the ability to live within one's means, an important political goal. The jury is still out about the economic impact of having deficits and debt. Deficits require the government to borrow from private investors, which makes less money available for private investment. Finally, the interest the government is paying on the national debt is money that cannot be spent on other government programs—it is money that in a sense is paying for nothing. Once the debt is reduced or eliminated, more money becomes available for other government programs or tax reductions. Years of deficit spending did not, however, seem to harm the nation's overall economic situation, so it is fair to ask whether ensuring balanced budgets is an important goal. Many Republican lawmakers supported the Bush administration's proposals to decrease taxes without major reductions in spending, which can increase the deficit and the national debt. Their stance on fiscal policy was unusual for conservatives, who more often than not argue against deficit spending.

The national debt has taken on new political importance in budget negotiations as the United States has had to increase its debt ceiling, which is in essence the legal limit on the amount of money the government can owe. Republicans, spurred on by conservative members and Tea Party supporters, dug in their heels about authorizing additional debt until President Obama and the Democrats agreed to address the federal deficit through significant government spending cuts and without raising taxes. Without raising the debt ceiling, many argued that the government would not be able to pay its bill and potentially could default on its loans. Most agreed that the economic consequences for the nation and even the world would be problematic.

For a few years, U.S. economic policy regarding deficits and debt appeared to be moving in the direction of decreasing debt, but as more recent events have shown, these policies can change quickly in different circumstances. Will strong economic growth return, or will the nation continue to have slower rates of growth—or even enter another recession? What about the ever-increasing demands on entitlement programs? It is clear that rosy forecasts about budget surpluses and debt reduction have changed dramatically and plunged the nation back into a situation where deficit policy—alternatives for how to decrease the deficit—may once again take on a dominant role in government policymaking.

Interrelationships of Economic Goals

It is difficult to discuss major economic policy goals without also considering how they interrelate. The relationship between inflation and full employment is a frequent subject of debate. For many years, economists assumed these two goals were in conflict because they believed a certain level of unemployment would keep inflation under control. This theory made economic sense: when a larger number of people are out of work, the demand for products should go down, and with a decrease in demand should come a decrease in prices. The opposite effect should occur when unemployment is low; more people with money to spend fuel the demand for products, and prices go up. The economic problems of the 1970s changed this view when the United States experienced high levels of both unemployment and inflation, and it has not been a major focus since then.

Another often discussed relationship is that of economic growth and inflation. This connection is of particular interest to the Fed, which is responsible for monetary policy in the United States. The Fed traditionally is concerned with inflation in the economy, and it often implements monetary policy to control it. In general, most policymakers (and citizens) see economic expansion in the United States as positive, but the Fed looks at the potential of higher prices as a possible negative consequence. If the economy is growing too fast, the Fed argues, people have more disposable income to spend, and the demand for products increases and leads to an increase in prices—inflation. The Fed therefore uses its powers to attempt to slow down the economy—for example, by raising the interest rate—to keep inflation in check.

The third relationship is between federal deficits (and debt) and the other economic indicators. With high deficits or debt, less money is available for private investment, which limits economic growth and perhaps exacerbates unemployment. The discussion here does not exhaust the relationships among these economic goals, but it should make clear that the government cannot conduct its economic policies in a vacuum; rather, it must take many factors into consideration before choosing to pursue a particular economic goal.

Tools of Economic Policy

Governments have a variety of policy tools to help them achieve their goals and deal with economic issues. Fiscal policy is a term that describes taxing and spending tools, but governments have other mechanisms, such as regulations or subsidies, that can also be effective. In addition, monetary policy, which is the Fed's responsibility, is another major tool of economic policy. The Fed tends to receive more media attention than other economic policymakers in the federal government, but it is only part of the picture. This section examines the various tools used to influence the economy and some of the consequences invariably associated with these choices.

Fiscal Policy

The president and Congress conduct fiscal policy when they make decisions concerning taxing and spending. At the federal level, major changes in fiscal policy often start with a presidential initiative. The president cannot act alone in this area but must work with Congress to make any major changes. The primary tool of fiscal policy is the budget process that the government goes through every year. During this process, policymakers decide how much money should be spent on government programs ranging from highway building and maintenance to national defense and education. Policymakers frequently reconsider provisions of the tax code, reducing some taxes and raising others. Tax changes and government expenditures are the major tools of fiscal policy, and policymakers use them to achieve certain economic and other public policy goals.

In a recession, for example, government policymakers typically would attempt to stimulate economic growth. To do this, the president and Congress have two basic choices: cut taxes or increase spending. Reducing the federal income tax puts more money into citizens' pockets—and, with that extra cash, people will likely buy more goods. The demand for products, in turn, requires companies to increase their production, which means hiring additional employees, driving down unemployment, and giving people paychecks so they can make purchases. Theoretically, these activities should promote economic growth and pull the nation out of recession. Similar to a tax cut, a tax rebate has been used in recent years to provide citizens with additional money in response to an economic downturn. A boost in government spending would have a similar impact. The increase in spending—for example, to build new highways—creates jobs, and these new workers are able to buy goods and services. Thus the cycle begins again. The Obama economic stimulus package in 2009, as one important example, included a number of provisions to rebuild infrastructure and invest in energy conservation activities that could produce jobs. When the economy is running "too hot," government can use the opposite tactics to address the situation. Raising taxes takes disposable income away from individuals and limits their purchasing power. The subsequent decrease in demand should reduce the level of inflation.

Although using fiscal policy makes sense from an economic perspective and appears to be a logical way to manage or control swings in the economy, elected officials may see the matter differently. A politician campaigning for office finds it easy to support lower taxes "to get the economy moving again," but what happens to a politician who campaigns on a platform of controlling inflation by *raising* taxes? The individual will probably face a hostile public and lose the election, even if the economic policy decision is sound in terms of its impact on the nation's economy.

Monetary Policy

Monetary policy is a pivotal component of economic policy in the United States. Indeed, the chair of the Federal Reserve Board, Janet Yellen in 2017, was widely considered to be among the most powerful positions in the nation's capital because of its influence on economic policymaking. Monetary policy differs from fiscal policy in several ways. First, it tries to deal with economic fluctuations by controlling the amount of money in circulation, also referred to as the "money supply." Second, the Fed implements the policy itself rather than responding to initiatives from the president and Congress. In other words, the Fed is relatively independent of the government's political institutions. Its independence is deliberate and intended to remove politics from these kinds of economic decisions. Third, the Fed's mechanisms typically affect the economy more quickly than the tools of fiscal policy. Fourth, unlike the decision making that occurs in Congress or the executive branch, most of the Fed's deliberations take place behind closed doors and outside of the political realm. This practice is controversial, given the American political culture of open decision making and political accountability. In light of that tradition, it was something of a surprise when former Fed chair Ben Bernanke agreed in March 2009 to be interviewed on the widely viewed television news program *60 Minutes*, the first such interview of a Fed chair in more than two decades. Bernanke clearly believed that the economic crisis at the time called for him to speak out to reassure the American public of the Fed's critical role in the economic recovery.

When trying to influence the economy, the Federal Reserve Board will either increase or decrease the amount of money in circulation. If the economy is in a recession, the Fed can make money available to stimulate growth. During times of inflation, the Fed may cut back the money supply. In general, the Fed tends to be an inflation hawk and will take action to curtail it even at the risk of hindering strong economic growth. The Fed has three primary tools at its disposal to try to influence the economy: open-market operations, changing the discount (interest) rate, and changing the reserve requirements. Figure 7-1 shows how the Fed uses these tools under different economic circumstances.

Open-market operations occur when the Fed decides to buy or sell U.S. Treasury bonds. The discount rate is the rate the Fed charges member banks to borrow money from the Federal Reserve Bank. Changes to this rate subsequently have an impact on the interest that banks charge their borrowers. The reserve requirement is the amount of money (a percentage of its deposits) that member banks must keep on reserve; in other words, the banks cannot use this money for any other purposes. Changes to the reserve requirement affect how much money banks can lend out and therefore either stimulate or suppress economic growth.

Regulation

Government regulation is rarely used explicitly to achieve economic goals, but it is a tool that can affect these goals, as we noted earlier with regard to food safety regulation and product recalls. The government has used regulatory policies for many years. In 1887, Congress created the Interstate Commerce Commission as a way of regulating the growing monopolistic railroad industry and to protect the public from unfair practices. Additional policies were developed throughout the

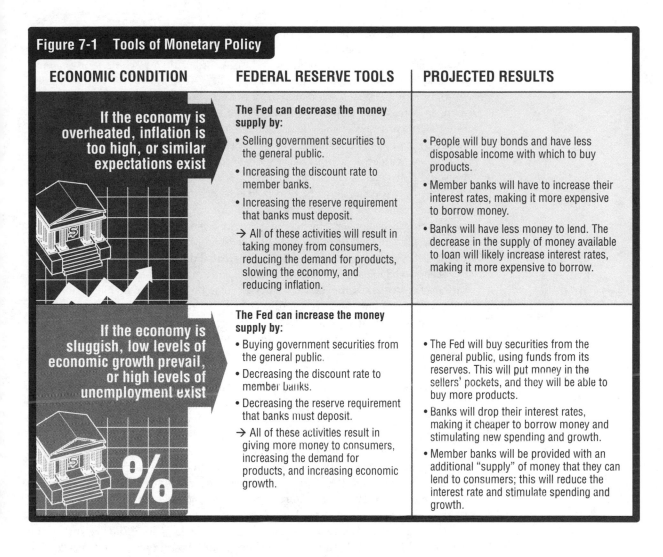

Figure 7-1   Tools of Monetary Policy

ECONOMIC CONDITION	FEDERAL RESERVE TOOLS	PROJECTED RESULTS
If the economy is overheated, inflation is too high, or similar expectations exist	**The Fed can decrease the money supply by:** • Selling government securities to the general public. • Increasing the discount rate to member banks. • Increasing the reserve requirement that banks must deposit. → All of these activities will result in taking money from consumers, reducing the demand for products, slowing the economy, and reducing inflation.	• People will buy bonds and have less disposable income with which to buy products. • Member banks will have to increase their interest rates, making it more expensive to borrow money. • Banks will have less money to lend. The decrease in the supply of money available to loan will likely increase interest rates, making it more expensive to borrow.
If the economy is sluggish, low levels of economic growth prevail, or high levels of unemployment exist	**The Fed can increase the money supply by:** • Buying government securities from the general public. • Decreasing the discount rate to member banks. • Decreasing the reserve requirement that banks must deposit. → All of these activities result in giving more money to consumers, increasing the demand for products, and increasing economic growth.	• The Fed will buy securities from the general public, using funds from its reserves. This will put money in the sellers' pockets, and they will be able to buy more products. • Banks will drop their interest rates, making it cheaper to borrow money and stimulating new spending and growth. • Member banks will be provided with an additional "supply" of money that they can lend to consumers; this will reduce the interest rate and stimulate spending and growth.

early twentieth century, but a major infusion of regulation occurred as a result of President Franklin D. Roosevelt's New Deal program. The New Deal created a number of programs and agencies whose goals were to manage the U.S. economy during the Great Depression of the 1930s. Most of these early actions were economic regulatory policies—those whose primary intention was to regulate the potential monopolistic practices of business. The policies were somewhat limited in that most of them tended to regulate a single industry.

Since the 1970s, government has produced more social or protective regulatory policies, which generally are not concerned with monopolies. The primary goals of social or protective regulation are not usually based on economics; rather, they are enacted to protect society from unsafe business practices and products (Harris and Milkis 1996). Social regulatory policies range from ensuring clean air and water to providing a safe workplace to ensuring a safe food supply. Social regulatory policies differ from economic ones in a number of ways. One major distinction is that these policies tend to affect multiple industries rather than just one. For example, a workplace safety standard developed by the Occupational Safety and Health Administration (OSHA) is a requirement placed upon all businesses. These policies tend to increase the scope of government and can affect business production. An unintended consequence may be an increase in the cost of doing business, which in turn may lead to price increases (inflation), unemployment, or a diminished ability to compete with other nations in the global economy. For these reasons, many analysts and policymakers, as noted in chapter 6, favor the use of cost-benefit analysis or cost-effectiveness analysis to help policymakers understand the consequences of regulatory policies or proposed regulations. Critics of regulation often point to the increased cost such policies create, but there are benefits gained as well. A 2016 draft report to Congress on the costs and benefits of major federal regulations completed by the Office of Management and Budget estimated that aggregate annual costs were between $74 billion and $110 billion, a significant amount to be sure. OMB estimated the benefits for these same rules at the aggregate to be between $208 billion and $672 billion, far outpacing the costs regardless of what number in the range is used.[11]

Many conservatives claim that excessive environmental regulation and health and safety regulation are responsible for holding back economic growth. The logic here is that businesses have to spend money to comply with environmental requirements, making fewer dollars available to them for investment and expansion (A. Freeman 2006). Such thinking had a powerful effect in shaping regulatory policy toward antiregulatory actions by different policymakers, and early indications from the newly elected Trump administration is that we can expect to see a rollback of regulatory policy.

Chapter 3 defined *regulation* as any government decree that forces or prevents a particular activity, but other kinds of government mandates can also directly or indirectly affect economic policy. For example, the United States has a minimum wage law that requires employers to pay at least a certain amount to their employees. The federal minimum wage in 2016 was $7.25. A number of states have minimum wages greater than the federal level. For example, the rate in California in 2016 was $10.00 per hour, the rate in Oregon was $9.25, and in Ohio it was $8.10. The policy exists for good reasons, but it clearly has economic policy ramifications. When the minimum wage goes up, employers may decide either to hire fewer people or to lay off a part of their workforce. If enough employers take these actions, the rate of unemployment goes up. On the other hand, higher wages will provide individuals with more income, spur economic growth, and perhaps lead to inflation. These results are not stated goals of minimum wage policy, but they could be the consequences.

Incentives, Subsidies, and Support

In addition to fiscal policy, monetary policy, and regulation, governments have other tools to achieve economic goals. These tools may be applied to a particular industry or individual businesses to promote that industry, or they may favor a particular location. State and local governments trying to encourage regional economic development and growth might provide a tax break to a company willing to locate in their area. They do this because they believe the additional jobs created by a new industry will make up for any loss in their tax base. Sometimes this projection is correct, and sometimes it is not.

At the federal level, Congress provides what is often called "corporate welfare" to large corporations to promote an industry. As noted earlier in the chapter, this assistance comes in the form of subsidies and tax incentives, sometimes called **tax expenditures**. While some may argue about how such an expenditure is defined, according to a study conducted by the Cato Institute, these cost taxpayers nearly $100 billion a year. The Cato report cites a number of examples of such expenditures, including $25 billion in agricultural subsidies that mainly go to agribusiness.[12] These kinds of support programs influence economic policy in a number of specific ways. First, government expenditures have a direct effect on the size of the budget and potentially affect deficit and debt policy. Second, tax incentives or breaks reduce the revenue the government collects, thereby limiting what it can spend. Third, if the policies are adopted to improve an industry's performance, they should lead to growth in a particular business or industry and to subsequent economic growth and higher employment rates. In the area of international trade, such programs may allow domestic companies to be more competitive abroad and perhaps improve the nation's balance of trade. Although many of these programs benefit certain businesses and industries, they also constitute another tool government has for managing the economy.

Tax Policy

Nothing generates as much political debate as discussions about raising taxes, in part because tax policy has important consequences for the public. Given their preferences, politicians would like to avoid the topic altogether. The Internal Revenue Service (IRS), the agency responsible for collecting the federal income tax, rarely receives high marks in public opinion polls. Still, compared to people in other developed nations, Americans are taxed at a lower rate. The reason is that the other nations have to tax at a high rate to provide for a much greater level of government-provided services, such as national health insurance and retirement benefits. According to the Organisation for Economic Co-operation and Development (OECD), the total tax rate in the United States in 2015, expressed as a percentage of GDP, was about 26 percent, while in Denmark it was 47 percent, and in the United Kingdom and Canada it was 33 and 32 percent, respectively.[13]

On its face, the goals of tax policy are quite simple. The government (at whatever level) wants to collect enough revenue to meet its expenditure demands. The problems arise when governments try to decide *how* to tax citizens and corporations. Governments have several different ways to raise revenue, such as income taxes, property taxes, and sales taxes. They might be able to collect similar amounts of revenue using different tax methods, but because other factors need to be considered, governments turn to policy analysis for help. Tax policy is highly susceptible to policy analysis because the criteria discussed throughout the book—effectiveness, efficiency, equity, political and administrative feasibility, and others—can clarify the effects of adopting one kind of taxation relative to another. What kinds of taxes are the most politically acceptable? Which are the most equitable in spreading the burden of taxation among different groups of citizens? Will any given tax generate enough revenue, a measure of effectiveness? Will it be administratively simple to collect? The box "Steps to Analysis: Variables in Making Tax Policy" defines the different factors policymakers need to consider when selecting an appropriate tax policy.

Another question analysts might ask is whether a proposed tax is regressive or progressive. A **regressive tax** applies the same rate of taxation to all individuals, regardless of their income or socioeconomic standing. A **progressive tax** is based on the philosophy that higher earners should pay higher taxes both in terms of actual dollars and as a percentage of income. Most sales taxes are regressive in nature because they treat all income the same. A poor person buying fifty dollars' worth of items pays the same amount in sales tax as a millionaire buying the same dollars' worth of goods. Payroll deductions such as Social Security and Medicare taxes are also regressive in that the rates of taxation do not vary by tax bracket, and these taxes in particular have major effects on take-home pay. Income taxes, on the other hand, tend to be progressive. As income increases, the wage earner not only pays more actual dollars in taxes but also may graduate to a higher tax bracket and pay taxes on a larger percentage of income. Recent changes in the tax system lowered the tax brackets and reduced their number as well, making the system less progressive than it used to be.

Subsidies for economic success. Among other tools, economic policy relies on the provision of incentives or subsidies to achieve the nation's goals, often through the tax code. The photo shows House Ways and Means Committee Chairman Kevin Brady (R-TX), who introduced the House Republicans' tax reform proposal at the U.S. Capitol on June 24, 2016. Among other provisions, the GOP wanted to get rid of the estate tax, a change that would benefit only the wealthiest families in the nation. *(Chip Somodevilla/Getty Images)*

Steps to Analysis

Variables in Making Tax Policy

The government has a number of ways to raise $1 million through taxes, but which is best? Policymakers must think about this question when designing tax policy, and many variables may affect the ultimate decision. B. Guy Peters (2016) notes five major characteristics of taxation: collectability, fiscal neutrality, buoyancy, distributive effects, and visibility. To these we can add the ideals of horizontal and vertical equity. Each addresses different policy analysis concerns.

Collectability: the ease of collecting the tax and its ability to generate the needed revenue. This is concerned with administrative feasibility and effectiveness, in this case meaning the ability to meet the goal of collecting enough revenue to meet expenditures.

Fiscal neutrality: whether the system gives preference to one kind of revenue or expenditure without good reason. Think of a tax loophole as something that is not fiscally neutral. As implied by the name, fiscal neutrality is an equity issue. Why should one kind of expenditure or revenue be treated differently?

Buoyancy: the ability of the tax to keep up with inflation and economic growth. Buoyancy is mainly an efficiency issue in that revenues increase automatically with inflation without any policy changes being necessary. This has political feasibility concerns as well

in that new tax proposals may not be necessary with a buoyant tax.

Distributive effects: the impact of the tax on different groups in the population. Who is most affected by the tax, for example, low-income or high-income households? This is mainly an equity criterion.

Visibility: the extent to which the tax is visible or acceptable to the general public. This is mainly a political feasibility criterion.

Horizontal and vertical equity: the degree to which the tax system is fair or equitable. Horizontal equity means that people who make the same amount of money pay the same amount in taxes. Vertical equity means that people with different income levels pay different amounts in taxes. As the name implies, this is an equity issue.

Think of some of the different kinds of taxes you currently pay or proposals about which you have heard. How do they stack up against these criteria? Some examples:

- Local property taxes
- Increases in federal and state gasoline taxes
- Movements to more consumptive taxes such as a national sales tax
- Increases in cigarette and alcohol taxes

Source: B. Guy Peters, *American Public Policy: Promise and Performance*, 10th ed. (Thousand Oaks, Calif.: CQ Press, 2016).

The Budget Process and Its Effect on Economic Policy

The budget process is so complex that even a book-length treatment of how it works would not exhaust the topic. The short introduction to the process provided here is intended to make the public policy student aware of the multitude of decisions that are made each year during the budget process and their implications. In addition, the politics of the budget often leads to activities that occur outside of the stated process. For example, high-level meetings and negotiations, often behind closed doors, may occur among congressional leaders and the administration and may include the president himself. These kinds of activities,

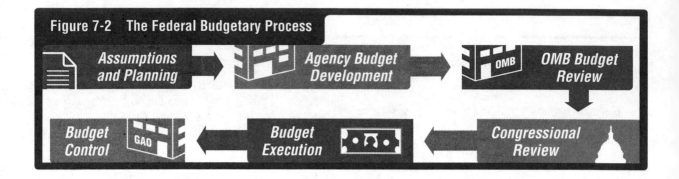

Figure 7-2   The Federal Budgetary Process

Assumptions and Planning → Agency Budget Development → OMB Budget Review → Congressional Review → Budget Execution → Budget Control

if they occur, will drive the rest of the budgetary process. The federal government's fiscal year begins on October 1 and ends on September 30 of the following year, but at any given time policymakers and government staff may be working on two or three different budgets for various years. Figure 7-2 provides a sketch of the major sequences of decisions in this process.[14]

Assumptions and Planning

The first major step in developing a budget occurs many months before the government implements the actual plan. During this stage, economic analysts in the executive branch and high-level policymakers begin the process of setting the budget's major taxing and spending goals. In addition, they develop assumptions about the economic conditions of the country, such as the growth rate and unemployment levels. These assumptions are necessary to sketch out a budget that will be implemented more than a year later. The problem with making assumptions is that conditions change and the assumptions may turn out to be wrong once the budget is implemented. For example, if policymakers assume that unemployment will be 4 percent and instead it is 6 percent, that difference has a major impact on the budget. Less revenue will be collected, and expenditures will likely rise to pay benefits to the unemployed. Another critical assumption is whether the economy will grow and by how much, which affects the anticipated revenues from income taxes. Eventually, however, the analysts develop their estimates of the total budget, and this information is communicated to the federal agencies so they can develop their individual budgets.

Agency Budget Development

Most of the specific work in budget development occurs at the agency level. Each agency is responsible for preparing the estimates for funding in the coming year based on its current programs as well as any new initiatives it would like to implement. Most agencies consist of bureaus or subagencies, and budget preparation begins with them and then is sent up the hierarchical chain until it reaches the highest level of the agency. Because agencies are enthusiastic about their programs, they will likely attempt to increase their budgets from year to year, a process often referred to as "incrementalism." They also recognize that they are part of a presidential team, and some will win and others will lose in the budget process. Once the agency has signed off on the budget proposal, it proceeds to the next step.

OMB Budget Review

The Office of Management and Budget (OMB) is a presidential agency that has the primary responsibility for reviewing all agency budgets and ensuring that they conform to the administration's policies and agenda. Inevitably, the agency's budget request will be higher than the amount OMB initially planned to provide it. At that point, OMB and the agency begin negotiations to settle on an amount. OMB holds hearings in which each agency defends its budget and provides a rationale for its programs and funding. The OMB director receives the final report of these hearings and negotiations and makes changes before delivering the entire package to the president for review. If agency heads are unhappy with the way OMB treated their submissions, they may attempt to make their case with the president.

The executive budget not only provides the financial information for and about the government and its programs but also sends a strong signal to Congress regarding the president's priorities for the coming year. For example, if the presidential budget includes an increase in environmental spending or a cut in defense spending, Congress can expect to see a number of substantive policy changes in these areas. Once the president and White House advisers complete their review, the presidential budget is delivered to Congress for the next stage of the process.

Congressional Review

The president initiates the budgetary process, but Congress's role in budget development is equally if not more important. Congress uses a two-step process for considering the president's budget recommendations. In the first step, the House and Senate Budget Committees formulate what is called a "concurrent budget resolution" that sets out the total amount of spending, the total revenues, and the expected surplus or deficit for the coming fiscal year. Part of this resolution specifies the total spending in nineteen categories, such as national defense, agriculture, and energy, with spending levels for each. This budget blueprint for the year is to guide the House and Senate Appropriations Committees as they formulate more detailed bills that specify how much money the government can spend on specific programs (Davidson et al. 2016). Usually, these committees rely on the president's budget as a baseline for starting the budget discussion, but sometimes a president's budget is declared DOA—dead on arrival. The two appropriations committees work primarily through their subcommittees, which are set up to mirror the functional units of government such as defense, energy and water development, agriculture, and education. The members of Congress who serve on the appropriations committees typically gain substantial expertise in their areas of specialization, and with this information they can influence budget and spending decisions. The subcommittees hold hearings on the budget proposals and mark up their respective budget areas. Upon completion of the subcommittee work, the appropriations bills, like other legislation, move to the full appropriations committee and then to the full House or Senate.

What Congress and the president contribute to budget development, in terms of which institution has the primary responsibility, has shifted back and forth throughout U.S. history based on the ebb and flow of power between these branches of government. Major changes occurred in 1974 with the passage of the Congressional Budget and Impoundment Control Act. Congress enacted this legislation to recapture some of the budget authority it had lost to the White House in previous years. The act had a number of noteworthy provisions. First, it created congressional budget committees to facilitate the coordination of budget development within the legislative branch and set the overall taxing and spending levels. Second, it created the CBO, a legislative agency responsible for providing Congress with economic and budget information. Prior to the creation of the CBO, Congress often had to rely on the president's OMB estimates and assumptions, and some members were concerned about the potential for political manipulation of the process. The CBO is a nonpartisan organization that most neutral observers believe provides the more accurate assessments of economic and budget issues. If nothing else, Congress now has its own independent assessment of economic assumptions and budget forecasts.

Once Congress passes the budget, the bill goes to the president for signature or veto in twelve separate appropriations bills that reflect the functional divisions in government. At this point, the president's options in regard to the budget are limited: accept and sign the appropriations bills or veto one or more of them. Many presidents have asked for **line-item veto** authority, a budgeting tool that would allow the president to delete specific items from an appropriations bill without rejecting the whole bill. Most state governors have this power. The Republican Congress in 1996 provided President Bill Clinton with a version of the line-item veto, sometimes referred to as "enhanced rescission authority," that he used a number of times in subsequent years. The Supreme Court, however, struck down the line-item veto law as unconstitutional, stating that it violated the constitutional provision requiring all legislation to be passed in the same form by both houses of Congress and sent to the president in its entirety for signature or veto. The Court said by vetoing part of a bill, the president was changing its form.[15]

In recent history, particularly under divided government, partisan politics has made enactment of the budget an excruciating task. The White House favors its version of federal spending priorities, and Congress may disagree strongly. If a president is prepared to exercise the veto option, the president can force Congress to negotiate or risk being held accountable for a breakdown in the budget process. If a budget is not passed by October 1, then technically the government must shut down.

A dramatic example of what can happen if both sides dig in their heels occurred in 2013 when the Republican-controlled House of Representatives attempted to get concessions on Obamacare as a condition to passing the budget. President Obama and the Democratic-controlled Senate refused to go along, and the result was that the government officially closed for over two weeks. The other trend in budget politics is for Congress to pass large omnibus bills, often pork laden, that include many programs the president supports and some he does not. Presidents find it almost impossible to veto these bills. Typically, however, the president and Congress are able to reach agreement on a budget, even if neither is completely satisfied with the outcome. Sometimes Congress enacts continuing resolutions that allow government agencies to operate while the budget negotiations carry on. When the president signs the final appropriations bills, the budget they represent becomes law, and the next step of the process begins.

Budget Execution and Control

Once Congress and the president approve a budget, the various government agencies execute it by spending the money to implement the programs receiving budget support. This spending goes for personnel, day-to-day supplies, and providing services and payments to those who qualify under the agency's programs, such as farm price supports or Social Security. Each agency typically decides what mechanisms to use to spend its allotted budget.

The final step in the process, and one to which most people pay little attention, is budget control. After the fiscal year is over, the Government Accountability Office (GAO) is responsible for ensuring that the money was spent legally and properly. In many ways, this amounts to an audit of the entire government. The GAO reports its findings to Congress, and the members may use the results to reward an agency or hold its metaphorical feet to the fire.

The steps discussed above assume a process that is working correctly. More commonly in recent history is that there tends to be major disagreement among policymakers, particularly during the congressional review aspect of the budget. The implication is often that a new budget does not get passed and instead Congress passes a continuing resolution that, in effect, locks spending and programs into what they were in the previous year. The policy impact of such practices is that there is little opportunity to adjust policies or their spending and think through what may be the more pressing priorities. Politically, it defers difficult decisions by those making them.

Economic Policy: Successes and Failures

In the past few decades, a number of economic policies have been proposed and implemented. These policies have enjoyed varying degrees of success in achieving their stated goals. Some also have had unintended consequences—that is, impacts that were neither planned nor foreseen when the policies were designed and implemented. This section considers several of the most significant of these economic policy actions.

Significant Income Tax Cuts

Tax cuts are always politically popular with citizens, but presidents will also make economic arguments for proposing such policies. When President Reagan took office in 1981, he faced an economy that by many measures was in a recession. Economic growth was low, both inflation and unemployment were high, the deficit was rising, and the country's morale was low. The Reagan administration introduced a different form of fiscal policy in 1981. Officials argued that a shortage of investment in the United States was the cause of the sluggish economy and rising deficits, and that the answer was supply-side economics. According to this theory, the government could increase economic growth by cutting taxes, especially for the richest individuals. The largest tax cuts went to the wealthy because, the administration assumed, they would use the additional resources to invest in the economy—building or expanding businesses, hiring more employees, and so forth—which would stimulate the economy, decrease unemployment, and increase the tax revenue collected. This theory continues to be supported by many conservatives and was a major policy perspective of former president George W. Bush.

Reagan's electoral mandate—he won 489 electoral votes to President Jimmy Carter's 49—was a major reason for his ability to secure passage of the Economic Recovery Tax Act of 1981. The $162 billion tax cut included a 23 percent reduction in personal income taxes, cuts in the highest tax rate, and major cuts in business taxes (Peterson and Rom 1988). The result was more money in the pockets of individuals, especially the wealthy. The hope of the supply-siders was that this new money would be used to invest in and expand the economy. After a recession in the early 1980s, the U.S. economy indeed began to grow in 1983. Unemployment decreased and inflation was held in check, so the tax cut and other Reagan economic policies achieved in part many of the administration's economic goals.

One criticism, however, lingers to this day. The president's policies, usually called Reaganomics, created unprecedented increases in the nation's deficit and debt. The national debt went from about $1 trillion in 1981 to well over $5 trillion by the late 1990s. The Reagan administration had hoped that the additional tax revenue generated through economic growth would pay for its spending priorities, including the rise in defense spending. This did not happen. Higher interest rates imposed by the Fed's monetary policy during the 1980s took back part of the money Reagan's fiscal policy had provided. In addition, domestic spending did not slow down enough to offset the potential loss in revenue created by the massive tax cuts. Although the Reagan administration redefined tax policy in many ways, it also helped to create a different problem in terms of economic goals. In fact, it was during this period that policymakers learned to pay more attention than ever before to deficit and debt management in economic policy.

Many proposals and policies were offered to address the deficit problem generated by the Reagan policies.

Taking office in 2001, President Bush, like President Reagan, faced a sputtering economy, and his vision for tax policy was an across-the-board tax cut. Much like the Reagan cuts, a significant portion of this cut would go to the nation's richest citizens, which Bush did not see as a problem because they pay a significant percentage of federal taxes. As president, Bush was able to work with the Republican-controlled Congress to enact tax legislation that not only lowered tax brackets but also provided a rebate check of $300 or $600 to many taxpayers. The weakening economy helped persuade Congress to approve the bill, as well as a similar one in 2008. The move was politically popular, and from an economic standpoint it could be an effective way to spur economic growth. Programs to further reduce taxes were implemented during the Bush administration, including a movement to repeal the estate tax (discussed in chapter 6). In most cases, such taxes only affect the richest 2 percent of the population.[16] In 2016, Republican presidential candidate Donald Trump also promoted a similar tax reduction proposal as part of his economic policy, and based on comments since the election, we can expect to see proposals and policies to reduce tax rates for the rich and businesses.

These tax cuts can have implications beyond the attempt to stimulate the economy. President Bush entered his second term of office with an increasing deficit. Administration officials said that the growing deficit was due to forces outside their control, such as a recession, slow recovery, and the September 11 attacks. But many analysts believe that a good portion of the shift from surplus to deficits that occurred under President Bush can be attributed to policy choices such as tax cuts, the wars in Afghanistan and Iraq, and a new prescription drug program for those on Medicare.[17] Through all of this, the administration had favored the maintenance or even an extension of these tax cuts. These rates continued into the Obama administration. Democrats and fiscal conservatives have been highly vocal in raising their concerns about these economic policies. Was it justifiable to give large benefits to the rich, especially in light of a growing gap between the rich and the poor? How will these decisions affect policymaking in the coming years? These are crucial questions that will continually need to be evaluated.

Responses to the Deficit

As mentioned, one consequence of the various tax cuts was a tremendous growth in the federal budget deficit. While fixing a deficit is theoretically a simple matter—either increase taxes or decrease government spending so that revenues are more in line with expenditures—politically, these two policy choices can be difficult. President Reagan was in office and holding the line against any significant tax increases. Democrats, on the other hand, were unwilling to go along with any additional cuts in the programs they supported. In essence, the political will to decrease

Economic recovery. Officials often debate which of many competing policy proposals will best promote economic growth and job creation. Republicans often favor corporate and individual tax cuts over alternative policies. In this photo, Donald Trump, the 2016 Republican presidential nominee, waves to the audience at an event to discuss his economic plans at the Detroit Economic Club in Detroit, Michigan, on August 8, 2016. Trump promised a big overhaul to the personal income-tax code and a deep cut in corporate tax rates as well as regulatory reforms. *(Sean Proctor/Bloomberg via Getty Images)*

the deficit was not there. In an effort to deal with the situation, in 1985 Congress enacted the Balanced Budget and Emergency Deficit Control Act to try to create a balanced budget over a five-year period. Supporters hoped that requiring relatively small reductions in the deficit (about $30 to $40 billion a year) might prove to be politically feasible, but if Congress did not do so, then a forced budget cut referred to as "sequestration" would ensure achievement of the deficit target.[18] In *Bowsher v. Synar* (1986), the Supreme Court ruled that sequestration by the General Accounting Office (now called the Government Accountability Office) unconstitutional, which led to the enactment of a revised law in 1987, which also failed to reduce the deficit, and in fact we saw increases. Many believed that sequestration would enforce discipline in the budget process because members of Congress or the administration would not want to see forced cuts in their programs. But the law provided too many loopholes to avoid sequestration. In addition, many legislators saw that forced percentage cuts in their favorite programs were better than targeted cuts that could be larger (Thurber 1996b).

In 1990, Congress and President George H. W. Bush tried again and formulated a new budget plan called the Budget Enforcement Act (BEA). The BEA also attempted to reduce the federal deficit, which was approaching $200 billion by then. Among the law's most important reforms was a "pay-as-you-go" provision that required all tax and spending legislation to be deficit neutral. In other words, if new legislation increased expenditures for a particular program, the new spending had to be offset either by subsequent increases in revenue or by decreases in expenditures in another program. The BEA also established spending ceilings for each discretionary spending category (defense, domestic, and international).

If spending went higher, the sequestration process would be applied only to the category of the offending area. The effectiveness of the BEA in reducing the deficit has been the subject of serious debate. On the one hand, the deficit was reduced during the late 1990s, and the Treasury had a surplus. Some credit the BEA and President Clinton's extension of its components through 1998 as the reason for the country's economic turnaround. On the other hand, others argue that credit for the deficit reduction should go to the nation's economic growth during this time. The reality is that a combination of both factors (and others) improved the country's deficit situation for a few years. One aspect of the BEA that has become more important over time is the definition of what constitutes an exemption under the law. The BEA always provided for exemptions, situations in which a budget ceiling could be exceeded. For most of the 1990s, these situations were limited to true natural or economic disasters. Since then, according to a former deputy director of the CBO, "the definition was discarded and any semblance of discipline abandoned."[19] By expanding the definition of an emergency, policymakers are able to spend well beyond the limits of the original budget.[20]

As part of the 2011 Budget Control Act, Congress once again attempted to address the deficit situation by mandating cuts through sequestration if Congress was unable to come up with a budget plan. But like the above examples, Congress ensured that many large programs were left untouched. Sequestration primarily hits discretionary spending, which is already a relatively small part of the overall budget.[21]

American Recovery and Reinvestment Act of 2009

The U.S. economy faced significant challenges during the Bush II administration and into the early years of the Obama administration as evidenced by the home mortgage crisis and the financial industry bailout. The result was a recessionary economy that has been very slow to recover fully. Upon taking office in 2009, Congress passed and President Obama signed the American Recovery and Reinvestment Act (ARRA) of 2009 as a response to the sluggish economy. The purpose of the act was to save or create jobs, spur economic activity, and foster accountability in government spending through tax cuts, federal spending for education and other entitlement programs, and making available money for contracts and loans. These fiscal policy measures—the cutting of taxes and the increases in government spending—are typical government responses to a recessionary economy and, as noted earlier in the chapter, are usually promoted as a way to spur economic growth.

The success of the Recovery Act or at least the level of its success has been debated over the past several years. In addition, many conservatives were uncomfortable with the overall expansion of government and its spending that resulted from this program (and the health care reform measure discussed in chapter 8). The CBO claimed in a February 2013 report that the ARRA was responsible for a 0.4 to 4.1 percent increase in the GDP during 2009 to 2012, and raised employment potentially as high as 4.7 million jobs beyond what it would have been without the act.[22] Gary Burtless of the Brookings Institution argued that the stimulus was a success and that "any reasonable grader would give the stimulus a B+." Unfortunately for supporters, the argument, as Burtless stated, that "it could have been much worse" is not a strong political statement.[23] Many Republicans have been quick to state that the stimulus was not effective, and they pointed to the continued high unemployment rate as evidence of this. In addition, those opposing the stimulus made claims of wasteful spending and stressed concerns about the increasing debt without noticeable progress. Not surprisingly, both parties took to the airwaves to put their own political spin on the success (or not) of the Recovery Act.

Economic Issues and Challenges

Looking at economic policy is always interesting because of the new or renewed challenges that must be faced from year to year. Market swings occur all the time, and changes in economic growth and inflation can affect the overall economy. In addition, what is termed *consumer confidence* plays a role in the health of the economy because consumer spending accounts for about 70 percent of economic activity in the United States. All of these factors point to the dynamic nature of the economy and economic policy. What might this term hold in regard to economic challenges and issues for the United States? In addition to the changing nature of budgetary politics, where surpluses can become deficits in a matter of months, there are many other issues to consider.

Maintaining Economic Growth

America's years of strong, sustained economic growth in the 1990s produced many positive benefits: tax receipts were up, unemployment was low, the deficit was eliminated, and there were decreases in the national debt. People across the nation saw the benefits of a strong economy as their wages rose and opportunities for personal advancement expanded. It is clear, however, that this kind of sustained growth does not go on forever.

Growth is a cornerstone not only of a strong economy but also of a satisfied electorate, which can translate to a stable political system. The economic growth of the 1990s facilitated action on many of the nation's problems such as the deficit. The strong economy also made possible the action on welfare reform in 1996 and related policies. Many analysts point out that states were able to meet the caseload reduction requirements of the law because of the strong economy and its effect on employment. When jobs are plentiful, people can move off the welfare rolls. The strong economy also allowed Congress to spend money on highway construction and maintenance, budget items that had been deferred because of deficits. These expenditures not only help local communities but also allow members of Congress to score political points with their constituents.

The real challenge for the United States and its economy is what to do when economic growth begins to lose momentum or the nation enters a recession.

Economic slowdowns that started in 2001—which eventually led to an economic recession—demonstrate that it is not realistic to expect a high level of growth to continue indefinitely. Changing economic conditions should cause policymakers to evaluate priorities and perhaps make changes. But doing so forces them to confront difficult political choices, and not everyone necessarily agrees on the best way to get the economy moving again. What types of expenditures might be directly linked to job creation and economic development? Is increased spending for higher education an investment in economic development, or is the effect too indirect? How do policymakers balance a perceived need for government intervention with an ever-increasing deficit? How does one cut or eliminate popular programs backed by an alert and powerful constituency? Can and should revenue be raised through tax increases? How much emphasis should be placed on reducing the federal deficit and debt? These are the kinds of questions policymakers ask when budget problems exist. The box "Working with Sources: Views on Economics and Budgeting" provides some additional sources of information from a variety of organizations interested in budget and economic policy.

Working with Sources

Views on Economics and Budgeting

Many of the economic and budget sites available on the web represent various partisan and ideological perspectives. Some focus on macrobudget issues, such as unemployment and inflation, while others are concerned with the budget's effects on specific programs and policy areas. Explore the sites and try to identify the partisan or ideological orientation of the organization that sponsors each of them. You can usually find this information in the site's "mission" or "about" links. A short comment from each organization's website follows below. How evident are the differences in political orientation? What kind of information tells you most reliably what each organization's political leanings are?

www.cbpp.org. Center on Budget and Policy Priorities
"A nonpartisan research and policy institute. We pursue federal and state policies designed both to reduce poverty and inequality and to restore fiscal responsibility in equitable and effective ways."

www.concordcoalition.org. Concord Coalition
"A nationwide, non-partisan, grassroots organization advocating generationally responsible fiscal policy."

www.nber.org. National Bureau of Economic Research
"A private, nonprofit, nonpartisan research organization dedicated to promoting a greater understanding of how the economy works. The NBER is committed to undertaking and disseminating unbiased economic research among public policymakers, business professionals, and the academic community."

www.taxfoundation.org. Tax Foundation
"The nation's leading independent tax policy research organization . . . informed smarter tax policy at the federal, state, and local levels."

www.whitehouse.gov/ (search for National Economic Council—as of March 2017, webpages were still being updated by the new administration). National Economic Council
"Established in 1993 . . . for the purpose of advising the President on matters related to U.S. and global economic policy."

Growth of Entitlements

Entitlement programs are very pronounced in the United States. An **entitlement** program is one with payment obligations determined by the law that created it, not by the budget associated with that program. Under an entitlement program, any person who meets the eligibility requirements is entitled to receive benefits from the program. The clearest example of an entitlement program is Social Security. When people reach a certain age, they are eligible to receive Social Security payments (see chapter 9). A major difference between an entitlement program and other government programs is how it is funded. The usual budget process does not apply; in other words, Social Security administrators do not determine their annual budgets as other agencies do. To change the amount of money spent on an entitlement program, Congress has to amend the authorizing law.

Entitlement programs account for a large portion of the federal budget. Unless policymakers decide to change the substance of the law, much of the federal budget is out of their hands at the start. Moreover, entitlements have grown tremendously. In 1968, entitlements made up approximately 28 percent of the budget; today they comprise over 60 percent of the federal budget. This is a dramatic increase that is expected to grow as the baby boom generation ages and increases demands on Social Security and Medicare. One of the major concerns about the ever-expanding entitlement programs is that they crowd out other budget expenditures. These other programs must go through the typical budget process and may take the brunt of any cuts because of their more precarious position. So-called discretionary spending, which includes funding for defense, the environment, national parks, and upgrading air traffic control systems, among other programs, has decreased significantly as a percentage of the budget partly because of the growing entitlement expenses. How likely is it that the government can get entitlements under control? Economically, it makes sense to do this because policymakers would probably want more authority over government spending. From an equity perspective, it seems only right that no government expenditures receive special treatment in the budget process. The real issue is political: why did policymakers decide to make programs such as Social Security and Medicare entitlements in the first place? The answer to this question explains why it is so difficult to make changes now.[24] Figure 7-3 shows where the money in the proposed fiscal 2017 federal budget comes from and where it is spent.

Income Inequality

As the national economy went through some improvements during 2011 to 2013, more discussion focused on who was benefiting from the economic uptick. The economic data indicated that the recovery was going well for the super-rich (often referred to as the top 1 percent), but less so for the lower and middle classes of the population. The United States has always had a somewhat unequal distribution of income and wealth, which is not unusual for a capitalist nation. But questions continue to arise regarding the degree of this inequity and its larger economic implications.

Figure 7-3 Fiscal 2017 Proposed Federal Budget by Category (in billions of dollars)

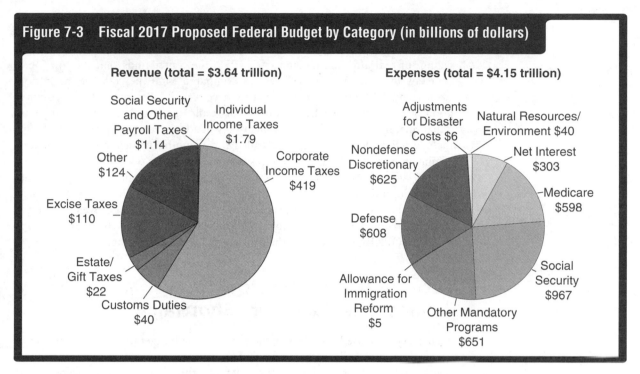

Revenue (total = $3.64 trillion)

- Social Security and Other Payroll Taxes $1.14
- Individual Income Taxes $1.79
- Other $124
- Corporate Income Taxes $419
- Excise Taxes $110
- Estate/Gift Taxes $22
- Customs Duties $40

Expenses (total = $4.15 trillion)

- Adjustments for Disaster Costs $6
- Natural Resources/Environment $40
- Nondefense Discretionary $625
- Net Interest $303
- Medicare $598
- Defense $608
- Social Security $967
- Allowance for Immigration Reform $5
- Other Mandatory Programs $651

Source: Office of Management and Budget, "The President's Budget for Fiscal Year 2017," available at https://obamawhitehouse.archives.gov/sites/default/files/omb/budget/fy2017/assets/tables.pdf (Table S-5).

Balancing priorities. State governments, much like the federal government, have had to contend with often difficult fiscal challenges that lead to some mix of changes in taxation and spending. The photo shows Governor Jerry Brown of California, right, discussing a proposed "rainy day" fund that he and then Assembly Speaker John Pérez, D-Los Angeles, supported during a hearing of the Assembly Budget Committee at the capitol in Sacramento in April 2014. The proposed constitutional amendment would force the state to set aside some revenues during boom years to better prepare for the inevitable economic downturns. *(AP Photo)*

Chapter 9 will discuss income inequality, one measure of which is the Gini coefficient. The Center on Budget and Policy Priorities provides a number of ways of looking at this issue on its website. For example, examining the percent change of real after-tax income since 1979, the center finds that the top 1 percent saw income gains of 192 percent compared to 46 percent for the bottom 20 percent.[25] Is such income inequality a concern? Does the overall economic good of the nation benefit or suffer as a result of such a variation in income? What role, if any, does the government play in addressing such inequality? Some, including President Obama, have called for a significant increase in the federal minimum wage to $10.10 per hour as one way to ensure what some call a "living wage." Conservatives and many business organizations oppose such an increase in the minimum wage as an unwarranted governmental intrusion into the marketplace that also may harm the economy. To see a discussion of wealth inequality in the United States, you can watch a YouTube video (www.youtube.com/watch?v=QPKKQnijnsM) and then review the issues with others.[26]

Focused Discussion: How to Address the Budgetary Shortfall

As has been stressed throughout the chapter, the budgetary picture can change quickly. In 2016, the nonpartisan CBO was projecting an annual deficit of nearly $600 billion and continued deficits throughout the projected years (2026). Former president Bush stated that he wanted to halve the size of the deficit by 2009. These claims came before the projected $200 billion to assist the recovery of New Orleans following Hurricane Katrina and before the true costs of the new Medicare prescription drug program were revealed. The financial and economic meltdown that occurred in 2007 and 2008 and the subsequent economic recovery packages passed in both the Bush and Obama administrations changed the picture again quite dramatically. Under current projections, deficits will continue to be hundreds of billions of dollars for many years to come.

The current size of the deficit and the changing political landscape have raised the salience of this issue, and it is clear that policymakers may need to rethink the deficit problem. Quick fixes are unlikely, and it will take a long-term strategy that may not be seriously considered until the current economic environment improves. The Brookings Institution highlighted the difficulty of balancing the budget and reducing the federal debt with an online exercise "The Fiscal Ship," with the expressed purpose of demonstrating the difficulty in making these decisions that often come down to values as well as economic impact.[27] President Obama created the bipartisan National Commission on Fiscal Responsibility and Reform, chaired by former Republican senator Alan Simpson and former Clinton chief of staff Erskine Bowles, to attempt to provide proposals to address the deficit. Using presidential commissions is common in such circumstances as presidents attempt to remove blatant politics from the discussions.[28] The commission generated and issued a report in December 2010, but a number of the members were unwilling to endorse the entire plan because parts of it conflicted with their ideological or political perspectives.

During the summer of 2011, serious talks began in regard to addressing deficit reduction, with leaders within the various parties, not surprisingly, having differences of opinion regarding how to move forward. Coming up with solutions to deficits is a common exercise among think tanks. Some have argued that a considerable amount of money would be saved if the government were just more efficient. There have been numerous reports, for example, of the rush to spend money in response to the September 11 attacks and in relief efforts following Hurricanes Katrina and Rita. In trying to respond quickly to these demands, policymakers probably wasted a substantial amount of money. These examples notwithstanding, it is hard to conceive of reducing a deficit this large through greater efficiency.

Generally, reducing the deficit requires that the government either bring in more revenue or cut expenditures. As noted earlier, neither of these options is politically popular. This focused discussion explores a few of the general alternatives—each with multiple choices—to reduce our federal deficit. These choices are relatively straightforward, and they are not necessarily mutually exclusive. In fact, one may want to explore all of these options:

- Decrease entitlement (or mandatory) expenditures
- Decrease discretionary expenditures
- Increase revenue through taxes or other devices

This section partially draws upon a CBO report "Choices for Deficit Reduction: An Update." Interestingly, the last section of the report discusses criteria to consider in evaluating the policy changes that may affect the deficit that sound similar to the criteria we have discussed throughout the book. These include the following:

- What role would the federal government play in society (political criterion)?
- What would be the economic impact in the short and long terms (economic criterion)?
- Who would bear the burden of proposed changes in policies (equity criterion)?[29]

Decreasing entitlement expenditures is an important option to explore because of the size of the entitlement budget in the United States. As mentioned earlier, over 60 percent of federal expenditures are entitlements, so it is in this category that one may be able to get significant reductions in federal spending. Upon entering office, President Obama stressed the importance of reforming Medicare and Social Security as one step toward long-term economic recovery, although to date not much has happened in these areas. Reducing discretionary spending is what generally has been occurring in the United States for the past thirty years as entitlements have grown. Discretionary funds include a wide range of expenditures such as those for the environment, most education, foreign aid, and a range of other programs. Most also classify military expenditures as discretionary, although typically within their own category—that is, defense versus nondefense discretionary spending. Together they represent a significant percentage of the budget. It is important to recognize that much of the 2009 economic stimulus plan would typically be characterized as discretionary expenditures. Critics of government waste and pork-barrel expenditures often look to this category to find cuts. Finally, there is always the option of bringing in more revenue. This may occur painlessly through economic growth, but more than likely, it may require an increase of taxes or fees. There have been increasing calls, including from the National Commission, to significantly reduce or eliminate "tax expenditures." As noted earlier, tax expenditures are tax earmarks that provide so-called tax breaks to certain parts of the population. One may be able to make the argument for increased taxes from the perspective that U.S. citizens are taxed at a far lower level than in other industrialized nations. Critics argue the additional taxes will probably just lead to more spending and slow down economic growth.

All of these choices involve complex economic relationships that need to be better understood in order to comprehend the arguments put forth and the consequences of each choice. We have stated that policy analysts can use a number of different criteria in evaluating policy alternatives including efficiency, effectiveness, and equity. For this case study on how to decrease the deficit, we use economic, political, and ethical criteria as we examine the three alternatives.

Economic Issues

The economic issues associated with how to decrease the federal budget deficit may be a bit different from those of the other public policy areas discussed in the following chapters. Here, the discussion does not necessarily attempt to address a problem of a market failure, such as a negative externality, but the budget has obvious economic implications that should be understood when considering the alternatives provided.

As stated earlier, one of the biggest economic arguments for decreasing entitlement spending is the overall size of this part of the budget. Of course, there are many entitlements from which to choose, including such popular programs as Social Security and Medicare, as well as a number of agricultural subsidies. Social Security is the government's largest program, and according to the CBO, the percentage of people sixty-five and older will be 19 percent of the total population by 2026. This will increase the number of beneficiaries for programs such as Social Security and Medicare.[30] There are a number of options available to reduce outlays for it. One would be to use an alternative measure of inflation when computing the **cost of living adjustment (COLA)** for benefits. The COLA occurs every year in response to the Consumer Price Index. According to the CBO, such an adjustment would save $108 billion over the 2014–2023 period. Another option might be to further increase the retirement age or to reduce benefits.

The CBO also suggests linking benefits to average prices rather than average earnings.[31] The downside to some of these options is that such reductions in benefits may have a detrimental effect on the economy because beneficiaries will have less money to spend. For Medicare, some have argued for an increase in the age at which one becomes eligible for the program. Similar changes have occurred in Social Security, which has slowly increased the required age for full benefits from sixty-five to sixty-seven. A similar change in Medicare could substantially reduce the program's outlays. Another idea would be to increase the premiums paid by beneficiaries.

Of course, reducing any of these entitlement programs may have economic impacts beyond reducing the deficit. Raising interest rates on federal student loans may decrease the number of students attending college, which would limit their future earning potential. The real problem with changing any entitlement program is that in order to make these adjustments, legislators have to change the authorizing statute. All of these programs either are very popular or have a well-represented constituency that benefits from the programs, which makes such changes difficult to make.

Reducing discretionary spending is another option. The CBO report stated that discretionary spending represents about 35 percent of federal outlays compared to 1973, when it represented 53 percent of the outlays. There was growth in such spending as part of the ARRA of 2009. Caps already exist on most discretionary spending as a result of the Budget Control Act of 2011, and there are assumptions that future legislation will adhere to these caps. Because of the relatively small percentage of the full budget, achieving any significant deficit reduction through cuts in discretionary spending can have dramatic effects on existing programs. Another issue is that the country rarely budgets for natural disaster assistance, though billions are spent every year in this area. A large variety of programs are categorized as discretionary, and it would be impossible to discuss every one of them as a proposal for elimination or decrease. Some have argued that too much is spent on military expenditures, which make up a sizable portion of the budget. According to the CBO, under the current caps, the funding for the Department of Defense is significantly below what is needed to implement its plans. Reduction in military spending is often difficult because of the strong support such spending generates from many in Congress as well as the Department of Defense. In addition, military spending acts as a major economic boost for local communities. A related area is homeland security. Military spending increased following the attacks of September 11 and the subsequent activities in Afghanistan and Iraq. Troop drawdowns may provide some budget relief, but it is unclear how much. Other choices for military savings include decreasing spending for specific programs such as reducing the building of hardware such as aircraft carriers or long-range bombers. These choices raise questions regarding the actual need of these programs, but also the economic impact of reducing spending.

As noted, there have been limited increases in discretionary spending in recent years. Because discretionary spending is just that—discretionary—it is easier for policymakers to ignore the needs of these areas compared to entitlement programs. As such, while some of these programs may have seen some increases in funding, the level of the increase may not have met program needs. A good example may be infrastructure funding. By just about every measure, the United States is underinvesting in maintaining its infrastructure. One often hears stories regarding the safety of the thousands of bridges on our nation's highways. These expenditures and others, such as for education and job training, may represent investments that could improve the nation's economic performance in the future. Others, such as environmental spending, protect important resources and the health of the nation's citizens, which also have economic value even if they are not calculated as part of the budget. In some situations, one could argue that the amount budgeted for an activity is insufficient to alleviate the existing market failure. For example, perhaps the amount budgeted for environmental protection is inadequate to address the negative externalities associated with the production of goods and services. Another example may be that the funds to ensure a capable military are currently insufficient and that it is the government's responsibility to provide this pure public good. All of this is to say that many times these decisions come down to the political priorities of those in office.

Increasing revenue through an increase in taxes or fees also has obvious economic implications. In a deficit situation, there is not enough revenue to meet expenditure demands, so one might think the best course of action would be to increase revenues. As discussed earlier in the chapter, a change in fiscal policy that increases taxes takes money out of the pockets of individuals. This could then lead to less spending and potentially a slowing down of the economy. Slower economic growth can then translate to less revenue generated through taxes. This is why many conservatives and antitax groups suggest decreasing taxes in order to increase economic growth and as an alternative way to increase revenue. As noted earlier, there have been calls to expand the tax base by eliminating most tax expenditures. This will also significantly simplify the tax code. Naturally, there are definite political implications to the tax question. These will be addressed in the next section.

Political Issues

To say that politics drives most of the debate surrounding the budget deficit alternatives would be a vast understatement. All of the alternatives being discussed have strong advocates and opponents both within government and in the interest group community. In addition, while sometimes the deficit itself does not generate much public interest, cutting desired programs or proposals to increase taxes will quickly gain the public's attention.

From a political standpoint, suggesting cuts to existing entitlement programs may be the most volatile option. This is especially true since many of these programs are projected to be underfunded in the future and not able to provide the current level of benefits. The political debate in cutting these programs is certain to be highly contentious, and because cuts in entitlement programs would require changes to the law itself, there is an extra burden placed on Congress for enacting such cuts. It is no secret that any suggestions to reform programs such as Social Security and Medicare are often met with accusations that the supporters of the so-called reforms are trying to harm senior citizens—a common accusation during political campaigns. By suggesting cuts in these popular entitlement programs, proponents are opening the door to intense criticism from politically active groups such as AARP. In addition, elected policymakers, because of the political sensitivity, are reluctant to suggest decreases in these programs for fear that they will lose their positions. Balancing the budget on the backs of the elderly is usually not seen as politically acceptable. It is a foregone conclusion that presidential backing is necessary for changes in these types of entitlements. During the budget talks in the summer of 2011, President Obama appeared willing to entertain discussion of and possible changes to what are often considered sacred programs such as Social Security and Medicare as long as Republicans were willing to consider revenue enhancers (for example, tax increases and/or reforms of the tax code) as well.

The same can be said for many other entitlement programs, such as agricultural subsidies. Policymakers do not want to be labeled "antifarmer," especially in a country that holds the family farmer in such high regard. It tends not to matter that a large proportion of these subsidies go not to the family farmer but to agribusiness. Significant cuts were made to the Agricultural Act of 2014, known as the Farm Bill, but a large portion of the cuts were in the Supplemental Nutrition Assistance Program (SNAP) or food stamp program that provides nutritional funding for the low-income population. On the other hand, because of the size of these programs, one could gain a lot of benefits with relatively modest changes, which can be appealing. In addition, since many people are not currently eligible for these entitlements, there could be a chance to gain public support for the cuts. Regardless, is it any wonder why policymakers tend to shy away from these kinds of choices?

Political debate about cutting discretionary programs can also be contentious. Generally, though, these debates are more limited because the programs are smaller and, depending on the program, may have less support and even some opposition. For example, a proposal to decrease spending in environmental protection programs will generate an uproar, particularly from environmental interest groups, but industry and property rights groups, as well as others who want to see limited government intervention, may applaud such a proposal. Likewise, suggestions to cut funding to advance the use of Amtrak and other high-speed railroad systems will be a concern to a few focused organizations but may be supported by the automobile and airline industries, which are worried about competition. In fact, in 2011, a number of state governors turned back federal funding for high-speed rail that was part of the stimulus package, claiming that it was wasteful and would potentially raise state costs later. The extent to which any discretionary spending can be labeled as "pork" or "wasteful" tends to maximize the chance of it being slashed. What constitutes "wasteful" is also up for political debate. Cuts in military spending or homeland security are politically more difficult. Policymakers do not want to be labeled weak on defense, and as noted earlier, the economic effects of some of this spending can be substantial.

In addition, politicians are not likely to stop trying to "bring home the bacon." More so than entitlements, discretionary programs are left to the preferences of those who are in power.

Raising taxes is never seen as a savvy political proposal, even if the result ultimately leads to a better economic outcome. Politicians have seen the political benefits of proposing tax cuts and the dire consequences for those who suggest tax increases. As such, this proposal may politically be the most difficult one to enact as a way to decrease the deficit. Such proposals are easy to attack in thirty-second sound bites, especially in an era where it appears that any budgetary problem should be addressed by a tax cut. On the interest group front, a number of organizations such as Americans for Tax Reform and the National Taxpayers Union continuously advocate for smaller government and lower taxes. These groups are also joined by conservative think tanks such as the Cato Institute and the Heritage Foundation. On the other hand, one rarely hears of interest groups that advocate tax increases. The general public seems to share distaste for tax increases, but when asked more specific questions regarding the use of tax increases, particularly on the rich, as a way to address the country's economic concerns, a significant majority of the population agrees that this option should be part of the overall package.[32]

One of the only areas related to revenue increases that sometimes generates public support is in the category of user fees and, to a lesser extent, calls for increases in "sin taxes" such as those on cigarettes. People are more willing to support user fee increases because the users are getting a particular service for which they pay (such as entry and use of a national park) or because others do not perceive that they will ever use the good, so the tax has no effect on them. Similarly, for nonsmokers, a proposal to increase the sales tax on cigarettes has no direct effect on them, so they are more likely to support it. Some user fee increases may make economic sense and garner public support. In areas such as grazing and mining on public lands, for example, it is generally accepted that these are government-subsidized programs; an increase in the fees to use these public lands would generate more revenue and would likely be supported by the general population, if not by the industries getting the subsidies. The difficulty of increasing the current tax base leads some to explore different tax options, such as eliminating tax expenditures or imposing a national sales tax as a way to generate more revenue. The current political environment suggests that any such proposals would not pass without decreasing the existing income tax.

Equity and Other Ethical Issues

As is often the case with equity and related ethical issues, people have different ideas of what is fair or moral. For example, is it fair to have the government increase taxes and take more revenue to cover expenditures? Is it moral to retreat from a promise made years ago by cutting entitlements? When the question is what the government should do about the deficit and how to decrease it, equity and ethics can inform the discussion.

Reducing the deficit by cutting entitlement programs may raise the strongest ethical argument, especially as it relates to Social Security and Medicare. Supporters of Social Security, for example, state that the program is a promise the government makes to the American public or a contract it has with workers: if employees contribute during their working lives, the program will pay benefits upon their retirement or disability. If the funds are not available because too many people have become eligible, has the government broken its word? Is its action unfair? On the other hand, some may argue that these programs have outlived their usefulness and the nation needs to turn to other ways of financing them that may better provide the necessary benefits. Why should certain segments in society such as the elderly receive so many government benefits without fully paying for them?

Fairness arguments to decrease discretionary spending come down to whether we should continue to underfund programs that over the past thirty years have already been subject to budget cuts according to proponents. For years, these programs have suffered from budget austerity. Proponents argue that now is the time to make up for their financial neglect, not to cut them further. The nation's infrastructure is in serious disrepair, education spending is not keeping pace with inflation, and, some argue, military spending and preparedness have suffered. Many believe it is these types of expenditures that will also lead to economic recovery through either immediate or long-term investment. On the other hand, some of these expenditures may include programs that some would say represent an oversized government or illustrate government intrusion. To the extent that one can show that some of these programs are unnecessary or wasteful, the ethical argument can be very persuasive, especially in times of budget austerity. What about military expenditures? It may be difficult to cut such funding during times of war. Policymakers want to ensure that the military has the necessary resources, especially if safety is an issue. Reports of understaffed and undersupplied troops in Iraq illustrate this. Once troops are committed, many argue that there is a moral obligation to ensure they have the necessary supplies.

Addressing the deficit by increasing taxes runs into issues of fairness and personal freedom. Typically, those supporting limited government also push for citizens to be taxed at the lowest possible level. It is easy to argue against this choice because it plays on many people's fears of an overzealous government that taxes too much and may intrude excessively into citizens' lives through a variety of public policies. On the other hand, people generally are asking for these programs, and there should be an obligation to pay for them. Many of the same people who decry taxes and would rally against a proposed tax increase oppose cuts in programs providing them with benefits. Some, for example, may argue that the government should not be spending money to fund renewable energy research, perhaps stating that the private sector should finance these efforts. Others, though, would say that the coal and oil energy industries have little incentive to fund such research, and it is up to the government to contribute to this effort. In addition, these energy industries have been and continue to receive their share of government support. If policymakers can increase revenue by decreasing taxes and thus spur economic growth, the equity issues shift to who should receive the tax cuts. While some argue that the rich should receive the greatest tax cuts because they pay the highest taxes, others counter that the poor will benefit most from the cuts. There is some debate as to which of these choices will better promote economic growth.

As noted earlier, there has been an increasing call to simplify the tax code and to eliminate a large number of tax expenditures or tax breaks. This is also an issue of equity and fairness. As discussed earlier in the chapter, fiscal neutrality—treating different types of revenue or expenditures the same—is something policymakers should consider in tax policy. Tax expenditures such as breaks for oil drilling, excluding capital gains at death, or even deductions for home mortgage interest are not necessarily fiscally neutral.

Clearly, all three of these alternatives for addressing the deficit have merit, and it is difficult to know which is best. From a political standpoint, policymakers have been reluctant to address the deficit at all because of what may befall them if they propose cutting a preferred program or increasing taxes. There is a strong incentive to do nothing and hope that strong economic growth returns and makes the problem disappear. Whether relying on economic growth to solve the deficit problem is realistic is something that will be evident only with the passage of time. If policymakers want to address the deficit using the alternatives suggested above, then ideally combining multiple policy alternatives might be the best choice. Sharing the pain through a wide range of program cuts and tax increases will lessen the overall effect on any one program and perhaps diffuse the political situation somewhat, and frankly may be the only real way to fully address the deficit issue. There is also an intuitive trait of fairness and equity with such a solution.

It is important to keep in mind that budget estimates for deficits or surpluses are just that—estimates. They are based on economic assumptions that may or may not prove to be reasonable. Minimal increases or decreases in economic growth, for example, can affect the deficit by billions of dollars. In addition, spending decisions change all of the time, as one can see from the increases in spending for homeland security, the changing international situations, natural disasters, and the economic stimulus plans. There are also political pressures to increase popular programs that policymakers may have a hard time ignoring. All of these issues require the public policy student to keep abreast of changes and be willing to continually ask questions and seek justification for program decisions.

Conclusions

This chapter is the first in the text to consider a substantive public policy issue. Its purpose is to demonstrate the different ways to examine problems, alternatives, and policies related to economic policy and budgeting. In other words, it shows how to apply the tools of policy analysis to real issues and the decisions policymakers make.

Economic policymaking is a bit different from most of the other substantive areas the next chapters discuss. It is almost always a starting point for other policy areas because money, or the lack of it, influences what government policymakers do at all levels. The best solutions to deal with issues such as providing health care for all, confronting terrorism within U.S. borders, or increasing the number of people pursing higher education cannot be adopted and implemented without adequate funding. This chapter shows that budget data and projections change frequently and that this information affects how policymakers address a particular problem or fail to do so.

Policy analysis can help policymakers make informed decisions about how to use a limited budget with a number of competing goals. It can also help citizens better understand how and why these decisions are made. Why, for example, did Congress spend billions of dollars on homeland security measures without any semblance of analytical thought? How can local leaders justify to their communities an increase in a sales tax to build a new professional sports stadium? Should the deficit be a concern, and if so, what is the best way to address it? Is it best to stimulate the economy through tax cuts or additional government spending? All of these fiscal and monetary tools of economic policy can lead to different outcomes and affect people in different ways. In addition, they often have different levels of political support depending on the action chosen.

Fiscal policy, controlled by the president and Congress, has to address the political issues most directly in order to even get proposals passed. Fiscal policy often occurs within the context of the budgetary process, which spans multiple years and relies heavily on analysis and projections of policy analysts within all parts of government. Knowing this process and who is involved can help citizens better understand the proposals pushed and ultimately approved. In most cases, there are bound to be unanticipated outcomes as a result of the decisions made. As noted throughout the chapter, economic indicators change often, and decisions are based on data and projections that ultimately may turn out to be wrong. Policy analysis of economic and budget matters can help people appreciate the difficulties of these kinds of questions and understand the policies proposed to address them. In the chapters that follow, students will find similar arguments about the importance of thinking critically and creatively about possible solutions to challenges in a range of policy areas.

SAGE edge™
for CQ Press

Sharpen your skills with SAGE edge at **http://edge.sagepub.com/ kraft6e**. SAGE edge for students provides a personalized approach to help you accomplish your coursework goals in an easy-to-use learning environment.

DISCUSSION QUESTIONS

1. Some consider the Federal Reserve Board to be more important than our elected leaders in affecting the economy. Do you think this is appropriate? What are the positives and negatives associated with such an independent organization having this much economic power?

2. Examine your state's current budgetary situation. Would you say the state budget picture is healthy? Why or why not? What are the largest budgetary issues affecting your state? How have these issues affected state programs?

3. Economic policy, as shown in this chapter, depends heavily on projections of future developments, for example, of economic growth and tax revenues. What questions would you ask about any such forecast to determine its reliability? Can these forecasts be used for political purposes? How so?

4. What issues should be taken into consideration when discussing the role of government in regulating aspects of our economy? Are the costs of regulations more important than the benefits they generate? Consider the different ethical and political perspectives that may enter into how one might answer this.

KEYWORDS

balance of trade   233
Consumer Price Index (CPI)   232
cost of living adjustment
   (COLA)   258
entitlement program   254

fiscal policy   236
full employment   230
line-item veto   246
monetary policy   237
national debt   234

progressive tax   242
regressive tax   242
supply-side economics   248
tax expenditures   241

MAJOR LEGISLATION

American Recovery and Reinvestment Act of 2009
Balanced Budget and Emergency Deficit Control Act
   of 1985 (Gramm-Rudman-Hollings)
Budget Enforcement Act of 1990

Congressional Budget and Impoundment Control Act
   of 1974
Economic Recovery Tax Act of 1981

SUGGESTED READINGS

Jeffrey H. Birnbaum and Alan S. Murray, *Showdown at Gucci Gulch: Lawmakers, Lobbyists, and the Unlikely Triumph of Tax Reform* (New York: Vintage, 1987). A journalistic account of the politics of tax reform and how interest groups try to get their most important goals enacted.

Scott Bittle and Jean Johnson, *Where Does the Money Go? Your Guided Tour to the Federal Budget Crisis*, rev. ed. (New York: HarperCollins, 2011).

Written by the editors of Public Agenda, this book is a very accessible discussion of the major issues associated with budgetary policy, with an emphasis on the issues brought about by the United States' current entitlement programs.

Marc Allen Eisner, Jeff Worsham, and Evan J. Ringquist, *Contemporary Regulatory Policy*, 2nd ed. (Boulder, Colo.: Rienner, 2007). One of the few books on regulatory policy, with a focus on the idea of regulatory change and why it occurs. Includes chapters on substantive regulatory policies, such as environmental protection, telecommunication, workplace safety, and consumer product safety.

James J. Gosling and **Marc Allen Eisner,** *Economics, Politics, and American Public Policy* (Armonk, N.Y.: Sharpe, 2013). The book discusses the interrelationship between politics and economics in the United States. It also discusses measures of the economic performance and why policymakers pursue certain policies to stabilize the economy.

John M. Rothgeb Jr., *U.S. Trade Policy: Balancing Economic Dreams and Political Realities* (Washington, D.C.: CQ Press, 2001). A concise text covering international trade, the political tensions related to it, and its historical roots.

Aaron Wildavsky and **Naomi Caiden,** *The New Politics of the Budgetary Process*, 5th ed. (New York: Longman, 2003). A classic in the field of budget politics and development. Promotes incrementalism as a way of government budget development.

SUGGESTED WEBSITES

www.cbo.gov. The Congressional Budget Office provides analysis of economic and budget issues. This site has a variety of data, projections, reports, and analyses on economic issues. This is also the place to get specific budget analysis publications on a range of government issues.

www.cbpp.org. The Center on Budget and Policy Priorities is a policy organization that examines how federal and state fiscal policies affect low- and moderate-income families.

www.epi.org. The Economic Policy Institute is a nonpartisan think tank that examines strategies to promote a fair and prosperous economy. The site contains reports relating to economic and budget

issues as well as other substantive policies and how they affect economic issues.

www.federalreserve.gov. The main website for the Federal Reserve Board provides a variety of information on monetary policy, how the Fed works, and how it uses its tools to affect the economy.

www.treasury.gov. The U.S. Department of the Treasury site provides general information on economic issues such as taxes, financial markets, and current events. Access the Bureau of the Fiscal Service site (www.fiscal.treasury.gov) to get information on the public debt, including what the debt is at a specific moment.

NOTES

1. See Pam Belluck, "Brain Scans of Brazilian Babies Show Array of Zika Effects," *New York Times,* August 23, 2016.

2. See Emmarie Huetteman, "Five Things to Know about Congress' Fight over Zika," *New York Times,* September 6, 2016.

3. Molly E. Reynolds, "What Emergency Zika Funding Tells Us about Congressional Dysfunction," Brookings Institution, May 18, 2016, available at www.brookings.edu/blog/fixgov/2016/05/18/what-emergency-zika-funding-tells-us-about-congressional-dysfunction/.

4. Ibid.

5. For a good and accessible discussion of these issues, see Scott Bittle and Jean Johnson, *Where Does the Money Go?* (New York: HarperCollins, 2008).

6. See U.S. Congressional Budget Office, "Budget and Economic Data: 10-Year Budget Projections," available at http://www.cbo.gov/about/products/budget_economic_data#3.

7. See U.S. Department of Labor, Bureau of Economic Analysis, "National Economic Accounts," 2016, available at www.bea.gov/national/index.htm#gdp.

8. See U.S. Department of Labor, Bureau of Labor Statistics, "Labor Force Statistics from the Current Population Survey," 2016, available at www.bls.gov/cps/tables.htm#annual.

9. Additional information can be found at Louis Uchitelle, "Economist's Survey Supports Theory That Inflation Is Overstated," *New York Times*, February 13, 1997.

10. To get information on the current federal debt and the interest on the public debt, see the following Department of the Treasury websites: www.treasurydirect.gov/NP/debt/current, for information on the public debt; www.treasurydirect.gov/govt/reports/ir/ir_expense.htm, for information on interest on the debt.

11. See U.S. Government Office of Management and Budget, Office of Information and Regulatory Affairs, "2016 Draft Report to Congress on the Benefits and Costs of Federal Regulations and Unfunded Mandates on State, Local, and Tribal Entities." https://obamawhitehouse.archives.gov/sites/default/files/omb/assets/legislative_reports/draft_2016_cost_benefit_report_12_14_2016_2.pdf. The report is no longer available online on the current White House webpage, but is currently accessible on the archived site above.

12. For more information, see Tad DeHaven, "Corporate Welfare in the Federal Budget," *Policy Analysis* 703 (July 25, 2012).

13. To see tax burdens for these and other countries, see Organisation for Economic Co-operation and Development, "Revenue Statistics—Provisional Data on Tax Ratios for 2015 Data," available at www.oecd.org/ctp/tax-policy/revenue-statistics-ratio-change-latest-years.htm.

14. There are many resources on the Internet regarding the budget process. If you want more detail, visit these websites for additional information: Anna Malinovskaya and Louise Sheiner, "The Hutchins Center Explains: Federal Budget Basics," Brookings Institution, June 1, 2016, available at www.brookings.edu/blog/up-front/2016/06/01/the-hutchins-center-explains-federal-budget-basics/;

James V. Saturno, "The Congressional Budget Process: A Brief Overview," Congressional Research Service, August 22, 2011, available at https://democrats-budget.house.gov/sites/democrats.budget.house.gov/files/documents/crs%20budget%20overview.pdf; and "Policy Basics: Introduction to the Federal Budget Process," Center on Budget and Policy Priorities, February 17, 2016, available at www.cbpp.org/cms/index.cfm?fa=view&id=155.

15. The Supreme Court case was *Clinton v. City of New York*. For a brief discussion of the line-item veto law, see www.congress.gov/bill/104th-congress/senate-bill/4.

16. For more information, see Jonathan Weisman, "Erosion of Estate Tax Is a Lesson in Politics," *Washington Post*, April 13, 2005.

17. See Jonathan Weisman, "The Tax-Cut Pendulum and the Pit," *New York Times*, October 8, 2004.

18. Although the spending cuts were split between defense and domestic spending, a large portion of the budget was considered off-limits in regard to sequestration. This part of the budget included most entitlement programs, such as Social Security, and interest payments on the debt (Thurber 1996b). The result was that sequestration had an even larger effect on those programs that could be sequestered.

19. See U.S. Congressional Budget Office, "CBO Testimony: Budgetary Discipline," 2002, available at www.cbo.gov/publication/13597.

20. For example, in fiscal year 1999, the total emergency appropriation was just over $34 billion—the largest since 1991, the year of Desert Storm. See U.S. Congressional Budget Office, "Emergency Spending under the Budget Enforcement Act: An Update," 1999, available at www.cbo.gov/publication/11589.

21. See Marcia Clemmitt, "Government Spending," *CQ Researcher* 23, no. 3 (July 12, 2013).

22. For more information, see Congressional Budget Office, "Estimated Impact of the American Recovery and Reinvestment Act on Employment

and Economic Output from October 2012 through December 2012," February 2013, available at www.cbo.gov/publication/43945.

23. See Gary Burtless, "Crisis No More: The Success of Obama's Stimulus Program," *Pathways* (summer 2010): 24–28.

24. For a larger and more accessible discussion of the issue of entitlements and their effect on the budget, see Scott Bittle and Jean Johnson, *Where Does the Money Go? Your Guided Tour to the Federal Budget Crisis* (New York: HarperCollins, 2008).

25. See Chad Stone, Danilo Trisi, Arloc Sherman, and William Chen, "A Guide to Statistics on Historical Trends in Income Inequality," Center on Budget and Policy Priorities, November 7, 2016, available at www.cbpp.org/cms/?fa=view&id=3629.

26. For perhaps a more comical perspective of this, see what comedian John Oliver has to say on this issue on his show at www.youtube.com/watch?v=LfgSEwjAeno.

27. You can try playing this game by going to fiscalship.org. Note that this website may not be available.

28. See FiscalCommission.gov for information about the commission, as well as a copy of its final report.

29. See Congressional Budget Office, "Choices for Deficit Reduction: An Update," December 20, 2013, available at www.cbo.gov/publication/44967.

30. See Congressional Budget Office, "The 2016 Long-term Budget Outlook," July 12, 2016, available at www.cbo.gov/publication/51580.

31. CBO, "Choices for Deficit Reduction."

32. For example, according to a national poll conducted by CBS News in July 2011, 66 percent of the respondents said they would want to see tax increases on the rich as part of a vote to raise the debt ceiling. See www.cbsnews.com/news/poll-most-americans-think-debt-deal-should-include-spending-cuts-and-tax-increases/.

Chapter 8

Chapter Objectives

- Understand the history and evolution of government involvement in health care.
- Explain major government health care programs.
- Identify important health care policy issues.
- Discuss concerns over and actions to address rising health care costs.
- Describe the role of managed care organizations.
- Explain measures that can be taken to reduce health care costs.
- Identify the role that quality of care plays in the health care system.
- Analyze selected issues in health care policy.

Promoting well-being. The United States spends twice as much per person on health care as does any other developed country yet, on average, gets worse results. A large portion of health care spending goes to treatment of preventable illnesses, so among the actions that could make a big difference is putting more money and effort into preventive health care and wellness activities. The photo shows Governor Andrew Cuomo of New York, center, signing legislation pertaining to breast cancer screenings while participating in a breast cancer awareness motorcycle ride in New York, June 27, 2016. *(AP Photo/Seth Wenig)*

Health Care Policy

U.S. spending on health care has been of great concern in recent years, and regularly is at the center of political debate. Yet from 2008 through 2013, health care spending grew by less than 4 percent annually, one of the lowest rates in more than fifty years, and well down from the annual average of more than 7 percent that prevailed from 2000 through 2008 and even higher rates of increase during the 1990s. In 2014, the rate increased somewhat from these levels, rising to 5.3 percent, following a 2.9 percent rise in 2013; and in 2015, the rate was slightly higher again, at 5.8 percent. The higher spending in 2014 and 2015 can be traced largely to expanded coverage for nearly twenty million people under the Affordable Care Act, and especially to enrollment of more people in the federal Medicaid program, and also to the continued increase in the cost of prescription drugs.

Even so, the broader picture is still a relatively low rate of growth in health care spending since 2008. The reasons include reduced growth in Medicare and Medicaid expenditures during that period and lingering effects of the economic recession of the late 2000s, which meant lower levels of employment and health insurance coverage and reduced demand for health care services such as physical examinations, emergency room treatment, and purchase of prescription drugs. So the news was not entirely good if lower expenditures reflected reduced access to health care, a trend that few would cheer.

The Centers for Medicare and Medicaid Services (CMS) reported that even with this reduced rate of increasing expenditures, overall spending on health care rose to a record high of $3.2 trillion in 2015, or nearly 18 percent of the nation's gross domestic product (GDP). The United States spent $9,990 per person for health care in 2015, a figure certain to grow substantially over the next decade. Indeed, the CMS projects that per capita spending on health care by 2025 will be an astonishing $16,032 and that overall health care spending will rise to $5.6 trillion, or nearly 20.1 percent of GDP. Given these costs, and the continuing challenge of ensuring broad access to vital health care services, it is no wonder that President Barack Obama spent so much of his first year in office championing his proposed policy changes that eventually became the Patient Protection and Affordable Care Act of 2010, also known as Obamacare. It is equally unsurprising that the president's detractors saw the new act as yet another costly expansion of governmental authority they believed was unjustified.[1]

It is likely, however, that the high cost of health care in the United States will remain a difficult challenge for the president and Congress regardless of which party is in control. This is particularly so as the nation's population ages, driving up health care costs, and it continues to struggle with federal deficits and a large national debt. Thus it needs to find ways to reduce overall federal spending and/ or adjust taxes to increase revenue.

Simply spending more money on health care, of course, is not necessarily the best way to deal with the nation's health care problems. The United States already spends twice as much per person on health care as most other industrialized nations, and achieves less for it. As the chief executive of the Mayo Clinic has stated: "We're not getting what we pay for. It's just that simple." Another health care expert put it this way: "Our health care system is fraught with waste," with as much as half of the money spent today doing nothing to improve health. The implication is that whether the money is spent through governmental programs or entirely in the private sector, fundamental changes are needed in the way the nation handles health and disease—that is, in the way we choose to structure and operate the health care system. As just one example, if more spending were shifted to preventive health care and wellness activities, the outcomes could be far better. This is because about 75 percent of health care costs go to treatment of preventable chronic illnesses, such as diabetes and heart disease.[2] Would you favor such a change in spending priorities that put more emphasis on wellness and disease prevention? Are there any reasons not to make such a seemingly sensible change? This chapter should help in answering such questions.

The long-recognized gap between health care spending and results remains as striking today as when it was first noticed. In a 2015 report, for example, the Commonwealth Fund found that the United States ranks poorly in terms of health care cost, access, and affordability compared to twelve other industrialized countries based on a series of measures of health system performance. The fund's president put it this way: "Time and again, we see evidence that the amount of money we spend on health care in this country is not gaining us comparable health benefits."[3] Many similar comparisons have come to the same conclusions. One reason for these findings is that prior to the Affordable Care Act, some eighty-four million people in the United States either lacked health insurance or were underinsured, and therefore have had limited access to health care services. Another is that the quality of health care people receive and what they pay for it depend on where they live and personal characteristics such as race, income, and education.[4]

What, if anything, should the nation do to correct such an important inequity? And who should pay for the added cost of doing so?

The combination of the high cost of and unequal access to quality health care has long been a major concern in public policy. In 2015, the average health insurance premium for a family of four under employer-provided health plans reached $17,322. Increasingly, workers also are forced to pay a higher percentage of these costs and to cope with higher deductibles and co-payments.[5] It is little wonder, then, that reform of health care policy has regularly appeared at the top of issues that voters consider important.

Most people rely on employer-provided health care insurance, for which they pay a portion of the cost, or on government programs to meet essential health care needs. Federal and state health care policies also affect the uninsured and those who pay for their own insurance. Government policies influence not only access to and quality of health services across the country, but also the pace of development and approval of new drugs and medical technologies and the extent of health research that could lead to new lifesaving treatments. Whether the concern is periodic medical examinations, screening for major diseases, or coping with life-threatening illnesses, health care policy decisions eventually affect everyone.

This chapter examines some of the problems associated with health care services and the public policies designed to ensure that citizens have access to them at a reasonable cost. The two major political parties disagree, often intensely, over the proper degree of government involvement and how much should be left to the private sector—to individuals, physicians, hospitals and clinics, insurance companies, and pharmaceutical houses. In addition, among the major controversies in health care are how best to deal with escalating costs, how to ensure sufficient access to health care services, and how to maintain the quality of health care services while containing costs. The chapter begins with background information about the evolution of major public policies, such as Medicare, Medicaid, and the veterans' health care system, and then turns to some of the leading policy disputes, including the rising costs of health care, the role of managed care, the regulation of prescription drugs, and the potential of preventive health care and other strategies to keep people healthy and save money. In this chapter, we give particular attention to the effectiveness of current public policies, and we use the criteria of economic efficiency and equity to examine these disputes and recommendations for improving health care policy.

Background

Health care policy includes all of the actions that governments take to influence the provision of health care services and the various government activities that affect or attempt to affect public health and well-being. Health care policy can be viewed narrowly to mean the design and implementation of the range of federal and state programs that affect the provision of health care services, such as Medicare and Medicaid. It also can be defined more broadly and more meaningfully by recognizing that government engages in many other activities that influence both public and private health care decision making. For example, the government funds health science research and public health departments and agencies; subsidizes medical education and hospital construction; regulates food, drugs, and medical devices; regulates health-damaging environmental pollution; and allows tax deductions for some health care expenditures (which makes them more affordable). The box "Working with Sources: Health Care Policy Information" lists some useful websites to begin a policy investigation.

As a government activity, health care policymaking is relatively recent, even though governments at every level long ago established what we call **public health agencies** to counter the threat of infectious diseases or unsafe food and to support medical research. The work of these agencies should be clearly differentiated from what we recognize today as health care policymaking, which involves how we as a society decide to deal with concerns such as access to health insurance and the provision and cost of health care services. These agencies dealt with such seemingly mundane but critical functions as providing safe drinking water supplies, sanitation, and waste removal. Many of the oldest of these public health agencies continue such work today, largely without much public notice. These include the Food and Drug Administration (FDA), the National Institutes of Health (NIH), and the Centers for Disease Control and Prevention (CDC).

Since 1862, when it employed a single chemist and was housed in the U.S. Department of Agriculture (USDA), the FDA has overseen the development of new drugs and medical devices as well as the nation's food supply (other than meat and poultry, which the USDA regulates). The modern FDA dates from 1906, when it was authorized by the Federal Food and Drugs Act and regulatory functions were added to the agency's scientific mission. The agency is now part of the Department of Health and Human Services (HHS). In addition to food and drugs, the agency is responsible for regulating biologics (vaccines and blood products); the labeling and safety of cosmetics once they come to market; medical devices, including contact lenses; and radiation in consumer products such as microwave ovens and cell phones. Later in the chapter we offer a "Steps to Analysis" exercise on how the FDA regulates the approval of new drugs.

The federal government also has been actively engaged in health science research for years. Generous budgets allowed the government to expand its research into the causes of various diseases and possible treatments. The NIH, the primary vehicle for federal health science research, was founded in 1887 and consists of twenty-seven separate institutes and centers. The NIH is one of eight health agencies of the U.S. Public Health Service, itself a component of HHS. The NIH supports health research across the nation at colleges and universities, at medical research centers, and on the NIH main campus in Bethesda, Maryland. The federal CDC has been part of the Public Health Service of HHS since 1973. The CDC was established in 1946 as the Communicable Disease Center. It focuses on the development and application of disease prevention and control, environmental health, and health promotion and education. The CDC has long been involved in programs dealing with immunization, the prevention and control of

AIDS and other infectious diseases, chronic disease prevention, birth defects and developmental disabilities, occupational safety and health, and the compilation of a treasure trove of national health statistics.

As the work of these three agencies shows, the federal government has been active in public health, if not the actual provision of health care services, for a very long time. The same is true of state and local governments. Government involvement in funding or provision of direct health care services, on the other hand, is relatively recent.

Working with Sources

Health Care Policy Information

As is the case with other public policy issues, there are hundreds of websites providing information on health care policy. The easiest way to learn about what information is available and its reliability is to visit one or more of the leading sites listed below and at the end of the chapter. Select one of the sites and try to find information about a major health care issue such as the ones highlighted below.

- How easily can you locate the information?

- Is coverage of the issue adequate or too limited to tell you what you need to know?

- Is the information provided at the site objective or biased in some way?

www.ahip.org. America's Health Insurance Plans, a leading industry trade association, has broad and excellent coverage of and links to the full range of health care policy issues. Select the link to Issues, and then Medicaid, where you can find the industry's views on the federal program, how well it works, and various suggestions for reform of it.

www.citizen.org/hrg. Public Citizen's Health Research Group site, with extensive links to policy issues and citizen activism. Select a topic such as drugs, devices, and supplements; health care delivery; or physician accountability.

www.cms.gov. The site for the federal Centers for Medicare and Medicaid Services, with links covering Medicare; Medicaid/CHIP; Medicare-Medicaid coordination; private insurance; the CMS Innovation Center; regulations and guidance; research, statistics, data, and systems; and outreach and education.

www.healthcare.gov. The leading federal government site for general information about health care and the Affordable Care Act, including topics such as enrolling in health insurance, saving money, and taxes, penalties, and exemptions.

www.kff.org. Kaiser Family Foundation, one of the premier online resources for coverage of health policy news and debate. Under Topics, select Health Reform, Medicare, Medicaid, Health Costs, Uninsured, Women's Health Policy, or Global Health Policy, among other subjects.

https://nam.edu/. The National Academy of Medicine, formerly the Institute of Medicine, a major source for reliable health care studies. Includes links to related sites for health care studies and reports. Find reports by the different categories on the main page, such as Programs, Initiatives, and Perspectives. Under the last, for example, you can find studies on obesity prevention, health inequities, and use of real-world evidence to guide new health treatments.

www.nytimes.com/section/health. The *New York Times* health news page. Select a specific news report.

www.policyalmanac.org/health/index.shtml. The *Almanac of Policy Issues* health care page, with many useful links to news, organizations, government agencies, health care statistics, and a range of health policy issues. Select a topic listed under the directory, such as abortion, health insurance, privacy, or medical professions.

Evolution of Health Care Policy

What we consider the core of health care policy developed in the United States only after the 1930s, with the idea of health insurance. Individuals could take out an insurance policy, much as they did for their lives, houses, or cars, that would defray the cost of health care should an illness develop or an injury occur. Most of those early policies covered only catastrophic losses. Health insurance works much the same way now, although instead of individual policies, most people are insured through their jobs, and the insurance policies cover routine medical services as well as preventive health care. Employer-sponsored health insurance became popular in the 1950s after the Internal Revenue Service ruled that its cost was a tax-deductible business expense. By the early 1960s, the push was on for federal health insurance policies, primarily to aid the poor and the elderly, two segments of the population that normally would not benefit from employer-provided health plans. It is clear that equity concerns in access to health care services were important as health care policy developed. Those efforts culminated in the enactment of the Social Security Act Amendments of 1965 that formally created the Medicare and Medicaid programs (Marmor 2000). These policies are discussed in detail later in the chapter.

Even with adoption of these two programs, the U.S. health care system remains distinctive in comparison to other industrialized nations, where **national health insurance**, also known as **single-payer insurance** (the government pays), is the norm; the Medicare program is one example of this in the United States. Campaigns to adopt national health insurance in the United States date back to 1948, when the Democratic Party platform endorsed the idea. Members of Congress began to introduce bills to create such a program, but they were unsuccessful until the decision in 1965 to establish insurance programs for the poor and the elderly through Medicaid and Medicare, respectively.

In 1993, President Bill Clinton submitted the Health Security Act to Congress after extensive analysis by a presidential health care task force headed by his wife, Hillary Rodham Clinton. The plan would have guaranteed health insurance to every American, including the thirty-four million who were uninsured at the time. It proposed doing so through a system of health care alliances that would function much like current managed care organizations. The plan called for individuals to pay about $1,800 a year for coverage, and families about $4,200; both amounts were less than private insurance rates at the time for most of the population. Most employers would have been required to cover their employees under the plan (a so-called employer mandate), with subsidies for small businesses that otherwise could not afford to pay.

Republicans in Congress criticized the Clinton plan as too expensive, bureaucratic, and intrusive, and the health insurance industry opposed it as well, and lobbied intensely against it. In the end, the Clinton recommendations failed to win congressional approval, as did the many alternatives members of Congress proposed (Hacker 1997; Patel and Rushefsky 2015).

With the election of Barack Obama and gains in Democratic seats in the House and Senate in the 2008 elections, national health care policy reform once again was in the spotlight, although with competing proposals that reflected deep differences between the two parties. President Obama had offered detailed proposals on his preferred approach to health care reform during the 2008 campaign, which he modified in 2009 in the face of Republican opposition and objections by the health insurance and pharmaceutical industries. In particular, the president abandoned what had been strong Democratic preference for a so-called public option, where the federal government would compete with private insurance companies in offering health care insurance. In 2009 and early 2010, Congress considered and eventually approved sweeping health care reforms, although on strict party-line votes. No Republican in either the Senate or the House voted for what became the Patient Protection and Affordable Care Act of 2010, and party members since then have vowed to repeal the act and replace it with an alternative policy.[6]

The **Affordable Care Act** is a highly complex and multifaceted policy in addition to being politically controversial. In recent years, most Republicans continued to call for its repeal, although with few concrete proposals for how they would replace it. Following their 2016 election success, both President Donald Trump and congressional Republicans vowed again to repeal the act, although also acknowledging that doing so might take several years. In an intriguing 2015 analysis, the Congressional Budget Office concluded that repealing the law would cost more than keeping it. Eliminating it entirely would add $137 billion to the federal deficit over the next decade.[7]

The 1,200-page law affects virtually every component of the U.S. health care system, and it survived a major legal challenge when the Supreme Court in 2012 upheld its constitutionality in a close vote.[8] Its major purpose was to increase health insurance coverage and access to health care services, and it does so through a number of key actions: (1) expanding Medicaid and the Children's Health Insurance Program (CHIP) and making eligibility and benefits more uniform across the states (although the Court allowed for states to opt out of the Medicaid expansion part of the law); (2) mandating that individuals who are not covered through their employers or by public programs purchase a minimal level of health insurance, with tiered plans that must offer standard packages of benefits, or pay a penalty for failing to do so; (3) subsidizing the costs of such insurance for low- to moderate-income families; (4) offering tax credits to encourage small businesses to provide health insurance to their employees and instituting a penalty for larger employers (with fifty or more employees) who do not offer health insurance benefits; and (5) creating new regulations for health insurers to deal with several long-standing concerns, such as prohibiting insurers from excluding children and eventually all individuals with preexisting medical conditions, preventing them from setting annual and lifetime limits on coverage, and requiring them to cover family members (such as college students) up to age twenty-six. Other provisions in the act set new limits on allowable administrative costs to encourage insurers to improve efficiencies in billing and health care management. The various components of the act were to take effect over a seven-year period between 2011 and 2018. A summary of them and how they apply to individuals can be found on the federal government's webpage (www.healthcare.gov), where the full text of the act is posted.[9]

Major Features of the Affordable Care Act

- Mandates that individuals not covered through their employers or by public programs purchase a minimal level of health insurance through state health insurance marketplaces

- Subsidizes the costs of health insurance for low- to moderate-income families

- Offers tax credits for small businesses to provide health insurance to their employees

- Removes annual and lifetime limits or caps on health insurance coverage

- Requires insurers to cover family members (such as college students) up to age twenty-six

- Expands Medicaid and the Children's Health Insurance Program

- Mandates free preventive services for those on Medicare and offers seniors savings on prescription drugs

- Creates accountable care organizations to help doctors and health care providers cooperate to deliver better care at lower cost

- Prohibits insurers from refusing coverage or charging higher rates due to gender or preexisting medical conditions

- Mandates that at least 80 to 85 percent of insurance premium dollars (depending on the plan) be spent on health care to reduce administrative costs

- Creates a new Patient's Bill of Rights to protect consumers from insurance industry abuses

- Establishes a new Center for Medicare & Medicaid Innovation to study improved ways to care for patients

Source: U.S. Department of Health and Human Services, "Key Features of the Affordable Care Act by Year," at www.hhs.gov/healthcare/facts-and-features/key-features-of-aca-by-year/index.html.

Among the act's more intriguing and promising elements are requirements to study ways to improve the efficiency of health care service delivery and to reduce costs. A new CMS Innovation Center is to oversee such studies and to devise ways to reward health care providers for improved quality and gains in efficiency. Similarly, a new independent federal advisory board is to identify cost savings in the Medicare program, and the new Patient-Centered Outcomes Research Institute is to conduct research on the comparative effectiveness of health care services—that is, to determine which procedures and drugs work best and at the least cost, a widely endorsed but still controversial proposal.[10] Other provisions in the act seek ways to reduce costly medical errors and hospital-acquired infections by rewarding hospitals with better patient outcomes, and to promote the use of disease management programs and preventive health care. Despite the partisan rancor over the bill, the two parties were largely in agreement on the need to increase emphasis on preventive health care through both governmental and private insurance programs.[11]

The costs of the Affordable Care Act are sizeable, and yet they are expected to be offset in part by a variety of new revenues, including a 0.9 percent increase in the Medicare payroll tax for high earners (household income of greater than $250,000 a year) and a new 3.8 percent tax on so-called passive income such as dividends and capital gains that took effect in 2013, also only for high-earning households. The act's critics, however, argue that net costs nonetheless are likely to rise because they believe that Congress may not agree to all of the new taxes and fees or make the expected reductions in some health care spending, and that younger people in particular might not sign up for insurance plans in sufficient numbers to balance older and less healthy segments of the population. In 2016, many critics also anticipated that prices some will pay for insurance coverage might well increase substantially, at least in the short term. The longer-term impacts are less clear, particularly in comparison to what might prevail without the act.[12]

As noted in chapter 6, implementation of the new act did not go as smoothly as the government had hoped. In addition, it soon became clear that each state would choose whether or not to offer a state insurance exchange or to defer to the federal government. Many states controlled by Republican legislators and governors chose not to offer their own exchanges as one expression of their dislike of the federal program.[13] In addition, following the Supreme Court's 2012 decision, many states chose not to expand Medicaid services under the Affordable Care Act even though the federal government was covering nearly all of the costs of doing so. These choices will affect the law's implementation, its success in persuading large numbers of people to sign up for insurance, and the anticipated cost savings.

Many of the uncertainties over how well the new provisions of the act will work, what they will cost, and how they will be paid for may well be reduced over the next several years as some of the remaining conflicts over the act's provisions are resolved and more individuals sign up for insurance plans under the law. In 2016, the Obama administration reported that enrollment in the new plans had exceeded expectations, with about 12.7 million in the marketplace itself, and about 20 million people total, if counting the Affordable Care Act marketplace, Medicaid expansion, young adults who stayed on their parents' plan, and coverage under other provisions of the act. The percentage of nonelderly Americans without health care insurance dropped from about 15.7 percent of the population (48.6 million people) to 9.2 percent (28.5 million), although young and healthy people more than others have resisted signing up for insurance under the act, thus jeopardizing the program's overall financial solvency.[14]

Continuing conflict over the law in Congress and the states tells us that we can expect persistent and sometimes intense disagreements between the two parties over what role the federal and state governments should play in health care insurance and the delivery of health services to the public. There also is no shortage of recommendations for how to improve the Affordable Care Act, and as noted earlier, major changes are likely in the Trump administration. Yet surveys conducted just after the 2016 elections, much as those taken before, showed that a large majority of Americans support the policy's major provisions, such as allowing children up to age twenty-six to stay on their parents' health plans, having the federal government help states to expand their Medicaid programs to cover a larger number of those in poverty, providing subsidies to low- and moderate-income people who use the government exchanges, and prohibiting insurers from denying coverage to those with preexisting medical conditions.[15]

A Hybrid System of Public and Private Health Care

Another way to consider the history of health care in the United States and the nation's present health care system is to emphasize that it relies largely on the private market and individual choice to reach health care goals, as we indicated in the chapter's opening paragraphs. Even following enactment of the Affordable Care Act, the U.S. government plays a smaller role in health care than, for example, the governments of Great Britain or Canada, nations that have national health insurance programs that provide comprehensive health services. Their systems have been criticized for delays in providing health services for some patients as well as the quality of care, although these weaknesses appear to be less important today than previously, and most citizens in these and other developed nations appear to be well served by such health care systems.[16]

In contrast to such government-run systems, most health care services in the United States are provided by doctors and other medical staff who work in clinics and hospitals that are privately run, even if some are not-for-profit operations. Indeed, the United States has long had the smallest amount of public insurance or provision of public health services of any developed nation in the world (Patel and Rushefsky 2015). The result is a health care system that is something of a hybrid. It is neither completely private nor fully public. It does, however, reflect the unique political culture of the nation, as first discussed in chapter 1. Americans place great emphasis on individual rights, limited government authority, and a relatively unrestrained market system. Those who favor a larger government role to reduce the current inequities in access to health care services are in effect suggesting that health care should be considered a so-called **merit good** to which people are entitled. In short, they tend to believe that normal market forces should not be the determining factor in the way society allocates such a good.

The majority of nonelderly U.S. adults have employer-sponsored, private health insurance, and others purchase similar insurance through individual policies. Those over age sixty-five are covered through Medicare, discussed later in the chapter. But with rising costs and a slow-growing economy, employer coverage is likely to be less widely available in the future. About 56 percent of employers offered health benefits to at least some of their employees in 2016; the rate was higher for companies with unionized employees and higher for larger firms.[17] The annual premium for covered workers in 2016 averaged $6,435 for single coverage and $18,142 for family coverage—an increase of about 3 percent over premiums in 2015. Family premiums have increased some 58 percent since 2006, and 20 percent since 2011. Employees with health insurance, on average, pay 18 percent of the insurance cost for single coverage and 30 percent for family coverage.[18] These premiums have been rising for the past several years, leading employers to cut back on some benefits and to shift more of the cost to employees. That trend will likely continue.

Employer and other private health insurance policies generally cover a substantial portion of health care costs, but not all. Some services, such as elective cosmetic surgery, generally are not covered, and only partial payment may apply to others. The federal government can specify particular services that must be included in private insurance plans, but there are major gaps in coverage, such as assistance with expensive prescription drugs and provision of long-term care in nursing homes and similar facilities that may follow a disabling injury or illness, or simple aging. People are living longer, and the demand for these services is expected to rise dramatically in the future as the U.S. population ages. Most policies historically also have had a lifetime cap on covered expenses that could be exceeded in the event of serious medical conditions, but the Affordable Care Act eliminated such caps.

The Perils of Being Uninsured

The number of individuals and families without any insurance coverage rose significantly between 1990 and 2010, and this was a major driver in congressional approval of the Affordable Care Act. In 2016, about thirty million individuals had no health insurance, a significant decline since adoption of the ACA in 2010. The percentage of people without health insurance, about 10 percent in 2016, is not uniform around the nation but instead varies widely from state to state. In some states (e.g., Georgia, Florida, and Texas), more than 15 percent of the nonelderly population was uninsured in recent years, but in several states (Connecticut, Vermont, Hawaii, and Massachusetts), the rate was less than 7 percent.[19]

As the cost of medical care continues to grow, what happens to the uninsured? The consequences for them can be devastating—a higher lifelong risk of serious medical problems and premature death. A widely cited review of the health consequences for uninsured, working-age Americans conducted by the National Academy of Medicine (NAM, previously the Institute of Medicine) in 2002 found that they are more likely than the insured to receive too little medical care, to receive it too late, to be sick, and to die prematurely. Indeed, they are 25 percent more likely to die than those with insurance coverage. That difference translates into an estimated eighteen thousand deaths per year that can be attributed to being uninsured. These estimates may even be too low. An Urban Institute study that sought in 2008 to update the NAM report put the number at twenty-seven thousand preventable deaths in the United States each year attributable to being uninsured.[20] Studies like these on the consequences of being uninsured played a role in consideration and enactment of the Affordable Care Act.

The uninsured also are more likely than the insured to receive less adequate care when they are in a hospital, even for acute care, such as injuries from an automobile accident. They are more likely to go without cancer screening tests, such as mammograms, clinical breast exams, Pap tests, and colorectal screenings, and therefore suffer from delayed diagnosis and treatment. That finding helps to explain why uninsured women with breast cancer have a 30 to 50 percent higher risk of dying than women with private health insurance (National Academy of Medicine 2002).

Prescription for health care.
Michelle Loose, a University of Denver accelerated nursing student, checks the blood pressure for patient Elife Bzuneh, during a medical clinic night at the DAWN clinic on August 9, 2016, in Aurora, Colorado. DAWN is a student-run clinic established to serve uninsured patients in Aurora at no cost. It opened in March 2015. The Patient Protection and Affordable Care Act of 2010, or Obamacare, was designed to improve access to health care for those without medical insurance, among other goals. *(Anya Semenoff/The Denver Post via Getty Images)*

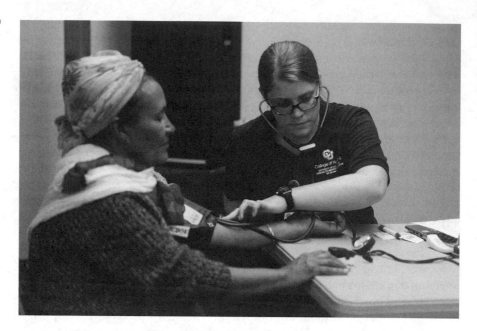

In addition, the uninsured tend not to receive the care recommended for chronic diseases such as diabetes, HIV infection, end-stage renal (kidney) disease, mental illness, and high blood pressure, and they have worse clinical outcomes than patients with insurance. "The fact is that the quality and length of life are distinctly different for insured and uninsured populations," the NAM report said. It added that if this group obtained coverage, the health and longevity of working-age Americans would improve (National Academy of Medicine 2002).

At least some policymakers are aware of some of these risks and the inequities they present to the U.S. public. As the failure of the Clinton health policy initiative in the 1990s and continuing controversy over the Affordable Care Act show, however, reaching agreement on extending insurance coverage to the entire population is not an easy task. The debate is likely to continue for years, and the rising costs of health care may force reconsideration of current policies that leave so many citizens without health care insurance.

Strengths and Weaknesses of the U.S. Health Care System

No one seriously doubts that the United States has one of the finest health care systems in the world by any of the conventionally used indicators, such as the number of physicians per capita, the number of state-of-the-art hospitals and clinics, or the number of health care specialists and their expertise. The United States also has a large percentage of the world's major pharmaceutical research centers and biotechnology companies, which increases the availability of cutting-edge medical treatments.

Despite these many strengths, however, patients and physicians alike frequently complain about the U.S. health care system. As noted at the beginning of the chapter, the United States is ranked well below the level of other developed nations despite spending far more than other nations on health care per person.[21] Such findings reflect the highly unequal access of the population to critical health care services, from prenatal care to preventive screening for chronic illnesses. The poor, the elderly, minorities, and those living in rural areas generally receive less frequent and less adequate medical care than white, middle-class residents of urban and suburban areas. Because of such disparities, among others, the fifty states vary widely in the health of their populations, with Massachusetts, New Hampshire, and Vermont at the top in recent rankings and Arkansas, Mississippi, and Louisiana at the bottom.[22]

As discussed earlier, comparisons of U.S. health care costs to those in other nations force the question of what U.S. citizens are getting for their money. Just how effective are current programs, and are health care dollars being well spent? How might the programs be modified to improve their effectiveness and efficiency and to ensure that there is equitable access to health care services? Plenty of controversy surrounds each of these questions, and they remain at the center of policymakers' concerns about the future of the U.S. health care system. The websites listed on page 275 in the box "Working with Sources: Health Care Policy Information" cover health care developments and policies and offer a wealth of information on these issues.

A Pluralistic Health Care System

Before we turn to a description and assessment of specific U.S. health care programs, we start with an overview of the health care system itself. The individual health care programs are complicated enough to confuse even the experts, but they do not represent the totality of government activities that affect the health and welfare of the U.S. public. A broad view of health care policy suggests that many other actions should be included as well. Table 8-1 lists the collection of agencies and policies at the federal, state, and local levels.

The table indicates the diversity of departments and agencies that are involved in health-related services, broadly defined, and shows that authority is highly diffused rather than concentrated and is shared among all levels of government. As we saw in the implementation of the Affordable Care Act, states have a great deal of discretion in what they choose to do under the act, as they have long had with state Medicaid programs. Moreover, as noted earlier in discussion of the hybrid U.S. health care system, health services are delivered through both the private sector and public programs. The programs most frequently in the public eye, such as Medicare and Medicaid, are only part of what governments do to promote the public's health. To put this in other terms, solutions to U.S. health problems are not to be found solely in either expanding or modifying the established Medicare, Medicaid, and veterans' health care programs. Other actions also are possible, including those that

TABLE 8-1   Major Government Health-Related Programs

Level of Government	Agency and Function
Federal	Department of Agriculture 　Food safety inspection (meat and poultry) 　Food stamp and child nutrition programs 　Consumer education Department of Health and Human Services Food and Drug Administration Agency for Healthcare Research and Quality Centers for Medicare and Medicaid Services Health Resources and Services Administration (health resources for 　underserved populations) Indian Health Service Substance abuse programs Health education Public Health Service (including the surgeon general's office, the National Institutes of Health, and the Centers for Disease Control and Prevention) Department of Labor 　Occupational Safety and Health Administration (regulation of 　　workplace safety and health) Department of Veterans Affairs 　Veterans Health Administration (VA hospitals and programs) Environmental Protection Agency (regulation of clean air and water, drinking water, pesticides, and toxic chemicals)
State	Medicaid and Children's Health Insurance Program (CHIP) State hospitals State mental hospitals Support of state medical schools State departments of health Health education State departments of agriculture and consumer protection State environmental protection programs
Local	City and county hospitals and clinics Public health departments and sanitation Emergency services City and county health and human services programs

rely on preventive health care. These include personal decisions related to diet and exercise, detection of disease at its earliest stages, health education, medical research, environmental protection, and a host of public and private programs to improve mental and physical health. We will return to a discussion of such preventive health care below.

Major Government Health Care Programs

The following sections describe the major federal and state programs that deal directly with health care services. In addition to the programs' goals and provisions, the discussion tries to evaluate them in terms of the major public policy criteria we set out earlier in the text: effectiveness, efficiency, and equity.

Medicare

The federal **Medicare** program began in 1965, following authorization by that year's amendments to the Social Security Act of 1935. It was intended to help senior citizens, defined as those age sixty-five and older, to meet basic health care needs. It now includes people under age sixty-five with permanent disabilities and those with diabetes or end-stage renal disease—for example, patients who need dialysis treatment or a kidney transplant. Medicare had over fifty-five million beneficiaries in 2016, a number certain to rise appreciably over the next two decades as the rest of the baby boom generation—those born between 1946 and 1964—reaches age sixty-five. In 2016, the three major entitlement programs—Social Security, Medicare, and Medicaid (including CHIP)—already accounted for about 48 percent of federal spending.[23]

Medicare Program Provisions. The Medicare program has two main parts, one standard and the other optional. Medicare Part A is the core plan, which pays partially for hospital charges, with individuals responsible for a deductible and co-payments that can be substantial. The program is paid for by Medicare trust funds, which most employees pay through a payroll deduction, much like the Social Security tax, which employers match. Part A also covers up to one hundred days in a nursing care facility following release from the hospital, but again with co-payments. Part A of Medicare covers people who are eligible for the federal Social Security system or Railroad Retirement benefits.

The optional part of the Medicare program, Part B, is supplemental insurance for coverage of health care expenses other than hospital stays. These include physician charges, diagnostic tests, and hospital outpatient services. The cost of Part B insurance is shared by individuals who choose to enroll in it (in 2016 they paid $121.80 per month, or more for those with higher incomes) and by the government, which covers about three-fourths of the cost from general federal revenues. Part B also has both deductibles and co-payments, and historically it did not cover routine physical examinations by a physician, but it now covers a yearly "wellness" visit that is designed to help prevent disease and maintain good health, and a variety of other preventive health services such as cardiovascular, cancer, and diabetes screenings. Many of these services were mandated by Congress under the Balanced Budget Act of 1997, and further changes have come with the Affordable Care Act.

Medicare uses a fee schedule of "reasonable" costs that specifies what physicians, hospitals, nursing homes, and home services should charge for a given procedure, and the government pays 80 percent of that amount. Some physicians choose not to participate in the Medicare system because they believe the fee schedule is too low and their options for raising patient fees are unrealistic.

Equally important is the fact that the regular Medicare program does not cover many other medical expenses, including prescription drugs used outside of the hospital, dental care, and eyeglasses. It also pays for only the first ninety days of a hospital stay and limited nursing home care. Because of these restrictions and the deductibles and co-payment charges, Medicare historically has covered only about two-thirds of the health care costs for the elderly. Individuals must therefore pay for the rest of the costs or purchase supplementary private insurance policies to cover the gaps in Medicare. Low-income elderly also may be eligible for state Medicaid programs, which cover some of these costs. Despite the many restrictions, Medicare is a bargain for the elderly, who would have to pay much higher fees for a full private insurance policy, considering the chronic and serious health problems they are likely to face.

As we discussed earlier, the costs of health care in general, including Medicare, continue to rise, and this trend poses major challenges to the solvency of the Medicare trust fund as the population ages and the ranks of Medicare recipients swell. With the enactment of the Medicare prescription drug benefit program in 2003, a previous Medicare + Choice program was replaced with Medicare Advantage (Part C), which consists of managed care programs that are run by private health insurance companies. In 2016, about 28 percent of those on Medicare signed up for a Medicare Advantage plan, with the rest choosing to remain with a traditional fee-for-service Medicare plan (Part B). Medicare Part D took effect on January 1, 2006. Approved by Congress in late 2003 in response to the rapid rise in drug prices, particularly for senior citizens, the Medicare Prescription Drug, Improvement, and Modernization Act of 2003 has several key elements. It is intended to provide discounts for routine prescription drugs and also to protect those who enroll against the extremely high costs that come with a serious illness. Prescription drug benefits depend on the plan that is selected.[24]

Fraud and Abuse under Medicare. A perennial problem in all government health care programs is fraud and abuse, especially notable under Medicare. Indeed, the Government Accountability Office (GAO) has declared both Medicare and Medicaid as "high risk" programs that are "particularly vulnerable to fraud, waste, abuse, and improper payments."[25] Less-than-scrupulous health care providers may charge the government for services that were not performed or order tests and procedures that may not be necessary but for which the health care provider knows Medicare will pay. The CMS has no official estimate of fraud, but the GAO has indicated that up to $60 billion a year, or about 10 percent of Medicare's budget, may be lost to a combination of fraud, waste, abuse, and improper payments.

Such improper payments have a long history. In a 1998 HHS investigation into abuses by community mental health centers, Donna Shalala, then secretary of the department, noted there was "extensive evidence of providers who are not qualified, patients who are not eligible, and services billed to Medicare that are not appropriate," including services "that weren't covered, weren't provided, or weren't needed."[26] More recent assessments of Medicare spending echo those concerns. The program continues to be deficient in its monitoring and enforcement of quality standards and in its oversight of spending even though it spends over $1 billion annually to combat fraud, waste, and abuse. Health care centers say that at least part of the problem lies in the government's complex billing procedures that contribute to errors. Federal agents who investigate Medicare fraud are not persuaded by such arguments. They charge that health care providers intentionally put services into a higher-paying category, or "up code" their billing, and engage in other illegal practices to increase profits. In addition, researchers at Dartmouth's medical school have estimated that as much as $1 of every $3 in the program is wasted by spending on inappropriate or unnecessary care; others have put the figure even higher.[27] Much of this kind of waste is the result not of fraudulent billing or similar abuse, but rather of the pattern of Medicare paying for procedures that provide little or no clear benefit to patients.[28]

Medicare's Future. Given the projections of an aging population, the cost of the Medicare program represents one of the most important issues in health care policy. It is a subject of regular debate in Congress, and some members, notably Speaker of the House Paul Ryan, R-Wis., have proposed dramatic changes, such as converting Medicare from a government-run insurance program to one where program participants are issued vouchers to purchase private health insurance on the open market. After the 2016 elections, many Republicans in Congress continued to press for such a major policy change. Aside from the prescription drug plan approved in 2003, there has been little agreement on how to modify Medicare to alter its benefits or improve its effectiveness and sustainability over time in light of the increasing demand for its services. There is no shortage of suggestions for how to reform the program, and these ideas are widely available.[29] However, bipartisan cooperation on health care policy, including Medicare reform, is made difficult by intense ideological disagreements over the role of government in health care and the different constituencies to which each of the major parties tries to appeal. The debate is certain to continue.

Medicaid

Medicaid is the second major program of the U.S. health care policy system. Like Medicare, it was established in 1965, as Title XIX of the Social Security Act. It is designed to assist the poor and disabled through a federal-state program of health insurance. It differs from Medicare in one critical way: Medicare serves all citizens once they reach age sixty-five, regardless of income, and is therefore a form of national health insurance for senior citizens, but Medicaid is a specialized health care program for the poor and disabled.

Medicaid Provisions and Controversies. Under Medicaid, the federal government establishes standards for hospital services, outpatient services, physician services, and laboratory testing, and it pays about half of the cost. States pay the remainder and set standards for eligibility and overall benefit levels, which have varied significantly from one state to another. If a state chooses to have a Medicaid program—and all have since 1982—it must also extend benefits to welfare recipients and to those receiving Supplemental Security Income because of blindness, another disability, or age. Medicaid provided health insurance coverage for over seventy million people in 2016, including thirty-three million children. By default, Medicaid has become the major payer for long-term health care provided in nursing homes and similar facilities, and it accounts for about half of the nation's spending for such services. Because of the rising demand and cost for these services, some states are changing their Medicaid programs to reduce use of nursing homes and to encourage health care in the home or community. These and other innovative approaches to help keep costs down will likely become more prevalent in the years ahead.[30]

In some respects, the state Medicaid programs are more generous than Medicare. The federal government requires states to cover hospitalization, nursing home services, physician services, diagnostic and screening tests, and X-rays. States may opt to cover prescription drug and other expenses, for which the cost can be exceedingly high. States are also required to cover children under the age of eighteen if the family income falls below the poverty level. Much like Medicare expenses, Medicaid costs continue to rise, in part because of expanded coverage under the Affordable Care Act. In 2014, spending stood at $496 billion, or about 16 percent of national health expenditures.

As might be expected in such a program, the states historically have been at odds with the federal government over the imposition of additional burdens. Medicaid is one of the largest programs in most state budgets. As states and counties spend more on Medicaid and face enormous resistance to raising taxes, they must cut back on the program's optional services, reduce the rate of reimbursement for physician and other services, and curtail funding elsewhere. Education, welfare, and other programs may suffer as Medicaid costs continue to rise, as they did in the 2008–2009 economic recession.

In response to concern over the rising costs of Medicaid, in late 2005 Congress approved broad changes that gave states new power to reduce their costs through imposition of premiums and higher co-payments for many of Medicaid's benefits; these include prescription drugs, physician services, and hospital services, such as use of emergency rooms for nonurgent care. Higher costs for beneficiaries are expected to reduce their demand for those services. States also were authorized to cap or eliminate coverage for many services that previous federal law guaranteed within the program. In addition, the new law made it somewhat more difficult for senior citizens to qualify for Medicaid nursing home care by transferring their assets to their children or other relatives.[31]

As part of the Balanced Budget Act of 1997, a new Title XXI was added to the Social Security Act to create the **Children's Health Insurance Program (CHIP)**, which helps to ensure that children living in poverty have medical coverage. The federal government provides funds to the states, which the states match. The states are free to set the eligibility levels, which can include families that earn up to three times the poverty level. More than eight million children have been covered under CHIP in recent years, but the states have varied widely in their ability to enroll children in the program. As has been the case for Medicaid in general, many states have reduced their funding of CHIP in recent years, as they have struggled with budget constraints and competing priorities. In 2007, Congress twice passed legislation to extend and expand CHIP, especially for families that work but remain too poor to pay for health insurance and make too much to enroll in Medicaid; the bills were vetoed by President George W. Bush. In 2009, Congress again took up similar legislation, with the cost to be financed largely by an increase in the federal tobacco tax. Both the House and Senate approved the measure by large margins and with bipartisan support, and President Obama signed it on February 4, 2009.[32] The Affordable Care Act made additional changes to the program.

Issues of Medicaid Fraud and Abuse. The Medicaid program, like Medicare, is vulnerable to fraud and abuse by service providers, such as filing inaccurate claims for reimbursement. Although the money lost to fraud is less than in the Medicare program, the costs are nevertheless substantial. The service providers defend themselves by arguing that they are the victims of an excessively complicated system of eligibility requirements and reimbursement procedures. In chapter 6, we cited the example of the New York State Medicaid program. The state failed to pursue many opportunities to reduce the program's high costs and to monitor its operation carefully. The result has been billions of dollars in fraud and abuse. One former state Medicaid investigator estimated that at least 10 percent of the New York program's dollars were spent on fraudulent claims and that another 20 to 30 percent had been wasted in "abuse," or unnecessary if not criminal spending. Thus as much as 40 percent of New York's Medicaid claims could be questioned, totaling some $18 billion each year in what may well have been wasteful spending. Following the highly visible criticism of its program, New York State pledged to substantially cut fraud over the next several years, and it seems to be making some progress.[33] It should be said that the states vary widely in how they administer the Medicaid program, and New York's experience does not imply that such waste exists in other states. The National Conference of State Legislatures lists an extensive number of actions that the states have taken and might take to reduce Medicaid fraud and abuse, and also recounts the many provisions of the Affordable Care Act that are directed at the problem.[34]

Veterans' Health Care

With all the attention paid to Medicare and Medicaid, policymakers and journalists sometimes forget that one of the oldest programs of federal health care service is similar to the national insurance programs that are the rule in Canada, Great Britain, and many other developed nations, but this one is for veterans only. The veterans' health care system is designed to serve the needs of U.S. veterans by providing primary medical care, specialized care, and other medical and social services, such as rehabilitation. The Veterans Health Administration operates veterans' hospitals and clinics across the nation and provides extensive coverage for veterans with service-related disabilities and diseases and more limited coverage for other veterans, particularly those with no private health care insurance. It also engages in diverse medical research.

One consequence of the wars in Iraq and Afghanistan became clear by 2011. There would be a major and costly expansion of service to veterans, many of whom suffered debilitating brain injuries and other serious battle wounds that would take years of treatment and recovery. The Pentagon has estimated that more than 200,000 troops have suffered from traumatic brain injury in the wars, chiefly from roadside bombs and similar devices, with long-term effects and treatment costs unknown.[35] According to the GAO, the number of veterans who have sought mental health care increased from 900,000 in 2006 to 1.2 million in 2010. The number of veterans of the Iraq and Afghanistan wars who entered therapy increased from 35,000 in 2006 to 139,000 in 2010, requiring the Department of Veterans Affairs (VA) to double its staffing for mental health care.[36] We do have some idea of the overall health care costs of the wars. In its tally of the long-term costs, the *New York Times* included an independent estimate that health care and disability payments for veterans of the wars over the next forty years will be nearly $590 billion.[37] Such projections are all the more reason to ensure that these health care programs are both effective in meeting veterans' needs and efficient in the use of federal health care dollars.

Congress expanded the existing veterans' health programs by enacting the Veterans' Health Care Eligibility Reform Act of 1996. That legislation created an enhanced health benefits plan that emphasizes preventive and primary care, but it also offers a full range of services, including inpatient and outpatient medical, surgical, and mental health services; prescription and over-the-counter drugs and medical and surgical supplies; emergency care; comprehensive rehabilitative services; and even payment of travel expenses associated with care for eligible veterans. The VA health care benefits extend to preventive care and include periodic physical examinations, health and nutrition education, drug use education and drug monitoring, and mental health and substance abuse preventive services. Medical needs attributable to service-related injuries and disease typically are free of individual deductibles and co-payments. VA uses a priority group structure and a financial means test to set co-payment charges for other veterans (see www.va.gov). Its medical system has undergone a major transformation in recent years, and many now consider it to be a model for a national health care system. This is especially so because of its use of electronic medical records, its strong focus on preventive care measures (for example, for cancer, diabetes, and heart disease), and its high scores on health care quality indicators.[38]

Despite its many strengths, the veterans' health care system has fallen short in delivery of timely health care services, partly because of soaring demand for services as wounded soldiers returned from Iraq and Afghanistan and as aging Vietnam-era veterans sought treatment for chronic diseases. The capacity of the system to treat patients (for example, the number of hospitals, clinics, doctors, and nurses) has not kept pace with the rising needs of veterans. In 2014, evidence mounted that the wait time for a medical appointment at some veterans' hospitals had grown significantly, prompting staff members at some facilities to alter waiting list records in an effort to disguise the problem. Congressional inquiries into the scandal led to the dismissal of top health care officials at VA and the resignation of the secretary of veterans' affairs, Eric Shinseki. Policymakers differ on the solutions needed, with some calling for improved management and efficiency at VA and others for increased spending. In 2016, the GAO found that VA had failed to fully address the wait time problem at a number of its facilities, and urged additional action.[39]

At the request of senior military leaders, in 2000 Congress approved another health care program for career military personnel. It expands the military's health plan, known as **Tricare**, to include retirees with at least twenty years of service once they become eligible for Medicare. Tricare pays for most of the costs for medical treatment that are not covered by Medicare, except for a yearly cap for out-of-pocket expenses. The plan also includes generous prescription drug coverage. Active-duty service members choose from a number of Tricare programs, depending on their status and needs, at a modest cost.[40]

Expansion in veterans' care. The care of military veterans has attracted much new attention with the return of thousands of military personnel from Iraq and Afghanistan, many of whom suffered serious injuries in the wars. The photo shows former U.S. Army sergeant Brendan Marrocco demonstrating pull-ups during occupational therapy at the Amputee Service Advanced Training Center at Walter Reed National Medical Center in May 2014. Marrocco was the first military service member to receive a double arm transplant *(Michel du Cille/The Washington Post via Getty Images)*

Other Health Care Policy Issues

Several major health care policy issues do not directly involve government insurance programs such as Medicare, Medicaid, and the veterans' health care system, but instead affect the way private medical insurance operates and the legal rights of policyholders. Two issues merit brief mention here: the portability of insurance as individuals leave one job for another, and the rights of patients to seek legal recourse for decisions made by a managed care or other health organization. Both are somewhat less important today than they were two decades ago, as health care policy has evolved and such rights have come to be acknowledged.

Portability

Given the large number of people whose health care services are provided under employer-sponsored insurance plans, the possible loss of benefits when an employee switches jobs was a long-time concern. One employer's plan might not be the same as another's in cost or quality. People with a preexisting medical condition, such as heart disease, hypertension, or cancer, might have found that a new employer's insurance company was unwilling to cover them at all or would charge higher premiums. To address some of these problems, in 1996 Congress approved the Health Insurance Portability and Accountability Act (HIPAA). The law guarantees that employees who change jobs have the right to insurance coverage, even if that coverage comes at a higher cost. That is, they have the right of **portability** for their insurance coverage. They can take guaranteed coverage with them if they change jobs, and they do not have to endure the waiting period that policies often impose to limit coverage of preexisting conditions. With enactment of the Affordable Care Act, portability is not as important today. Similarly, a federal act approved in the mid 1980s, the Consolidated Omnibus Budget Reconciliation Act (COBRA), was designed to allow employees to remain on an employer's health insurance policy for up to eighteen months, although the employee pays for the insurance premium, and it is no longer as important given insurance coverage under the Affordable Care Act.

Patients' Rights

Historically, one of the most common complaints about managed care health systems, such as HMOs (discussed below), was the inappropriate denial of care. Congress approved the Employee Retirement Income Security Act of 1974 (ERISA) to support **patients' rights**, particularly by allowing individuals to sue health insurance companies for such decisions, although only in federal court. ERISA says that federal regulations supersede state laws governing employee health plans and that no punitive damages may be sought beyond compensation for actual medical expenses. Once again, enactment of the Affordable Care

Act set in place new expectations for insurance company coverage, and behavior builds on the heritage of ERISA but also makes it less important today.

Rising Health Care Costs

As this chapter has emphasized, one of the most difficult issues in health care policy disputes is cost. To make matters worse, the cost of providing health care services is rising inexorably even if more slowly today than a few years ago. Health care is expensive enough that individuals whose employers do not provide full coverage can easily find themselves unable to pay for private insurance or for all the medical services they need. The result can be financially devastating should a major medical emergency arise from an acute illness or an accident. Indeed, such circumstances often are a major reason for personal bankruptcy filings. Even those with relatively generous health care insurance policies can find themselves facing enormous medical bills because of required deductible expenses and co-payment fees, for example, for prescription drugs and hospital stays.

Table 8-2 shows the trend in health care costs. It lists total U.S. health care expenditures for the years 1980 to 2014 (with projections out to 2025), as well as per capita expenditures, indicating that health care costs rose substantially over this period and are projected to rise much more in coming years, in part because of increases in the number of people served by Medicare and Medicaid and expected increases in those enrolled in private health insurance plans purchased through the new health insurance exchanges created by the Affordable Care Act.

As might be expected, rising costs deeply affect the leading federal health care programs. Medicare expenditures alone totaled about $620 billion in 2016, and the overall cost for federal and state spending on Medicaid was over $500 billion, for a total of more than $1 trillion. As noted in the chapter opening, costs have

TABLE 8-2 National Health Expenditures, 1980–2025 (in current dollars)

Item	1980	1990	2000	2014	2025 (estimated)
Total national health care expenditures (in billions)	$255.30	$721.40	$1,369.70	$3,031.00	$5,631.00
Per capita health care expenditures	$1,108	$2,843	$4,857	$9,523	$16,032
Health care expenditures as percentage of GDP	8.9%	12.1%	13.3%	17.5%	20.1%

Sources: Drawn from current and historical tables prepared by the Centers for Medicare and Medicaid Services, Office of the Actuary website (www.cms.gov), October 12, 2016. Projections of health expenditures are offered for ten years out from the time of publication, or through 2025, for the most recent year of data (2014). The documents are updated annually.

been rising more slowly in recent years than previously, and the growth may slow even more as the Affordable Care Act is more fully implemented. Indeed, in 2014, the Congressional Budget Office reported that Medicare spending on a per capita basis was falling, and new economic analyses suggested that much of the cost of giving children health care coverage under Medicaid is likely to be recovered over time in federal and state taxes that the individuals pay.[41]

Rising expenditures for drugs are part of this larger picture of health care expenditures. As many television viewers have noted, pharmaceutical manufacturers have changed their marketing strategies and now advertise drugs directly to consumers, instead of only to health professionals. Among developed nations, the United States stands nearly alone in allowing such advertising. In sometimes deceptive advertisements, viewers are urged to ask their doctors for the new medications. The practice has been a success for the pharmaceutical companies, as the public demand for expensive new prescription drugs grew, even though many of them are only marginally more effective than cheaper, over-the-counter medications and generic versions of similar drugs, and sometimes come with significant risks of side effects.[42]

What is the future of health care costs? As shown in Table 8-2, the CMS offers projections for U.S. health care costs through 2025, and they show no change in the overall upward trend. Total health care expenditures are expected to grow at a substantially higher rate than the economy as a whole, rising from $3.0 trillion in 2014 to $5.6 trillion in 2025, per capita expenditures from $9,523 to $16,032, and expenditures as a percentage of GDP from 17.5 percent to 20.1 percent.[43] The federal government anticipates that pressure will increase on both public and private payers to cover accelerating health care costs, and it anticipates additional need to reconsider health care priorities in the years ahead. These projections are based on the assumption that all major provisions of the Affordable Care Act remain in effect, but even if they do not, there will still be substantial increases in overall health care spending, and there will be a continuing need to find ways to greatly improve the efficiency of the health care system.[44]

State Policy Innovations

The federal government is not the only policy actor trying to contain health care costs; the states also have a role to play, and some states have adopted innovative public policies. For example, as we pointed out in chapter 6, Oregon approved a state health plan that offered Medicaid recipients and others universal access to basic and effective health care. Based on a public-private partnership, the plan included state-run insurance pools, insurance reforms, and a federal waiver allowing for the expansion of Medicaid. The system featured rationing of services based on a ranking of medical procedures that the state and its residents believed to be cost-effective.

Other states have long promoted policy innovation. California, for example, developed an aggressive antismoking media campaign and raised tobacco taxes

"Mind if I smoke?"

"Care if I die?"

California Department of Health Services. Funded by the Tobacco Tax Initiative.

Public campaigns. As an illustration of the capacity of state governments to develop innovative public policies when the federal government often cannot or will not do so, some states have targeted smoking as a preventive health measure, and they have used creative ways to do so. The photo shows an e-card from the Tobacco-Free California website, produced for the California Department of Public Health. The site also has ads, videos, message boards, and other information about quitting smoking and the harmful effects of tobacco. *(Centers for Disease Control and Prevention Media Campaign Resource Center)*

in an effort to get people to stop smoking, a preventive health care action. The goal is to reduce the number of people needing expensive medical services in the future, and thus to improve the economic efficiency of health care programs. By all accounts, the effort has been successful. States also have taken measures to deal with rising rates of obesity, such as limiting access to calorie-laden fast food in public schools. One notable success story under the Affordable Care Act was the formation of accountable care organizations for coordinating patient care, where doctors are rewarded for keeping patients healthy rather than for how many procedures they perform. In Rio Grande Valley in Texas, the change meant that preventive care, such as encouraging change in diet and lifestyle, became a key focus of the Medicare program there. The change saved money and improved patients' health.[45]

Some states, as noted early in the chapter, have gone well beyond these limited measures to adopt comprehensive health care plans. Most notably, a landmark plan enacted in Massachusetts in 2006 requires all state residents to purchase health insurance coverage and imposes a financial penalty on those who do not. There is a state subsidy for low-income residents, the poorest of whom are enrolled automatically into the program. The plan also requires employers with eleven or more employees to make a "fair and reasonable" contribution toward their health insurance coverage or to pay a "fair share" contribution annually per employee. Although the plan is potentially costly, supporters point to its coverage of more than 350,000 state residents who previously did not have health insurance. They also highlight the plan's Health Care Quality and Cost Council, which sets goals for improving quality, containing costs, and reducing inequities in health care. Despite its many successes and serving as a model for what became the national policy under the Affordable Care Act, critics continue to fault the Massachusetts plan for its level of government involvement and costs.[46]

These and many other examples illustrate the pivotal role that the states can play in finding solutions to the emerging health care crisis. Where the federal government has often been unable to act because of the constraints on policymaking that we discussed in chapter 2, states have been able to try different approaches and demonstrate their merits.

Regulation of Prescription Drugs

Given the already high and rapidly rising cost of prescription drugs, another way to control health care costs is to change the way the federal government and drug manufacturers develop and approve new medicines. The current process of drug development is long and expensive, forcing drug manufacturers to charge high prices to cover their cost of research and development. For example, Neulasta, a drug used in some cancer treatments to improve the immune system, costs $5,000 per injection. The new drug Harvoni, used to treat hepatitis C, costs over $1,000 per pill, or more than $94,000 for a twelve-week course of treatment. Mylan, at the time the only maker of the widely prescribed EpiPen used for severe allergy and asthma attacks, raised the price of its two-pack nearly fivefold since 2010, reaching $608 in 2016. The increase sparked a public outcry and a congressional hearing.[47] In defense of their pricing policies, the drug companies note that, for every successful product, dozens of others never make it to market despite millions of dollars in development costs. Moreover, even drugs that are approved have patent protection against generic competition for only about eleven years.

Is there a way to reduce such costs without jeopardizing the public's health? Or is it more important to maintain a rigorous and demanding drug approval process regardless of the time and cost it imposes? Congress addressed the need for such balancing when it passed legislation in 2007 aimed at expanding the FDA's regulatory powers and budget, particularly for its monitoring of prescription drugs and medical devices.[48] Adding to the concerns that prompted the policy change, some news accounts in 2008 questioned the validity of new drug studies, with allegations that pharmaceutical companies often were ghostwriting medical research studies about their own drugs that were later published in medical journals as objective scientific evaluations.[49] The box "Steps to Analysis: Regulation of New Drug Approval" deals with these kinds of issues. It focuses on the difficult trade-offs that the FDA faces in trying to move new drug treatments to market. How carefully should it review the safety and effectiveness of new drugs prior to their approval? Is it better to err on the side of caution or to help ensure that we have early access to new medical treatments?

Managed Care Organizations

Managed care, now a fixture of modern health care services and policy, was proposed as one way to contain rising health care costs that had soared under the old system of unrestrained fee-for-service, in which the patient or an insurance company pays for the medical service rendered. Over the past several decades, the United States has shifted from fee-for-service to a system dominated by managed care, typically with the costs borne by third-party payers,

Steps to Analysis

Regulation of New Drug Approval

The Food and Drug Administration (FDA) requires pharmaceutical and biotechnology companies to conduct elaborate, lengthy, and costly testing of new drugs before they can be approved for patient use. The justification for this process is to ensure the safety and effectiveness of new drugs prior to marketing. Drug manufacturers have often complained that the FDA procedures are too demanding and delay the availability of new treatments, prevent some of them from reaching the market at all, and contribute to the high cost of new drug development. They also report that a new drug may take as long as ten to fifteen years to develop, with research and development costs reaching $800 million or more.

In response to some of these concerns, Congress enacted the Prescription Drug User Fee Act in 1992, which imposed tight deadlines for new drug evaluation at the agency but also required pharmaceutical companies to pay fees that would permit the agency to hire more drug reviewers, thus reducing the time needed to evaluate and approve new drugs. Reviews are now expected to be completed within ten months, half the time that was common before the act. Priority drugs may be reviewed even more quickly. Yet one consequence of the new procedures is that some drugs are approved even when questions remain about their safety, efficacy, or quality.

Has the United States struck an acceptable balance between the need for a speedy approval process and the necessity to ensure drug safety and efficacy? Has the FDA been too lax in its approval of new drugs? Should the agency use a special, expedited procedure to approve so-called breakthrough drugs that offer great promise for serious illnesses, such as cancer and heart disease, as members of Congress favored when voting for the 21st Century Cures Act in 2016? What about drugs that might be used to combat bioterrorism?

To explore this question, consider this example. In 1999, the FDA approved the pain relief drug Vioxx, a nonsteroidal anti-inflammatory medication. Vioxx was widely used, even though the majority of those taking it could have chosen instead to use safer, more effective, and cheaper drugs that had long been on the market. Then, in 2004, new information appeared on serious side effects of using the drug; those taking Vioxx for a long time faced a doubled risk of heart attack or stroke. The manufacturer, Merck, withdrew Vioxx from the market, and the FDA issued a public health advisory to warn patients to consult with their physicians about use of the drug. Merck faced at least seven thousand lawsuits over the drug, with a potential financial liability of perhaps $50 billion. In 2007, it settled the cases for nearly $5 billion. Was the FDA approval process insufficient in this case? Was its post-approval monitoring of the drug's safety inadequate?[a]

Consider a related concern: that the ingredients in cosmetics and food supplements require no FDA approval at all despite what are sometimes serious health effects, such as liver damage. In 1994, after intense lobbying by the food supplement industry, Congress approved the Dietary Supplement Health and Education Act, which weakened the capacity of the FDA to oversee the safety of products advertised as nutritional supplements. Before the act, the FDA could keep a product off the market until its manufacturer proved it was safe, but the new law forced the FDA to prove a product was unsafe, which it was ill equipped to do.[b] Was this policy change a good idea? Should the makers of both food supplements and cosmetics be required to prove their safety before they are marketed, or does doing so place too great a burden on them? Should consumer rights trump such cost concerns? What information would you need to answer these questions?

---

a. For a review of similar problems with the FDA approval process, see "Prescription for Trouble," *Consumer Reports*, January 2006, 34–39. For the Vioxx settlement as well as allegations that drug studies may not be as valid as once thought, see Stephanie Saul, "Merck Wrote Drug Studies for Doctors," *New York Times*, April 16, 2008.

b. See Eric Lipton and Rachel Abrams, "Their Hair Fell Out. Should the F.D.A. Have the Power to Act?" *New York Times*, August 15, 2016; and Anahad O'Connor, "'Supplements and Safety' Explores What's in Your Supplements," *New York Times*, January 19, 2016.

such as health insurance companies or the government. By most measurements, the transition has been successful, particularly in holding down health care costs and promoting preventive health care.

Managed care organizations provide health care by forming networks of doctors, other health care providers, and hospitals associated with a given plan; monitoring their treatment activities; and limiting access to specialists and costly procedures. The best-known type of managed care organization is a **health maintenance organization (HMO)**. Along with other managed care companies, such as a **preferred provider organization (PPO)**, HMOs promote health services that are the most cost effective, such as ensuring regular physicals and certain medical screening tests, limiting access to costly services and specialists, and negotiating lower fees with health care providers. PPOs differ from HMOs in that enrollees have a financial incentive to use physicians on the preferred list but may opt to see other health professionals at a higher cost. By most accounts, HMOs and PPOs save the nation billions of dollars a year in health care costs, an important achievement.

Managed care still has its critics, even if by most indications it has been a highly successful design that balances quality health care service with the concern over how to constrain costs. Recent criticism of HMOs has focused on limits placed on patients' stays in hospitals—routinely, only twenty-four hours following childbirth, for example—and denying or limiting coverage for certain procedures. HMOs counter that they are trying to ensure that limited health care dollars are spent efficiently and fairly and that patients be provided with only safe and proven treatments. They fear that expanding patients' rights might lead to the use of unnecessary and possibly dangerous procedures, resulting in higher insurance fees and injuries to patients. They also argue that laws guaranteeing patients the power to select physicians and to sue their health care plans will raise premium costs and leave more people uninsured and vulnerable to health risks.

Following patient complaints and adverse publicity in the 1990s and early 2000s, however, managed care companies changed some of their policies to become more accommodating than in the past. The evidence suggests they are not denying care in many cases, even though the occasional horror story to that effect pops up in a movie or on television. Indeed, some states, including Connecticut, New Jersey, and New York, require managed care plans to report incidents of care denial and how they were resolved. In these states, plan administrators seem to be reluctant to second-guess physicians, but the plans still deny access to physicians outside of their networks and nonessential or experimental treatments.

Reducing Health Care Costs

If managed care has not succeeded in restraining the rise in health care costs, other strategies may emerge to reach that goal. Four of these merit brief mention:

(1) passing on additional costs to health care consumers, (2) setting up personal health accounts, (3) managing disease more effectively, and (4) using preventive health care.

Everyone complains about the cost of health care, but the fact is that few people ever see the full price tag because insurance plans take care of most of it. Of course, even simple surgeries can cost thousands of dollars, and many prescription drugs can run to hundreds of dollars per month. So these relatively low burdens on individuals can escalate quickly if a major health care need arises. But under more normal circumstances, these modest costs borne by individuals suggest that one way to reduce rising demand for health care services and prescription drugs is to pass along more of the cost to them. For example, if employees had to cover more of the costs now paid by their employers' insurance policies, they might have an incentive to reduce their demand for health services that are not essential, such as visiting a hospital emergency room for a nonemergency situation, demanding exotic new drugs when less expensive alternatives exist, or requesting expensive diagnostic tests that a physician believes are unnecessary. Raising the policyholder's share of the cost with higher deductibles and higher levels of co-payments would inject "market discipline" into health care coverage.[50]

A variation on this theme is that individuals who use health services more frequently than average should pay more of the cost, for example, through higher insurance premiums. In other words, the sicker should pay more, just as those with more driving citations or accidents pay higher automobile insurance premiums and those with safe driving records get a break. Is this proposal fair? It might be if the health care consumers brought on their conditions through poor choices over which they had reasonable control. But what about individuals with inherited diseases, or accident victims, or those who simply have the misfortune of suffering from a rare (and expensive) illness? Is it ethical to pass the costs of treatment along to them and their families?

Many employers seeking ways to cope with rising premium costs are setting up personal health accounts for their workers. The employers deposit money into an account that is used to pay for each employee's health expenses that the regular insurance does not cover. The money can be used for prescription drugs, physician visits, dental work, and other health-related bills. Employees make their own decisions about how best to spend the limited funds. Once the money is gone, the employee is responsible for any additional charges that year. These plans may come with a very high deductible, which would make them essentially catastrophic insurance policies; if so, the employee is better off using the plan for a highly unusual major medical need, not routine services. Those who make poor choices, or are unlucky and suffer from a serious injury, or need continuing medical care, may be worse off under such a plan. Is this kind of plan likely to be effective as a compromise to control costs and still cover catastrophic illness or injury?

Disease management programs focus on a few chronic diseases associated with high costs. The programs promise to reduce employers' costs by bringing employee diseases under control more effectively than is likely through conventional medical treatment. Managed care organizations have led the way in developing these kinds of programs. Surveys indicate that a majority of them have implemented programs for managing conditions such as asthma, diabetes, heart disease, end-stage renal disease, cancer, and depression. Their goal is to train patients to take better care of themselves by monitoring their diseases, watching their diets, and seeking appropriate and timely medical care. Some critics are concerned that singling out employees with chronic conditions for the training programs may pose a threat to them. Even some insurance programs believe that disease management of this kind raises difficult ethical issues involving medical privacy and employee-employer relationships. But few question that such programs make many individuals healthier and also reduce health care costs. How would you weigh the ethical issues of disease management?

The compelling logic of preventive care is addressed more fully at the end of the chapter. All agree that if people take good care of themselves throughout their lives, they are likely to be healthier and need less medical care than those who do not. Preventive care health plans usually allow regular physical examinations and diagnostic tests; education and training in diet, exercise, and stress management; and smoking cessation programs.

Quality of Care

The issue of quality in medical care is easy to understand. At a minimum, every patient should expect to receive professional and competent care that is consistent with good medical practice. The physician or other health care professional should be well trained, up-to-date on new research and treatments, and able to spend sufficient time with a patient to properly diagnose and treat medical conditions that arise. These expectations are particularly reasonable in the United States, given the vast amounts of money invested by government, insurance companies, and individuals in one of the best medical care systems in the world.

The evidence suggests, however, that quality care is not as routinely available as many would like to believe. Patients complain about poor-quality care, and even the American Medical Association concedes that errors in diagnosis and treatment occur at a significant rate.[51] In addition, studies indicate that many physicians rely excessively on costly medical technology and drugs, in part to increase revenues for physician offices and hospitals and in part as "defensive medicine," to guard against liability in malpractice claims. Indeed, a 1991 study put the cost of defensive medicine in the United States at $25 billion per year.[52] Another study in 2002 by the Juran Institute, a group representing large employers, found that $390 billion a year was wasted on outmoded and inefficient medical procedures. The authors argued that poor quality in health care at that time cost the average employer some $1,700 to $2,000 for each covered employee each year. More recently, studies by Dartmouth's medical school questioned the effectiveness of aggressive medical care found in some regions of the country. Patients receiving such care were at increased risk of infections and medical errors, and they didn't benefit appreciably compared to those who received less aggressive care.[53]

If, as patients in HMOs sometimes complain, doctors spend less time with them and access to specialists is limited, are these problems evidence of lower-quality care? They might be, if physicians and other health care professionals are too busy to properly diagnose and treat their patients. It is true that, to cope with rising patient demand and to compensate for lower rates of reimbursement, medical professionals must see more patients per day than they did in the past. Still, it is difficult to measure the quality of medical care.[54] The issue is not likely to go away because the amount of care and patients' perceptions of its quality are closely tied to the factors that escalate health care costs, such as seeing physicians more frequently, gaining access to specialists, benefiting from new medical technology and treatments, and using the latest prescription drugs.

Medical Errors

One element of the concern about the quality of medical care is more concrete and disturbing—the incidence of medical errors. A widely circulated and influential report released in 1999 by what is now the National Academy of Medicine estimated that between 44,000 and 98,000 patients die each year as a result of medical errors made in hospitals. A 2016 study put the number at over 250,000 lives a year lost to medical errors in hospitals and other health care facilities, which would make such errors the third leading cause of death in the United States.[55] The errors include operations on the wrong patient or the wrong side of a patient, incorrect drug prescriptions or administration of the wrong dosages, malfunctioning mechanical equipment, and nursing and other staff errors, such as poor communication of medical information. Neither study included the more than 700,000 infections acquired in the nation's hospitals each year, which the CDC claims lead to some 75,000 deaths annually. The CDC findings have led many hospitals to adopt new procedures to try to cut infection rates, with some measure of success.[56]

Following the 1999 NAM study of medical errors, Congress approved, and President Bush signed, legislation that establishes procedures for voluntary and confidential reporting of medical errors to independent organizations that are to submit the information to a national database. Many recommendations for improving hospital safety have been made since that time, and greater attention to reducing medical errors came also after the federal Medicare program announced that it would no longer pay for medical errors—what it called "reasonably preventable" conditions on a list it made available to hospitals. Some of the nation's largest health insurance companies also announced that they would not pay for what they called "never events"—that is, medical errors that should never occur.[57] As noted earlier, the Affordable Care Act is likely to be yet another force for reducing medical errors.

Focused Discussion: Should There Be Greater Emphasis on Preventive Health Care?

Throughout the chapter, we have highlighted many of the weaknesses of the U.S. health care system, particularly its high costs and the forecasts for increasing costs as the baby boom generation ages. Much of the debate over health care policy actions, from government programs such as Medicare and Medicaid to employer-provided health insurance plans, focuses on how to pay for expensive health care services. One of the most promising ways to constrain health care costs and also to keep people healthy would be to give greater emphasis to **preventive health care**, or the promotion of health and prevention of disease in individuals. This would include routine screening for serious diseases such as diabetes, heart disease, and high blood pressure; better treatment of chronic illnesses; improved health care education; and more attention to the role of diet, exercise, smoking, and other lifestyle choices that can affect individuals' health. Put otherwise, ill health and premature death are not merely functions of genetics or exposure to disease-causing microbes or environmental pollutants over which individuals have little control. They also reflect choices people make in their daily lives.

For this focused discussion, we turn to selected efforts of this kind, particularly those involving smoking and diet. We evaluate them in terms of the criteria we have emphasized in the chapter and throughout the book: effectiveness, economic efficiency, and equity and other ethical issues. That is, we want to see how effective preventive health care measures might be in improving health, what they might save in costs to the nation, and how we can appraise the wisdom of such policy actions in terms of ethical issues, including possible infringement on individuals' right to behave as they choose without government regulations or pressures to change their lifestyles.

Effectiveness

One way to appreciate the importance of preventive health care is to consider the leading causes of death in the United States. Heart disease and cancer are dominant, followed by chronic respiratory diseases such as emphysema and cerebrovascular diseases or stroke. Among the leading contributing factors in all of these cases are smoking, diet, lack of exercise, stress, and exposure to environmental pollutants. Moreover, even where the causes can be found elsewhere (such as in genetic predisposition to certain diseases), early detection and treatment can both save lives and lower the costs of treatment. For chronic diseases such as diabetes and high blood pressure, regular monitoring of those conditions and use of appropriate medical treatments could improve the quality of patients' lives, reduce premature death rates, and save money, all at the same time.

Take the issue of smoking. It is widely recognized to be the single most preventable cause of premature death in the United States, accounting for more than 480,000 deaths annually, nearly one in five deaths, according to the CDC. Another 16 million suffer from a disease attributable to smoking. Secondhand smoke takes an additional health toll, accounting for an estimated 42,000 deaths a year. Roughly half of those who smoke die prematurely from cancer, heart disease, emphysema, and other smoking-related diseases, and the CDC estimates that on average smokers die ten years earlier than nonsmokers.[58] If there is good news related to smoking, it can be found in the number of Americans who have quit. An estimated 48 million people have stopped smoking, while about 40 million people continue to smoke. Of those eighteen years of age or older, smokers account for about 16.8 percent, the lowest level since the mid 1960s. The U.S. surgeon general's reports indicate that smoking cessation at any age conveys health benefits; for example, quitting even at age sixty-five can reduce the risk of dying from some diseases by as much as 50 percent.[59] The recent marketing of e-cigarettes that deliver nicotine without the harmful ingredients may help some to quit smoking, and they are rising sharply in popularity. Yet experts continue to debate their safety, and some are concerned that, at least for some users, e-cigarettes may prolong their habit of smoking. Because of those concerns, in 2016 the FDA adopted major new rules that extend federal regulation over e-cigarettes.[60]

Or consider the role of diet and insufficient exercise to prevent excessive weight gain. The surgeon general has observed that, left unabated, "overweight and obesity may soon cause as much preventable disease and death as cigarette smoking."[61] Recent studies by the CDC indicate that over 36 percent of U.S. adults age twenty or older are obese, as are 17 percent of children and adolescents. Another 33 percent of the adult population is overweight, and the number of young people who are overweight has tripled since 1980. However, after increasing for years, the prevalence of obesity among children 2 to 5 years of age decreased significantly; it fell from 13.9 percent in 2003–2004 to 8.4 percent in 2011–2012. The finding was important because children who are overweight between the ages of three and five are five times as likely as others to be either overweight or obese when they reach adulthood.[62]

As might be expected, the rates of obesity and overweight vary substantially from state to state, with some states such as Colorado, California, and Massachusetts having comparatively low obesity rates (25 percent or less) and others such as Mississippi, Alabama, and West Virginia having relatively high rates (more than 35 percent). (See Figure 8-1.)[63] Being overweight, which for some is beyond their control because of genetic and other factors, increases the risk of many health problems. Among them are hypertension, high cholesterol levels, type 2 diabetes, coronary heart disease, and stroke. Taken together, these are so important that recent studies suggest an eventual decline in U.S. life expectancy because of obesity trends and their associated health problems.[64]

The American diet is a strong contributing factor in obesity for both children and adults, with increasing reliance on prepared foods high in calories, fat, and cholesterol. Some critics single out the nation's food industry for much of the blame, saying it undermines good nutrition by strongly promoting sales of unhealthy food (Nestle 2002, 2015). Not surprisingly, the food industry rejects the charge, and it has fought hard in Congress and state legislatures to protect itself against any legal liability for the nation's collective weight gain.[65] Some analysts have favored the imposition of taxes on unhealthy food, such as sugary soft drinks, much as we have taxed and regulated cigarettes to discourage their use, and the idea has gained some traction in recent years, both in the United States and in other nations. Even without taxes, governments can try to discourage unhealthy diets. In 2016, the federal government issued new dietary guidelines that urged Americans to reduce their intake of sugar, and to consume more fruits and vegetables, whole grains, lean cuts of meat, and lower-fat foods while cutting back on foods with high levels of saturated fat, trans fats, and cholesterol. In addition, in a move praised by nutritionists, in 2014 the FDA issued new rules

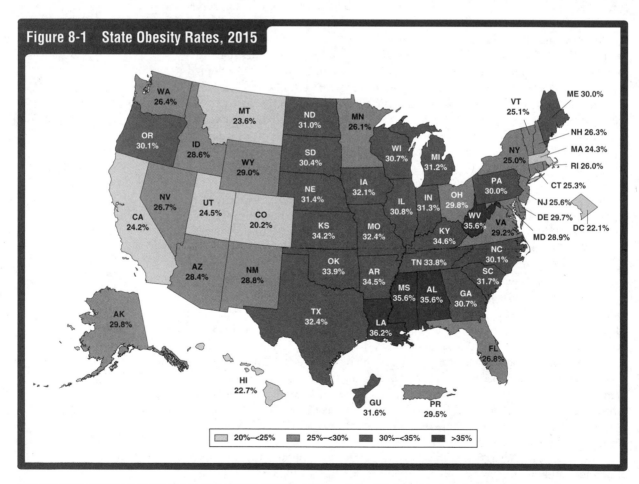

Figure 8-1   State Obesity Rates, 2015

Source: The State of Obesity, "Adult Obesity in the United States," September 1, 2016, available at http://stateofobesity.org/adult-obesity/.

that require chain restaurants and some other establishments to indicate calorie content on their menus, an action stimulated by the Affordable Care Act.[66] Some studies indicate that once obese or overweight, many people find it extraordinarily difficult to lose the extra pounds and keep them off, thus suggesting the logic of early intervention in obesity prevention programs.[67]

By most accounts, Americans also fall well short of the recommended levels of physical exercise and fitness, and they drink too much alcohol. Both habits contribute to poor health. Indeed, recent studies suggest that low levels of fitness may be nearly as bad for health and longevity as smoking.[68] At least a portion of the national weight gain can be attributed to declining physical activity at work, as more jobs become sedentary or require only very light activity—for example, being seated at a desk and using a computer for much of the workday.[69] About one in ten adults reports consuming alcohol excessively, with higher percentages among younger adults. Despite these habits, life expectancy in the United States reached an all-time high of 78.9 years in 2014—which, however, placed it only number twenty-six among the thirty-six Organisation for Economic Co-operation and Development (OECD) nations, behind Canada and Germany but close to the Czech Republic and Turkey. However, in 2015, it declined for the first time since 1993, falling to 78.8. Life expectancy is slightly higher for women and somewhat lower for men, and there are large and growing disparities between rich and poor citizens, which parallels growth in U.S. income inequality over the past several decades.[70] It is reasonable to assume that average life expectancy would be even higher if people took better care of themselves throughout their lives, and also higher if more people had regular access to health care services.

Economic Efficiency Issues

Consistent with the information provided in the previous section, many advocates of preventive health care defend such initiatives as providing economic benefits. That is, spending money on preventive health care would pay substantial dividends, both financially and in improved health and well-being. For example, a 2009 article in *Health Affairs* put the cost of obesity at $147 billion per year in 2008, up from $78 billion in 1998, and another study in 2012 estimated that obesity accounted for $190 billion in U.S. health care costs at that time. These studies indicate the potential savings if the nation found effective and acceptable ways to reduce our collective waistlines.[71] In addition, some studies make clear that health care for obese and overweight individuals can cost considerably more (about 37 percent more on average) than for those of normal weight.[72] As one example, type 2 diabetes, strongly associated with being overweight, currently ranks number one in direct health care costs, at more than $275 billion a year in the United States in 2012; this number is projected to rise to $500 billion a year by 2020, when half of Americans are expected to have diabetes or prediabetes.[73]

Excessive weight also has been linked to more than a hundred thousand cancer deaths per year.[74] Studies like the ones cited here have helped convince the federal government to spend more on antiobesity therapies and to increase support for research on obesity.

Experience at the state level tells much the same story. The state of West Virginia, for example, found that the cost of obesity for its state employees more than doubled since 1995, and consumed more than one-fifth of the health plan's cost. An even more striking study comes from California. In 2005, a report put the cost of obesity to businesses and the state itself at $22 billion per year in lost productivity, increased medical costs, and higher insurance payments. The report was the first to link such weight problems to increases in employer costs. The study concluded that a 5 percent increase in physical activity could save businesses and the state $6 billion each year; a 10 percent increase could save nearly $13 billion.[75] Numbers like these suggest that both state governments and businesses would be wise to give serious thought to programs that promise to reduce weight gain. Analysts have long made similar arguments about the costs of smoking, which are estimated to result in about $156 billion in health-related economic productivity losses each year.

Equity and Other Ethical Issues

As suggested in the box "Working with Sources: Ethical Issues in Health Care," taking action on preventive health care should be evaluated not only on the grounds of effectiveness and efficiency but also in terms of ethics. One of the concerns is equity, or fair treatment for all groups in the population, and another is whether governments (or employers) are justified in taking actions that may impinge on individual rights.

Consider the case of smoking. Do the statistics presented above make for a strong case for further government intervention to reduce smoking and therefore smoking-related disease? For example, should government further raise the price of cigarettes to discourage their use? Studies show that increasing the price of cigarettes can substantially decrease the number of young people who become smokers, and that restrictions on smoking in workplaces and public places can decrease smoking by young adults (Tauras 2005). But does this mean that it is right for government to restrict smoking, particularly among adults who choose to smoke? Should state and local governments become more aggressive in restricting smoking in public places? What about using the kind of graphic warning labels on cigarette packs that are common in more than eighty other nations, with good evidence that they work, but which are rejected in the United States? Or, would it be right for employers to refuse to hire employees who smoke, or to fire those who do, based on the impact on their health and the cost to the employer? In all of these illustrations, it is easy to see that smokers might well feel they are being treated unfairly as a group even if they acknowledge the possible health care costs of their habit.

Working with Sources

Ethical Issues in Health Care

Some of the most contentious issues in health care involve ethical rather than economic issues. One of the prominent debates in recent years concerned provisions of the Affordable Care Act that related to insurance coverage for contraceptive services. The act requires group health insurance plans to offer Food and Drug Administration–approved contraceptive methods, sterilization procedures, and patient education and counseling for women with reproductive capacity (not for men), and to do so without a co-pay or deductible. The law exempted health plans that are sponsored by certain religious organizations or nonprofit organizations with religious objections to contraception, such as churches. In addition, the federal government provided some accommodation for eligible organizations that voiced religious objections to such coverage, with the insurance companies rather than the religious organization paying for the contraceptive coverage.

Some organizations and businesses objected to the new mandated coverage even with this accommodation, saying that the requirement to provide cost-free contraceptive coverage violated their religious freedom. That is, they did not want to provide such coverage for their employees. Among the dozen or so businesses objecting to the new law was the arts and crafts store Hobby Lobby, with some twenty-one thousand employees. In November 2013, the U.S. Supreme Court agreed to hear two cases brought by such secular, for-profit corporations, whose owners sought an exemption under the law based on their religious beliefs, and in late June 2014, the Court ruled 5 to 4 in favor of the corporations.

To examine some of the arguments for and against the Affordable Care Act's contraceptive coverage mandates, go to the federal government's website for preventive health care services for women at www.healthcare.gov/what-are-my-preventive-care-benefits/#part=2 to see a review of the services that are covered under the act. For an overview of Planned Parenthood's perspective on the act's contraceptive coverage rules, see www.plannedparenthood.org/about-us/newsroom/press-releases/planned-parenthood-statement-final-birth-control-rule-new-report-impact. For the perspective of religious organizations on the new contraceptive coverage rules, go to the website for the United States Conference of Catholic Bishops at www.usccb.org/issues-and-action/human-life-and-dignity/health-care and follow the Contraception link to the Health and Human Services contraceptive services rule.

- What do you see as the main points of contention?

- Is one view more persuasive than another?

- Do you think the ethical issues involved in either support for or opposition to the rules are stated clearly enough?

Lifestyle choices and wellness activities also are part of the equity question when it comes to provision of generous prescription drug coverage or other health care insurance benefits. Some would argue that heavily subsidized coverage of drugs and other medical expenses discourages individuals from making sensible lifestyle decisions regarding diet, weight, exercise, and smoking. Individuals may believe that medical science will be able to treat any resulting illness with no cost to them, so they have little incentive to take responsibility for such choices. However, if they were responsible for more of the eventual cost, they might make different choices.[76]

Given the arguments here for effectiveness, efficiency, equity, and other ethical issues, would you favor a major shift on the part of government, employers, and insurance companies toward emphasizing preventive health care? What reasons do you find most persuasive? What reasons might lead you to challenge such a recommendation?

Conclusions

This chapter traces the evolution of government health care policies and examines the leading programs. It emphasizes issues of cost, access, and quality, and the diverse ways government activities affect the public's health and well-being. The present array of health care programs, from Medicare and Medicaid to innovative state preventive health measures and provisions of the Affordable Care Act, may seem complex and confusing to many, and it strikes health care professionals the same way. Students of public policy, using the criteria discussed in the text, can evaluate all of these programs against standards of effectiveness in delivering quality health care services, efficiency of present expenditures in terms of the benefits received, and equity in access to and payments for those services. Many analysts, policymakers, health care professionals, and patients alike find strengths and weaknesses in this system in terms of all three criteria. The strengths merit the praise they have received, but the weaknesses need to be addressed as well.

Rising costs alone suggest the imperative of change. As we have shown, the costs threaten to bankrupt the Medicare system as the baby boom generation ages. Employers and individuals face similar hurdles in meeting the anticipated increases in insurance policy premiums and almost certainly higher deductibles and co-payments. Health care policy therefore would profit greatly from critical assessments that point to better ways of providing affordable and high-quality health care to the U.S. public in the future. The questions posed throughout the chapter encourage such assessments, from how best to reform Medicare and Medicaid to the effectiveness of many state efforts to constrain costs to the promotion of health education, wellness training, and other preventive health care measures. Fortunately for the student of public policy, information to help design more appropriate health care policies and institutions is widely available on the Internet through government and independent sites.

DISCUSSION QUESTIONS

1. Consider the data provided in this chapter on the rising cost of health care services. What are the most effective ways to control these costs? Try to think of several alternative ways to do so, and then compare them in terms of the criteria of effectiveness, efficiency, and equity.

2. In light of the chapter's discussion of the consequences of being uninsured, what should governments do to meet the needs of Americans without health care insurance beyond what the Affordable Care Act does?

3. Should employers continue to carry the burden of providing health care benefits to employees, or should the government institute a form of national health insurance instead? What difference might this make for the ability of U.S. companies, such as automobile manufacturers, to compete internationally when most other developed countries provide national health insurance?

4. Was Congress right to approve the new Patient Protection and Affordable Care Act in 2010 despite unanimous opposition by Republicans and considerable doubt about it among the American public? What provisions in the act ought to be kept, and which would you favor repealing or replacing with something else, and why?

5. What kinds of public policies might be designed to give individuals more incentives to remain healthy and reduce demand for costly health care services?

KEYWORDS

Affordable Care Act   277
Children's Health Insurance
    Program (CHIP)   289
fee-for-service   296
health maintenance
    organization (HMO)   298
managed care   296
Medicaid   287

Medicare   285
merit good   280
national health insurance   276
patients' rights   292
portability   292
preferred provider organization
    (PPO)   298
preventive health care   302

public health agencies   274
single-payer insurance   276
third-party payers   296
Tricare   291
veterans' health care
    system   290

MAJOR LEGISLATION

Balanced Budget Act of 1997
Children's Health Insurance Program Reauthorization
    Act of 2009
Consolidated Omnibus Budget Reconciliation Act of
    1985 (COBRA)
Employee Retirement Income Security Act of 1974 (ERISA)
Health Insurance Portability and Accountability Act
    of 1996 (HIPAA)

Health Security Act
Medicare Prescription Drug, Improvement, and
    Modernization Act of 2003
Patient Protection and Affordable Care Act of 2010
Social Security Act Amendments of 1965
Veterans' Health Care Eligibility Reform Act of 1996

SUGGESTED READINGS

Thomas S. Bodenheimer and Kevin Grumbach, *Understanding Health Policy*, 7th ed. (New York: McGraw-Hill, 2016). A broad introduction to the field of health care policy.

Jacob S. Hacker, *The Road to Nowhere: The Genesis of President Clinton's Plan for Health Security* (Princeton, N.J.: Princeton University Press, 1997). A review of the failure of Clinton's national health care plan of 1993.

Lawrence R. Jacobs and Theda Skocpol, *Health Care Reform and American Politics: What Everyone Needs to Know*, revised and updated edition (New York: Oxford University Press, 2012). A history and assessment of the politics of the Affordable Care Act of 2010.

Theodore R. Marmor, *The Politics of Medicare*, 2nd ed. (Hawthorne, N.Y.: Aldine de Gruyter, 2000). An insightful assessment of Medicare's history and success.

Kant Patel and Mark E. Rushefsky, *Health Care Politics and Policy in America*, 4th ed. (New York: Routledge, 2015). A major text in health care policy that covers the full spectrum of issues.

SUGGESTED WEBSITES

www.citizen.org/hrg. Public Citizen's Health Research Group, with extensive links to policy issues and citizen activism.

www.cms.gov. Centers for Medicare and Medicaid Services within the Department of Health and Human Services, with extensive links to federal and state health care programs.

www.hhs.gov/healthcare/about-the-law/index.html. The federal government's portal for health care information, particularly related to the Affordable Care Act.

www.kff.org. Kaiser Family Foundation, respected by both liberals and conservatives for its reliable health care studies and reports. Written for the general public.

www.rwjf.org/en/library/collections/health-policy.html. Robert Wood Johnson Foundation's health policy page. Research and policy analysis on health care issues, with a progressive leaning.

NOTES

1. The cost estimates come from the federal Centers for Medicare and Medicaid Services, Office of the Actuary, and are based on the National Health Expenditure Accounts, with detailed reports available at www.cms.gov/Research-Statistics-Data-and-Systems/Statistics-Trends-and-Reports/NationalHealthExpendData/Downloads/Proj2012.pdf.

2. Ceci Connolly, "'We're Not Getting What We Pay For': Experts Say U.S. Health Care Is Inefficient, Wasteful, and Sometimes Dangerous," *Washington Post National Weekly Edition*, December 8–14, 2008; Elizabeth Rosenthal, "The 2.7 Trillion Medical Bill," *New York Times*, June 1, 2013; and Annie Lowrey, "Study of U.S. Health Care System Finds Both Waste and Opportunity to Improve," *New York Times*, September 11, 2012.

3. See Reed Abelson, "While the U.S. Spends Heavily on Health Care, a Study Faults the Quality," *New York Times*, July 17, 2008; Connolly, "'We're Not Getting What We Pay For'"; and Rosenthal, "The $2.7 Trillion Medical Bill." The Commonwealth Fund study can be found at the group's website: www.commonwealthfund.org. For an account of how the U.S. health care

system compares to that of other nations, see T. R. Reid, *The Healing of America: A Global Quest for Better, Cheaper, and Fairer Health Care* (New York: Penguin Books, 2010).

4. Kevin Sack, "Research Finds Wide Disparities in Health Care by Race and Region," *New York Times*, June 5, 2008.

5. The data come from the website for the Kaiser Family Foundation: www.kff.org. The foundation staff regularly survey employers nationwide on the costs of health insurance for employees and report the results. See the report "Average Family Premium per Enrolled Employee for Employer-Based Health Insurance" at http://kff.org/other/state-indicator/family-coverage/?currentTimeframe=0.

6. See, for example, Reed Abelson, Gardiner Harris, and Robert Pear, "Whatever Court Rules, Major Changes in Health Are Likely to Last," *New York Times*, November 14, 2011. See also Lawrence R. Jacobs and Theda Skocpol, *Health Care Reform and American Politics: What Everyone Needs to Know* (New York: Oxford University Press, 2010); and a compilation by the staff of the *Washington Post*, *Landmark: The Inside Story of America's New Health-Care Law and What It Means for Us All* (New York: Public Affairs/Perseus Books, 2010).

7. See Philip Ellis, "Budgetary and Economic Effects of Repealing the Affordable Care Act," Congressional Budget Office, June 19, 2015, available at www.cbo.gov/publication/50252.

8. See Adam Liptak, "Supreme Court Upholds Health Care Law, 5–4, in Victory for Obama," *New York Times*, June 28, 2012.

9. For a detailed summary of the act, see Marian Jarlenski and Richard Rubin, "Health Care Overhaul's Key Parts," *CQ Weekly*, April 12, 2010, 914–922. A summary of the act's provisions also can be found on the Henry J. Kaiser Family Foundation website: kff.org/health-reform/fact-sheet/summary-of-the-affordable-care-act/.

10. See, for example, Sharon Begley, "The *Best* Medicine," *Scientific American*, July 2011, 50–55; and Jocelyn Kaiser, "Health Bill Backs Evidence-Based Medicine, New Drug Studies," *Science* 327 (March 26, 2010). The U.S. Government Accountability Office released an initial and positive assessment of the institute in March 2015: "Comparative Effectiveness: Initial Assessment of the Patient-Center Outcomes Research Institute" (GAO-15-301).

11. See Robert Pear, "New Health Initiatives Put Spotlight on Prevention," *New York Times*, April 5, 2010.

12. See a special report, "Questioning the Cost of the Health Care Overhaul," *New York Times*, April 3, 2010.

13. See, for example, "In Florida, Opposition by the State and Snags in Signing Up on the Web," *New York Times*, October 10, 2013. See also Emily Ethridge, "Medicaid Expansion a Tough Call for GOP," *CQ Weekly*, June 17, 2013, 1037–1038.

14. Enrollment numbers are taken from obamacarefacts.com, retrieved on October 10, 2016, and from the Kaiser Family Foundation report "Key Facts about the Uninsured Population," September 29, 2016, available at kff.org. On the reluctance of younger people to sign up for insurance plans, see Abby Goodnough and Reed Abelson, "Health Care Law's Beneficiaries Reflect Its Strengths, and Its Faults," *New York Times*, October 14, 2016.

15. Ashley Kirzinger, Elise Sugarman, and Mollyann Brodie, "Kaiser Health Tracking Poll: November 2016," December 1, 2016, available at www.kff.org.

16. For a revealing picture of health care around the world that includes a review of the British system, see the PBS *Frontline* documentary "Sick around the World," available with discussion, interviews, and analysis at www.pbs.org/wgbh/pages/frontline/sickaroundtheworld.

17. The data come from the annual Employer Health Benefits Survey conducted by the Kaiser Family Foundation, available at its website: www.kff.org.

18. Ibid.

19. The numbers come from the Kaiser Family Foundation website (http://kff.org/statedata/) and represent the uninsured from ages zero to sixty-four for 2015–2016. The data are regularly updated.

20. Stan Dorn, "Uninsured and Dying Because of It: Updating the Institute of Medicine Analysis on the Impact of Uninsurance on Mortality," Tax Policy Center, January 8, 2008, available at tpcprod .urban.org/publications/urlprint.cfm?ID= 411588.

21. World Health Organization, *World Health Statistics 2016*, available at the WHO website: www.who.int/gho/publications/world_health_ statistics/en/.

22. Taken from "America's Health Rankings," 2016, available at www.americashealthrankings.org. The data are presented on an interactive map of the United States, allowing quick access to individual state health care data.

23. The precise percentage depends on which programs are counted. The estimate used here is taken from a Henry J. Kaiser Family Foundation report, "The Facts on Medicare Spending and Financing," July 20, 2016, available at http://kff .org/medicare/issue-brief/the-facts-on-medicare-spending-and-financing/.

24. For a clear discussion of all these provisions, see Mary Agnes Carey, "Provisions of the Medicare Bill," *CQ Weekly*, January 24, 2004, 238–243. It is interesting that Congress chose to devise such a complex drug plan when the federal government already has one that is widely considered a model. This is housed within the veterans' health care program. See Robert Pear and Walt Bogdanich, "Some Successful Models Ignored as Congress Works on Drug Bill," *New York Times*, September 4, 2003.

25. Government Accountability Office, "Medicare and Medicaid Fraud, Waste, and Abuse: Effective Implementation of Recent Laws and Agency Actions Could Help Reduce Improper Payments" (GAO-11–409T), March 9, 2011; and a follow-up study, "Medicare Fraud: Progress Made, but More Action Needed to Address Medicare Fraud, Waste, and Abuse" (GAO-14–560T), April 30, 2014.

26. Robert Pear, "Cost of Rampant Mental Health Care Fraud Soars in Medicare," *New York Times*, September 30, 1998.

27. Gilbert M. Gaul, "Medicare's Chronic Condition," *Washington Post National Weekly Edition*, August 1–7, 2005, 6–9.

28. See, for example, Rita F. Redberg, "Squandering Medicare's Money," *New York Times*, May 25, 2011.

29. For one account, see the Center for Medicare Advocacy's extensive discussion of reform proposals at www.medicareadvocacy.org/medicare-info/medicare-and-health-care-reform/. As noted earlier, the Affordable Care Act includes many provisions aimed at improving care under both Medicare and Medicaid and controlling rising costs.

30. A comprehensive review of Medicaid and its future can be found in Julia Paradise, "Medicaid Moving Forward," March 9, 2015, available at the Henry J. Kaiser Family Foundation website: kff.org/health-reform/issue-brief/medicaid-moving-forward/.

31. Robert Pear, "Budget Accord Could Mean Payments by Medicaid Recipients," *New York Times*, December 20, 2005.

32. Alex Wayne, "Congress Defies Bush on SCHIP," *CQ Weekly* online edition, October 1, 2007; and Robert Pear, "Health Bill for Children Is Passed by Senate," *New York Times*, January 30, 2009.

33. Clifford J. Levy and Michael Luo, "New York Medicaid Fraud May Reach into Billions," *New York Times*, July 18, 2005.

34. The report can be found at www.ncsl.org/ research/health/medicaid-fraud-and-abuse.aspx.

35. Greg Miller, "Engineering a New Line of Attack on a Signature War Injury," *Science* 335 (January 6, 2012).

36. Government Accountability Office, "VA Mental Health: Number of Veterans Receiving Care, Barriers Faced, and Efforts to Increase Access" (GAO-12–12), Oct 13, 2011.

37. See Shan Carter and Amanda Cox, "One 9/11 Tally: 3.3 Trillion," *New York Times*, September 8, 2011. For another view of the costs of veterans' health care resulting from the wars, see David Herszenhorn, "Estimates of Iraq War Cost Were Not Close to Ballpark," *New York Times*, March 19, 2008. For a much fuller

treatment of the subject, see Government Accountability Office, "VA Health Care: Long-Term Care Strategic Planning and Budgeting Need Improvement," January 2009.

38. Gilbert M. Gaul, "Back in the Pink: The VA Health Care System Outperforms Medicare and Most Private Plans," *Washington Post National Weekly Edition*, August 29–September 4, 2005. On the history of the VA program and its many successes, see Colin D. Moore, "Innovation without Reputation: How Bureaucrats Saved the Veterans' Health Care System," *Perspectives on Politics* 13, no. 2 (June 2015): 327–344.

39. See Michael E. Shear and Richard A. Oppel Jr., "V.A. Chief Resigns in Face of Furor over Delayed Care," *New York Times*, May 30, 2014. The GAO's report is "VA Health Care: Actions Needed to Improve Newly Enrolled Veterans' Access to Primary Care" (GAO-16-328), March 18, 2016.

40. The various Tricare plans are described at the program's website: www.military.com/benefits/tricare.

41. The program cost data come from the Kaiser Family Foundation and are available at its website: www.kff.org. More detailed reports are available from the Centers for Medicare and Medicaid Services at www.cms.gov. See also Margot Sanger-Katz, "Per Capita Medicare Spending Is Actually Falling," *New York Times*, September 3, 2014; and Sanger-Katz, "How Medicaid for Children Recoups Much of Its Cost in the Long Run," *New York Times*, January 12, 2015.

42. Robert Pear, "Investigators Find Repeated Deception in Ads for Drugs," *New York Times*, December 4, 2002. The article summarizes findings from a GAO report. See also Elisabeth Rosenthal, "A Push to Sell Testosterone Gels Troubles Doctors," *New York Times*, October 15, 2013; and Rosenthal, "Ask Your Doctor If This Ad Is Right for You," *New York Times*, February 27, 2016.

43. Extensive data on these trends can be found at www.cms.gov. The CMS actuary staff also offer a detailed discussion of the economic models, assumptions, and calculations that lie behind these kinds of cost projections.

44. For an overview of reform ideas for controlling health care spending, see Marilyn Werber Serafini, "Bending the Curve," *National Journal*, October 3, 2009, 22–28; and Ezekiel J. Emanuel, "Saving by the Bundle," *New York Times*, November 16, 2011.

45. See Bob Kocher and Farzad Mostashari, "A Health Care Success Story," *New York Times*, September 23, 2014.

46. The plan and its implementation are described in a May 2012 report by the Kaiser Family Foundation, "Massachusetts Health Care Reform: Six Years Later," available at http://kaiserfamily foundation.files.wordpress.com/2013/01/8311 .pdf. See also Kevin Sack, "With Health Care for Nearly All, Massachusetts Now Faces Costs," *New York Times*, March 16, 2009; and Marilyn Werber Serafini, "The Lessons of Massachusetts," *National Journal*, July 18, 2009, 20–27.

47. See Eric Lipton and Rachel Abrams, "EpiPen Maker Lobbies to Shift High Costs to Others," *New York Times*, September 16, 2016.

48. Drew Armstrong, "FDA Bill Clears after Intense Negotiations," *CQ Weekly* online edition, September 24, 2007.

49. See Stephanie Saul, "Merck Wrote Drug Studies for Doctors," *New York Times*, April 16, 2008.

50. Cited in "The Unraveling of Health Insurance," *Consumer Reports*, July 2002, 48–53. See also Charles Morris, "The Economics of Health Care," *Commonweal* 132 (online edition, April 8, 2005), for insightful analysis of the need to find more creative ways to limit overuse and misallocation of health care resources.

51. See, for example, "Misdiagnosis Is More Common Than Drug Errors or Wrong-Site Surgery," *Washington Post*, May 6, 2013.

52. See Richard E. Anderson, "The High Cost of Defensive Medicine," available at www.thedoctors .com/TDC/PressRoom/IntheMedia/CON_ID_ 000697.

53. Milt Freudenheim, "Study Finds Inefficiency in Health Care," *New York Times*, June 11, 2002. The Dartmouth study is reported in "Too Much Treatment? Aggressive Medical Care Can Lead to

More Pain, with No Gain," *Consumer Reports*, July 2008, 40–44.

54. For research on health care quality and discussions of national commitment to quality health care, see the website for the Agency for Healthcare Research and Quality: www.ahrq.gov/professionals/quality-patient-safety/index.html.

55. See Ariana Eunjung Cha, "Researchers: Medical Errors Now Third Leading Cause of Death in the United States," *Washington Post*, May 3, 2016. The study was published in a leading medical journal. A 2013 study put the number of medical errors even higher, at 440,000 a year. See David Bornstein, "Reducing Preventable Harm in Hospitals," *New York Times*, January 26, 2016.

56. Bornstein, "Reducing Preventable Harm in Hospitals."

57. Tina Rosenberg, "To Make Hospitals Less Deadly, a Dose of Data," *New York Times*, December 4, 2013; and Bornstein, "Reducing Preventable Harm in Hospitals."

58. The figures come from the CDC, which reports regularly on smoking-related deaths and economic losses, and are available at www.cdc.gov/tobacco.

59. These statistics are taken from the surgeon general's extensive report of 2004, and are available at the CDC website: www.cdc.gov/tobacco.

60. Sabrina Tavernise, "A Hot Debate over E-Cigarettes as a Path to Tobacco, or from It," *New York Times*, February 23, 2014; Matt Richtel, "Selling a Poison by the Barrel: Liquid Nicotine for E-Cigarettes," *New York Times*, March 23, 2014; and Tavernise, "F.D.A. Tightens Rules for E-Cigarettes in a Landmark Move," *New York Times*, May 5, 2016. For a thorough discussion of the regulation of e-cigarettes, see a "point-counterpoint" review in the *Journal of Policy Analysis and Management* 35, no. 2 (2016): 472–495.

61. Quoted in a review of Marion Nestle's *Food Politics: How the Food Industry Influences Nutrition and Health* (Berkeley: University of California Press, 2002), by Ben Geman, *National Journal*, June 22, 2002, 1899.

62. The new data can be found at the CDC site on overweight and obesity: www.cdc.gov/obesity. Obesity is defined as having a body mass index (BMI) of 30 or greater, and being overweight is defined as having a BMI of 25 or higher.

63. Reed Abelson, "F Is for Americans Getting Fatter," *New York Times*, July 7, 2011.

64. See the National Institutes of Health for a summary of some of the data: www.nih.gov/news-events/news-releases/nih-study-finds-extreme-obesity-may-shorten-life-expectancy-14-years.

65. Melanie Warner, "The Food Industry Empire Strikes Back," *New York Times*, July 7, 2005.

66. Anahad O'Connor, "New Dietary Guidelines Urge Less Sugar for All and Less Protein for Boys and Men," *New York Times*, January 7, 2016; and Sabrina Tavernise, "F.D.A. to Require Calorie Count, Even for Popcorn at the Movies," *New York Times*, November 24, 2014.

67. Tara Parker-Pope, "The Fat Trap," *New York Times Magazine*, December 28, 2011. See also David H. Freedman, "How to Fix the Obesity Crisis," *Scientific American*, February 2011.

68. The study is summarized in Anne Lise Straden, "Being Unfit Nearly as Harmful as Smoking," *Real Clear Science*, August 16, 2016. The original research was published in the *European Journal of Preventive Cardiology*.

69. Tara Parker-Pope, "Less Active at Work, Americans Have Packed on Pounds," *New York Times*, May 25, 2011.

70. The National Center for Health Statistics in the CDC releases these figures each year. The OECD numbers come from https://data.oecd.org/healthstat/life-expectancy-at-birth.htm.

71. Neil Munro, "The End of Obesity," *National Journal*, February 6, 2010, 36–42. The 2012 study is J. Cawley and C. Meyerhoefer, "The Medical Care Costs of Obesity: An Instrumental Variables

Approach," *Journal of Health Economics* 31, no. 1 (2012): 219–230.

72. The cost estimates come from the journal *Health Affairs* and are reported on its website: www .healthaffairs.org.

73. The estimates come from the American Diabetes Association (www.diabetes.org) and from Mark

Bittman, "How to Save a Trillion Dollars," *New York Times*, April 12, 2011.

74. Munro, "The End of Obesity."

75. David M. Drucker, "A Fat and Lazy State: Obesity Costly for California," *LA Daily News*, April 13, 2005.

76. Morris, "The Economics of Health Care."

Chapter 9

Chapter Objectives

- Describe issues related to poverty and different perspectives about why it occurs.

- Explain the differences between social insurance programs and means-tested programs.

- Understand the basics of the Social Security program and different policy options offered to improve it.

- Assess both past and current welfare-related programs.

Struggling to make ends meet. Debate continues over setting higher federal and state minimum wages, which have not kept up with inflation. The photo shows California governor Jerry Brown signing a bill that will raise the state's minimum wage to $15 an hour by 2022 while surrounded by supporters and politicians on stage at the Ronald Reagan State Building in downtown Los Angeles, California, on April 4, 2016. (AFP/FREDERIC J. BROWN)

Welfare and Social Security Policy

How well do you know and understand the issue of poverty in the United States? Who are the poor? Are particular demographic groups affected more than others? How do our current economic system, minimum wage, and other factors affect poverty rates and individuals trying to make ends meet?

Poverty continues to be a major concern for the nation. Over forty-three million Americans (15 percent of the population) lived in poverty in 2015, and millions more are only one disaster away from also falling into poverty. Some of the characteristics of those in poverty may surprise you: 35 percent are children, 25 percent are people within the workforce, 10 percent are senior citizens or disabled, and 7 percent are students.[1] There are numerous programs that attempt to address poverty and its impacts on individuals. Programs such as food stamps (the Supplemental Nutrition Assistance Program, discussed later) try to ensure that people have enough to eat. Housing and medical assistance programs provide help in these critical areas for those without the means to provide it themselves. Even a program such as Social Security has an important element to ensure that the elderly and disabled have sufficient financial resources. As noted in chapter 7, programs such as Social Security are considered entitlements and represent a significant portion of the federal budget.

Note that many of those in poverty are senior citizens despite their receipt of Social Security benefits. The Social Security program served nearly sixty million people in December 2015. Most receive benefits that are tied to their age or to being a surviving spouse of a beneficiary, which are the programs people most associate with Social Security; most people also expect to receive such benefits upon their retirement. This is a sizable portion of the U.S. population, and it is also a significant political force in American politics. Over the past two decades, many analysts and policymakers have suggested changes to the program, particularly to address demographic shifts (such as retirement of the baby boom generation), budgetary concerns, and questions of sustainability, and yet the program continues on with only minimal changes having been made. Budget and economic crises often bring Social Security reform to the forefront, but rarely is anything significant done.

Social Security is one of those programs in which economics, politics, and ethics intersect, leading to a variety of opinions about the program and what, if anything, to do about it. More broadly, Social Security is considered an income maintenance program—and such programs are put in place partially to address concerns about poverty and to ensure an adequate income. There are a number of government policies geared toward income maintenance and support in the United States. Some of these, such as Temporary Assistance for Needy Families (TANF) or welfare, are programs that require recipients to meet a certain income test. As noted above, other policy changes, such as an increase to the minimum wage, also can affect income. Social Security is considered a program that provides financial stability, and most of its recipients meet their eligibility requirements in other ways. This chapter examines the issue of poverty generally and some of the major programs implemented by the United States to address concerns related to low income levels. As you will see, the general population often perceives these programs quite differently, and as a result, the politics surrounding them varies as well.

Background

As noted, Social Security is one of a number of federal programs designed to help individuals maintain a minimal level of income after retirement or, if they are unable to continue working, before they reach retirement age. The other major program associated with income maintenance is the welfare system, currently administered under the Personal Responsibility and Work Opportunity Reconciliation Act of 1996 (PRWORA) and reauthorized in 2006. This law was a major reform of the old Aid to Families with Dependent Children (AFDC), and it provides support to individuals with low incomes. These two programs are the chief components of social welfare in the United States, and they are designed largely to help combat poverty. The programs differ on a number of levels, however, including general public acceptance, sources of financing, and potential challenges they face in the future.

To better understand the social welfare programs, one first needs to know something about poverty in the United States. With the United States' large economic engine, it can be difficult to believe that a substantial number of Americans live in poverty. The fact is that poverty exists and needs to be addressed, and it becomes an even greater concern during times of economic downturns as we have seen in recent years. This chapter begins with some information about poverty in the United States and then discusses Social Security and welfare programs.

Poverty

The United States has always had different viewpoints regarding poverty. The American cultural and social perspective that encourages individualism and promotes equality of opportunity leads to a tendency to blame the poor for their own circumstances. On the other hand, some say there really is inequality of opportunity that prevents many from increasing their standard of living. Hurricane Katrina and its aftermath, as well as the recent economic recessions and slow recovery, once again have focused America's attention on persistent poverty and inequality. This may be particularly problematic for those considered to be in extreme or deep poverty. Deep poverty is defined as a household case income less than half of the federal poverty amount. Over 6 percent of the population lives under these conditions.[2]

There are a number of different ways to examine poverty in the United States, starting with the official definition, as noted in chapter 5. For 2016, the federal government placed a family of four below the poverty line if its annual income was less than $24,300 in the forty-eight contiguous states. This rate is adjusted based on factors such as the number of people in a family, the composition of a family, and inflation from year to year. According to the Census Bureau, in 2015, over 43.1 million people were considered to be impoverished. This was down from 46 million in 2012.[3] Others look at poverty from an income distribution perspective: the more unequal the distribution of income, the greater the potential poverty problem. Still others examine poverty in terms of demographic characteristics such as race, gender, and age (see Figure 9-1).

As an issue, poverty in the United States came to a head during the mid 1960s when President Lyndon Johnson declared the War on Poverty. The government initiated a number of programs to deal with the problem. Between 1965 and 1973, the poverty rate fell from 17.3 percent to 11.1 percent, and it appeared that the nation was winning the war. Unfortunately, the United States has not achieved a poverty rate this low since 1973. The rate has improved significantly in certain demographic categories; for example, the elderly and intact minority families have made definite advances. Single mothers, children, and poorly educated young people, however, still have a hard time rising out of poverty.

Some statistics concerning children in poverty help to drive this point home. In 2007, 18 percent of all children in the United States were poor, and this percentage increased to 21.8 in 2012, and decreased to 19.7 percent in 2015. Children make up only 25 percent of the population, but they comprise 35 percent of the nation's poor. Moreover, minority populations in the United States also suffer higher poverty rates than whites,[4] which may indicate something about the weaknesses of government programs to reduce poverty as well as those aimed at improving the status of minorities. Figure 9-2 shows the United States' poverty rate by age over the past fifty years.

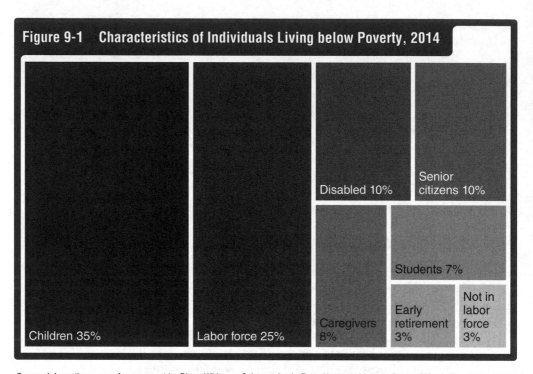

Figure 9-1   Characteristics of Individuals Living below Poverty, 2014

Disabled 10%

Senior citizens 10%

Students 7%

Children 35%

Labor force 25%

Caregivers 8%

Early retirement 3%

Not in labor force 3%

Source: Information comes from a report by Diane Whitmore Schanzenbach, Ryan Nunn, and Lauren Bauer, "Who Is Poor in the United States?" Brookings Institution, June 17, 2016, available at www.brookings.edu/research/who-is-poor-in-the-united-states/.

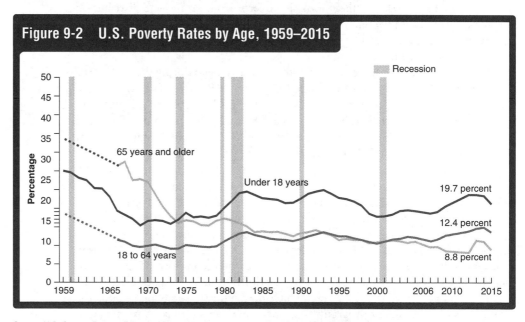

Figure 9-2   U.S. Poverty Rates by Age, 1959–2015

Recession

65 years and older

Under 18 years

19.7 percent

12.4 percent

18 to 64 years

8.8 percent

Source: U.S. Census Bureau, "Historical Poverty Tables: People and Families—1959 to 2015," Annual Social and Economic Supplements. Available at www.census.gov/data/tables/time-series/demo/income-poverty/historical-poverty-people.html.

Note: The data points are placed at the midpoints of the respective years. Data for people aged eighteen to sixty-five and sixty-six and older are not available from 1960 to 1965.

Many look at poverty as an income distribution problem. In other words, a large number of people are living on limited resources, while a smaller percentage of people earn a large proportion of the nation's combined income. Economists often use the **Gini coefficient** (see Figure 9-3) as a way of demonstrating a nation's income equality and inequality. Income equality is represented by a forty-five-degree line, on which each percentage of the population is making the same percentage of the income. As a curve deviates away from the forty-five-degree line, it shows an increase in income inequality. The implicit interpretation of the curve is that if a few people are making a large percentage of the income, more people are put at risk of poverty.

Based on 2015 data from the Census Bureau, the richest 20 percent of the population makes 51 percent of all of the income in the United States, and the poorest 20 percent makes only 3.1 percent. Another way to state this is that the top quintile is making more than the other 80 percent of the population (see Table 9-1). This gap is even more pronounced when you look at the top 5 percent, which earns more than 22 percent of all income. Some analysts and policymakers have begun to look at the poverty problem in a way they believe will change the debate on the issue. Although levels of poverty, as defined by the Census Bureau, have been decreasing, as we noted just above, in 2010 they reached the highest level in over fifty years, in part because of the prolonged economic downturn and high levels of unemployment or underemployment (working only part time or for low wages).

Even before these recent changes, some data indicated that the poor increasingly faced real challenges. For example, the U.S. Conference of Mayors announced in 2013 that almost all cities reported an increase in emergency food assistance over the past year. Similar findings were reported for homelessness.[5] While the Census Bureau has considered revising its definition of poverty, no real changes occurred until 2011, when the bureau introduced a supplementary measure of poverty. While the bureau will continue to use the "official" measure,

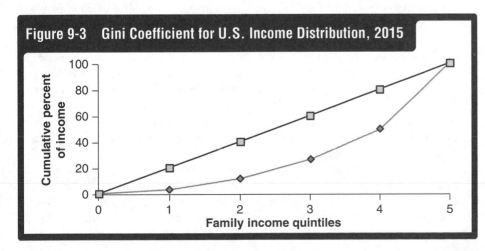

Figure 9-3   Gini Coefficient for U.S. Income Distribution, 2015

Source: U.S. Census Bureau, "Historical Income Tables: Income Inequality."

TABLE 9-1   Income Distribution in the United States, 2015

Income Quintiles	Percentage of Income	Cumulated Percentage
Lowest	3.1%	3.1%
Second	8.2	11.3
Third	14.3	25.6
Fourth	23.2	48.8
Highest[a]	51.1	100.0

Source: Bernadette D. Proctor, Jessica L. Semega, and Melissa A. Kollar, "Income and Poverty in the United States: 2015," U.S. Census Bureau, September 2016, available at https://www.census.gov/content/dam/Census/library/publications/2016/demo/p60-256.pdf.

[a]The distribution of income in the United States is even more unequal than the data in the table suggest. If one examines the gain in income over the past thirty years of the top 10 percent of Americans, one discovers that most of the gain went to the top 1 percent of taxpayers, and 60 percent of the gains of the top 1 percent went to the top 0.1 percent. The disparity between the very rich and the average American has been growing significantly in recent years. For a commentary about the erosion of equality in income distribution over the past several decades, see Paul Krugman, "We Are the 99.9%," *New York Times,* November 24, 2011.

it will also publish this supplementary measure that will attempt to take into consideration "social and economic realities and government policies."[6] In essence, the new measure takes into account a fuller range of variables related to both revenue and expenditures. Changing definitions can dramatically affect poverty statistics, which is probably why this supplemental measure will not be used to determine eligibility for programs.

The new measure of poverty also could significantly affect the political stakes. As an example, based on analyses using some different definitions of poverty, the income threshold in 2015 would be $25,930, or nearly $2,500 greater than the stated rate. Thus use of a different definition of poverty could increase the poverty rate substantially.[7] Such changes in the poverty-line calculations may be necessary because the original poverty line is based on a number of assumptions made in the mid 1960s that may no longer be valid. In addition, the poverty level is the same for the lower forty-eight states and does not take into consideration what are often substantial cost-of-living differentials across the country. The supplemental measure discussed above represents the first major effort to reconsider this measure. It is probably safe to say that even the proposed increase in the income threshold and the resulting additional assistance may not be sufficient to cover a family's expenses—housing, food, clothing, child and medical care, and everything else.[8]

On the other hand, more recently a number of pundits and politicians, particularly conservatives, have argued that perhaps poverty may not be what it once was, and that even the poor enjoy a better quality of life than was the case decades ago. For example, they say that a large proportion of the population may not be paying any income taxes at all. Their claim is that everyone, even the poor, should be helping the nation address its fiscal challenges, and that they can afford to do so because they are living with what might be called luxury items in comparison to how many families lived in the 1960s.[9]

Another way to examine poverty is from an ideological perspective, or what some might say are the root causes of poverty. Is poverty due to broad economic circumstances or to individual behavior and choices not to work? Liberals and conservatives have different ideas about why poverty exists and consequently make different proposals for addressing the problem. Conservatives see poverty in part as a personal choice; they believe that little poverty exists in the United States that is involuntary. Some may also believe in the **culture of poverty**, meaning that those brought up in poverty learn how to be poor and work the current system to their benefit, and that they choose to remain poor as adults. In addition, conservatives tend to blame government programs for encouraging people to remain poor, in part by not requiring any kind of responsibility in exchange for received benefits. Liberals, on the other hand, see poverty as a problem brought on by economic and social conditions over which individuals have little or no control. Liberals recognize that not everyone has the same opportunity for quality education or job training, and they favor government intervention to help equalize the playing field. They believe as well that the high number of minorities who are poor indicates that discrimination also contributes to poverty.

As discussed in chapter 6, equity is one of the criteria used to analyze problems or policies, but the word can have multiple meanings. In the case of poverty, should the concern be whether the processes by which people gain an education and jobs, and thus a certain income, are fair, and thus whether the nation's overall distribution of income is fair? Conservatives tend to think this way about income distribution and poverty. On the other hand, liberals would ask whether equity means moving toward a more equal distribution of resources in the nation.

In 2011 and 2012, the Occupy Wall Street and related movements tended to emphasize the latter perspective. That is, supporters viewed the current income distribution between the top 1 percent of the population and the remaining 99 percent as unfair or inequitable. The strong support for Senator Bernie Sanders during the Democratic primaries, particularly among college students, was built in part on the continuing level of inequality in the U.S. economy. Moreover, analysts pointed to new studies that showed significant constraints on social mobility—that is, on the ability of people to rise from the lower income levels. Recent research indicates that the United States now provides less mobility of this kind than do comparable nations. For example, 42 percent of American men raised in the bottom fifth of the income distribution remain there in adulthood. This persistent disadvantage is higher than in Denmark (where it is 25 percent) and Britain (where it is 30 percent).[10] Some saw the rise and eventual victory of the Trump candidacy in 2016 as linked strongly to the perception and perhaps the reality of economic stagnation and the "left behind" white working class.[11] Even with such data, of course, liberals and conservatives might disagree about whether inequality of this kind is acceptable or not. As we have argued throughout the book, students of public policy know that, depending on how one sees the causes of a problem and defines the evaluative criteria, various alternatives to address it will seem more or less appealing. Some will conclude that the United States continues to offer a reasonable degree of social and income mobility and thus the situation is fair, while others will interpret it as showing an unacceptable degree of inequality.

Many of the social programs developed throughout U.S. history have attempted to deal with the poverty issue from different perspectives. Social Security, for example, was developed specifically to address poverty among the elderly. By this measure, the program has been somewhat successful. According to an analysis conducted by the Center on Budget and Policy Priorities using U.S. Census Bureau data, 40.5 percent of the elderly would be in poverty without Social Security benefits. With these benefits, the number in poverty drops to 8.8 percent.[12] One of the goals of the food stamp program is at least to address issues of severe hunger that could occur as a result of poverty. The Earned Income Tax Credit (discussed later in this chapter) supplements wages of the working poor to lift recipients out of poverty. Programs such as AFDC and the newer TANF have attempted to deal with the poverty of all individuals who happen to fall below a certain income level or who have no income at all.

Social Security

Social Security is the single largest federal government program today, providing money for retired workers, their beneficiaries, and workers with disabilities. While almost everyone these days is covered by Social Security, some federal, state, and local government employees and certain agricultural and domestic workers are not. For beneficiaries over the age of sixty-five, however, Social Security provides the largest component of their total income, and it is the largest share of income for the aged (see Figure 9-4). The presidential budget request for Social Security for fiscal year 2017 was $967 billion,[13] which provides some idea of the size and budgetary impact of the program. Social Security was enacted in 1935 during the New Deal period as a way to ensure that certain segments of society were guaranteed an income after their working years. The perception of Social Security both at its birth and today is that it is a social insurance program. Other examples of such programs are unemployment insurance and workers' compensation. With these programs, citizens pay into a fund from which they expect to receive money back when they are eligible. Because of this designation, the public has always looked upon Social Security as more acceptable than other government welfare programs. Social Security is regarded not as a government handout but as money returned based on an individual's contribution or investment. It should be noted, however, that in most cases a Social Security recipient eventually receives more money than he or she contributed as a worker.

Social Security is typically classified as a redistributive policy program. Money is being redistributed across generations—that is, from workers to nonworkers

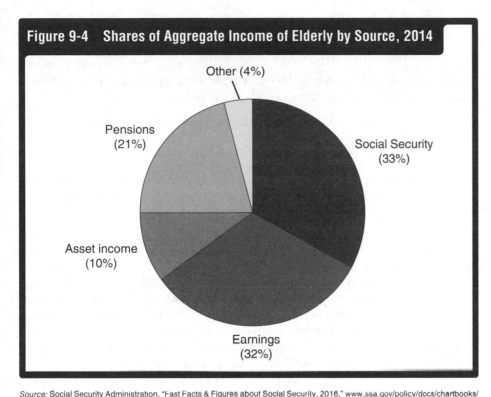

Figure 9-4   Shares of Aggregate Income of Elderly by Source, 2014

Other (4%)

Pensions
(21%)

Social Security
(33%)

Asset income
(10%)

Earnings
(32%)

Source: Social Security Administration, "Fast Facts & Figures about Social Security, 2016," www.ssa.gov/policy/docs/chartbooks/fast_facts/2016/.

Note: Social Security provides the largest share of income for the aged. Aggregate income for the aged population comes largely from four sources: Social Security, earnings, pensions, and asset income. As the figure shows, only 4 percent comes from other sources.

or young to old—rather than between economic classes. Many people believe that their personal contributions are going into a benefits account to be paid out upon retirement, but that is a misconception. Social Security is a pay-as-you-go program; someone's current contributions are paying for someone else's current benefits. The program is also considered an entitlement. That is, if a person meets any of the eligibility requirements for Social Security, he or she is entitled to its benefits. The program is typically associated with payments to the elderly, and in fact this is the system's largest outlay, but other people are eligible as well.

Who is entitled to Social Security? Qualifying for the program is based partially on the number of years one has worked and contributed to the program. As individuals work, they earn "credits" toward Social Security. They can earn a maximum of four credits a year, and most people need forty credits to be eligible for benefits. Benefits fall into five major categories:

1. Retirement: Full benefits are currently provided at age sixty-six plus a few months. The minimum age will gradually increase to sixty-seven for those born in 1960 or later.

2. Disability: Benefits are provided to people who have enough credits and have a physical or mental condition that prevents them from doing "substantial" work for a year or more.

3. Family: If an individual is receiving benefits, certain family members such as a spouse or children may also be eligible for benefits.

4. Survivor: When individuals who have accumulated enough credits die, certain family members—for example, a spouse aged sixty or older—may be eligible for benefits.

5. Medicare: Part A (hospital insurance) is paid through part of the Social Security tax. Typically, if individuals are eligible for Social Security, they also qualify for Medicare.

The Social Security Administration also administers the Supplemental Security Income benefits program for low-income individuals who are at least sixty-five years old or disabled. The program is not financed through Social Security taxes.

The Social Security program has two major goals, and in some ways, these goals conflict with each other. First, the level of benefits individuals receive is related to the amount they put into the system. In other words, the greater their contributions, the higher their benefits. Second, the program was supposed to ensure that lower-income individuals had at least minimal financial protection (Derthick 1979; Light 1995). Both goals are included in the benefits formula, and although the rich receive higher total benefits, the amounts are not proportionally higher. The poor, on the other hand, get a much greater return on their investment.

Most of Social Security is financed by a specific tax on income. The rate of this tax has remained stable since 1990, with no significant increases since 1985. Currently, the government taxes individuals and employers 7.65 percent of their income.[14] Theoretically, this tax is earmarked, meaning the money collected goes specifically toward the benefits; these taxes also are the only source for these benefits. In reality, the federal government collects more revenue through Social Security taxes than it is currently spending to pay benefits. The government uses the excess dollars for various purposes—most commonly to reduce the size of the federal deficit.

The Social Security tax is capped at an annual income of $118,500 (the 2016 amount, which normally increases each year based on inflation) for a maximum contribution total of $7,347 per year. If an individual's income is greater than $118,500, he or she pays the maximum tax and no more for that year. In other words, a person making $1 million or $10 million pays the same amount of Social Security taxes as a person making $118,500. And everyone is paying the same rate of tax; as discussed in chapter 7, this formula makes the Social Security tax regressive. Is the Social Security tax fair in light of some of the considerations on tax policy introduced in chapter 7? Keep in mind that there are also limits imposed on the amount of money that each person can receive each month from the program. Some progressives have argued that one way to better ensure the long-term stability of Social Security is to raise the maximum income level or to not put a cap on it at all. This would represent a Social Security tax increase on upper-income individuals, but it would generate additional revenue.

Social Security is often referred to as the political "third rail" because of the potential political danger associated with attempts to reform it, a reference to the subway that receives its power from this rail. Politicians foolish enough to touch the issue of Social Security reform will likely find themselves voted out of office—in other words, "fried." Whenever policymakers suggest changes, intense debate arises, and the proposals often anger the people who are currently benefiting from the program or expect to benefit in the near future. From a political standpoint, there are two closely related reasons for the controversial nature of any proposal to change the Social Security system. First, the majority of the recipients are senior citizens, who are demographically the people most likely to vote in the United States. Politicians are necessarily wary about crossing such a politically active group. Second, the power of AARP, the major interest group representing the concerns of seniors, is formidable. AARP claims a membership of more than thirty-seven million people, and it is one of the most influential interest groups in the nation. It also has a large professional staff involved in lobbying. With these political resources, it should be clear why efforts to make major reforms to Social Security can be challenging. The box "Steps to Analysis: AARP as an Advocacy Group" suggests some ways to become familiar with the group's activities. Nevertheless, almost everyone believes that something must be done to reform Social Security, because it is not sustainable under its current model.

Steps to Analysis

AARP as an Advocacy Group

AARP is an advocacy organization adept at developing and using policy analysis to promote its positions on issues such as Social Security reform and health care for the elderly. Visit AARP's Public Policy Institute website at www.aarp.org/ppi. Under the Issues tab, you will find a number of reports, video discussions, and responses to reports on Social Security. Other issues of interest are available on this site as well such as Medicare, consumer protection, and others. Click on Social Security and you can examine the various reports and positions to determine the major concerns the organization has regarding this program. Based on the material on this site, examine these materials with the following issues and questions in mind:

- What type of issues is AARP spotlighting and providing information about? Why are these issues highlighted compared to some other type? Does AARP do a good job presenting the options in an unbiased way?

- Select one of the organization's issue reports. Can you discern what AARP's preferred position is on reform? What is it, and what is the basis of the group's support?

Now turn to the Concord Coalition site at www.concordcoalition.org. Select the Issues and Social Security links. What does this organization say about Social Security and its reform? Do its ideas match those of AARP? Go to the home pages of members of Congress, particularly those for your home state. What do they say on the issue? Given these similarities and differences, how much influence does AARP seem to have on policymaking on this issue?

Social Security's Changing Demographics

The Social Security program and the number of people eligible for it have changed dramatically since its inception in 1935. In 1945, the program had fewer than five million beneficiaries, but by 2016, the number had grown to over sixty-five million.[15] The reason for this increase is simple: life expectancy is higher today than it was fifty years ago. As more people live beyond the age of sixty-five, larger numbers are entitled to Social Security benefits. What this has meant is that Social Security, as a program, has grown enormously since the New Deal years and, by all estimates, will continue to grow well into the future. Analysts are especially worried about the impending retirement of the baby boom generation. The first wave of Americans born between 1946 and 1964 started retiring in 2011.

Social Security is obviously larger now in terms of total dollars. But it also makes up a larger percentage of government expenditures; it grew from about 14 percent of the federal budget in 1969 to almost 23 percent in 2017.[16] More problematic for Social Security is that while the number of beneficiaries is growing larger, the number of workers contributing to the program is becoming smaller, leaving fewer workers per beneficiary. In 2015, the ratio of workers to retirees was approximately 2.8:1; that is, 2.8 workers were supporting each recipient. Compare this to 1960, when the ratio was 5.1:1, or to 1950, when the ratio was

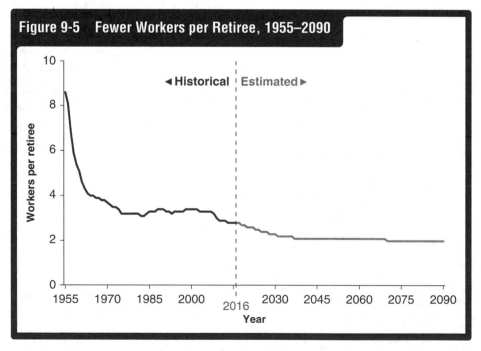

Figure 9-5   Fewer Workers per Retiree, 1955–2090

Source: Social Security Administration, "Fast Facts & Figures about Social Security, 2016," www.ssa.gov/policy/docs/chartbooks/fast_facts/2016/fast_facts16.pdf.

16.5:1, and the problem becomes apparent. Projected estimates indicate that with no change to Social Security, by 2037 each recipient will be supported by only 2.1 workers,[17] when the typical 2017 college graduate will be only in midcareer. The graying of the U.S. population is actually quite staggering when examined over time. Figure 9-5 shows the ratio of workers to Social Security beneficiaries since 1955 and the dramatic decrease in that ratio.

Because of these changing demographics, projections suggest that the amount of revenue coming into the Social Security system will finance only 75 percent of the benefits. For younger workers today to receive full benefits, it might be necessary to increase the withholding tax. This issue will affect people not only in the long term upon their retirement, but also in the short term if Social Security taxes go up. Another option that has been raised primarily by Republicans would be to continue to raise the retirement age as high as seventy years of age. Would these moves be fair and equitable? If not, what are the alternatives to increasing the Social Security tax?

Problems with Social Security

Beneficiaries and policymakers have acknowledged for years that even though the government has addressed some of its problems, Social Security as it currently exists has a number of flaws. In 2000, Congress and the president changed the rule regarding the employment of retired workers and how it affects their Social Security benefits. Under the old rules, beneficiaries who chose to work to supplement their income would lose part of their Social Security benefits if they made more than a certain amount of money during the year. With the change, everyone sixty-six and over (the full-benefit or normal retirement age for those born between 1943 and 1954) can earn as much as they want without forfeiting part of their Social Security benefits. Naturally, this change in the law benefits only those senior citizens who continue to work.

Another Social Security issue the government addressed is the fixed retirement age. Historically, the official age for collecting Social Security benefits was sixty-five, but changes to the law have gradually raised the age of eligibility to between sixty-six and sixty-seven, depending on the year of birth, in recognition of the population's longer life expectancy and people's tendency to continue to work.[18] Raising the age provides two major benefits for Social Security's solvency. First, if people cannot receive full benefits until sixty-seven, they will not receive as much money over their lifetimes. Second, if they continue to work, they will also continue to contribute to the program.

Increasing the retirement age raises other issues, however, such as equity. Is it fair to the members of the current working generation to demand that they work until age sixty-seven when their parents or grandparents could retire at sixty-five? What about quality of life? If people cannot retire until relatively late in life, they may be less able to enjoy their retirement years because of illness or physical limitations. Some social commentators have already raised concerns about the amount of time people spend working in American society, compared to most European countries. In addition, a policy that encourages later retirement may exacerbate problems affecting family life and employment opportunities for younger people.

A third major problem with Social Security is the potential gender inequity built into the system. When Social Security was enacted, few married women worked outside the home, but by the mid 1990s, more than 60 percent did, and the number today is higher still.[19] Why is this a concern? First, women generally earn about 20 percent less money than men,[20] which will affect their benefits upon retirement. Second, women tend to stay at home for parts of their career to raise families, which again will affect benefits. Women also tend to outlive men by a few years, which can be a further financial disadvantage.

Financing Social Security

Obviously, the biggest problem with Social Security and the one that gets the most attention is the financing of the program and the projections showing the system running out of money. The strong economy during the 1990s partially improved the situation of Social Security by increasing its solvency. Recent projections by the Social Security Administration, however, show that benefits and expenses are more than the taxes collected by the program. By 2033, the trust funds, which are in reality a promise to pay, will be depleted, and the revenue coming into the program will pay only about 75 percent of the benefits that are due to retirees and other recipients.[21] These kinds of numbers spark concern among many younger Americans, who say they do not believe that Social Security will be around when they are eligible to collect it after they paid a lifetime of taxes into the system.

Solutions to financing Social Security are particularly problematic from a political perspective. Like any other budget problem, the "simple" solution to deal with the coming deficit in Social Security would be to increase revenues flowing into the program or to cut expenditures. In the context of Social Security, how might that be done? To bring in more money, policymakers could increase the tax on individuals and employers by raising either the withholding percentage or the maximum income that can be taxed, or both. If, however, the government made a subsequent change in the benefits to which retirees are entitled, then the additional revenues would be partially offset. As discussed in other chapters, Congress always finds it politically difficult to raise taxes even to protect a popular program such as Social Security.

The other course of action is to reduce expenditures, which can be done in a number of ways. As discussed earlier, the age of eligibility for benefits has already gone up, which postpones the outlay of funds for a number of years. Another idea, which has been used in the past, is to delay the cost of living adjustment (COLA). Social Security benefits go up annually, and the amount is linked to changes in inflation, as measured by the Consumer Price Index (CPI). By not implementing the COLA for a period of time, the Social Security Administration could save billions of dollars. Another solution would be to decrease the COLA outright. In other words, it might only be a partial, not a full, inflationary adjustment.

The reasons for exploring the COLA option are worth considering. First, many workers in the United States do not receive inflationary adjustments in their wages. Is it fair that retirees get regular increases in their income while those who are working do not? Second, as discussed in chapter 7, many policy analysts believe the government's current indicators, such as the CPI, overstate inflation. There is not uniform agreement regarding this, though. For example, some prices for goods purchased by the elderly in areas such as health care and drugs rise faster than the CPI. If the CPI is overstated, the COLAs are actually higher than the true rate of inflation. For the sake of illustration, if Social Security paid out $400 billion in benefits this year and the inflation rate was determined to be 3 percent, it would mean an automatic increase in benefit payments the following year (disregarding new beneficiaries or deaths) to $412 billion. Delaying the payment of the COLA increase for six months would save $6 billion a year. Adjusting the COLA down by 1 percent would save $4 billion a year. If either of these proposals were adopted for a number of years, significant savings in the program would materialize. Some have advocated for a different, and more generous, COLA for seniors since their "basket of goods" is quite a bit different from others. For example, seniors may be spending more on prescription drugs, but may drive less and therefore use less gasoline.

Privatization is another approach to Social Security financing. The idea here is that individuals would be allowed to invest some of their withholding tax in mutual funds of their choosing, or the government might be permitted to invest Social Security funds in the stock market or other private instruments to generate a higher rate of return than is now possible. Currently, the money collected for Social Security is invested in government bonds with a relatively low yield (albeit with little risk). Many people believe that a partially privatized system would increase the return and extend the financial life of the system.

Privatization has been proposed by a number of people and organizations. Former president George W. Bush proposed the idea of personal accounts that would allow workers to contribute up to four percentage points of their payroll taxes into a larger range of account options that potentially would have provided them with a greater return upon their retirement. President Bush's proposal would have partially changed the structure of Social Security from pay-as-you-go to more of a 401(k) plan; it sets up a private account for each person from which he or she can draw upon retirement. The Social Security Advisory Council (1997) included it as one of its proposals, although not all of the committee members supported it.[22] In addition, the National Commission on Retirement Policy (1999), which addressed a number of issues on how to fund retirement, included a plan to allow for private investment of a portion of the withholding tax. Much of the Bush plan was based on the commission's proposal, which would direct approximately one-quarter (or two percentage points) of the current 7.65 percent payroll tax into individual savings accounts for which people could make choices about investment strategies for their money.

There are some things to consider with this kind of Social Security reform. A system that permits individual retirement accounts and siphons off a portion of the Social Security withholding tax changes the investment picture. These accounts would be specifically earmarked for the individual retiree. In other words, the four percentage points withheld, plus interest, would be dedicated directly to each worker, who would want to get the largest return possible on these investments. Doing so would likely mean investing outside of government securities, particularly in the stock market. Is this a good idea? Related to this, in the absence of other policy changes, and with four percentage points of the withholding tax going into individual accounts, the solvency of the current Social Security funds becomes even more fragile. The funds would be depleted earlier than under current projections. The Center on Budget and Policy Priorities estimated that such a change would deplete the reserves in 2030 rather than 2041.[23] On the positive side, if individuals make good investment choices, they will receive a higher rate of return from Social Security and subsequently a higher standard of living upon retirement.

The negative effects are equally obvious, and the most important of these is the impact on financial markets of a prolonged economic downturn. For example, the markets suffered some of the steepest losses in 2008 when the economy soured in the United States and abroad. The losses demonstrated that there are large potential risks associated with these kinds of investments. This situation raises new questions: Will people be able to manage their investments? How many will make poor choices on where to invest their money? Will financial advisers pressure people to make unwise decisions? Under this proposal, the investment part of people's Social Security donations will not be protected, and retirees could receive less money than they would under the current plan. Would society be willing to redirect money into programs to ensure that people can make ends meet? Will action be taken to provide any protection for these self-invested funds? If the answer is yes to either of these questions, it may require so much money from the federal budget that the purpose of the legislation is defeated.[24]

The politics of Social Security reform also merits attention. We have already mentioned the sensitive politics associated with Social Security and potential reform efforts. Senior citizens are an attractive target for politicians because, as a group, they turn out to vote in large numbers. Not surprisingly, seniors and the interest groups representing them, such as AARP, have been wary of Social Security reform efforts that may decrease their benefits. According to AARP, its members should be concerned about privatization reform plans for two reasons: the potential unpredictability of the stock market and fears that such accounts will take money out of the Social Security account and pass the bill along to future generations.[25] It seems clear that any reform option that includes a form of privatization will need to proceed cautiously, assuring the current beneficiaries and people close to retirement that their benefits will continue at the same rate. Privatization programs tend to be more popular with younger voters who have the time to take advantage of these investments, are more likely to invest in the market, and are concerned about the current pay-as-you-go system and

©Taylor Jones - Hoover Digest

cagecartoons.com

its future solvency. But there is one problem with this analysis. While the young should be more supportive of such a plan, they are likely to be the least engaged in the political debate because it is a program from which they will not see benefits for decades.[26]

Each of the numerous and conflicting perspectives on proposals to privatize Social Security comes with plenty of supporting data and reports, but the debate is not only about personal retirement and investment but also, and perhaps more important, about how the program will continue to survive for future generations. Social Security has been, and will continue to be, a highly politicized issue, which makes major reforms exceedingly difficult. Any reform effort, whether it is privatization or less drastic changes such as increasing the withholding tax or changing the benefit structure, also has multiple economic implications for individuals and for the nation as a whole. In addition, the perceived success of the program in providing for the elderly and those who cannot work raises important equity issues. All of these problems will become even more significant both to individuals and to the nation as more and more baby boomers retire. We will return to this issue in the "Focused Discussion" section later in the chapter.

Welfare

Welfare policies, as most Americans think about them, concern **means-tested programs**. To qualify for a means-tested program, a potential recipient usually must meet an income test—perhaps better described as a lack-of-income test. These programs include food stamps, job training, housing benefits, and direct cash payments to the poor. Means-tested programs differ from social insurance programs such as Social Security: eligibility for these programs is based on need rather than contributions made to the program.

Because of this distinction, welfare programs do not engender the same level of public support as Social Security. Most people see welfare not as a social insurance program but as a government handout or charity, which has different connotations for many. Welfare programs are also redistributive, but in this case funds are being transferred to the poor from those who are paying taxes.

The Supplemental Nutrition Assistance Program

One of the largest federal programs for the poor is the **Supplemental Nutrition Assistance Program (SNAP)**, formerly known as the **food stamp program** and administered by the Department of Agriculture (USDA). The plan provides low-income households with financial resources to purchase food. Eligible recipients, who need to meet certain resource and income requirements, are allotted a dollar amount based on the size of their household. In 2015, SNAP served nearly forty-five million people at a cost of nearly $74 billion. One of the changes made to the welfare program is that SNAP recipients are expected to register for work and take available employment. In 2014, Congress passed and President Obama signed the Farm Bill, which cut food stamps by $800 million over the next decade (about 1 percent per year)—an amount that was much less than what Republicans were originally seeking. These cuts reflected conservative criticism of the program, including concerns they raised about overreliance on the program by beneficiaries as well as numerous accusations of fraud in the way benefits are sought and distributed under the program. On the other hand, many potential beneficiaries do not seek benefits to which they are entitled because of complex bureaucratic rules associated with the program; therefore, they either do not get adequate nutrition or turn to other sources for help.[27]

Federal Assistance for Food. SNAP is only one of many public programs geared to meet the nutritional requirements of individuals. The USDA also administers the federally assisted national school lunch and school breakfast programs, which provide well-balanced, nutritional meals at either no cost or reduced cost to children from low-income households. The school lunch program was first aimed at assisting schools to purchase food for nutritious lunches. The passage of the National School Lunch Act in 1946 gave the program a permanent funding basis and stipulated how funds would be apportioned to the states. The purpose of the law was to ensure the "safety and well-being of the nation's children" through a program that encouraged consumption of nutritious commodities and assisted states to provide such food and necessary facilities.[28] The program, as it is currently conceived, started in 1971, when subsidized meals were tied directly to the poverty guidelines. Today, children in a family at or below 130 percent of the poverty level ($24,300 for a family of four in fiscal year 2016) are eligible for free meals. Nearly thirty-one million lunches are provided or subsidized by the program.[29] This program is clearly directed at children living below or near the poverty line, but it is also part of the government's larger effort to provide valuable nutrition education to all Americans, including yet another revamping of the food pyramid in 2005 and again in 2011 with the introduction of the MyPlate campaign.[30] Providing information and education is one tool policymakers use to address public problems. The federal government has even set up a centralized website (www.nutrition.gov) where anyone can access nutrition information.

Aid to Families with Dependent Children

For years, the nation's major means-tested program was AFDC, which was what most people referred to as "welfare." AFDC was intended to provide financial aid to low-income mothers and children. The program benefited about fourteen million people in its last year in existence and cost about $14 billion annually (Peters 2000).

Critics denigrated the AFDC program for years on numerous grounds. First, AFDC provided funds to individuals but expected little in return. Welfare programs are not popular with voters in the first place, because they believe the recipients are getting something for nothing. Widespread media accounts of people taking advantage of the system in various ways made the public angry. Although

Need for human services. The photo shows patrons being served food at the Broad Street Ministry on July 27, 2016, in Philadelphia, Pennsylvania. An estimated forty-seven million Americans saw their food stamp benefits cut starting that day as temporary relief to the federal program ended with no new budget from Congress to replace it. Under the new Supplemental Nutrition Assistance Program (SNAP), a family of four that used to receive $668 per month was likely to see the amount cut by $36. (Spencer Platt/ Getty Images)

little systematic evidence existed to prove that these practices were common, the stories persisted and helped lead to the program's elimination. Other critics disapproved of several of the program's practices. In particular, they said AFDC stigmatized the beneficiaries by requiring them to respond to personal questions, home inspections, and other administrative intrusions to qualify for the benefits (Cochran et al. 1999; Peters 2000). Another frequently raised issue was that AFDC seemed to provide a disincentive to work. Under AFDC, beneficiaries could work only so many hours a month. If they earned more than the specified amount, they would lose a part of their benefits. The incentive therefore was to work only up to the point of losing benefits. A related problem was that attempts to move off welfare by taking a job were not necessarily a rational solution for beneficiaries. By the time individuals paid for child care, transportation, and perhaps health care, they often had little money left, especially if they were being paid **minimum wage**. The smart financial decision, therefore, was to remain in the government welfare program.

Staying on public assistance may have been a rational decision for individuals, but it did not mean that the money provided was adequate. Statistics showed that the purchasing power of AFDC payments and food stamps had declined over time. During the 1980s and 1990s, the gap between the government poverty line and the welfare benefits provided grew wider (Cochran et al. 1999).

The Earned Income Tax Credit

The Earned Income Tax Credit (EITC) is a refundable federal income tax for low-income working individuals and families. For those who qualify, if the EITC is greater than the amount owed in taxes, the beneficiary receives a tax refund. The government implemented the EITC over thirty years ago as a way to encourage work and to provide recipients with some tax relief and in some cases even a tax refund. In 2016, the maximum tax credit was $6,242 for a family with three or more qualifying children. For those in deep poverty, the tax credit is probably not significant enough to provide much improvement to living conditions, but it could make a difference for low-wage workers. Some have argued for an expansion in the EITC, and President Obama's 2015 budget request did just that. Such an increase could protect families from short-term monetary problems. It could also decrease the number of people who need other government support programs.

Increases in the EITC would raise budgetary concerns that the government would need to take into consideration, particularly in times with large deficits. While the program encourages work and is generally supported, an expansion of it could have budgetary effects. In the current political climate, some also raise the question of how much of a role government should play in ensuring that people do not live in poverty. These issues are also obviously tied to the ethical questions associated with poverty.

All of the welfare programs discussed above have raised difficult questions for the United States throughout its history. Should we be comfortable with a segment of the population living in poverty? What role should government play, if any, to address this? What are the most appropriate or effective programs to address this problem? This brings us to one of the major changes in welfare that occurred in 1996.

Welfare Reform Options

The concerns with AFDC led to calls for reform from many ideological perspectives. Liberals saw the program as inadequate to provide enough benefits to ensure an adequate standard of living and protect the children who were supposed to be the primary beneficiaries. Conservatives, on the other hand, were more interested in correcting the disincentives for adult beneficiaries to work and try to become self-sufficient. R. Kent Weaver (2000) discussed this conflict as the "dual clientele trap" associated with calls for welfare reform:

> Policymakers usually cannot take the politically popular step of helping poor children without the politically unpopular step of helping their custodial parents; they cannot take the politically popular steps such as increasing penalties for refusal to work or for out-of-wedlock childbearing that may hurt parents without also risking the politically unpopular result that poor children will be made worse off. (45)

During the 1990s, major forces came together to get welfare reform onto the government agenda, and the result was a new policy. As Randall B. Ripley and Grace A. Franklin (1986) state, in the U.S. system of government, presidential leadership is often needed to propose any major changes to redistributive programs. The election of President Bill Clinton in 1992 and the subsequent Republican victories in the 1994 congressional elections set the stage for change. On the issue of public support for the poor, Clinton said he wanted to "end welfare as we know it" (Clinton and Gore 1992). His ideas to require work to receive benefits and "demand responsibility" (Clinton and Gore 1992, 164) were in some ways more in line with Republicans than with traditional Democratic constituencies. The Republicans had made welfare reform a tenet of their Contract with America, a set of proposals that formed the basis of their campaign. Their version of welfare reform emphasized work even more firmly than the Clinton proposals (Weaver 2000). The ideological changes in Congress likely also forced some movement in Clinton's position. The eventual outcome, after much negotiation, political posturing, and strong opposition by many liberal interest groups, was PRWORA.

Welfare Reform Law

PRWORA ended the old AFDC program and welfare as most people know it, replacing it with the block grant program TANF, which provided state governments with additional flexibility to run their welfare programs. The law also imposed work requirements for beneficiaries and put lifetime limits on receiving benefits (Weaver 2000). The law included the following new rules:

- Teenage parents are required to live with their parents or in an adult-supervised setting.
- States are required to ensure people are moving off the welfare rolls and into work. For example, 50 percent of the families were to be working thirty hours a week by 2002. States not meeting the requirements are penalized by reductions in their TANF block grant funds.
- Adult recipients are limited to a total of five years of receiving federal TANF funds, and states can either impose additional limits or use their own money to fund recipients beyond the five-year period.
- The entitlement structure would change from a system in which individuals who meet the eligibility requirements are entitled to AFDC funds to one in which the states receive the entitlement based on a federal block grant formula (Weaver 2000).

As part of the Deficit Reduction Act of 2005, which became law in 2006, Congress reauthorized TANF and approved changes that made the program stricter, made it more difficult for states to meet the established goals, and took away some state flexibility. These changes included the following:

Working with Sources

Welfare and the Weakening Economy

The economy can have major implications for the general population, particularly as it relates to people eligible for welfare. High levels of unemployment and underemployment can lead to more people qualifying for welfare programs such as Temporary Assistance for Needy Families and the Supplemental Nutrition Assistance Program. Oftentimes, it is left up to state governments to implement such programs, and this may occur differently across the country. Go to the following sites and see what they are saying about welfare and the economy and how states may be reacting:

Center on Budget and Policy Priorities (www.cbpp.org/research/index.cfm?fa=topic&id=42)

National Conference of State Legislatures (www.ncsl.org/research/human-services/welfare-and-poverty.aspx)

Urban Institute (www.urbaninstitute.org/welfare/index.cfm)

Consider the following questions:

- What are these organizations saying about the effectiveness of welfare programs to address need in less-than-ideal economic times?

- How is this affecting states and their populations differently? What concerns are being raised by these organizations?

- What is your assessment of what should happen? What improvements might you recommend, and why?

- Work participation rates are based on caseload declines after 2005 rather than 1995. Since significant case reductions occurred particularly in the late 1990s, the result was that it was more difficult for states to meet the goals.
- Work participation rates are based on both TANF and state-funded programs. In the past, state-funded programs did not count toward the work rate.
- Uniform methods for reporting hours, type of work accepted, and other issues are adopted.
- A new penalty of up to 5 percent is established for states that do not implement internal procedures and controls consistent with the secretary of Department of Health and Human Services (HHS) regulations.[31]

In 2015, over 3.1 million people were receiving TANF benefits according to the HHS Administration for Children and Families. The box "Working with Sources: Welfare and the Weakening Economy" presents opportunities to examine this issue in more depth.

Analysis of the Welfare Reform Law

The welfare reform policy incorporated a number of components of interest to public policy students. In terms of economic efficiency, the Congressional Budget Office (CBO, 1996) estimated that the new law would save $54 billion by fiscal year 2002, with most of the savings coming from reductions in benefits to legal immigrants and other changes to existing programs such as food stamps (Weaver 2000). These savings obviously pleased many in the Washington community, especially conservatives who wanted to cut funding for welfare programs. It is also interesting to note, however, that many of the suggestions for reforming welfare, such as providing job training, child care benefits, or medical care to ensure that adults can work, would actually be more expensive to implement in the short run than the previous AFDC program. Kent Weaver calls this problem the "money trap." PRWORA, however, did not fully endorse many of the high-cost provisions being pushed by advocates of the work requirement.

Politically, the public supported and continues to agree with the changes to the welfare program. Remember, most of the general public is wary of a program that gives benefits with no strings attached. The public also supported the work requirement that would provide people with the skills they needed to become self-sufficient, not to mention the reduction of the number of out-of-wedlock births that seemed to come as a result (Weaver 2000). On the other side of the fence, many individuals and groups worried about the welfare reforms. Liberal politicians and interest groups, especially child advocacy groups, expressed concerns that the reforms would lead to higher levels of poverty for the affected populations because of their inability or unwillingness to follow the new requirements such as finding work. The supporters of welfare reform, however, constituted a much larger coalition, which included nearly all Republicans and conservative and moderate Democrats. Moreover, the Clinton administration was feeling pressured to follow through on one of its major policy proposals, especially as the president was running for a second term.

Looking at the law from the point of view of individual freedom, it is clear that in some ways the welfare reforms impinged on a measure of the beneficiaries' freedom. In fact, many parts of the law reflected what has been called "new paternalism," whose adherents had found the permissiveness in the welfare state appalling (Mead 1986). Requiring work to receive benefits not only takes away part of an individual's freedom but also imposes a different set of values—the government's values—over how people should live. On the other hand, taxpayers prefer a program that has clear guidelines and requirements for what it takes to receive benefits. Ethically, the questions that inevitably arise ask what happens to children under this program if their parents do not meet their obligations or if they exceed their time limits for receiving benefits. Is the nation willing to cut off benefits to this vulnerable population?

Ultimately, one needs to evaluate the success of welfare reform based on the goals of the program. According to Lawrence Mead (2007), three major goals were associated with welfare reform based on what the government did: (1) enforce work requirements, (2) reduce dependency, and (3) promote marriage. A fourth goal, to reduce poverty, would follow from the previous conditions. Goals one and two relate very explicitly to the important question of whether PRWORA has been effective at removing people from the welfare rolls. The initial numbers showed a dramatic decrease in the welfare caseloads since the enactment of the law in 1996. By the end of 1998, for example, caseloads had decreased by 38 percent, and many states experienced caseload reductions higher than 50 percent. These decreasing trends in the welfare rolls continued into 2008, even with a sluggish economy and increases in unemployment and poverty, but saw an increase in 2009 and then reductions again starting in 2011.[32] The changes to TANF made in 2006 that link program goals and caseload reductions made it more difficult for states to claim success or perhaps to make some hard decisions regarding how they will meet the new work rules. States could choose to assist fewer poor families in order to meet new requirements.[33]

The initial positive caseload numbers led many to announce that welfare reform was a major success. Even initially the Government Accountability Office cautioned against making such grand assessments at this stage. According to the GAO (1998), the success documented by its studies might be a factor of the positive economic conditions that prevailed during the mid to late 1990s. In addition, the first beneficiaries who moved from welfare to work were likely to have been the easiest people to place.

Moreover, much "remains unknown about how families fare after leaving welfare with respect to economic stability and child and family well-being" (U.S. Government Accountability Office 1998, 8). Another GAO report (1999) found that people were indeed getting jobs after being on the welfare rolls, but the jobs paid so little that the families were still relying on other forms of aid, such as food stamps and the EITC, to maintain a semblance of economic stability. One analyst at the Urban Institute described the situation as follows:

> Figuring out whether welfare reform is a success means looking beyond how families that recently left welfare are faring today. For those families that have left welfare and joined the workforce, success will depend on whether they move into jobs with higher wages and benefits so that they can be not just better off than when they were on welfare but move further toward self-sufficiency.[34]

Evaluation of PRWORA and debate about its effectiveness continues. As is often the case in determining the impact of public policies (Sabatier and Jenkins-Smith 1993), sufficient time must pass before analysts can accurately assess how well the act is working. Is twenty years after its passage "sufficient"? There have clearly been different studies regarding the law from many sides of the debate. A major test of the law occurred during the country's economic slowdown. As the unemployment rate inched upward, advocates for the poor were concerned that this would cause problems with the TANF program and its beneficiaries and increase the number eligible for cash assistance.[35] Many states had used their TANF funds to provide services to people who moved off the welfare rolls into work. These funds supported services such as child care and medical care and have helped former recipients move into jobs. If more people need cash assistance because jobs are scarce, will these services be reduced? Another issue that merits

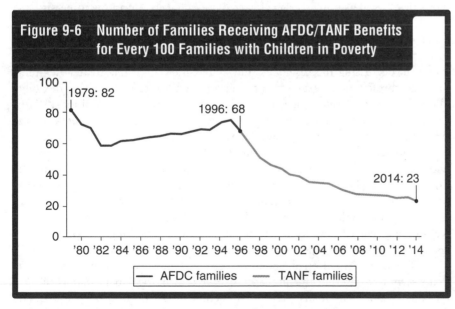

Figure 9-6 Number of Families Receiving AFDC/TANF Benefits for Every 100 Families with Children in Poverty

Source: Material created by the Center on Budget and Policy Priorities (www.cbpp.org).

Note: TANF = Temporary Assistance for Needy Families, AFDC = Aid to Families with Dependent Children.

serious thought is the time limit imposed on beneficiaries. Whenever the country experiences recessions or economic slowdowns, these kinds of questions are raised anew. The left-leaning Center for Budget and Policy Priorities argues that the block-grant-oriented TANF program is problematic in that it does not increase even with growth in the number of eligible people. The result has been a series of negative consequences such as (1) TANF providing fewer families with cash assistance, (2) TANF playing a lesser role in reducing poverty than AFDC, and (3) TANF serving few families in need.[36] Figure 9-6 shows how TANF is supporting fewer families in poverty. The longer it takes for the economy to recover, the greater the likelihood of adverse effects if the program is not funded at a level to meet the needs. A 2012 GAO report on the TANF program suggests that while the program provides a "basic safety net to many families and helped many parents step into jobs," questions remain regarding the "strength and breadth of the TANF safety net."[37] Is the public willing to entirely cut off benefits to needy individuals, especially children?

Other studies of welfare reform showed a level of success, but also raised cautions. While former welfare recipients were entering the job market in higher numbers and seemed financially better off, much of the reason had to do with the financial support provided by other programs such as food stamps and the EITC. Yet, while economically more comfortable than before, many of these people still hovered around the poverty line (Rodgers 2005). The poorest households may continue to have particular concerns in that the TANF cash benefits are losing value. According to the Center on Budget and Policy Priorities, cash assistance benefits are 20 percent below the original 1996 levels in thirty-seven states. The U.S. Census Bureau also found that those most vulnerable had the greatest hardships.[38] And as noted earlier, issues of deep poverty continue to persist.[39]

The question of effectiveness is critical as policymakers decide what may be the next step in addressing poverty and welfare issues. Did welfare reform work? From the federal government's perspective, the stricter requirements were paramount in decreasing the caseloads. But state officials see the greater flexibility provided through block grants as a primary reason for its success. This flexibility allowed states to develop their own solutions based on local conditions.[40] How this question is resolved can affect future decisions. Should requirements be even stricter to receive benefits, or should states be provided with additional funding and flexibility? Additional data and analysis are critical to better understand the wide range of issues. The Urban Institute has suggested five major areas for additional research: (1) improving data capacity, (2) understanding changes in welfare participation, (3) tracking current and former welfare recipients to identify persistent needs and problems, (4) understanding how specific state initiatives affect the well-being of current and former recipients, and (5) expanding beyond TANF to learn more about how other public programs are serving low-income families.[41]

While there are different opinions regarding the success of welfare reform, many seem to agree that the direction welfare reform took in 1996 was the correct one. Welfare caseloads went down significantly from the early 1990s, and more people are working for their benefits. But are these changes the best way to evaluate success? Remember that the purpose of these programs was to lift people out of poverty. Did that happen? As mentioned earlier, poverty continues to be a problem in the United States, and deep poverty seems to be increasing. As stated earlier, the 2015 Census Bureau reported forty-three million people in the United States were living below the poverty line. There are other problematic signs regarding the state of the poor. Families leaving the TANF rolls more recently seem less likely to find a job, and caseloads for other poverty programs, such as food stamps, were increasing for a time particularly during the recessionary period.[42] Growing poverty rates with continued decreases in TANF caseloads seem counterintuitive and may suggest a need for a different standard to measure the success of these programs (K. Murray and Primus 2005). A large number of people, even those who found work as a result of welfare reform, still remain impoverished. In addition, what remains unclear is how well the families that left welfare are doing economically.[43]

It is of interest that the original PRWORA had no requirements to track these families, a serious matter from the perspective of policy design and evaluation. Instead, the only available data came from the states, and only from states that chose to present the information. These data may display only snapshots of welfare recipients and their conditions (McQueen 2001). They continue to come in, but if the information is inadequate, how will policymakers know what changes to make in welfare programs? Are former welfare recipients better off or worse off? Should work requirements be increased? On the positive side, think tanks and other nonprofit groups are also collecting and analyzing data on these problems.

Focused Discussion: Can We Do Better? Addressing Poverty

This chapter addresses issues of income maintenance and different programs that try to ensure that our population has a safety net to protect individuals from falling into poverty. As noted throughout the chapter, though, poverty continues to be a major concern for a significant percentage of Americans, many of whom are children. Such poverty has obvious implications on those affected and trying to make ends meet, but it also causes a drag on the economy and perhaps as importantly raises significant moral considerations for us as a citizenry.

Policymakers, analysts, and many others engaged in the search for solutions to these looming problems have come up with several answers. In 2015, two of the largest and most well-known think tanks, the American Enterprise Institute (AEI) and the Brookings Institution, published a joint report titled "Opportunity, Responsibility, and Security: A Consensus Plan for Reducing Poverty and Restoring the American Dream."[44] The report puts forward a series of recommendations to address the continued issue of poverty in America. Remember from earlier in the book that these two think tanks typically represent two ideologically different perspectives in policy development, but they occasionally publish joint reports such as this in areas where they see common ground to move forward. The report itself provides information regarding what we know about poverty, current policies, and what the two organizations call "three domains of life that interlock so tightly that they must be studied and improved together." These domains—family, work, and education—are those from which the AEI/Brookings' recommendations emanate. AEI/Brookings frames these areas as such:

- To strengthen families in ways that will prepare children for success in education and work
- To improve the quantity and quality of work in ways that will better prepare young people—men as well as women—to assume the responsibilities of adult life and parenthood
- To improve education in ways that will better help poor children avail themselves of opportunities for self-advancement (p. 5)

From this base, AEI/Brookings puts forward twelve recommendations. While we cannot examine each of the twelve, we will focus on a few of these proposals in the discussion of our policy analysis criteria of economic and effectiveness, political, and ethics and equity issues.

Economic and Effectiveness Issues

The AEI/Brookings report sees the issue of work as an important element in addressing poverty. One recommendation is to "make work pay more for the less-educated," and within this area two specific proposals are to expand

Drawing attention to income inequality. Hundreds of environmentalists and Bernie Sanders supporters march through downtown before the start of the Democratic National Convention (DNC) on July 24, 2016, in Philadelphia, Pennsylvania. Income inequality became a major issue in the 2016 presidential campaign. *(Spencer Platt/Getty Images)*

federal childless EITC and to raise the minimum wage. The EITC was discussed earlier in the chapter and has been a successful program for many years, but as the report points out, it offers little to support to childless adults. Such a policy would provide a bit more money to this population. An expansion in the program would therefore put additional money in the wallets of these recipients. Proponents of the EITC also point out that this program may provide families with the ability to "save for a rainy day" and protect them from short-term monetary problems. At the macroeconomic level, more money can lead to additional expenditures or savings, both of which can have a positive effect on the overall economy. In addition, families may be less likely to enter other, more expensive government support programs. To prevent a disincentive to work, some might suggest a minimum number of hours of work.

Raising the federal minimum wage is the second related proposal put forth by the AEI/Brookings report. An increase in the minimum wage would also put additional money in the wallets of those working at this wage and would have similar individual and macro-level benefits. President Obama suggested an increase to $10.10 an hour over a period of time and then indexing it to inflation.

Both of these proposals have economic and potential deficit effects. The EITC is an appropriated item in the budget, and any expansion of the tax credit will have budgetary implications and potentially increase the federal deficit unless it is offset in some way. Increasing the minimum wage has always generated different opinions regarding the economic impacts. A minimum wage is similar to setting a price floor—the minimum price at which a product can sell. In this case, individuals represent a supply of workers, and setting a minimum wage could lead to a situation where the number of workers is greater than the demand for those workers. More simplistically, employers may be less willing to hire workers when wages are higher because of the additional costs. Opponents to minimum wage increases have often raised this issue as a burden, particularly on small businesses, that would have adverse economic consequences. We do know that a number of states have set minimum wages higher than the federal level, and there seems to be little or no effect on the number of jobs or the states' overall economy. Another common argument for those opposing a minimum wage increase is that it has a limited effect on those in poverty who really need relief. They argue that a low percentage of workers actually earns this wage, and those that do are mainly teenagers working for extra spending money, not to make ends meet. In addition, opponents state that an increase in the wage will lead to employee layoffs, particularly in entry-level positions. Therefore, the policy would actually do more harm to those it is intended to aid because they will not have the skills necessary for higher-wage positions.

The economics of these proposals not only highlight disagreements about their effects—they also show differing political positions. In addition, there are differing opinions regarding how effective these policies would be in dealing with poverty problems in the United States. Some relate directly to how the problem has been defined for purposes of this focused discussion.

Another proposal from the AEI/Brookings report is to "increase investments in two underfunded stages of education," in which they are referring to early childhood and postsecondary education. Looking at one of these—early childhood—we know that the path to quality education starts prior to entering kindergarten. Development is critical at the early childhood stage, and there are few efforts provided by government in this area. Most of the focus of government education policy is on the K–12 years. Proposals to increase funding for quality child care, particularly for low-income people, and state expansion of preschool education are examples to address this concern. The argument is that we need to ensure all students are entering into the K–12 years adequately prepared and not allow those without such access to fall behind. Such policies, theoretically, would lead to an overall positive gain in education throughout the children's lifetimes, which would help address poverty concerns. Public education has always been considered a public good, and one of the economic arguments often made for its funding is that all of society gains from a well-educated population. In other words, there is a positive externality that society gains from education.

Clearly the other side of the economic issue is most directly related to budgets at different levels of government. Education funding is generally a discretionary expense within budgets, and as noted in chapter 7, this is a decreasing portion of the federal budget. Changes in the overall budget spending priorities or increases in revenue would likely be necessary to fund such programs. This is equally true at the state and local levels, which are also seeing much of their discretionary budgets reduced due to increases in Medicare and Medicaid budgets and spending in other areas.

Political Issues

The politics of the proposals introduced above are relatively straightforward. Both expanding the EITC and increasing the minimum wage have the political advantage of being related to work requirements, so they could have a bit more support than a traditional welfare program that may not have any requirements. General population support is important because the beneficiaries of these programs often are not adequately represented by interest groups and have a more difficult time getting their voices heard. Political organization can be difficult when those in poverty are worrying about their next meal or whether they may be out on the street. While there are organizations, such as the National Coalition for the Homeless, that represent the poor, mobilizing this population for political purposes can be difficult. These types of policies are generally classified as "redistributive programs," meaning that as one group of people benefits, some other group may lose. In the case of minimum wage, for example, those getting a higher minimum wage are benefiting at the expense of the employer paying the wage.

On the other side of the political equation will likely fall those stressing free-market economies that would set wages based on the supply and demand of the labor market. These groups and individuals would argue that government should not be involved, particularly in minimum wage policies. Organizations such as the National Small Business Association argue that increases in the minimum wage will force small businesses to cut their workforce because of the increased cost not just of minimum wage workers but of all workers.[45]

The EITC raises more general budgetary issues that the government needs to take into consideration, as well as potential concerns by organizations worried about the federal deficit. While the program encourages work and is generally supported, an expansion of it could have budgetary effects, particularly an increase in the federal deficit. As noted above, this will require some important discussions regarding government priorities, including just how much of a role government should play in ensuring that people do not live in poverty.

The politics of education funding at all levels has a number of elements. First, there is the question of whether the amount of money being spent is leading to positive outcomes—in other words, the effectiveness argument. Second, there are different opinions about whether education should be considered a public or a private good. This argument is particularly relevant in terms of higher education, but occurs at all levels. You see evidence of this when local school referendums call for new or improved facilities. Some question how they will benefit from this if their children are grown and out of school. Another somewhat political issue as it relates to poverty is drawing and understanding the line of causality between education and poverty, and the fact that it is circular. In other words, poverty can hinder efforts to provide a quality education, and less education increases the likelihood of poverty. It is a complex problem to understand and address.

Ethics and Equity Issues

At first glance, one might think the ethics and equity issues associated with programs dealing with poverty would be somewhat simple and agreed to by all. Shouldn't we live in a society where people no longer need to live in poverty? Who could argue against this or, for that matter, the programs that address poverty? Of course, as is true with most public policy questions, especially as they relate to issues of ethics and equity, matters are never quite so simple. The devil is in the details, and your perspective on this issue may depend on how a problem is defined and the types of solutions that are offered.

One policy recommendation from the AEI/Brookings report is to promote delayed, responsible childbearing. Research suggests that children born from unplanned pregnancies or to nonmarried people are more likely to be in poverty. The medical technology exists to address this issue, but its use is often met with ethical controversies. Those supporting policies geared toward more intensive counseling on the issue of childbearing or making birth control more available point to data and research regarding the benefits in reducing unwanted pregnancies and how this will potentially lead to better lives for all. Opponents suggest that such policies encourage young women and men to partake in premarital sex. Many also believe that government funding should not be used for such activities. This is clearly one recommendation where there are interconnections between personal responsibility and government action, which also can raise additional ethical or "too much government" concerns. Programs such as these often fall to state and local government to develop, pay for, and implement.

In terms of increases in the EITC or minimum wage, there are also potential equity concerns. Questions of equity often examine the difference between equality of opportunity and equality of results; and the United States has focused historically more on equality of opportunity. Do programs such as the EITC and increases in the minimum wage provide individuals with additional opportunities to increase their income status and lead them out of poverty? Equity questions often arise regarding the role of government in the free market, and programs that require a specific minimum wage directly insert the government into matters of employer-employee contracts as they relate to a fair wage based on supply and demand. Of course, the other equity issue that should be considered is what effect these policies have on businesses or employees if they find themselves out of a job as a result of a minimum wage requirement. Should government step in if a person is willing to work for less than the minimum wage? Isn't a low wage better than no wage?

In considering education funding, the lack of government funding in early childhood raises equity concerns due to the differences between the rich and poor in accessing prekindergarten education and development. This difference can carry through to a child's continued preparation and education in the future. Not providing such opportunities for all seems to go against our nation's perspective of equality of opportunity. On the other hand, education funding at all levels continues to get crowded out due to other perceived priorities with arguments very much turning to private benefits—why should I pay more for early childhood programs if I don't have children or my children are older? Society needs to come to terms with the question of whether public education and its funding provides a societal benefit in which we share the costs.

Addressing ongoing poverty in the United States raises complex concerns. While no one wants high levels of poverty, the individualistic perspective of our society and culture, along with the difficult politics surrounding poverty, make it a difficult problem to adequately address.

Conclusions

This purpose of this chapter is to examine the challenge of poverty and some of the major programs designed to address it. These programs aim to ensure an adequate income to make ends meet, and they have enjoyed different levels of support from the general public. Social Security is often heralded as a prime example of successful government intervention to deal with a public problem. While most agree that the nation needs to maintain a guaranteed income for senior citizens based on their previous working lives, they would also agree that the current Social Security program has some deficiencies and faces serious problems. Welfare programs, on the other hand, have not experienced the same level of public support, and this attitude is apparent in the debates over welfare programs and subsequent changes in how they are administered.

Poverty continues to exist in the United States, despite the programs aimed at relieving it and getting people into the workforce. It is important to understand not only the statistics of poverty but also the political dimensions in order to see the types of choices our government systems make to address the issue. Addressing poverty from the perspective of individual responsibility, for example, will lead government in a different direction than if we believe the issue is more about equitable opportunities and the role of the economic market. Many of the programs developed to address poverty are characterized as means tested and, as noted, typically not as politically supported. One reason why it is important to evaluate such polices is because of this lesser support. Understanding if the programs (past, present, and future) are addressing issues of poverty and allowing citizens to be successful is important for political support as well as ensuring that the nation uses its resources in the best way possible. Poverty continues to be a concern, and finding and evaluating ways to address this issue requires the type of analysis discussed throughout the book. Likewise with Social Security, what type of choices are people willing to accept in order to ensure its financial stability? Every student of public policy needs to understand the issues and know how to find and assess the available data to make informed decisions about these programs.

Sharpen your skills with SAGE edge at **http://edge.sagepub.com/ kraft6e. SAGE edge for students** provides a personalized approach to help you accomplish your coursework goals in an easy-to-use learning environment.

DISCUSSION QUESTIONS

1. Why do you think it has been so difficult to address issues of entitlement spending? What is necessary in order to get policymakers to move on these issues?

2. What explains the continued relatively high levels of poverty across the nation? How might the United States address issues of poverty other than through its means-tested programs?

3. The level of individual income subject to the Social Security tax was capped at $118,500 in 2016. Should the income level be raised to help address anticipated shortfalls in the Social Security trust fund? Would doing so constitute an unfair taxation on current workers? Would it be more equitable to meet anticipated future demand for Social Security by reducing the level of benefits?

4. There has been a lot of debate recently regarding the level of public assistance that should go to the poor and the related question of personal responsibility. Should we move in the direction of less public support for the poor? If so, what are the implications? If not, what should be done?

KEYWORDS

culture of poverty 323
Earned Income Tax Credit
   (EITC) 336
food stamp program 334

Gini coefficient 321
means-tested programs 333
minimum wage 336
poverty 319

Social Security 324
Supplemental Nutrition
   Assistance Program
   (SNAP) 334

MAJOR LEGISLATION

Aid to Families with Dependent Children (AFDC)
Deficit Reduction Act of 2005
National School Lunch Act of 1946

Personal Responsibility and Work Opportunity
Reconciliation Act of 1996 (PRWORA)

SUGGESTED READINGS

AEI/Brookings Working Group on Poverty and Opportunity, "Opportunity, Responsibility, and Security: A Consensus Plan for Reducing Poverty and Restoring the American Dream," 2015, available at www.brookings.edu/wp-content/uploads/2015/12/full-report.pdf.

Richard V. Burkhauser, ed., "Welfare Reform: A 20-Year Retrospective," *Journal of Policy Analysis and Management* 35, no. 1 (2016): 223–244. A point/counterpoint set of commentaries and data on welfare reform over the past two decades.

Maria Cancian and Sheldon Danziger, eds., *Changing Poverty, Changing Policies* (New York: Russell Sage Foundation, 2009). Carefully documents how economic, social, demographic, and public policy changes since the 1970s have affected poverty, and shows that thoughtful policy reforms can reduce poverty and promote economic opportunities.

Kenneth A. Couch, ed., "The War on Poverty: 50 Years Later," *Journal of Policy Analysis and Management*, 34, no. 3 (2014): 593–638. A review of actions taken in the War on Poverty, with abundant data on the effects over time and with commentary by highly regarded analysts.

Kathryn J. Edin and H. Luke Shaefer, *$2.00 a Day: Living on Almost Nothing in America* (New York: Houghton Mifflin, 2015). A book that documents the deep poverty that many Americans are experiencing often right under our noses. It brings to light these issues.

David Hosansky, "Social Security," *CQ Researcher*, June 3, 2016. Provides a good introduction to Social Security and the major issues affecting it focusing on the continued financing of the system.

Theodor R. Marmor, Jerry Mashaw, and John Pakutka, *Social Insurance: America's Neglected Heritage and Contested Future* (Thousand Oaks, Calif.: CQ Press, 2013). Examines a number of social insurance programs within the United States and provides the history, politics, and economics of them and why we have the programs we do.

Joe Soss, Jacob S. Hacker, and Suzanne Mettler, eds., *Remaking America: Democracy and Public Policy in an Age of Inequality* (New York: Russell Sage Foundation, 2007). Reviews the trends in inequality of income and wealth in the United States, the public policies that have affected these trends, and what might be changed for the future.

SUGGESTED WEBSITES

www.aarp.org. AARP is an advocacy group for senior citizens. The site contains data and research on a variety of issues of concern to this constituency.

www.acf.hhs.gov. HHS site for the Administration for Children and Families, with links, data, and information on welfare issues.

www.cbpp.org. Center on Budget and Policy Priorities is a "nonpartisan research and policy institute" that examines policies associated with reducing poverty and income inequality.

www.concordcoalition.org. The Concord Coalition is a nonpartisan think tank advocating fiscal responsibility for programs such as Social Security and Medicare. The site contains data and analysis concerning Social Security and reform options.

www.ssa.gov. U.S. Social Security Administration site, with a wide range of information on the Social Security program and its history; also reports and data on projections for the future.

www.urban.org. The Urban Institute is a policy research organization. The site contains analyses of Social Security and welfare issues.

NOTES

1. Information comes from a report by Diane Whitmore Schanzenbach, Lauren Bauer, and Ryan Nunn, "Who Is Poor in the United States?" Brookings Institution, June 17, 2016, available at www.brookings.edu/research/who-is-poor-in-the-united-states/.

2. See Emily Cuddy, Joanna Venator, and Richard V. Reeves, "In a Land of Dollars: Deep Poverty and Its Consequences," Brookings Institution, May 7, 2015, available at www.brookings.edu/research/in-a-land-of-dollars-deep-poverty-and-its-consequences.

3. Bernadette D. Proctor, Jessica L. Semega, and Melissa A. Kollar, "Income and Poverty in the United States: 2015," U.S. Census Bureau, Report Number: P60-256, September 13, 2016, available at www.census.gov.

4. This and additional information regarding poverty statistics can be found at the U.S. Census Bureau website: www.census.gov/topics/income-poverty/poverty.html.

5. See U.S. Conference of Mayors, *Hunger and Homelessness Survey*, December 2013, available at www.usmayors.org.

6. For more information, see the U.S. Census Bureau website: www.census.gov/hhes/povmeas/methodology/supplemental/overview.html.

7. See the U.S. Census Bureau website: www.census.gov/hhes/www/povmeas/tables.html.

8. There has been a great deal of research done on the question of how best to calculate poverty. For more information, see the Welfare Reform Academy site, particularly the Income and Poverty link: www.welfareacademy.org/pubs/poverty.

9. Not surprisingly, this line of thinking was lampooned mercilessly by Jon Stewart on the *Daily Show* when conservative pundits stated that over 99 percent of the poor have refrigerators and 81 percent have microwaves. The not-so-subtle comment is that these are luxury items. To view this *Daily Show* skit, go to http://thedailyshow.cc.com/videos/jfmt11/world-of-class-warfare—the-poor-s-free-ride-is-over.

10. The studies are summarized in Jason DeParle, "Harder for Americans to Rise from Lower Rungs," *New York Times*, January 4, 2010.

11. See Thomas Edsall, "How Falling Behind the Joneses Fueled the Rise of Trump," *New York Times*, July 7, 2016.

12. See Kathleen Romig and Arloc Sherman, "Social Security Keeps 22 Million Americans Out of Poverty: A State-by-State Analysis," Center on Budget and Policy Priorities, October 25, 2016, available at www.cbpp.org.

13. U.S. Office of Management and Budget, "Budget of the United States Government, Fiscal Year 2017," available at https://obamawhitehouse.archives.gov/omb/budget/.

14. The 7.65 percent is made up of 6.2 percent for Social Security and the remainder (1.45 percent) for Medicare.

15. See U.S. Social Security Administration: www.ssa.gov/policy/docs/quickfacts/stat_snapshot.

16. See "The President's Budget for Fiscal Year 2017," available at https://obamawhitehouse.archives.gov/omb/budget/.

17. See U.S. Social Security Administration, "Fast Facts & Figures about Social Security, 2016," available at www.ssa.gov/policy/docs/chartbooks/fast_facts/2016/fast_facts16.pdf.

18. The full-benefit or normal retirement age for those born between 1955 and 1960 increases slowly from sixty-six to sixty-seven. For those born in 1960 or later, the full-benefit or normal retirement age is sixty-seven.

19. See U.S. Government Accountability Office, *Social Security: Issues Involving Benefit Equity for Working Women* (Washington, D.C.: U.S. Government Printing Office, 1996).

20. See Claire Cain Miller, "As Women Take Over a Male-Dominated Field, the Pay Drops," *New York Times*, March 18, 2016.

21. See U.S. Social Security Administration, "Fast Facts & Figures about Social Security, 2016," available at www.ssa.gov/policy/docs/chartbooks/fast_facts/2016/fast_facts16.pdf.

22. For further information on this report, see www.ssa.gov/history/reports/adcouncil/index.html.

23. You can review the report by Jason Furman, "The Impact of the President's Proposal on Social Security Solvency and the Budget," Center on Budget and Policy Priorities, May 10, 2005, available at www.cbpp.org/5-10-05socsec.htm#fig.

24. Several reports go into further detail on the potential economic impacts of the private investment plan. For details, see Alan S. Blinder, Alicia H. Munnell, Henry J. Aaron, and Peter R. Orszag, "Governor Bush's Individual Account Proposal: Implications for Retirement Benefits," Brookings Institution, June 5, 2000, available at www.brookings.edu/research/papers/2000/06/05saving-aaron; and Barry P. Bosworth and Gary Burtless, "The Effects of Social Security Reform on Saving, Investment, and the Level and Distribution of Worker Well-Being," Center for Retirement Research at Boston College, January 1, 2000, available at www.brookings.edu/research/papers/2000/01/01saving-bosworth.

25. You can find a variety of research reports on this issue prepared by AARP at www.aarp.org.

26. For information regarding the pros and cons of privatizing Social Security, see ProCon.org, "Should Social Security Be Privatized?" available at http://socialsecurity.procon.org.

27. For more information on hunger and the food stamp program, see Kathy Koch, "Hunger in America," *CQ Researcher*, December 22, 2000. Other articles addressing hunger from a poverty and farm policy perspective include Peter Katel, "Child Poverty," *CQ Researcher*, October 28, 2011, and Jennifer Weeks, "Farm Policy," *CQ Researcher*, August 10, 2012.

28. This information comes from the U.S. Department of Agriculture's National School Lunch Program website: www.fns.usda.gov/nslp/history.

29. See U.S. Department of Agriculture, "National School Lunch Program: Participation and Lunches Served," available at www.fns.usda.gov/sites/default/files/pd/slsummar.pdf. Also see Sam Dillon, "Lines Grow Long for Free School Meals, Thanks to Economy," *New York Times*, November 29, 2011.

30. See the USDA website on MyPlate information at www.choosemyplate.gov.

31. See Center on Budget and Policy Priorities and Center for Law and Social Policy, "Implementing the TANF Changes in the Deficit Reduction Act: 'Win-Win' Solutions for Families and States (Second Edition)," February 9, 2007, available at www.cbpp.org/2-9-07tanf.htm. This site also provides more details on the changes to welfare as a result of the Deficit Reduction Act of 2005.

32. See U.S. Department of Health and Human Services, Administration for Children and Families, Office of Family Assistance, "Temporary Assistance for Needy Families Program (TANF): Eleventh Report to Congress," April 7, 2016, available at www.acf.hhs.gov/sites/default/files/ofa/eleventh_report_to_congress.pdf.

33. See Sharon Parrott and Arloc Sherman, "TANF's Results Are More Mixed Than Is Often Understood," *Journal of Policy Analysis and Management* 26, no. 2 (2007): 374–381.

34. See Pamela Loprest, "Long Ride from Welfare to Work," *Washington Post*, August 30, 1999.

35. This information comes from a report by Zöe Neuberger, Sharon Parrott, and Wendell Primus, "Funding Issues in TANF Reauthorization," Center on Budget and Policy Priorities, February 5, 2002, available at www.cbpp.org/archiveSite/1-22-02tanf5.pdf.

36. For more information and a discussion of additional effects, see "Chart Book: TANF at 20," Center on Budget and Policy Priorities, updated August 5, 2016, available at www.cbpp.org/research/family-income-support/chart-book-tanf-at-20.

37. See U.S. Government Accountability Office, "Temporary Assistance for Needy Families: Update on Program Performance" (GAO-12-812T), June 5, 2012, available at http://gao.gov/products/GAO-12-812T.

38. See Ife Floyd and Liz Schott, "TANF Cash Benefits Continued to Lose Value in 2013," Center on Budget and Policy Priorities, October 21, 2013, available at www.cbpp.org/cms/index.cfm?fa=view&id=4034; and Julie Siebens, "Extended Measures of Well-Being: Living Conditions in the United States: 2011," U.S. Census Bureau, September 2013, available at www.census.gov/library/publications/2013/demo/p70-136.html.

39. For additional information and discussion regarding deep poverty, the reader may want to consult Kathryn J. Edin and H. Luke Shaefer, *$2.00 a Day: Living on Almost Nothing in America* (New York: Houghton Mifflin Harcourt, 2015).

40. For more information, see Corine Hegland, "What Works for Welfare?" *National Journal*, January 10, 2004, 106.

41. This study provides a comprehensive summary of a number of welfare reform studies and also conducts its own analysis of some welfare issues. See Gregory Acs and Pamela J. Loprest, "TANF Caseload Composition and Leavers Synthesis Report," Urban Institute, September 28, 2007, available at www.urban.org/UploadedPDF/411553_tanf_caseload.pdf.

42. See Dottie Rosenbaum and Brynne Keith-Jennings, "SNAP Costs and Caseloads Declining," Center on Budget and Policy Priorities, March 8, 2016, available at www.cbpp.org/research/food-assistance/snap-costs-and-caseloads-declining.

43. For further studies on the evaluation of PRWORA, see *Review of Policy Research* (May 2005), which examines a number of areas relating to welfare reform.

44. You can find a copy of this report at www.brookings.edu/wp-content/uploads/2015/12/full-report.pdf.

45. See National Small Business Association, "Minimum Wage," available at www.nsba.biz/docs/minimum_wage.pdf.

Chapter 10

Chapter Objectives

- Describe issues associated with the government's role in both K–12 and higher education.

- Understand some of the common concerns associated with K–12 and higher education.

- Identify education policy reform efforts to address quality concerns.

- Discuss the issues surrounding various policy choices that could be used to address problems in higher education.

- Assess policy reforms that have been suggested to address school quality issues.

Educated in debt. Reports in recent years show that about three-quarters of recent graduates had finished school with a loan debt, and the average debt is now over $29,000. The photo illustrates how many students feel the weight of this debt. *(PAUL J. RICHARDS/AFP/Getty Images)*

Education Policy

I n 2016, more than forty million Americans held some form of student debt, with total loans equaling $1.3 trillion.[1] Student debt has been in the news often over the past few years, particularly in accounts about how this debt affects individuals' dreams and futures, both subjects of rising concern. In January 2014, the White House convened a higher education summit that included over one hundred college and university presidents and members of the administration to discuss the issue of increasing access to college for low-income students. During the summit, participants presented what their institutions were doing as a commitment to improving opportunities for poor students to access a higher education and develop themselves for a better future. Both President Barack Obama and First Lady Michelle Obama addressed the summit and shared their own stories regarding the importance of a college education. Ms. Obama stated, "Right now, we're missing out on so much potential because so many promising young people simply don't believe that college can be a reality for them."[2] There are many factors that may lead one to believe that college may not be a reality, particularly for a low-income student, but one of the more important factors must be the increasing cost of college.

During his presidency, President Obama raised concerns about the increasing cost of college a number of times, and he attempted as well to use his bully pulpit to drive home this point and convince state governments to reverse the trend of decreasing public support of higher education and encourage colleges and universities to be more cognizant of cost increases that so greatly affect their students. State support for higher education is much lower than in the past, and among the reasons are the rising costs in other areas of state spending such as Medicare and state prisons, and a desire to keep taxes low. These are seen as higher priorities than spending on public higher education.

Many high school students and their parents are well aware of the plethora of college ranking systems—perhaps the most well known being the assessment provided by *U.S. News and World Report*, although such rankings also are done by publications such as *Forbes*, the *Princeton Review*, and others. But how visible is one of the most important aspects of higher education: its cost? Colleges are ranked, of course, on everything from academic quality to prettiest campus to which ones are the biggest party schools, and there are multiple problems with measuring academic quality. Academic quality is difficult to define, and it is perhaps even more difficult to collect the appropriate data. Yet as concerns about the value of higher education have become more pronounced, policymakers have started paying more attention not only to these indicators, but also to the importance of costs.

In 2013, the president set forth a new agenda to attempt to address rising college costs. His plan included a new ratings system for college performance, which would include "college value" as a major data point that can be accessed by students. Indicators might include data such as access by low-income students, affordability, and outcomes such as graduation rates and earnings. While the rating system would be significant, the real innovative part of the proposed plan is to base student aid on this college value measure. So, for example, students attending higher-value colleges could receive higher amounts of aid.[3] Such a policy would require new legislation, but it was an indication of the seriousness that the president placed on expanding college opportunity and addressing cost and value concerns.

As noted, the cost and value of higher education have frequently been in the news in recent years, and became a major theme in the 2016 presidential elections, particularly in the primary contests between Senator Bernie Sanders and former secretary of state Hillary Clinton. Each sought to offer a concrete plan to address rising student debt, a vivid sign that both understood well how much the issue affects younger voters. Others have spoken out as well in many different ways. Former secretary of education Arne Duncan, for example, was very vocal in regard to higher education costs, and he urged college officials to "think more creatively and with much greater urgency" in addressing college cost containment.[4] These rising college costs not only affect low-income families who may not be able to afford higher education, but they also can hamstring students with high levels of debt that they need to repay after graduation. While the federal government recently placed this issue on the agenda, some question remains as to what it can really do to solve the problem. Terry Hartle, senior vice president for the American Council on Education, an organization that advocates for higher education, commented that "the federal government can ease the burden of tuition increases with financial aid, but there is no mechanism for it to force the states to maintain funding for higher ed."[5] Similarly, then University of Michigan president Mary Sue Coleman, while welcoming the attention to the issue, put much of the responsibility for public higher education back on state governments that have been decreasing their support.[6] On the other hand, Suzanne Mettler (2014) argues that while the states play an important role in keeping tuition down, there have been changes to the political and policy system at the federal level as well. These changes have shifted much federal higher education aid toward tax breaks and loan programs that have advantaged the rich and the lenders and have saddled students with an increasing amount of debt.

The issue of higher education cost is critical. Education has always been considered the great equalizer in the United States, and an important aspect of its egalitarian and individualistic culture. A good education allows for social mobility and success, according to this perspective. If this access is decreased in the area of higher education—a level of education that more and more people believe is essential in our increasingly high-tech and changing world—then what happens to an individual's ability to make ends meet and to the country's ability to remain competitive in a global economy? Concerns about access to a quality education are also relevant for our students in the primary and secondary schools, but sometimes for different reasons.

Education is one of the many public services that people take for granted. For some students, it provides the knowledge and skills that enable them to continue their studies in college. For many others, however, receiving a quality education is a difficult, if not impossible, task. Since the release of the federal report *A Nation at Risk* in 1983, concern has been growing about the quality of education in the United States. Although most people living in the United States are products of a public education system that has existed for almost as long as the nation itself, critics claim that the system is broken and that students are suffering from its inadequacies. Indeed, statistics suggest that U.S. students are not performing at the same levels as their counterparts in other countries. This chapter explores a number of different concerns associated with education in the United States at all levels including its quality, the costs of providing it, and the role of the federal and state governments in supporting it.

Background

Education, especially public education, fulfills many of the nation's basic goals and has done so since the country's founding. First, according to the beliefs of Thomas Jefferson, it provides an avenue to ensure the continuation of U.S. democracy (Mayo 1942). How can people be active, engaged participants in democratic processes if they lack the ability to read and understand the issues? Second, education helps to assimilate large numbers of immigrants. Finally, it is the primary mechanism for social mobility in the United States, as the educated are better able to secure jobs that raise their economic and social status. This goal fits nicely with the American ideal of upward mobility and rewarding those who work hard. An educated population has a better chance of being productive and taking care of itself. Such people are less likely to need government assistance.

Government took it upon itself to provide education for both moral and political reasons. Morally, education was seen as a way to help individuals and groups in the population understand the nation's ideals and to give them a chance to better themselves. Politically, education not only informed people about the U.S. system of government but also imparted the nation's political culture. In addition, it served the needs of certain political parties and helped those running for office to get elected. As we pointed out in chapter 1, public education also has been a response to market failure in that it is an example of a positive externality. Society benefits from a well-educated population, which justifies the government's involvement and support. The reasons for providing public education that existed years ago are still relevant as government policymakers deal with education policy today.

Traditionally, public education has been in the hands of state and local government. Policymakers at these levels have guarded this responsibility throughout the years and raised concerns whenever the federal government has attempted to interfere in education policy, especially in primary and secondary schools. State governments have the major responsibilities in education policy with respect to curriculum, teacher training and certification, and—to a greater degree than before—funding public schools. And a great deal of education policy remains under local control. Schoolteachers employed by local government comprise the largest category of public workers. There are over thirteen thousand local school boards across the United States, all shaping education policy to some degree within their districts.[7]

This is not to say that the federal government has been completely absent from public education, but its involvement is relatively recent, and growing. Congress passed the Elementary and Secondary Education Act (ESEA), its first major education legislation, in 1965. That law raised the amount of federal funding for primary and secondary education (N. Thomas 1975). According to the Department of Education, the federal government provided about 8 percent of all funding for levels K–12 in 2012–2013.[8] Multiple agencies within the government are the sources for these funds, and they do not all come from ESEA.[9] With federal funding came a variety of contentious issues, including whether the federal government could dictate what was taught and whether parochial schools should receive funding. ESEA also signaled the beginning of increased federal interest in public education. In fact, many elected officials and candidates for office from both political parties regard education as a high-priority issue and want to enact programs designed to improve it.

Historically, however, the federal government has demonstrated a greater interest in higher education than in primary or secondary education. Because education is associated with positive externalities, policymakers want to encourage individuals to attend college and to help defray the cost of doing so; in the end, the better-educated population stimulates economic growth. The national government also provides billions of dollars in research grants that cover nearly all disciplines to universities every year. These grants support basic research in the biomedical and other sciences through the National Institutes of Health (NIH) and the National Science Foundation (NSF). Grants from the NSF and other agencies fund applied research in support of space exploration, national defense, and environmental protection, among other goals.

Among the early programs in support of higher education was the Morrill Act, approved in 1862. It helped to develop the nation's land-grant college system, which in turn contributed significantly to economic development during the nineteenth and twentieth centuries. Land-grant colleges focused initially on practical fields such as agriculture and engineering, but they eventually broadened their scope to include the full range of arts and sciences. Institutions such as Cornell University, Rutgers University, and the University of Wisconsin were first established to foster research, development, and training to improve the practice and productivity of agriculture. These schools, and many others with similar backgrounds, have since blossomed into major centers of higher education. In addition, the federal government fully funds the service academies, such as the U.S. Military Academy at West Point, New York, and the U.S. Naval Academy at Annapolis, Maryland. This support is not cheap; it costs the government over $97,000 per year for each student attending the naval academy.[10]

The federal government also assists the general student population and specific categories of individuals by making money available through direct payments, subsidized loans, and tax breaks. Programs such as the GI Bill and the Pell Grant provide money directly to eligible students to make attending college more affordable. The GI Bill, originally the Servicemen's Readjustment Act of 1944, was instrumental in the decision of tens of thousands of veterans to attend college after World War II. Congress continues to update the law to help fund higher education programs for eligible veterans, and many veterans today rely on these funds to pay for their college education. The Pell Grant program offers awards—not loans—of as much as $5,815 (the 2016–2017 amount) to eligible undergraduates, depending on financial need and costs of attending college. Many other students benefit from guaranteed student loan programs. With federal guarantees for the loans, private financial institutions agree to lend money to students at a reduced interest rate, making college more accessible.

As even this brief introduction indicates, the federal government typically pays more attention to higher education than to elementary and secondary education, which state and local governments traditionally control. In recent years, however, the federal government has begun to respond to the problems in public education at all levels. For example, student performance statistics show wide variation in the quality of education from state to state, and the government has attempted to impose higher standards where needed. The federal government's participation has raised not only suspicion on the part of policymakers who oppose it but also questions about equity and freedom. Does increased federal involvement represent a genuine concern about the quality of education for all students? Or is it an unwarranted intrusion by federal policymakers into an area of public policy where state and local government officials are better able to determine public needs?

The federal government's role in primary and secondary education brings up many issues relating to the goals of education policy and the government's obligations in ensuring an educated public. In today's world, what are, or should be, the goals and objectives of education policy regardless of the level of government

Steps to Analysis

What Successful Education Programs Require

The UNESCO requirements for a successful education program include

1. healthy, well-nourished, and motivated children;

2. well-trained teachers and active learning techniques;

3. adequate facilities and learning materials;

4. relevant curriculum that can be taught and learned in a local language and builds upon the knowledge and experience of teachers and learners;

5. an environment that encourages learning and is welcoming, gender-sensitive, healthy, and safe;

6. clear definition and accurate assessment of learning outcomes including knowledge, skills, attitudes, and values;

7. participatory governance and management; and

8. respect for and engagement with local communities and cultures.

As you examine the details of these elements, think about the type of measures that might be used to help evaluate whether or not success has been achieved. Think about these kinds of questions:

- How does a school or community determine if a teacher is "well trained"?

- Who determines whether a curriculum is "relevant" or not?

- Is the learning of foreign language relevant?

- What about art and music?

Note how closely number 6 relates to our discussion of policy analysis.

How do you think the United States is performing in meeting these kinds of standards? Information on other kinds of educational data that may answer this question can be accessed at the Department of Education's site on research and statistics at www2.ed.gov/rschstat/landing.jhtml. You may also want to visit sites for the National Center for Education Statistics and the National Assessment of Educational Progress. As you read these goals, also consider whether there may be other ways to measure success.

with primary responsibility? It would be easy to say that the goals of education policy are to provide a high-quality education to all students, but that statement raises many additional questions, the most basic of which is, what constitutes "high quality"? The United Nations Educational, Scientific and Cultural Organization (UNESCO) has its own perspectives regarding what a high-quality education should entail. These requirements can be found in the box "Steps to Analysis: What Successful Education Programs Require."

Problems Facing Education

To provide the means for elementary and secondary schools to do the best they can for each student, policy analysts and policymakers need to address a number of problems and issues. Among them are funding for public schools, the separation of church and state, the quality of education, school vouchers, and the merit of a host of proposals—such as teacher standards and testing requirements—for improving the performance of public schools.

Funding

Traditionally, a significant portion of funding for public schools in the United States comes from local property taxes. In fact, it is this characteristic of education policy that has ensured that state and local governments maintain a large measure of control over school curriculums in their jurisdictions. This form of financing, however, has run into problems. First, in general, the property tax does not keep pace with the inflationary costs of providing an education; or, to use a tax policy term discussed in chapter 7, it is not *buoyant*. So while teacher salaries, textbooks, school supplies, and other costs continue to increase, the amount of money provided through property taxes remains unchanged. In essence, schools find themselves having to provide more services with fewer resources. This can be particularly problematic with increasing costs and an unwillingness of local or state government to increase revenue by raising property or state taxes.[11]

The second problem is equity. Property tax revenue directed to public schools varies considerably among the fifty states and within states. For example, in 2014, New York spent $20,610 per student on public education, while Utah spent only about $6,500.[12] The result is that students from some states or poor areas within

Steps to Analysis

State Education Funding

The discussion of how states fund their public education systems suggests the importance of the different evaluative criteria discussed throughout the book. Questions of equity, political feasibility, economics, and effectiveness are particularly pertinent to this discussion. Which criteria do you think are the most important in examining education funding? Is one typically the "driving force" in making decisions regarding funding sources? States use a variety of ways to finance public education. Policy analysis can help you learn about these systems and what issues may be most important for specific states. Using the criteria discussed throughout the text, examine how two states fund their educational systems (elementary and secondary) and what criteria seem to be driving these decisions.

Search a particular state with the words *school funding* to get a listing of sites that address this issue. For each state you select, respond to the following questions:

- How does the state finance its public education system? What kinds of taxes or funding mechanisms are used?

- What criteria do you believe were the most important in making these funding decisions for the state?

- What challenges does the state now face regarding funding? What about future challenges?

- How has the state balanced issues of effectiveness, equity, and politics in making these decisions?

a state may be receiving a lower-quality education. Many believe that financing education with local property taxes is inequitable and should be replaced with a system of state or federal funding to ensure greater equality. Education funding is a topic ripe for policy analysis. The box "Steps to Analysis: State Education Funding" provides some guidance for engaging this topic.

School funding has a direct bearing on the quality of education. School districts have to deal with growing costs and flat budget resources; some have to face the low end of unequal funding. Without adequate resources, schools cannot hire well-qualified teachers and other staff, provide the needed books and supplies, make use of computers and other technological resources, or even give students a clean and safe building in which to learn.

Separation of Church and State

The First Amendment to the U.S. Constitution provides, among other strictures, "Congress shall make no law respecting an establishment of religion, or prohibiting the free exercise thereof." These two clauses dealing with freedom of religion, the Establishment Clause and the Free Exercise Clause, established the concept that church and state are separate in the United States. Certain policies have come into conflict with these First Amendment clauses, and the conflicts continue to this day. Prayer in public schools and government funding of religious institutions of learning are the two leading areas of education policy that have caused disagreements and have led to Supreme Court cases.

The issue of prayer in public schools relates to both religion clauses. Opponents to school prayer argue that it represents an establishment of religion by government. If a public school or an official of the school, such as a teacher or principal, requires prayer in the classroom, then, according to judicial interpretations, the practice is state sponsorship of religion and a violation of the Establishment Clause. Even though a majority of the public supports some form of prayer in the schools, since the Supreme Court case *Engel v. Vitale* (1962), the courts have consistently ruled against any kind of school-sponsored prayer. The prohibition extends to student-led prayer in an officially sanctioned event such as a football game, as the Court ruled in *Santa Fe Independent School District v. Doe* (2000). The courts also have dealt with the so-called moment of silence or moment of reflection, and whether this practice also violates the Constitution's Establishment Clause. Politically, the moment of silence may be more acceptable because it involves no established prayer that could violate an individual's religious freedoms. It should also protect an individual's rights for the same reasons. Is there any reason to be opposed to school use of a moment of silence? Are the issues similar to school requirement of a prayer?

But what about school prayer and the Free Exercise Clause, which states that the government cannot prohibit the practice of religion? In theory, students who choose to pray on their own should have that right; that is, the school cannot prohibit students from engaging in prayer. In the *Santa Fe* case, the school district argued that preventing students from expressing their views amounted to an unconstitutional censorship of their speech. The Court did not agree with the argument, saying that the practice not only constituted an endorsement of religion but also was coercive in that it forced students who wished to attend school-sponsored activities, such as football games, to conform to a state-sponsored religious activity.[13]

Public funding of religious schools is the other major issue related to the separation of church and state in education, and here the courts have been more lenient than on school prayer, despite some contradictory rulings. In general, if public money is being used for a secular purpose and the money is being provided to students rather than to the religious institutions that run the schools, the courts have ruled public funding allowable. This issue took on added importance because of the growing popularity of school vouchers. The voucher program provides parents with public funds in the form of vouchers that they can use to send their children to private schools. Proponents of the voucher movement see it as a way to introduce competition into education and improve the quality of education across the board (Chubb and Moe 1990). The constitutional question is whether parents can use these publicly funded vouchers to send their children to parochial schools. The Supreme Court said yes, they could, when in *Zelman v. Simmons-Harris* (2002) it upheld the Cleveland voucher system, which the justices said did not violate the First Amendment. Even with the Supreme Court's ruling, though, this issue continues to be raised at the state level, where voucher opponents have brought suit in states such as Florida, stating that these programs violate state constitutional protections.

It should be clear that even a constitutional issue, such as the separation of church and state, relates to concerns about educational quality, especially public funding for parochial schools. Parents who believe their children are trapped in a poor public school have a strong incentive to look for alternative ways to improve their education and opportunities for the future.

Quality

Certain statistics support the concern about the quality of education in the United States, but like many types of data, it partially depends on the specific criteria analysts examine. Data collected from the 2015 Trends in International Mathematics and Science Study showed that eighth graders in the United States performed below those in eight other countries but above those in twenty-four. These math scores show a gradual increase since 1995.[14] Another test, the National Assessment of Educational Progress (NAEP), showed slight increases for fourth and eighth graders in 2013 in reading and math compared to previous years, but the 2015 results were slightly lower than 2013.[15] Yet, the most recent results from the Program for International Student Assessment (PISA) found that fifteen-year-olds scored in the "middle of the developed world in reading and science while lagging in math."[16] These results seem contradictory on their face, but notice that they are presenting information on different groups of students and in some cases different subjects; you can see why you can report both good and bad news regarding educational quality. In addition, SAT scores, often used as a measure of college preparedness, went down for a number of years during the 1980s. Scores rebounded slightly during the 1990s and continued into the new century, but more recent years (2006–2014) have seen small decreases in performance in the reading score and the math scores holding steady.[17] Although these statistics may be questioned in terms of the validity of the measurements used, they do correspond with qualitative accounts of public education's failings in the United States. Does the information in the box "Steps to Analysis: Civic Knowledge" prove that the lack of competence extends to social studies?

One problem is that defining a quality education is not so easy, but as public policy students have learned, it is necessary. The way a public problem is defined affects the appraisal of it, the alternatives that are considered, and the policies that might be adopted to deal with it. In that regard, education is no different from any other policy area. One positive measure for quality is the increasing

Steps to Analysis

Civic Knowledge

The standards movement may be a direct result of national surveys of academic material that educators (and others) believe everyone in the population should know. But there has also been a strong emphasis placed upon English and math skills and knowledge development that may be hindering education in other important areas. According to a study by the National Center for Education Statistics (NCES), eighth- and twelfth-grade students have not made any significant progress (and twelfth graders have actually decreased) in their knowledge of civic education since 1998, when their scores were already quite low. In a democratic society, civic education is extremely important to ensure active and meaningful engagement in the political and governmental process. To give you a sense of the kind of information that students were being tested on, we provide some of the standards as determined by the NCES for different levels of proficiency. Eighth graders at the "Proficient" level should be able to understand the separation and sharing of powers among the branches of government, know how citizens influence government, and describe events that have international consequences.

- Why do you think students may not have a thorough knowledge of civics?

- How important is this kind of knowledge?

- Do the results suggest that students are not prepared to exercise their roles as citizens?

- As a policymaker, how could you respond to such a report?

- What initiatives are currently in place to address civic education, and what could be done to strengthen them?

- Do you think you could score at an eighth-grade proficiency level?

We encourage you to go to the Nation's Report Card website and drill down into the information provided. The Civics area is available at http://nationsreportcard .gov/hgc_2014/#civics. You can even see some of the questions asked.

Sources: U.S. Department of Education, National Center for Education Statistics, "2014 Civics Assessment," available at http://nationsreportcard.gov/hgc_2014/#civics.

percentage of high school graduates, which hit 82 percent in 2013–2014. But other information suggests that a high school diploma is not a guarantee that students are academically prepared to enter college or have the skills necessary to enter the workforce.[18] Education traditionalists suggest that quality is decreasing because schools are not emphasizing the basics such as math, English, reading, writing, and science in their teaching. By offering flexibility and electives, especially for secondary school students, the traditionalists say that the education system has moved away from its responsibilities of teaching the fundamental skills and subject matter and allowed quality to slip. Others argue that students need to be encouraged to learn and provided with opportunities to pursue their interests. The abilities to access, understand, and judge information; be critical thinkers; and work with others are more important than simply memorizing geometric theorems, chemical formulas, and the steps for how a bill becomes a law. These kinds of skills, proponents argue, create lifelong learners and will ultimately be of greater value to society.[19] Such goals are much more difficult to measure and typically are not "tested" through the traditional quality measures. PISA attempted this in 2012, and students in the United States did not fare well compared to those in other nations; they scored 508 compared to 562 in Singapore, 526 in Canada, and 510 in Italy.

So is the quality of education in the United States better or worse than in the past? This question may get a different answer, depending on what the respondent believes are the ultimate goals of the education system. But if quality *is* a problem compared to the past, what variables might be explored to improve the education system? What can be changed to help students learn more effectively?

One area of exploration is **teacher quality.** Some analysts assert that current teachers have less skill and knowledge than teachers in the past. There were a number of reports prior to the passage of No Child Left Behind (NCLB) of a significant number of instructors teaching in fields in which they were not trained. The Education Trust reported in 2010 that while there have been significant improvements in the area of out-of-subject teaching, the nation had not yet reached the nation's goal of 100 percent of the instructors teaching in areas within their specialty.[20]

If the quality of teachers is lower today, what are the reasons? Another study provided a different perspective. It showed that one in five teachers leaves the profession after only three years, and those who do so are more likely to have been in the top of their education classes when they graduated.[21] A 2014 study conducted by the National Center for Education Statistics did not find such a large number of "leavers" of the profession, but did show an increasing percentage of leavers over the past twenty-five years. They also note that over half of those who left the profession reported that "the manageability of their workload was better in their current position than in teaching."[22] Workload and another common explanation, that teachers are paid far less than those in other professions with comparable educational requirements, are both often put forth as reasons why it may be difficult to find high-quality teachers. From an economic standpoint, why should good students become teachers and earn lower starting salaries when they can choose another field and make substantially more money? Another reason may be the level of respect for the teaching profession. The old adage "Those who can, do; those who can't, teach" suggests that people become teachers by default because they cannot succeed in other professions. Outsiders may see teaching as an easy job because teachers get the summers off. What they do not see is that teachers are on nine-month contracts and get paid accordingly. Moreover, teachers may become discouraged with their jobs. The classroom atmosphere is difficult and may include school violence, crowded classrooms, and pupils' unstable family situations that make it more difficult to learn, and hence fewer are inspired to become teachers than in the past.[23]

Another issue regarding teacher quality often raised by reformers is the teacher tenure system. In essence, once teachers have worked a certain number of years within a public school district, they have significant job security. Supporters say that tenure protects teachers from unfair decisions based on a variety of factors that affect student success but are outside the control of an individual teacher. Others see the system as flawed in that it provides protections for individuals who truly are not serving the needs of the students. Removing such an individual is a long, drawn-out process that can be very expensive.[24]

Another explanation for the disappointing quality of education centers on the students themselves. Teachers who have been in the field for some time often compare the present situation to how things "used to be." Students today spend more time watching television, working, texting, going online and "Facebooking" with friends, and playing video games, and less time reading and focusing on schoolwork.[25] In addition, the increase in families headed by one parent or in which both parents work, along with other changes in home life, has likely hindered students' ability to learn.

One response to poor-quality education has been moving toward increased testing requirements for students. In order for students to move on to the next grade or perhaps to graduate, they must meet the appropriate standards. President George W. Bush's signing of NCLB in 2002 ushered in this movement at the federal level and involved the federal government more directly in educating the nation's children than in the past. NCLB required student testing as one mechanism to try to close the education gap. The law required states and school districts to be accountable for student performance. Under its provisions, all states administered a single test, the NAEP, to determine if the schools were meeting the appropriate standards. Schools that failed to improve for two years in a row could receive more federal funds, but if improvement still did not occur, the money could be used to provide tutoring or to move students to different schools. One goal of the standards movement was to prevent "social promotions." According to the testing proponents, the requirements ensure that students are promoted based on their understanding of the material.

The Obama administration came into office with plans to reform NCLB. Not surprisingly, many Democrats, organizations such as the National Education Association (NEA), and many states supported these efforts. While many lauded some of the goals of NCLB, it became increasingly clear that the implementation of the law, including its inflexibility, was causing a variety of problems for the states. One program adopted by the Obama administration was the Race to the Top initiative. Under the program, the federal government provided significant levels of funding (over $4 billion to eleven states) to states that pledged to

- adopt statewide learning standards and assessments;
- build data systems to measure achievement;
- recruit, retain, and reward effective teachers and principals through measures such as merit pay and retention bonuses;
- foster education innovation through such means as laws encouraging charter school development; and
- focus on turning around the lowest-performing schools.[26]

The Obama administration set forth a "blueprint" related to the reauthorization of ESEA, and by extension NCLB. The major points of the blueprint include ensuring that all students complete high school and are prepared for college and a career, providing for great teachers and leaders in every school, creating equity and opportunity for all students, raising the bar and rewarding excellence, and promoting innovation and continuous improvement.[27] The proposals discussed in the blueprint provide a bit more flexibility to state governments and seem to focus more on incentives than on penalties. Saying this, some of the ideas such as promoting charter schools and supporting some elements of merit pay are not necessarily backed by the traditional public school advocates.

As part of the rollout of these ideas, the administration also provided opportunities for states to get some relief from the existing NCLB requirements as long as they pursued President Obama's education reform agenda.[28] The administration also promoted the Common Core State Standards as one way to improve education and also provide a sense of consistency regarding standards in the states. These standards were developed through state leaders tied to the National Governors Association and the Council of Chief State School Officers in 2009. They set "grade-specific goals" for English and math. While the development of the standards occurred outside of the federal government, the Common Core became a politically charged issue as many politicians argued that it removed the control of education standards from the states and would have created a more centralized assessment. Many states that had earlier adopted the standards subsequently moved to reverse that decision.[29] Indeed, in 2015, President Obama signed a new version of the federal education law (ESEA) called the Every Student Succeeds Act (ESSA), which reversed much of the federal government's control of public education and returned control to the states and local districts.

Many other issues affect the quality of education. Inadequate facilities, increases in student violence, and high student-faculty ratios are just a few of the many variables frequently associated with school quality. All are fruitful areas for investigation and public policy analysis.

Education Policy Reforms

It is not surprising that many of the education reforms that policymakers and others have proposed, debated, and implemented originated as a response to their concern over the quality of education. This section assesses some of these ideas for reform and their potential impact.

Merit Pay

One of the most divisive issues concerning education and quality is the system most public schools use to pay their teachers. In general, teachers get raises based on their years of service. Although there may be good reasons to provide raises based on longevity, critics say that teachers have little incentive to change their methods to improve their teaching. To correct what they see as a flaw in the system, some reformers have promoted the idea of tying teacher salary increases to merit. **Merit pay,** according to supporters of this plan, should lead to better education as teachers improve themselves to be eligible for greater raises or promotions. Some states have implemented merit pay systems in their school districts with varying success.

Opponents raise several issues about linking pay increases to performance. First, no objective or agreed-upon measurement has yet been formulated for what constitutes an effective or quality teacher. Using student performance as an indicator of quality disregards other factors that may affect how students perform in the classroom. In addition, tying merit pay to student performance may produce some possibly undesirable incentives in the education system as the pressure mounts on schools to ensure high scores or for teachers to receive bonuses. This appears to have been the case in Atlanta where a former school superintendent and principals and teachers in a number of schools were implicated in a cheating scandal. According to investigators, some administrators held "erasing parties" to change wrong answers.[30] Without some agreement as to what makes a quality teacher, bias and inequity could taint the assessments. Second, many argue that until teacher salaries are competitive with those of other occupations, merit pay will not succeed in attracting and retaining highly qualified people. Third, opponents point out that merit pay does not achieve the stated goal. A report from the California State University Institute for Education Reform found that merit pay systems reward a small percentage of the teachers as individuals (in contrast to recognizing the value of team-based activities) without addressing the overall problems of education quality. In addition, the study reported that funding for such programs is not maintained, resulting in "pervasive cynicism among teachers about new pay schemes."[31]

The American Federation of Teachers has promoted a proposal that would provide significant salary increases to those who become board certified by the National Board for Professional Teaching Standards (NBPTS). This nonprofit organization has set standards for teacher excellence and is analogous to boards that certify doctors.[32] By having specific standards that teachers must meet and demonstrate, this process not only is objective but also offers a monetary incentive for teachers to pursue excellence in the classroom. In addition, it brings an element of professional status that sometimes is lacking in the education field. For more information regarding the standards, access the organization's website at www.nbpts.org.

Teacher Standards, Certification, and Salaries

Related to merit pay are proposals for teachers to meet certain standards to become and remain certified in the profession. Requiring a uniform level of competency for teaching should ensure a better-quality education for the students. For example, the standards would end the practice of assigning teachers to courses in fields that are not among their specialties. There continues to be an issue in the United States in that certification varies from state to state and the training and development that is done for our incoming teachers occurs at over one thousand different colleges and universities around the country. While such a system may provide for flexibility and specialization, it ensures a wide range of content. With such diversity, can we ensure quality? Much has been written about how other countries, such as Finland, develop their teachers with more rigorous training and often are pulling from the top college graduates.[33]

Some have suggested using a **competency test** for teachers, but this is not without its problems. The validity of any kind of standardized test, for example, can be questioned. One can also ask which kind of expertise is more important: knowledge of the content (substance), or ability to transmit that knowledge (pedagogy)? The quick answer is that they are equally important. Rather than using a test to certify teaching competence, states such as Indiana and Connecticut have focused on programs that help current teachers improve their skills. The development of more stringent standards can be part of this process. Indiana, for example, adopted a rigorous set of standards developed by the NBPTS as part of its licensing system. School districts need to maintain a balance because if the standards become too onerous, the schools may not have enough qualified teachers, at least in the short term. A report by the Organisation for Economic Co-operation and Development (OECD) states that many countries are pursuing multiple avenues to ensure high-quality teacher education, and in some cases, these ideas go beyond the content-versus-pedagogy dichotomy. The report provides a few best practices, which include clear and concise profiles of what teachers are expected to know, models that focus more on preparing professionals for school settings and less on academic preparation, and flexible structures that allow teachers to be more reflective and research based in addressing what is going on in the classroom.[34]

Few would dispute the importance of ensuring that the nation's children receive a quality education and develop a capacity to participate actively in the economy and government, and few doubt that the majority of U.S. residents

TABLE 10-1   Median Salaries of Selected Occupations, 2015

Occupation	Median Salary
Computer programmer	$79,530
Electrical engineer	95,230
Chemical engineer	97,360
Accountant	67,190
Mathematician	111,110
Teacher	57,200

Source: U.S. Bureau of Labor Statistics, *Occupational Outlook Handbook*, 2015, available at www.bls.gov/ooh/home.htm.

strongly support a better education system. Even so, teacher salaries continue to seriously lag behind what other professionals earn. Table 10-1 shows median salaries for selected occupations in 2012. Proponents of higher teacher salaries argue that if teachers are professionals, their school districts must pay them as such. This is what occurs in a number of other developed nations around the world. It is not so much that teachers are paid all that much more in other countries as that

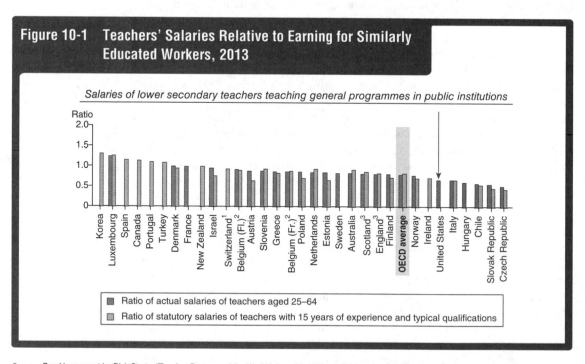

Figure 10-1   Teachers' Salaries Relative to Earning for Similarly Educated Workers, 2013

Salaries of lower secondary teachers teaching general programmes in public institutions

■ Ratio of actual salaries of teachers aged 25–64
■ Ratio of statutory salaries of teachers with 15 years of experience and typical qualifications

Source: Brookings report by Dick Startz, "Teacher Pay around the World," June 20, 2016, available at https://www.brookings.edu/blog/brown-center-chalkboard/2016/06/20/teacher-pay-around-the-world/.

the pay differential between teachers and other occupations is not as great. This large differential in the United States is noted in Table 10-1. Figure 10-1 shows the pay differential between teachers and similarly educated workers across a number of industrialized countries. A ratio of 1.0 would mean that teacher pay is equal to the pay of a similarly paid worker. The United States' ratio is 0.71, and quite far down the line compared to other countries.

School Vouchers, School Choice, and Charter Schools

Local school boards have traditionally drawn district lines that determine which school each student attends. Unless parents decide to send their children to a private school, or to homeschool, students generally go to the school closest to where they live in the district. One way to look at the students in a particular school district is as a captive market whose single provider (a monopoly) supplies their public school education. Americans traditionally mistrust business monopolies, believing that they can increase prices indiscriminately or offer lower-quality goods and services, but consumers have little or no choice. Monopolies are seen as inefficient in a market system, and such companies have no incentive to improve on quality if consumers have nowhere else to turn. Some analysts see the same lack of competition in education (Chubb and Moe 1990). Schools do not need to improve their product because they have a guaranteed market. In essence, public schools are a government-sponsored monopoly.

Many have argued that in order to break up the public school monopoly, society needs to reform the system in a way that gives parents options about where to send their children to school. Among the suggested reforms are school choice, school vouchers, and charter schools. Supporters argue that when parents can exercise choice, the schools will compete for students by providing higher-quality education, and the competition will raise the level of quality for everyone. NCLB brought school choice to the forefront by giving parents the ability to switch schools if their original school does not meet the appropriate standards. The offending schools must take on the financial burden of transporting these students to new schools.

School choice programs allow parents to send their children to any public school in a particular area. The competition is among public schools only, not between public and private schools, but these programs do foster competition. With school choice programs, school selection is based no longer on school districts but on where the child might get the kind of education desired. If the chosen school also receives government funding associated with the child, then this arrangement should spur competition. The various schools might try to improve the education they offer to maintain or even increase the size of their student body. It should be noted that many education reformers use the term *school choice* to encompass all reform efforts that provide parents with options about where to send their children, including charter schools and voucher programs.

School vouchers, theoretically, are also intended to improve education by promoting competition among schools. The major difference is that with school vouchers, the government provides a certain dollar amount that parents can then apply to private or parochial school tuition or as part of the full cost of a public school education. The government voucher may not be enough to cover the full cost of tuition, but it allows parents the choice of sending a child to a private school by relieving the family of part of the financial burden. In this way, the government encourages competition by bringing private schools into the education market. In addition, proponents argue that the voucher system will improve the quality of all schools; to entice students to enroll, administrators will do everything they can to improve their schools and compete in this open market.

Most school voucher systems currently in place in the United States, including the best-known plans in Cleveland and Milwaukee, are limited in that they are aimed at assisting low-income students. For example, to be eligible for a voucher in the Milwaukee program, a family of four must have an income no higher than 300 percent of the poverty level, or about $80,401 in 2016.[35] School voucher purists would support a universal voucher system in which every family would receive a designated amount of money for their children's education.

The school voucher programs became politicized when opponents, who see them as unconstitutional, took the school boards to court asserting that the programs could violate an individual's religious freedom and the principle of separation of church and state. They argued that giving public money to parents to send their children to parochial schools is a clear violation of the First Amendment because, no matter the religious denomination, the funds are being used to promote religion. *Zelman v. Simmons-Harris*, the Supreme Court's 2002 decision regarding Cleveland's voucher system, perhaps has clarified the legal environment surrounding school voucher programs. Voucher opponents had hoped that the constitutional issues would be resolved in their favor. With that option gone, the debate moved into other policymaking arenas, such as state courts, state legislatures, and referendums.[36] A number of questions remain regarding school vouchers: Are resources being transferred from the public to the private schools, and is this equitable? Who should be eligible for vouchers? Should it be based on need?

Of course, a primary issue must be whether voucher programs have been successful. Opponents cite a number of studies suggesting that voucher programs have minimal effects at best in improving education programs.[37] Studies by John F. Witte (1997, 2000) and John F. Witte et al. (1995), Cecilia E. Rouse (1997, 1998), and Kim Metcalf et al. (1998) all find that voucher programs are not as effective as proponents claim and that other, more accessible programs can provide better results. Naturally, supporters of school voucher programs point to their own set of studies, or even parts of the same studies, that contradict the arguments of their opponents. The Heritage Foundation, for example, cites studies by Kim Metcalf (1999) and Paul E. Peterson, William G. Howell, and Jay P. Green (1999) that found positive effects associated with voucher programs. According to Heritage, the Metcalf study found that "Cleveland scholarship students show a small but statistically significant improvement in achievement scores in language and science," and Peterson et al. claim that parents are more satisfied with many aspects of the school they chose (Shokraii Rees 2000). As vouchers have continued to be debated, studies have continued. Some of these continue to suggest only small gains for voucher school students, and these results are often not statistically significant (Rouse and Barrow 2009). Others suggest more positive outcomes.[38] One major study conducted by William G. Howell and Paul E. Peterson (2002) found that the use of vouchers had a significant impact on the success of African American students. Using this measure of effectiveness—that is, whether the program improves educational success for a particular demographic group—is another way that researchers can present their results and voucher proponents can claim success. When making policy, one must be careful with the results of such studies. Researchers later found the study by Peterson et al., for example, to be inconclusive in terms of improving scores.[39] Unfortunately, organizations with a particular bias will take advantage of some of these nuances when making their claims in support of or in opposition to the voucher programs.[40]

The charter school is another way of introducing choice into education. Charter schools are unique in that they are government supported but independent. A state board of education gives an independent entity the responsibility of establishing a school and delivering education services with limited control by the school board. The state funds these schools, but the regulations that typically govern public schools are significantly reduced to allow the schools to have a particular focus. Some examples of charter schools in Illinois illustrate their variety. The Academy of Communications and Technology seeks to prepare students for careers in communications and computer technology. The Young Women's Leadership Charter School follows the small school model and focuses on academic achievement. It offers a rigorous career and college preparatory curriculum that emphasizes math, science, and technology; leadership; and personal and social development. Charter schools may choose to pursue certain educational needs or strategies to improve student performance, and they are responsible for meeting the standards they develop. The number of charter schools is growing, with more than six thousand operating in 2016.[41] Some see charter schools as just another form of voucher system because the state is paying for them while perhaps reducing the funding for traditional public schools. The question of whether charter schools are a more effective way to educate students is still open to debate, and the evidence to date is mixed. The other question relates to whether the existence of these schools may be improving educational effectiveness for the public schools; the evidence here is also mixed.[42]

It is interesting to note that President Donald Trump has been a strong supporter of public school choice and has proposed $20 billion in federal funds to expand voucher programs.[43] As noted, most existing programs target lower-income families. Trump's choice for the Department of Education secretary is Betsy DeVos, who is a strong advocate for school choice. It will be interesting to watch how this issue proceeds under the Trump presidency.

School Testing

When enacted in 2002, NCLB represented a dramatic shift in the role of the federal government in public education. The testing requirement was one of the largest changes to education policy and, in some ways, probably the most controversial. This controversy increased as states complained about inadequate federal funding and many educators questioned the relevance of standardized testing in improving education quality. The Obama administration was willing to provide more flexibility in the context of meeting the standards dictated by NCLB, but still demanded a certain level of assessment and accountability. Former president Bush defended the testing requirement and even advised incoming president Obama not to make any major changes to the law. Bush argued that without tests or some other form of measurement, how can one be sure that students are getting the appropriate education? Shouldn't parents be made aware if their children's schools are not adequate? Not everyone agrees, however, that testing—or perhaps the term is *overtesting*—is the right policy choice. Do increases in testing lead to less classroom instruction? Do teachers "teach to the test" to be sure the children will pass? What do such high-stakes tests do the internal environment of a school or district?

Standardized testing creates its own problems. First, the way the exams are written and graded may introduce racial or cultural bias. Second, is the imposition of such standards an infringement on state and local education? Third, the testing is expensive. Could the resources be put to better use in the classroom? A related issue is the amount of classroom time devoted to testing, which can then not be used for content instruction. The federal requirements encouraged states to reassess their existing standards or issue new ones that students must meet in specific subject areas. Given that these state standards may differ considerably from one another, is it wise to allow such variation, given that people frequently move to pursue employment opportunities or for other reasons?[44] Anna Quindlen argued in a *Newsweek* column that "constant testing will no more address the problems of our education system than constantly putting an overweight person on the scale will cure obesity."[45] Her point was that testing is occurring for the sake of testing and not to make curricular changes that may improve learning. But what if the results of these tests are being used to improve the curriculum?

As noted earlier, the conflict regarding testing led to a large rewrite of No Child Left Behind that was signed by President Obama at the end of 2015. The ESSA had a number of areas that walked back the role of the federal government that NCLB championed. These included

- returning power to states and local districts to determine how to address failing schools;
- leaving it up to states and localities to set performance goals and school rating;
- eliminating the federal consequences for schools that perform poorly; and
- barring the federal government from imposing academic requirements.

While hailed by many on both sides of the political aisle, groups representing the poor and underrepresented populates claimed it went too far in eliminating federal oversight and worried about a return of inconsistent education standards that might particularly affect the poor.[46]

The policy analysis framework used throughout the book can be used to explore the major questions in this ongoing debate. In this case, some of the major analytic criteria used to study this issue include economic costs or efficiency, politics and political feasibility, effectiveness, and equity. What are the economic impacts of these testing programs on state governments? Is this an appropriate area for the federal government to become involved, or should it be left to the states? Perhaps most important, are such testing programs effective in improving education? It is clear that President Obama's signing of ESSA represented a rare situation where Democrats and Republicans came to an agreement regarding a major federal policy. Whether the political victory leads to a more effective K–12 education system remains to be seen.

Charters for choice. The photo shows first-grade teacher Tony Ring-Dowell chatting with a student during class at Rocketship Sí Se Puede Academy, a public elementary school, in February 2014 in San Jose, California. The school includes Grades K–5 and uses a blended-learning method of teaching. *(Melanie Stetson Freeman/The Christian Science Monitor via Getty Images)*

Higher Education Issues

Unlike primary and secondary education, attending college is not a requirement; rather, it is a student's personal choice. But it is becoming increasingly clear that a higher education may be necessary for a wider range of careers and jobs than before. Perhaps this is one reason why governments get involved by encouraging students in many ways to continue their education. President Obama made higher education a policy priority. In his first speech to Congress as president, he stated his goal of having the highest proportion of college graduates in the world by 2020; he also emphasized the necessity of providing a range of postsecondary educational opportunities for students other than a traditional four-year college degree. The achievement of that goal is directly affected by one of the issues discussed below—the cost of going to college. The other issue concerns doing a better job in making higher education a goal for a wider diversity of people in the United States.

Affirmative Action

For years, many colleges and universities, in the name of promoting diversity in their student bodies, have given admissions preferences to certain demographic groups such as African Americans and Hispanic Americans. Many administrators and faculty members argued that a more diverse student body adds value to the education of all the students at a college or university. For that reason, they believed it was justifiable, indeed essential, to admit some students whose academic work or test scores may not have been at the same level as others but whose other qualities enriched the campus community.

A number of states have moved to eliminate these kinds of preference programs from their state institutions. Many college administrators believe that racial diversity is critical to the goals of education. At most schools, the effect of eliminating these programs is likely to be minor. It is at the more selective institutions—the elite schools—where they currently have the greatest effect.[47] Do declines in minority admissions, especially at elite schools, pose a significant problem? Some worry about fostering even greater inequalities between elite and non-elite universities than have existed for some time. Those who favor the abolition of affirmative action programs, however, see nonaffirmative action admissions practices as more equitable to all the applicants. The students who score lower on SATs and other admissions criteria are not being denied a higher education, but they may have to choose a less competitive institution.

From a policy analysis perspective, how might one examine the issue of affirmative action programs in higher education? There are obvious ethical and fairness issues associated with affirmative action, but naturally, proponents and opponents of affirmative action programs both defend their positions in terms of equity. Proponents of affirmative action might point out that in the past minorities were excluded from many institutions of higher learning. In addition, many minorities have faced discrimination and inadequate preparation to attend elite schools, and affirmative action programs help to level the playing field. Opponents argue that it is unfair to give preferences just because of racial characteristics. They strongly defend the position that admission to college should be based on individual abilities rather than demographic characteristics. Any other method, they say, is unfair.

Have affirmative action programs been effective? That depends on one's definition of the problem. More minorities are attending college than ever before, and these increases are across the board in terms of the quality of the institution. A study by William G. Bowen and Derek C. Bok (1998) found that affirmative action programs in highly selective institutions have been successful in educating and promoting the students who benefited from the admissions policy. This particular study, however, is somewhat limited because it concentrates on selective institutions rather than a broader range of schools. Many institutions assert that affirmative action programs are effective because they reach the goal of diversified student bodies. But are the programs effective if they also deny admission to qualified students?[48]

College admissions are partially a zero-sum game. In any given year or program, each university has only so many openings, and competition can be fierce for the highly selective schools. One person's admission results in another's denial. In June 2003, the Supreme Court ruled on two University of Michigan cases dealing with affirmative action admission procedures. The ruling was somewhat complex: it stated that minorities could be given an edge for admissions but limited the extent that race could play as a factor in selecting students. Subsequent years have found that schools such as the University of Michigan and The Ohio State University saw only slight decreases in the number of minority students accepted, but that they spent considerably more time on the applicant evaluation process.[49] The Court heard the case of *Fisher v. University of Texas* twice and in 2016 upheld the legality of such procedures but put the burden on schools to show that "race-neutral alternatives do not suffice" to ensure a diverse student population.[50] In April 2014, the Court ruled on yet another affirmative action case. In *Schuette v. Coalition to Defend Affirmative Action*, the Court upheld the right of Michigan's citizens to ban race-conscious admissions at their state colleges and universities.

Costs of Higher Education

Most readers of this text need no reminder that the costs of college education are substantial and continue to rise. For much of the past several decades, they have been rising faster than the rate of inflation. In a thirty-year period between 1986 and 2016, the inflation-adjusted tuition and fees for public schools increased 310 percent. For private institutions, the increase was 229 percent. (See Figure 10-2 for inflation-adjusted tuition and fees.) There are regional variations for these increases. In the previous decade, the Middle States region has seen increases of 27 percent, but during that same period, the Western region has increased 66 percent.[51] Because a college education is regarded as essential for a competitive and productive workforce and for maintaining economic growth, the ever-higher price tag for a college degree is alarming. The cost of attending a private college or university can be prohibitive. For example, at Princeton University, the 2016–2017 comprehensive fee (tuition, room, board, and expenses) was nearly $64,000—although, as with other private institutions, scholarships often lower the cost. Many students who might have considered private institutions have turned instead to public colleges and universities, which almost always cost less. Attending the University of Wisconsin in 2017–2018, for example, has an estimated cost of more than $25,000 for tuition and room and board for in-state residents, and more than $48,000 for out-of-state residents.[52] See the box "Steps to Analysis: 'I'm a Student Debt Slave'" for some additional information regarding how the costs of college are affecting students and the amount of debt they take.

Given the costs, one of the most important issues in higher education is the level of state support provided to students, especially those attending state

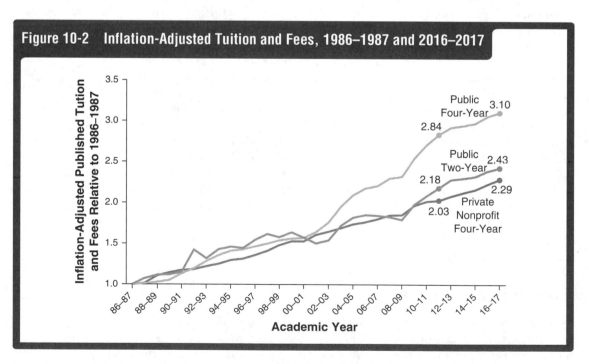

Figure 10-2   Inflation-Adjusted Tuition and Fees, 1986–1987 and 2016–2017

Source: College Board, *Trends in College Pricing*, 2016, Figure 5, page 14, https://trends.collegeboard.org/sites/default/files/2016-trends-college-pricing-web_0.pdf.

Note: The figure shows published tuition and fees by sector, adjusted for inflation, relative to 1986–87 published prices. For example, a value of 3.10 indicates that the tuition and fee price in the public four-year sector in 2016–17 is 3.1 times as high as it was in 1986–87, after adjusting for increases in the Consumer Price Index. Average tuition and fee prices reflect in-district charges for public two-year institutions and in-state charges for public four-year institutions.

Steps to Analysis

"I'm a Student Debt Slave"

During the past decade, there have been an increasing number of stories regarding the amount of college debt held in the United States. As noted earlier in the chapter, this number approaches $1.3 trillion. A majority of graduates leave school owing more than $25,000, and nearly seven million have defaulted on their loans.[a] Some have raised particular concerns in regard to for-profit schools, which have been accused of targeting veterans and poorer students through aggressive recruiting tactics.[b] Table 10-2 shows the amount of federal loans and Pell Grants going to different school types. According to the College Board, loans for students enrolling in for-profit schools increased from 13 percent of the total loan balance in 2003–2004 to 21 percent in 2013–2014.[c]

in that students who do not finish school, or who take on more debt than is necessary, raise the possibility of debt. Consider these and other issues related to student debt:

- What role should government play in addressing student debt? Part of your discussion should focus on the idea of whether higher education is a public or a private good.

- Most research suggests that higher education is one of the best investments you can make to improve your financial situation. If this is the case, at what point does debt become overbearing?

- Some have suggested that students' payoff of their debt should be based on the level of their salary. What are the pros and cons of such a system?

TABLE 10 2   Federal Loans and Pell Grants Awards by Type of Institution, 2013–2014

School Type	Federal Loans	Pell Grants
For-profit	$9,619,525,300 (19%)	$5,837,724,315 (19%)
Private, nonprofit	$12,328,929,207 (25%)	$4,699,647,614 (15%)
Public	$28,109,523,681 (56%)	$20,622,409,885 (66%)
TOTAL	$50,057,978,188 (100%)	$31,199,781,814 (100%)

Politicians, policy organizations, and journalists are taking notice of this issue and are increasingly discussing it. Take a look at the NPR story "I'm a Student-Debt Slave" (available at http://www.npr.org/sections/ed/2016/07/11/484364476/im-a-tudent-debt-slave-howd-we-get here?utm_source=npr_news letter&utm_medium=email&utm_content=20160711&utm_campaign=npr_email_a_friend&utm_term=storyshare).

There are a variety of potential reasons for increasing student debt. Some have put the blame on colleges and universities for continuing increases in their prices. Others state that governments, particularly at the state level, are not doing enough to invest in college. There also is some personal responsibility

a. See Tom Price, "Student Debt," *CQ Researcher*, November 18, 2016.
b. One study found that the for-profit colleges accounted for a disproportionate number of student loan crises. See Adam Looney and Constantine Yannelis, "A Crisis in Student Loans? How Changes in the Characteristics of Borrowers and in the Institutions They Attended Contributed to Rising Loan Defaults," *Brookings Papers on Economic Activity*, September 10–11, 2015, available at www.brookings.edu/wp-content/uploads/2016/07/ConferenceDraft_LooneyYannelis_StudentLoanDefaults.pdf.
c. See College Board, "Aggregate Outstanding Federal Student Loan Balances by Sector over Time," *Trends in Higher Education*, available at https://trends.collegeboard.org/student-aid/figures-tables/aggregate-outstanding-federal-student-loan-balances-sector-over-time.

For-profit costs and defaults. For-profit colleges have proliferated across the nation, competing directly with public colleges and universities. Yet for-profit colleges typically charge much more for tuition and often are criticized for serving their students poorly, for example, in not preparing them for the job market. Students who have attended for-profit colleges are much more likely to default on their government-funded higher education loans. Recent changes in federal policies have attempted to address these concerns and have led to some high-level institutional closures such as ITT and Corinthian Colleges. This 2005 file photo shows real estate mogul, TV star, and now president Donald Trump, left, listening as Michael Sexton introduces him to announce the establishment of Trump University at a press conference in New York. Sexton was president and cofounder of the now-defunct business education company. *(AP Photo/Bebeto Matthews)*

institutions. Students may consider such support to be unexceptional, much as they expect the public to pay for the cost of elementary and secondary education, but public support for higher education raises important questions of equity. Should state governments be providing such subsidies for individuals to attend college? Or should individuals be responsible for paying their own college costs on the grounds that they are getting the benefits, such as enhanced social and economic status, that a college education usually provides? The "Focused Discussion" section addresses some of these questions in more detail.

Focused Discussion: Higher Education Affordability, Cost, and Value

The chapter opened with a discussion of a topic that should be near and dear to almost everyone reading this book. As noted earlier in the chapter, the costs of getting a college degree continue to increase and are typically greater than the rate of inflation. There are a number of reasons for these cost increases, some of which are true for almost all types of institutions (e.g., public and private). For example, higher education is an industry that relies heavily on personnel to run its operations. Thus whenever there is a cost increase associated with personnel, those costs may be passed along to the consumers. Wage increases are one such cost, but even in times of austerity, when raises are rare or very small, there are other labor costs. Like any other employer, colleges and universities have had to adjust to continuing increases associated with health care and insurance. Other costs include new buildings and facilities that colleges build in order to stay competitive with their peers and be successful in recruiting students. Most campuses also want to ensure state-of-the-art technology, with a number of campuses providing Wi-Fi access to all on their campus.

With public schools, the issue of cost to students is directly related to the decreasing support coming from state governments for higher education. Even though the states continue to subsidize state colleges and universities, they cover a smaller percentage of school operating budgets than they did in the past. State support for higher education has gone down over the past twenty-five years as competition for funding has increased, particularly from the prison systems and state support for Medicaid and other social service programs. Colleges and universities therefore raise tuition to make up for the shortfall. Stories abound regarding the continued decrease of state support of public higher education in most states. Some relief was provided by the American Recovery and Reinvestment Act, but these funds were spent by 2012. As shown in Figure 10-3, on a per-pupil spending basis, states provided, on average and controlling for inflation, 2.4 percent less in 2015 than they did in 2010. It is important to note that this decrease is actually lower than it was a few years ago. Many states have made attempts during the economic recovery to provide some reinvestment in higher education or at least slow the decrease. Even so, the largest decrease was in Louisiana at 28.5 percent and the largest increase in Illinois at 32.5.[53] In fact, compared to previous years when only a few states saw increases, this most recent report shows thirteen states with appropriation increases over the past five years. To consider this from a

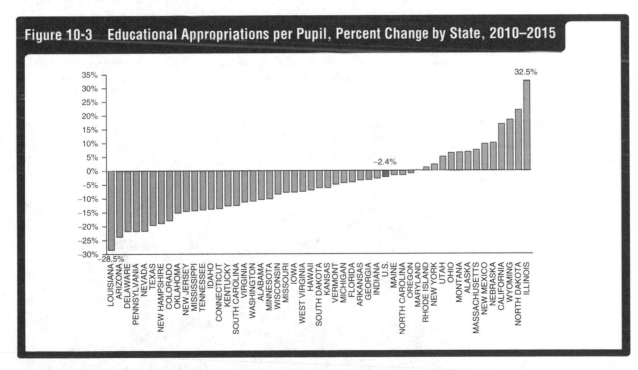

Figure 10-3 Educational Appropriations per Pupil, Percent Change by State, 2010–2015

Source: By permission of the State Higher Education Executive Officers Association, *State Higher Education Finance: FY 2015*, available at http://sheeo.org/sites/default/files/project-files/SHEEO_FY15_Report_051816.pdf.

Notes: Dollars adjusted by 2015 Higher Education Cost Adjustment, Cost of Living Adjustment, and Enrollment Mix Index. For Illinois, a $1.08 billion back payment in fiscal year 2015 to the state's historically underfunded higher education pension program resulted in past legacy pension funds accounting for 37 percent of all educational appropriations.

longer-term perspective, according to the *Postsecondary Education Opportunity*, between fiscal years 1980 and 2011, nearly every state had cut its appropriations for higher education from a low of 14.8 percent to as much as 69.4 percent. The average cut across all states was 39.9 percent.[54] As many colleges and universities have attempted to compete for students, there has also been a tendency to provide more scholarship money based on merit than on need. In addition, there has been a decided shift in college aid from grants to loans, which students eventually need to pay back. While it is difficult to argue against merit-based scholarships, it is also clear that a larger proportion of these dollars is likely to go to middle- to upper-income families, thus providing less financial help for low-income students. Is the decrease of government funding, coupled with the increase in merit-based financial aid, pricing some students out of going to college? Are we in danger of a college education being a good only the elite can afford?

How we as a nation finance a college education partially gets at the issue of what type of good higher education is. In other words, is it a private good or a public good? If it is a private good, meaning that most of the benefits of higher education are bestowed upon the individual and he or she receives a higher wage as a result, then pushing more cost to that individual may make sense. But if higher education is seen as a public good, since the additional education will make society as a whole better through better citizenship, more economic development, and less need for social services, then public support for education is appropriate. It is clear that both the individual and the greater society are the beneficiaries, which then raises the question of what is the appropriate level of public support. An article in the *Atlantic* suggests that the federal government already spends enough money on

A public good with rising costs. With the rising costs of college education, the availability of scholarships and loans becomes more important than ever to students. The photo shows Michael Adams, a sophomore at Berea College, tutoring freshman Enchanta Jackson at the school's Learning Center in Berea, Kentucky. All students at Berea get a full-tuition scholarship, and families pay for housing, meals, and books based on what they can afford. In exchange, all students must work for the university at least ten hours a week, receiving a stipend below minimum wage with the rest of their earnings directed toward their education costs. *(AP Photo/Brian Tietz)*

grants, loans, and college tax breaks to allow students to attend public school for nearly free.[55] This section examines the issue of public support of higher education.

Economic Issues

A typical argument made to provide public support to higher education, and specifically to students seeking such an education, is that such support leads to larger public benefits. As noted earlier, education can be considered a positive externality in that society benefits from a more educated population. Individuals typically will make more money with a college degree, but what about the return on a state's investment through tuition subsidization? A number of studies have examined the economic impact of higher education spending, and they suggest that such spending is a good investment for the state. For example, it is estimated that the state of Texas receives a $5.50 return for every dollar spent on higher education. Another study, of the University of Wisconsin system, found a number of positive economic benefits as a result of state support. These included a $9.5 billion economic contribution, direct and indirect job creation, and positive state tax revenue generation. This economic benefit of over $9 billion compares to an approximate $1 billion state expenditure provided to the University of Wisconsin system, which would suggest that state support for the university is a good economic investment.[56] These represent tangible returns to a state economy and may justify political movements to try to stop the downward trend of state support for higher education. It is interesting to note that one sees such studies more prominently featured on college websites, perhaps indicative of the economic and political environment where state funding is decreasing.

Although higher education costs and funding provoke considerable debate, the value of a college education from an individual's perspective cannot be overestimated. On average, students with a bachelor's degree or higher earn substantially more than those who only complete high school. Table 10-3 shows the mean salaries of males and females in 2015 at different levels of educational attainment. Based on 2015 data, both men and women over the age of twenty-five with a bachelor's or higher degree earn over twice as much than those without a college degree.[57]

TABLE 10-3   2015 Mean Salaries of Males and Females over Age Twenty-five, by Educational Attainment

Educational Attainment	Male	Female
No high school diploma	$29,394	$16,777
High school diploma	$42,160	$24,440
Bachelor's degree or more	$92,921	$55,663

Source: U.S. Census Bureau, "Historical Income Tables: People," available at www.census.gov/data/tables/time-series/demo/income-poverty/historical-income-people.html.

It is also evident that many students place a high value on attending some of the most prestigious colleges and universities despite what other people believe are exorbitant costs. Clearly, they think their investment in such a college degree will prove to be worth it over time. Much the same is true of students who pay high tuition costs to attend professional graduate programs in law, medicine, or business administration. They expect to recoup their investment many times over once they graduate and begin to work. The financial impact of getting a college degree on students is quite clear.

What is less clear is just what the public value is to higher education; or, in other words, how much public investment should there be in this area? Policymakers, politicians, and higher education officials often raise the importance of universities in preparing a workforce and aiding a state in the midst of an economic recession.[58] Often, these choices come down to priorities: Is public funding for higher education more important than maintaining the criminal justice and prison systems? Or funding state Medicaid programs? Or maintaining funding for K–12 education? Or decreasing taxes? Like all public policy choices, there is often more need than there are resources. What is clear, though, is that public support for higher education, particularly from state governments, has decreased dramatically. Many public institutions are stating that they are "state-assisted" or "state-located" rather than public universities. As a result, students and parents are picking up a larger share of the bill.

Higher education appears to be becoming much more of a private good. If this is the case, then the other issue that may need further discussion is how this will affect low-income people who want to pursue a college degree. Public colleges and universities, including community colleges, have traditionally been an option for those without financial means. Tuition discounting and need-based financial aid may always be options, but they can be somewhat limited. The federal Pell Grants, one of the primary federal programs for low-income students, continue to be an important source of funding. Unfortunately, the purchasing power of these grants has decreased significantly since the early 1980s. If public support is decreasing and being replaced by higher tuition, it could have a deadening effect on access.

Political Issues

The political issues surrounding public support of higher education are not as straightforward as some of the other content areas that we have discussed. One reason may be that the service being provided is not necessarily controversial. Most would agree that more education is generally better for individuals and society. As noted earlier, there is a strong recognition that higher levels of education can promote economic development, encourage citizen engagement, and provide other benefits. How can one not support these ideas? At the state government level, the conflict likely comes from a decision regarding priorities. Should higher education be funded at a particular level instead of some other public policy option? This is where the politics of higher education funding occurs.

Earlier in the book, we discussed the importance of public opinion, interest groups, and the popular vote in the lives of policymakers, particularly politicians, and subsequently the policies they promote. In a democratic society where politicians rely upon the vote to keep their jobs, one expects members of a state legislature, for example, to pay attention to who is affected by their decisions. Support for higher education has decreased dramatically over the past thirty years, and many state colleges and universities have had to turn to higher tuition to make up for lost revenue and continue to operate as they did before. As such, students (and their parents) have felt the brunt of this decreased state support in their wallets. One then might ask what type of political pressure can be placed upon state policymakers.

In the fall of 2014, undergraduate enrollment was over 17 million students, and over 13 million of these were attending public institutions.[59] Let's look at a few state examples. According to data provided by the Integrated Postsecondary Education Data System, the fall 2014 total enrollment for all public four- and two-year schools in California was over 2.1 million students; in New York, this number was over 725,000; and in Texas, the number was over 1.3 million.[60] These are quite large numbers, even within the context of individual states. One might expect that with this many people affected, it would represent a large voting block or even a potential interest group that could provide political pressure on government to adequately fund higher education. Add to this parents and those who work within the higher education field, and these numbers increase quite a bit. And yet, funding has decreased, and in many ways, the potential political power of this group has never been realized. Why is that? One reason may be that the traditional-age student (eighteen to twenty-four) is a demographic having one of the lowest voting turnout rates. According to the U.S. Census Bureau, only 16 percent of this age group reported voting in the November 2014 elections, over 10 percent less than the next group (twenty-five to forty-four), and 35 percent below the group with the highest reporting (sixty-five to seventy-four).[61] With voting turnout statistics such as these, is it any wonder that state politicians may not see this as a priority?

As noted earlier, many higher education institutions, particularly those in the public sector, do their own lobbying to protect their public financing. This often is done by providing data regarding the economic or financial benefit that a school provides to the local or state economy, or by linking the need for a well-educated workforce to promote economic growth and provide a well-prepared workforce. A report regarding the economic impacts of the University of California, for example, found that it generated $46.3 billion in economic activity for California and, for every $1 in taxpayer support, generated $13.80 in economic output.[62] It is important to note that such studies are not just for large university systems such as the University of California or the State University of New York (SUNY). Many individual campuses, both public and private, are conducting similar studies of economic effect, partially to provide the political argument for increased or continued support.

The other side of the political argument for continued public support for higher education will raise the issue of priorities, or why public dollars should support what is a private benefit. We noted earlier that typically more education will lead to higher salaries for individuals. If that is the case, then those higher earnings could pay the additional cost necessary for college. In an era when it seems that the answer to every public policy question is to cut taxes, many might ask why their taxes should be used to support these endeavors. The other part of the political argument has to do with the ever-increasing cost of higher education and a question by some if the college industry's appetite can ever be satiated. They see ever more elaborate student-life facilities, high salaries for administrators, and exorbitant costs for college sports, and question if this is the best use of public tax dollars.

The political debate surrounding the issue of funding higher education has a number of different elements. What is clear, though, is that the rich will always be able to afford to go to college and be able and willing to pay a premium for this service. But what about the poor and middle class? We now turn to the equity and ethics questions associated with public financing.

Equity and Ethical Issues

One of the major arguments for supporting education generally is the belief that it is the great equalizer within U.S. society. Education provides a mechanism for success. This is also true for higher education, but the major difference is that there are significant individual costs associated with higher education that must be paid by the recipient. How do we ensure equity in access to students who may not have the means to afford the tuition and other costs associated with a university education?

Federal Pell Grants are one program that addresses the needs of low-income individuals. As noted above, these grants provide up to $5,815 (for 2016–2017) based on need, cost of attendance, and your student status. There is concern, though, that these grants do not provide the same purchasing power as they used to, and that more people are turning to loan programs to help meet their college costs and hence all the concerns about student debt (see Table 10-4). First, you will note that the percentage of students taking out loans has increased over the ten-year period shown in the table. Second, note the increase in the average loan level. While federal loans are capped by legislation, students can turn to other sources, including private loans, to finance their education. As you can see, the average loan debt has increased by 35 percent during this period. It is also important to note that private loans generally charge higher interest rates and are not as forgiving as federal student loans. The point is that more and more students are finding themselves with a significant level of debt upon graduation, and this is going to affect the low- to middle-income student to a greater degree.[63] The issue of the ever increasing student debt raises significant issues because it could hamstring students to the point where they have a difficult time making ends meet.[64]

TABLE 10-4 Number of Loans and Loan Amounts for First-Time, Full-Time Undergraduate Students for Their First Year in College (in constant 2013 dollars)

	2003–04	2013–14
Total number of first-time, full-time undergraduate students	2,104,959	2,436,276
Number of these students receiving student loans	872,869	1,111,946
Percent of these students receiving student loans	41%	46%
Total amount of loans awarded to first-time, full-time undergraduate students (2013 dollars)	$4,480,474,748	$7,688,172,555
Increase from 2003 to 2013 in the total amount loaned to these students for their first year of college		72%
Average amount of loans awarded to these students for their first year of college (2013 dollars)	$5,133	$6,914
Increase from 2003 to 2013 in average loan amount		35%

Source: "Student Financial Aid of Full-Time First-Time Degree or Certificate-Seeking Undergraduate Students." Data Set: Integrated Postsecondary Education Data System, available at IPEDS Data Center (National Center for Education Statistics), https://nces.ed.gov/ipeds/Home/UseTheData, accessed and summarized November 21, 2016.

Some have argued for a system that provides for free or significantly reduced college. President Obama argued for free community college. Both Hillary Clinton and Bernie Sanders, the two major Democratic candidates for the 2016 election, proposed free tuition at public institutions, particularly for certain income levels, or in Clinton's words "having no-debt tuition."[65]

There have been other kinds of programs implemented to help alleviate college costs, such as the HOPE (Helping Outstanding Pupils Educationally) Scholarship program in Georgia. Under the program, students must maintain a B average in high school and keep this average in college to qualify for state grants to pay for college. Given state financial issues, many of these types of programs have had to decrease funding. Like other forms of state aid, though, critics may bemoan these programs because they are redistributing tax dollars to particular beneficiaries. These merit-based programs may have other equity concerns related to the quality of the schools the students are attending as well as their socioeconomic status. Which students are more likely to achieve a B average or higher, and thus qualify for the HOPE Scholarship program? Students from a middle- or upper-middle-class background or from a working-class or blue-collar background? Students from cash-strapped inner-city schools or from well-supported suburban high schools? Given a perceived interest to make college accessible, can such programs be justified on the basis of equity or fairness?

So the issue of equity in the financing of higher education really comes down to a couple of different perspectives. One is whether one considers higher education to be a public or a private good. If public, then perhaps public support is appropriate and a good use of taxpayer dollars. If private, then one might consider such support unnecessary. The other perspective to consider relates to how the country ensures sufficient education to low- and middle-income students who may not be able to afford the costs of higher education. If education is an equalizer and a way for people to better themselves, then perhaps supporting this system makes sense. In this case, the question may come down to what is the appropriate level of public investment to ensure such access, and whether these needs rise above other public policy issues and problems.

Conclusions

This chapter examines education policy and a number of associated issues. The heart of the debate, particularly for the K–12 schools, is this question: What is the best way to improve the quality of education in the nation's schools? Whether it is raising standards for students and/or teachers, increasing teachers' pay, or providing additional choices for parents, all of the alternatives address what is perceived to be a problem of less-than-adequate quality. Within the higher education environment, much of the discussion has been toward access to a college education, which often comes down to cost and affordability issues.

This chapter examined the role that government plays in the education policy area along with a number of issues that it has focused on, including ensuring a quality education. Since state and local governments fund a good portion of school budgets, there is much local control, but that can lead to differences of quality. As noted, many reform efforts, including merit pay, school choice, and student testing, have been attempted as ways to address educational quality. The passage of NCLB saw federal policymakers much more involved in education issues, particularly around quality, and taking a greater interest in this policy area. Their rhetoric on the subject reflects differing partisan and ideological views, and the conflicts over education policy show little sign of dissipating. Given the high level of public concern over education, this response by federal officials was not surprising, but many continue to be guarded about the federal role in education policy and thus you saw the pendulum swing back toward state and local control with the passage of ESSA. Both NCLB and ESSA started as bipartisan efforts and showcased the changing nature of the role of the federal government in education. The Common Core, while first supported by the National Governors Association, has also been pulled into the partisan rhetoric. It is clear that finding the appropriate balance between local control and consistent quality will continue.

Within the higher education environment, the major issues will continue to be cost, affordability, and value. State financing of public higher education continues to be stressed by other priorities and an interest to keep tax rates low. As noted earlier in the chapter, though, there have been some major changes regarding the type of support the federal government is providing as well. Support from the federal sector continues, but a larger amount of this support comes through loans, which will increase student debt, or through tax breaks, which tend to favor the better-off. Many continue to want to see an increase in the number of college graduates, and to do that, more needs to be done to address issues of affordability and debt. One might typically consider education policy to be an area where the parties, our different governments, and the public could come together, but partisan differences remain. Like many areas of public policy, how programs are developed and implemented affect how people may react to them.

$SAGE edge™
for CQ Press

Sharpen your skills with SAGE edge at **http://edge.sagepub.com/ kraft6e. SAGE edge for students** provides a personalized approach to help you accomplish your coursework goals in an easy-to-use learning environment.

DISCUSSION QUESTIONS

1. Should education policy remain primarily a state and local government concern, or should the federal government be involved? What are the arguments for the federal government to be more involved in education policy? What advantages do states have in maintaining their responsibility in this policy area?

2. Should government continue to support higher education and students who attend college? If so, is this a federal or state responsibility? What factors should be considered when making such a policy decision? What are the arguments for and against such government support? What about the role of the for-profit sector? Are these schools a good option when comparing their costs and

success rates? What role should government have in overseeing these types of higher education institutions?

3. Why do you think the United States underpays teachers compared to other nations and other professionals needing equal education?

4. Should there be income limits associated with school voucher programs? Why or why not? How would you design such a program so that it can address most of the criticisms? Is this an issue of improving education quality, or is it related more to moral questions in our education system?

5. Should higher education be considered a private or public good? What are the elements for both?

KEYWORDS

MAJOR LEGISLATION

SUGGESTED READINGS

A. J. Angulo, *Diploma Mills: How For-Profit Colleges Stiffed Students, Taxpayers, and the American Dream* (Baltimore: Johns Hopkins University Press). Explores the history of the for-profit higher education institutions—their growth and evolution to where they are today.

John E. Chubb and **Terry M. Moe**, *Politics, Markets, and America's Schools* (Washington, D.C.: Brookings Institution, 1990). One of the first scholarly books to discuss the issues of the nation's public school systems and how these monopolies could be improved by the introduction of school choice and voucher programs.

Michael Fabricant and **Stephen Brier**, *Austerity Blues: Fighting for the Soul of Public Higher Education* (Baltimore: Johns Hopkins University Press, 2016). The book discusses the growth of public higher education following World War II primarily due to state public investment and how the disinvestment, along with other changes in the market, has affected the industry and students it serves.

R. Kenneth Godwin and **Frank R. Kemerer**, *School Choice Tradeoffs: Liberty, Equity, and Diversity* (Austin: University of Texas Press, 2002). An overview and appraisal of school choice; examines a number of issues related to this education policy alternative and the trade-offs associated with it, such as equality of opportunity and religious freedoms.

Sara Goldrick-Rab, *Paying the Price: College Costs, Financial Aid, and the Betrayal of the American Dream* (Chicago: University of Chicago Press, 2016). A study of students in public colleges and universities needing federal programs to help meet need, and how these programs failed the students and left many in debt.

William G. Howell and **Paul E. Peterson**, *The Education Gap: Vouchers and Urban Schools* (Washington, D.C.: Brookings Institution, 2002). A comprehensive analysis of different school voucher programs around the country. The study finds, among other things, that voucher programs have a consistent positive benefit for African American students who participate in such programs.

Suzanne Mettler, *Degrees of Inequality: How the Politics of Higher Education Sabotaged the American Dream* (New York: Basic Books, 2014). The book examines both the changing political and policy scene within the higher education area and how these changes have led to a situation of actually increasing inequality, which is counterintuitive to why we want students to pursue college.

Tom Price, "Student Debt," *CQ Researcher*, November 18, 2016. Discusses the reasons for increases in debt and the issues associated with such debt.

SUGGESTED WEBSITES

www.acenet.edu. The American Council on Education is the coordinating organization for higher education. It also conducts research on issues of higher education and provides a clearinghouse for news related to higher education.

www.aft.org. Site of the American Federation of Teachers, an advocacy group that conducts research and publishes studies on a range of education issues.

www.cep-dc.org. Site of the Center on Education Policy, a national, independent advocate for public education and for more effective public schools. The center conducts a range of research on the issue of public education, which can be accessed at this site.

www.ed.gov. U.S. federal government site for the Department of Education, with links to resources, news, policies, and statistics. Users can also access information about No Child Left Behind and other federal programs.

http://edtrust.org. The Education Trust is a nonprofit organization that focuses on schools in low-income areas and schools with high numbers of

minority students. Reports, data, and news on these issues are provided on this site.

www.heritage.org/Issues/Education. Heritage Foundation portal to reports and information regarding its ideas on education policy.

www.nbpts.org. National Board for Professional Teaching Standards site. Provides information regarding professional standards for the teaching profession.

http://nces.ed.gov. The National Center for Education Statistics is part of the U.S. Department of Education. A wide range of information is available at this site.

www.nea.org. Site for the National Education Association, a major organization representing teachers and supporting public education. Reports and information are available on a number of education issues.

www.pta.org. Site for the National Parent Teacher Association, a child advocacy group that promotes engagement in the school system as a way to help children. Resources, news, and links to other organizations are available.

NOTES

1. See Jason Furman, "The Truth about Higher Education and Student Loans," *The Huffington Post*, July 19, 2016; and Eric Westervelt, "I'm a Student-Debt Slave. How'd We Get Here?" *NPR*, July 11, 2016.

2. See Kelly Field, "Obamas Urge Colleges and Students to Step Up on Access and Success," *The Chronicle of Higher Education*, January 16,

2014, available at http://chronicle.com/article/Obamas-Urge-Colleges-and/144057/.

3. See White House Office of the Press Secretary, "Fact Sheet on the President's Plan to Make College More Affordable: A Better Bargain for the Middle Class," August 22, 2013.

4. See Tamar Lewin, "Official Calls for Urgency on College Costs," *New York Times*, November 29, 2011.

5. Ibid.

6. See this letter at the University of Michigan website: http://michigantoday.umich.edu/a8118/.

7. This information is from the National School Boards Association website: www.nsba.org.

8. See U.S. Department of Education, "The Federal Role in Education," available at www2.ed.gov/about/overview/fed/role.html?src=ln.

9. For more information, see U.S. Government Accountability Office, "Federal Education Funding: Overview of K–12 and Early Childhood Education Programs" (GAO-10–51), January 2010, available at www.gao.gov/assets/310/300246.pdf.

10. This figure is based on 2012 data provided by the U.S. Department of Education's IPEDS Data Center and can be accessed at https://nces.ed.gov/ipeds/Home/UseTheData. The subsidy is calculated by dividing the total expenditures of the academy by the enrollment total.

11. For more information on school financing in different states, see "Rankings of the States 2013 and Estimates of School Statistics 2014," available at the National Education Association site: www.nea.org/home/rankings-and-estimates-2013-2014.html.

12. Information about state school funding can be found at U.S. Census Bureau, "Public Elementary-Secondary Education Finance Data," available at the bureau's website: www.census.gov/govs/school.

13. It should be noted that although the Court has ruled relatively consistently on this issue since the *Engel* case, there are a number of districts and schools where critics of organized prayer and similar issues claim there are blatant violations. As an example, see Erik Eckholm, "Battling Anew over the Place of Religion in Public Schools," *New York Times*, December 27, 2011.

14. See U.S. Department of Education, National Center for Education Statistics, "Highlights from TIMSS and TIMSS Advanced 2015," November 2016, available at http://nces.ed.gov/pubs2017/2017002_timss_2015_results.pdf.

15. See "The Nation's Report Card: 2015 Mathematics and Reading Assessments," available at www.nationsreportcard.gov/reading_math_2015/#?grade=4. Note that you can get results on a variety of subject areas that the NAEP tests at http://nces.ed.gov/nationsreportcard/subjectareas.aspx.

16. These reports were all published in the *New York Times* and written by journalist Motoko Rich. The articles are "Better News in New Study That Assesses U.S. Students," October 23, 2013; "U.S. Reading and Math Show Slight Gains," November 7, 2013; and "American 15-Year-Olds Lag, Mainly in Math, on International Standardized Tests," December 3, 2013. You can also access the reports directly by going to the sites for the NAEP at http://nces.ed.gov/nationsreportcard/ and PISA at http://nces.ed.gov/surveys/pisa/.

17. See U.S. Department of Education, National Center for Education Statistics, "Fast Facts: SAT Scores," available at https://nces.ed.gov/fastfacts/display.asp?id=171.

18. For an interesting perspective of this concern see Motoko Rich, "As Graduation Rates Rise, Experts Fear Diplomas Come Up Short," *New York Times*, December 26, 2015.

19. See Marcia Clemmitt, "Teaching Critical Thinking," *CQ Researcher*, April 10, 2015.

20. Additional information can be found at American Council of Education, "To Touch the Future: Transforming the Way Teachers Are Taught," 1999, available at https://eric.ed.gov/?id=ED471782; and "Touching the Future: Final Report," 2002, available at http://eric.ed.gov/?id=ED478818. See also Craig D. Jerald and Richard Ingersoll, "All Talk, No Action: Putting an End to Out-of-Field Teaching," *The Education Trust*, August 2002, available at http://repository.upenn.edu/gse_pubs/142; and Sarah Almy and Christina Theokas, "Not Prepared for Class: High Poverty Schools Continue to Have Fewer In-field Teachers," *The Education Trust*, November 18, 2010, available at https://edtrust.org/resource/not-prepared-for-class-high-poverty-schools-continue-to-have-fewer-in-field-teachers.

21. See Kenneth J. Cooper, "'Best and Brightest' Leave Teaching Early, Study Says," *Washington Post*, January 13, 2000.

22. Some more detailed information is found in "Teacher Attrition and Mobility: Results from the 2012–13 Teacher Follow-up Survey," National Center for Education Statistics, September 2014, available at http://nces.ed.gov/pubs2014/2014077.pdf.

23. In a country like Finland, teachers are held in much higher regard and considered professional much in the same way as lawyers, doctors, and engineers. Those interested in the issue of teacher turnover may want to refer to Liz Riggs, "Why Do Teachers Quit?" *The Atlantic*, October 18, 2013, available at www.theatlantic.com/education/archive/2013/10/why-do-teachers-quit/280699/.

24. See a quote from Terry Moe, education policy specialist, in Marcia Clemmitt, "School Reform," *CQ Researcher*, April 29, 2011, 392.

25. According to the Bureau of Labor Statistics' American Time Use Survey, the average American spends 2.78 hours per day watching television. You can access this report at www.bls.gov/news.release/atus.nr0.htm.

26. See Clemmitt, "School Reform."

27. For more information on the blueprint, see Arne Duncan and Carmel Martin, "A Blueprint for Reform: The Reauthorization of the Elementary and Secondary Education Act," U.S. Department of Education Office of Planning, Evaluation, and Policy Development, March 2010, available at www2.ed.gov/policy/elsec/leg/blueprint/blueprint.pdf.

28. See Sam Dillon, "Obama Turns Power of Education Back to States," *New York Times*, September 23, 2011.

29. Information on the Common Core State Standards can be found at www.corestandards.org.

30. For more information, see Kim Severson and Alan Binder, "Test Scandal in Atlanta Brings More Guilty Pleas," *New York Times*, January 7, 2014.

31. See California State University Institute for Education Reform, *Paying for What You Need: Knowledge- and Skill-Based Approaches to Teacher Compensation*, September 1997, 9.

32. See American Federation of Teachers, "Raising the Bar: Aligning and Elevating Teacher Preparation and the Teaching Profession," April 2013, available at www.aft.org/sites/default/files/news/raisingthebar2013.pdf.

33. See Jal Mehta, "Teachers: Will We Ever Learn?" *New York Times*, April 13, 2013.

34. See Organisation for Economic Co-operation and Development, 2011, "Building a High-Quality Teaching Profession: Lessons from around the World," available at www2.ed.gov/about/inits/ed/internationaled/background.pdf.

35. This amount is for a married family of four. For additional information, see www.chooseyourschoolwi.org/.

36. For more information regarding the role of state constitutions, their legal environments, and the effect on school vouchers, see R. Kenneth Godwin and Frank R. Kemerer, *School Choice Trade-offs: Liberty, Equity, and Diversity* (Austin: University of Texas Press, 2002). Information on policies of different states regarding vouchers can be found at the National Conference of State Legislatures site at www.ncsl.org/research/education/voucher-law-comparison.aspx.

37. The NEA provides a list of studies suggesting either zero or minimum positive effects of voucher programs (see www.nea.org/home/16378.htm).

38. See Greg Foster, "A Win-Win Solution: The Empirical Evidence on School Vouchers," Foundation for Educational Choice, 2011, available at http://eric.ed.gov/?id=ED517753.

39. There was quite a bit of controversy surrounding the results by Peterson et al. and their interpretation. For more information, see Michael Winerip, "What a Voucher Study Truly Showed, and Why," *New York Times*, May 7, 2003.

40. For more information, students should see Brian Gill, P. Mike Timpane, Karen E. Ross, Dominic J. Brewer, and Kevin Booker, *Rhetoric Versus Reality: What We Know and What We Need to Know about Vouchers and Charter Schools* (Santa Monica, Calif.: RAND Corporation, 2007), available at www.rand.org/pubs/monograph_reports/MR1118-1.html.

41. Additional information on charter schools can be found at the National Alliance for Public Charter Schools, available at www.publiccharters.org.

42. See Gill et al., *Rhetoric Versus Reality*.

43. See Emily Deruy, "Donald Trump and the Future of Education," *The Atlantic*, November 9, 2016, available at www.theatlantic.com/educa tion/archive/2016/11/donald-trump-on-education/ 507167/.

44. Kenneth Jost discusses many of the issues regarding standardized testing in "Testing in Schools," *CQ Researcher*, April 20, 2001.

45. See Anna Quindlen, "Testing: One, Two, Three," *Newsweek*, June 13, 2005, 88.

46. See Julie Hirschfeld Davis, "President Obama Signs into Law a Rewrite of No Child Left Behind," *New York Times*, December 10, 2015. You can also find information on ESSA at the Department of Education site at www .ed.gov/esea.

47. Research by Kate Antonovic and Ben Backes focused on the University of California system and found that removing the racial preferences as part of the admission decision lowered the admission rates of underrepresented minorities at the most selective UC schools. See "The Effect of Banning Affirmative Action on College Admissions Policies and Student Quality," *Journal of Human Resources* 49 (2014): 295–358.

48. For more information, see Peter Katel, "Affirmative Action," *CQ Researcher* 18, no. 36 (October 17, 2008), available at http://library .cqpress.com/cqresearcher/cqresrre2008101711.

49. See Greg Winter, "After Ruling, Three Universities Maintain Diversity in Admissions," *New York Times*, April 13, 2004.

50. See Eric Hoover, "*Fisher* Happened. Now What?" *Chronicle of Higher Education*, June 27, 2013, for information regarding the first case; and Arthur Coleman, "5 Lessons to Take from the *Fisher* Decision," *Chronicle of Higher Education*, June 24, 2016, for information on the second case.

51. More detailed information on college pricing can be found at College Board, *Trends in College Pricing*, 2016, available at https://trends.college board.org/sites/default/files/2016-trends-college- pricing-web_0.pdf.

52. For certain low-income, high-quality students, attending a private school could be cheaper than attending a public school, particularly as tuition has continued to increase at public universities and they often do not have the same resources to provide aid to these students.

53. See State Higher Education Executive Officers Association, *State Higher Education Finance: FY 2015*, available at http://sheeo.org/sites/default/ files/project-files/SHEEO_FY15_Report_051816 .pdf.

54. These percentages are based on the amount of state tax funds for operating expenses of higher education per $1,000 of personal income. Two states during this time period, Wyoming and North Dakota, saw small increases of 2.3 and 0.8 percent. This information comes from Thomas G. Mortenson, "State Fiscal Support Higher Education FY1961–FY2011," *Postsecondary Education Opportunity*, February 2011.

55. See Jordan Weissmann, "Here's Exactly How Much the Government Would Have to Spend to Make Public College Tuition-Free," *The Atlantic*, January 3, 2014; and "How Washington Could Make College Tuition Free (Without Spending a Penny More on Education)," *The Atlantic*, March 8, 2013.

56. See Texas Comptroller of Public Accounts, "The Impact of the State Higher Education System on the Texas Economy," February 2005; and Dennis K. Winters and William A. Strang, "The Economic Impact of the University of Wisconsin System," *NorthStar Economics*, September 12, 2002, available at www.wisconsin.edu/news/2002/ sept_bor/study.pdf.

57. This information is based on U.S. Census Bureau data from its historical data tables. To access this information, go to http://census.gov/data/tables/ time-series/demo/income-poverty/historical- income-households.html.

58. As an example, the University of Wisconsin system has been promoting a "2020FWD" for

Wisconsin with an emphasis on providing more graduates in the state. Some of the primary goals of the plan include serving the needs of the Wisconsin businesses and communities. Information on this plan can be found at www.wisconsin.edu/2020FWD/.

59. This number comes from U.S. Department of Education, National Center for Education Statistics, "The Condition of Education 2016," available at http://nces.ed.gov/pubsearch/pubsinfo.asp?pubid=2016144.

60. This information was extracted from the U.S. Department of Education, National Center for Education Statistics, Integrated Postsecondary Education Data System.

61. This percentage increases during a presidential election year. For example, in 2012, the rate was 38 percent. Early indications for 2016 suggested youth turnout (ages eighteen to twenty-nine) of about twenty-four million, which is about 50 percent. See Meteor Blades, "Estimates Put Youth Vote Turnout at 50 Percent," *Daily Kos*, November 11, 2016, available at www.dailykos.com/story/2016/11/11/1596789/-Estimates-put-youth-vote-turnout-at-50-percent-heavily-for-Clinton-except-among-whites.

62. See Economic and Planning Systems, Inc., *The University of California's Economic Contribution to the State of California*, September 12, 2011, available at www.universityofcalifornia.edu/regents/regmeet/sept11/f7attach.pdf.

63. It is also interesting to note the differences in these data by race. For example, in 2011–2012, 66 percent of white students had loan debt with an average of $25,800, whereas the Hispanic student numbers were 72 percent and $24,700, and for African Americans they were 90 percent and $30,400.

64. Chapter 7 provided information about the National Debt Clock, you can see the federal student loan debt clock here www.finaid.org/loans/studentloandebtclock.phtml.

65. See Abby Jackson, "Hillary Clinton Has a Plan to Make College Debt Free—Here's How," *Business Insider*, October 1, 2016.

Chapter 11

Chapter Objectives

- Explain the nature of environmental and energy policies and the key concepts associated with them.

- Understand the history of government involvement in environmental and energy policy.

- Identify areas of consensus and conflict in addressing environmental and energy concerns.

- Compare major U.S. environmental policies and their impacts.

- Discuss major U.S. energy policies and their impacts.

- Analyze select issues in environmental and energy policy.

Effects of climate change. In this August 16, 2016, photo, Danny and Alys Messenger paddle a canoe away from their flooded home after surveying the damage in Prairieville, Louisiana. Scientists estimate that climate change about doubled the chances for the type of heavy downpours that caused devastating Louisiana floods that month. "We are now actually able to objectively and quantifiably say 'Yes, climate change contributed to this event,'" Climate Central Chief Scientist Heidi Cullen said of the August downpours in Louisiana. "It's unequivocal." *(AP Photo/Max Becherer, File)*

Environmental and Energy Policy

In the spring of 2014, the United Nations–sponsored **Intergovernmental Panel on Climate Change (IPCC)** issued two of its most sobering reports to date, attracting a great deal of media attention and bringing a greater sense of urgency to the debate over climate change policy. One report stated bluntly that **climate change**, a shift in climate patterns characterized by rising temperatures, increased storm intensity in some locations, and persistent droughts in other areas, already is having significant effects throughout the world. It noted as well that the problem is certain to grow much worse unless the United States and other nations sharply reduce their greenhouse gas emissions, most of which come from burning of fossil fuels: coal, oil, and natural gas.

The report focused on how climate change is likely to affect human society in addition to its adverse environmental impacts, citing high risks of death and injury and effects on public health to drive home its point. "Throughout the 21st century, climate-change impacts are projected to slow down economic growth, make poverty reduction more difficult, further erode food security, and prolong existing and create new poverty traps, the latter particularly in urban areas and emerging hot spots of hunger." Then secretary of state John Kerry, who had been actively seeking global cooperation on climate change initiatives as a major U.S. foreign policy priority, spoke forcefully about the report's conclusions: "There are those who say we can't afford to act. But waiting is truly unaffordable. The costs of inaction are catastrophic."[1] The second of the two IPCC reports focused on mitigation strategies, including public policy actions, and strongly endorsed a rapid shift to low-carbon energy sources and putting a price on greenhouse gas emissions to encourage reduction in their release.[2]

The IPCC and related studies arrived at an opportune time, as the United States and other nations, and the fifty states, continued to debate how they should respond to the challenge of climate change, widely considered to be the most important environmental problem of the twenty-first century. In June 2009, the U.S. House of Representatives approved landmark legislation that sought to create a "cap-and-trade" system for reducing the release of greenhouse gases such as carbon dioxide, but intense partisan conflicts and aggressive lobbying by industry prevented the Senate from acting on the bill through the end of the 111th Congress (2009–2011).[3] By 2013, the Obama White House concluded that action by a Republican Congress on climate change was so unlikely that its only viable strategy was to forge ahead with administrative decisions that needed no congressional approval. Over the past decade, many states and cities, unwilling to wait further for the national government, acted on their own to develop energy and climate change policies (Betsill and Rabe 2009; Karapin 2016; Rabe 2004, 2016).

As noted in the introduction to chapter 6, the Obama administration acted where it could on the problems of energy use and climate change. In 2012, it finalized new vehicle fuel efficiency regulations that set a fleet average target of 54.5 miles per gallon for cars and light trucks by 2025, and it did so with the full cooperation of the automobile industry. In 2016, it did much the same for heavy-duty trucks, vans, and buses.[4] The administration also fostered extensive investment in energy research and development, particularly for energy efficiency and renewable energy sources such as wind and solar power. Many of these investments will likely reduce U.S. greenhouse gas emissions, and despite criticism from the president's detractors, they appear to be achieving their objectives.[5]

Two other steps President Obama took are even more important than the fuel efficiency rules and energy investments. First, he strongly backed a new international agreement on climate change that was finalized in Paris in December 2015, in which the United States pledged to make significant reductions in greenhouse gas emissions over the next several decades (discussed later in the chapter). Second, his **Environmental Protection Agency (EPA)** developed a far-reaching and politically contentious plan to reduce emissions from coal-fired power plants, which release about 40 percent of the nation's total energy-related greenhouse gas emissions. The EPA issued the final rules for its **Clean Power Plan** in August 2015. That plan seeks to reduce carbon pollution from electric power generation by 32 percent below 2005 levels when fully in place by 2030, and thereby to facilitate a transition to cleaner sources of energy. The plan also will significantly lower emissions of sulfur dioxide and nitrogen dioxides, major contributors to air pollution and thus a risk to public health. The plan's critics, including more than half the states, coal producers, and many electric utilities, remained unhappy with the EPA plan, and they filed suit in federal court to block it. Assuming they survive legal challenge and a seeming determination by the Trump administration and congressional Republicans to reverse the decision, the rules require the fifty states to create and implement their own individual plans, and the states have considerable discretion in how they meet the new goals. For example, they may choose to reduce energy demand through conservation measures, improve energy efficiency, expand use of renewable energy resources such as wind and solar power, or rely more on nuclear power in addition to or instead of closing coal-generating facilities. Each state also has the option to join existing "cap-and-trade" programs in California or the Northeast.[6]

These varied policy developments of the past few years capture the momentous changes now under way in the nation's use of energy and the impacts they will have on the environment and public health. We can add to the pot one other striking change in energy technology and the economy: the impacts coming from rapidly expanding oil and gas drilling in shale rock formations. While hydraulic **fracturing**, or fracking of shale deposits to produce oil and natural gas, remains a controversial practice, there is no question that the resulting abundant and inexpensive natural gas is reshaping the economy and also helping to moderate the effects the new EPA rules will have in phasing out older coal-fired power plants. The coal plants will likely be replaced by far cleaner natural gas facilities with about half of the carbon emissions and few of the toxic air pollutants, such as mercury, that come from burning coal.[7]

What should we make of these changes in energy policy and the environment? Are they all good news? Certainly, the coal industry doesn't think so. The American Coalition for Clean Coal Electricity, a pro-coal group, urged members of Congress to overturn the EPA regulations on carbon emissions. Long before the final rule was issued, the House passed a bill by a margin of 229–183 to do just that, as it often has over the past few years in the face of new environmental rules.[8] Others worry that by phasing out so many coal-fired power plants the United States will face a shortage of electricity-generating facilities that will lead to higher prices for electricity. These effects are likely to be particularly important in states that are heavily dependent on coal plants, such as Ohio, Kentucky, and Missouri, and on coal mining states such as West Virginia; hence the political arguments advanced about an alleged "war on coal."

These recent decisions underscore the strong relationship between energy and environmental policy; that is, the amount of energy Americans use and its sources—especially fossil fuels—can have profound environmental impacts, including climate change, oil spills on land or offshore (such as the massive 2010 BP Deepwater Horizon spill in the Gulf of Mexico), increased urban air pollution, production of toxic chemicals and hazardous wastes, and damage to ecosystems. Environmental policy itself, such as air and water quality regulations, can significantly influence the production and use of energy by setting high standards that can affect which sources of energy may be used and what they will cost. This is one reason why critics of environmental policy in recent years have favored lowering those standards to promote increased drilling for oil and natural gas in offshore and other public and private lands and construction of oil pipelines such as the highly controversial Keystone XL pipeline that was to bring Canadian tar sands oil to U.S. refineries in Texas; in February 2015, President Obama successfully vetoed legislation to authorize the pipeline.

This chapter describes and evaluates U.S. environmental and energy policies. It discusses their evolution, especially since the 1970s and 1980s, when most of the key policies were approved. Political disagreements over time and today center on the costs and burdens these policies impose on industry and the economy, the promise of alternative policies, and the potential for integrating economic and environmental goals through sustainable development in the United States and around the world. In keeping with our emphasis throughout the text on several core criteria for judging policy alternatives, the chapter gives special consideration to the effectiveness of current policies and to economic, political, and equity issues in evaluating policy ideas and proposals.

Background

Environmental policy is not easy to define. As is the case with health care policy, its scope is much broader than one might see at first glance. Many people believe the environment, and therefore environmental policy, refers only to humans' relationship to nature—which they see as wilderness and wildlife, parks, open space, recreation, and natural resources such as forests. Or perhaps they understand that much environmental policy deals with human health concerns; the Clean Air Act and Safe Drinking Water Act, for example, just as easily could be described as public health laws. The widely reported contamination of drinking water in Flint, Michigan, and other cities around the nation with unsafe levels of lead reminds us of the public health focus of environmental policies.[9]

Environmental scientists argue that a more useful way to understand the environment is to see it as a set of natural systems that interact in complex ways to supply humans and other species with the necessities of life, such as breathable air, clean water, food, fiber, energy, and the recycling of waste products. To put it another way, humans are intimately dependent on environmental systems to meet their essential needs. People cannot survive without these systems but often fail to recognize their functions or to place a reasonable value on the natural services that almost everyone takes for granted (Daily 1997).

Many scientific reports in recent years also tell us that human beings are now so numerous and use nature to such an extent to meet their needs that they threaten to disrupt these natural systems and lose the services on which life depends, such as a reliable supply of freshwater and productive agricultural land. In the late 1990s, Jane Lubchenco, President Obama's selection to head the National Oceanic and Atmospheric Administration and a former president of the American Association for the Advancement of Science, observed that "humans have emerged as a new force of nature." She argued that people are "modifying physical, chemical, and biological systems in new ways, at faster rates, and over larger spatial scales than ever recorded on Earth." The result of these modifications is that humans have "unwittingly embarked upon a grand experiment with our planet" with "profound implications for all of life on Earth" (Lubchenco 1998, 492).

At the 1992 United Nations Conference on Environment and Development (the Earth Summit), delegates from 179 nations pledged support for an elaborate plan of action for the twenty-first century called Agenda 21 (United Nations 1993). It addresses environmental concerns by emphasizing **sustainable development**, or economic growth that is compatible with natural environmental systems and social goals. The objective of sustainable development is "meeting the needs of the present without compromising the ability of future generations to meet their own needs" (World Commission on Environment and Development 1987, 43). Given the continued growth of the human population and the economic expansion that must occur to provide for the nearly 9.8 billion people who are expected to inhabit the planet by 2050 (up from 7.4 billion in early 2017), that will be no easy task. In September 2002, on the tenth anniversary of the Earth Summit, a new World Summit on Sustainable Development was held in Johannesburg, South Africa, and continued to define that challenge in light of persistent worldwide poverty, and in June 2012, the United Nations (UN) held a Rio+20 Conference on Sustainable Development to consider what additional steps need to be taken in the twenty-first century. The box "Steps to Analysis: Sustainable Development" suggests some ways to study and evaluate issues raised at the 2012 conference and similar sustainability initiatives taken by cities and

Steps to Analysis

Sustainable Development

Visit the webpage for the United Nations Sustainable Development Knowledge Platform at https://sustainabledevelopment.un.org/. Click on the tab for 2030 Agenda for Sustainable Development and the Sustainable Development Goals, and then on any of the goals, such as No Poverty, Zero Hunger, Affordable and Clean Energy, Climate Action, Responsible Consumption and Production, Gender Equality, or Sustainable Cities and Communities.

- What do you make of these? Do you see them as desirable or not?

- Do you consider the goals to be economically or politically feasible?

- How would you compare these goals to what most people are willing to consider or embrace as desirable directions for government or society today?

- How do you think political conservatives would react to these goals? Would they see them as desirable or not? As giving too much power to government?

For an example of U.S. actions on the topic of sustainable cities, visit the websites for those communities with an especially strong commitment to sustainability goals, such as Seattle, Washington (www.seattle.gov/environment); Portland, Oregon (www.portlandoregon.gov/bps/67121); Santa Monica, California (www.smgov.net/departments/ose); New York City (www1.nyc.gov/site/sustainability/index.page); or Boulder County, Colorado (http://bouldercountysustainability.org). Go to the website for one of these cities or counties and read about what it has done to date and its plans to foster sustainability in the future. Does the community seem to have a clear understanding of and commitment to sustainability? Are its various actions consistent with its stated goals? Can you tell from the description provided on its website how well the city or county is doing in moving toward those goals?

other local governments that promote energy conservation and efficiency, use of renewable energy resources, recycling, water conservation, improved growth management, use of mass transit, and similar actions (Mazmanian and Kraft 2009; K. Portney 2013, 2016).[10]

Put in this broader context, **environmental policy**, both in the United States and globally, can be defined as government actions that affect or attempt to affect environmental quality and the use of natural resources. The policy actions may take place at the local, state, regional, national, or international level. Traditionally, environmental policy was considered to involve the conservation or protection of natural resources such as public lands and waters, wilderness, and wildlife. Since the late 1960s, however, the term has also been used to refer to governments' environmental protection efforts that are motivated by public health concerns, such as controlling air and water pollution and limiting exposure to toxic chemicals. In the future, environmental policy is likely to be tightly integrated with the comprehensive agenda of sustainable development at all levels of government. Environmental policy will extend to government actions affecting human health and safety, energy use, transportation and urban design, agriculture and food production, population growth, and the protection of vital global ecological, chemical, and geophysical systems (Brown 2010; Chasek, Downie, and Brown 2017; Mazmanian and Kraft 2009; Vig and Kraft 2016; Worldwatch Institute 2012). Almost certainly, environmental policy is going to have a pervasive and growing impact on human affairs in the twenty-first century.

To address these challenges effectively, however, policy analysts, policy-makers, and the public need to think in fresh ways about environmental and energy policies and redesign them as needed. Many existing policies were developed nearly five decades ago, and criticism of their effectiveness, efficiency, and equity abounds. Not surprisingly, some complaints come from the business community, which has long argued that stringent laws dealing with clean air, clean water, toxic chemicals, and hazardous wastes can have an adverse impact on business operations and constrain their ability to compete internationally (Kraft and Kamieniecki 2007). Others, however, are just as likely to find fault, including state and local governments that must handle much of the routine implementation of federal laws and pay a sizable part of the costs. Critical assessments come as well from independent policy analysts who see a mismatch between what the policies are intended to accomplish and the strategies and tools on which they rely (Davies and Mazurek 1998; Eisner 2007; Fiorino 2006; Kamieniecki and Kraft 2013; Kraft 2018).

For more than three decades, environmental policy has been bitterly contested, with no clear resolution on most of the major policies; energy policy has been similarly disputed. Piecemeal and incremental policy changes have improved some existing environmental programs, such as regulating pesticides and providing safe drinking water, but what remains is a fragmented, costly, often inefficient, and somewhat ineffective set of environmental and energy policies. During the 1990s, President Bill Clinton's EPA tried to "reinvent" environmental regulation to make it more efficient and more acceptable to the business community and to congressional Republicans. For example, it experimented with streamlined rulemaking and more **collaborative decision making,** in which industry and other stakeholders worked cooperatively with government officials. The experiments were only moderately successful. Clinton's successor, George W. Bush, likewise proposed a "new era" of flexible and efficient regulation and a greater role for the states, but few experts thought Bush's efforts were more effective than Clinton's. Clinton and Bush preferred different kinds of reforms of the major environmental laws to make them more appropriate for the twenty-first century, but political constraints prevented both of them from realizing their goals. As discussed earlier, much the same was true during the Obama administration when Republicans in Congress sought to constrain the EPA's rulemaking and to block efforts on climate change they believed to be unjustified (Fiorino 2006; Kraft 2018; Vig and Kraft 2016).

As this brief review suggests, environmental policy has reached an important crossroads, as have energy policies, particularly as they relate to the use of fossil fuels and climate change. More than ever before, policymakers and analysts need to figure out what works and what does not, and to remake environmental policy for the emerging era of sustainable development both within the United States and internationally. How Congress, the states, and local governments will change environmental and energy policies in the years ahead remains unclear, particularly as the partisan divide over these issues has widened in the last several years (Dunlap, McCright, and Yarosh 2016). Much depends on the way leading policy actors define the issues and how the media cover them, the state of the economy, the relative influence of opposing interest groups, and whether political leadership can help to forge a national consensus. Until policy breakthroughs occur, however, today's environmental and energy policies are likely to continue in much their present form. Yet some of the most innovative and promising policy actions, rooted in the kind of comprehensive and coordinated thinking that is associated with sustainability, are taking place at the regional, state, and local levels, and they provide a glimpse of what might eventually be endorsed at higher levels of government (Klyza and Sousa 2013; Mazmanian and Kraft 2009; K. Portney 2013, 2016; Rabe 2016).

The Evolution of Environmental and Energy Policy

Modern environmental policy was developed during the 1960s and shortly thereafter became firmly established on the political agenda in the United States and other developed nations. During the so-called environmental decade of the 1970s, Congress enacted most of the major environmental statutes in effect today. Actions in states and localities paralleled these developments, as did policy evolution at the international level (Axelrod and VanDeveer 2015; Chasek, Downie, and Brown 2017; Kraft 2018; McCormick 1989). Energy policy experienced a somewhat different history, but here too it has been considered in a comprehensive manner only since the 1970s (Rosenbaum 2015).

Early Environmental and Energy Policies

Although formal environmental policy in the United States is a relatively recent development, concern about the environment and the value of natural resources can be traced back to the early seventeenth century, when New England colonists first adopted local ordinances to protect forestland (Andrews 2006a). In the late nineteenth and early twentieth centuries, conservation policies advanced to deal with the excesses of economic development in the West, and new federal and state agencies emerged to assume responsibility for their implementation, including the U.S. Forest Service in 1905 and the National Park Service in 1916. In 1892, Congress set aside two million acres in Idaho, Montana, and Wyoming to create Yellowstone National Park, the first of a series of national parks. Many of the prominent conservation organizations also formed during this period. Naturalist John Muir founded the Sierra Club in 1892 as the first broad-based environmental organization, and others followed in the ensuing decades.

Following a number of natural disasters, most memorably the Dust Bowl of the 1930s, President Franklin Roosevelt expanded conservation policies to deal with flood control and soil conservation as part of the New Deal. Congress also created the Tennessee Valley Authority (TVA) in 1933 to stimulate economic growth by providing electric power development in that region. The TVA demonstrated a critical policy belief: that government land-use planning could further the public interest.

Prior to the 1970s, energy policy was not a major or sustained concern of government. For the most part, it consisted of federal and state regulation of coal, natural gas, and oil, particularly of the prices charged and competition in the private sector. The goal was to stabilize markets and ensure both profits and continuing energy supplies. The most notable exception was substantial federal support for the commercialization of nuclear power. Beginning in the late 1940s, Congress shielded the nascent nuclear power industry from public scrutiny, spent lavishly on research and development, and promoted the rapid advancement of civilian nuclear power plants through the Atomic Energy Commission and its successor agencies, the Nuclear Regulatory Commission and the Department of Energy (DOE).

The Modern Environmental Movement and Policy Developments

By the 1960s, the modern environmental movement was taking shape in response to changing social values. The major stimulus was the huge spurt in economic

For the health of planet and populace. The dome of the U.S. Capitol is seen behind the smokestacks of the Capitol Power Plant on March 10, 2014. It is the only coal-burning power plant in the nation's capital. Later that day, twenty-six Democratic and Independent senators spoke through the night on the need to confront climate change. As noted in the chapter opening, such coal-burning power plants face new EPA regulations in an effort to cut the nation's greenhouse gas emissions, although the Trump administration has indicated it will seek to end the agency's Clean Power Plan. *(Andrew Harrer/ Bloomberg via Getty Images)*

development that followed World War II (1941–1945). During the 1950s and 1960s, the nation benefited further from the rise in consumerism. An affluent, comfortable, and well-educated public began to place a greater emphasis on quality of life, and environmental quality was a part of it. Social scientists characterize this period as a shift from an industrial to a postindustrial society. In this context, it is easy to understand a new level of public concern for natural resources and environmental protection. Scientific discoveries also helped. New studies, often well publicized in the popular press, alerted people to the effects of pesticides and other synthetic chemicals. Rachel Carson's influential book *Silent Spring*, which documented the devastating effects that such chemicals had on songbird populations, was published in 1962, and for many, it was an eye-opener.

The initial public policy response to these new values and concerns focused on natural resources. Congress approved the Wilderness Act of 1964 to preserve some national forestlands in their natural condition. The Land and Water Conservation Fund Act, also adopted in 1964, facilitated local, state, and federal acquisition and development of land for parks and open spaces.[11] In 1968, Congress created the National Wild and Scenic Rivers System to preserve certain rivers with "outstandingly remarkable" scenic, recreational, ecological, historical, and cultural values.

Action by the federal government on pollution control issues lagged in comparison to resource conservation, largely because Congress deferred to state and local governments on these matters. Congress approved the first modest federal water and air pollution statutes in 1948 and 1955, respectively. However, only in the late 1960s and 1970s did it expand and strengthen them significantly.

International environmental issues also began to attract attention in the 1960s. In his 1965 State of the Union message, for example, President Lyndon Johnson called for federal programs to deal with "the explosion in world population and the growing scarcity in world resources." The following year, Congress authorized the first funds to support family planning programs in other nations (Kraft 1994).

These early policy developments were a prelude to a wholesale shift in the political mood of the nation that led to the present array of environmental protection, natural resource, and energy policies. Public opinion was the driving force in most of this policy advancement. Membership in environmental organizations such as the Sierra Club and the Audubon Society surged during the 1960s, reflecting a growing public concern about these issues. By the early 1970s, newer groups, such as the Natural Resources Defense Council (NRDC), were established, and almost all of them saw their budgets, staffs, and political influence soar. As a result, policymakers became aware of a concerned public that demanded action, and they were eager to respond and take political credit (Bosso 2005; Dunlap 1995).

Congress approved most of the major federal environmental laws now in effect between 1969 and 1976 in a stunning outpouring of legislation not repeated since that time. Policymakers were convinced that the public favored new federal regulatory measures that would be strong enough to force offending industries to clean up. In many respects, this development illustrates the kind of market failure discussed in chapter 1. The public and policymakers demanded that the federal government intervene to stop rampant pollution by industry that constituted a market externality. Most of the states also were constrained from taking action. As we noted in chapter 2, either the states lacked the necessary policy capacity at that time, or they chose not to act because of pressure from local industry. Eventually, Congress decided that only national policy action would suffice (Davies and Davies 1975). The development of environmental and resource policies during the 1960s and 1970s, therefore, grew out of the same factors that led to other public policies: market failures (economic reasons), a belief that government action was the right thing to do (ethical reasons), and the eagerness of elected officials to respond to strong public demand (political reasons). Table 11-1 lists the most important of the federal environmental laws enacted between 1964 and 2016. Comparable policy developments took place at the state level and abroad (Axelrod and VanDeveer 2015; Rabe 2016; Steinberg and VanDeveer 2012; Vig and Faure 2004).

Policymakers also appeared to believe at the time that pollution problems and their remedies were fairly simple. Few would make such assumptions today, because they understand the complexity of environmental problems and the difficulty of solving them. But in the 1960s and 1970s, policymakers and the public had more confidence that the chosen solutions would work. They thought that application of technological or engineering know-how would do the trick and that little or no change would be required in human behavior, for example, in using

TABLE 11-1   Major U.S. Environmental Laws, 1964–2016

Year Enacted	Legislation
1964	Wilderness Act, PL 88-577
1968	Wild and Scenic Rivers Act, PL 90-542
1969	National Environmental Policy Act (NEPA), PL 91-190
1970	Clean Air Act Amendments, PL 91-604
1972	Federal Water Pollution Control Act Amendments (Clean Water Act), PL 92-500 Federal Environmental Pesticide Control Act of 1972 (amended the Federal Insecticide, Fungicide, and Rodenticide Act [FIFRA] of 1947), PL 92-516 Marine Protection, Research, and Sanctuaries Act of 1972, PL 92-532 Marine Mammal Protection Act, PL 92-522 Coastal Zone Management Act, PL 92-583 Noise Control Act, PL 92-574
1973	Endangered Species Act, PL 93-205
1974	Safe Drinking Water Act, PL 93-523
1976	Resource Conservation and Recovery Act (RCRA), PL 94-580 Toxic Substances Control Act, PL 94-469 Federal Land Policy and Management Act, PL 94-579 National Forest Management Act, PL 94-588
1977	Clean Air Act Amendments, PL 95-95 Clean Water Act, PL 95-217 Surface Mining Control and Reclamation Act, PL 95-87
1980	Comprehensive Environmental Response, Compensation, and Liability Act (Superfund), PL 96-510
1982	Nuclear Waste Policy Act, PL 97-425 (amended in 1987 by the Nuclear Waste Policy Amendments Act, PL 100-203)
1984	Hazardous and Solid Waste Amendments (RCRA amendments), PL 98-616
1986	Safe Drinking Water Act Amendments, PL 99-339 Superfund Amendments and Reauthorization Act (SARA), PL 99-499
1987	Water Quality Act (CWA amendments), PL 100-4
1988	Ocean Dumping Act, PL 100-688
1990	Clean Air Act Amendments, PL 101-549 Oil Pollution Act, PL 101-380 Pollution Prevention Act, PL 101-508
1992	Energy Policy Act, PL 102-486 Omnibus Water Act, PL 102-575
1996	Food Quality Protection Act (amended FIFRA), PL 104-120 Safe Drinking Water Act Amendments, PL 104-182
2002	Small Business Liability Relief and Brownfields Revitalization Act, PL 107-118
2003	Healthy Forests Restoration Act of 2003, PL 108-148
2005	Energy Policy Act of 2005, PL 109-58
2007	Energy Independence and Security Act of 2007, PL 110-140
2009	American Recovery and Reinvestment Act of 2009 (for its funding of energy policy), PL 111-5 Omnibus Public Lands Management Act of 2009, PL 111-11
2016	Frank R. Lautenberg Chemical Safety for the 21st Century Act, PL 114-182

Note: For a more complete list, with a summary description of major features of each act, see Norman J. Vig and Michael E. Kraft, eds., *Environmental Policy*, 9th ed. (Thousand Oaks, Calif.: CQ Press, 2016), Appendix 1.

personal automobiles in urban areas or in creating far-flung suburbs (Paehlke 2013). These policy beliefs dominated legislative debates, although it was evident to some even then that the necessary technical knowledge did not always exist and that government agencies sometimes lacked the necessary resources and skills to take on the many new responsibilities mandated by these laws (Jones 1975; Mazmanian and Sabatier 1983).

On the one hand, these policy actions are a remarkable testimony to the capacity of government institutions to move quickly to approve major legislation when public and partisan consensus demands a policy such as pollution control. On the other hand, this history of policy development suggests why so many of these environmental laws later came under forceful criticism from business groups and conservatives, and why economists worried about the cost they imposed on society, not to mention their limited success in reaching the ambitious policy goals they embodied (Higgs and Close 2005; P. Portney and Stavins 2000).

Some thoughtful environmental philosophers offer a different perspective, which is more closely attuned to current concepts of sustainable development. They argue that environmental policies of this kind can never succeed as long as human population growth and material consumption continue and society's institutions remain unchallenged. Mere reformist policies of pollution control and ecological management, they say, are doomed to failure because they do so little to alter human attitudes and behavior or to confront the economic and political systems that contribute to environmental degradation in the first place (Ophuls and Boyan 1992). In chapter 4, we referred to one of the dilemmas facing policy analysts—whether to deal with fundamental or root causes of public problems or to focus on the more manageable proximate causes. Environmental policies to date have dealt primarily with the latter.

From Consensus to Conflict in Environmental Policy

If consensus on environmental policy was the norm during the 1970s, by the 1980s political conflict became the new standard in policymaking. The shift in perspective had many causes, but chief among them were the conservatives' growing concern about the strong role of government and its implications for the private sector, increasing doubts among policy analysts about the effectiveness and efficiency of the dominant command-and-control regulation, and the business community's resentment over the burdens and costs of the new policies. Industry representatives frequently argued that the costs could not be justified by what they saw as the limited benefits produced in improved public health or environmental quality.

These new ideas about environmental policy rose to prominence during Ronald Reagan's presidency (1981–1989), when environmental agencies suffered deep budget cuts, lost experienced professional staff members, and saw their program activities slow down. Reagan's agenda was largely one of providing temporary relief to the business community and to western resource development interests such as mining, logging, and ranching. His administration demonstrated little persistent interest in genuine reforms of environmental programs to make them more effective and efficient (Vig and Kraft 1984). That goal would have been much tougher. To work toward it would have meant rewriting the basic environmental laws, and that in turn would have required broad agreement among the major policy actors, which did not exist. One such rewrite that was successful occurred when Reagan's successor, George H. W. Bush, worked closely with Congress to enact the Clean Air Act Amendments of 1990. That law was a major expansion of the original 1970 act, and it is discussed below. Environmentalists cheered their success in keeping the policies and programs of the 1970s intact and in some instances expanding them. But policy analysts continued to argue that additional reform of those policies was essential to make them more effective and to control their substantial and rising costs (Durant, Fiorino, and O'Leary 2017; Eisner 2007; Fiorino 2006; P. Portney and Stavins 2000).

Partisan conflict had much to do with the inability to focus seriously on the real reform agenda and to chart new environmental policy directions for the future. The two major political parties grew further apart over environmental policy, even though they had worked together in the 1970s to advance environmental protection. By the 1990s, a widening gulf divided the parties on fundamental issues such as the legitimacy of government regulation to protect the public's welfare, the sanctity of private property rights, and even whether environmental problems posed a real and substantial risk to the public's health and well-being (Vig and Kraft 2016).

These differences were particularly evident in congressional voting on environmental protection and natural resource issues. Comprehensive analyses of voting records in Congress compiled by the League of Conservation Voters show that the gap between the parties grew from the early 1970s through the late 1990s, and then continued to widen in the 2000s and 2010s (Dunlap, McCright, and Yarosh 2016; Shipan and Lowry 2001). Clearly, the two major parties no longer saw eye to eye on environmental issues. The box "Steps to Analysis: Voting Records on the Environment" (pp. 410–411) explains how these scores are compiled and points to the website where students can find the environmental voting record of any member of Congress.

Major Federal Environmental Policies

Environmental policy consists chiefly of the many different statutes enacted during the 1960s and 1970s and their later amendments, but there is no single consolidated policy on the environment that describes the nation's goals and the strategies needed to reach them. Nor is environmental policy concentrated in one executive department or agency; rather, at the national level, responsibility for the environment is divided among twelve cabinet departments and the EPA, the Nuclear Regulatory

Steps to Analysis

Voting Records on the Environment

The League of Conservation Voters (LCV) is a leading environmental organization. For almost five decades, it has kept tabs on how members of Congress vote on the environment. Each year, the group compiles the National Environmental Scorecard, which records members' choices on ten to fourteen key votes. Go to the league's website (www.lcv.org) to see a recent scorecard. You can view the full report as a pdf file or see the scores of individual members or state delegations as HTML files. Look up the voting records for one or more members of the House of Representatives and Senate from your state or a state you find interesting. If using the full report, you can see how these votes compare to the average for the member's state, the scores of the chair and ranking minority member on each of the leading environmental policy committees of the House and Senate, and each party's House or Senate leaders. For comparison, Figure 11-1 reports the changes over time in each party's LCV scores from 1970 to 2015. The annual LCV reports also indicate which issues and particular votes were used to compile the scores. Why do you think the member you selected has the score he or she does? Does it reflect the nature of the constituency, the locally active environmental or business groups, or the member's own political philosophy or ideology?

The LCV scores reported on the site represent how often a member of Congress voted in accordance with the position taken by the league and the coalition of environmental group leaders on which it relies to select an annual list of important environmental votes. Look at the votes the LCV selected in a particular year and the way it

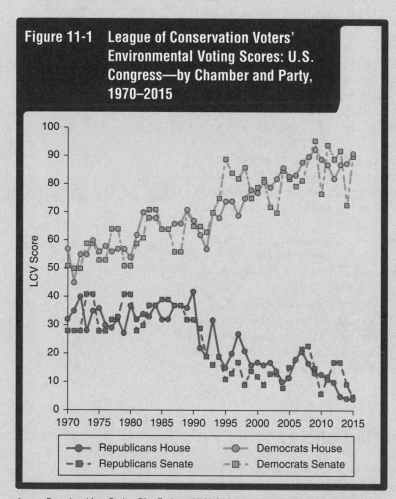

Figure 11-1   League of Conservation Voters' Environmental Voting Scores: U.S. Congress—by Chamber and Party, 1970–2015

Legend:
- Republicans House
- Republicans Senate
- Democrats House
- Democrats Senate

Source: Reproduced from Dunlap, Riley E., Aaron M. McCright, and Jerrod H. Yarosh. 2016. "The Political Divide on Climate Change: Partisan Polarization Widens in the U.S." *Environment* 58, no. 5 (September/October), p. 7. Copyright Taylor & Francis.

compiles the environmental voting score. These are described at the beginning of the full report.

- Do you think the score fairly represents the voting record of members of Congress on environmental and energy issues?
- Compare the voting records of Democrats and Republicans, either nationwide or within your own state, or as reported in

Figure 11-1. Why do you think Republicans consistently have much lower LCV scores than Democrats?

- Do you think there is a bias in the way votes are selected and the scores calculated?
- Do the differences in scores reflect the nature of the constituencies within each of the major parties? Their political philosophies? Something else?

Commission, and other agencies. The EPA has the lion's share of responsibility, but it must work with other departments and agencies, especially the Departments of Agriculture, Energy, and the Interior, to carry out its mission.

Because so many agencies contribute to U.S. environmental policy, the best way to survey the subject is to highlight the major elements within each of three areas: environmental protection policy or pollution control, natural resource policy, and energy policy. Only one major statute, the National Environmental Policy Act, cuts across these categories. For each of the three categories, this chapter emphasizes the broad goals that policymakers have adopted and the policy strategies or means they use to achieve them. It also evaluates selected policy achievements and considers policy options for the future. Students who want a more complete description of the major environmental or energy policies should consult the suggested readings listed at the end of the chapter or visit the websites of the implementing agencies, where summary descriptions as well as the full statutes are usually available. The box "Working with Sources: Executive Agencies with Environmental Responsibilities" lists the websites for the leading executive agencies with environmental responsibilities and suggests how public policy students might evaluate the information they find at those sites.

The chapter focuses on national environmental and resource policies, even though, as noted earlier, some states, such as California, Minnesota, Oregon, and Vermont, often have been at the forefront of policy innovation. One of the best ways to compare state environmental policies is to visit the website for the Council of State Governments (www.csg.org) for links to all the state home pages. Those pages in turn describe environmental policy within the state. Another source for state environmental policy is the website for the Environmental Council of the States (www.ecos.org), a national nonpartisan association of state environmental commissioners that reports on a range of issues concerning state environmental policy activities and federal-state relations.

Working with Sources

Executive Agencies with Environmental Responsibilities

Visit one or more of the webpages of the leading federal environmental and natural resource departments and agencies to learn more about their missions, the laws they administer, the agencies and programs under their jurisdiction, and their programs' achievements or shortcomings. The Department of the Interior, for example, includes the U.S. Geological Survey, Fish and Wildlife Service, National Park Service, and Bureau of Land Management. The U.S. Forest Service and the Natural Resources Conservation Service are parts of the Department of Agriculture. The Department of Energy (DOE) sponsors a large number of energy research and development programs and has broad responsibilities for cleaning up former defense installations, including heavily contaminated nuclear weapons production facilities.

All of the agency websites have links to current programs and issues, studies and reports, internal organization issues, related programs at other departments and agencies, or White House positions on the issues. In interpreting information provided by these sites regarding program accomplishments, you should bear in mind that government agencies—federal or state and local—almost always offer a positive assessment of their activities and say little about their weaknesses or failures.

To find environmental and natural resource agencies at the state level, visit the website for the Council of State Governments (www.csg.org) and search for "state pages," where all fifty state governments are listed. Once on the state government home page, look for agencies dealing with the environment, natural resources, or energy.

As you examine these pages, consider what might be the telltale signs that the agency is providing only one side of an issue or putting a positive spin on the agency's achievements or current actions. For example, in 2016, the DOE site (www.energy.gov) described in very positive terms President Obama's initiatives that were part of the economic stimulus package of early 2009 as well as expansion of renewable energy on public lands in the West. Click on the tab for Science and Innovation, and then Energy Sources, and then Renewable Energy or Nuclear.

- What does the agency have to say about the potential contribution of wind power, solar power, or nuclear power?

- Can you tell from these descriptions how effective the action taken has been and what its promise is for the future?

www.doi.gov (U.S. Department of the Interior)

www.energy.gov (U.S. Department of Energy)

www.epa.gov (U.S. Environmental Protection Agency)

www.nrc.gov (U.S. Nuclear Regulatory Commission)

www.usda.gov (U.S. Department of Agriculture)

The National Environmental Policy Act

One law that might appear to constitute a coherent national policy on environmental issues is the National Environmental Policy Act of 1969 (NEPA). The enactment of this six-page statute signified the beginning of the modern era in environmental policy. NEPA acknowledged the "profound impact of man's activities on the interrelations of all components of the natural environment" and the "critical importance of restoring and maintaining environmental quality" for human welfare. The instrument for achieving these goals, however, is procedural rather than substantive: the preparation of an **environmental impact statement** (EIS), which is then used in government agency planning and decision making. Such statements are required for major federal actions "significantly affecting the quality of the human environment." They are intended to offer a detailed and systematic assessment of the environmental effects of a proposed action, such as building a highway, and alternatives to the action that might be considered. New guidelines now require that these statements also assess the impact of agency actions on climate change. Put otherwise, NEPA mandates that agencies engage in policy analysis before they make decisions. Its real effect, however, comes less from the preparation of these impact statements than from a requirement that they be made public. Doing so means that agencies have to give serious consideration to the consequences of their decisions and anticipate how critics of those decisions might respond.

NEPA requires only that such EISs be prepared and be subject to public review; it does not prevent an agency from making an environmentally harmful decision. Nevertheless, most evaluations of the policy find that it has had a substantial effect on decision making by government agencies such as the U.S. Forest Service, the Federal Highway Administration, and the Army Corps of Engineers (Bartlett 1989; Caldwell 1998). In a way, NEPA symbolized environmental policy action during the late 1960s and the 1970s by establishing new decision-making procedures that opened the policy process to public scrutiny and ensured widespread consultation with affected parties, including environmental groups and local governments. The old subgovernments that we described earlier in the text had long dominated many areas of natural resource management such as logging, mining, and ranching, and they were forever changed as a result of these procedural requirements.

NEPA also created a presidential advisory body for environmental issues called the Council on Environmental Quality (CEQ). The CEQ is charged with supervising the EIS process, and it works with executive agencies to define their responsibilities under the act. As might be expected, not all agencies adapted quickly to the new requirements for impact statements and public review, but over time, most have significantly altered their decision making. Still, about one hundred court challenges to agency decisions under NEPA are filed every year. The most common complaints are that no EIS was prepared when one should have been or that the EIS was inadequate. Many states have adopted "little NEPAs," or NEPA-like statutes, with much the same purpose—to assess the likely environmental impacts of development projects such as highways. This is yet another reminder that states have considerable independent authority to act on environmental protection challenges, and many have gone well beyond what the federal government has done (Rabe 2016).

Environmental Protection Statutes and the EPA

Congress has enacted and, over time, strengthened with amendments seven major environmental protection, or pollution control, statutes: the Clean Air Act; Clean Water Act; Federal Insecticide, Fungicide, and Rodenticide Act; Safe Drinking

Water Act; Resource Conservation and Recovery Act; Toxic Substances Control Act; and Comprehensive Environmental Response, Compensation, and Liability Act (Superfund). This is a diverse set of public policies, but they have much in common: the EPA develops regulations that affect the current and future use and release of chemicals and pollutants that pose a significant risk to public health or the environment.[12]

The Clean Air Act Amendments of 1970 (CAA) required for the first time the development of national ambient air quality standards that were to be uniform across the country, with enforcement shared by the federal and state governments. These standards were to "provide an adequate margin of safety" to protect human health, and cost was not to be a consideration in setting standards. The CAA also set emissions standards for cars, trucks, and buses—the mobile sources of pollution—and it regulated fuels and toxic and hazardous air pollutants. In addition, it set emissions limits on stationary sources of pollution such as power plants, oil refineries, chemical companies, and other industrial facilities. The extensive 1990 amendments added acid rain controls and set new deadlines for improving urban air quality and controlling toxic air pollutants.

The Clean Water Act of 1972 (CWA) is the major federal program regulating surface water quality. Like the CAA, the CWA established a national policy for water pollution control. It set 1985 as the deadline for stopping the discharge of pollutants into navigable waters (a stipulation that allows federal jurisdiction) and sought to make all surface water "fishable and swimmable" by 1983. The act encouraged technological innovation and comprehensive regional planning for attaining water quality. And like the CAA, the CWA gave to the states primary responsibility for implementation as long as they followed federal standards and guidelines. Essentially, these involve water quality standards and effluent limits set by a permit system that specifies how much each facility is allowed to discharge and the control technologies it will use, but the act has been far less attentive to what are called nonpoint sources of water pollution, such as agricultural and urban runoff, which today are bigger problems for surface water quality than point sources such as industrial facilities. For years, the CWA also provided substantial subsidies and loans to the states to help construct new wastewater treatment plants.

The Federal Environmental Pesticide Control Act of 1972, which modified the Federal Insecticide, Fungicide, and Rodenticide Act of 1947, was similarly ambitious and limited. It required the EPA to register (regulate) the pesticides used commercially in the United States. The pesticides had to not pose "any unreasonable risk to man or the environment," but the law allowed consideration of the economic and social costs and benefits of pesticide use. The EPA had to balance the benefits of using pesticides against their impact on public health, and the government had the burden of proof to show harm if it attempted to ban an existing pesticide. The pesticide control act was modified significantly by the Food Quality Protection Act of 1996, which required the EPA to apply a new, uniform "reasonable risk" approach to regulating pesticides used on food, fiber, and other crops. The new standard is more stringent than the old one. In addition, the agency is required to give special consideration to the impact of pesticide residues on children and to set higher standards for these residues. The law gives the EPA greater authority to suspend a pesticide believed to pose a public health hazard, and the agency must review all pesticide registrations at least once every fifteen years.

The Safe Drinking Water Act of 1974 was designed to ensure the quality and safety of drinking water by specifying minimum health standards for public water supplies. The EPA sets the standards for chemical and microbiological contaminants for tap water. The act required regular monitoring of water supplies to ensure that pollutants stay below safe levels, and it regulated state programs for protecting groundwater supplies that many areas use for drinking water. To assist states and localities in meeting these goals, the act provided loans and grants to defray the costs. A 1996 amendment established a flexible approach to regulating water contaminants based on their risk to public health and allowed consideration of the costs and benefits of proposed regulations. It also added a "right to know" provision that requires water systems to provide customers once a year with a report of any contaminants in the local water supply.

The Resource Conservation and Recovery Act of 1976 (RCRA) is the nation's main hazardous waste control policy. The law was intended to regulate existing hazardous waste disposal practices and promote the conservation and recovery of resources through comprehensive management of solid waste. It required the EPA to develop criteria "necessary to protect human health and the environment" for the safe disposal of solid waste and to set standards for the treatment, storage, and disposal of hazardous wastes. The 1984 amendments to RCRA made the act even more demanding and set tight new deadlines, largely because the EPA had made insufficient progress toward the goals that Congress initially set.

The Toxic Substances Control Act, also approved in 1976, gave the EPA comprehensive authority to identify, evaluate, and regulate risks associated with commercial chemicals. The idea was to help develop a national database of chemicals posing an "unreasonable risk of injury to health or the environment," but without unduly burdening industry or impeding technological innovation. Policymakers combined these two competing goals and saddled the EPA with a difficult and time-consuming set of procedural requirements that greatly limited the act's effectiveness. After years of complaints, in 2016, Congress finally modernized the law and gave more power to the agency to act.

The last of the seven statutes, the Comprehensive Environmental Response, Compensation, and Liability Act of 1980, also known as Superfund, is perhaps the most criticized of the lot. It was enacted after the public became alarmed about toxic waste dumps, such as the one at Love Canal in New York. Superfund is directed at the thousands of abandoned or uncontrolled hazardous waste sites in the nation. Congress gave the EPA responsibility to respond to the problem by identifying, assessing, and cleaning up these sites. If necessary, the EPA can draw from a special fund for that purpose, which is how the program got its nickname. The fund originally was financed through a tax on the petrochemical industry and other chemical manufacturers. One of the central principles of Superfund is that polluters should pay the costs of cleanup, and the act's financial liability provisions have caused controversy for years.[13] In 1986, Congress strengthened the act, put more money into the fund, and added an entirely new provision on the public's right to know about toxic chemicals made by, stored within, or released through local businesses. The **Toxics Release Inventory (TRI)** is published each year and can be accessed on the EPA's website and elsewhere. The TRI describes toxic chemicals that industrial facilities release to the air, water, and land in communities across the country, and the information can be displayed on a local map that shows the location of each facility (Hamilton 2005; Kraft, Stephan, and Abel 2011). After 1995, Congress declined to renew the taxes on chemical and oil companies that support the Superfund trust fund, resulting in a slowdown of action on site cleanups and a shifting of the financial burden to the public through general tax revenue.

Common Themes in Environmental Protection Policy. Separately and collectively, these seven policies created diverse regulatory actions that touch virtually every industrial and commercial enterprise in the nation. They also affect ordinary citizens by regulating air, food, and water quality, and the cars and other consumer products everyone buys. In other words, almost every aspect of daily life is affected by the way these statutes were written and how the EPA and the states implement them. It should not be surprising, therefore, that routine implementation of the policies and their periodic renewal in Congress usually spark contentious debates. People argue over the extent of the risks that citizens face, the appropriate standards for protecting public health and the environment, the mechanisms used to achieve these standards, and how the benefits of these policies should be weighed against the costs of compliance and other social and economic values. The box "Working with Sources: Environmental Policy Advocacy" lists some of the environmental and industry groups that have been active in these policy debates. Their websites are included as well.

These disagreements put the EPA, whether fairly or not, at the center of fractious political fights. The agency is a frequent target of criticism by members of Congress, the business community, and environmental groups, all of whom often fault its scientific research and regulatory decision making (Andrews 2016; Rosenbaum 2013). The EPA is an independent executive agency, but its administrator reports directly to the president, and its decision making tends to reflect White House priorities. The agency is the largest of the federal regulatory agencies, with a staff of about fifteen thousand people and a budget in 2017 of about $8 billion. By most accounts, the EPA handles its job fairly well and is among the most professional of the federal environmental agencies. Policy analysts have long observed, however, that the EPA's resources are insufficient to handle its vast responsibilities. They have also concluded that to succeed at its demanding tasks, the agency must adopt new policy approaches and work with Congress to ensure that it has the authority and tools it needs (Durant, Fiorino, and O'Leary

Working with Sources

Environmental Policy Advocacy

Many organizations play an active role in shaping environmental policy in Congress, federal executive agencies, federal courts, and state and local governments. To learn more about what positions they take and what they do, visit some of the following websites. We list environmental groups first and then several groups that normally oppose the environmentalist position. Comparable groups are involved at state, local, and regional levels, and you might try the same exercise in these locales for advocacy organizations.

Environmental Groups

www.edf.org (Environmental Defense Fund)

www.nrdc.org (Natural Resources Defense Council)

www.nwf.org (National Wildlife Federation)

www.sierraclub.org (Sierra Club)

Industry Groups

www.nam.org (National Association of Manufacturers)

www.nfib.com (National Federation of Independent Business)

www.uschamber.com (U.S. Chamber of Commerce)

2017; Fiorino 2006; National Academy of Public Administration 1995, 2000; Rosenbaum 2013; Vig and Kraft 2016).

The core environmental protection policies have over time produced substantial and well-documented environmental and health benefits, which are especially evident in dramatically improved urban air quality and control of point sources of water pollution. Not every policy has been equally effective, however, and those dealing with control of toxic chemicals and hazardous wastes have been the least successful. Moreover, existing policies barely touch some substantial environmental risks, such as indoor air pollution, even though the cost of these policies has been relatively high. In 1992, the U.S. Government Accountability Office estimated that between 1972 and 1992 the cumulative expenditures for pollution control exceeded $1 trillion. By the late 1990s, the EPA put the continuing cost to both government and the private sector at more than $170 billion per year, and by most estimates, more than half of that cost is paid by the private sector, which no doubt passes it along to consumers as higher product prices.

What does the nation get for such expenditures? In a detailed assessment of the CAA alone, economists at the EPA estimated that the value of public health benefits between 1970 and 1990 was about $22 trillion, and the direct costs of compliance were about $523 billion. That is, the benefits greatly exceeded the costs. In a follow-up study in the late 1990s, the agency's analysts pegged continuing benefits of the act through 2010 at four times the annual compliance costs. Finally, in the latest study, released in 2011 and containing estimates through 2020, the agency concluded that the "direct benefits to the

American people . . . vastly exceed compliance costs." The benefits were estimated to be $2 trillion in 2020, or more than thirty times the estimated costs in the medium projection, and ninety times the costs in the high projection; even in the low projection model, the benefits were three times the costs.[14] Is such analysis persuasive? Could the costs be reduced if the nation used different policy approaches, such as market incentives or flexible regulation? What else would you need to know to judge how well the CAA or any of the other environmental protection laws is working well?

The seven major environmental protection statutes share a common approach to problem solving. All rely on a regulatory policy strategy, or what critics call **command and control**; economists would call it a system of **direct regulation**. What this means is that environmental quality standards are set and enforced according to the language of each statute, and each specifies how the agency is to make its decisions. Generally, Congress gives the EPA discretion to set standards that are consistent with the law, and the EPA is expected to base its decisions on the best available science. Invariably, however, setting environmental quality standards involves an uncertain mix of science and policy judgment about how much risk is acceptable to society (Andrews 2006a, 2016; Kraft 2018; Rosenbaum 2013). The cost of implementing the standard is also usually considered. These kinds of judgments are necessary whether the issue is the amount of pesticide residues allowed on food, the level of lead or arsenic in drinking water, or how much ground-level ozone in the air is acceptable. That is, the laws do not aim for the elimination of risks to public health or the environment; instead, they seek to reduce the level of risk to a point that is reasonable in light of the costs.

For example, in its 2011 proposal on mercury and other toxic chemicals emitted from coal-fired power plants, the EPA calculated that the new rules would prevent up to 11,000 premature deaths, 130,000 asthma attacks, 4,700 heart attacks, and 5,700 hospital and emergency room visits each year. It put an estimated value of $37 to $90 billion annually on these and other human health benefits of the rules, and also argued that the rules would avoid some 540,000 missed work or "sick" days, thus enhancing workplace productivity and reducing health care costs. Moreover, it argued that the technology was readily available and its use would create tens of thousands of jobs in construction and the utility industry. Yet the power industry objected nonetheless to the new rules, citing what it considered to be excessively high costs of compliance, the possible closing of some power plants, an increased cost of electricity, and the loss of thousands of jobs. As we argued in previous chapters, the benefits of regulations like these flow to the broad public while the costs tend to be concentrated on electric power industry and the communities in which plants are located. This is one reason for the varied responses to new rules.[15]

Because the science is almost never complete or definitive, agency officials must make policy or political judgments about how stringent a standard ought to be, as this example illustrates. These kinds of decisions are never easy to make, and they invariably cause disagreements. Business groups typically criticize the standards for being too stringent and costly while environmental and public health groups often say they are too weak. One side or the other in a dispute, and sometimes both, may decide to challenge the standard in court. As might be expected, and as noted earlier in the chapter, EPA decision making operates under somewhat different expectations in Democratic and Republican administrations. For example, Clinton's EPA was more likely than Bush's EPA to adopt tough environmental standards, and the Obama administration was far more like Clinton's than Bush's. Once a standard is set, the EPA and the states take various actions, through issuing rules and regulations and enforcing them, to ensure that it is met (Rinfret and Furlong 2013).

How Well Do Environmental Protection Programs Work? With all the criticism that has been directed at environmental protection policy and command-and-control regulation, one would think the programs have been dismal failures. But the evidence suggests that they have been quite successful on the whole. Granted, environmental policies are difficult to evaluate, in part because they entail long-term commitments to broad social values and goals that are not easily quantified. Short-term and highly visible costs tend to attract more attention than long-term gains in public and environmental health—another source of debate over the value of environmental programs.

Some environmental conditions, such as air and water quality, are regularly monitored, but it is still difficult to assess how well present programs are achieving other objectives. For many critical natural resource concerns, such as protection of biological diversity, accurate measures are still being developed, and national inventories are not yet available. The uncertainties over environmental trends mean that scientists and policy advocates frequently debate whether the environment is deteriorating or improving. Many state-of-the-environment reports addressing such conditions and trends can be found on websites for government agencies and environmental research institutes. The box "Working with Sources: Evaluating Environmental and Energy Policy" lists some of the most useful sources of such data and analysis of what the information means.

Fairly good information is available for air and water quality even if disagreement exists over which measures to use. For example, the EPA estimates that, between 1980 and 2014, aggregate emissions of the six principal, or criteria, air pollutants decreased by 63 percent even while the nation's gross domestic product (GDP) increased by 153 percent, its population grew by 41 percent, vehicle miles traveled rose by 106 percent, and energy consumption grew by 25 percent, all of which would likely have increased air pollution without federal laws and regulations.[16] See Figure 11-2. Progress generally continues as measured by substantial declines between 2000 and 2014 in the atmospheric levels of all six of the key pollutants the EPA measures regularly. In addition, between 1990 and 2011, emissions of toxic chemicals to the air dropped by over 60 percent as a result of implementing air quality regulations. Despite these impressive gains in air quality, as of 2015, over 121 million people lived in counties with pollution

Working with Sources

Evaluating Environmental and Energy Policy

As stated throughout the text, it is important to evaluate how well public policies have worked and what they have achieved. The organizations and websites listed here offer such information from many different perspectives. Government websites usually have official reports and databases, such as the annual Environmental Protection Agency (EPA) report on air pollution and periodic reports on surface water quality. The Government Accountability Office conducts independent evaluations of executive agencies and programs for Congress. Many other groups evaluate environmental and resource programs in terms of economic costs, efficiency, and effectiveness (Resources for the Future); the role of government and regulatory burdens (Cato Institute, Competitive Enterprise Institute, and Heritage Foundation); environmental science and public health (Environmental Defense Fund, Natural Resources Defense Council, and Union of Concerned Scientists); or some combination of these criteria.

> www.cato.org (Cato Institute)
>
> www.cei.org (Competitive Enterprise Institute)
>
> www.doi.gov (Department of the Interior)
>
> www.edf.org (Environmental Defense Fund)
>
> www.epa.gov (Environmental Protection Agency)
>
> www.gao.gov (Government Accountability Office)
>
> www.heritage.org (Heritage Foundation)
>
> www.nrdc.org (Natural Resources Defense Council)
>
> www.rff.org (Resources for the Future)
>
> www.sierraclub.org (Sierra Club)
>
> www.ucsusa.org (Union of Concerned Scientists)

Go to the EPA website for climate change (www.epa.gov/climatechange) and click on Basic Information to see the agency's overview of the nature of climate change, its major causes, and the implications for public policy.

- How does the EPA portray scientific knowledge about climate change? Is the description persuasive?

- Now click on the link for What EPA Is Doing. Under the heading of Developing Commonsense Regulatory Initiatives, look at the agency's description of its Clean Power Plan for regulating coal-fired power plants under the Clean Air Act. Is the EPA persuasive in arguing for what the Clean Power Plan can do to limit greenhouse gas emissions in a "reasonable" way? Are any significant concerns missing from the agency's description of the proposal?

Now visit one or more of the other sites to see how environmental organizations and industry view climate change and energy issues. For example, visit the Natural Resources Defense Council (www.nrdc.org) and click on Our Work, then on Climate Change, and finally on Dirty Energy to see its description of coal-fired power plants. Is the argument persuasive? Do you think that anything important is missing from the NRDC's description? Now compare the NRDC position on climate change and energy to that of a conservative think tank such as the Heritage Foundation (www.heritage.org). Click on Issues, then Energy and Environment, and finally on one of the links to reports about climate change, coal, or "unlocking America's vast oil and gas reserves." How would you describe the group's position on climate change and energy? Are the arguments presented here convincing? For a highly skeptical view of the science and actions taken on or proposed for climate change, see the website for Climate Depot (www.climatedepot.com). How would you describe the arguments you see here? Do you think there is any scientific basis for the organization's views? What statements on the page lead you to your conclusion?

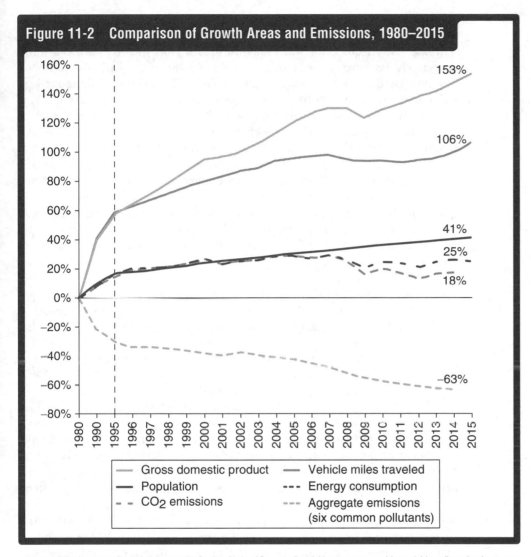

Figure 11-2   Comparison of Growth Areas and Emissions, 1980–2015

Legend:
— Gross domestic product
— Population
- - CO$_2$ emissions
— Vehicle miles traveled
- - - Energy consumption
- - - Aggregate emissions (six common pollutants)

Source: U.S. Environmental Protection Agency, "Air Quality—National Summary," available at www.epa.gov/air-trends/air-quality-national-summary.

Note: Carbon dioxide emissions estimates are for 2013 and are taken from the 2014 U.S. Greenhouse Gas Inventory Report.

levels above the standards set for at least one of these criteria pollutants, typically for ozone and fine particulates. Do such figures tell you that the Clean Air Act is working well? Should the nation have done even better more than forty years since its enactment? Are the critics right to say that the cost of improving air quality can be too high and that the EPA must base its standards and enforcement on what is economically acceptable?

The nation's water quality also has improved since passage of the 1972 CWA, although more slowly and more unevenly than has air quality. Monitoring data are less adequate for water quality than for air quality, with the states collectively assessing, for example, only 32 percent of the nation's rivers and streams. Based on these inventories, 45 percent of the surveyed river and stream miles were considered to be of good quality and 55 percent impaired. Some 71 percent of lakes, ponds, and reservoirs also were found to be impaired. A classification as "impaired" means that water bodies are not meeting or fully meeting the national minimum water quality criteria for "designated beneficial uses" such as swimming, fishing, drinking-water supply, and support of aquatic life. These numbers indicate some improvement over time, yet they also tell us that many problems remain.[17] Prevention of further degradation of water quality in the face of a growing population and strong economic growth could be considered an important achievement. At the same time, water quality clearly falls short of the goals of federal clean water acts. Would you draw a different conclusion?

Policy Options for the Future. What kinds of policy alternatives should be considered for the future to replace or, more likely, to complement environmental regulation? Critics of regulation frequently mention the greater use of market incentives or market-based approaches, more reliance on public information disclosure, flexible and more cooperative approaches to regulation, and further decentralization of power to the states (Dietz and Stern 2003; Eisner 2007; Fiorino 2006). Such alternatives may be especially appropriate where conventional regulation works poorly. Two examples are reducing indoor air pollution and cleaning up nonpoint water pollution, which cannot be traced to a single source. In both cases, there are too many sources to regulate or regulation simply is impractical; for example, no government can regulate indoor air quality in every U.S. dwelling. What might work instead are subsidies, public education campaigns, and tax credits, which are a form of market incentive. The federal government and the states have experimented with such policy options.

The 1990 CAA revision incorporated market incentives by allowing marketable permits for emissions of sulfur dioxide. The idea behind the permits is that some companies will find it cheaper than others to make needed changes to reduce emissions, and they can then sell the "extra" permits to other companies. The program operates in two ways: the market incentives improve economic efficiency by reducing the overall cost of environmental improvement, and the government reduces the number of permits over time to ensure that the goal of lower emissions is reached. Although the federal program is thought to have worked well, a similar effort in the Los Angeles metropolitan area through a regional air quality management system has not entirely lived up to expectations (Mazmanian and Kraft 2009). Nevertheless, environmental economists have high hopes for these efforts because they provide important economic incentives for industry to work toward environmental goals, even to go "beyond compliance" to make greater improvements than the law requires (P. Portney and Stavins 2000). Is their assessment persuasive?

As a policy strategy, information disclosure is another useful supplement to regulation. The nation uses this strategy by compiling the TRI; by publishing automobile fuel efficiency standards, which are also attached to the windows of new cars; by promoting appliance efficiency standards, developed as part of the federal ENERGY STAR program; and in many other ways (Kraft, Stephan, and Abel 2011).[18] The hope here is that individuals and organizations will use the information to press industry and government to move more aggressively on environmental and energy improvements than they might otherwise be inclined to do. Or, acting proactively to avoid embarrassment, those same parties might undertake initiatives to head off criticism, such as reducing pollution or improving fuel efficiency.

The use of flexible regulatory approaches and collaborative regulatory approaches was a hallmark of the Clinton administration's EPA, and the Bush and Obama administrations also favored these techniques (Vig and Kraft 2016). The general idea is to reduce conflict between regulators and those being regulated and to work cooperatively to develop appropriate environmental standards, regulations, and action programs. The intention is to move from the contentious, legalistic system of regulation to one in which the various stakeholders work together to seek solutions. Environmentalists are sometimes skeptical of these arrangements, fearful that they will endanger what has been achieved in environmental quality, but business interests, state and local governments, and many policy analysts think highly of the promise of flexible regulations and collaborative decision making (Bennear and Coglianese 2013).

Further decentralization of environmental responsibilities to the states is also controversial. Over the past three decades, a major transfer of environmental authority from the federal government to the states has taken place. How much more is desirable and what the likely effects will be are questions yet to be answered. Policymakers in both parties favor increased decentralization, but many analysts are skeptical about whether giving additional powers to the states will improve policy effectiveness. They also raise questions of equity. Many states have a greater capacity for environmental policy than they did four decades ago, but the performance from state to state is highly uneven. As noted, California, Minnesota, and Oregon have been leaders in environmental policy innovation and enforcement, but other states lag behind and may be subjecting their citizens to preventable health risks. The tendency of states to compete with one another economically could constrain enforcement of environmental laws. In addition, many environmental problems—including acid rain, toxic air pollutants, and water pollution—cross state lines, suggesting that a national or regional approach might be both more effective and more equitable than leaving the solution to the states. Ultimately, what is needed is a sorting out of which environmental functions are best suited for state and local governments and which require national, or even international, management (Rabe 2016).

Natural Resource Policies

Many of the concerns that arise in environmental protection or pollution control policy also pertain to natural resource policies that govern the management of public lands, forests, and parks, and the efforts to protect species and biological diversity. Public policies for the management of natural resources developed in response to concerns over their abuse. After more than a century of policies that encouraged exploitation of resources in the vast federal lands of the West, the twentieth century brought a new ethic of **environmental stewardship**, the protection of resources for the future. That change has taken effect only slowly, however, and the resource development interests, such as timber, ranching, agriculture, mining, and oil and gas drilling businesses, often disagree with conservation organizations over what policies best promote the public's welfare.

Most of the current federal natural resource policies are grounded in the principle of **multiple use**, which Congress intended to use to help balance competing national objectives of economic development and environmental preservation. Should old-growth forests in the Northwest be cut for timber or preserved as wildlife habitat? To what extent should mining for gold, silver, and other minerals, which can cause extensive environmental damage, be permitted on public lands—and how much should developers pay the Treasury for the right to do it? Should the government protect particularly sensitive public lands from oil and gas drilling, or is expansion of energy sources a more important priority? Using the guidance found in the various natural resource laws, the officials in federal resource agencies, mostly in the Interior and Agriculture Departments, are charged with answering these questions (Lubell and Segee 2013; C. Thomas 2013).

Two major statutes, the Federal Land Policy and Management Act of 1976 (FLPMA) and the National Forest Management Act of 1976 (NFMA), have helped to change the way the government makes natural resource decisions. These acts set out new procedures for government planning and management of resources, including extensive public participation, and they established a mission for long-term stewardship of public resources. In effect, these policies required government officials to consider diverse values in managing resources, not just the highest dollar return (Clarke and McCool 1996; Davis 2001).

These two policies did not end the disputes over public lands and forests. Environmentalists continue to battle with timber, ranching, mining, and oil and gas interests, and the winners often depend on which party is in the White House. Republican administrations tend to side more often with the forces of development, and Democratic administrations with those of land preservation. For example, President Clinton used his executive authority under the Antiquities Act of 1906 to establish nineteen new national monuments and enlarge three others. In all, he protected more than six million acres of public land this way. In addition, just before he left office, Clinton issued an executive order protecting nearly sixty million acres of roadless areas in the national forests from future development. President Bush challenged Clinton's policies, reversed many of his initiatives, and was far more receptive to development interests than to conservation (Lowry 2006; Lubell and Segee 2013; Vig 2016). Indeed, a comprehensive examination of Bush's natural resource policies after his first year in office found that he was "aggressively encouraging more drilling, mining, and logging on much of the seven hundred million acres controlled by the Interior Department and the Forest Service."[19] President Obama's approach was much like Clinton's. He established over thirty new national monuments under the Antiquities Act and protected large areas of public land and ocean preserves, much to the consternation of his critics.[20]

One of the most controversial of the natural resource policies is also one of the toughest. The Endangered Species Act of 1973 (ESA) in many ways symbolizes the nation's commitment to resource conservation goals, and perhaps for that reason, it has become a lightning rod for forces opposed to environmentalists. The ESA broadened federal authority to protect threatened and endangered species and established procedures to ensure the recovery of all species threatened with extinction. It prohibited the "taking" of such species by fishing, hunting, or habitat alteration or destruction whether the species inhabited state, federal, or private land. The U.S. Fish and Wildlife Service (FWS) implements the ESA for land-based species, and the agency has struggled to achieve its goals amidst frequent congressional criticism and perennially inadequate budgets. Despite condemnation from conservatives who see the ESA as a threat to property rights, most decisions under the act have been made without much controversy, and the act has prevented few development projects from going forward. In recent years, the FWS has made good use of collaborative decision making in developing habitat conservation plans to avoid such confrontations.

Evaluating Success. As is the case with pollution control policies, evaluating the success of natural resource policies is not easy. The kinds of measurements available, such as the number of acres of protected lands set aside in national monuments and parks, are not good indicators of what really matters. Still, these laws have brought about considerable achievements. For example, the national park system grew from about 26 million acres in 1960 to over 84 million acres by 2016, and the number of units or parks in the system doubled. Since adoption of the 1964 Wilderness Act, Congress has set aside 109 million acres of wilderness through the National Wilderness Preservation System. Since 1968, it has designated over 12,000 protected miles in the National Wild and Scenic Rivers System (Kraft 2018).

Protection of biological diversity through the ESA has produced some success as well, although far less than its supporters believe essential. By 2016, forty-one years after passage of the 1973 act, more than 1,594 U.S. plant and animal species had been listed as either endangered or threatened. Over 700 critical habitats have been designated, more than 1,000 habitat conservation plans have been approved, and more than 1,500 recovery plans have been put into effect. Yet only a few endangered species have recovered fully. The FWS reported in 2008 that 551 species, or 43 percent of those listed, were considered to be stable or improving, but that 389 species, or 30 percent, were considered to be declining in status, and for 301 species, or 24 percent, their status was unknown (Kraft 2018).

The true measurement of success or failure is whether an ecosystem is healthy or sustainable, but even ecologists cannot agree on precisely what that means or what indicators to use. Ecologists are attempting to develop such standards so that communities across the nation can determine whether, or to what extent, a lake, river, bay, or land area should be preserved or restored to a healthy condition. Many communities are already trying to make those kinds of decisions. Massive federal and state efforts to restore damaged ecosystems such as the Great Lakes, the Florida Everglades, and the Chesapeake Bay testify to the need for accurate ecological indicators.

Policy Options for the Future. Even without the most accurate indicators to judge the success of natural resource policies, suggestions abound for reforming the policies to make them more effective, efficient, and fair. Among the most frequently proposed are reduction or elimination of subsidies for resource development or exploitation; the imposition of **user fees**, which are a form of market

A policy to protect. One of the most recognized of the natural resource policies is the federal Endangered Species Act (ESA), enacted in 1973. It was designed to identify and help protect those species that might be lost, most often from human activities that adversely affect their habitat. Over more than forty years, the U.S. government has spent billions of dollars trying to save nearly 1,600 species deemed endangered, like this gray wolf at the Wildlife Science Center in Forest Lake, Minnesota. House Republicans say that's translated into just 2 percent of protected species being recovered, and they want to overhaul the ESA. Environmentalists and many Democrats credit the act with saving species from extinction. *(AP Photo/Dawn Villella)*

incentive; the use of ecosystem-based management; and greater reliance on collaborative decision making and collaborative planning.

Natural resource policies have long incorporated generous resource subsidies to users—such as ranchers, mining and timber companies, and oil and gas drilling companies. Often, the user pays the government less in fees than the cost to taxpayers of providing services to these businesses. For example, for years the Forest Service realized less money from timber sales than it cost the agency to build and maintain the access roads for loggers. Because of the General Mining Law of 1872 (little has changed since its adoption), the mining industry has paid only nominal sums for the right to mine public lands and has paid no royalty on the minerals extracted from them; moreover, it has caused extensive environmental damage, particularly to western rivers. Critics argue that the government should reduce or end resource subsidies. These subsidies are hard to defend on equity or efficiency grounds, and often they contribute to environmental degradation.[21] Environmentalists say that development interests should pay the full cost of access to public resources through higher user fees. Although the argument seems reasonable, the developers stoutly defend their long-standing subsidies, arguing that changing the rules at this time would be unfair to them and the industries they represent and would harm the economy in many rural areas of the West.

The idea of imposing user fees extends to charges for entering national parks and other federal lands. Historically, visitors paid a small fee that was well below what they would pay for comparable recreation on private lands and hardly sufficient to cover the costs of park maintenance. Fees have gone up over time, but is this fair? Some argue that people already pay for the national parks with their federal taxes. Should they have to pay again when they enter a park? From the perspective of equity, the answer might be, "Yes, those who use public services should pay a premium for them. Otherwise, taxpayers who do not use the parks are subsidizing those who do." What is fair in this case?

As a policy, ecosystem-based management means a shift in emphasis toward principles of protecting habitat and maintaining biological diversity. Among its supporters are natural scientists, particularly biologists and ecologists concerned about the loss of biological diversity and the fragmentation of ecosystems that do not coincide with the boundaries of national parks and wilderness areas. Essentially, ecosystem-based management is a long-term, comprehensive approach to natural resource management, with a priority on ecosystem functioning rather than human use (Cortner and Moote 1999; Layzer 2008). Critics of ecosystem-based management include economic development interests that predict less access to natural resources and conservatives who question the wisdom of increasing government agencies' authority over public and private lands. Some policy analysts also question just how effective ecosystem-based management has been, reminding us that even good ideas do not always translate into effective policy. Much depends on how programs are designed and implemented (Layzer 2008, 2013).

Collaborative decision making and planning aspires to resolve conflicts over local and regional natural resource issues. It brings the various stakeholders together in an ad hoc and voluntary process characterized by cooperation and consensus building. Policymakers have used it to develop successful habitat conservation plans, protect and restore damaged ecosystems, and plan for the future of river basins, among many other activities (Sabatier et al. 2005; Weber 2003; Wondolleck and Yaffee 2000). The parties have an incentive to cooperate because collaboration may speed up the decision-making process and allow them to avoid costly litigation. Although the principle is generally applauded, critics of collaboration argue that not all interests are necessarily represented and that the most powerful interests may dominate the process. Nevertheless, such collaboration holds considerable promise for the future, and its use is likely to continue (Gerlak, Heikkila, and Lubell 2013; Lubell and Segee 2013).

Energy Policy

Energy policy is part environmental protection and part natural resource policy, but most analysts would probably agree that the United States has no real or comprehensive energy policy. Instead, individual and corporate decisions in the marketplace largely determine energy use, with each sector of energy influenced to some extent by a variety of government subsidies and regulations. For example, since the 1940s, nuclear power has benefited substantially from government subsidies; indeed, the financial aid made its commercial development possible. Other subsidies have promoted coal, natural gas, and oil, often in ways that those outside the industries barely recognize.[22] As discussed below, even more recent energy policies continued this pattern, although President Obama gave far greater emphasis to renewable resources such as wind and solar energy.

Energy policy is something of an anomaly compared to the collection of broadly supported environmental policies listed in Table 11-1. For energy, the prevailing pattern was policy stalemate or gridlock from the 1970s through the early 2000s. Presidents Richard Nixon, Gerald Ford, and Jimmy Carter all attempted to formulate national energy policies to promote energy independence by increasing domestic supplies, primarily fossil fuels. Following the oil embargo imposed by the **Organization of the Petroleum Exporting Countries (OPEC)** in 1973 and the subsequent sharp increases in the cost of oil, Carter, who was elected in 1976, undertook the most sustained and comprehensive of these presidential policy efforts, but for the most part, they failed. The reasons were Carter's inability to overcome public disinterest in energy issues, the combined force of organized group opposition to policy action, and his poor relations with Congress on energy and other issues (Kraft 1981). Congress did create the DOE in 1977 to consolidate previously independent energy agencies, but its chief mission was national defense (nuclear weapons development), not development of energy resources.

The other major outcomes from the energy policy debates of the 1970s were enhanced federal research support for energy conservation and efficiency and automobile fuel efficiency requirements. Congress did finally raise the **Corporate Average Fuel Economy (CAFE) standards** (originally approved in 1975) in a 2007 energy act, and, as noted in the chapter opening, the Obama administration negotiated with the automobile industry to set far higher standards for the future. Another kind of policy approach to achieve the same goal of reducing use of imported oil or reducing greenhouse gas emissions would be to impose a higher tax on gasoline or on all fossil fuels, what is usually called a **carbon tax**. Such a carbon tax could be combined with a reduction in other taxes to create what is called a revenue-neutral carbon tax that imposes no net increase on individuals or corporations. Which policy strategy is preferable: setting higher fuel economy standards or imposing a higher tax? Is one more politically feasible than the other? Is one more likely to be fair to the American public? Would you expect there to be any difference in overall effectiveness of such policies?

In the more than four decades since energy issues rose to prominence on the national agenda, a number of energy policies have been approved, and yet the nation does not have a comprehensive national energy policy. The reasons can be found in partisan and regional disagreement over energy policy goals and the often intense opposition by energy interests that fear a loss of government subsidies or a reduced market share in a changing energy economy. With the newer challenge of climate change, debate on energy issues has become even more contentious as energy and climate change policies are closely intertwined.

Among the most notable energy policies that Congress has managed to approve, the Energy Policy Act of 1992 created new energy conservation programs aimed at electric appliances, lighting, plumbing, and heating and cooling systems, as well as efficiency programs for alternative-fuel fleet vehicles. A decade later, the George W. Bush White House began a major energy policy initiative. The president's plan called for an increase in the production and use of fossil fuels. It also favored a greater reliance on nuclear energy, gave modest attention to the role of energy conservation, and sparked intense debate on Capitol Hill with its emphasis on oil and gas drilling in the Arctic National Wildlife Refuge (ANWR).

Four years of partisan conflict in Congress followed, with agreement seemingly out of reach. Yet in 2005, Congress approved much of the president's proposal, other than oil and gas drilling in ANWR. Consistent with White House preferences, the Energy Policy Act of 2005 emphasized greater production and use of oil, natural gas, and coal, and strongly boosted federal support for nuclear power. It also streamlined—some would say weakened—environmental requirements as they affect energy production. In addition, it required utilities to modernize the nation's electricity grid to ensure reliable delivery of electric energy. Even the president conceded that the complex law, running to over 1,700 pages, would do little to lower gasoline or other energy costs, or U.S. dependence on imported oil, in the short term.[23] Two years later, Congress approved the Energy Independence and Security Act of 2007, which increased auto fuel efficiency standards and mandated an increase in use of biofuels via a renewable fuel standard. Most of the biofuel to date has been ethanol derived from corn crops, although research and development projects continue on other forms of biofuels. As noted in the chapter's opening, President Obama gave far greater emphasis to funding of energy research and development, and his administration sought to advance renewable energy facilities, such as wind and solar power projects, on public lands in the West.

Perhaps the greatest challenge for the future of energy policy lies in its connection to climate change, which many authoritative studies link strongly to use of fossil fuels: coal, oil, and natural gas (DiMento and Doughman 2014; IPCC 2013; Selin and VanDeveer 2016). In effect, the nation needs to choose whether and how to reduce greenhouse gas emissions, by how much, and over what time period. This in turn implies some choices over what mix of energy sources best meets the public's interest and the world's interests, and what kinds of policy tools should be used to reach the goals that are agreed upon. For example, should we rely on regulation (such as fuel economy standards), imposition of taxes (such as a carbon tax), use of market incentives (a cap-and-trade system), investment in research and technology development, or some mix of these tools? The focused discussion that follows explores some of these questions.

Focused Discussion: Climate Change and Energy Policy Alternatives

Climate change is probably the most important environmental challenge of the twenty-first century, and U.S. policymakers are only just beginning to deal with it seriously, particularly at the federal level. As indicated in the chapter opening, each new study or report illustrates continuing controversy over the extent of the problem and its possible solutions. The vast majority of climate scientists (and environmentalists) are convinced that enough is already known about the risks of climate change to justify taking strong measures now to reduce future harm to people and the environment (DiMento and Doughman 2014). So too are the national intelligence agencies and the military; both say that climate change is among the most serious national security threats that the nation faces.[24] Yet skeptics have argued that climate science is inadequate to forecast such risks with much precision. They support more research on the subject and voluntary efforts by industry, but they oppose most other policy actions as premature and excessively costly. Some of the more extreme skeptics deny that the world is experiencing any climate change at present or that it is likely to in the future, while others acknowledge that some changes are under way but challenge the idea that human activities (such as the use of fossil fuels) are a major cause. Some climate change critics also argue that the United States can adapt to any climate change that does occur, and therefore that the nation need not be overly concerned about preventing it, particularly if doing so is viewed as too costly (Dunlap and McCright 2015).[25]

As we have stated throughout the text, perhaps the most common basis for judging whether public policy action is needed or how well it is doing is effectiveness.

In the case of climate change, the question is what government might do to reduce the likelihood that severe climate change will occur in the future, to minimize the impacts it will have, and to facilitate adaptation to changing climatic conditions, such as increased frequency of severe storms and flooding. That is, governments might rely on prevention, mitigation, or adaptation strategies. Most scientists would say it is too late for preventive solutions other than to reduce the risks of future change, since the world already has released enough greenhouse gases to set climate change in motion and that cannot really be undone. Thus, nearly all discussion focuses on mitigation and adaptation responses.

Although commentators and public officials do not always make the link clear, climate change policy is closely tied to energy policy. Acting on climate change means that we must reduce the world's emissions of greenhouse gases, with attention focused on carbon dioxide that is produced when fossil fuels are burned. Both the United States and the rest of the world rely on fossil fuels for about 80 percent of the energy used today. Hence we face the challenge of reducing such reliance in a relatively short period of time.

In its April 2014 report discussed at the beginning of the chapter, the IPCC called for a minimum reduction in greenhouse gas emissions by the world's major economies of between 40 and 70 percent below 2010 levels by 2050; doing so, it argued, should keep mean temperatures from rising more than the target of 3.6 degrees Fahrenheit by that date. Further reductions, probably to zero emissions, would be needed by 2100. Most experts, including those who work under the auspices of the IPCC, say that one of the surest ways to slow the rate of climate change and reduce its harmful effects is to cut back on the use of fossil fuels, which produce large amounts of carbon dioxide when burned.[26] If coal, oil, and natural gas remain the dominant energy sources, carbon dioxide emissions will continue unless carbon capture and storage technologies become technically and economically feasible. Because we are so heavily dependent on fossil fuels, many policymakers are reluctant to endorse a substantial reduction in their use for fear that doing so will significantly harm the economy if energy prices rise too quickly. They also argue that the nation at this time has no other major fuel sources to substitute for fossil fuels other than nuclear power, and nuclear plants are very costly and continue to face public opposition; that opposition increased to some extent after the catastrophic 2011 accident at the Fukushima Daiichi plant in Japan. Concern also continues over the unresolved issue of how to dispose of the spent fuel rods (nuclear waste) that result from the operation of nuclear power plants.

The Paris Agreement on climate change was approved in late 2015 and went into effect in November 2016. It seeks to keep global temperatures from rising more than 2 degrees Celsius, or 3.6 degrees Fahrenheit, beyond which scientists believe we will be locked into a future of severe warming, rising sea levels, extensive flooding and droughts, food and water scarcity, and extreme storms. The agreement consists of individual plans by each nation to lower its greenhouse gas emissions by 2025 or 2030 by an amount sufficient to achieve about half of the required reduction needed. The other half relies on a requirement that each nation ratchet up its plans every five years in a manner to be negotiated at international meetings beginning in 2020. In addition, each nation is to take stock of its emissions reduction actions, which it is required to monitor, verify, and report on publicly. As is apparent, the agreement relies heavily on voluntary action by nations, but with some legally binding elements. The Trump administration has indicated that it might not follow through on these commitments.[27]

As this overview of climate change and international agreements suggests, many questions remain. Has the scientific community supplied enough credible information about climate change and its effects on public health and the environment for policymakers to take action? What kinds of public policies should be considered, and which of them is likely to be the most effective? Which is likely to be the least costly? How can the benefits of taking action be balanced against the costs, particularly when policymakers consider very long-term costs and benefits that are difficult to measure? What about ethical issues? Is it fair for people today to continue their dependence on fossil fuels and to pass along the risks of climate change to future generations? The discussion below addresses some of the economic issues, questions of political feasibility, and equity and other ethical issues. We focus on these three criteria because they are at the heart of most debates today. However, it is equally important to ask how climate change actions stand up to other criteria, such as probable effectiveness and environmental impacts.

Economic Issues

If policymakers focused solely on reducing the use of fossil fuels to cut carbon dioxide emissions, what actions might they suggest? Among the most common

Regulation in need. One of the biggest changes in U.S. energy use in recent years has been the rapid development of natural gas supplies across the country through a process called hydraulic fracturing or fracking. Highly pressurized water, chemicals, and sand are injected deep underground through a wellbore drilled into rock formations that contain natural gas. The practice has been only loosely regulated to date, raising concerns about possible contamination of water supplies, threats to public health, and release of methane to the atmosphere, adding to the risk of climate change. The photo shows a typical hydraulic fracking rig in Weld County, Colorado. *(Matthew Staver/Bloomberg via Getty Images)*

policy recommendations are to increase taxes on fossil fuels such as through a carbon tax, to reduce their use (a market incentive approach), and to raise energy efficiency standards that apply to motor vehicles and other products (a regulatory approach), which we discussed at the chapter's opening. Other proposals include government support to encourage use of renewable energy sources such as wind and solar power, increased spending on energy research and development to speed the arrival of new technologies, tax credits for buying energy-efficient appliances and cars, and approval of tougher building codes to improve energy efficiency. Many bills introduced in Congress in the late 2000s emphasized the use of a market-based cap-and-trade policy that would resemble the one for sulfur dioxide under the 1990 CAA. Such a program might give away and/or sell through auctions various credits for the right to release greenhouse gases, which could be bought and sold by coal-fired power plants, oil refineries, and manufacturers. Money generated by the government's sale of such credits could be distributed to industries, states, and consumers to encourage use of renewable energy, conservation, and energy efficiency. But to keep things simple, let us consider the first two approaches.

Should the federal government, for example, raise gasoline taxes by a substantial amount, perhaps fifty cents to a dollar per gallon, or more? Gasoline in the United States would still be far cheaper than it is in most other industrialized nations, where it is usually two to three times higher because of government taxes. Raising gasoline taxes has several benefits, including providing additional revenues for government support of other environmental and energy programs. Of course, higher gas prices can hurt some segments of the public that can ill afford the cost. So one alternative is what we discussed earlier as a revenue-neutral gas tax—or a broader carbon tax—in which all fees are rebated or returned to the public. A ballot proposal in Washington State in 2016 was based on that idea. A carbon tax that rises over time would be offset by a reduction in the state sales tax, thus eliminating a tax on manufacturers in the state, and also providing up to $1,500 in tax credits for low-income residents; however, the measure was defeated in part because of concern over inequities of the financial impacts.[28]

The assumption behind such proposals is that the higher cost of gasoline or other fossil fuels would be a strong incentive for consumers and manufacturers to change their behavior. With higher gas prices, for example, consumers might look for fuel-efficient vehicles, or perhaps use mass transit or find other ways to use their cars less often. Traffic congestion in the 2000s cost the nation more than $78 billion a year in wasted fuel and extra travel time, a figure that is expected to soar over the next twenty years as the U.S. population grows and the number of vehicles keeps pace.[29] Reducing the use of motor vehicles could bring many economic benefits, as well as improve air quality in urban areas.

What about raising automobile fuel efficiency standards once again? As noted in the chapter's opening, the Obama administration and the auto industry agreed to a fleet average of 54.5 miles per gallon by 2025. Should the standards be set at an even higher level? Many economic analyses have reached skeptical conclusions about the benefits of higher fuel economy standards in comparison with their costs to the economy, but their authors also acknowledge that great uncertainty surrounds such calculations (Parry 2005).

Even without new standards, consumers can choose higher-efficiency vehicles. New gas-electric hybrid vehicles, and particularly plug-in hybrids that can be recharged overnight in a home garage, come close to being fully electric vehicles and get substantially higher mileage than conventional cars, although at a premium in purchase price. That price has been offset to some extent by generous federal and state tax credits, $2,500 to $7,500 in federal tax credits in 2016, and in some states such as California as much as another $2,500. But because most vehicles sold over the next twenty years or so will run on gasoline engines, higher efficiency standards could make a big difference in greenhouse gas emissions. Should the government adopt tougher fuel efficiency standards that go beyond those set in 2012 to force automakers to build vehicles that use even less gasoline, or are the new standards already high enough? Would you be willing to pay more for a car that got better mileage but otherwise had the same performance and safety features as cars currently on the market?

Political Feasibility

During debates in recent Congresses on national energy policy, proposals to raise automobile fuel efficiency standards did not fare well until 2007. When Congress acted at that time, the CAFE standards had not changed since 1990 except for the minor increase in the light truck requirements noted earlier, and the average gas mileage of vehicles sold in the United States continued to drop. Policymakers also had shown no enthusiasm for raising gasoline taxes by any substantial amount. Automobile manufacturers, with the exception of Honda and newer companies such as Tesla Motors (which makes only electric vehicles), historically had adamantly opposed higher fuel economy standards as an unwarranted intrusion into the marketplace.[30] Their multimillion-dollar lobbying and advertising campaigns, in association with autoworkers' unions, emphasized the importance of individual choice and implied that, if such standards were adopted, people would be forced to drive small and unsafe cars.

As for gasoline taxes, policymakers fear the voters' wrath over any tax increase, especially one that will annoy them every time they fill their gas tanks. When gas prices have risen sharply from time to time in recent years, many policymakers reacted with horror at the possible political implications, and they promised to take any number of actions to ensure that prices dropped. As they discovered, however, there is little that policymakers can do to affect world oil prices and thus the price of gasoline in the short term.[31] Previous legislative debates indicate that a large gasoline tax increase is not politically feasible at this time, but would it be more acceptable if it were clearly linked with a decrease in other taxes—a move known as "tax shifting"? In other words, if the gas tax had a neutral impact on overall taxation rates, would the public accept it? What about if the tax increases were linked in the public's mind with action on energy policy or climate change? Would that make a difference, and would policymakers be more likely to favor some kind of gas tax hike under these circumstances?

A 2006 *New York Times*/CBS News poll addressed such questions. If asked directly whether they favored an increase in the federal tax on gasoline, only 12 percent of the public did, hardly a surprise. But if told the increased tax would "reduce the United States' dependence on foreign oil," 55 percent were in favor. And if told the increased tax would "cut down on energy consumption and reduce global warming," 59 percent were in favor. What is the message here? On this and many other issues, we should be careful not to dismiss policy alternatives that we think would not attract public or political support. Circumstances can change quickly, and policymakers may find the public more amenable to some ideas than they imagined would be the case. Much depends on the context and how policymakers explain a proposal to the public.[32]

Democrats have supported raising fuel efficiency standards more than Republicans typically have, but neither party has favored higher gasoline taxes. With intense partisan disagreement over some aspects of national energy policy and with no consensus so far on how to reduce the use of fossil fuels and greenhouse gas emissions, state legislators have taken on energy issues themselves, and with some success.

In addition to California's unique approach, many other states (and cities) have adopted or are considering policies to reduce greenhouse gas emissions, including, as noted above, offering subsidies for the purchase of alternative-fuel vehicles. Indeed, several recent analyses conclude that the states were taking the lead on climate change policies by offering more innovative and far-reaching policies than the federal government (Rabe 2004, 2010, 2016; Rabe and Mundo 2007; Selin and VanDeveer 2016). By 2016, the states had enacted dozens of laws that established specific strategies, from electricity generation to building standards, transportation initiatives, and new approaches to forestry and agriculture, all of which might reduce greenhouse gases and sometimes with significant economic savings for consumers. Oregon, for example, established a tough standard for carbon dioxide releases from new electric power plants. Massachusetts also set limits on carbon dioxide emissions for many of the state's power plants. California established its own cap-and-trade program. Dallas, Denver, Phoenix, Los Angeles, and Salt Lake City all put new money into mass transit in recent years in an effort to reduce highway congestion, improve air quality, or reduce greenhouse gas emissions. New studies of these states and opportunities for action at both the state and national level suggest that there may well be reasons for greater optimism on political feasibility than most commentators have assumed (Karapin 2016; Rabe, forthcoming; Raymond 2016).

Ethical Issues

The ethical issues of climate change and energy policy concern how the various policy proposals affect different groups of citizens now and in the future. For example, many point out that the gasoline tax is regressive, that it has an adverse effect on the poor. Will raising this tax make driving to work prohibitively expensive? What about people who live in sparsely populated rural areas and need to drive farther to work and for other necessities, or who need to use heavy-duty pickup trucks and vans that get lower mileage? Will adding new technologies to make cars more fuel efficient push the price of already expensive vehicles beyond the reach of many people?

Some of the most intriguing ethical issues relate to the U.S. role in climate change. The United States, which comprises less than 5 percent of the world's population, uses almost 25 percent of its commercial energy and produces more than 20 percent of global greenhouse gas emissions. Was its refusal to sign the **Kyoto Protocol** and decision to defer action on climate change under the Bush administration justifiable on equity or other ethical grounds? What about the decision by the Obama administration in 2015 to join the historic Paris Agreement on climate change? While environmentalists applauded the move as both ethically correct and critical to the success of the global agreement, conservative critics argued that the agreement was not in the interest of U.S. citizens. Pope Francis weighed in on these questions in 2015 in his encyclical on climate change, "Laudato Si,'" where he called for what the press described as a "radical transformation of politics, economics and individual lifestyles to confront environmental degradation and climate change."[33]

Also to be considered in this debate is **intergenerational equity**, or what is fair to future generations. Climate change forecasts suggest that the adverse impacts will be felt mostly by people fifty to one hundred years or more in the future. Taking action on climate change, however, would impose economic burdens on those living now. Is it more equitable to defer action on climate change to improve economic well-being today or to take action now to protect future generations from an unreasonable risk of climate change and its effects? What obligations does the present generation have to the future in this regard? A related concern is the role of the United States as an international leader. As the wealthiest and most powerful nation in the world, does the United States have an obligation to take a leadership role on climate change and promote sustainable development, as President Obama argued was the case with the Paris Agreement? Without U.S. support, it was highly unlikely that other nations would have joined the pact to reduce greenhouse gas emissions.

Those opposed to a strong climate change policy for the United States raise a different kind of equity concern. Why should the United States lead in these efforts when so little has been required (as was true, for example, under the Kyoto Protocol) of rapidly developing nations such as China and India? The United States and other developed nations have been the main generators of greenhouse gases and thus could fairly be said to be obliged to play a greater role in reducing emissions now. Yet in the future, Brazil, China, India, Indonesia, and other developing nations may well exceed the U.S. level of emissions. So does equity call for those nations to take substantial action today rather than to place most of the burden on the United States and other rich nations? These kinds of issues have been debated for years at international meetings on climate change and likely will continue to be at the center of concern in the future.

Conclusions

This chapter defines and explains the nature of U.S. environmental and energy policy and introduces key concepts associated with this policy area. It describes the major policies and how they came to be adopted, and also how they became increasingly controversial over time. Knowing this history is important for understanding why the policies are evaluated so differently by Democrats and Republicans and by the major organized groups active in this policy area, particularly environmental and business organizations.

As we have argued throughout the text, it is important to assess environmental and energy policies in terms of effectiveness in achieving their long-term goals, but also how efficiently and fairly they do so, and the societal impacts they have, both positive and negative. It is equally important to seek out the best available information in making these kinds of judgments. These tasks are especially difficult when facing new and complex challenges such as climate change, but the principles of policy analysis apply here as much as they do in other policy areas.

It is clear that the U.S. public is concerned about environmental and health risks and continues to support strong public policies. When a Gallup poll in 2000 asked people to name what they thought would be the most important problem facing the United States twenty-five years in the future, more people named the environment than any other issue. Nonetheless, in the short term, environmental problems, including climate change, remain a low-salience concern, as they have been for much of the past several decades.[34]

The chapter also emphasizes the need to modernize environmental, resource, and energy policies for the twenty-first century. From many perspectives, including that of policy analysis, the policies are neither as effective nor as economically efficient as they could be with some adjustments in the policy strategies that are used. Policymakers need to evaluate current policies and consider alternative approaches that hold more promise for better performance. Among the changes the U.S. environmental policy system needs is a set of priorities that is more in tune with the reality of risk to public and environmental health, including policies to deal with climate change. Ultimately, these and other policy changes must also be consistent with the widely recognized, long-term goal of sustainable development.

DISCUSSION QUESTIONS

1. What do you see as the greatest strengths and weaknesses of U.S. environmental policies? What policy elements do you think are most in need of change? For example, should the nation rely more on the use of market incentives than on regulation? More on information disclosure? More on what is often termed "flexible regulation" that gives more latitude to industry to reach an agreed-upon set of goals? Should more responsibility for environmental policy be devolved to the states?

2. Consider a specific environmental protection policy, such as the Clean Air Act, Clean Water Act, or CERCLA (Superfund). What kind of information would allow you to determine how successful the policy has been?

3. Consider a specific natural resource policy, such as the Endangered Species Act or the National Environmental Policy Act. Answer the same question posed above. What kind of information would you need to have to determine how effective the policy has been?

4. What approach should be at the heart of a U.S. national energy policy? Increasing energy supplies? Decreasing demand? Shifting emphasis to renewable energy resources such as wind and solar? Relying more on nuclear power? Whichever goal you consider to be most important, which policy alternatives are most promising? For example, should policy be based on provision of market incentives (such as higher gasoline taxes) or regulation (such as CAFE standards)?

5. What should the United States do about climate change? Should it adopt strong policies to reduce the use of fossil fuels and thus to limit the emissions of greenhouse gases? Or should it encourage more research for now, and hold off on adopting strict requirements until the scientific evidence about climate change and its effects is much more certain than at present? Other than requirements or incentives for reducing fossil fuel use, what kinds of policies should the federal or state governments consider?

KEYWORDS

cap-and-trade policy   433
carbon tax   429
Clean Power Plan   398
climate change   397
collaborative decision
    making   403
command and control   418
Corporate Average Fuel
    Economy (CAFE)
    standards   429
direct regulation   418

ecosystem-based management   427
environmental impact statement
    (EIS)   413
environmental policy   402
Environmental Protection Agency
    (EPA)   398
environmental stewardship   424
hydraulic fracturing   399
intergenerational equity   436
Intergovernmental Panel on
    Climate Change (IPCC)   397

Kyoto Protocol   436
multiple use   424
Organization of the Petroleum
    Exporting Countries
    (OPEC)   428
resource subsidies   426
sustainable development   401
Toxics Release Inventory
    (TRI)   416
user fees   426

MAJOR LEGISLATION

American Recovery and Reinvestment Act of 2009
Antiquities Act of 1906

Clean Air Act Amendments of 1970
Clean Air Act Amendments of 1990

Clean Water Act of 1972

Comprehensive Environmental Response, Compensation, and Liability Act of 1980 (Superfund)

Endangered Species Act of 1973

Energy Independence and Security Act of 2007

Energy Policy Act of 1992

Energy Policy Act of 2005

Federal Environmental Pesticide Control Act of 1972

Federal Land Policy and Management Act of 1976

Food Quality Protection Act of 1996

General Mining Law of 1872

Land and Water Conservation Fund Act of 1964

National Environmental Policy Act of 1969

National Forest Management Act of 1976

Resource Conservation and Recovery Act of 1976

Safe Drinking Water Act of 1974

Toxic Substances Control Act of 1976

Wilderness Act of 1964

SUGGESTED READINGS

Joseph F. C. DiMento and Pamela Doughman, eds., *Climate Change: What It Means for Us, Our Children, and Our Grandchildren*, 2nd ed. (Cambridge, Mass.: MIT Press, 2014). A short and highly readable collection that clearly explains climate change and societal responses to it.

Michael E. Kraft, *Environmental Policy and Politics*, 7th ed. (New York: Routledge, 2018). A concise text that focuses on the major environmental problems and their consequences for society, the policymaking process, the evolution of U.S. policies, and current issues and controversies.

Judith A. Layzer, *The Environmental Case: Translating Values into Policy*, 4th ed. (Thousand Oaks, Calif.: CQ Press, 2016). A collection of intriguing case studies in environmental politics and policy that emphasizes conflicts in values and how they are resolved in pollution control and natural resource management.

Christopher McGrory Klyza and David J. Sousa, *American Environmental Policy: Beyond Gridlock*, updated and expanded ed. (Cambridge, Mass.: MIT Press, 2013). An original and detailed study of environmental policymaking in the United States that emphasizes alternative pathways to problem solving when partisanship and legislative gridlock prevent passage of new national laws.

Patrick M. Regan, *The Politics of Global Climate Change* (Boulder, Colo.: Paradigm, 2015). A comprehensive and succinct overview of the challenge of climate change and the politics that will shape how we design and adopt solutions to it.

Norman J. Vig and Michael E. Kraft, eds., *Environmental Policy: New Directions for the Twenty-first Century*, 9th ed. (Thousand Oaks, Calif.: CQ Press, 2016). A collection of original studies covering U.S. political institutions and policymaking, the role of the states and local communities, natural resource policies, climate change, global population growth and economic development, Chinese environmental policy, and environmental security.

SUGGESTED WEBSITES

www.api.org. American Petroleum Institute, a trade association representing the oil and natural gas industry, with much information on U.S. energy issues. Includes valuable links to energy statistics, industry statistics, and policy issues.

www.doi.gov. Department of the Interior portal, with news links and access to the department's agencies such as the National Park Service, U.S. Geological Survey, Fish and Wildlife Service, and Bureau of Land Management.

www.energy.gov. Department of Energy portal, with news links and access to DOE studies and reports on energy and the environment, and debates over national energy policy.

www.epa.gov. Home page for the U.S. Environmental Protection Agency. Contains the full text of the agency's major laws and their associated rules and regulations. Includes useful links to all major environmental problems and current government activity on them.

www.ipcc.ch. Website of the Intergovernmental Panel on Climate Change, the leading international organization for the assessment of climate change; provides periodic reports on the current state of scientific knowledge about the changing climate and socioeconomic and environmental impacts.

www.nam.org. National Association of Manufacturers site; includes a page on resources and environmental issues that provides business commentary on a range of current policy disputes.

www.nrdc.org. Natural Resources Defense Council site, with an extensive set of links to environmental issues, recent events, news releases, and reports.

www.ucsusa.org. Union of Concerned Scientists portal, with extensive reports and analyses related to the use of scientific information in environmental and energy policy.

NOTES

1. See Justin Gillis, "Panel's Warning on Climate Risk: Worst Is Yet to Come," *New York Times*, March 31, 2014; and Gillis, "U.N. Panel Warns of Dire Effects from Lack of Action over Global Warming," *New York Times*, November 2, 2014. See also the Risky Business Project, which focuses on the risks posed by climate change for the U.S. economy, available at www.riskybusiness.org. The IPCC report itself, from the panel's Working Group II, *Climate Change 2014: Impacts, Adaptation, and Vulnerability*, can be found on the organization's website, along with many other studies and reports: www.ipcc.ch. For background on Kerry's efforts to build international support for climate change, see Coral Davenport, "Climate Study Puts Diplomatic Pressure on Obama," *New York Times*, March 31, 2014.

2. See Justin Gillis, "U.N. Climate Panel Warns Speedier Action Is Needed to Avert Disaster," *New York Times*, April 13, 2014. This report, *Climate Change 2014: Mitigation of Climate Change*, also is available at the IPCC webpage, both in its complete version and in a "summary for policymakers." Yet another detailed report, this one by the National Climate Assessment, came in May 2014 and also received extensive media coverage. See Justin Gillis, "Climate Change Study Finds U.S. Is Already Widely Affected," *New York Times*, May 6, 2014.

3. See Coral Davenport and Avery Palmer, "A Landmark Climate Bill Passes," *CQ Weekly*, June 29, 2009, 1516; and Ryan Lizza, "As the World Burns," *The New Yorker*, October 11, 2010. Lizza in particular also faults the Obama White House for doing too little to build support for the bill in the Senate.

4. Brady Dennis, "White House Sets New Fuel-Efficiency Standards for Heavy-Duty Trucks, Vans, and Buses," *Washington Post*, August 16, 2016.

5. Eric Lipton and Clifford Krauss, "A Gold Rush of Subsidies in the Search for Clean Energy," *New York Times*, November 11, 2011; and Justin Doom, "U.S. Expects $5 Billion from Program That Funded Solyndra," *Bloomberg*, November 12, 2014.

6. See the EPA page on the Clean Power Plan at www.epa.gov/cleanpowerplan. The plan's details, its history, and the economic analyses are all available at the EPA website. The consolidated lawsuit, reflecting opposition by 28 states and 120 companies and organizations, is *State of West Virginia et al. v. EPA*. Of special note is that most people in the states that are party to the lawsuit actually favor the plan. The survey results are reported on WorldPublicOpinion.org, September 12, 2016. On the Trump administration's possible actions, see "Up in Smoke? What Will Happen If America's President-Elect Follows

through on Pledges to Tear Up Environmental Laws?" *The Economist*, November 26, 2016, available at www.economist.com.

7. The EPA also is targeting coal plants for their release of air toxics. See the agency's fact sheet on the Mercury and Air Toxics Standards (MATS), "Benefits and Costs of Cleaning Up Toxic Air Pollution from Power Plants," available at www.epa.gov.

8. Leslie Kaufman, "Republicans Seek Big Cuts in Environmental Rules," *New York Times*, July 27, 2011. On the 2014 House vote, see Valerie Volcovici, "U.S. House Advances Bill Curbing EPA Power Plant Emissions Limits," Reuters, March 25, 2014. Most of these House votes are largely symbolic. House members knew the Senate would not go along, and the president would never sign such legislation. For a review of these and other actions on the environment in Congress, see Kraft 2016.

9. Michael Wines and John Schwartz, "Unsafe Lead Levels in Tap Water Not Limited to Flint," *New York Times*, February 8, 2016.

10. See also Ann Rappaport, "Campus Greening," *Environment* 50, no. 1 (January/February 2008): 7–16.

11. For a fascinating history of land acquisition, see Fairfax et al. (2005). The authors critically assess the potential and limitations of both public and private land acquisition strategies.

12. For a fuller description of each of these statutes and recent changes either proposed or approved, see Kraft (2018). These and other environmental protection statutes, and the regulations used to implement them, are also available in full at the EPA website: www.epa.gov/laws-regulations.

13. In 2002, the Bush administration announced it would not seek reauthorization of the Superfund tax. It would sharply curtail the number of Superfund sites to be cleaned up and cover the costs through general Treasury funds. In an op-ed article, former Clinton EPA administrator Carol Browner called the Bush action "an enormous windfall for the oil and chemical companies." See "Polluters Should Have to Pay," *New York Times*, March 1, 2002.

14. These and similar studies are available at the EPA website on the benefits and costs of the Clean Air Act: www.epa.gov/clean-air-act-overview/progress-cleaning-air-and-improving-peoples-health#cost.

15. The EPA estimates come from the agency's "Benefits and Costs of Cleaning Up Toxic Air Pollution from Power Plants," while the industry estimates are noted in Steve Davidson, "Pace Quickens for Extinction of Coal-Fired Electric in the U.S.," *Communities Digital News*, March 25, 2014.

16. EPA, "Air Quality—National Summary" available at www.epa.gov/air-trends/air-quality-national-summary.

17. See the EPA's "National Summary of State Information: Assessed Waters of United States," available at http://ofmpub.epa.gov/waters10/attains_nation_cy.control.

18. See Mary Graham and Catherine Miller, "Disclosure of Toxic Releases in the United States," *Environment* 43 (October 2001): 8–20; and Mary Graham, "Regulation by Shaming," *Atlantic Monthly*, April 2000, available at www.theatlantic.com.

19. See Margaret Kriz, "Working the Land: Bush Aggressively Opens Doors to New Mining, Drilling, and Logging on Federal Lands, as Green Activists Despair of Even Keeping Track," *National Journal*, February 23, 2002, 532–539.

20. A summary of Obama's actions can be found in Douglas Brinkley, "Obama the Monument Maker," *New York Times*, August 27, 2016.

21. See Robert M. Hughes and Carol Ann Woody, "A Mining Law Whose Time Has Passed," *New York Times*, January 11, 2012.

22. *National Energy Policy: Inventory of Major Federal Programs and Status of Policy Recommendations*, GAO-05–379 (Washington, D.C.: U.S. Government Accountability Office, 2005).

23. See Ben Evans with Joseph J. Schatz, "Details of Energy Policy Law," *CQ Weekly*, September 5, 2005, 2337–2345.

24. See a list of key reports on national security and climate change at the Center for Climate and

Energy Solutions, www.c2es.org/science-impacts/national-security. See also Coral Davenport, "Pentagon Says Global Warming Presents Immediate Security Threat," *New York Times*, October 13, 2014. In September 2016, President Obama ordered all security agencies to incorporate climate change effects into their planning processes. See Erika Bolstad, "Obama Demands That Security Agencies Consider Climate Change," *ClimateWire*, September 22, 2016, available at www.eenews.net/climatewire/2016/09/22/stories/1060043251.

25. For current updates on climate change and policy action, see the website Inside Climate News, at https://insideclimatenews.org/, and Climate Science and Policy Watch, at www.climatesciencewatch.org/. For a fossil fuel industry perspective, see the American Petroleum Institute's page on climate change, at www.api.org/oil-and-natural-gas/environment/climate-change.

26. The IPCC reports can be found at www.ipcc.ch. The IPCC issues a new report about every five years, with separate studies on the scientific aspects of climate change, the impacts that such change could have, and policy actions that could mitigate those impacts. As noted early in the chapter, several new reports were issued in 2013 and 2014.

27. For an overview of the agreement, see Coral Davenport, "195 Nations Near Landmark Deal to Cut Emissions," *New York Times*, December 13, 2015. The details can be found at the UN site for the climate change agreement, at http://unfccc.int/paris_agreement/items/9485.php. On the position of the Trump administration and the likely impacts its decisions will have, see Coral Davenport, "Donald Trump Could Put Climate Change on Course for 'Danger Zone,'" *New York Times*, November 10, 2016.

28. New York Times Editorial Board, "Washington State's Ambitious Carbon Tax Proposal," *New York Times*, October 24, 2016.

29. See Mark Murray, "Road Test," *National Journal*, May 25, 2002, 1548–1553; and estimates from 2008 at www.infrastructurereportcard.org/slides/roads/.

30. Honda's unique role in supporting higher fuel economy standards, even for SUVs, is detailed by Danny Hakim in "Honda Takes Up Case in U.S. for Green Energy," *New York Times*, June 12, 2002. On the broader industry opposition to fuel economy standards, see John Lancaster, "Debate on Fuel Economy Turns Emotional," *Washington Post*, March 10, 2002; and David Rosenbaum, "Senate Deletes Higher Mileage Standard in Energy Bill," *New York Times*, March 14, 2002.

31. Martin Kady II with Isaiah J. Poole, "Record Gas Prices Immune to Any Legislative Magic," *CQ Weekly*, June 12, 2004, 1388–1396.

32. The poll was published in the *New York Times* on February 28, 2006, and it was conducted in February of that year. Most recent polls show continued public opposition to raising the gasoline tax, even if doing so would help to reduce greenhouse gas emissions. See Barry G. Rabe and Christopher Borick, "The Decline of Public Support for State Climate Change Policies: 2008–2013" (Center for Local, State, and Urban Policy, Gerald R. Ford School of Public Policy, University of Michigan, March 2013). Yet polls by the Yale Project on Climate Change Communication indicate strong public support for specific actions to deal with climate change. See the report "Americans' Actions to Limit Global Warming November 2013" (February 19, 2014), available at the project's website: http://climatecommunication.yale.edu/publications/americans-actions-to-limit-global-warming-november-2013/.

33. See Jim Yardley and Laurie Goodstein, "Pope Francis, in Sweeping Encyclical, Calls for Swift Action on Climate Change," *New York Times*, June 18, 2015.

34. Andrew C. Revkin, "Environment Issues Slide in Poll of Public Concerns," *New York Times*, January 23, 2009. See also Guber and Bosso (2013a).

Chapter 12

Chapter Objectives

- Explain the nature of foreign policy and homeland security and the key concepts associated with them.

- Describe major issues in foreign policy and homeland security.

- Evaluate significant foreign and defense policy actions taken since the end of World War II.

National security and citizen rights. Former security contractor Edward Snowden speaks via video link at a news conference for the launch of a campaign calling for President Obama to pardon him on September 14, 2016, in New York City. Snowden released classified documents exposing U.S. domestic data collection on phone calls and Internet use and foreign surveillance, sparking a controversial debate over privacy and security, and straining diplomatic relations. *(Spencer Platt/Getty Images)*

Foreign Policy and Homeland Security

T hroughout 2013, the nation was gripped by news of the National Security Agency's extensive and secretive domestic surveillance operations that far exceeded what the public and policymakers thought was taking place. Most Americans recognize the need to keep close tabs on potential terrorists at home or abroad, particularly in the aftermath of the September 11, 2001, attacks and more recent incidents, such as the mass shooting at a nightclub in Orlando, Florida, in 2016. But how much authority should the NSA have to gather information about ordinary Americans in its search for telling patterns that might alert the agency to risks of terrorism? Should all phone calls and all e-mail messages be monitored for such patterns? What about web browsing and postings to social network sites such as Facebook and Twitter? At what point does such government surveillance cross the line and become an invasion of privacy or even a violation of federal laws that are designed to protect citizens' civil liberties even as the nation pursues its national security goals?

Many of the news stories in 2013 followed the release of thousands of classified documents by Edward J. Snowden, a then twenty-nine-year-old former NSA contractor who worked for the consulting company Booz Allen Hamilton. By one recent estimate, more than three million federal employees and nine hundred thousand contractors hold security clearances, making it difficult to oversee their actions. In fact, some of Booz Allen's twenty-five thousand employees, about half of whom hold top secret security clearances, actually work inside the highly secretive facilities of the NSA, and others are located in nearby office buildings.[1] There they work as policy analysts, gathering and analyzing information and advising government policymakers.

Snowden and his supporters say that he released classified data to journalists because he had no confidence that the NSA itself would take action against what he viewed as excessive and illegal domestic surveillance operations. In effect, they said he became a whistle-blower, hoping that by releasing evidence of NSA's mass collection of phone records and Internet use he would help to end the practices. Some of his supporters called him a hero. Snowden's detractors offered a much less positive interpretation. They said that he was not a whistle-blower at all, but a traitor, and that his release of classified documents did enormous damage to the ability of the NSA and other intelligence agencies to do their jobs and protect the nation from terrorism. They argue that rather than leak classified information to the press, he should have informed his superiors about the surveillance abuses and allowed them to deal with the matter.

Snowden left the United States, with the NSA computer files, and resided briefly in Hong Kong while he sought political asylum in more than a dozen nations. Ultimately he settled in Russia, which provided him with a one-year renewable asylum, while he sought more permanent asylum in Europe. As of early 2017, Russia extended the asylum, and Snowden remained there while the U.S. government continued to seek his return to the United States to face criminal charges.[2] He has been charged with violation of the Espionage Act for unauthorized communication of classified material, and also for theft of government property, the files that he transferred to his computer. Other charges are likely to be added to these, probably ensuring that should Snowden ever return to the United States and be convicted, he would spend the rest of his life in a federal prison.[3] His supporters argued that President Obama should pardon him before leaving office, but the White House did not do so.

In yet another twist in the story, in April 2014, two of the newspapers that published stories based on the NSA documents that Snowden provided to them, the *Washington Post* and the *Guardian*, won the prestigious Pulitzer Prize for public service. At the height of the controversy, both newspapers were strongly criticized by the American and British governments for the harm they were said to inflict on national security by publishing the information. Yet the Pulitzer committee indicated that it gave the award because of the papers' "revelation of widespread secret surveillance by the National Security Agency, marked by authoritative and insightful reports that helped the public understand how the disclosures fit into the larger framework of national security."[4]

The sharply varying assessments of Snowden's release of classified documents and of the NSA's massive domestic surveillance operations illustrate well the contemporary challenge of providing for the nation's security. As many observers noted in the aftermath of the September 11 terrorist attacks, "the world has changed." As a result, the goals of U.S. foreign policy, national defense, and homeland security need fresh and critical examination. Policy tools that were widely used in the past, from diplomacy and international economic assistance to weapons procurement and military intervention abroad, need to be rethought as well. At the same time, use of new policy tools, including the NSA's elaborate electronic surveillance programs, clearly calls for careful analysis

Steps to Analysis

The National Security Agency and Domestic Surveillance

To learn more about the National Security Agency and its activities, go to the website for the agency at www.nsa.gov/index.shtml. Click on the tab for About Us, and then on Mission & Strategy.

- How does the agency view its purpose and its activities?

- What conclusions do you draw about the legitimacy of the agency's domestic surveillance work?

Now click on the tab for What We Do, and then Understanding the Threat. How does the NSA describe current national security threats? What in particular does the agency highlight as important? Do you have any concerns about the threats that the agency identifies? Are any important threats not listed here?

- For an alternative perspective, see the American Civil Liberties Union page on domestic surveillance at www.aclu.org/issues/national-security/privacy-and-surveillance/nsa-surveillance.

- What concerns about surveillance does the ACLU highlight?

- Do you agree or disagree with the group's concerns over such NSA activity as a possible violation of individuals' right to privacy?

- Do you think government agencies such as the NSA should be allowed to access cell phone records as one way to deter terrorist activity or to examine locked phones that were owned by terrorists?

Note: At the time when Edward Snowden's activities became known (2013), the Congressional Research Service issued a brief (sixteen pages) but important report: "CRS: NSA Surveillance Leaks: Background and Issues for Congress." It can be found at the CRS website. www.cfr.org/intelligence/crs-nsa-surveillance-leaks-background-issues-congress/p31676.

and reassessment, and that process is under way in Congress and the administration as well as in organizations outside of the government.

Similarly, government agencies and offices responsible for foreign and defense policy, such as the Departments of State and Defense, the Central Intelligence Agency, and the **Department of Homeland Security (DHS)**, created through an executive agency reorganization in the aftermath of the 2001 attacks, need to be thoroughly examined to make sure they are as capable as they can be of carrying out U.S. policy and protecting the nation from security threats.[5] Aside from capacity to do their jobs well, it is imperative that these agencies be able to weigh and balance their missions against long-standing concern for the rights of citizens. As we will see at the end of the chapter, critics have questioned the trade-offs between security and liberty in debates over the USA PATRIOT Act, both at the time of its adoption in 2001, just a few weeks after the terrorist attacks, and during its renewal by Congress in later years. The box "Steps to Analysis: The National Security Agency and Domestic Surveillance" explores these concerns.

Because of the scope of the topic, this chapter is organized differently from those that precede it. Instead of the major policies and programs, we emphasize key issues in foreign policy and homeland security and address questions about the effectiveness of new policies adopted in the years following the terrorist attacks of 2001. We also place those policies within the larger context of new and complex global challenges that confront the United States in the twenty-first century, including national security threats posed by the growth of international terrorism, often defined as the unconventional use of violence for political gain. In addition, we provide a brief historical overview of U.S. foreign and defense policy since the end of World War II in 1945 that helps to explain the changing policy agenda in recent years, particularly following the collapse of the Soviet Union in 1991 and the end of the Cold War that dominated U.S. thinking about foreign policy for decades.

We emphasize as well that policy analysis can help in understanding contemporary challenges in foreign policy and homeland security, much as it can in domestic policy areas such as education, the environment, and health care. Analysts and policymakers need to be alert to the available policy tools and think about which are most likely to be effective, which are justifiable in terms of economic costs and efficiency, and which are likely to be fair or acceptable on ethical grounds. There is an obvious need to think clearly and imaginatively about such questions, yet much of the current political debate over foreign policy and homeland security continues to be grounded in simplistic assessments of the situation faced. If this pattern continues, it will serve the nation poorly in the years ahead.

Background and Policy Evolution

We start this section with some basic definitions. **Foreign policy** refers to the collection of government actions that affect or attempt to affect U.S. national security as well as the economic and political goals associated with it. Foreign policy can deal with matters as diverse as international trade, economic assistance to poor nations, immigration to the United States, building of political alliances with other nations, action on human rights abuses around the world, global environmental and energy issues such as climate change, and strategic military actions abroad. As the list of topics suggests, foreign policy involves a great diversity of policy actors, among the most important of which are the president, the secretary of state, the president's national security adviser, the National Security Council (see below), and key congressional committees. Among the most commonly used policy tools are diplomacy (high-level communication among policymakers), economic relations (such as imposing trade restraints or providing economic assistance), and threats of military intervention. Foreign policymaking also has some distinctive qualities, among them a greater need than in other policy areas for secrecy or a lack of transparency, more of a reliance on policy professionals (for example, in the State Department and in intelligence and defense agencies), considerably less opportunity for public input, greater involvement by foreign policy actors, and dominance by the president over Congress.

Defense policy, considered part of foreign policy, refers to the goals set (usually by civilian policymakers in the White House and Congress) and the actions taken by government officials directed at the conduct of military affairs.

Here too the issues are diverse, ranging from decisions to build and deploy a variety of strategic weapons systems such as nuclear missiles and manned bombers to the maintenance of suitable military force levels, domestically and abroad, and the planning and conduct of military operations such as the wars in Iraq and Afghanistan. Among the major policy actors in defense decisions are the secretary of defense, other members of the National Security Council, and the Joint Chiefs of Staff (representing the military services). The National Security Council (NSC) is chaired by the president, and the regular attendees (both statutory and non-statutory) include the vice president, secretary of state, secretary of the Treasury, secretary of defense, and assistant to the president for national security affairs (also called the president's national security adviser). The chair of the joint chiefs by statute is the military adviser to the council, and the director of national intelligence is the intelligence adviser. The Obama administration altered the NSC substantially by extending its scope beyond traditional foreign policy issues (for example, to climate change and energy concerns) and including other agencies in its work. Members of Congress who serve on defense-related committees also are influential policy players.[6] In one of his first actions as president, Donald Trump issued a controversial executive order that changed the membership of the Principals Committee of the NSC by putting his top political operative, Stephen K. Bannon, on the committee while downgrading the role of the Chairman of the Joint Chiefs of Staff and the director of national intelligence.[7]

Although it is something of a simplification, the chief purpose of U.S. foreign policy since the end of World War II can be described as the promotion of national security through a diversified economic, political, and military strategy. The United States emerged from the war in 1945 as one of the world's leading military and economic powers, and it sought to ensure that the security it won at such a high price in World War II would not be lost. For most of the postwar era, that goal was associated with five essential activities: (1) the rebuilding of a war-devastated Europe through the Marshall Plan and the formation of the North Atlantic Treaty Organization (NATO), (2) the formation of and support for the United Nations, (3) a military buildup to ensure adequate capacity to deal with potential enemies, (4) the development and growth of the nation's intelligence agencies to provide reliable knowledge about security threats, and (5) the initiation of economic and military assistance to other nations for humanitarian and strategic purposes. We briefly review each of these in turn.

The Marshall Plan, NATO, and the Cold War

The Marshall Plan, named after Secretary of State George Marshall, was authorized by the Economic Cooperation Act of 1948 to help rebuild Europe after the defeat of Nazi Germany by the Allied forces, which included the United States and the Soviet Union. Europe continued to suffer greatly from the effects of the prolonged war, which had caused unprecedented loss of life and destruction across the continent. The plan was to offer humanitarian aid to assist in

Europe's recovery and to encourage nations in Europe to work together to improve economically. This was an early form of economic cooperation that led decades later to the European Union. The United States offered up to $20 billion in aid, and by 1953, it had spent some $13 billion, enough to put Europe back on its feet.[8] The United States also was aware that a stronger Europe could help to block the expansion of communism from the East as well as stimulate the U.S. economy, because so much of what European nations bought was made in the United States. The plan was one of the first clear demonstrations after the war that foreign policy could reflect idealistic goals but also be grounded in *realpolitik*, a hardheaded or practical appraisal of national interests that emphasizes competition among nation-states.

By 1949, in response to the threat of aggression by the Soviet Union, the United States and Western European nations created a formal alliance to pursue their security interests cooperatively: the **North Atlantic Treaty Organization (NATO)**, also called the North Atlantic Alliance or the Western Alliance, which was signed in Washington, D.C., in April. By 1955, NATO welcomed West Germany to the pact, but East Germany remained under the domination of the Soviet Union. The divided Germany would come to symbolize the deep ideological and political differences between NATO nations and the Soviet Union and its satellite states, the communist nations of Central and Eastern Europe. In response to West Germany's entry into NATO, and with Soviet concern about a "remilitarized" West Germany, in 1955, these nations formally established their counterpart, called the Warsaw Pact. The two collections of nations, West and East, were on opposing sides during the rest of the Cold War. The Warsaw Pact itself was formally dissolved in 1991 with the end of the Soviet Union (the Union of Soviet Socialist Republics, or USSR).

The **Cold War** was so named because the conflicts between the United States and the Soviet Union never emerged into direct military confrontation between the two, or a "hot" war. Rather, the conflicts that were fought were between surrogate nations, such as North and South Korea in the early 1950s and North and South Vietnam in the 1960s and early 1970s. This is not to say there was an absence of real warlike activities. In place of military engagement between the two superpowers, the Cold War relied on a variety of other policy tools. These included diplomatic actions, communication strategies (propaganda), economic and military aid to nations to secure their support, and covert intelligence and military operations in advance of each nation's interests. The Cold War lasted from 1947 until the collapse of the Soviet Union in 1991 (Gaddis 2006).

The United Nations and Globalization

At the end of World War II, the United States and its European allies concluded that future conflicts might be resolved without war through the establishment of an international organization. In 1945, the United States and fifty other nations formed the **United Nations (UN)**, headquartered in New York City and governed under the United Nations Charter, its constitution. Today, the UN is often described as a "global association of governments facilitating cooperation in international law, international security, economic development, and social equity."[9] In 2017, the UN consisted of 193 member states, and it had a vast array of agencies and programs to further its purposes, such as the World Health Organization, the United Nations International Children's Emergency Fund (UNICEF), and the United Nations Development Programme. In addition to these agencies, the UN sponsors periodic international conferences on issues of special importance such as the Conference on Sustainable Development (discussed in chapter 11) and the Fourth World Conference on Women (held in Beijing, China, in 1995).

Several affiliated organizations work toward goals similar to those of the UN, especially economic development of poor nations. Most prominent among them are the **World Bank** and the **International Monetary Fund,** which are controlled by leading developed nations, such as the United States. The World Bank was created at about the same time as the UN, in 1945, and loans money to developing nations for certain kinds of development projects. As is the case with the UN itself, these organizations often are criticized for a variety of reasons. Some argue that they impose Western political and economic values on developing nations, such as a demand for democratic institutions and free-market economic systems that do not necessarily benefit the people of those nations. Others complain that they have worsened environmental conditions by fostering wasteful and damaging projects, such as the construction of large hydroelectric dams. There is no question, however, that the World Bank remains a highly regarded financial institution with an enormous impact on world economic development strategies. The same could be said of its related financial institutions.

As we discussed in chapter 7, one of the most important economic aspects of foreign policy, though not restricted to work through the United Nations, is an attempt to manage the effects of **globalization,** defined here as the growing interrelationship of all nations through global trade and other kinds of interaction and communication. Increasingly, national barriers to trade, such as tariffs (customs duties or taxes imposed on imports), have been lowered, facilitating the development of an international marketplace in what one journalist has called an increasingly "flat" or connected world (Friedman 2006, 2008). Yet the nations that compete in this marketplace do so with greatly varied economic circumstances, particularly their cost of labor and reliance on different national health, safety, and environmental regulations. These variations can lead to conflicts over what is considered to be fair trade, which became a major issue in the 2016 U.S. presidential election.

Today such conflicts often are presented to the **World Trade Organization** (WTO). The WTO was established in 1995 and administers trade agreements among 164 nations (as of 2017), representing about 97 percent of the world's population, to settle conflicts over trade disputes, such as imposing unreasonable restrictions on other nations' trade with the United States. Its very existence testifies to the global marketplace of the twenty-first century, the effects of which sometimes become topics of intense debate. One example is the United States' increasing reliance on importation of Chinese-made goods, which are ubiquitous in discount department stores across the nation such as Walmart and Target. Concerns have been raised about issues as disparate as China's record on human rights abuses; its lax environmental, health, and safety protection; and the economic impact on the United States when importation of goods greatly exceeds purchase of U.S.-made products in China and other nations (thus contributing to the United States' trade deficit).

The membership of the UN Security Council—the most important of the UN policymaking bodies—reflects the history of the UN's formation. The council has a rotating membership of ten nations selected from the UN General Assembly (which consists of all member states) in addition to five permanent members: China, France, the Russian Federation (Russia, replacing the former Soviet Union), the United Kingdom, and the United States; each of the five has veto power over the council's actions.

Military Buildup and Nuclear Weapons

Following the end of World War II, the most expensive war in U.S. history, military spending declined somewhat but remained high for decades.[10] Measured as a percentage of the federal budget, spending rose in the early 1950s during the Korean War (1950–1953) and stayed at high levels during the 1950s and 1960s. It then declined steadily after the formal end of the Vietnam War in 1975. In 1960, defense spending was over 52 percent of the federal budget, and it remained at over 40 percent by 1965. By 2016, however, the Department of Defense budget and other security-related activities stood at about $535 billion, or one-sixth of all federal spending—a reduced level of spending as a percent of the federal budget explained in part by the breakup of the Soviet Union and the end of the Cold War and in part by the soaring costs of federal entitlement programs such as Social Security, Medicare, and Medicaid.[11] Federal defense spending in President Obama's 2017 budget request to Congress was $632 billion, making it one of the most costly programs in the budget even with some decline in spending and troop levels compared to previous years.[12] Another $53 billion is budgeted for the National Intelligence Program, and about $50 billion for diplomacy and foreign aid through the Department of State and the Agency for International Development. In 2017, the defense budget supported nearly 1.3 million active-duty military personnel and over 800,000 in the National Guard or other military reserves.[13]

Those with a serious interest in defense programs and spending levels might peruse the federal budget documents for the Department of Defense (www.defense.gov) and related programs in the Departments of State (www.state.gov), Energy (www.energy.gov), and Homeland Security (www.dhs.gov). The annual budget documents provide elaborate descriptions of defense programs and priorities. These also include an accounting of homeland security funding by each department and agency.[14]

The high cost of defense and the increasing reliance on technologically advanced weapons systems, as well as the corporations that manufacture them, became a prominent issue as early as the 1950s and 1960s. In his farewell address to the nation in January 1961, President Dwight Eisenhower, who had served as commanding general of U.S. forces in Europe in World War II, famously complained about the nation's "military-industrial complex," a form of iron triangle discussed in chapter 2. It was, he said, a "permanent armaments industry of vast proportions," and with great political influence. Even if no dominance by military or industrial elites is suspected, cumulative military spending during this period was without precedent.

Today, defense contractors work closely with members of Congress and the Pentagon and continue to press for costly weapons systems, even when the Pentagon seeks to shift spending to newer and more appropriate technologies. For example, in 2016, Congress approved $400 million for an extra littoral combat ship despite opposition by Secretary of Defense Ash Carter and the Obama White House to doing so. Both "strongly objected" because of multiple problems that the ship had to date and a preference to spend the money on other military priorities.[15]

An even more astonishing example is the long resistance by members of Congress to proposals to end production of the obsolete F-22 Raptor fighter jet that was first conceived during the Cold War, in large part because of the tens of thousands of jobs in some forty-four states linked to the F-22. Finally, in 2009, Congress agreed to cease funding for the F-22 and instead looked to the F-35 Joint Strike Fighter to replace it, deferring to Defense Department preferences. Yet even the F-35 will be very costly, with separate versions of the jet for each of the services. The Defense Department estimates the cost of developing, testing, and building the problem-plagued F-35 fighter jet at $400 billion if the government builds the anticipated 2,457 jets; the amount is twice the initial estimate. An additional $1.1 trillion is anticipated for operating and sustaining the planes over the next fifty years.[16] At this cost, the F-35 is likely to become the most expensive Pentagon weapons procurement project in history.

In addition to the problem of congressional defense earmarks, an ongoing challenge has been dealing with the authorization and acquisition of expensive weapons and other national security systems. A 2009 Government Accountability Office study of ninety-six major defense acquisition programs found that nearly two-thirds of them involved significant cost overruns and delays that cost close to $300 billion.[17] A similar comprehensive study by Reuters in 2013 concluded that the Pentagon is "largely incapable of keeping track of its vast stores of weapons, ammunition and other supplies," because it relies on a "tangle of thousands of disparate, obsolete, largely incompatible accounting and business-management systems."[18]

As one example of how such management deficiencies affected spending and the war in Afghanistan, in 2013, U.S.-funded contractors working for the Defense Department completed work on a sixty-four-thousand-square-foot and elaborately equipped headquarters building that cost some $34 million. Yet for years before its construction, senior U.S. officers in Afghanistan repeatedly informed the Pentagon that they had no need for the building, and with the impending withdrawal of U.S. troops, they saw no reason to move into it. Many other construction projects in that nation were similarly wasteful because of poor planning, communication, and management. As one journalist summed up the military's reaction to the new headquarters building, it is "the whitest elephant in a war littered with wasteful, dysfunctional and unnecessary projects funded by American taxpayers."[19] In 2015, another report surfaced of the Pentagon's Afghanistan reconstruction program spending $43 million to build a compressed natural gas station that was 140 times as expensive as a similar one built in Pakistan.[20]

In short, there are continuing questions about some very basic matters of budgetary management and housekeeping that must be addressed if the nation is to get what it seeks with the current level of military spending. These needs become even more important if the Pentagon budget shrinks over the next few years as part of the larger national effort to reign in federal spending.[21]

Issues related to the use of nuclear weapons no longer get the attention they once did, with the exception of concern over their possible use by rogue nations such as Iran and North Korea, yet they remain among the most important in foreign and defense policy. The potential of nuclear weapons was vividly demonstrated by their use in Japan at the end of World War II, and the United States and the Soviet Union began a decades-long effort to achieve superiority in the number and destructive potential of nuclear weapons. This part of the arms race between the two nations was intended to serve one major purpose: to deter an attack by one against the other by creating fear of a counterattack. The key idea is that of mutually assured destruction, and it is based on an application of the rational choice theory that we discussed in chapter 3. In such strategic and foreign policy decisions, policymakers need to understand the interests, perceptions, and motivations of nation-states and other international actors, whether they are terrorists or multinational corporations. In the case of nuclear weapons, the assumption is that a strike by one nation would likely be followed by an equal strike by the other, so that both nations are assured of destruction. If the nations are rational actors, neither should be motivated to engage in a first strike. Hence, having sufficient weapons would promote deterrence, and there would be no nuclear war.[22] The United States relied on the policy of deterrence to prevent the outbreak of such a war.

The number, increasing power, and location of these weapons on land and on or under the sea were some of the most closely protected military secrets during the Cold War and a vital component of defense strategy. Each side was attentive to the possibility that the other might acquire more or better weapons or place them in areas where they could not easily be destroyed in a nuclear strike, such as within reinforced missile silos, on manned bombers, or in nuclear-powered submarines that could remain hidden for long periods of time under the sea. Thus pressure on both nations led to an enormous investment in the building of nuclear stockpiles and the vehicles that would deliver them. The United States also placed nuclear weapons in strategic locations throughout Europe in the 1950s and 1960s, with over seven thousand nuclear warheads at the peak in 1971.[23]

Beyond the stockpiled weapons in internationally recognized "nuclear weapons states" (China, France, Russia, the United Kingdom, and the United States),

The high cost of military weapon systems. A Lockheed Martin Corp. F-35A jet flies during a training mission in Hill Air Force Base, Utah, on October 21, 2016. Critics fault the F-35 fighter jet refuels between missions aboard the USS *Wasp* off the coast of Virginia during sea trials in October 2011. Critics fault the F-35 as an ill-conceived and excessively expensive multipurpose aircraft. Part of the high cost of the jet is attributable to its use of stealth technology and other advanced and highly complex systems, which also add to the difficulty of maintaining the planes for combat. Advocates, however, believe that the jet is well worth the cost and that it will revolutionize the way America fights. (*George Frey/Bloomberg via Getty Images*)

there is continuing concern over nuclear proliferation; this is the spread of nuclear weapons knowledge and technology to new nations such as India and Pakistan. The interest is particularly great over those nations that are politically unstable or that for other reasons may pose a threat to regional or world peace. The U.S. government is alert to the possibility that nations such as Iran and North Korea might eventually be able to threaten others with nuclear weapons. The U.S. decision to deploy a still-developing missile defense system was based in part on concern over the possibility of such an attack.[24]

The enormous buildup of nuclear stockpiles led over time to a number of talks and treaties to try to reduce their numbers. The manufacture and maintenance of those weapons were costly and inefficient uses of defense funds, and their numbers posed a continuing security risk. Both the United States and the Soviet Union had a reason to favor arms limitations, but they also distrusted each other, so the various arms talks went slowly and yielded mixed results. Eventually, the United States and the Russian government agreed to limit their nuclear weapons arsenals to 1,700 to 2,200 warheads each. Critics have complained, however, that such agreements are only loosely enforced, with no provisions for verification. Thus despite considerable progress in reducing the number of nuclear weapons, concern persists over the risk posed by the existence of so many old weapons and the security of the stockpiles, especially in nations of the former Soviet Union.

During his campaign for the presidency, President Obama proposed setting a goal of eliminating all nuclear weapons in the world, in part to lower the risk of terrorism. In doing so, the president added his support to a bipartisan effort to rethink the nation's reliance on nuclear weapons that has become "increasingly hazardous and decreasingly effective." In April 2009, shortly after a North Korean missile test, the president called for reducing the role of nuclear weapons in U.S. national security policy and urged other nations to do the same. He also began negotiations with Russia to decrease the number of warheads and stockpiles of nuclear weapons in both nations, and the two nations signed a nuclear arms reduction pact in 2010.[25] The Obama administration also persuaded North Korea to suspend work on long-range missile launches and to permit inspections of its weapons program in exchange for U.S. food aid to the nation, which has long suffered from an insufficient food supply.

A related question, still unresolved, is the extent to which the nation's aging nuclear weapons arsenal should be modernized. Current plans call for spending $350 billion over the next decade, which President Obama sought to cut back over congressional opposition. Members of Congress argued that a failure to upgrade the weapons would weaken the nation's nuclear deterrent. The estimated cost for the full thirty-year plan to modernize nuclear weapons and production facilities for the second half of the twenty-first century is $1 trillion. The plan calls for redesigning nuclear warheads and for building new nuclear bombers, submarines, land-based missiles, weapons laboratories, and production facilities. Critics question whether such an enormous expenditure can be justified as the threat of nuclear war has diminished.[26]

The Intelligence Agencies and the War in Iraq

In addition to the formation of NATO and the United Nations, and the buildup of military forces, the post–World War II era saw a transition from temporary intelligence services during the war to the organizations that operate today. The National Security Act of 1947 created the **Central Intelligence Agency (CIA)** to replace the Office of Strategic Services that had performed more limited operations during World War II. The act also established the National Security Council to advise the president on security issues. Under the act, the CIA was charged with coordinating the nation's intelligence activities and "correlating, evaluating, and disseminating intelligence which affects national security."[27] Other intelligence agencies were created as well, many operating in relative secrecy for much of their existence. For example, according to the website for the Office of the Director of National Intelligence, the **National Security Agency (NSA)** "coordinates, directs, and performs highly specialized activities to protect U.S. government information systems and produce foreign signals intelligence information."[28] Created by President Harry Truman to unify the nation's codemakers and codebreakers, the agency began operating in 1952, during the Korean War. It is widely viewed as one of the most secretive of the intelligence agencies, working on the cutting edge of intelligence data analysis.

For years, the intelligence agencies were considered to be highly professional and effective in their work. Yet the terrorist attacks of 2001 cast them in a completely different light. Several major assessments of their organization and decision making were launched, including one by a joint congressional panel representing the House and Senate intelligence committees. It reported in July 2003 with a scathing critique of the Federal Bureau of Investigation (FBI) and the CIA, saying they had failed to pay attention to repeated warnings that the terrorist organization al-Qaeda was planning to attack the United States. It said the attacks might have been prevented if the agencies had been more alert to such information and had conducted more thorough analysis of intelligence data.[29] A second, nineteen-month investigation was undertaken by a bipartisan commission chaired by former New Jersey Republican governor Thomas H. Kean, called the 9/11 Commission; it issued its report on July 23, 2004. It too focused on the many failures of the FBI, the CIA, the Pentagon, the NSC, and almost every other agency charged with defending the nation. The commission called for a major overhaul of the intelligence agencies, and it argued that without such a restructuring the United States would be vulnerable to an even more damaging attack in the future.[30]

In response to the 9/11 Commission report, Congress enacted a sweeping overhaul of the agencies, called the Intelligence Reform and Terrorism Prevention Act of 2004. It was the most extensive reorganization of the intelligence community since World War II. The law focused on establishing a new management structure to coordinate and oversee the disparate agencies. The director of national intelligence is to develop the budgets of the nation's seventeen military and civilian intelligence agencies (said to employ about one hundred thousand people and to have a budget of more than $50 billion a year, although the budgets have long been secret), advise the president on intelligence matters, coordinate intelligence activities worldwide, and set an overall strategic direction for the U.S. intelligence system.[31] The agencies themselves are to improve their analysis of intelligence data and develop mechanisms for coordinating activities and sharing their information with one another. The law also calls for a variety of new efforts to improve transportation and border security and to better protect the nation against terrorism.[32]

Time will tell if the new institutional arrangement will succeed in improving what was widely thought to be unacceptably weak performance and lack of coordination by the CIA, FBI, and other agencies in anticipating the 2001 attacks and communicating critical information to policymakers. Directors of national intelligence have emphasized their own views on what changes are needed to improve performance. Generally, all of them call for use of a mix of policy tools, including so-called soft power (diplomacy and economic development assistance) and the "hard power" of tough counterterrorism efforts. One reason for the mix of policy tools is a growing recognition that global instability and terrorism can be linked to economic and social unrest in developing nations as well as to the independent actions of terrorist organizations.[33]

Where does the nation now stand in relation to possible future terrorist attacks? Much has been done to improve the nation's capacity to gather a wide array of information about diverse terrorist threats and to respond to them. Yet in a report issued on the tenth anniversary of the attacks, the 9/11 Commission still found serious shortcomings that could leave the country vulnerable to new and "likely successful" attacks, including congressional "dysfunction" in addressing security and intelligence issues, government procrastination in setting federal identification standards, and the "outrageous" failure by Congress to address continuing communication problems faced by first responders.[34]

By some accounts, the serious weaknesses in the intelligence agencies also played a large role in U.S. decisions regarding how to mount the global war on terrorism. Flawed intelligence as well as misuse of intelligence data led to the Bush administration's assertion that Iraq was linked directly to al-Qaeda and that it possessed weapons of mass destruction (nuclear, chemical, or biological) that could be used to attack the United States. A five-year inquiry by a U.S. Senate committee drew essentially these conclusions in 2008.[35] At about the same time, however, on the fifth anniversary of the war, President Bush acknowledged that its costs in lives and money were higher and that it lasted longer than he had anticipated, but he nonetheless remained convinced that the 2003 invasion was justifiable and had made the world and the United States safer: "The answers are clear to me. Removing Saddam Hussein from power was the right decision, and this is a fight that America can and must win."[36]

The case against Afghanistan was far stronger than the one the president made against Iraq. It clearly did harbor and support those responsible for the attacks. In October 2001, the United States sent troops to Afghanistan in what the U.S. military called Operation Enduring Freedom. It was the beginning of the U.S. war on terrorism. U.S. forces sought to remove the Taliban organization from power and to track down and capture the leaders of al-Qaeda responsible for the 9/11 attacks, especially Osama bin Laden. U.S. forces worked intensely with the Afghan Northern Alliance and with a number of Western allies. President Obama substantially increased U.S. forces in Afghanistan in an effort to improve the ongoing war's success against Taliban fighters, and in May 2011, U.S. forces tracked bin Laden to a large compound in Abbottabad, Pakistan, and killed him. The Obama administration set a deadline of late 2014 for withdrawal of most U.S. troops from Afghanistan, and 2016 for the withdrawal of the remaining 9,800 troops, whose mission is to train Afghan forces and support continuing operations against al-Qaeda. However, in October 2015, the president indicated that about 5,500 troops would remain in that nation through the end of his presidency in January 2017.[37]

The Iraq war itself was equally if not more controversial during its turbulent eight years. On March 20, 2003, after Iraqi president Saddam Hussein refused to agree to U.S. terms (particularly to surrender suspected weapons of mass destruction) or to adhere to a UN demand for disarmament, the United States invaded Iraq. It was supported by a number of coalition allies, chief among them the United Kingdom, in what the United States called Operation Iraqi Freedom. Hussein's elite Republican Guard troops were quickly defeated, and the Iraqi capital, Baghdad, fell on April 9. On May 1, 2003, President Bush declared the end of major combat operations in Iraq, a statement that would later prove to be wildly optimistic. The coalition forces eventually captured Saddam Hussein in December 2003, and he was brought to trial in late 2005 and later executed.

Following the military success of the first few weeks of the war in 2003, the situation quickly deteriorated. Iraq came to be plagued by continuing violence, much of it launched by the Sunni Muslim insurgency and its supporters, including al-Qaeda. If al-Qaeda was not active in Iraq prior to the war, there was little question that the war itself, and hatred for the United States in many Muslim nations, made it easier for the terrorist group to recruit volunteers in that nation and in neighboring states. As many analysts have argued, one of the greatest weaknesses of the U.S. war on terrorism in Iraq and elsewhere has been a failure to truly understand the adversaries that the United States faces, and thus to determine what would be most effective in countering the threats they pose.[38] By 2016, critics pointed to the U.S. failure to deal adequately with the aftermath of the Iraq war as one reason for the rise of the Islamic State in Iraq and Syria or ISIS, also known as ISIL. After 2011, ISIS became a powerful force in Iraq and neighboring Syria, which faced a civil war. Over the next few years, ISIS captured territory in Syria and Iraq, where it fought Syrian government forces, some rebel groups, Iraqi military forces, and Kurdish Peshmerga troops.[39]

Over time, public support for the Iraq war withered, and the United States withdrew all of its combat forces in December 2011. By that time, 4,486 Americans had lost their lives in Iraq, and over 32,200 had been wounded. At the height of the Iraq war in 2007, the United States had more than 170,000 military personnel in that country and maintained some 505 military bases.[40] Beyond the obvious human toll, there have been varying estimates of the costs of the Iraq war, some higher than $3 trillion when short-term and some long-term costs (such as medical care and disability payments for veterans and interest on the national debt) are included.[41] Most of these cost estimates do not attempt to put a value on the number of Americans and other coalition forces killed or wounded, or the very large number of Iraqi civilians who died as a result of the war.

The box "Steps to Analysis: What Is the Cost of the Global War on Terrorism?" raises questions about how best to measure the costs of the Iraq war. In light of the objectives of the war, the successes and failures, and the overall costs, would you say the war was worth fighting, or not? Can the methods of cost-benefit analysis be applied to questions like this, or are such methods not really suitable for determining whether a war is justifiable or not?

By 2008, both policy analysts and elected officials began asking questions like this, in effect asking what else the country might have done with the money being spent on the Iraq war. On the campaign trail in West Virginia in March 2008, for example, then candidate Barack Obama made that argument: "Just think about what battles we could be fighting instead of this misguided war." For their part, journalists and policy analysts began counting what the roughly $12 billion per month spent on the war during 2008 would buy in other federal programs, such as health care reform, relief for homeowners unable to pay their mortgages, development of renewable energy sources, or fixing the Social Security system. The congressional Joint Economic Committee examined the same kinds of questions that year, concluding in one example that the money spent on the war in one day would be enough to enroll an additional 58,000 children in the Head Start program, make a year of college affordable for 160,000 low-income students through Pell Grants, or pay for 14,000 more police officers.[42] Do you think these are fair comparisons to make in trying to decide to continue a war?

Steps to Analysis

What Is the Cost of the Global War on Terrorism?

Although decisions to go to war rarely are based on economics alone, the costs of war are hardly insignificant. Here we look at several different estimates for the Iraq war. Before the war's launch in 2003, the Bush administration offered a worst-case estimate of $200 billion, and in September 2005, the Government Accountability Office (GAO) reported that the Pentagon's estimate for what had been spent by that date on the global war on terrorism (most of which was for the Iraq war) was $191 billion. This estimate did not include the cost of rebuilding war-torn Iraq and many other indirect costs of the war; the GAO also expressed concern that the Pentagon's cost estimates were of "questionable reliability."[a] By December 2005, military outlays alone totaled over $250 billion, a number that rose considerably over the next several years.

In late 2005, two independent economic analyses of the cost of the war in Iraq were completed. They reached different conclusions, both offering much higher estimates of the war's costs. This is chiefly because they included not only direct expenditures such as payments for military hardware and supplies and support for the troops, but some indirect and long-term costs as well. These included lifelong disability and health care payments to injured soldiers, the effects of the war on the price of oil, and interest payments on the national debt (money borrowed to pay for the war). Both studies acknowledged the difficulty of making such calculations with all of the intangible factors involved, such as loss of life and the value of a

stable and democratic Iraq. They also stated that many assumptions have to be made in the conduct of such analysis, as we discussed in chapter 6. Still, the conclusions were remarkable. One of the studies, noted in the text, put the cost at $3 trillion to $4 trillion by 2008, far higher than the initial 2005 estimate. A comprehensive tally by the *New York Times* on the tenth anniversary of the 9/11 attacks put the total U.S. costs of the global war on terrorism at a similar $3.3 trillion by counting both short-term and long-term costs, and both direct and indirect spending.[b]

- Which of these different ways of measuring the costs of the war makes the most sense?

- Is it fair to consider indirect and long-term costs when trying to estimate what a nation pays for a war, or should only direct costs be counted? Why do you think so?

a. U.S. Government Accountability Office, "Global War on Terrorism: DOD Needs to Improve the Reliability of Cost Data and Provide Additional Guidance to Control Costs" (GAO-05–882), September 2005.

b. Linda Bilmes and Joseph E. Stiglitz, "The Economic Costs of the Iraq War: An Appraisal Three Years after the Beginning of the Conflict" (New York: Columbia University, 2005). The study was updated in 2008 and reported in an editorial by the authors and a book: Linda J. Bilmes and Joseph E. Stiglitz, "Day of Reckoning," *Washington Post National Weekly Edition*, March 17–23, 2008, 27; and *The Three Trillion Dollar War: The True Cost of the Iraq Conflict* (New York: Norton, 2008). Excerpts from these studies can be found on Professor Stiglitz's webpage: www8.gsb.colum bia.edu/faculty/jstiglitz/. The *New York Times* summary can be found in Shan Carter and Amanda Cox, "One 9/11 Tally: $3.3 Trillion," *New York Times*, September 8, 2011.

Economic and Military Assistance: Foreign Aid

One of the most recognizable aspects of U.S. foreign policy today is economic and military assistance to other nations, or foreign aid. The United States has long helped other countries in need, and for many reasons. The one that is easiest to understand is humanitarian assistance, for example, following a natural disaster such as the catastrophic earthquake that struck Haiti in January 2010, the earthquake and tsunami that devastated parts of coastal Japan in March 2011, the typhoon that struck the Philippines in late 2013, and the Syrian refugee crisis in the Middle East in 2015 and 2016.

However, U.S. assistance more often than not has also served the nation's strategic interests. That is, aid often is given to nations where it can help to support U.S. foreign policy goals. For many years, a large percentage of foreign aid went to the Middle East, especially to Egypt and Israel, and a similar pattern continues today, with Israel, Egypt, Afghanistan, Jordan, Pakistan, and Kenya receiving large shares of the pie (see Figures 12-1 and 12-2).

According to figures compiled by the Congressional Research Service, in recent years about 28 percent of foreign aid money has gone for military purposes (for example, to acquire U.S. military equipment and training), about 32 percent for development purposes (such as health, family planning, environmental protection, and economic reform), about 16 percent for humanitarian ends (such as assistance for refugees and for food), about 6 percent for multilateral aid through international organizations, and most of the remainder (about 18 percent) for other political, economic, or security purposes (for example, to advance U.S. strategic goals in the Middle East). These allocations reflect presidential and congressional policy priorities, which can shift from year to year.[43]

The Clinton administration, for example, gave special emphasis to the promotion of sustainable development as a new strategy in the post–Cold War period, with attention to achievement of broad-based economic growth, stabilization of the world population, protection of human health, sustainable management of natural resources, and building of human capacity through education and training. The Bush administration modified these goals to focus on three "strategic pillars": (1) economic growth, agriculture, and trade; (2) global health; and (3) democracy, conflict prevention, and humanitarian assistance. Later, the administration identified five "core" elements of U.S. foreign assistance:

- Promoting transformational development, especially in the areas of governance, institutional capacity, and economic restructuring
- Strengthening fragile states
- Providing humanitarian assistance
- Supporting U.S. geostrategic interests, particularly in countries such as Afghanistan, Egypt, Iraq, Israel, Jordan, and Pakistan
- Mitigating global and international ills, including HIV/AIDS[44]

Early in his administration, President Obama signaled his intention to change U.S. foreign policy and foreign aid significantly, and a new set of goals and

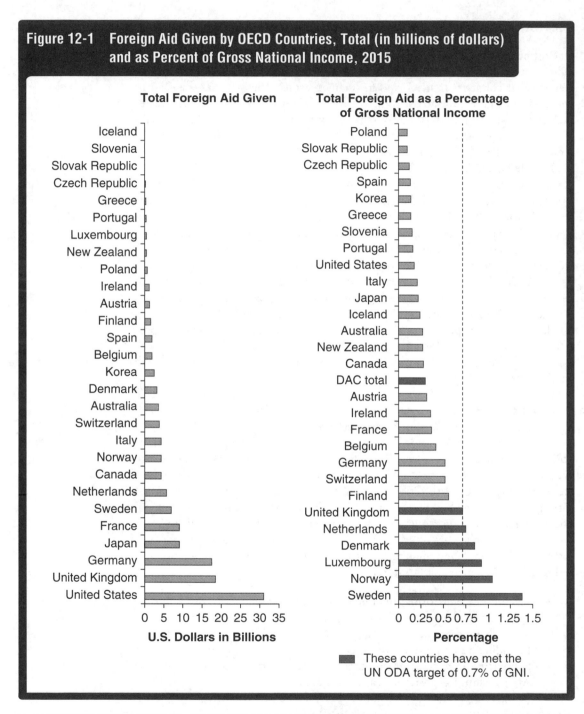

Figure 12-1   Foreign Aid Given by OECD Countries, Total (in billions of dollars) and as Percent of Gross National Income, 2015

Total Foreign Aid Given

Iceland
Slovenia
Slovak Republic
Czech Republic
Greece
Portugal
Luxembourg
New Zealand
Poland
Ireland
Austria
Finland
Spain
Belgium
Korea
Denmark
Australia
Switzerland
Italy
Norway
Canada
Netherlands
Sweden
France
Japan
Germany
United Kingdom
United States

0   5   10   15   20   25   30   35
U.S. Dollars in Billions

Total Foreign Aid as a Percentage of Gross National Income

Poland
Slovak Republic
Czech Republic
Spain
Korea
Greece
Slovenia
Portugal
United States
Italy
Japan
Iceland
Australia
New Zealand
Canada
DAC total
Austria
Ireland
France
Belgium
Germany
Switzerland
Finland
United Kingdom
Netherlands
Denmark
Luxembourg
Norway
Sweden

0   0.25   0.5   0.75   1   1.25   1.5
Percentage

■ These countries have met the UN ODA target of 0.7% of GNI.

Source: OECD (2016), "Compare Your Country—Official Development Assistance 2015," ODA 2015, available at www.oecd.org/dac/development-aid-rises-again-in-2015-spending-on-refugees-doubles.htm and www.oecd.org/dac/stats/ODA-2015-complete-data-tables.pdf (accessed on January 26, 2017).

Background and Policy Evolution

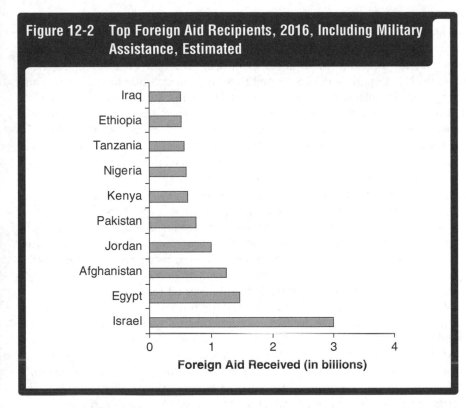

Figure 12-2 Top Foreign Aid Recipients, 2016, Including Military Assistance, Estimated

Source: Susan B. Epstein and Marian Leonardo Lawson, "State, Foreign Operations and Related Programs: FY2017 Budget and Appropriations" (Washington, D.C.: Congressional Research Service, October 5, 2016), www.fas.org/sgp/crs/row/R44391.pdf.

Notes: These are all requested amounts in Obama's fiscal year 2017 budget, not final congressionally authorized figures. Amounts for 2017 are not expected to differ much from the last year with confirmed figures, 2016.

priorities emerged. The president placed a high priority on reestablishing American leadership and standing around the world, particularly through more cooperation and partnerships with other nations than was evident in the Bush administration. He addressed some of the emerging global challenges more firmly as well, particularly climate change, population growth, the global financial crisis, and sustainable development. Former secretary of state Hillary Clinton, for example, emphasized the administration's commitment to renewed funding for reproductive health care through the UN Population Fund, as well as the bilateral family planning and reproductive health care programs, at the highest level in more than a decade. She also launched a new Global Health Initiative that committed the United States to spending $63 billion over six years to improve global health through investment in programs to prevent maternal and child mortality and unintended pregnancies, among other goals (Hook and Scott 2011). Donald Trump's administration is likely to change direction once again in its economic and military assistance programs.

The U.S. Agency for International Development (USAID) is the principal vehicle for the distribution and management of what is called bilateral economic aid—that is, money the United States sends directly to other nations. Most multilateral (or multination) aid is handled by the U.S. Treasury Department, and the U.S. Departments of State and Defense separately administer military and other security-related aid programs. Some of the multilateral aid goes to the UN or to other international organizations, which in turn distribute it through their own programs. The history of foreign aid dates back to the Marshall Plan and the reconstruction of Europe after World War II, and the agency took its current name in 1961 when President John F. Kennedy signed the Foreign Assistance Act and created USAID by executive order. USAID is an independent federal agency but works closely with the Department of State.

There is widespread misunderstanding over the level of foreign aid today, which also explains why the program is so often criticized as being excessive. Polls taken over the past decade have shown that most people think the amount the nation spends on foreign aid is too much; however, they have also believed that the nation devotes far more than it does to such programs. When told the United States spent about 1 percent of the federal budget on foreign aid, a large majority said that was about the right amount, if not too little; few thought it was too much. Over the past three decades, the United States spent between one-quarter and one-half of 1 percent of the nation's gross domestic product (GDP) on foreign aid; the Congressional Research Service puts this amount at about 1.3 percent of total federal budget authority.[45] Recent polls have found that a strong majority of Americans favored spending at least 0.7 percent of the nation's GDP—the UN target level—on foreign aid, or about four times recent levels of spending.[46]

Such findings are important for several reasons. It is clear that foreign aid is not popular, even if there is much misunderstanding about it. People tend to argue that unmet needs at home (e.g., health care, education, job training, improving the nation's highways, and much more) require that the money be spent here rather than abroad. There is also a widely shared belief that foreign aid does not reach those in need abroad but goes instead to corrupt officials or is simply wasted on inefficient and ineffective projects. It has been extremely difficult, therefore, to build public support for ambitious new goals to end world destitution, such as those adopted at the 2002 World Summit on Sustainable Development and set out in the UN Sustainable Development Goals that we described in chapter 11 (Sachs 2005, 2015). Many analysts believe that at least one solution is to improve the way foreign aid resources are used, particularly to fund only those projects with measurable, provable results (called "paying for results"). There are many such projects in developing nations that could meet such a test in areas as diverse as ensuring primary education for children, providing essential childhood vaccinations, delivery of vital health care services, supplying clean water, and improving agricultural productivity.[47]

U.S. spending on foreign aid is substantially lower today than it has been historically, particularly when viewed as a percentage of the nation's GDP, and yet the nation is still among the leading contributors to developing countries. According to the Organisation for Economic Co-operation and Development (OECD),

Challenges of foreign aid during times of war. Decisions on foreign aid can be complicated by ongoing and intense military actions, as made clear in Syria in 2016. The photo from December 2016 shows a Syrian boy who had been evacuated from eastern Aleppo, waiting to receive food aid inside a shelter in government controlled Jibreen area in Aleppo, Syria. *(Xinhua/Yang Zhen via Getty Images)*

shown in Figure 12-1, in 2015, the United States gave 0.17 percent of its gross national income to developing nations, well below the UN target level of 0.7 percent. This put the United States below most other developed nations in the world, down sharply from the level of 0.54 percent it donated in 1960 and the 1 to 2 percent it gave during the Marshall Plan era.[48] However, the actual dollar amount of U.S. aid was easily the highest in the world, at about $31 billion a year. How would you interpret these data? Should the United States be applauded for providing more money in aid than any other developed nation, or should we focus on the amount of aid given as a percentage of a country's overall economy, which suggests that the United States is not as generous as many other countries?

Selected Issues in Homeland Security

Homeland security as a focus of public policy did not begin with the terrorist attacks of September 2001. It has always been an important component of foreign and defense policy and of law enforcement activity at all levels of government. However, the level of government activity in homeland security and the kinds of efforts made were completely transformed after the 2001 attacks. In this section, we review the major activities and programs not already touched on earlier and examine several of the most prominent issues that have arisen in the past few years. Among these are the diverse responsibilities of the DHS, the varied homeland security threats that the nation faces, the special case of transportation security, and the conflict between pursuit of security goals and protection of citizens' civil liberties.

Most people probably associate the term *homeland security* with antiterrorist actions of the nation's intelligence agencies, military, and law enforcement bodies. Yet even the DHS defines its job in broader terms. It is responsible for dealing with natural disasters, protecting the nation's borders, handling immigration services, managing transportation security at airports, directing the movement of international trade across U.S. borders in ports and waterways, and supporting scientific and technological research that could improve the nation's capacity for security protection. Even the Secret Service is now part of the massive new department.

This form of organization and the preoccupation with international and domestic terrorism is problematic. The department is an awkward conglomeration of offices and programs, and many of its component agencies appear to have lost the professional capabilities they once had. One consequence can be seen in the ineffective response of the Federal Emergency Management Agency (FEMA), made part of the DHS at its creation, to Hurricane Katrina in September 2005. With its massive toll in lives lost and economic damage, Katrina was a sign to many not only that FEMA was ill prepared to deal with natural disasters but that the DHS itself was organizationally dysfunctional and unable to handle similar threats to the nation's citizens. Many hope fervently that the department gains greater administrative capabilities over time, learns better how to communicate with the American public, and figures out how to set meaningful priorities in homeland security.

Comparing Homeland Security Threats: How Vulnerable Are We?

As the DHS itself openly acknowledges, the nation must learn how to identify and measure the various security risks it faces and also find a way to set priorities among them. No agency or government can possibly protect the United States fully against all threats to its security. So which ones are most important? For which might government action realistically prove to be effective? Which can be addressed at moderate cost? To its credit, the DHS is beginning to grapple seriously with such questions, which we can think of as the application of risk analysis, discussed in chapter 6, to a set of related public problems.

Consider the following list, which is derived from one account that the DHS developed over a decade ago, but which remains, as it said at the time, "troubling vulnerabilities that have yet to be seriously addressed" by the nation despite the great attention to security issues and the large investment of public funds:

- Large chemical plants that could endanger one million or more individuals in a worst-case attack. The Environmental Protection Agency identified 123 such plants, but little has been done to protect them. The chemical industry has resisted the imposition of stronger safety measures.
- Use of a so-called dirty bomb, a compact nuclear device, in a major urban center. The concern here is the international capacity to identify and secure nuclear materials, especially in nations of the former Soviet Union.

- Nuclear power plants or nuclear waste storage facilities that could become the focus of an attack from the air or ground. Current security measures may prove ineffective.
- Insufficient security at the nation's ports. The question is whether sufficient security exists to prevent a weapon of mass destruction from being brought into the country through one of the millions of shipping containers that arrive every year, mostly without inspection (discussed below).
- Hazardous waste transport, in trucks and on rails, much of it through populated urban areas. How adequate are the regulatory measures for the movement of such material?
- Bioterrorism, especially release of a deadly toxin in an urban area. The concern here is the adequacy of security at laboratories that house such materials.[49]

Is one of the risks of greater importance than the others? How would you go about determining that? Recall the discussion in chapter 6 on risk assessment as you consider these issues.

The DHS itself has lent support to such expressions of concern, and it is beginning to try to address the issues. In March 2005, one of its internal studies that the department did not intend for public release was inadvertently posted on a state government website and picked up by the press. The National Planning Scenarios identified fifteen possible threats to the nation, some by terrorists, some by natural disasters, and some by disease outbreaks. It then estimated the likely economic and human costs of each. At the upper end of the scenarios was a biological disease outbreak not related to terrorism, a flu pandemic that could kill eighty-seven thousand people, hospitalize three hundred thousand, and cost the nation $70 to $160 billion in economic impacts. Several natural hazards could be equally devastating, such as a 7.2 magnitude or higher earthquake in a large city, or severe flooding following intense rainstorms. Yet various forms of terrorism could exact a very high toll as well, particularly actions directed at chemical storage tanks near urban areas or detonation of a small nuclear device.[50]

One thing that such a comparison of risks and costs tells us is that despite the many actions taken since 9/11, the nation remains vulnerable to a variety of harmful events, many of which have not been directly addressed with current federal priorities. The bombing of the Boston Marathon in April 2013 reminded the nation that terrorist threats remain real. Three people were killed and more than 260 injured, many severely. The number of those killed and injured puts the Boston attack in the ranks of the most notable of such actions in recent American history, including the 1993 World Trade Center attack, the Oklahoma City bombing of 1995, and the 9/11 attacks. Other attacks since that time in San Bernardino, California, and Orlando, Florida, resulted in even more deaths. By some measures, the decade following 9/11 saw far fewer attacks than the decade prior to it. No doubt the greatly enhanced level of security one sees today and the many ways in which law enforcement has been improved account for a good part of the decline.[51]

Nonetheless, is the United States today adequately prepared to protect the public against terrorists who might be wielding biological agents or using other exotic technologies? Some assessments over the past decade have expressed doubt about that.[52] Increasingly, analysts also worry about new kinds of threats, such as cyberterrorism, where terrorists gain access to governmental or private sector computer networks that are critical to maintaining the nation's economy and infrastructure. Possible targets include power plants, trains, oil and gas pipelines, financial institutions, and the electrical grid. However measured, it is now evident that cybersecurity risks have risen substantially in recent years. Indeed, controversy over hacked e-mail communications of the Democratic Party became a significant issue in the 2016 presidential election.[53] Luckily, so far the attacks have focused on gaining information rather than sabotaging the operation of these computer systems.[54] In sum, the DHS and other federal, state, and local agencies have learned much since 9/11 about how to prevent terrorist attacks and how to respond to them should they occur. Yet it is equally clear that much more could be done.

The Case of Transportation Security

One way to assess the effectiveness to date of antiterrorism efforts is to examine transportation security, which was made a high priority following the hijacking of the airliners used in the 9/11 attacks. Since that time, airport security has undergone a dramatic transformation, as anyone who has traveled by air in recent years is well aware. Airport security was federalized, and the number of airport security agents increased substantially. There is now elaborate, costly, and time-consuming screening of baggage and passengers. Other airport personnel have undergone special training, airliners have been retrofitted to greatly reduce the risk of hijacking, and armed federal agents now travel on selected flights. The task is massive. The Transportation Security Administration (TSA) at the DHS has a 2017 fiscal year budget of $7.6 billion, employs over forty thousand transportation security officers at more than 450 airports and other transportation centers in the nation, and screens nearly two million passengers each day, or about seven hundred million people per year as well as hundreds of millions of pieces of luggage. These are impressive numbers, but do they tell us how effective the TSA has been in reducing security risks? Is it even possible to know that?

By one important measure, the TSA has been remarkably effective. As of early 2017, there have been no further hijackings of U.S. aircraft and no terrorist incidents at airports, although there have been such incidents at other airports around the world. But the added security for U.S. aviation comes at a substantial price and does not necessarily protect the United States adequately.

First, because of the rush to secure the nation's airports, a great deal of money was wasted. Numerous reports indicate that the TSA in effect "lost control of the spending" in an effort to meet a congressional deadline for added safety. High costs also have been linked to reliance on private contractors and a lack of sufficient management of them, much as we saw for the Iraq war effort.[55]

Second, the TSA itself reports that in recent years it has spent far more on airport security than for any other form of transportation. For example, in the 2000s, it spent nearly $5 billion on aviation security but only a small fraction of that amount on passenger rail service, buses, and other modes of surface transportation. Currently, the TSA spends about 80 percent of its budget on aviation security and only 2 percent on surface transportation security, that is, on trains, buses, highways, and marine transportation.[56] Is such an imbalance in security spending warranted in light of the different levels of risk for various modes of transportation? Would the nation be better served by spending a greater share of the funds on other forms of transportation that might also become terrorist targets?[57] The box "Steps to Analysis: Should Passenger Aircraft Be Equipped with Antimissile Defense Systems?" explores a terrorist risk that most people probably have not thought much about: possible attacks on passenger aircraft in the United States.

The DHS also has reported that there are about eleven million trucks and two million railcars that cross into the nation each year, and also some 7,500 foreign flagships that make over fifty thousand calls in U.S. ports annually. Some of those vessels carry shipping containers, a common way to move goods around the world today. More than twelve million cargo containers enter the United States annually at 360 seaports around the nation, reflecting the fact that about 90 percent of global trade is shipped via such containers. The newest and largest of these ships are up to 435 yards long and carry up to eighteen thousand containers. Until recently, relatively few of those containers, were inspected—and for good reason. U.S. Customs and Border Protection has said that inspecting the average twenty- to forty-foot container would take four customs inspectors four hours. With over thirty thousand containers entering the country *every day*, routine manual screening is not feasible.

Congress enacted the Security and Accountability For Every Port Act (SAFE Port Act) of 2006 to require that 100 percent of U.S.-bound ocean containers be scanned before they leave their foreign port of origin, but the act has yet to be fully implemented. Moreover, U.S. importers continue to urge Congress to eliminate the scanning requirement because they believe it adversely affects the flow of commerce. The DHS also has a Container Security Initiative that is to prescreen shipping containers at their point of origin at some fifty-eight ports around the world to identify high-risk shipments that might then be physically inspected or scanned. Development of new scanning technologies might improve the effectiveness of these kinds of actions.[58] Do you think we should do more to scan or inspect containers reaching U.S. ports? Can government agencies enhance security by doing so without harming the import of goods?

Some of the same kinds of concerns have arisen over protection of U.S. borders, which is one reason why immigration has become such a hot topic in the last few years. U.S. Customs and Border Protection says it is intent on "keeping terrorists and terrorist weapons from entering the United States," and that as the nation's unified border agency, it is "strategically positioned at and between our ports of entry to prevent further terrorist attacks on our nation." According to

Steps to Analysis

Should Passenger Aircraft Be Equipped with Antimissile Defense Systems?

There is rising concern about the spread of shoulder-fired missiles around the world (also called man-portable air defense systems, or MANPADS), and particularly after the fall of Muammar al-Qaddafi in Libya in 2011 where many such missiles were left unguarded. More than seven hundred thousand such missiles have been manufactured worldwide, and many thousands are unaccounted for, including some that the United States sent to Afghanistan during that nation's fight against the Soviet Union in the 1980s. An attack using any of these missiles could kill several hundred passengers on an airliner and also create an enormous economic impact on the nation, because airline travel would likely be severely restricted following such an attack.

Given these possible consequences, some have argued that the nation should seriously consider equipping passenger aircraft with defensive systems to guard against such missiles. The concern increased after September 11, 2001, for obvious reasons. There are several ways to thwart an attack through use of lasers to jam a missile's guidance system and other technology, and some are currently used for military aircraft. But none of these antimissile systems would be cheap. There are also many technical issues that would have to be resolved to make such systems workable for commercial airliners.

Would it be a good idea to better protect passengers on commercial aircraft by making such antimissile systems available or even mandating that airlines use them? The RAND Corporation, a policy analysis institute widely respected for its work on defense and foreign policy concerns, studied the proposal during 2004. It concluded that such systems are both too expensive and too unreliable to justify such action. Its calculations are interesting. RAND researchers found that installing such systems on the entire fleet of commercial airlines (about 6,800 planes at the time) would require up to $11 billion, with operating costs running an additional $2.1 billion per year. Over twenty years, it said, the cost could be as high as $40 billion. To put that amount into perspective, the federal government in recent years has spent a little over $7 billion annually for all operations of the Transportation Security Administration.

These numbers force the question of whether it would make sense to spend such large amounts of money on an unproven technology when spending funds in other ways could do much more to safeguard the nation. The director of RAND's homeland security program emphasized the need to consider such efficiency criteria: "Resources available for homeland security are limited, so we must strive to get the most benefit from our investment," he noted. "There may well be other strategy alternatives that could prove to be less expensive and considerably more effective." One alternative to the airliner-equipped antimissile defense system is to install systems at the nation's major airports. Shoulder-fired missiles are only effective during an airliner's take-off or landing (where they are close enough to strike the plane), so a land-based system might work as well.

By 2008, the Department of Homeland Security (DHS) had funded the first-ever tests of shoulder-fired missile defense systems for commercial aircraft carrying passengers. The DHS signed a $29 million contract for the laser systems, which were being installed on selected American Airlines aircraft flying between New York and California.[a] By 2014, Israel had completed its own tests of such systems and decided to begin deployment of its SkyShield system on commercial aircraft. But would such a system make sense in the United States, particularly given its very high costs?

Sources: Drawn from a news release from the RAND Corporation, "RAND Study Says Airliner Anti-missile Systems Too Expensive and Unreliable," January 25, 2005; and other news accounts. See Nancy Scola, "Should Passenger Jets Have Missile Defense Systems?" *Washington Post*, July 18, 2014.

a. The government has not been forthcoming about the results of these tests, but see one report in a private aviation journal: "Countering MANPADS," *Aviation Today*, November 15, 2010, at www.aviationtoday.com/regions/usa/Countering-MANPADS_71564.html#.U1klrss06po.

the agency, it is adopting a number of initiatives to live up to those expectations. Yet, according to independent accounts, costly programs involving the use of new technology have not proved to be very effective to date. Indeed, critics have complained that the use of new and untested (and expensive) technology, as well as continued reliance on computer systems that are out of date and ineffective, has created an "illusion of security," and that more needs to be done. Members of Congress also have called for strengthening of border defenses, even if money for transportation security has to be decreased to provide for it. In one such initiative, as discussed in chapter 5, the DHS worked for several years to construct a seven-hundred-mile fence along the U.S.-Mexican border, an effort that attracted plenty of critics who doubted its effectiveness.[59]

Focused Discussion: Civil Liberties in an Age of Terrorism

Following a terrorist attack in San Bernardino, California, in late 2015 that killed fourteen people, the FBI sought to unlock an iPhone used by one of the attackers to learn more about his connections and activities. Apple challenged a court order to unlock the phone as an "unprecedented step" that could jeopardize its assurances to iPhone owners of personal security through its exceptionally strong encryption technology. The dispute was a classic case that pitted the government's need to protect the nation from terrorists against citizens' right to privacy. It also illustrated well that law enforcement agencies need to devise new ways to investigate terrorism risks that reflect the technological advances in the twenty-first century we all take for granted.[60]

As discussed earlier in the chapter, a perennial issue for any national security action beyond its actual success in protecting the nation's security and whether the money is spent efficiently is the degree to which it may infringe on the civil liberties of citizens. As noted in the chapter's opening, sharp disagreement over publication of secret documents related to the NSA domestic surveillance system speaks to the continuing controversy and underscores how policymakers and the public appraise the trade-offs between security and liberty in very different ways. These conflicts concern the use of surveillance technology as authorized by the USA PATRIOT Act and other legislation whose chief purpose is to detect possible terrorist activity. We examine arguments related to the likely effectiveness of such surveillance as well as legal and ethical concerns.

Effectiveness and Efficiency

There are few direct measures of effectiveness in the nation's war on terrorism, including policy actions to improve homeland security through the use of surveillance technology. That is, government agencies such as the FBI, CIA, and NSA make thousands of decisions and accumulate untold quantities of data on possible terrorists and their activities. But it would be exceptionally difficult to determine just how effective these efforts have been or whether the investments of agency budgets and staff time are worth the results achieved. Consider this possibility. The vast majority of actions taken by the NSA and FBI, including the kind of surveillance of citizens' e-mail and web browsing that has become common since the terrorist attacks of 2001, are not very effective in producing useful knowledge, but a few of them turn out to be critically important in identifying and apprehending suspected terrorists. Would you say that the overall effort is effective, or at least defensible? What about the efficiency of having government agents spending so much time on actions that prove to be fruitless? Is this of concern? The difficulty of evaluating the effectiveness or efficiency of many anti-terrorist policy efforts has significant implications. It means that policy proposals and defense or criticism of existing policies, such as the PATRIOT Act, often are framed in terms of support for the intelligence or law enforcement agencies, a determination to stop terrorism at any cost, or an equal determination to defend the civil rights of citizens under any circumstances that may exist.

Rep. F. James Sensenbrenner Jr., R-Wis., has been one of the most fervent supporters in Congress of the PATRIOT Act and as a high-ranking member of the House Judiciary Committee held an influential policymaking position. "It is not by luck that the United States has not been attacked since September 11, 2001," he said in July 2005, following terrorist bombings in London. "It is through increased cooperation and information sharing among law enforcement and intelligence agencies as well as the enhanced domestic security and investigative tools contained in legislation such as the PATRIOT Act."[61]

Like Sensenbrenner, the Bush administration was convinced that the act was working, and in 2005, it sought congressional approval to make all of its provisions permanent, without any major changes. Indeed, it asked for additional legal authority to track terrorists. Former attorney general Alberto Gonzales put the case this way in his testimony before the Senate Judiciary Committee in April 2005: "The tools contained in the USA PATRIOT Act have proven to be essential weapons in our arsenal to combat the terrorists, and now is not the time for us to be engaging in unilateral disarmament [by not renewing the act's provision]." At least some members of Congress were not persuaded, in part because the administration was reluctant to share information with Congress about just how it had used the act and what effects its provisions had. Said longtime critic of the act, then senator Russell D. Feingold, D-Wis.: "I do think the administration, by its lack of candor and its unwillingness to provide basic information, has caused the movement across the country against the PATROIT Act to grow."[62] Based on these kinds of statements, how effective do you think the PATRIOT Act has been? What kind of information would you need to determine that with some confidence?

These debates have recurred each time the PATRIOT Act has come up for renewal. For example, in 2005, as Congress was deeply immersed in debates over renewal of the act, President Bush made a startling announcement. He acknowledged that he had ordered the NSA to conduct electronic eavesdropping on individuals *without* first requesting a warrant from judges who serve on the special

Foreign Intelligence Surveillance Court as the law seems to require. He claimed the action was essential in the war on terrorism, and that his authority for such orders came from his role as commander in chief: "I think most Americans understand the need to find out what the enemy's thinking," the president said.[63] His actions meant that the NSA could intercept international communications of those with known links to al-Qaeda and other terrorist organizations, which Bush defended as a "vital tool in our war against the terrorists." That is, the president strongly believed that such surveillance was not only effective in reaching its goals but also critical to the nation's security. Another assessment, mandated by Congress and produced by inspectors general in five federal agencies in 2008, reached a quite different conclusion. It found that other intelligence tools provided more timely and detailed information than that coming from warrantless wiretapping, which it concluded was of "limited value" in the war on terrorism.[64] Particularly in light of the new study, was the Bush administration justified in its decision to authorize such wiretapping? Do you think the policy was effective enough to keep it?

Concerns about the efficiency of such surveillance also have long been voiced, particularly by the FBI, which had the task of dealing with massive amounts of information sent to it by the NSA. According to news accounts, in the months after the September 11 attacks, FBI officials "repeatedly complained to the spy agency that the unfiltered information was swamping investigators." The agency reported that virtually all of the thousands of tips it received each month led to "dead ends or innocent Americans," and thus diverted agents from counterterrorism work that they considered to be more important. The NSA itself, however, has continued to view the surveillance program as a valuable source of information that was not available anywhere else.[65] As noted in the chapter's opening, it was precisely the NSA's surveillance activities of this kind that led Edward Snowden to leak information about the agency's actions. In 2013, the Obama administration ordered a review of surveillance policy, yet the president continued to defend both domestic surveillance and the gathering of intelligence on foreign leaders, including U.S. allies. Some members of Congress, however, including Sen. Patrick Leahy, D-Vt., and Rep. Sensenbrenner, introduced legislation designed to end what the press has called the "bulk collection of Americans' communications data." The administration said that such data collection is authorized by the PATRIOT Act.[66]

Legal and Ethical Concerns

In addition to judgments about the effectiveness or efficiency of government efforts in the war on terrorism, policy debates turn on questions of legality with respect to several elements of current law and the Constitution. Closely aligned with these questions are concerns over one of the ethical aspects of policy that we have discussed throughout the text. This relates to individual rights, or liberty in the face of government actions to pursue policy goals.

The USA PATRIOT Act is the short name (and acronym) for the Uniting and Strengthening America by Providing Appropriate Tools Required to Intercept and Obstruct Terrorism Act of 2001. This law, rushed through Congress forty-five days after the 2001 terrorist attacks, has sweeping implications for both national security and civil liberties, as the statements above suggest. There was limited debate over its provisions at that time, but a belief among policymakers that something extraordinary was needed to protect the nation after the shocking experience of 9/11. In particular, President Bush argued that the administration needed additional tools to combat terrorism, including expansion of federal investigating authority. Congress approved the act after extended and difficult negotiations both within Congress and between Congress and the administration. There was, however, a great deal of concern expressed within Congress over how the act would be implemented and how it would affect both presidential power and individual rights (Wolfensberger 2005).

The PATRIOT Act emphasized empowering the government to monitor communications, detect signs of terrorist activities, and take action against suspected terrorists. Clearly, there was a belief in Congress and in the White House that such surveillance would help in the difficult task of identifying suspicious individuals, gaining critical information about them and their activities, and preventing possible terrorist attacks. A minority of members expressed concern about the implications for civil liberties and the necessity to place limits on the exercise of executive authority.

Well before the news of late 2005 regarding presidential approval of NSA surveillance practices, and the renewed concerns sparked by Snowden's release of NSA files in 2013, many critics of the PATRIOT Act had voiced these concerns about civil liberties. For example, the American Civil Liberties Union (ACLU) pointed to a "lack of due process and accountability [that] violates the rights extended to all persons, citizens and non-citizens, by the Bill of Rights." Among other complaints, it said the PATRIOT Act threatened a return to illegal actions taken by the FBI in the 1950s, 1960s, and 1970s, when it "sought to disrupt and discredit thousands of individuals and groups engaged in legitimate political activity."[67] Some four hundred resolutions expressing some kind of opposition to parts of the act were approved by state and local governments around the nation, from both political parties and all points on the ideological spectrum. Although they had varying reasons for their opposition, opponents included civil libertarians, gun rights advocates, the American Conservative Union, librarians, doctors, and business organizations. As the press reports put it, the biggest complaint about the act was that it would not sufficiently protect civil liberties. Critics also raised the same concerns during the 2013 controversies over the NSA's activities.[68]

When the controversies both in 2005 and in 2013 hit the newspapers, many members of Congress raised other legal and political issues. For one thing, some charged that the president's actions were illegal under current law, the Foreign Intelligence Surveillance Act of 1978 (FISA), unless first authorized by the Foreign Intelligence Surveillance Court. In early 2006, after several members of Congress asked it to weigh in on that particular dispute, the nonpartisan Congressional Research Service concluded that Congress did not appear to have given the president the legal authority to order such surveillance without a court-issued warrant.[69] President Bush's defense of his actions in 2005 did little to convince his opponents in Congress, and the year ended with only a temporary extension of the act. The debate continued in 2006 and is ongoing today, although it was much less visible until the extensive media coverage of domestic surveillance activities following Snowden's release of NSA documents. In March 2006, Congress voted overwhelmingly to renew the PATRIOT Act, giving the Bush administration most of what it had sought. However, critics in Congress also promised an investigation into the president's use of domestic surveillance without court approval.

In 2007 and 2008, Congress considered several key amendments to FISA to bring it up to date by explicitly covering Internet communication, which was not addressed in the original 1978 legislation. That action raised anew the many conflicts between the Bush administration and Congress over the president's assertion that he had the legal authority to intercept any telephone calls or e-mail communications from citizens without first obtaining a warrant. The revised law also protected telecommunications companies that cooperated with the Bush administration's warrantless wiretapping program by granting immunity from lawsuits. Ultimately, however, Congress acquiesced to most of the president's demands, making it easier for the government to wiretap U.S. phone and computer lines in its search for possible terrorists. This was the most significant revision of the law in a generation. Yet, as a political compromise, it skirted some of the most controversial elements, and even people familiar with the issues reported that they found the new policy hard to understand. In 2011, Congress once again approved and President Obama signed into law an extension of key provisions of the USA PATRIOT Act, with the Senate voting, 73–23, for the renewal, and the House approving by a margin of 250–153. The act continued surveillance powers until June 1, 2015, and shortly after that date, Congress once again approved extension of the act (voting by 67–32 in the Senate and 338–88 in the House). President Obama signed the USA Freedom Act in June 2015.[70]

The debate over precisely what legal rights exist in such circumstances is not new. A balance of sorts had been reached in earlier years to govern such actions by the NSA. After the end of the Vietnam War, where government surveillance of opponents of the war was a common practice, a new policy was set. Government spying on citizens would be prohibited unless very special circumstances required it. Those circumstances were to be examined, and the process regulated and supervised, by the courts to ensure that there was no abuse of power on the part of the executive branch. By one tally in 2004, the Foreign Intelligence Surveillance Court had issued more than 1,700 warrants since the September 11 attacks and had turned down only a handful of government requests for wiretaps. In an updated tally requested by then Senate majority leader Harry Reid, D-Nev., the Department of Justice reported that the court approved every single request made during 2012: 1,719 requests were made for wiretaps, and the court did not reject any of them, leading critics to doubt that the court exercised much, if any, independent judgment over the Justice Department or the NSA.[71] Would you be inclined to give the president the benefit of the doubt in these kinds of disputes, or to question the need to act without a court warrant? What might be done to help ensure that the Foreign Intelligence Surveillance Court exercises independent judgment and thus helps to limit unreasonable activities on the part of intelligence agencies or the Justice Department?

In a parallel development that did not attract quite as much attention in the nation's press, much concern was expressed in 2005 about the FBI's increasing use of so-called national security letters (NSLs) to gather data on U.S. citizens. Recently, the FBI has issued about twenty-five thousand NSLs each year—one hundred times the historical rate—in what one assessment called "a growing practice of domestic surveillance under the USA PATRIOT Act."[72] A single such letter—for example, to a librarian—can be used to mine or acquire data on many people at once, including the books they borrow from libraries and the websites they browse. Recipients of NSLs are permanently barred from disclosing their content, making it difficult to determine whether they are being used responsibly.[73]

The point of such data mining is to look for evidence of terrorist activities. However, the FBI needs no approval by a prosecutor, grand jury, or judge to issue such letters; nor is there any review of their use after the fact by the Department of Justice or Congress. Moreover, the data gathered in such broad searches are deposited into government databases, which are widely shared within the federal government and beyond it with state, local, and tribal governments, and even with private sector entities. The data gathered on innocent citizens and companies are not destroyed, but are kept in this system.

Is the FBI justified in using such NSLs in the search for terrorist activities? What potential is there for abuse of the information by the FBI or other agencies and organizations that have access to it? Are such broad sweeps of data collection a threat to the nation's civil liberties? It is no surprise that groups such as the ACLU have denounced the practice as potentially having "a profound chilling effect" on people's behavior. But does the war on terrorism require such unusual methods?

Even though they draw the line differently, both liberals and conservatives agree that it is imperative that the nation improve its gathering of information related to possible terrorism, including domestic intelligence. The essential question they must address is how best to balance competing needs of security and civil liberties. As the nation's intelligence agencies chart a new path under the reorganization plans discussed earlier, both the agencies and their overseers in Congress and the White House will be struggling to figure out how to combat the threat of terrorism without weakening the nation's historic commitment to citizens' rights. Concerns like these extend to homegrown security threats, including domestic antigovernment groups. According to the Southern Poverty Law Center, a group that tracts extremist organizations, the antigovernment militia movement has grown significantly in recent years. Partly in response to these trends, in 2014, then attorney general Eric Holder reestablished the Domestic Terrorism Task Force.[74]

There was little doubt that President Obama would change many of the Bush administration's policy choices on these issues. The president made this clear on his first day in office, when he ordered the closure of the Guantánamo Bay detention facility in Cuba—long a source of criticism for its treatment and prosecution of prisoners in the war on terrorism; however, Congress blocked the closure.[75] In addition, at the end of 2011, Congress enacted and the president signed the National Defense Authorization Act, which contained a controversial provision on the detention of persons suspected of aiding terrorism. Specifically, the act grants to the president (and to the military) the authority to indefinitely detain and interrogate such suspects, even if they are U.S. citizens who are arrested on American soil. That grant of authority was strongly opposed by civil liberties and human rights groups, among others. The president initially threatened to veto the bill, but ultimately he agreed to sign it as he faced a deadline for the expiration of military funding and after Congress made some changes in the measure that he sought. He also issued a statement upon signing the bill indicating that he had "serious reservations" about the provision. However, if the law stands, any president in the future could use that provision to justify such indefinite detention.[76]

It is not fully evident how President Obama changed domestic surveillance operations, but as of 2014, his administration generally drew the line much closer to civil liberties than did President Bush. For example, in his first few months in office, Attorney General Holder indicated that he would critically review the practice of warrantless surveillance and run the Justice Department with "transparency and openness." He also stated that he saw no reason why the war on terrorism could not be pursued without sacrificing American freedoms. Consistent with these beliefs and goals, in April 2009, Holder authorized the release of secret Justice Department documents that were used during the Bush administration to guide the CIA's interrogation of terrorism suspects (including the use of torture), an era that President Obama referred to as a "dark and painful chapter in our history."[77] In 2012, however, Holder asserted that it is lawful for the U.S. government to kill U.S. citizens if federal officials consider them to be operational leaders of al-Qaeda who are plotting attacks on the United States and when capturing them and conducting a trial is not feasible. That is, when terrorists present what the attorney general called an "imminent threat of violent attacks," the government has the "clear authority to defend the United States with lethal force."[78]

Throughout 2013, the Obama White House was highly critical of Snowden's release of classified NSA documents, and stoutly defended the need for continued domestic surveillance by the NSA and other intelligence agencies. However, by early 2014, the president acknowledged that the new high-tech surveillance programs could threaten civil liberties. He called for overhauling NSA's bulk collection of Americans' phone call records, but also wished to maintain many other components of the nation's intelligence programs, defending them as essential in the continuing war on terrorism.[79]

In 2016, Democratic presidential nominee Hillary Clinton suggested the creation of a national commission to examine both legal and practical questions surrounding surveillance and encryption technologies, and she indicated a desire to work with Silicon Valley technology leaders in developing new approaches that better balance these national security needs and individual rights to privacy. The Republican nominee and winner of the election, Donald Trump, did not address these concerns substantively, but he did propose several highly controversial steps during the campaign. The *New York Times* called them "draconian, unconstitutional measures to keep the nation safe, including carrying out surveillance of mosques and creating a database of Muslims."[80] The first year of the Trump administration should make clear what direction the new president decides to take.

Conclusions

This chapter surveys the evolution of U.S. foreign policy and the key institutions involved in its formation and implementation, and examines selected issues in homeland security. In keeping with the overall purpose of the text, it emphasizes questions of policy effectiveness, the efficiency with which government funds are invested in a diversity of competing programs, and ethical and political concerns that invariably arise as nations try to balance foreign and national security policy needs against the rights of citizens, as evident in the debates over the USA PATRIOT Act and the activities of the National Security Agency that were brought to light with release in 2013 of classified documents.

The implication is that students of public policy need to be knowledgeable about the major issues in foreign policy and homeland security, and also need to be able to evaluate key policy actions as well as the capabilities of the agencies charged with implementing them. To do that, you need to know how different types of policy analysis can build understanding of the issues and of the agencies themselves. In addition to questions of economic efficiency, such as the cost of weapon systems and wars, the chapter underscores the importance of political, legal, and ethical criteria, such as concern for civil liberties when governments engage in extensive domestic surveillance of citizens' phone calls and Internet use.

Although they appraise the risks differently and call for varied forms of action, analysts of all stripes point to a similar set of international problems with which the nation must now come to terms. These include economic globalization and its consequences for the United States; worldwide threats of diseases that spread more easily today than in earlier years; rising global use of energy, particularly fossil fuels that contribute to climate change; persistent poverty in developing nations; increasing demands on the world's natural resources to meet rising human needs; cultural and religious conflicts that threaten regional and world peace; and escalating international terrorism. All of these current and future challenges call for creative thinking, better analysis, and stronger leadership to discover viable solutions and to build public and political support for a new generation of public policy actions.

DISCUSSION QUESTIONS

1. Consider the widespread surveillance of citizens' phone calls and Internet use described in the chapter's opening and the concluding section. Is the NSA collection of this kind of data essential to protect the nation, or is it an intrusion on citizens' civil liberties? Why do you think so?

2. Based on the changes made in airport security since 9/11, do the more elaborate security systems appear to be working well? On the whole, do the new procedures seem to be justifiable? Does the emphasis on airport security appear to be excessive in light of other threats to transportation security, as discussed in the chapter?

3. Should the nation continue to try to reduce its stock of nuclear weapons and to work with other nations to do the same? Would doing so jeopardize the nation's security? What information

would you need to answer these questions with confidence?

4. Was the war in Iraq a success? What about the war in Afghanistan? Or efforts in recent years to combat ISIS in Iraq and Syria? How would you go about determining success in any of these cases? What standards would you use, and what kinds of information do you think you would need to make that judgment?

5. Review the data on foreign economic and military assistance provided in the chapter. Is the United States providing the right kind of foreign assistance to developing nations, and doing enough to address the problems that they face? Should the nation do more? What do you think is the best way to determine an appropriate level of foreign aid?

KEYWORDS

MAJOR LEGISLATION

Economic Cooperation Act of 1948 (the Marshall Plan)

Foreign Intelligence Surveillance Act of 1978 (FISA)

Intelligence Reform and Terrorism Prevention Act of 2004

National Security Act of 1947

Security and Accountability For Every Port Act (SAFE Port Act) of 2006

Uniting and Strengthening America by Providing Appropriate Tools Required to Intercept and Obstruct Terrorism Act of 2001 (USA PATRIOT Act)

USA Freedom Act of 2015

SUGGESTED READINGS

CQ Researcher, Issues for Debate in American Foreign Policy: Selections from CQ Researcher, 2nd ed. (Thousand Oaks, Calif.: CQ Press, 2012). Covers major topics in foreign policy, including drone warfare, terrorism and the Internet, turmoil in the Arab world, U.S.-China relations, the future of globalization, and climate change.

Katherine Hibbs Pherson and Randolph H. Pherson, *Critical Thinking for Strategic Intelligence*, 2nd ed. (Thousand Oaks, Calif.: CQ Press, 2017). An introduction to the use of critical thinking within the intelligence community.

Stephen W. Hook, *U.S. Foreign Policy: The Paradox of World Power*, 5th ed. (Thousand Oaks, Calif.: CQ Press, 2017). An introduction to U.S. foreign policy that addresses topics such as the global economy, friction between world powers, the influence of nonstate actors, and the domestic factors that affect U.S. policymaking.

Steven W. Hook and John Spanier, *American Foreign Policy Since World War II*, 20th ed. (Thousand Oaks, Calif.: CQ Press, 2016). A classic and comprehensive text on U.S. foreign policy that covers both traditional and newer issues, such as the Arab Spring uprisings and the shifting balance of global power today.

Mark M. Lowenthal, *Intelligence: From Secrets to Policy*, 7th ed. (Thousand Oaks, Calif.: CQ Press, 2017). An intelligence veteran writes about the sources and uses of intelligence in government policymaking.

Jeffery D. Sachs, *The Age of Sustainable Development* (New York: Columbia University Press, 2015). A leading development economist offers a broad introduction to global sustainable development ideas and practices, based on a massive open online course of the same name.

SUGGESTED WEBSITES

www.brookings.edu. Brookings Institution home page. Brookings releases many studies on defense strategy, homeland security, military organization and management, and military technology issues.

www.cia.gov. Central Intelligence Agency home page, with information about the agency, its history, its organization, its activities, and a variety of agency publications.

www.csis.org. Home page for the Center for Strategic and International Studies, a major independent research organization that studies defense and security policy, international affairs, and world trends.

www.defense.gov. U.S. Department of Defense home page, with links to the war on terrorism, military news, U.S. military forces and capabilities, a variety of fact sheets on the military and the Pentagon, and links to each of the military services and other defense-related agencies.

www.dhs.gov. U.S. Department of Homeland Security portal, with links to major issues such as immigration and borders, emergencies and disasters, security threats and protection, and travel and transportation.

www.fbi.gov. Federal Bureau of Investigation home page. Select the Terrorism link for detailed information about FBI programs and activities related to homeland security.

www.rand.org. Portal for the RAND Corporation, an independent policy analysis organization that has long studied military and national security threats. Does extensive and high-quality work on terrorism, international affairs, defense, and science and technology issues.

www.state.gov. U.S. Department of State home page, with links to a variety of international issues, the department's bureaus and offices, press and public affairs, travel and living abroad, countries and regions, and more.

www.un.org/en. United Nations portal, with extensive links to UN programs and activities, from the establishment of Sustainable Development Goals to actions of the World Health Organization in combating disease and promoting public health in developing nations.

http://worldpublicopinion.org. A website sponsored by the Program on International Policy Attitudes located at the University of Maryland that provides information and analysis of public opinion on international issues.

NOTES

1. Binyamin Applebaum and Eric Lipton, "Leaker's Employer Became Wealthy by Maintaining Government Secrets," *New York Times*, June 9, 2013; Charlie Savage, Edward Wyatt, and Peter Baker, "U.S. Confirms That It Gathers Online Data Overseas," *New York Times*, June 6, 2013; and Charlie Savage, "U.S. Outlines N.S.A.'s Culling of Data for All Domestic Calls," *New York Times*, July 31, 2013. On the estimate of security clearances, see Scott Shane and Jo Becker, "N.S.A. Appears to Have Missed 'Big Red Flags' in Suspect's Behavior," *New York Times*, October 29, 2016. The story explored how another Booz Allen employee who worked at the NSA, Harold T. Martin III, removed massive quantities of classified documents and digital files over a decade, and stored them at his home for unknown reasons.

2. Andrew E. Kramer, "Russia Extends Edward Snowden's Asylum," *New York Times*, January 18, 2017.

3. Editorial, "Edward Snowden, Whistle-Blower," *New York Times*, January 1, 2014.

4. Ravi Somaiya, "Pulitzer Prizes Awarded for Coverage of N.S.A. Documents and Boston Bombing," *New York Times*, April 14, 2014.

5. The DHS, with some 240,000 employees in 2016, was assembled in 2002 from twenty-two different federal agencies, many of which had never worked together. Surveys of federal employees regularly find high levels of dissatisfaction among its staff. In addition, scholars have characterized the department and its activities as constituting an "anemic policy regime" (May, Jochim, and Sapotichne 2011).

6. See the NSC website for a description of its work, membership, and history: https://obamawhitehouse.archives.gov/administration/eop/nsc/.

7. See Glenn Thrush and Maggie Haberman, "Bannon Is Given Security Role Usually Held for Generals," *New York Times*, January 29, 2017.

8. The numbers come from the U.S. State Department's history of the Marshall Plan, available at https://history.state.gov/milestones/1945-1952/marshall-plan.

9. See www.newworldencyclopedia.org/entry/United_Nations.

10. For an account of the cost of all U.S. wars in constant 2011 dollars, see Stephen Daggett, "Costs of Major U.S. Wars" (Washington, D.C.: Congressional Research Service, June 29, 2010). The CRS estimate of war cost includes only direct military operations and not the costs of veterans' benefits, interest on war-related debt, or assistance to allies.

11. These estimates come from the Center on Budget and Policy Priorities, and are available on its website: www.cbpp.org.

12. See the Obama White House Budget proposal for 2017 at the Office of Management and Budget: https://obamawhitehouse.archives.gov/omb/budget/.

13. The Congressional Budget Office offers a comprehensive overview of defense and national security spending at www.cbo.gov/topics/defense-and-national-security.

14. The budget documents can be found at https://obamawhitehouse.archives.gov/omb/budget/. Click on the latest fiscal year budget. Budget documents include "Historical Tables" that can provide a good idea of how spending has changed over time.

15. Lauren Chadwick and R. Jeffrey Smith, "Congress Buys the Navy a $400 Million Pork Ship," *Politico*, July 5, 2016.

16. See Christian Davenport, "The Air Force Is Close to Declaring the Controversial F-35 Ready for Combat," *Washington Post*, July 28, 2016; and Clyde Haberman, "Despite Decades of Stealth, Sticking Points Bedevil F-35 Jet," *New York Times*, January 24, 2016.

17. R. Jeffrey Smith and Ellen Nakashima, "Pentagon's Unwanted Projects in Earmarks," *Washington Post*, March 8, 2009; John Arquilla and Fogelson-Lubliner, "The Pentagon's Biggest Boondoggles," *New York Times*, March 13, 2011; and Christopher Drew, "Audit of Pentagon Spending Finds $70 Billion in Waste," *New York Times*, March 30, 2011. The $70 billion in waste was over just two years, according to a GAO study summarized in the article. See also Sydney J. Freedberg Jr., "Fix It. Again," *National Journal*, April 25, 2009, 38–41.

18. Scot J. Paltrow, "Unaccountable: The High Cost of the Pentagon's Bad Booking," *Reuters*, November 18, 2013.

19. See Rajiv Chandrasekaran, "A Brand-New U.S. Military Headquarters in Afghanistan. And Nobody to Use It," *Washington Post*, July 11, 2013. On flawed and unnecessary construction projects, see also Matthew Rosenberg, "Report Links Failed Afghan Project to Soldiers' Deaths," *New York Times*, July 23, 2013; and Erin Cunningham, "The U.S. Spent Billions Building Roads in Afghanistan. Now Many of Them Are Beyond Repair," *Washington Post*, October 30, 2016.

20. Christian Davenport, "How the Pentagon Spent $43 Million on a Single Gas Station," *Washington Post*, November 2, 2015.

21. Elizabeth Bulmiller and Thom Shanker, "Defense Budget Cuts Would Limit Raises and Close Bases," *New York Times*, January 26, 2012. See also Craig Whitlock and Bob Woodward, "Pentagon Buries Evidence of $125 Billion in Bureaucratic Waste," *Washington Post*, December 5, 2016.

22. Of course, part of the concern in strategic analysis is that not all nations are rational in this way. One might think it can win with a first strike despite the likelihood of severe retaliation. Similarly, some nations may be so motivated by ideology or other political and cultural beliefs that they are prepared to launch such an attack despite the consequences.

23. Steven Pifer, "NATO, Nuclear Weapons and Arms Control" (Washington, D.C.: Brookings Institution Arms Control Series, Number 7, July 2011), available at www.brookings.edu/research/papers/2011/07/19-arms-control-pifer.

24. John M. Donnelly, "Debate Yields to Deployment as Missile Defense Takes Off," *CQ Weekly*, September 11, 2004, 2090–2096.

25. Peter Baker and Dan Bilefsky, "Russia and U.S. Sign Nuclear Arms Reduction Pact," *New York Times*, April 8, 2010. For an update through 2014, see Stephen Pifer, "How U.S.-Russia Relations Complicate Obama's Nuclear Arms Legacy," April 2, 2014, available at the

Brookings Institution: www.brookings.edu/blog/
up-front/2014/04/02/how-u-s-russia-relations-
complicate-obamas-nuclear-arms-legacy/. For a
thorough and frequently updated account of how
many nuclear warheads each nation has, see the
website of the Arms Control Association: www
.armscontrol.org/factsheets/Nuclearweapons
whohaswhat.

26. For both sides on the debate, see "Room for
Debate: A Nuclear Arsenal Upgrade," *New York
Times*, October 26, 2016.

27. Central Intelligence Agency, "History," available
at www.fas.org/irp/cia/ciahist.htm.

28. Taken from the Office of the Director of National
Intelligence website: www.dni.gov/index.php/
intelligence-community/members-of-the-ic#nsa.

29. David Johnson, "Report of 9/11 Panel Cites
Lapses by C.I.A. and F.B.I," *New York Times*,
July 25, 2003, A12–A13.

30. See also Philip Shenon, "9/11 Report Calls for a
Sweeping Overhaul of Intelligence," *New York
Times*, July 23, 2004. The full report of the 9/11
Commission is available at www.9-11commis
sion.gov. See also a harsh critique of the various
intelligence failures as well as the proposed and
adopted reforms in Paul R. Pillar, *Intelligence and
U.S. Foreign Policy: Iraq, 9/11, and Misguided
Reform* (New York: Columbia University Press,
2011).

31. Greg Miller, "Budget 2012: CIA/Intelligence
Agencies," *Washington Post*, February 14, 2011.
Some critics also charge that a sizeable portion
of the intelligence budget is outsourced, going to
private-sector contractors and consultants such
as Booz Allen and SAIC—many of whom are
exempt from public oversight. See Harry Hurt III,
"The Business of Intelligence Gathering," *New
York Times*, June 15, 2008.

32. See Philip Shenon, "Next Round Is Set in Push
toward Intelligence Reform," *New York Times*,
December 20, 2004. A summary of the law
can be found in Martin Kady II, "Details of
the Intelligence Overhaul Law," *CQ Weekly*,
February 21, 2005, 464–468. The website for
the Office of the Director of National Intelligence

provides considerable detail about the new
programs: www.dni.gov.

33. Scott Shane, "Blair Pledges New Approach to
Counterterrorism," *New York Times* online
edition, January 23, 2009; and Joby Warrick,
"A New Wave of Threats," *Washington Post
National Weekly Edition*, November 24–30,
2008, 6. The website for the Office of the Director
of National Intelligence contains a vast amount
of information on the seventeen intelligence agencies and organizations and their activities: www
.dni.gov.

34. See a summary of the report in an editorial,
"What Remains to Be Done," *New York Times*,
September 4, 2011. On intelligence failures to
detect a terrorist plan to blow up a passenger
plane in flight, see Mark Mazzetti and Eric Lipton,
"U.S. Spy Agencies Failed to Collate Clues on
Terror," *New York Times*, December 31, 2009;
and Shane Harris, "Too Much Information,"
National Journal, January 30, 2010, 35–39.

35. See Mark Mazzetti and Scott Shane, "Bush
Overstated Evidence on Iraq, Senators Report,"
New York Times, June 6, 2008.

36. Steven Lee Myers, "Marking 5 Years, Bush
Insists U.S. Must Win in Iraq," *New York Times*,
March 20, 2008.

37. See Philip Ewing and Edward-Isaac Dovere,
"Obama to Keep 9,800 Troops in Afghanistan,"
Politico, May 27, 2014, available at www
.politico.com/story/2014/05/obama-afghanistan-
troops-after-2014-us-107105.html; and Mark
Landler, "U.S. Troops to Leave Afghanistan by
Late 2016," *New York Times*, May 27, 2014.

38. See, for example, Bruce Hoffman's *Inside
Terrorism* (New York: Columbia University Press,
1999), and work by the RAND Corporation's
Center for Terrorism Risk Management Policy.
Hoffman directs RAND's Washington, D.C.,
office.

39. For an account of ISIS's history and actions that
is regularly updated, see a Stanford University
site called Mapping Militant Organizations, at
http://web.stanford.edu/group/mappingmilitants/
cgi-bin/groups/view/1.

40. Thom Shanker, Michael S. Schmidt, and Robert F. Worth, "In Baghdad, Panetta Leads Uneasy Moment of Closure," *New York Times*, December 15, 2011.

41. David M. Herszenhorn, "Estimates of Iraq War Cost Were Not Close to Ballpark," *New York Times*, March 19, 2008; and Shan Carter and Amanda Cox, "One 9/11 Tally: $3.3 Trillion," *New York Times,* September 8, 2011. Nobel Prize–winning economist Joseph E. Stiglitz has one of the higher estimates. As noted in chapter 6, these estimates include long-term health care and disability costs for veterans, the impact of the rising national debt attributable to the war, and wider economic effects, such as part of the cost of rising oil prices. Linda Bilmes and Stiglitz are the authors of *The Three Trillion Dollar War: The True Cost of the Iraq Conflict* (New York: Norton, 2008), and they also maintain a website on the subject, including what they describe as "lessons from Iraq," at http://threetrilliondollar war.org. Some analysts say the long-term total cost could grow to over $6 trillion if interest over the next four decades is counted.

42. John M. Broder, "Views on Money for Iraq War, and What Else Could Be Done with It," *New York Times*, April 14, 2008; and Bob Herbert, "The $2 Trillion Nightmare," *New York Times*, March 4, 2008.

43. Taken from Curt Tarnoff and Marian L. Lawson, "Foreign Aid: An Introduction to U.S. Programs and Policy" (Washington, D.C.: Congressional Research Service, June 17, 2016). The original sources of the data are USAID and the Department of State.

44. Ibid.

45. Tarnoff and Lawson, "Foreign Aid."

46. See Ezra Klein, "The Budget Myth That Just Won't Die: Americans Still Think 28 Percent of the Budget Goes to Foreign Aid," *Washington Post*, November 7, 2013.

47. See Tina Rosenberg, "How to Protect Foreign Aid? Improve It," *New York Times*, March 14, 2011.

48. Celia W. Dugger, "Discerning a New Course for World's Donor Nations," *New York Times*, April 18, 2005.

49. The list comes from the *New York Times*, February 20, 2005, but similar lists have been compiled by other sources. On the risk of bioterrorism, see Wil S. Hylton, "How Ready Are We for Bioterrorism," *New York Times Magazine*, October 26, 2011. On the continuing risks presented by hundreds of chemical plants and similar facilities, see Christine Todd Whitman, "The Chemical Threat to America," *New York Times*, August 29, 2012.

50. See Eric Lipton, "U.S. Lists Possible Terror Attacks and Likely Toll," *New York Times*, March 16, 2005. See also Daniel Benjamin and Steven Simon, *The Next Attack: The Failure of the War on Terror and a Strategy for Getting It Right* (New York: Times Books/Henry Holt, 2006), on the failure of the war on terrorism and a review of continuing terrorist threats.

51. Scott Shane, "Bombings End Decade of Strikingly Few Successful Terrorism Attacks in U.S.," *New York Times*, April 16, 2013.

52. John Mintz and Joby Warrick, "Are Our Biodefenses Up?" *Washington Post National Weekly Edition*, November 15–21, 2004, 6–7.

53. David E. Sanger and Charlie Savage, "U.S. Says Russia Directed Hacks to Influence Elections," *New York Times*, October 7, 2016; and Sanger, "Under the Din of the Presidential Race Lies a Once and Future Threat: Cyberwarfare," *New York Times*, November 6, 2016.

54. John Seabrook, "Network Insecurity: Are We Losing the Battle against Cyber Crime," *New Yorker*, May 20, 2013, 64–70. The DHS maintains an extensive webpage on cybersecurity threats and its actions on them: www.dhs.gov/topic/cybersecurity.

55. Scott Higham and Robert O'Harrow Jr., "Securing the Homeland: The Government's Rush to Private Contracting Led to Abuse and Fraud," *Washington Post National Weekly Edition*, May 3–June 5, 2005, 6–7.

56. Justin Bachman, "After New York Attack, Congress Wants TSA to Secure Amtrak, Buses," *Bloomberg*, September 26, 2016.

57. For a comprehensive analysis of the risk and priority setting across different modes of transportation, see a March 2009 Government Accountability Office study, "Transportation Security: Comprehensive Risk Assessments and Stronger Internal Controls Needed to Help Inform TSA" (GAO-09-492).

58. "Countering MANPADS," *Aviation Today*, November 15, 2010, at www.aviationtoday .com/regions/usa/Countering-MANPADS_71564 .html#.U1klrss06po. See also the U.S. Customs and Border Protection webpage for a description of the Container Security Initiative: www.cbp .gov/border-security/ports-entry/cargo-security/csi/ csi-brief. For a critical appraisal of the container initiative, see the GAO report "Supply Chain Security: DHS Could Improve Cargo Security by Periodically Assessing Risks from Foreign Ports" (GAO-13-764), September 16, 2013.

59. Robert O'Harrow Jr. and Scott Higham, "'An Illusion of Security': Technology Problems Limit the Effectiveness of a Costly Program to Screen Visitors," *Washington Post National Weekly Edition*, June 6–12, 2005; and Tim Starks, "Committee Realigns Homeland Priorities," *CQ Weekly*, June 20, 2005, 1652. On the fence project, see Randal C. Archibold and Julia Preston, "Homeland Security Stands by Its Fence," *New York Times*, May 21, 2008; and Preston, "Border Patrol Seeks to Add Digital Eyes to Its Ranks," *New York Times*, March 21, 2014.

60. Katie Benner and Eric Lichtblau, "Apple Fights Order to Unlock San Bernardino Gunman's iPhone," *New York Times*, February 17, 2016; and Susan Landau, "The Real Security Issues of the iPhone Case," *Science* 352 (June 17, 2016): 1398–1399.

61. Quoted in Keith Perine, "Attacks Loom over Anti-Terrorism Law," *CQ Weekly*, July 8, 2005, 1902.

62. Ibid.

63. David E. Sanger, "In Speech, Bush Says He Ordered Domestic Spying," *New York Times*, December 18, 2005, 30; and Eric Lichtblau, "Bush Defends Spy Program and Denies Misleading Public," *New York Times*, January 2, 2006.

64. See Eric Lichtblau and James Risen, "U.S. Wiretapping of Limited Value, Officials Report," *New York Times*, July 11, 2009. The bulk of the study's findings were classified; only a thirty-eight-page summary was released. The five agencies included the Justice Department, the NSA, the CIA, the Defense Department, and the Office of the Director of National Intelligence. For an update on the Obama administration's position on how best to balance privacy and security, see Editorial Board, "Surveillance in the Post-Obama Era," *New York Times*, October 9, 2016.

65. Lowell Bergman, Eric Lichtblau, Scott Shane, and Don Van Natta Jr., "Spy Agency Data after Sept. 11 Led F.B.I. to Dead Ends," *New York Times*, January 17, 2006.

66. See New York Times Editorial Board, "The White House on Spying," *New York Times*, October 28, 2013; and Savage, Wyatt, and Baker, "U.S. Confirms That It Gathers Online Data Overseas"; and Savage, "U.S. Outlines N.S.A.'s Culling of Data for All Domestic Calls." See also James Risen and Laura Poitras, "N.S.A. Examines Social Networks of U.S. Citizens," *New York Times*, September 29, 2013.

67. The language comes from a flyer on the ACLU webpage: "The USA PATRIOT Act and Government Actions That Threaten Our Civil Liberties," available at www.aclu.org/FilesPDFs/ patriot%20act%20flyer.pdf.

68. Perine, "Attack Looms"; Michael Sandler, "Another Setback for Anti-terrorism Law," *CQ Weekly*, December 9, 2005, 3325; Charlie Savage and Edward Wyatt, "U.S. Is Secretly Collecting Records of Verizon Calls," *New York Times*, June 5, 2013; Risen and Poitras, "N.S.A. Examines Social Networks of U.S. Citizens."

69. Eric Lichtblau and Scott Shane, "Basis for Spying in U.S. Is Doubted," *New York Times*, January 7, 2006.

70. For a description of the new surveillance law, see Shane Harris, "Explaining FISA," *National Journal*, July 19, 2008, 66–70. For a history of a two-decades-long battle over domestic surveillance or wiretapping and limits placed on government's authority, see Shane Harris, "Surveillance Standoff," *National Journal*, April 5, 2008, 21–27. The 2011 renewal of key provisions is described in Paul Kane and Felicia Sonmez, "Congress Approves Extension of USA Patriot Act Provisions," *Washington Post*, May 26, 2011; and in Ellen Nakashima, "Senate Approves Measure to Renew Controversial Surveillance Authority," *Washington Post*, December 28, 2012.

71. The report to Sen. Reid is available in many locations on the Internet. One of them is the site for Common Dreams, "1,856 to Zero: Secret Spy Court Authorizes 100% of US Government Requests," available at www.commondreams .org/headline/2013/05/03-2. Interesting enough, the John Birch Society (www.jbs.org) also published the report on its site, with an equal expression of outrage about the court's actions. Nationwide, about twenty thousand requests a year are made by law enforcement for court orders approving searches of individuals' phone, e-mail, or online communications activities. See Spencer S. Hsu, "This Judge Just Released 200 Secret Government Surveillance Requests," *Washington Post*, September 23, 2016.

72. Barton Gellman, "The FBI Is Watching," *Washington Post National Weekly Edition*, November 14–20, 2005.

73. Barton Gellman, "FBI Mines Records of Ordinary Americans," *Washington Post*, November 6, 2005. For an updated account, see Maria Bustillos, "What It's Like to Get a National Security Letter," *New Yorker*, June 28, 2013, available at www .newyorker.com/tech/elements/what-its-like-to-get-a-national-security-letter.

74. Ron Nixon, "Homeland Security Looked Past Anti-Government Movement, Ex-Analyst Says," *New York Times*, January 8, 2016. The Southern Poverty Law Center regularly follows actions of antigovernment groups, and posts reports on its website: www.splcenter.org/.

75. Mark Mazzetti and William Glaberson, "Obama Issues Directive to Shut Down Guantánamo," *New York Times*, January 21, 2009. By late 2013, the closure seemed more likely to take place. See Stacey Kaper, "Obama, Congress Bring Guantanamo Bay Prison Closer to Closed," *National Journal*, December 23, 2013.

76. David Nakamura, "Obama Signs Defense Bill, Pledges to Maintain Legal Rights of U.S. Citizens," *Washington Post*, December 31, 2011.

77. Greg Miller and John Meyer, "Memos Reveal Harsh CIA Interrogation Methods," *New York Times*, April 17, 2009. See also Jane Mayer, *The Dark Side: The Inside Story of How the War on Terror Turned into a War on American Ideals* (New York: Doubleday, 2008).

78. Charlie Savage, "U.S. Law May Allow Killings, Holder Says," *New York Times*, March 5, 2012.

79. Mark Landler and Charlie Savage, "Obama Outlines Calibrated Curbs on Phone Spying," *New York Times*, January 17, 2014; and Savage, "Obama to Call for End to N.S.A.'s Bulk Data Collection," *New York Times*, March 24, 2014.

80. Editorial Board, "Surveillance in the Post-Obama Era."

PART IV

Conclusions

Chapter 13

Vote protection or suppression? North Carolina State University students wait in line to vote in the primaries at Pullen Community Center on March 15, 2016, in Raleigh. The North Carolina primaries are the state's first use of its voter ID law, which excludes student ID cards, and Wake County was among the highest in use of provisional ballots, where voters had home addresses on or near campuses. The Board of Elections was to review those ballots to determine if the vote should count. The state's voter ID law was still being argued in federal court in 2017. *(Sara D. Davis/Getty Images)*

Politics, Analysis, and Policy Choice

In May 2011, the Wisconsin legislature approved Act 23, which required that residents present an acceptable photo identification card in order to vote in state and federal elections. Republicans in the state had long sought to enact such a voter ID requirement, but Democrats consistently blocked their efforts. Republicans had argued that the measure would protect the state from voter fraud at the polls and inspire confidence in the integrity of the electoral process, while Democrats said the new law would suppress voting by minorities, college students, and the poor, elderly, and disabled. With the 2010 elections giving Republicans the governorship and both houses of the state legislature, the party had the votes to approve the new voter ID requirement and did so. Democrats decried the law, enacted at a time of political turmoil in the state as protests mounted against the newly elected conservative governor, Scott Walker.

The League of Women Voters of Wisconsin, the state chapter of the American Civil Liberties Union, and other groups and individual voters filed suit in both state and federal courts to overturn the voter ID law. They argued that it violated the Constitution's guarantee of equal protection under the law as well as the federal Voting Rights Act. At the time of its adoption in Wisconsin, eleven states had such a voter ID requirement, and over thirty states were considering adding or strengthening voter identification requirements, according to the National Conference of State Legislatures. By the 2016 elections, thirty-two states had such laws in effect, although legal challenges in a number of them constrained their use at that time. Many of these state efforts were inspired by draft legislation that was prepared by the American Legislative Exchange Council (ALEC), a conservative advocacy group active on a range of electoral policy issues that critics argued were designed to make it harder for citizens to vote and to erect barriers to direct democracy via ballot initiatives.[1]

The new Wisconsin law was one of the strictest in the nation, and it was explicit about the kinds of ID cards that could be used, with minimal exceptions allowed. They included a state driver's license, a state ID card, an ID card issued by a military service (but not a veteran's ID card), an ID card issued by a federally recognized Indian tribe in Wisconsin, a U.S. passport, a U.S. certificate of naturalization issued within two years of the election, or documentation showing that the individual has an application pending for one of the above. The law also allowed an unexpired ID card issued by an accredited Wisconsin university or college, but only if the card contained the date of issuance, the individual's signature, and an expiration date no later than two years from the date of issuance; if a student ID card is used, the individual also must present evidence that she or he is currently enrolled. At the time the law was approved, student ID cards at the University of Wisconsin campuses did not meet these conditions.[2] An official state ID card could be issued upon application, but certain documentation, including a birth certificate, would be required, and the cards were only available with a personal visit to a Division of Motor Vehicles (DMV) service center, and normally with an $18 fee unless a fee waiver is explicitly requested. DMV service centers are located in most of the cities within the state, but not in small towns, and they are open only between 8:30 A.M. and 4:45 P.M. on weekdays, and not on weekends. Were these overly restrictive requirements that could have kept the state's citizens from exercising their right to vote? Or were they a reasonable way to protect the integrity of elections and inspire confidence in the process of voting and vote counting?[3]

Supporters of the election law argued that a photo ID is needed for a wide variety of other activities, such as boarding a commercial aircraft, and that most individuals already have such a card, particularly a driver's license; hence, they say, the law imposed no substantial burden on potential voters. Opponents said that those without the ID cards faced unacceptable hurdles to voting, and also unreasonable barriers to ordering a state ID card that would allow them to vote. They noted as well that the only kind of voter fraud addressed by such legislation, voter impersonation fraud, is virtually nonexistent both in the state and across the nation. Indeed, one comprehensive assessment of election fraud in all fifty states between 2000 and 2012 found only ten cases in the country of voter impersonation fraud, or one case per year for the entire nation; more recent studies confirmed the extreme rarity of such voter fraud.[4]

All states must meet the minimum requirements that were set by the federal Help America Vote Act (HAVA) of 2002, which was enacted in the wake of the 2000 presidential election, with its many irregular procedures in the way ballots were counted. The voting in Florida was particularly controversial, and ultimately the U.S. Supreme Court had to resolve the election outcome in that state, giving George W. Bush the state's electoral vote and the presidency. Partly because of HAVA, about twenty states, much like Wisconsin, chose to require a photo ID for voting; another ten states required or requested some form of identification in order to vote. Such voter ID laws, as well as similar measures to restrict voter registration and absentee, early, and weekend voting, have been particularly favored in states with Republican legislatures and governors, and they got a big boost with the party's success in the 2010 midterm elections.[5]

Do such laws, as their supporters say, help to inspire confidence in elections and their outcomes? If some citizens are denied the right to vote because they lack an acceptable form of identification, is this fair? Or are these kinds of laws, as opponents argue, merely a partisan effort to reduce voting by those likely to vote for Democratic candidates? Despite the partisan warfare over these election laws, the Pew Research Center in 2012 reported that they enjoy broad public support. The center's survey found that fully 77 percent of registered voters in the nation agreed that citizens who are voting should be required to show a photo ID. The center also noted that this finding has changed little in recent years. Indeed, Gallup found in a 2016 survey that 80 percent of Americans favor a photo ID requirement.[6] Does public support for the laws mean that they are a good idea, or merely that most people are not well informed about the intention and impact of these laws?

These kinds of controversies reached the presidential election in 2016. When the Republican nominee Donald Trump was behind in pre-election polls, he argued forcefully that the election was "rigged" because of rampant voter fraud that he was convinced would prevent his success. Trump won the Electoral College vote, and thus the presidency, but he lost to Hillary Clinton in the popular vote count by nearly 2.9 million votes (2.1 percent), the largest raw vote margin of any losing presidential candidate in U.S. history. President Trump said he lost the popular vote only because "millions of people" voted illegally, an assertion immediately dismissed by state election officials and experts as having no basis in fact. As recounts initiated and paid for by Green Party nominee Jill Stein were under way or pending in three states (Wisconsin, Michigan, and Pennsylvania), Trump supporters filed suit in federal court to halt them. It is fair to say that none of these statements or actions was likely to inspire confidence in the electoral process.[7]

Even before the 2016 elections, the voter ID law in Wisconsin and similar laws in North Carolina, Texas, and other states faced multiple court challenges after their adoption. In Wisconsin, U.S. District Judge Lynn Adelman struck down Wisconsin's law in April 2014, saying that it violated the federal Voting Rights Act and the U.S. Constitution.[8] Adelman ruled that the state did not offer a convincing rationale for imposing the voter ID requirement because, in his words, "virtually no voter impersonation occurs in Wisconsin, and it is exceedingly unlikely that voter impersonation will become a problem in Wisconsin in the foreseeable future." He also said there is no empirical evidence that photo ID requirements have any effect on confidence or trust in the electoral process. Of special importance for this text, in drawing these conclusions, Judge Adelman cited and discussed recent social science and legal research and summarized the views of political scientists and other experts. He noted as well that as many as three hundred thousand residents, or about 9 percent of all registered voters, might be denied the right to vote under the new law because they lack a qualifying

ID, and he observed that this number exceeded the margin of victory in the most recent races for governor and U.S. senator in the state.[9] He found that the state's interest in mandating a photo ID to prevent voter impersonation fraud could not be justified in light of its likely impact on voting. In short, the judge relied heavily on policy analysis, as well as legal precedent, in making his decision in the case.

The groups supportive of the initial suit challenging the law celebrated Adelman's analysis of voter ID requirements and his ruling in the case. News of the judge's decision spread quickly across the nation's media, sparking a new round of debate over the necessity of such voter ID laws and their likely effects on the electoral process. Adelman's decision was overturned by the Seventh Circuit Court of Appeals in Chicago, but in 2016, another federal judge in Wisconsin, James Peterson, ruled against the state's law a mere four months before the November elections, calling it "a cure worse than the disease." He too expressed deep concern over possible voter disenfranchisement, and he demanded that the state take actions to minimize adverse impacts of the law. His ruling came on the same day that a federal appeals court overturned a similar voter ID law in North Carolina, and a week after a comparable decision against a Texas photo ID law. In contrast to these efforts to limit voting, some states have tried to make registration and voting easier, most notably Oregon, California, Vermont, West Virginia, and Illinois. As analysts continue to examine voting patterns in the 2016 elections, we should learn more about what impact the various voter ID laws had on the outcomes that year, as well as whether accusations of voter fraud or any other form of election fraud have sufficient merit to warrant changing election laws or procedures.[10]

Policy Analysis, Citizen Participation, and Policy Change

The controversies over voter ID laws and other state actions to alter electoral processes illustrate several themes that we address in this concluding chapter. The first concerns the substance of policy choices and the critical nature of policy design. As we have shown throughout the text, the way policymakers (or interest groups such as ALEC) design and advocate for public policies can make them more or less effective, efficient, and fair, and also spark intense opposition by those who object to the policy goals or the particular means to achieve those goals. There is no guarantee that policies will work or have the impact for which policymakers and the public hope. Even if they do, some other interest group or segment of the population might find their effects unacceptable, as was clearly the case for Wisconsin's voter ID law, and those in North Carolina, Texas, and other states where citizens mounted challenges to them. Sometimes careful thought and design of public policies at the earliest stages, and genuine efforts to seek bipartisan support for them, make a big difference and avoid unexpected consequences as well as the kind of partisan disagreements all too evident over voter ID laws.

Cases like this also illustrate the need for policy analysis and critical appraisal of governmental actions, whether at the local, state, or federal level. Just because some assert that a new law will improve state elections or governance—or the economy, education, or health care service delivery—does not make it so. It is always important to seek out other points of view and credible assessments by professional analysts or other nonpartisan observers. Whether applied to contemporary challenges, such as how best to promote the nation's economic recovery, how to ensure that the nation's food supply is safe, or how to make college education affordable, or to problems that will arise in the future, analysis can help to define the issues more sharply, focus public debate, and help the public and policymakers find the best solutions.

The case of voter ID laws also reminds us that public policy changes over time. What prevails in one time period may or may not continue to be favored by elected officials or by the American public. Voters can change their minds, or they can change the composition of the state legislature or Congress, sparking a new round of policy proposals and actions. One need only look to the varied state actions, some of them by state legislatures and others by state voters, that have brought about major changes recently in laws on marijuana use, the legality of same-sex marriage, collective bargaining by public employee unions, energy use and climate change, and more (Karapin 2016; Rabe 2016). Policy changes like those seen in the new state voter ID laws remind us as well that we may see more frequent and abrupt changes in public policy in part because state legislatures and Congress are increasingly characterized by sharply divergent party positions. Hence, election of a new party majority may bring with it a policy agenda that differs greatly from that favored by the previous one. Certainly that was the anticipation among voters who supported Donald Trump in the 2016 elections, but also in many ways among supporters of Hillary Clinton.

Finally, the voter ID case demonstrates the dynamics of the policymaking process as well as the opportunities that it affords to citizens. As we have stated often throughout the text, policymaking never really ends. It is an ongoing process of defining problems, developing solutions to them, selecting what we prefer to do, putting those solutions into effect, and then considering whether to continue or modify those policies depending on how well they are working and whether collectively we find the results to be acceptable or not. Precisely because policy decisions can have important effects on people's lives, those who feel aggrieved by a decision are moved to take action to amend it or overturn it. Individuals and organized groups on either side of a given dispute will make the best case they can and use whatever arguments and data—and political tactics—they believe will strengthen their position.[11] The political parties and elected officials are, of course, deeply involved in this process of policymaking, and ultimately politics in this sense strongly affects what kinds of public policies and governance we have.

All this is mostly good news for all of us. It means that at all levels of government we can choose to play an active role in decision making, sometimes by the simple act of voting on a ballot initiative and sometimes through deeper involvement in the political process, in government decision making, in judicial lawsuits over voter ID and other statutes, and in civic or community affairs in general. Initiatives and referenda, such as the Colorado marijuana legalization amendment that voters approved in November 2012 and similar actions by voters in California, Massachusetts, and Nevada in 2016, are unusual in that they offer citizens the chance to vote directly on public policy measures. But even if they are less directly involved in other kinds of policymaking, individuals can choose to participate in countless ways, particularly at state and local levels, where opportunities often are abundant.

Reversal of previously approved policy is not as unusual as might be thought. In November 2011, for example, voters in Ohio overturned the state's new law that limited collective bargaining rights for public employees. A union-backed citizen drive, We Are Ohio, put the measure on the ballot shortly after the Republican legislature and Gov. John Kasich approved it. After spending a reported $30 million on the campaign to reverse the policy, the citizen coalition won by 61 to 39 percent.[12] After the Wisconsin legislature and newly elected governor Scott Walker approved a similar and even more contentious state policy to eliminate nearly all collective bargaining rights for state employees (including most public school teachers), opponents gathered more than one million signatures to force a recall election for the governor (only the third in U.S. history) and hundreds of thousands of additional signatures to try to recall the lieutenant governor and four Republican state senators in special elections that were held in mid 2012. The governor won the recall election, but the state remained sharply divided on his performance throughout his four years in office, during his campaign for reelection in 2014, and well into his second term.[13]

As the presidential election of 2008 clearly showed, modern Internet technologies facilitate a much greater level of citizen involvement, even in national elections and governing. Voter turnout in 2008 was the highest in decades, especially among Democratic voters excited about their candidate, Barack Obama. Interest in the election, participation in the campaign, and voting in 2008 were particularly strong among younger voters, indicating an emerging potential for political activism among this segment of the electorate (McKenna and Han 2014).[14] By 2012, however, much of the enthusiasm of younger voters for the president had diminished, and the trend did not change appreciably in the 2016 election, although Bernie Sanders's campaign for the Democratic Party nomination in 2016 did spark great enthusiasm among millennial voters.

At the other end of the political spectrum, supporters of the Tea Party movement enjoyed considerable success in the 2010 midterm elections as well as in elections in 2012, and many were just as energized during Republican primary contests in 2013 and 2014, and beyond. They too relied increasingly on Internet technologies and reflected a new approach to grassroots political organizing (Skocpol and Williamson 2012; Williamson, Skocpol, and Coggin 2011). Moreover, pundits were suggesting that much of the political advertising and mobilization of voters in elections would take place on social network sites such as Facebook and Twitter, and that seemed to be the case for the 2016 elections. Equally important, however, is the increasing role played by fake news and extremist sites that propagate conspiracy theories and advance fringe perspectives on politics and political leaders. One analysis by *BuzzFeed News* showed that in the last three months of the presidential campaign, twenty fake news stories posted on Facebook led to more reader engagement (that is, shares, likes, and comments) than a comparable number of leading stories from genuine news websites.[15] Thus future campaigns may well take on a very different character compared to recent political contests.

Equally worrisome is that coverage by the leading television news shows in 2016 continued a trend of focusing on candidate characteristics to the near exclusion of reporting on their issue positions, which arguably are equally if not more important for advancing voters' interests. According to one accounting, from January through early November 2016, the three network evening news shows devoted a total of only thirty-two minutes to candidates' positions on public policy. Eight years previously, the figure was nearly seven times higher. Moreover, the news networks focused overwhelmingly on Clinton's use of a private e-mail server while serving as secretary of state but gave little attention to her policy positions.[16]

In the remaining sections of this chapter, we revisit the core arguments of the book and extend them to several contemporary challenges, especially as they relate to government's capacity to act on public problems and what might be done to improve that capacity as well as to build a vital democratic process for the future. The questions are exceptionally important today. Experience in both the Bush administration and the Obama administration made clear that government is not always well prepared to deal with the problems it faces, whether they concern global terrorism, financial market collapses, health care reform, or climate change. Policymakers do not always fully understand the causes of the problems, as was evident in the initial financial rescue plans directed at Wall Street banks in 2008, and they may be incapable of designing a coherent and comprehensive approach that stands much chance of working—simply because of the enormity and complexity of the economic system today. Even the economic experts are unsure of what to do in such cases. Much the same is true of climate change, as we saw in chapter 11, and many other challenging problems facing government today.

At the same time, at least some analysts and policymakers viewed the dire economic conditions of early 2009 as offering a unique opportunity to institute major policy changes. For example, the economic recovery plan that Congress approved in February 2009—the American Recovery and Reinvestment Act—and the budget message that Obama delivered to Congress shortly thereafter offered an ambitious policy agenda to "build a new foundation for lasting prosperity." It included sweeping changes in the nation's use of energy resources, a long-delayed plan to address climate change, a proposed overhaul of the nation's health care system, and plans to sharply increase spending on childhood education and college loan programs to "ensure that every child has access to a complete and competitive education, from the day they are born to the day they begin a career." The president clearly did not get everything that he sought, and the two parties were deeply divided by many proposed solutions, and remained divided in subsequent years. Yet the seriousness of the national economic predicament also sparked some new and creative ways of thinking about long-standing concerns such as rising federal spending and deficits, the costs of entitlement programs such as Social Security and Medicare, ways in which defense spending might be constrained, and the elements of an equitable tax system.

Public Policies and Their Impacts

Chapter 1 defined public policy as what governments and citizens choose to do or not to do about public problems. Such choices are made at every level of government through the kinds of policymaking processes outlined in chapter 3 and elsewhere in the book. General descriptions of policymaking are somewhat abstract, however, and do not convey how important those choices can be, especially the great impact they can have on people's lives. The examples are myriad. Social Security policy has enormous consequences for the ability of senior citizens to live in dignity and meet their most essential needs during what is often a financially difficult period in their lives. So too do health care policies such as Medicare and Medicaid, which provide insurance coverage when health care is urgently needed, expensive, and often beyond the means of many individuals. Education policies can affect every public school in the country, what children learn, and how well prepared they are for college or employment. Economic and environmental policies that shape human well-being in the short term can also have serious long-term effects, as the discussion of energy policy and climate change in chapter 11 indicated. In short, even though many people may not be aware of it, government and public policy matter a great deal.

Because policymaking involves a specification of policy goals as well as the means used to achieve them, a natural part of it is disagreement in every policy area. What should we do about the high levels of student loan debt that many college graduates face, and even those who didn't complete a program of study? Many proposals have been offered, but little agreement has emerged about what is acceptable. For Medicare, Medicaid, and the veterans' health care system, what rules or regulations might the government adopt to control the rising cost of health care services? What about the case of texting and other uses of cell phones while driving that we discussed in chapter 4? Should more be done to prevent texting while driving, and if so, should states make the practice illegal or use other ways to curtail the practice? To deal with climate change, should the nation put a price on carbon, a so-called carbon tax that would discourage the use of fossil fuels, and if so, should the tax be revenue neutral? That is, should other taxes be lowered at the same time so there is no net increase in the tax burden that citizens face? If renewable energy technologies are to be encouraged, what is the best way to do that? As these and countless other examples illustrate, policy design can make a big difference in how much policies cost and how well they work to meet people's needs. Particular statutory or regulatory provisions can have significant effects on the way policies are implemented, how individuals and institutions comply with the law, and the impacts those laws have on society.

Policy Conflicts and Incremental Decision Making

Conflict arises when policy actors have differing views about the substance of public policies or whether government intervention is justifiable at all. Conflicts over the role of government and public policy underscore the inherently political nature of policymaking. Inevitably, policymaking involves choices about social values as well as calculations about policy design. In the heat of public debate, the differences are not always clear, even to those most directly involved. Policymakers and interest groups may disagree intensely about whether government intervention is warranted and about broad policy goals such as homeland security, access to quality health care, or equality in the workplace. Forging consensus is more difficult on fundamental goals and values than it is on the specific policy tools that might be used, such as provision of market incentives, regulation, privatization, or government management. The history of policy gridlock in areas as diverse as energy policy, economic stimulus measures, health care reform, and taxes and spending in general reflects the inability of policymakers to resolve some of these deep conflicts, particularly when organized groups on each side subject the policymakers to intense lobbying (Mann and Ornstein 2012; Persily 2015; Thurber and Yoshinaka 2015).

Because political conflict is endemic to policymaking, almost all policies represent a compromise on the goals being sought as well as the policy tools proposed to achieve them. Compromise means that the policies are likely to be only partially effective and that the debate over further changes will continue. Thus elected officials enact policies to remove agricultural subsidies, only to put them back again a few years later when farmers complain that the free market that policymakers anticipated is not working well. In 2010, Congress approved the new Affordable Care Act, although without a single Republican in either the House or the Senate voting for it. Will the act survive future Congresses, or additional legal challenge in the courts? Republicans in the House voted more than sixty times to repeal the act, and President Donald Trump promised to do the same during his 2016 campaign. Will they do so now that voting for repeal will be more than a politically symbolic act, and will have major real-world consequences for citizens? Almost certainly members of Congress will revisit many components of the law in an effort to fine-tune them as well as to respond to continuing partisan differences over the measure.

It is also evident that the nation alternates between periods when policymakers impose tough requirements on food safety, auto safety, and the marketing of drugs, for example, and when there is little effective regulation. When weak policies result in public exposure to unreasonable risks of contaminated food, as happened with a variety of food products between 2008 and 2011, the pendulum swings the other way as public outrage convinces policymakers to take action. In 2010, Congress responded to the spate of food contamination problems by approving the Food Safety Modernization Act, the first major overhaul of the food safety system since 1938. President Obama signed the act in January 2011. Yet as we noted in chapter 3, in recent years, members of Congress remained divided over the appropriate level of funding to implement the new law, and by many accounts, funding is well below what is needed for the law to be effective.[17] Public outrage spread across the country over lead contamination in Flint, Michigan's drinking water, and later in the water in many other cities and in public schools. Yet, conservative candidates for office regularly denounce environmental regulations for the burdens and costs they impose. Which view will win out?

These and other characteristics of U.S. politics mean that most of the time public policy change occurs in small steps, with only modest alterations made at the margins of existing policy. Incremental policymaking of this kind can be a sensible way to act on public problems, although not always. On the positive side, it can provide short-term political stability by minimizing conflict over social values and policy goals. It can forge compromises that help diverse policy actors gain something that they want while delivering needed services to the public. It subjects policy proposals to careful evaluation of their likely effectiveness, costs, and impacts, thus reducing the risk of serious mistakes. It can help to build political legitimacy and confidence in the policymaking processes. Finally, it can encourage policy experimentation and learning, the kind of trial-and-error decision making that allows policymakers, especially at the state level, to try new approaches to see how they work before committing to a particular course of action (Lindblom and Woodhouse 1993). Programs that are successful or broadly supported, such as Head Start, can be expanded over time, and those that fall short can be curtailed or modified in other ways.

Policy Strategies with No Crystal Ball

Incremental policymaking, the dominant style in the U.S. political system, is suitable for many public problems and circumstances, but it also has its limitations. Some critics suggest that it may be least appropriate when governments face new problems for which they are ill prepared and where considerable uncertainty exists over the risks, the costs of trying to reduce them, and the likely effectiveness of policy measures (Ophuls and Boyan 1992). Others may be tempted to say that this is precisely when incremental policy change makes more sense than a radical departure from the status quo.

Global climate change offers a context in which to consider the relative advantages of incrementalism and change that is broader or brought about quickly. Climate science continues to advance, and yet forecasts of future climate scenarios are necessarily somewhat uncertain given the time frames for such projections. The uncertainties lead some to assume that climate scientists are in serious disagreement on the basics of the changes that are occurring and why, when in fact consensus exists on the reality of the problem. Scientific assessments from the Intergovernmental Panel on Climate Change (IPCC) and the U.S. National Academy of Sciences, among others, clearly point to human actions, particularly use of fossil fuels such as coal, oil, and natural gas, as the chief contributors to release of greenhouse gases, and also to changes in the global forest cover and agricultural practices. So what should be done? Opting for taking minimal policy actions while awaiting more definitive scientific evidence, an incremental approach, could result in catastrophic consequences for many countries around the world, particularly those with the fewest resources available to permit adaptation to a changing climate. On the other hand, adopting strong measures to force a rapid change in fossil fuel use to try to prevent climate change from occurring could be very costly, and doing so could pose a very different kind of risk to society—that of spending money that might be better used for other purposes (DiMento and Doughman 2014; IPCC 2013; Selin and VanDeveer 2016). What constitutes prudent government action under such circumstances? Reasonable people can disagree about what to do even if they accept the reality of climate change.

Much the same could be said of policy efforts as diverse as fixing the federal entitlement programs (Medicare, Medicaid, and Social Security), reforming the U.S. tax code, reshaping campaign finance laws, and improving health care. That is, incremental changes might be more politically acceptable than bold or far-reaching changes, but sometimes going well beyond incrementalism is essential to deal effectively with the problem at hand and to minimize the costs to society of current policies. Given the high federal deficits in recent years, the ever-increasing national debt, and a reluctance to increase taxes, policymakers might judge bold proposals for policy change more favorably than they would in normal times. So too might policymakers at the state and local levels.

Luckily, in many instances, a middle course is available. Many recent proposals in a range of policy areas have emphasized the value of policy flexibility and adaptive management, meaning that policymakers can continue to evaluate the situation while taking incremental policy steps that make sense. For climate change, this type of policymaking might mean a strong effort to promote energy efficiency and conservation, which are relatively cheap to achieve and for which technologies already exist. Or it might mean funding a research program to further develop alternatives to fossil fuels such as wind and solar power, as President Obama favored in 2009 as part of his economic stimulus measure and budget proposals. Or it might mean building additional nuclear power plants, which are one of the few mature energy technologies not based on fossil fuel use in the operation of the facilities. Whatever policies are adopted could have enough built-in flexibility to allow program changes as new knowledge develops. Administrators might be given the discretion to alter course when conditions justify doing so. Policymakers can always revisit the policy when they have enough evidence to warrant a change in direction.

In this vein, one of the most frequently observed limits of decision making is that it tends to focus on events or developments that are closest to people in time and space. Commentators often criticize policymakers for having a short-term time horizon as well as a local or parochial rather than a broader perspective on the problem at hand. By this they mean that elected officials tend to think about impacts only through the next election and to view the consequences of public problems or policies in terms of effects on their own states, districts, or localities.

This is a common explanation for why the president and Congress have been unable to reform entitlement programs, such as Social Security and Medicare, or to resolve their differences over reducing the federal deficit and the national debt, or to invest in a large-scale infrastructure repair program to address clear needs for rebuilding highways, tunnels, bridges, rail lines, and airports, as well as to modernize the electrical grid. The effects of the shortened time horizons are particularly notable. The dire consequences of the many challenges or public policies, such as the national debt, entitlement programs, and climate change, will be felt in the future, and often in the distant future. Yet any attempts to address the problems or to revise the policies invite political controversies over short-term costs and burdens.

This kind of bias, even if exaggerated, exists throughout society. Corporations, for example, focus heavily on short-term profits shown in quarterly and annual financial reports. As a result, they may lose sight of long-term goals, which are not highly valued in the marketplace. The financial meltdowns of 2008 and 2009 clearly showed major banks and other financial institutions taking on enormous risks for short-term gains, a gamble that turned extremely negative for them, but only after they profited handsomely from those very calculations.

As understandable as such a fixation on the short term is, public policy of necessity must look ahead. It must also adopt a broader perspective that includes people and institutions located at some distance, geographically and culturally, from policymakers and citizens. As the nation has learned since September 11, 2001, fighting global terrorism means more than guarding domestic airports or taking military action against specific targets in other countries. It involves trying to understand and respond to cultural and economic forces around the world that breed resentment toward the United States and sympathy and support for terrorists (Kavanagh 2011).

The 2012 United Nations Conference on Sustainable Development (Rio+20), mentioned at the beginning of chapter 11, is a good example of forward-looking and wide-ranging policymaking. The world's population is expected to climb to some 9.8 billion by 2050, and the Census Bureau projects a U.S. population of close to 400 million by then. To provide for all the people, nations will have to foster more economic development to meet rising demands for energy, food, water, clothing, housing, transportation, jobs, and other essentials. To be sustainable, economic development around the globe will have to be designed to avoid the severe environmental, economic, and social strains that would likely come with reliance on conventional growth strategies. The 1992 conference on sustainable development, as well as its 2012 counterpart, was arranged to try to identify and build support for this new kind of economic development.

Because the targets of public policy are always shifting, analysts, policymakers, and citizens need to be alert to changing situations and consider new policy ideas. As the substantive policy chapters showed, too often old policies continue long after they are outdated. If the nation truly values effective and efficient public policies, it must be open to evaluating those policies and changing them as needed. The same argument applies to addressing new concerns about the equity of public policies, whether the concerns are over environmental justice for poor communities or equal access to opportunities in education.

Policy Analysis and Policy Choices

Making public policies more effective, efficient, and equitable raises once again the subject of policy analysis and its role in policymaking. As we discussed in chapters 4 through 6, policy analysis can bring greater clarity to public problems and their solutions than might otherwise be the case. Analysts acknowledge the political character of the policymaking process, but they also believe that objective knowledge can reveal the nature of problems and their causes and help guide the search for public policies that promise a measure of success. If nothing else, policy analysis can clarify the issues and sharpen political debates. The potential for using policy analysis in state and local problem solving may be even greater than at the national level because state and local governments often lack the level of expertise seen in the federal government.

Wisconsin's voter ID law discussed in the chapter opening indicates that potential. Each side in the debate brings a different set of values and priorities, but ultimately their arguments must be grounded in reliable evidence to succeed. For example, what impact does a voter ID requirement have on potential voters? Does such a requirement offer real promise of reducing voter fraud, and is that potential great enough to compensate for the law's possible disenfranchisement of many more voters? In this case and many others like it, policymakers and ordinary citizens interested in a fair electoral process would benefit from unbiased information that addresses such questions.

Evaluating Public Policy

Among other evaluative criteria, this book has placed special emphasis on three: effectiveness, efficiency, and equity. Effectiveness, or how well a policy works or might work, is always difficult to address, but it is obviously an important consideration at a time when many critics doubt the capacity of government to solve any problem. At the earliest stages of the policy process, when policy alternatives are proposed, effectiveness is necessarily based on various assumptions and projections of the future that may or may not come to pass.

At periodic stages of the policy process, effectiveness is the criterion analysts use to determine how well a policy has lived up to expectations. Did it succeed in producing the desired results? Even after a reasonable period of time, it is not easy to identify and measure a policy's impacts and compare them to the initial policy goals. Policymakers and independent analysts in and out of government conduct such evaluation studies, which have great value, despite their limitations. Whether use of school vouchers or the operation of charter schools is effective in improving educational outcomes, for example, depends on what one measures. Should analysts consider parental support, improvement by participating students, or progress of all students? The difficulty in measuring success means that students of public policy need to think critically about such studies and their findings.

Cases are easy to find. For the much-criticized Affordable Care Act, critics say it is a failure, and cite rising premium costs, or some flaws in its implementation. Yet the act's supporters note its many achievements, such as providing health insurance to twenty million individuals who previously lacked it and promoting greater efficiencies in health care delivery. Similarly, conservative critics frequently highlight long-term financial concerns for the Medicare program and call for it to be converted into a voucher system where individuals buy their insurance on the private market. Yet Medicare is remarkably efficient as a government program, and recipients of its services and others regularly applaud its effectiveness. Long-term fiscal stability could easily be assured with modest reforms of the program.

Efficiency is probably the criterion most likely to receive attention in contemporary policymaking as policy alternatives and existing programs are assessed. The reasons are clear. Government budgets are almost always under tight constraints, and it is a rare politician or taxpayer who favors tax increases, so policymakers want to ensure a good return on the money spent. This has long been true, but with continuing federal deficits and a rising national debt, the constraints on spending today are far greater than they were in the past (see chapter 7). Policymakers almost certainly will want to know how much proposed programs cost and where the money will come from to pay for them. They will demand some kind of comparison of the costs with the benefits of government action. They may even compare different programs according to which are most efficient in producing good results for the same dollar amount invested; increasingly, we want to see such questions addressed in health care, for example, where some very expensive drugs or costly medical procedures may not produce improvements that justify the costs. Policy analysis can contribute to answering those questions. While this is all well and good, public policy students already know that measuring and comparing costs and benefits is rarely simple; not all can be identified and measured, and it is difficult to compare them over time. Policymakers and the public need to exercise care in the way they use such studies and pay attention to their assumptions and methods so that they understand the studies' limitations. Unfortunately, this kind of consideration often takes place today in a deeply divided and highly partisan atmosphere, which greatly compounds the challenge of weighing the evidence in a rational or dispassionate manner (Campbell 2016).

Equity issues and personal freedom are addressed less frequently than effectiveness and efficiency, but they are no less important in public policy. As we have seen, equity can be defined in several different ways. Therefore, it may include concerns that range from protecting individual freedom to regulating how policy costs and benefits are distributed among groups in a population, such as urban and rural residents or rich and poor taxpayers, or, as popularized in recent years, between those in the top 1 percent of income earners and the rest of the population (the 99 percent). The issue of individual (or corporate) freedom arises frequently when a new program is proposed or an old one expanded. For example, federal health care policies offer benefits to Medicare and Medicaid recipients, but they impose constraints on health insurance companies and health professionals. Federal and state environmental regulations can help to protect the public's health, but at some cost to the rights of corporations to make decisions about the technologies they use and the kinds of products they make. As we saw in chapter 12, surveillance of individuals' phone calls and Internet use might allow the intelligence agencies to track potential terrorists, but is doing so fair to citizens who place a high value on their privacy? Policy analysis can facilitate policy choices by clarifying these kinds of trade-offs. Analysis can be similarly useful in describing the way many programs, such as Social Security, welfare, the tax system, and education policies, either redistribute wealth in society or try to promote equity in some other ways.

Improving Policy Capacity

Policy analysis also can help improve the performance of government and its responsiveness to citizen concerns. Policy capacity refers to the ability of government to identify and act on public problems within a reasonable period of time. One element of such a capacity is public trust and confidence in government because such trust affects the ability of policymakers to work together on policy

A spectrum of citizen engagement. Public participation through protests can be seen on both the left and the right side of the political spectrum. This photo shows hundreds of U.S. military veterans vowing to defend the Standing Rock protest camp and march through a winter blizzard to the scene of recent clashes with state police and the national guard just outside of the Lakota Sioux reservation of Standing Rock, North Dakota, December 5, 2016. The protests were over the Dakota Access Pipeline, which was to be built under the Missouri River adjacent to the reservation. The gathering was the largest meeting of Native Americans since the Little Bighorn camp in 1876. *(Andrew Lichtenstein/Corbis via Getty Images)*

solutions. Yet public trust in governmental institutions fell almost steadily from the 1960s to the late 1990s, with a small upward trend only in the fall of 2001, following the terrorist attacks on the United States and the U.S. response to them (Mackenzie and Labiner 2002). Following the financial crisis of 2008 and 2009, and growing public frustration over government's seeming ineptitude in figuring out what to do, it would be remarkable if trust and confidence in government returned to its former levels anytime soon. On the campaign trail in 2008, then candidate Obama pledged to "make government cool again." In support of such a goal, some policymakers and citizen activists supported a new civilian service academy, analogous to the military academies but devoted to training a new generation of public servants. The United States Public Service Academy would have offered a free four-year college education if individuals who attended were prepared to commit to five years of government service. In early 2009, the idea was attracting support, and legislation was pending in Congress to create such a program, but it was not approved.[18]

By 2016, public confidence had fallen to new lows, and public attitudes of this kind bolstered the campaign of Donald Trump, whose rhetoric often focused on government ineptitude and disregard for the concerns of many Americans. Polls confirmed that public assessments of Congress reached historic lows, and the public clearly disapproved of the performance of both major political parties. Much the same was true in many states where governments faced similar partisan divisions, a rising level of political incivility, and policy stalemate. As many studies have shown, there has been a significant decline in public trust in government since the late 1950s. To make matters worse, this loss of public trust and confidence extends to many other institutions over the same time period. These include newspapers, television news, big business, financial institutions, organized labor, public schools, and the criminal justice system. These trends have exacerbated political polarization and incivility in the nation and show few signs of abating anytime soon.[19]

Despite the many criticisms of government performance, the evidence on how well government programs have done is clearly mixed. Some programs have indeed fallen short of expectations, but others, as we have shown in previous chapters, have produced significant benefits to the public, from public education and environmental protection to health care services delivered through Medicare, Medicaid, and the veterans' health care system. A 2007 article in the *National Journal* on ten notable successes in public policy put it this way: "Not every problem is intractable. Progress *is* possible."[20] In a similar vein, in 2000, the Brookings Institution released a study of government's greatest achievements of the past half-century. Among the most notable were rebuilding Europe after World War II; expanding the right to vote; promoting equal access to public accommodations, such as hotels and restaurants; reducing disease; ensuring safe food and drinking water; increasing older Americans' access to health care through Medicare; enhancing workplace safety; increasing access to higher education; and reducing hunger and improving nutrition. The study's point was simple: it is easy to ignore some of the most important public policy actions because they are not very visible as they become routine parts of American life; yet examining such a list confirms the important role that government and public policy has played throughout American history and that it can play today in improving everyday life.[21]

Still, there is little doubt from public commentary and political rhetoric that many people believe, to the contrary, that government is not working well (Bok 2001; Hacker and Pierson 2016). In response to this skeptical public mood, policymakers at all levels of government have struggled with how to improve public policies and programs and better meet citizens' needs and expectations. Various efforts to "reinvent" government and to improve its efficiency were tried during the 1990s, and they continue today. Yet, as noted, the public remains distrustful of government, and partisan divisions in the nation continue over what role government should play in our lives, from health care and food safety to environmental protection and energy policy. To some extent, the rise of the Tea Party movement reflected this broad discontent, as did Donald Trump's campaign. Both were fueled by increasingly partisan news shows, social media, and talk radio (Jamieson and Cappella 2008).[22] It is clear that any meaningful change in the public's view of government and public policy will require more than a determined White House and comparable leadership at the state and local levels. It will mean developing a broader policy capacity to define and respond effectively to public problems, both present and future, and ensuring that government agencies, from the military to Social Security, are as well managed as they can be.

How can policy analysis contribute to improving the policy capacity of government? One way is through the analysis of proposed institutional reforms, such as changes in the electoral process, campaign finance reform, and opportunities for citizens to participate in decision making. This is a task at which political scientists excel (Levi et al. 2008). Yet too often their analyses fail to reach the public or even policymakers, who then must act without benefit of what the analysis has uncovered. The box "Steps to Analysis: Money in Politics" illustrates these needs.

Other chapters have suggested that policy capacity can also be improved through better evaluation of the agencies charged with implementing policies and programs. Thanks to the Government Performance and Results Act of 1993, the federal government is likely to conduct more evaluations of this kind than in the past, though probably of varying quality (Radin 2006). For many reasons, think tanks and other independent bodies carrying out external evaluations may be better able to identify institutional strengths and weaknesses and to suggest meaningful paths to reform. For example, chapter 11 noted that a series of studies by the National Academy of Public Administration (1995, 2000) identified many elements of the U.S. environmental protection system that could be changed to improve the effectiveness and efficiency of the Environmental Protection Agency (EPA) and other agencies. Studies by Resources for the Future have reached similar conclusions (Davies and Mazurek 1998). Chapter 12 highlighted a number of studies by the Government Accountability Office

Steps to Analysis

Money in Politics

Particularly since the controversial Supreme Court decision in *Citizens United v. Federal Election Commission* that removed limits on corporate and union spending in elections, the role of money in the political process has attracted great attention. Conservatives applaud the decision as a defense of constitutionally protected free speech while liberals argue that treating corporations as persons entitled to such deference makes little sense and can distort political campaigns. President Obama, for example, called the *Citizens United* decision "a major victory for big oil, Wall Street banks, health insurance companies and the other powerful interests that marshal their power every day in Washington to drown out the voices of everyday Americans." Was he right?

One way to address these arguments is to look directly at campaign contributions to candidates. The website of the Center for Responsive Politics, www .opensecrets.org, says that it is the "most comprehensive resource for federal campaign contributions, lobbying data and analysis available anywhere." Here you can find news and analysis of campaign financing, assessment of the impact that the *Citizens United* decision has had, the top individual and organizational donors to political campaigns, and details of all campaign spending reported to the Federal Election Commission. This kind of information can give voters insight into the politics of policymaking. The center argues that turning the "sunshine" on these activities will get policymakers thinking about how they go about making decisions and just who is supplying not only the money but also the information they use to make them.

The website also provides research and reports on political and electoral issues, and you can make your own assessments of the information. For example, early in the 2014 election cycle, the center reported that so-called dark money, funds contributed by groups that do not have to report the sources of their money under the law (groups classified by the Internal Revenue Service as having a "social welfare" purpose under section 501(c)(4) of the tax law), already was more than three times the amount spent at the same point in the 2012 campaign. The 2016 election likely set new records as well, continuing concern that, as critics put it, American elections are being hijacked by a small number of wealthy citizens (Mayer 2016).

To learn which groups are contributing the most to election campaigns, go to www.opensecrets.org and click on Menu, then Influence & Lobbying, and then Interest Groups. You will see the total contribution by each sector to each of the major parties, such as financial services, lawyers and lobbyists, communications/electronics, health, and energy/natural resources. Then select Finance/Insurance/Real Estate to see how companies within this sector contributed to election campaigns. Beyond the first box on contribution totals, you will find graphics that show the level of contributions by the sector over time, the total amount spent on lobbying, which parties received the funds, and the top recipients by name of those funds, among other information. This information is continuously updated during each election cycle.

Examine the data presented in the table and figures for this sector or one of the other business sectors.

- Which political party received the majority of money from this industry in the most recent election cycle?

- Which companies contributed the most?

- How does recent spending on elections compare to spending in previous years?

Return to the main page of the site and select Politicians & Elections from the Menu. Then select the tab for Congress. You can examine any of the members in leadership positions whose names and photos are on the main page. Or you can find your member of Congress, or the candidate who challenged that member, by using the box on the left and entering part of the member or candidate's name.

- How much did he or she spend on the last election campaign, and where did the money come from?

- Click on the member's name to see the leading contributors to the campaign. What conclusions would you draw?

- To what extent do you think the sources of election funding might affect decisions on public policy issues before Congress?

and the Congressional Research Service on foreign economic assistance, domestic electronic surveillance, the risks of terrorism, and military weapons acquisition and spending. And chapter 8 highlighted studies on health care issues from the Kaiser Family Foundation and the National Academy of Medicine, among others, on the costs of health care, the effects of being uninsured, and the promise of various policy initiatives.

One of the central tasks in improving policy capacity in government is in the hands of the people. If citizens lack interest in public affairs and fail to educate themselves on the issues, government is likely to continue to respond chiefly to organized groups and special interests. What citizens see as faulty performance in government often reflects the influence of organized groups that work to ensure that policies affecting them are *not* effective, or that they inflict minimum constraints on their activities. A well-known example from the late 1990s was the influence of corporations in weakening government oversight of their financial operations. The weaker financial regulations provided the opportunities for corporate abuses at companies such as Enron and WorldCom that shocked and disgusted the public in 2002. Much the same kind of organized opposition to financial regulation helped to weaken the 2010 Dodd-Frank Act and its implementation that was designed to make Wall Street and other financial institutions more accountable to the public. In the aftermath of the 2016 election, the Dodd-Frank Act once again was under attack by those who argued that it unreasonably burdened financial institutions, even if many of its provisions helped protect ordinary citizens from unreasonable financial risks.[23] The best way to counter such self-serving actions by special interests is for citizens to pay close attention to these debates and to get involved. Continued public vigilance is essential to ensure strong policies and consistent implementation of the policies. Otherwise those interests with most at stake will likely bide their time and intervene quietly to try to reverse the actions taken at the height of public concern over their practices. Studies of interest group behavior point to the efficacy of such strategies (Kraft and Kamieniecki 2007).

Citizen Participation in Decision Making

The final perspective this chapter emphasizes is the politics of policymaking—that is, how policy choices are made and the political values they represent. The decision-making process affects what kinds of decisions are made and, ultimately, what impacts they have on society. The policy outcomes reflect who participates in the process, who does not, and the different resources that each policy actor brings to the decision-making arena. In a democracy, one would expect public policies to be consistent with public preferences and to meet the needs of citizens. As noted, however, policymakers are often more responsive to organized interests—the agriculture industry, the mining industry, the oil and gas industry, health insurance companies, or the music recording industry—than they are to the general public. The discussion of subgovernments, elites, and the role of interest groups in chapters 2 and 3 highlighted these patterns.

Citizen Capacity and Policy Engagement

How might that situation be changed? One way is to strengthen **citizen capacity** to participate in policymaking processes. With some notable exceptions as evident in recent Tea Party activism, the level of public participation in policy processes, whether voting in elections or taking active roles in civic affairs, has declined over the past several decades (Putnam 2000; Skocpol 2003; Skocpol and Fiorina 1999; Skocpol and Williamson 2012). Of all the age groups, the youngest—including college students—generally has had the lowest level of interest in politics and policymaking and active participation in these processes. However, as stated earlier, there are some contrary indicators of citizen interest in public affairs, especially in local communities. The movement toward sustainable communities often involves extensive citizen involvement in local decision making, and it captures recent interest in redesigning communities in terms of mass transit, energy efficiency, use of open space, and rehabilitation of older buildings and neighborhoods (Mazmanian and Kraft 2009; K. Portney 2013). There also are encouraging signs from surveys by the Pew Partnership for Civic Change, demonstrating that Americans have a "profound sense of connectivity to their communities and neighbors" and are willing to work with others to solve problems.[24] Additional evidence comes from recent election campaigns, where candidates proved they could spark intense interest and participation by younger voters.[25] As indicated by the recall campaigns in Wisconsin and citizen action on initiatives in other states, such as Ohio, under the right circumstances citizens can and do become mobilized to get involved in political processes.

There is no shortage of analyses about why the American public has been so disengaged from politics and civic affairs for so long. At least part of the explanation lies in the disconnect between the policy process and people's daily lives. That is, either most citizens do not see how government affects their lives, or they do not believe they can do much to change either governmental processes or public policies. As we have argued, public policies unquestionably have a great impact on people's lives. The question is whether people see these impacts, and also whether they believe their opinions and actions can make a difference. Some will say that the 2016 elections constituted something of a rebirth of citizen enthusiasm about government and politics, although this may be truer for those on the right side of the political spectrum than for those in the middle or on the progressive side. Compared to the 2012 elections, overall turnout was about the same, but it was lower among Democratic constituencies and higher among Republicans.[26]

In addition to making the connection between policy choices and individual lives clearer, improving the public's access to government information might encourage more people to participate. Consider the activities of the public interest group Environmental Working Group (EWG), which in 2002 became heavily involved in congressional debates over agricultural subsidies, among many other issues. Frustrated by the lack of public attention to what

Steps to Analysis

Using Websites to Influence Public Opinion and Policy Debate

In the early 2000s, the groups Public Citizen and Government Accountability Project analyzed testing records from the U.S. Department of Agriculture (USDA) for salmonella bacteria found at ground-beef processing plants. They acquired the data with a Freedom of Information Act request. The groups' report cited many plants that failed the tests, some repeatedly, because of lax USDA enforcement. They placed the list of failing plants on the Public Citizen website to highlight what they considered to be a serious threat to public health.

In 2008, another public health scare received enormous media attention. This again involved salmonella bacteria, but this time the concern was tainted peanut butter at a plant in Georgia whose ingredients wound up in thousands of food products across the country. Eventually, the Food and Drug Administration (FDA) recall of those products became the largest in U.S. history. The FDA set up a special webpage on the recalls as a way to provide important information for the public.[a] Since that time, there have been many additional concerns over food safety, prompting the FDA to establish several different webpages devoted to illnesses related to food and cosmetic products. Visit the site that lists recalled foods and dietary supplements (www.fda.gov/Food/RecallsOutbreaksEmergencies/Recalls/default.htm).

- How understandable are the FDA's product lists?

- Review the other topics on this page, including foods, drugs, cosmetics, and medical devices. What conclusions can you draw from the information provided here?

- Do you believe the FDA did a good job on the peanut butter recall action or on previous product recalls or comparable agency actions? Should the agency have done even more to protect public health and to keep the public alert to the potential for food-borne illness?

According to the U.S. Centers for Disease Control and Prevention, improperly handled ground beef, eggs, chicken, and other foods contaminated with pathogens such as salmonella, listeria, and *E. coli* bacteria are implicated in an estimated 48 million illnesses, 128,000 hospitalizations, and 3,000 deaths each year. Illness and death are particularly high among newborn infants, the elderly, and those with weakened immune systems. The figures can be found at (www.cdc.gov/foodborneburden).

- In light of these numbers, why do you think the United States has not done more to reduce the risks of food-borne illness and death?

a. For an overview of the contaminated peanut butter story and related problems with food safety inspections, see Michael Moss and Andrew Martin, "Food Safety Problems Slip Past Private Inspectors," *New York Times*, March 5, 2009; and Sabrina Tavernise, "F.D.A. Says Importers Must Audit Food Safety," *New York Times*, July 26, 2013.

it believed were inequitable payments to wealthy farmers, the group secured access to the raw data for the government's farm subsidy payments and placed the information on its website (www.ewg.org). Members of Congress frequently cited the data and the EWG website when considering the bill, probably because they had heard from their constituents on the subject. Particularly important was the revelation that hundreds of farmers and absentee landlords were receiving millions of dollars in subsidies.[27] It is noteworthy that by early 2009 President Obama made a point of urging Congress to end such subsidies. Whether one thinks that the group's efforts were praiseworthy or not, its strategy suggests the potential political power of web-based citizen education and lobbying. The box "Steps to Analysis: Using Websites to Influence Public Opinion and Policy Debate" illustrates yet another group effort to shape public opinion and policy debate.

New Forms of Citizen Participation

Public participation in the policy process can go well beyond voting, writing letters or e-mail messages to policymakers, and discussing policy issues. Historically, only a small percentage of the public is even this active. But the percentage could rise as technology makes public involvement easier and as policymakers become more interested in raising public participation in government.

As discussed in previous chapters, some government agencies already make a concerted effort to promote the use of their websites, to offer information and public services through "e-government," and to invite the public to engage in the issues (West 2005). The opportunities to become involved in policymaking are even greater at the state and local levels. In addition to inviting people to public meetings and hearings and asking the public to submit comments on proposed government actions, policymakers ask citizens to serve on advisory panels and assist them in making often difficult choices.

In the world of campaign and advocacy politics, recent elections demonstrated the enormous potential for candidate fund-raising and citizen mobilization through Internet technology. The use of specialized networks and blog sites has greatly expanded, and the potential for citizen involvement in politics and public policy continues to grow. With nearly universal access to the Internet and increasing use of high-speed and wireless connections via smartphones and tablet computers, citizens should find it even easier to become active in public affairs (Bimber, Flanagin, and Stohl 2012; Fox and Ramos 2011; Gainous and Wagner 2011; Kamarck, Ciulla, and Nye 2002).[28]

Of course, there is also a downside to these developments. Citizens face a veritable flood of political and public policy commentary, much of which is biased and partisan, and sometimes blatantly manipulative and misleading.[29] The same could be said for many Internet news sites that bear little relationship to real journalism. The trend is made worse as Americans' interest in news from all sources has declined steadily in recent years.[30] Without an ability to compare information from different sources, and evaluate it objectively, citizens have little protection against the onslaught.

One of the forms of citizen involvement that is most vulnerable to these kinds of risks is voting on ballot propositions. A highly contentious one, Proposition 23 in California in 2010, asked voters whether or not to suspend the state's Global Warming Solutions Act of 2006. The two sides in that dispute spent over $40 million to sway voters' opinions, with much of the support for the measure coming from out-of-state oil companies and much of the opposition funded by environmental groups and Silicon Valley investors who had backed clean energy technologies. The ballot measure lost by a vote of 61 percent to 39 percent.[31] In a related action in 2016, voters in Washington State were presented with a ballot measure that would have imposed the nation's first carbon tax, and they rejected it after opposition by environmental justice advocates who feared that it would adversely affect working people and the poor. That stance put them in the same position as the fossil fuel industry that opposed the measure for quite different reasons.[32]

States and cities increasingly also are approving ballot measures that tax sugary soft drinks as a way to raise much-needed local revenue. In 2016, voters in San Francisco, Oakland, and Albany, California, and in Boulder, Colorado, approved such measures, as did Cook County, Illinois (Chicago metropolitan area). Soft-drink companies such as Coca-Cola and Pepsi have long fought hard and successfully against such ballot propositions. But soda-tax advocates are winning of late with arguments that the increased revenue can be used for funding early childhood education, public safety, and other local programs, and also to reduce consumption of beverages linked to obesity.[33]

Consider another example that also gained national media attention but involved some new twists on the way such campaigns on voter initiatives and referenda are conducted today. In 2008, voters in California approved Proposition 8, a ballot measure that revised the state's constitution to restrict the definition of marriage to a union between a man and a woman. The vote was close, with 52 to 48 percent in favor, and its approval reversed a decision by the state's supreme court earlier that year permitting marriage by same-sex couples; the court had ruled that banning such marriages was discriminatory under the state's constitution. The two sides in the state ballot campaign had spent about $40 million each, making it the costliest state ballot measure ever and, except for the presidential election, the highest-funded election campaign in 2008. In early 2009, that same court heard legal challenges to Proposition 8 that sought to declare it invalid, and in 2010, a federal district court judge in California ruled that Proposition 8 was indeed an unconstitutional form of discrimination. Early in 2012, a three-judge federal appeals court in California upheld that decision (by a vote of 2 to 1), and in 2013, the U.S. Supreme Court ruled narrowly that the proponents of Proposition 8 did not have legal standing to defend the law in federal court. Thus the Court dismissed the appeal and ordered the Ninth Circuit Court of Appeals to vacate its decision, which upheld the initial district court ruling against Proposition 8. Thus, in the end, California's constitution was not changed to ban nontraditional marriage as supporters of Proposition 8 had sought to do.[34]

Conclusions

Throughout this book, we have emphasized an integrated approach to the study of public policy rather than focusing on policy history and program details. Although this kind of information is clearly important, policy and program particulars change quickly, and the knowledge learned may be of limited use over time. In the long run, the perspectives and approaches of policy analysis are more helpful in understanding how the nation's policies evolved into their present state and considering what alternatives might work better. The book stresses how to think about policy issues, where to find pertinent information, and how to interpret it. It also underscores the need to develop a robust capacity for critical and creative thinking about public problems and their solutions.

This last chapter revisits some of these points in the context of the policy challenges governments face as they try to make difficult decisions about the future. It focuses on the way policy decisions can affect people's lives, how policy analysis can clarify public problems and possible solutions, and the role of citizens in the policymaking process. For example, the case of voter requirements nicely illustrates how such analysis can bring some clarity to the debate over alleged voter impersonation fraud and the justification for requiring IDs to vote as well as the impact on minority voters and others.

The chapter also illustrates how citizens as well as analysts can evaluate policy proposals for their effectiveness, efficiency, and equity, among other concerns, and it emphasizes the need to improve the government's capacity for problem solving at all levels of government. As we have emphasized throughout the text, the capacity for problem solving is not always as high as it might be, and it is important to try to build that capacity as the nation struggles to deal with problems as diverse as climate change, continuing poverty and economic inequality, and national security threats. We need a more robust way to identify problems promptly, build support for acting on them, and develop appropriate solutions.

The chapter also focuses on the dynamics of policymaking, including how policy is changed over time, and the opportunities that the policy process presents for citizens to participate in decision making.

Despite a prevailing sense of cynicism toward government and politics, we believe that we live in a time of exceptional opportunity for citizens to get involved in public affairs. New technologies, particularly those based in the Internet, greatly facilitate access to a vast range of policy information. Governments at all levels are welcoming citizen involvement, giving new vitality to the promise of American democracy. We urge you to take advantage of these opportunities and play an active role in designing and choosing public policies for the future.

DISCUSSION QUESTIONS

1. Consider the case presented at the beginning of the chapter on voter ID policy in Wisconsin and other states. Are such requirements for photo IDs a good idea? That is, should everyone have to present an acceptable form of photo ID in order to vote, or are such requirements an unreasonable burden on state residents who otherwise qualify to vote?

2. Why do you think most citizens do not take more interest in politics and public policy? What might increase their level of interest and participation? Their level of knowledge of public policy? What would motivate you to become more active?

3. How much potential do you see in Internet-based political mobilization of citizens, either during election campaigns or for specific advocacy campaigns between elections? What particular kinds of actions are most likely to be successful in reaching voters, especially younger ones? Based on the examples and discussion offered in this chapter, what concerns, if any, do you have?

4. Consider this chapter's discussion of California's Proposition 8 banning same-sex marriage in the state, or the Washington State proposition on a carbon tax. Should these kinds of highly controversial questions be placed on the ballot for citizens to vote on directly, or should they be decided instead by state legislators?

5. Consider one or more major policy challenges, such as reforming health care, reforming the major federal entitlement programs (Social Security, Medicare, and Medicaid), redesigning the tax code, or developing a national energy or climate change policy. What do you see as the major advantages or disadvantages of incremental policy change? Similarly, what do you think are the major advantages or disadvantages of pursuing policy change that is more far-reaching or radical, whether the ideas are endorsed by the left or right side of the political spectrum?

KEYWORDS

citizen capacity   508

public participation   510

MAJOR LEGISLATION

Food Safety Modernization Act of 2010

Help America Vote Act (HAVA) of 2002

SUGGESTED READINGS

Russell J. Dalton, *The Good Citizen: How a Younger Generation Is Reshaping American Politics*, 2nd ed. (Thousand Oaks, Calif.: CQ Press, 2016). Charts how young Americans are creating new norms of citizenship and engagement, including evidence from Barack Obama's 2008 and 2012 presidential campaigns.

Stephen E. Frantzich, *Citizen Democracy: Political Activists in a Cynical Age*, 3rd ed. (Boulder, Colo.: Rowman & Littlefield, 2008). Addresses the myriad ways in which citizens can participate in the political process despite today's prevailing cynicism about government and politics.

Jason B. Gainous and Kevin M. Wagner, *Rebooting American Politics: The Internet Revolution* (Lanham, Md.: Rowman & Littlefield, 2011). Offers a careful examination of the growing use of the Internet in American politics and how it changes the way voters acquire information and act politically.

Samara Klar and Yanna Krupnikov, *Independent Politics: How American Disdain for Parties Leads to Political Inaction* (New York: Cambridge University Press, 2016).

Paul Rogat Loeb, *Soul of the Citizen: Living with Conviction in Challenging Times*, 2nd ed. (New York: St. Martin's Press, 2010). Describes how ordinary citizens can make their voices heard on a range of social issues during a time of widespread political cynicism.

Bernie Sanders, *Our Revolution: A Future to Believe In* (New York: Thomas Dunne Books, 2016). A restatement of the Democratic Party candidate's arguments that he advanced during the presidential nomination race.

Carmen Sirianni, *Investing in Democracy: Engaging Citizens in Collaborative Governance* (Washington, D.C.: Brookings Institution, 2009). Clearly explains how citizens can work together to help solve the many challenges facing American society and government today.

SUGGESTED WEBSITES

www.apsanet.org/RESOURCES/For-Students. American Political Science Association site for student resources, including internships, career resources, and options for graduate study.

www.ash.harvard.edu. Ash Center for Democratic Governance and Innovation at Harvard, which promotes innovations in government. The site offers a number of programs of interest to students.

www.citizen.org. Public Citizen home page, with many links to policy issues and activism.

www.icma.org. International City/County Management Association citizen involvement page, with examples of how citizens can get involved in local government across the nation.

www.pewinternet.org. Pew Research Center site for Internet, Science, and Technology, which covers developments in the use of social networks for political organizing and action.

www.usa.gov. The federal government's citizen portal, with links to public action and e-government services.

NOTES

1. John Nichols, "ALEC Exposed: Rigging Elections," *The Nation*, August 1–8, 2011. On the monitoring of state voter ID laws and proposals, see the National Conference of State Legislatures, "Voter ID: 2012 and 2011 Legislation," available at www.ncsl.org. A similar state photo ID law in Texas enacted in 2013 also disallowed student ID cards.

2. Rick Lyman, "Texas' Stringent Voter ID Law Makes a Dent at Polls," *New York Times*, November 6, 2013. The apparent targeting of college students occurred in many other states as well and led to some unusual legal challenges to voter ID laws that were grounded in an allegation of age discrimination. See Matt Apuzzo, "Students Joining Battle to Upend Laws on Voter ID," *New York Times*, July 6, 2014.

3. It has not been unusual in Wisconsin and other states for individuals to be turned down for such a request for a state voter ID card because of clerical errors, such as a misspelled name on a birth certificate. Getting corrected documents may well involve considerable additional time and money on the individual's part.

4. Natasha Khan and Corbin Carson, "New Database of US Voter Fraud Finds No Evidence That Photo ID Laws Are Needed," *NBC News*, August 11, 2012, available at www.nbcnews .com. The team of investigators from News21 sent thousands of requests to election officials in all fifty states, asking about all cases of any kind of fraudulent activity, including registration fraud, absentee ballot fraud, campaign fraud, and voter impersonation fraud. For a summary of other studies and concerns about such laws, see Michael Wines and Manny Fernandez, "Stricter Rules for Voter IDs Reshape Races," *New York Times*, May 1, 2016.

5. Alexander Keyssar, "Who Gets to Vote," *New York Times*, October 2, 2016; and Emily L. Mahoney, "Voters in Wisconsin, Other States Navigate Maze of New Voting Rules," Wisconsin Center for Investigative Journalism, September 4, 2016, available at http://wisconsinwatch.org/2016/09/voters-in-wisconsin-other-states-navigate-maze-of-new-voting-rules/.

6. Pew Research Center, "Broad Support for Photo ID Voting Requirements," November 2, 2012, available at www.pewresearch.org. On the Gallup poll finding, see "Four in Five Americans Support Voter ID Laws, Early Voting," August 22, 2016, available at www.gallup.com/poll/194741/four-five-americans-support-voter-laws-early-voting.aspx. The same poll found that 63 percent favor

automatic voter registration and 80 percent favor early voting. Some 95 percent of Republicans favor voter ID requirements versus 63 percent of Democrats, and 83 percent of Independents.

7. Michael E. Shear and Maggie Haberman, "Trump Claims, with No Evidence, That 'Millions of People' Voted Illegally," *New York Times*, November 27, 2016. After Trump singled out several states, including California, for having "serious voter fraud," the state's top election official, its secretary of state, insisted that no evidence existed for such an unprecedented assertion by a president-elect. See Adam Nagourney, "California Official Says Trump's Claim of Voter Fraud Is 'Absurd,'" *New York Times*, November 28, 2016. Once in office, Trump continued to assert that three to five million illegal votes had been cast in the presidential race. He also called for a "major investigation" of the alleged voting fraud despite repeated assurances by election officials and voting experts that the allegations had no basis in fact. See Michael E. Shear and Peter Baker, "After His Claim of Voter Fraud, Trump Vows 'Major Investigation,'" *New York Times*, January 25, 2017.

8. Patrick Markey, Jason Stein, and Bruce Vielmetti, "Federal Judge Strikes Down Wisconsin's Voter ID Law," *Milwaukee Journal Sentinel*, April 29, 2014. Judge Lynn Adelman's ninety-page opinion in the case can be found at www.jsonline.com/news/judge-adelmans-ruling-striking-down-wisconsins-voter-id-law-257210301.html. The U.S. Justice Department has challenged similar state laws, such as ones in North Carolina and Texas that impose strict photo ID requirements. See Charlie Savage, "Justice Department Poised to File Lawsuit over Voter ID Law," *New York Times*, September 30, 2013; and the *New York Times* Editorial Board, "Voter ID Is the Real Fraud," *New York Times*, April 29, 2014.

9. The 2016 election produced a close victory in Wisconsin in the presidential race, with Donald Trump beating Hillary Clinton by only about twenty-two thousand votes. Yet in the U.S. Senate race, Ron Johnson, the Republican

incumbent, defeated former senator Russ Feingold, the Democrat, by nearly one hundred thousand votes.

10. Patrick Marley and Jason Stein, "Judge Strikes Down Wisconsin Voter ID, Early Voting Laws," *Milwaukee Journal Sentinel*, July 29, 2016; and Michael Wines, "Jury Out on Impact as Some States, Bucking a Trend, Make Voting Easier," *New York Times*, June 5, 2016. After federal intelligence agencies accused Russia of trying to meddle in the 2016 U.S. elections via WikiLeaks disclosures of stolen e-mails, circulation of fake news stories on the Internet, and other actions, one concern is whether voting machines used across the nation are vulnerable to hacking and, if so, how to design new machines that are more robust against such cyberattacks. See David Sanger and Charlie Savage, "U.S. Says Russia Directed Hacks to Influence Elections," *New York Times*, October 7, 2016; Sanger, "U.S. Officials Defend Integrity of Vote, Despite Hacking Fears," *New York Times*, November 25, 2016; and Craig Timberg, "Russian Propaganda Effort Helped Spread 'Fake News' during Election, Experts Say," *Washington Post*, November 24, 2016.

11. Direct citizen participation of this kind is often fraught with risk. Both sides in such disputes may be tempted to distort the facts, a good deal of money can be spent in ways that can easily mislead voters, and the outcome does not always represent what citizens or the state legislature might choose to do with greater deliberation. The risks of direct policymaking by citizens have not gone unnoticed by scholars. See, for example, Richard J. Ellis, *Democratic Delusions: The Initiative Process in America* (Lawrence: University Press of Kansas, 2002).

12. Sabrina Tavernise and Steven Greenhouse, "Ohio Vote on Labor Is Parsed for Omens," *New York Times*, November 9, 2011.

13. Monica Davey, "Organizers Say 1 Million Signed Petition to Recall Wisconsin Governor," *New York Times*, January 17, 2012.

14. Scott Helman, "For Democrats, a New Electorate," *Boston Globe*, January 30, 2008.

15. John Herrman, "What We've Learned about the Media Industry during This Election," *New York Times*, November 8, 2016; Editorial Board, "Facebook and the Digital Virus Called Fake News," *New York Times*, November 19, 2016; and Timberg, "Russian Propaganda Effort Helped Spread 'Fake News' during Election, Experts Say." For a broader treatment of how use of the Internet is affecting politics, see Gainous and Wagner (2011).

16. David Dayen, "How Low Can Political Journalism Sink?" *New Republic*, November 2, 2016; and Eric Boehlert, "How the Media's Email Obsession Obliterated Clinton Policy Coverage," *Media Matters for America*, November 23, 2016. Christopher Achen and Larry Bartels (2016) argue that the model of thoughtful citizens carefully considering the policy positions of candidates is misguided and that voters today tend to choose parties and candidates more on the basis of social identities and partisan preferences rather than policy stances.

17. Ron Nixon, "Food Safety Law's Funding Is Far below Estimated Requirement," *New York Times*, April 7, 2015.

18. Jason DeParle, "A Plan to Lift the Lowly Bureaucrat to a Status of Cherished Public Servant," *New York Times*, January 7, 2009.

19. See, for example, reports at the Pew Research Center, such as the April 2010 report "Distrust, Discontent, Anger and Partisan Rancor," available at http://pewresearch.org/pubs/1569/trust-in-government-distrust-discontent-anger-partisan-rancor, and the October 2013 report "Trust in Government Nears Record Low, but

Most Federal Agencies Are Viewed Favorably," available at www.people-press.org/2013/10/18/trust-in-government-nears-record-low-but-most-federal-agencies-are-viewed-favorably/. A summary account of recent surveys of this kind can be found in Jeff Zeleny and Megan Thee-Brenan, "New Poll Finds a Deep Distrust of Government," *New York Times*, October 25, 2011; and Lynn Vavreck, "The Long Decline of Trust in Government, and Why That Can Be Patriotic," *New York Times*, July 3, 2015. On the phenomenon of political incivility, see a special symposium, "Political Civility," *PS: Political Science and Politics* (July 2012): 401–434. See also Mann and Ornstein (2012).

20. See "10 Successes, 10 Challenges," *National Journal*, January 20, 2007, 18–40. Among the successes were support for higher education, clean air and clean water, the food stamp program, and action against AIDS.

21. The Brookings study, "Government's Greatest Achievements of the Past Half Century," by Paul C. Light, is available at www.brookings.edu/research/governments-greatest-achievements-of-the-past-half-century/.

22. See Jeffrey M. Berry and Sarah Sobieraj, "Understanding the Rise of Talk Radio," *PS: Political Science and Politics* (October 2011): 762–767.

23. Michael Corkery, "Trump Expected to Seek Deep Cuts in Business Regulations," *New York Times*, November 9, 2016.

24. The Pew study, "Ready, Willing, and Able: Citizens Working for Change," is available at www.civicchange.org. The site includes similar studies and recommendations for civic engagement.

25. Melissa Dahl, "Youth Vote May Have Been Key in Obama's Win," *MSNBC*, November 5, 2008, available at www.nbcnews.com/id/27525497.

26. See David Leonhardt, "The Democrats' Real Turnout Problem," *New York Times*, November 17, 2016; and Carl Bialik, "No, Voter Turnout Wasn't Way Down from 2012," *FiveThirtyEight*, November 15, 2016, available at http://fivethirtyeight.com/features/no-voter-turnout-wasnt-way-down-from-2012/.

27. Elizabeth Becker, "Accord Reached on a Bill Raising Farm Subsidies," *New York Times*, April 27, 2002.

28. One of the most active liberal groups to have exploited the potential of the Internet for citizen mobilization is MoveOn.org (www.moveon.org). See David Karpf, *The MoveOn Effect: The Unexpected Transformation of American Political Advocacy* (New York: Oxford University Press, 2012).

29. For an argument that the Republican Party has been especially guilty of such manipulation of the American public, see Jacob S. Hacker and Paul Pierson, *Off Center: The Republican Revolution and the Erosion of American Democracy* (New Haven, Conn.: Yale University Press, 2005). Republicans would counter that liberals and Democrats also manipulate language and political symbols that can mislead the public on policy issues in much the same way.

30. See Frank Ahrens, "Hard News to Digest," *Washington Post National Weekly Edition*, February 28–March 6, 2005, 19–20.

31. The list of contributors to each side can be found at the website for MapLight, a nonpartisan group that collects data on contributions to political campaigns: http://maplight.org/content/california-prop-23-nov-2010. See also Todd Woody, "Foes Outspend Backers of Proposition 23," *New York Times*, October 11, 2010.

32. Marianne Lavelle, "Washington State Voters Reject Nation's First Carbon Tax," *Inside Climate News*, November 9, 2016.

33. Anahad O'Connor and Margot Sanger-Katz, "Soda Taxes Gain Acceptance, City by Revenue-Hungry City," *New York Times*, November 27, 2016.

34. Maura Dolan, "California Supreme Court Looks Unlikely to Kill Proposition 8," *Los Angeles Times* online edition, March 6, 2009; Adam Nagourney and John Swartz, "Backers of Prop. 8 Can Challenge Court Ruling," *New York Times*, November 17, 2011; and Nagourney, "Court Strikes Down Ban on Gay Marriage in California," *New York Times*, February 7, 2012.

Glossary

advocacy coalition framework: A policymaking theory developed by Paul Sabatier and Hank Jenkins-Smith that focuses on the "interactions of competing advocacy coalitions," particularly within a policy subsystem, such as agriculture or environmental protection. Each coalition consists of policy actors from different public and private institutions and different levels of government that share a particular set of beliefs about the policies that government should promote.

Affordable Care Act: The Patient Protection and Affordable Care Act, enacted in 2010, which significantly altered health care policy in the United States, and also deeply divided the nation over its expansion of the federal role in health care.

agenda setting: A step in the policy process whereby policy actors attempt to get an issue seriously considered for public action.

assessing alternatives: Determining the merit of possible policy choices, often through use of policy analysis.

balance of trade: An economic goal related to the role of the United States in an international economy; examines the value of a nation's exports compared to its imports.

bicameral: The term used to describe a two-house congress. In the United States, this consists of the House of Representatives and the Senate.

block grants: Transfers of federal dollars to the states, where the states have substantial discretion in how to spend the money to meet the needs of their citizens.

brainstorming: Used to foster creativity in consideration of policy alternatives. In a small group setting, individuals are encouraged to think of possible solutions without imposing constraints on the discussion or criticizing ideas as they are offered.

cabinet-level departments: Offices within the executive branch, such as the Department of the Treasury, that implement policy in specialized areas.

cap-and-trade policy: A policy action that relies on market-based mechanisms in which an overall cap or ceiling is set and trading of permits or allowances is allowed within that cap. The cap may be lowered over time.

carbon tax: A tax on gasoline or on all fossil fuels, often proposed as a revenue-neutral tax in which other taxes are lowered by the same amount as the new tax on carbon.

categorical grants: Transfers of federal dollars to the states where the funding must be used for specific purposes.

causes: The factors that are thought to bring about a given situation or problem. Used in problem analysis to identify how a problem came to exist and why it continues.

Central Intelligence Agency (CIA): The federal agency established in 1947 to collect, evaluate, and distribute information and analysis related to national security, and to coordinate the nation's intelligence activities.

charter school: A school reform idea in which a school is government supported but independent. A state board of education gives an independent entity the responsibility for establishing a school and delivering education services with limited control by the school board.

Children's Health Insurance Program (CHIP): A program that helps to ensure that children living in poverty have medical coverage. The federal government provides the states with funds, which the states match. States are free to set eligibility levels.

circuit court of appeals: At the federal level, one of thirteen courts responsible for hearing appeals from the federal district courts; circuit courts have only appellate jurisdiction.

citizen capacity: The ability of citizens to participate in policymaking processes; that is, their level of interest and knowledge, and their ability to understand issues and play an active role.

Clean Power Plan: Issued by the EPA in August 2015, a plan that seeks to reduce carbon pollution from electric power generation by 32 percent below 2005 levels when fully in place by 2030, and thereby to facilitate a transition to cleaner sources of energy. The plan also will significantly lower emissions of sulfur dioxide and nitrogen dioxides, major contributors to air pollution and thus a risk to public health.

climate change: A change in global climate patterns, characterized by rising temperatures, increased severity of storms, and persistent droughts, caused largely by greenhouse gas emissions from burning of fossil fuels: coal, oil, and natural gas.

Cold War: The period of persistent hostility, but not overt "hot" war, between the former Soviet Union and the United States that lasted from 1945 until the Soviet Union's collapse in 1991.

collaborative decision making: An approach to environmental or resource decision making in which industry and other stakeholders work cooperatively with government officials. Thought to be more effective and less conflict ridden than more conventional regulation.

collective good: The general good of all people in a community, state, or nation. Also refers to goods, such as national defense, that could in principle be private but instead are provided by government because private markets cannot do so. Also called a public good.

command and control: The traditional approach to environmental regulation (also called direct regulation) in which government sets and enforces standards for air quality, water quality, and other resources.

common pool resources: Resources that are shared by a society and available to all to consume, such as oceans, lakes, rivers, and public lands. Also represents a type of market failure in which a good is defined by its ability not to be jointly consumed and for which exclusion is not feasible.

competency test: An exam used to determine teachers' pedagogical skills or knowledge base.

competitive regulation: Regulatory policies that are mostly associated with the regulation of specific industries and their practices.

Consumer Price Index (CPI): An economic statistic used to measure the inflation rate. The index is calculated by examining percent price changes for a typical market basket of goods.

contingent valuation methods: The use of surveys to determine the economic value that people place on certain goods or services for which there is no market value. Used in cost-benefit analysis to consider intangible costs or benefits, such as a safe community or clean water.

cooperative federalism: A theory that states that the national government is more involved in different policies through collaboration between the national and state governments.

Corporate Average Fuel Economy (CAFE) standards: A federal program that mandates achievement of an average level of fuel efficiency for a given automaker's line of vehicles. That is, it sets minimum fuel economy standards, but only for the average of all vehicles produced.

cost-benefit analysis: A form of policy analysis in which the costs and benefits of proposed policy actions are considered carefully. Often, although not always, the major costs and benefits are measured quantitatively by their value in dollars.

cost-effectiveness analysis: A comparison of the relative value of policy alternatives in terms of a given benefit that is delivered; a method for comparing policy alternatives when a dollar value cannot easily be placed on the benefits of action, such as the value of lives that are saved by requiring safer automobiles.

cost of living adjustment (COLA): Programs with COLAs have benefits tied to the inflation rate so that benefits increase as inflation increases.

creative thinking: Refers to a way of analyzing public problems and their solutions that goes beyond conventional ideas. Important for imagining and proposing unusual solutions.

culture of poverty: A term used by some to describe how those living in poverty learn to work the welfare system to their benefit and pass this information on to their children, who remain poor.

decentralization: The transfer of policy authority from the federal government to the states.

defense policy: A major component of foreign policy that encompasses the conduct of military affairs, such as choice of weapons systems and deployment of troops. Intended to achieve policy goals set by civilian policymakers in the White House and Congress.

democratic political processes: Opportunities for citizen involvement in decision making and ensuring public review of policy ideas.

Department of Homeland Security (DHS): The federal executive department created in 2002 and charged with diverse responsibilities related to protection of the nation from security threats.

deterrence: A policy strategy used most often in national defense in which the object is to deter or prevent a potential enemy from taking actions harmful to the nation. The strategy of nuclear deterrence, for example, was based on the assumption that no nation would engage in a preemptive, or first-strike, war because the likely retaliation would be too massive to accept.

direct regulation: Also called command and control, or simply regulation. Government regulates or controls environmental, health, and safety performance of industry or other facilities through the setting and enforcement of standards and sometimes through requirements for certain technologies to be used.

discount rate: A calculation made in conducting cost-benefit analysis that takes into account the changing value of a dollar over time. Future costs and benefits are "discounted" to present value by using estimated inflation rates.

distributive policies: Individual programs or grants that a government provides without regard to limited resources or zero sum situations (in which one group's gain is another's loss).

dual federalism: A theory that states that the functions or responsibilities of each level of government are distinct; little integration of the two levels of government exists.

Earned Income Tax Credit (EITC): A tax credit for people who work but have low wages; it reduces the amount of taxes they owe or provides a tax refund.

ecosystem-based management: A comprehensive approach to natural resource management that emphasizes the integrated treatment of entire ecosystems and their functions. Contrasted with efforts to deal with a specific species or body of land or water.

effectiveness: An analytical criterion that refers to whether a current policy or program or one that is being considered is likely to work—or the likelihood that the policy's goals will be achieved.

efficiency: An analytical criterion that refers to what a policy or policy proposal costs in relation to its expected benefits to society; or a desire to realize the greatest possible benefit out of the dollars that the government spends.

elite theory: A policymaking theory that emphasizes how the values and preferences of governing elites, which differ from those of the public at large, affect public policy development.

entitlement program: A program in which payment obligations are determined by the law that created it, not by the budget associated with that program. Under entitlement programs, any person who meets the eligibility requirements is entitled to receive benefits from the program.

environmental impact statement (EIS): A form of impact assessment in which government agencies must provide details on the environmental consequences of major actions, such as highway construction, and make them public prior to a final decision on the project.

environmental policy: Government actions that affect or attempt to affect environmental quality and the use of natural resources. The policy actions may take place at the local, state, regional, national, or international level.

Environmental Protection Agency (EPA): An independent federal regulatory agency charged with enforcement of most environmental protection (such as pollution control) laws.

environmental stewardship: A philosophy of governance based on the belief that the natural environment should be protected for future generations—that is, that the government is the steward of such protection.

equity: An analytical criterion that refers to the consideration of what constitutes a fair or equitable policy choice, how a program's costs and benefits are distributed among citizens, or a way to think about who is allowed to participate in policymaking processes.

Establishment Clause: The part of the First Amendment to the Constitution that states that Congress cannot establish a state religion.

ethical analysis: Policy analysis that is based on ethical principles or norms, such as personal freedom or equality. It can supplement analysis based largely on economic, political, or administrative concerns.

Every Student Succeeds Act (ESSA): A new version of the federal education law (ESEA), signed by President Obama in 2015, that reversed much of the federal government's control of public education and returned control to the states and local districts.

Executive Office of the President (EOP): A "mini bureaucracy" that consists of the White House offices and agencies, such as the Office of Management and Budget, that assist the president in the development and implementation of public policy and provide the president and the president's staff with vital information and policy ideas in their respective areas.

federal district courts: The federal (national) courts primarily responsible for conducting trials—in the original jurisdiction—for national laws.

federalism: A system of government in which sovereignty is divided between a central government and another government unit.

fee-for-service: The traditional way to pay for medical services, whereby the patient or health insurer pays for the services rendered with no restraint on overall costs. Managed care programs are offered as an alternative.

filibuster: The senatorial procedure whereby a single senator or group of senators can talk for an extended period of time in hope of delaying, modifying, or defeating a proposal.

fiscal policy: A term that describes the taxing and spending tools at the government's disposal to influence the economy.

food stamp program: A plan administered by the Department of Agriculture that provides low-income households with coupons that they can use to purchase food. Also called the Supplemental Nutrition Assistance Program, or SNAP.

foreign policy: The collection of government actions that affect U.S. national security and the economic and political goals associated with it. Encompasses issues as diverse as international trade, economic assistance to poor nations, immigration to the United States, and action on human rights abuses around the world.

Free Exercise Clause: The part of the First Amendment to the Constitution that states that Congress cannot prevent the exercise or belief of a particular religion.

full employment: A goal of economic policy generally defined as the lowest level of unemployment that can be sustained in light of the structure of the overall economy. Also described as the condition in which everyone who wishes to work at the prevailing wage rates can find a job.

Gini coefficient: A graphical way to demonstrate a nation's income equality/inequality by charting the percentage of income made by quintiles of families.

globalization: The growing interrelationship of all nations through global trade. Facilitates the development of an international marketplace in an increasingly connected world.

group theory: A policymaking theory that sees public policy as the product of a continuous struggle among organized interest groups; tends to believe that power in the U.S. political system is widely shared among interest groups, each of which seeks access to the policymaking process.

health maintenance organization (HMO): A form of managed care in which an individual chooses or is assigned to a health care provider network that contracts with physicians to deliver health care services. HMOs promote cost-effective health care

by negotiating lower fees with health care providers, limiting access to expensive services, and often emphasizing preventative health care.

hydraulic fracturing: Rapidly expanding oil and gas drilling in shale rock formations in which water, sand, and chemicals are injected under pressure to release the oil and natural gas.

ideal situation: A reference used in policy analysis whereby a highly preferable or ideal goal or solution to a problem might be set.

impact assessment: A form of policy analysis that examines the likely effects or impacts of proposed or adopted policies. These may be environmental, social, economic, or other significant impacts.

implementation analysis: A form of policy analysis that examines the process and effects of implementing public policy. Can be used to anticipate likely implementation problems prior to adoption or to document actual problems after a policy has been put into effect.

incremental decision making: A way of making decisions that emphasizes consideration of a limited number of policy alternatives and their effects.

incremental policymaking: Policy changes that occur in small steps; adjustments are made at the margins of existing policies through minor amendments or the gradual extension of a program's mandate or the groups it serves.

independent executive agency: An executive branch organization, such as the EPA, that differs from cabinet-level departments chiefly because it is responsible for a more focused policy area.

independent regulatory commission (IRC): Another type of executive agency whose commissioners are appointed by the president and confirmed by the Senate for fixed and staggered terms; most IRCs are responsible for the economic regulation of certain industries.

information failure: A type of market failure that occurs when willing buyers and sellers do not possess all of the information needed to enter into a transaction or exchange.

institutional or government agenda: Issues to which policymakers give active and serious consideration.

institutional theory: A policymaking theory that emphasizes the formal and legal aspects of government structures. Institutional models look at the way governments are arranged, their legal powers, and their rules for decision making.

intergenerational equity: An ethical principle that emphasizes fairness or equity among generations. Important for environmental policies that have substantial effects far into the future, such as actions on climate change.

Intergovernmental Panel on Climate Change (IPCC): The United Nations' scientific body charged with periodic assessment of global climate change and its effects. Its reports are widely considered to reflect scientific consensus on the subject.

International Monetary Fund (IMF): An international financial institution that promotes international trade by increasing the exchange stability of the major currencies. Similar to the World Bank, the IMF also lends money to developing nations.

issue framing: The practice in which policymakers and interest groups do whatever they can to set the policy agenda in their favor by defining problems their way.

issue networks: A term coined by political scientist Hugh Heclo to describe informal arrangements or relationships among policy actors in the making of public policy.

Kyoto Protocol: The major international treaty that commits signatory nations to reducing their greenhouse gas emissions by a specified amount as a way to reduce the risk of global climate change or global warming.

line-item veto: A budgeting tool that allows chief executives to delete specific items from an appropriations bill without rejecting the whole bill.

literature review: A review or assessment of available analyses or writings about a given subject. This can be a way to discover what has been written on a subject and what policy approaches have been tried in various settings.

lobbying: Activities through which interest groups attempt to persuade policymakers to agree with their points of view or support policy proposals they favor, oppose those the group does not, or keep certain issues or policy alternatives off the legislative agenda.

logic of collective action: An interest group theory that suggests that a single individual would be irrational to join an interest group when almost no personal gain would follow.

managed care: A variety of efforts to organize and manage health care services, for example, through health maintenance organizations. Designed as one way to contain rising health care costs that had soared under the old, unrestrained "fee-for-service" system.

market failure: A term used when the private market is not efficient; some argue that such a failure provides a justification for government intervention.

Marshall Plan: The plan adopted in 1947 for the economic rebuilding of Europe after the end of World War II. Named for Secretary of State George Marshall.

means-tested programs: Social programs in which recipients must meet an income test in order to qualify for benefits.

Medicaid: A federal state health insurance program that assists the poor and disabled. The federal government sets standards for services and pays about half the cost. States pay the rest, and set standards for eligibility and overall benefit levels.

Medicare: A national health insurance program for senior citizens. Covers basic medical care for those age sixty-five and older, and others with permanent disabilities, diabetes, or end-stage renal disease.

merit good: A good or service to which people are entitled as a right. Some argue that health care should be considered a merit good and as such be provided by either employers or government regardless of ability to pay.

merit pay: The idea that teacher pay increases should be based on performance in the classroom; this is sometimes linked to how students perform on standardized exams.

minimum wage: The lowest wage, typically by the hour, that employers may legally pay to employees or workers; the states may set a level for this wage that is higher than the federal minimum.

monetary policy: A tool used by the Federal Reserve Board to influence economic policy goals; it attempts to control economic fluctuations (through tools such as changes to the reserve requirement) by controlling the amount of money in circulation, also referred to as the money supply.

multiple use: The principle that any natural resource, such as public forestland, can be used simultaneously for multiple purposes or uses, for example, timber harvesting and recreation. A long-standing element of federal land and forest policies.

National Assessment of Educational Progress (NAEP): The test that is required by the No Child Left Behind Act to determine whether schools are meeting appropriate standards.

national debt: The accumulation of all of the deficits the nation has run historically.

national health insurance: A common health care policy in industrialized nations in which the national government provides health insurance to all citizens. Also called a single-payer system.

National Security Agency (NSA): A secretive intelligence agency created in 1952 to coordinate, direct, and perform activities to protect U.S. government information systems as well as assess a diversity of foreign communications related to national security.

National Security Council (NSC): A White House advisory body that focuses on issues of national security. Chaired by the president, it includes the vice president, the secretary of state, the secretary of the Treasury, the secretary of defense, and the assistant to the president for national security affairs (also called the president's national security adviser).

negative externality: A type of market failure that occurs when two parties interact in a market and a third party is harmed as a result, and does not get compensated.

no-action analysis: A policy alternative that considers the advantages or disadvantages of taking no new action, and thus keeping a current policy in place. Maintains the status quo.

North Atlantic Treaty Organization (NATO): A formal alliance of the United States, Canada, and Western European nations created in Washington, D.C., in 1949 to pursue common security interests. During the cold war, NATO stood in opposition to actions by the Warsaw Pact, representing the communist nations of Central and Eastern Europe.

nuclear proliferation: The spread of nuclear weapons knowledge and technology to new nations such as India and Pakistan. The United States and other nuclear powers often express concern over such proliferation because it may increase security risks.

operational measures: A specific way to define and measure a policy problem, such as a rate of poverty or unemployment. Often useful when quantitative measures of problems are needed.

opportunity costs: Common in economic analysis; one considers the value of opportunities that are forgone when time or resources are spent on a given activity. It is what people might have done with the same time or resources if they had had the choice.

Organization of the Petroleum Exporting Countries (OPEC): An association of oil-producing and -exporting nations that was established to help fuse their mutual interests, particularly the price of oil on the world market and the stability of oil production and consumption.

parallel situation: A similar condition in a related policy area that might provide ideas for what actions might be undertaken to address a problem.

passive collection: Finding out what others have suggested in a given policy area by speaking with a program's clients or administrators, advocates of various positions, and organizations that have taken a position on the issues.

patients' rights: A privilege of patients to see medical specialists or have a specific medical treatment, or to sue their health care provider in order to gain those services or be compensated for their loss. This became a legal issue when a 1974 federal law (ERISA) allowed such suits in federal court only.

policy capacity: The ability of government to identify and evaluate public problems, and to develop suitable policies to deal with them.

policy change: The modification of policy goals and/or the means used to achieve them.

policy cycle: A term sometimes used to describe the policy process to indicate that the steps of the process can be continuous and cyclical.

policy design: A form of policy analysis that occurs during policy formulation, where an analyst considers how the various components of a proposed policy fit together and how they are likely to work to solve a problem. Involves consideration of what actions government will take and how they will affect "target populations," or the people most affected by the policy.

policy evaluation: A step in the policy process that assesses whether policies and programs are working well. Also called program evaluation.

policy formulation: A step in the policy process that results in the development of proposed courses of action to help resolve a public problem.

policy gridlock: When political decision makers are unable or unwilling to compromise in a way that permits public policy action.

policy implementation: The actual development of a program's details to ensure that policy goals and objectives will be attained; it is during this part of the policy process when one sees actual government intervention and real consequences for society.

policy instrument: The tool, such as regulation or education, that government uses to intervene in a given problem or issue.

policy legitimation: A step in the policy process that gives legal force to decisions or authorizes or justifies policy action.

policy outcomes: The effects that policy outputs, such as the passing of a law, have on society.

policy outputs: The formal actions that governments take to pursue their goals.

policy stream: What might be done about a problem—that is, the possible alternative policies.

political culture: Widely held values, beliefs, and attitudes, such as trust and confidence in government and the political process.

political feasibility: A calculation of the likely acceptability to policymakers of proposed policy ideas or alternatives. Refers to whether elected officials are likely to support the idea. This is assumed to reflect a broader social acceptability of the same ideas or alternatives.

political stream: A political climate or public mood, evident in public opinion surveys, the results of elections, and the activity and strength of interest groups.

political systems theory: A policymaking theory that stresses the way the political system responds to demands that arise from its environment, such as public opinion and interest group pressures. Systems theory emphasizes the larger social, economic, and cultural context in which political decisions and policy choices are made.

politics: The exercise of power in society or in specific decisions over public policy; used to refer to the processes through which public policies are formulated and adopted, especially the role played by elected officials, organized interest groups, and political parties. Politics can also be thought of as how conflicts in society are expressed and resolved in favor of one set of interests or social values over another.

portability: A right guaranteed by a 1996 federal law in which employees can take their guaranteed insurance coverage with them (that is, the insurance is portable) if they change jobs.

positive externality: A type of market failure that occurs the same way as a negative externality, but the third party gains something from the two-party interaction and does not have to pay for it.

poverty: Defined by the Census Bureau as falling below a specified level of annual income that is adjusted each year to reflect the rising cost of living.

precedent: The legal doctrine in which judges rely on prior court decisions in the making of current decisions.

preferred provider organization (PPO): An alternative to an HMO, in which enrollees have a financial incentive to use physicians on an approved list but may opt to see other health professionals (preferred providers) at a higher cost.

preventative health care: The promotion of health and prevention of disease in individuals through such actions as routine screening for serious diseases, better treatment of chronic illnesses, improved health care education, and more attention to the role of diet, exercise, smoking, and other lifestyle choices.

problem: The existence of an unsatisfactory set of conditions for which relief is sought, either through private means or from the government. Commonly used in discussion of societal issues that call for a governmental response in the form of public policy.

problem analysis: A series of methods that can be used to analyze the causes of public problems, where they exist, what effects they have, and what might be done about them.

problem definition: The step in the policy process whereby a particular issue is defined or explained in a particular way that people can understand. Problems can be defined in a number of ways.

problem stream: The various bits of information available on a problem, whom it affects, and in what ways.

program evaluation: Focuses more on policy results or outcomes than on the process of implementation, but the two go together. Evaluation of any program may be an essential part of long-term implementation success, and there are many different ways to evaluate a program.

progressive tax: A tax that is based on the philosophy that higher earners should pay higher taxes both in terms of actual dollars and as a percentage of income.

protective or social regulation: Regulatory policies that protect the general public from activities that occur in the private sector.

proximate causes: Those causes of public policy problems that are most direct or immediate, and sometimes easier to handle. Often contrasted with underlying, or root, causes of problems.

public attitudes and habits: The collective opinion or practice of the public, which can become entrenched due to long-standing habits and can influence policy action.

public good: *See* collective good.

public health agencies: Government-established agencies to counter the threat of infectious diseases or unsafe food, and to support medical research.

public opinion: What the public thinks about a particular issue or set of issues at any point in time.

public participation: The involvement of the public in political or governmental processes. It can refer to voting, writing letters or e-mail messages to policymakers, talking with others about policy issues, or assuming a direct role in governmental decisions.

public policy: What public officials within government, and by extension the citizens they represent, choose to do or not do about public problems. This can include passing laws or approving regulations, spending money, or providing tax breaks, among other things.

punctuated equilibrium model: Suggests that we can get dramatic policy change when the conditions are right. Thus we may have long periods in which policy stability is the norm, in part because those who dominate the policy process are "privileged groups of elites" who are largely satisfied with the status quo.

pure private good: A good or service where the consumer enjoys all the benefits and bears all the costs.

pure public goods: A type of market failure in which a good, such as police protection, is defined by its ability to be jointly consumed and for which exclusion is not feasible.

quick survey: Talking with people in a particular policy network or searching through hearings transcripts, minutes of meetings, newspaper accounts, and the like for pertinent information about a problem and policy alternatives.

rational choice theory: A policymaking theory that draws heavily from economics; assumes that in making decisions, individuals are rational actors who seek to attain their preferences or further their self-interests. The goal is to deduce or predict how individuals will behave under a variety of conditions.

rational-comprehensive approach: A way of making decisions that considers all significant policy alternatives and all of their major consequences. Often contrasted with incremental decision making, which is thought to be more realistic and practical.

rational decision making: An approach to decision making that attempts to follow a series of logical or rational steps: defining a problem, identifying goals and objectives to be sought, evaluating alternative solutions, and recommending one that best achieves the goals and objectives.

realpolitik: A hardheaded or practical appraisal of national interests that emphasizes competition among nation-states.

redistributive policies: Policies that provide benefits to one category of individuals at the expense of another; often reflect ideological or class conflict.

regressive tax: A tax that, when applied, taxes all individuals at the same rate regardless of their income or socioeconomic standing.

regulatory policy: Government restriction of individual choice to keep conduct from transcending acceptable bounds. Often used in health, safety, and environmental policies.

resource subsidies: Government policies that provide financial incentives (subsidies) to develop and use specific resources, such as land, water, minerals, and forests. Traditionally a major component of federal natural resource policies.

risk assessment: A calculation or estimate of the risks to society posed by a given situation, such as terrorism or natural hazards—for example, hurricanes. A specialized and technical form of policy analysis that can identify risks and estimate their severity.

risk evaluation: Use of various methods to determine the level of risk that is acceptable to the public and policymakers. For example, to what extent should the nation protect its citizens against the risk of air pollution or unsafe food or water? Risk evaluation addresses the question of how safe is safe enough.

risk management: Describes public policies that are adopted to manage or control various risks. For example, antiterrorist policies are designed to lower the risk that terrorism presents for public safety, and pollution-control policies aim to reduce risk to public health posed by various chemicals.

root causes: The basic or fundamental causes of public problems, sometimes referred to as underlying causes. Often contrasted with proximate causes.

school choice: The term used to describe any school reform effort that provides parents with options regarding where to send their children, including charter schools and voucher programs. Sometimes the term is used more specifically to describe programs in which parents can send children to public schools in a particular area.

school vouchers: A school reform idea in which the government provides individuals with a certain amount of money that can be applied to a student's education; often associated with a way to provide people with a private school option they may not have been able to afford in the past.

sensitivity analysis: A way to adjust policy analysis by making it sensitive or responsive to changes in any one variable so that the consequences can be better understood under varying assumptions. For example, forecasting can be made sensitive to different assumptions about economic growth or inflation.

single-payer insurance: A common health care policy in industrialized nations in which the national government provides health insurance to all citizens. Also called national health insurance.

Social Security: A government entitlement program that provides money for retired workers and their beneficiaries and disabled workers.

solutions: Proposed alternatives to solve a given problem once the causes have been identified.

subgovernments: The term used to describe how policymaking occurs in less formal settings or venues and involves policy actors within particular issue areas, such as national defense.

Supplemental Nutrition Assistance Program (SNAP): *See* food stamp program.

supply and demand perspectives: Two views on how to think about public problems. One focuses on the quantity of the good or service that is, or can be made, available (supply) and the other on its use by the public (demand)—which might increase or decrease. For example, energy policy could try to increase the supply or decrease the demand through conservation.

supply-side economics: An economic theory that states that the government can increase economic growth by cutting taxes, especially for the richest individuals.

sustainable development: Economic growth that is compatible with environmental systems and social goals.

systemic agenda: Issues the public is aware of and may be discussing. Also referred to as the societal or social agenda.

tax expenditures: Tax subsidies, such as an investment credit or deduction, designed to favor a particular industry, activity, or set of persons. Called an expenditure because such a subsidy reduces government revenue and thus is like spending money. Also sometimes called corporate welfare.

teacher quality: An issue in education policy that concerns a teacher's ability in the classroom.

terrorism: Usually defined as the unconventional or unlawful use or threat of violence to achieve political or social ends. Terrorism encompasses the strategies and tactics of diverse groups around the world.

third-party payers: In health care policy, refers to insurance companies, employers, governments, or other parties that pay for most health care expenses.

toll goods: A type of market failure whereby a good is defined by its ability to be jointly consumed, and exclusion is feasible. An example is cable television services.

Toxics Release Inventory (TRI): A report published each year and that can be accessed on the EPA's website and elsewhere. The TRI describes toxic chemicals that industrial facilities release to the air, water, and land in communities across the country.

Tricare: A health insurance program offered by the U.S. Department of Defense. Includes substantial benefits for retirees with at least twenty years of military service when they become eligible for Medicare.

unfunded mandates: Federal requirements placed upon the state governments without sufficient funds for implementation.

United Nations (UN): Established in 1945 by the United States and fifty other nations as a global association of governments to facilitate cooperation in international law, security, economic development, and social equity. Headquartered in New York City.

UN General Assembly: Made up of all member states, it oversees the budget of the United Nations, appoints the nonpermanent members to the Security Council, receives reports from other parts of the United Nations, and makes recommendations in the form of General Assembly Resolutions. All member nations have equal representation.

UN Security Council: The most important of the UN policymaking bodies, which focuses on maintaining peace and security. The council has a rotating membership of ten nations selected from the UN General Assembly in addition to five permanent members: China, France, the Russian Federation, the United Kingdom, and the United States.

U.S. Agency for International Development (USAID): The principal office charged with the distribution and management of U.S. economic aid, or foreign aid. USAID is an independent federal agency that works closely with the Department of State.

user fees: Specific fees or charges that the user of a natural resource pays. Could be fees for entering a national park, harvesting timber from public lands, or mining minerals on public lands.

veterans' health care system: A medical system designed to serve the needs of American veterans by providing primary medical care, specialized care, and other medical and social services, such as rehabilitation.

veto: A presidential power to reject a bill approved by Congress; Congress may override the president's veto with a two-thirds vote in both houses.

World Bank: Loans money to developing nations for certain kinds of development projects.

World Trade Organization (WTO): The WTO was established in 1995 and administers trade agreements among about 150 nations to settle conflicts over trade disputes. Its existence reflects the global marketplace of the twenty-first century.

References

Achen, Christopher H., and Larry M. Bartels. 2016. *Democracy for Realists: Why Elections Do Not Produce Responsive Government*. Princeton, N.J.: Princeton University Press.

Adams, Rebecca. 2002. "OIRA Directs Guidelines on Data Quality," *CQ Weekly*, March 23, 827.

Almy, Sarah, and Christina Theokas. 2010. "Not Prepared for Class: High Poverty Schools Continue to Have Fewer In-field Teachers." *Education Trust*, November 18. Available at https://edtrust.org/resource/not-prepared-for-class-high-poverty-schools-continue-to-have-fewer-in-field-teachers/.

American Council of Education. 1999. "To Touch the Future: Transforming the Way Teachers Are Taught." Available at https://eric.ed.gov/?id=ED471782.

Ammons, David N. 2009. *Tools for Decision Making: A Practical Guide for Local Government*. 2nd ed. Washington, D.C.: CQ Press.

Amy, Douglas J. 1984. "Why Policy Analysis and Ethics Are Incompatible." *Journal of Policy Analysis and Management* 3: 573–591.

Anderson, Charles W. 1979. "The Place of Principles in Policy Analysis." *American Political Science Review* 73: 711–723.

Anderson, James E. 2011. *Public Policymaking*. 7th ed. Florence, Ky.: Wadsworth/Cengage.

———. 2015. *Public Policymaking*. 8th ed. Stamford, Conn.: Cengage Learning.

Andrews, Richard N. L. 2006a. *Managing the Environment, Managing Ourselves: A History of American Environmental Policy*. 2nd ed. New Haven, Conn.: Yale University Press.

———. 2006b. "Risk-Based Decision Making: Policy, Science, and Politics." In *Environmental Policy*. 6th ed. Edited by Norman J. Vig and Michael E. Kraft. Washington, D.C.: CQ Press.

———. 2016. "The Environmental Protection Agency." In *Environmental Policy*. 9th ed. Edited by Norman J. Vig and Michael E. Kraft. Thousand Oaks, Calif.: CQ Press.

Antonovic, Kate, and Ben Backes. 2014. "The Effect of Banning Affirmative Action on College Admissions Policies and Student Quality." *Journal of Human Resources* 49: 295–358.

Asher, Herbert. 2017. *Polling and the Public: What Every Citizen Should Know*. 9th ed. Thousand Oaks, Calif.: CQ Press.

Axelrod, Regina S., and Stacy D. VanDeveer, eds. 2015. *The Global Environment: Institutions, Law, and Policy*. 4th ed. Thousand Oaks, Calif.: CQ Press.

Bardach, Eugene, and Eric M. Patashnik. 2016. *A Practical Guide for Policy Analysis: The Eightfold Path to More Effective Problem Solving*. 5th ed. Thousand Oaks, Calif.: CQ Press.

Bartlett, Robert, ed. 1989. *Policy through Impact Assessment: Institutionalized Analysis as a Policy Strategy*. New York: Greenwood Press.

Baumgartner, Frank R., and Bryan D. Jones. 1993. *Agendas and Instability in American Politics*. Chicago: University of Chicago Press.

Baumgartner, Frank R., and Bryan D. Jones, eds. 2002. *Policy Dynamics*. Chicago: University of Chicago Press.

Baumgartner, Frank R., and Beth L. Leech. 1998. *Basic Interests: The Importance of Groups in Politics and Political Science*. Princeton, N.J.: Princeton University Press.

Behn, Robert D., and James W. Vaupel. 1982. *Quick Analysis for Busy Decision Makers*. New York: Basic Books.

Beierle, Thomas C., and Jerry Cayford. 2002. *Democracy in Practice: Public Participation in Environmental Decisions*. Washington, D.C.: Resources for the Future.

Bennear, Lori S., and Cary Coglianese. 2013. "Flexible Approaches to Environmental Regulation." In *The Oxford Handbook of U.S. Environmental Policy*. Edited by Sheldon Kamieniecki and Michael E. Kraft. New York: Oxford University Press.

Berman, Evan, and XiaoHu Wang. 2017. *Essential Statistics for Public Managers and Policy Analysts*. 4th ed. Thousand Oaks, Calif.: CQ Press.

Berry, Jeffrey M. 1997. *The Interest Group Society*. 3rd ed. New York: Longman.

———. 1999. *The New Liberalism: The Rising Power of Citizen Groups*. Washington, D.C.: Brookings Institution.

Berry, Jeffrey M., Kent E. Portney, and Ken Thomson. 1993. *The Rebirth of Urban Democracy*. Washington, D.C.: Brookings Institution.

Betsill, Michele M., and Barry G. Rabe. 2009. "Climate Change and Multilevel Governance: The Evolving State and Local Roles." In *Toward Sustainable Communities: Transformations and Transition in Environmental Policy*. 2nd ed. Edited by Daniel A. Mazmanian and Michael E. Kraft. Cambridge, Mass.: MIT Press.

Billitteri, Thomas J. 1997. "Teacher Education." In *Issues for Debate in American Public Policy*. Edited by Sandra L. Stencel. Washington, D.C.: CQ Press.

Bimber, Bruce, Andrews J. Flanagin, and Cynthia Stohl. 2012. *Collective Action in Organizations: Interaction and Engagement in an Era of Technological Change*. New York: Cambridge University Press.

Birkland, Thomas A. 1997. *After Disaster: Agenda Setting, Public Policy, and Focusing Events*. Washington, D.C.: Georgetown University Press.

———. 2016. *An Introduction to the Policy Process: Theories, Concepts, and Models of Public Policy Making*. 4th ed. New York: Routledge.

Bittle, Scott, and Jean Johnson. 2011. *Where Does the Money Go? Your Guided Tour to the Federal Budget Crisis*. Rev. ed. New York: HarperCollins.

Blinder, Alan S., Alicia H. Munnell, Henry J. Aaron, and Peter R. Orszag. 2000. *Governor Bush's Individual Account Proposal: Implications for Retirement Benefits*. Available at www.brookings.edu/research/papers/2000/06/05saving-aaron.

Boardman, Anthony, David Greenberg, Aidan Vining, and David L. Weimer. 2011. *Cost-Benefit Analysis: Concepts and Practices*. 4th ed. New York: Pearson.

Bok, Derek. 2001. *The Trouble with Government*. Cambridge, Mass.: Harvard University Press.

Borins, Sandford. 1998. *Innovating with Integrity: How Local Heroes Are Transforming American Government*. Washington, D.C.: Georgetown University Press.

Bosso, Christopher J. 2005. *Environment Inc.: From Grassroots to Beltway*. Lawrence: University Press of Kansas.

Bosworth, Barry P., and Gary Burtless. 2000. "The Effects of Social Security Reform on Saving, Investment, and the Level and Distribution of Worker Well-Being." Center for Retirement Research at Boston College. Available at http://crr.bc.edu/working-papers/the-effects-of-social-security-reform-on-saving-investment-and-the-level-and-distribution-of-worker-well-being/.

Bowen, William G., and Derek C. Bok. 1998. *The Shape of the River: Long-term Consequences of Considering Race in College and University Admissions*. Princeton, N.J.: Princeton University Press.

Bowman, Ann O'M., and Richard C. Kearney. 2011. *State and Local Government*. 8th ed. Boston: Houghton Mifflin.

Bowman, James S., and Frederick A. Elliston, eds. 1988. *Ethics, Government, and Public Policy*. Westport, Conn.: Greenwood Press.

Brennan, Timothy J. 2001. *The California Electricity Experience, 2000–2001: Education or Diversion?* Washington, D.C.: Resources for the Future.

Brick, Philip D., and R. McGreggor Cawley, eds. 1996. *A Wolf in the Garden: The Land Rights Movement and the New Environmental Debate*. Lanham, Md.: Rowman and Littlefield.

Brown, Lester R. 2010. *Plan B 4.0: Mobilizing to Save Civilization*. New York: Norton.

Caldwell, Lynton Keith. 1998. *The National Environmental Policy Act: An Agenda for the Future*. Bloomington: Indiana University Press.

California State University Institute for Education Reform. 1997. *Paying for What You Need: Knowledge- and Skill-based Approaches to Teacher Compensation*.

Campbell, James E. 2016. *Polarized: Making Sense of a Divided America*. Princeton, N.J.: Princeton University Press.

Cawley, R. McGreggor. 1993. *Federal Land, Western Anger: The Sagebrush Rebellion and Environmental Politics*. Lawrence: University Press of Kansas.

Chasek, Pamela S., David L. Downie, and Janet Welsh Brown, eds. 2017. *Global Environmental Politics*. 7th ed. Boulder, Colo.: Westview Press.

Chubb, John E., and Terry M. Moe. 1990. *Politics, Markets, and America's Schools*. Washington, D.C.: Brookings Institution.

Chubb, John E., and Paul E. Peterson, eds. 1989. *Can the Government Govern?* Washington, D.C.: Brookings Institution.

Cigler, Allan J., and Burdett A. Loomis, eds. 2015. *Interest Group Politics*. 9th ed. Thousand Oaks, Calif.: CQ Press.

Clarke, Jeanne Nienaber, and Daniel McCool. 1996. *Staking Out the Terrain: Power and Performance among Natural Resource Agencies*. 2nd ed. Albany: State University of New York Press.

Clemmitt, Marcia. 2011. "School Reform." *CQ Researcher*, April 29, 392.

Clinton, Bill, and Al Gore. 1992. *Putting People First*. New York: Times Books.

Cobb, Clifford, Ted Halstead, and Jonathan Rowe. 1995. "If the GDP Is Up, Why Is America Down?" *Atlantic Monthly*, 276, no. 4 (October), 59–78.

Cobb, Roger W., and Charles D. Elder. 1983. *Participation in American Politics: The Dynamics of Agenda-Building.* 2nd ed. Baltimore: Johns Hopkins University Press.

Cochran, Clark E., Lawrence C. Mayer, T. R. Carr, and N. Joseph Cayer. 1999. *American Public Policy: An Introduction.* 6th ed. New York: Worth.

College Board. 2011. *Trends in College Pricing, 2011.* Available at http://trends.collegeboard.org/sites/default/files/College_Pricing_2011.pdf.

Concord Coalition. 2005. "Social Security Series-Reform Should Not Wait for a Crisis." Available at http://concordcoalition.org/publications/2005/0304/social-security-series-reform-should-not-wait-crisis.

Congressional Budget Office. 1996. *Federal Budget Implications of H.R. 3734, The Personal Responsibility and Work Opportunity Reconciliation Act of 1996* (August 9).

Congressional Budget Office. 2013. "Choices for Deficit Reduction: An Update." Available at www.cbo.gov/publication/44967.

Cooper, Kenneth J. 2000. "'Best and Brightest' Leave Teaching Early, Study Says." *Washington Post,* January.

Cortner, Hanna J., and Margaret A. Moote. 1999. *The Politics of Ecosystem Management.* Washington, D.C.: Island Press.

Cronin, Thomas E. 1989. *Direct Democracy: The Politics of Initiative, Referendum, and Recall.* Cambridge, Mass.: Harvard University Press.

Daily, Gretchen, ed. 1997. *Nature's Services: Societal Dependence on Natural Ecosystems.* Washington, D.C.: Island Press.

Dalton, Russell J. 2004. *Democratic Challenges, Democratic Choices: The Erosion of Public Support in Advanced Industrial Democracies.* New York: Oxford University Press.

———. 2009. *The Good Citizen: How a Younger Generation Is Reshaping American Politics.* Rev. ed. Washington, D.C.: CQ Press.

Davidson, Roger H., Walter J. Oleszek, Frances E. Lee, and Eric Schickler. 2016. *Congress and Its Members.* 15th ed. Thousand Oaks, Calif.: CQ Press.

Davies, J. Clarence, ed. 1996. *Comparing Environmental Risks: Tools for Setting Government Priorities.* Washington, D.C.: Resources for the Future.

Davies, J. Clarence, III, and Barbara S. Davies. 1975. *The Politics of Pollution.* 2nd ed. Indianapolis: Bobbs-Merrill.

Davies, J. Clarence, and Jan Mazurek. 1998. *Pollution Control in the United States: Evaluating the System.* Washington, D.C.: Resources for the Future.

Davis, Charles, ed. 2001. *Western Public Lands and Environmental Politics.* 2nd ed. Boulder, Colo.: Westview Press.

deLeon, Peter. 1997. *Democracy and the Policy Sciences.* Albany: State University of New York Press.

Delisio, Ellen R. 2003. "Pay for Performance: It Can Work—Here's How." *Education World.* Available at www.educationworld.com/a_issues/issues374c.shtml.

Derthick, Martha. 1979. *Policymaking for Social Security.* Washington, D.C.: Brookings Institution.

———. 2005. *Up in Smoke: From Legislation to Litigation in Tobacco Politics.* 2nd ed. Washington, D.C.: CQ Press.

Dietz, Thomas, and Paul C. Stern, eds. 2003. *New Tools for Environmental Protection: Education, Information, and Voluntary Measures.* Washington, D.C.: National Academy Press.

DiMento, Joseph F. C., and Pamela Doughman, eds. 2014. *Climate Change: What It Means for Us, Our Children, and Our Grandchildren.* 2nd ed. Cambridge, Mass.: MIT Press.

Dionne, E. J. 1997. "Welfare Reform: The Clues Are in Wisconsin." *Washington Post,* September.

Dodd, Lawrence C., and Bruce I. Oppenheimer, eds. 2013. *Congress Reconsidered.* 10th ed. Thousand Oaks, Calif.: CQ Press.

Donahue, John D. 1997. *Disunited States.* New York: Basic Books.

Duffy, Robert J. 1997. *Nuclear Politics in America: A History and Theory of Government Regulation.* Lawrence: University Press of Kansas.

Dunlap, Riley E. 1995. "Public Opinion and Environmental Policy." In *Environmental Politics and Policy.* Edited by James P. Lester. Durham, N.C.: Duke University Press.

Dunlap, Riley E., Michael E. Kraft, and Eugene A. Rosa, eds. 1993. *Public Reactions to Nuclear Waste: Citizens' Views of Repository Siting.* Durham, N.C.: Duke University Press.

Dunlap, Riley E., and Aaron M. McCright. 2015. "Challenging Climate Change: The Denial Countermovement." In *Climate Change and Society: Sociological Perspectives.* New York: Oxford University Press.

Dunlap, Riley E., Aaron M. McCright, and Jerrod H. Yarosh. 2016. "The Political Divide on Climate Change: Partisan Polarization Widens in the U.S." *Environment* 58, no. 5 (September/October): 4–22.

Dunn, William J. 2016. *Public Policy Analysis: An Introduction.* 5th ed. New York: Routledge.

Durant, Robert, Daniel Fiorino, and Rosemary O'Leary, eds. 2017. *Environmental Governance Reconsidered: Challenges, Choices, and Opportunities,* 2nd ed. Cambridge, Mass.: MIT Press.

Dye, Thomas R. 2001. *Top Down Policymaking*. New York: Chatham House.

Easton, David. 1965. *A Systems Analysis of Political Life*. New York: Wiley.

Eberstadt, Nicholas. 1995. *The Tyranny of Numbers: Mismeasurement and Misrule*. Washington, D.C.: AEI Press.

Edin, Katherine J., and H. Luke Shaefer. 2015. *$2.00 a Day: Living on Almost Nothing in America*. Chicago: Houghton Mifflin.

Eisner, Marc Allen. 2007. *Governing the Environment: The Transformation of Environmental Regulation*. Boulder, Colo.: Lynne Rienner.

Eisner, Marc Allen, Jeff Worsham, and Evan J. Ringquist. 2007. *Contemporary Regulatory Policy*. 2nd ed. Boulder, Colo.: Lynne Rienner.

Elazar, Daniel J. 1984. *American Federalism: A View from the States*. 3rd ed. New York: Harper and Row.

Ellis, Richard J. 2002. *Democratic Delusions: The Initiative Process in America*. Lawrence: University Press of Kansas.

Eulau, Heinz, and Kenneth Prewitt. 1973. *Labyrinths of Democracy*. Indianapolis: Bobbs-Merrill.

Fairfax, Sally K., Lauren Gwin, Mary Ann King, Leigh Raymond, and Laura A. Watt. 2005. *Buying Nature: The Limits of Land Acquisition as a Conservation Strategy, 1780–2004*. Cambridge, Mass.: MIT Press.

Fideler, Elizabeth F., Elizabeth D. Foster, and Shirley Schwartz. 2000. *The Urban Teacher Challenge: Teacher Supply and Demand in the Great City Schools*. Washington, D.C.: Recruiting New Teachers.

Figlio, David N. 1995. "The Effect of Drinking Age Laws and Alcohol-Related Crashes: Time Series Evidence from Wisconsin." *Journal of Policy Analysis and Management* 14: 555–566.

Fiorino, Daniel J. 2006. *The New Environmental Regulation*. Cambridge, Mass.: MIT Press.

Fletcher, Michael A. 2002. "A Cap and Gown Gender Gap." *Washington Post National Weekly Edition*, July, 30.

Fox, Richard L., and Jennifer M. Ramos, eds. 2011. *iPolitics: Citizens, Elections, and Governing in the New Media Age*. New York: Cambridge University Press.

Freeman, A. Myrick, III. 2000. "Economics, Incentives, and Environmental Regulation." In *Environmental Policy*. 4th ed. Edited by Norman J. Vig and Michael E. Kraft. Washington, D.C.: CQ Press.

———. 2006. "Economics, Incentives, and Environmental Policy." In *Environmental Policy*. 6th ed. Edited by Norman J. Vig and Michael F. Kraft. Washington: D.C.: CQ Press.

Freeman, J. Leiper. 1965. *The Political Process: Executive Bureau–Legislative Committee Relations*. Rev. ed. New York: Random House.

Fremstad, Shawn. 2004. "Recent Welfare Reform Research Findings." Center on Budget and Policy Priorities, January 30. Available at www.cbpp.org/1-30-04wel.pdf.

Friedman, Thomas. 2006. *The World Is Flat: A Brief History of the Twenty-first Century*. New York: Farrar, Straus and Giroux.

———. 2008. *Hot, Flat, and Crowded: Why We Need a Green Revolution and How It Can Renew America*. New York: Farrar, Straus and Giroux.

Fritschler, A. Lee, and Catherine E. Rudder. 2007. *Smoking and Politics: Bureaucracy Centered Policymaking*. 6th ed. New York: Longman.

Furman, Jason. 2005. "The Impact of the President's Proposal on Social Security Solvency and the Budget." Center for Budget and Policy Priorities, May 10. Available at www.cbpp.org/5-10-05socsec.htm#fig.

Gaddis, John Lewis. 2006. *The Cold War: A New History*. New York: Penguin.

Gainous, Jason, and Kevin M. Wagner. 2011. *Rebooting American Politics: The Internet Revolution*. New York: Rowman and Littlefield.

Gerlak, Andrea K., Tanya Heikkila, and Mark Lubell. 2013. "The Promise and Performance of Collaborative Governance." In *The Oxford Handbook of U.S. Environmental Policy*. Edited by Sheldon Kamieniecki and Michael E. Kraft. New York: Oxford University Press.

Gilens, Martin, and Benjamin I. Page. 2014. "Testing Theories of American Politics: Elites, Interest Groups, and Average Citizens." *Perspectives on Politics* 12: 564–581.

Gill, Brian, P. Mike Timpane, Karen E. Ross, Dominic J. Brewer, and Kevin Booker. 2007. *Rhetoric versus Reality: What We Know and What We Need to Know about Vouchers and Charter Schools*. Available at www.rand.org/pubs/monograph_reports/MR1118-1.html.

Goggin, Malcolm L., Ann O'M. Bowman, James P. Lester, and Laurence J. O'Toole Jr. 1990. *Implementation Theory and Practice: Toward a Third Generation*. Glenview, Ill.: Scott Foresman/Little, Brown.

Goldenberg, Jacob, David Mazursky, and Sorin Solomon. 1999. "Creative Sparks." *Science*, September 3, 1495–1496.

Gonzales, Patrick, Juan Carlos Guzman, Lisette Partelow, Erin Pahlke, Leslie Jocelyn, David Kastberg, and Trevor Williams. 2004. *Highlights from the Trends in International Mathematics and Science Study (TIMSS) 2003* (NCES 2005-005). U.S. Department of Education,

National Center for Educational Statistics. Washington, D.C.: U.S. Government Printing Office.

Gormley, William T., Jr. 1987. "Institutional Policy Analysis: A Critical Review." *Journal of Policy Analysis and Management* 6 (March): 153–169.

Graham, Mary. 2002. *Democracy by Disclosure: The Rise of Technopopulism*. Washington, D.C.: Brookings Institution.

Graham, Mary, and Catherine Miller. October 2001. "Disclosure of Toxic Releases in the United States." *Environment* 43: 6–20.

Grant, Darren, and Stephen M. Rutner. 2004. "The Effect of Bicycle Helmet Legislation on Bicycling Fatalities." *Journal of Policy Analysis and Management* 23, no. 3: 595–612.

Green, Donald P., and Ian Shapiro. 1994. *Pathologies of Rational Choice Theory: A Critique of Applications in Political Science*. New Haven, Conn.: Yale University Press.

Guber, Deborah Lynn, and Christopher Bosso. 2013a. "Past the Tipping Point? Public Discourse and the Role of the Environmental Movement in a Post-Bush Era." In *Environmental Policy*. 7th ed. Edited by Norman J. Vig and Michael E. Kraft. Thousand Oaks, Calif.: CQ Press.

_____. 2013b. "Issue Framing, Agenda Setting, and Environmental Discourse." In *The Oxford Handbook of U.S. Environmental Policy*. Edited by Sheldon Kamieniecki and Michael E. Kraft New York: Oxford University Press.

Gupta, Dipak K. 2011. *Analyzing Public Policy: Concepts, Tools, and Techniques*. 2nd ed. Washington, D.C.: CQ Press.

Hacker, Jacob S. 1997. *The Road to Nowhere: The Genesis of President Clinton's Plan for Health Security*. Princeton, N.J.: Princeton University Press.

Hacker, Jacob S., and Paul Pierson. 2016. *American Amnesia: How the War on Government Led Us to Forget What Made America Prosper*. Princeton, N.J.: Princeton University Press.

Hamilton, James T. 2005. *Regulation through Revelation: The Origin, Politics, and Impacts of the Toxics Release Inventory Program*. New York: Cambridge University Press.

Harris, Richard A., and Stanley M. Milkis. 1996. *The Politics of Regulatory Change: A Tale of Two Agencies*. 2nd ed. New York: Oxford University Press.

Heclo, Hugh. 1978. "Issue Networks and the Executive Establishment." In *The New American Political System*. Edited by Anthony King. Washington, D.C.: American Enterprise Institute.

Hedge, David M. 1998. *Governance and the Changing American States*. Boulder, Colo.: Westview Press.

Hibbing, John R., and Christopher W. Larimer. 2005. "What the American Public Wants Congress to Be." In *Congress Reconsidered*. Edited by Lawrence C. Dodd and Bruce I. Oppenheimer. Washington, D.C.: CQ Press.

Hibbing, John R., and Elizabeth Theiss-Morse. 1995. *Congress as Public Enemy: Public Attitudes toward American Political Institutions*. New York: Cambridge University Press.

_____. 2002. *Stealth Democracy: Americans' Beliefs about How Government Should Work*. New York: Cambridge University Press.

Higgs, Robert, and Carl P. Close, eds. 2005. *Re-thinking Green: Alternatives to Environmental Bureaucracy*. Oakland, Calif.: The Independent Institute.

Hill, Stuart. 1992. *Democratic Values and Technological Choices*. Stanford, Calif.: Stanford University Press.

Hird, John A. 2005. *Power, Knowledge, and Politics: Policy Analysis in the States*. Washington, D.C.: Georgetown University Press.

Hogwood, Brian W., and Lewis A. Gunn. 1984. *Policy Analysis for the Real World*. Oxford, U.K.: Oxford University Press.

Hook, Steven W., and James M. Scott, eds. 2011. *U.S. Foreign Policy Today: American Renewal?* Washington, D.C.: CQ Press.

Howell, William G., and Paul E. Peterson. 2002. *The Education Gap: Vouchers and Urban Schools*. Washington, D.C.: Brookings Institution.

Huber, Peter. 1999. *Hard Green: Saving the Environment from the Environmentalists (A Conservative Manifesto)*. New York: Basic Books.

Ingram, Helen, and Steven Rathgeb Smith, eds. 1993. *Public Policy for Democracy*. Washington, D.C.: Brookings Institution.

Intergovernmental Panel on Climate Change (IPCC). 2013. *Climate Change 2013: The Physical Science Basis. Summary for Policymakers. Working Group I Contribution to the IPCC Fifth Assessment Report*, September 27, available at www.ipcc.ch.

Jamieson, Kathleen Hall, and Joseph N. Cappella. 2008. *Echo Chamber: Rush Limbaugh and the Conservative Media Establishment*. New York: Oxford University Press.

Jaschik, Scott. 2011. "The Sinking States." *Inside Higher Ed*, January 24. Available at www.insidehighered.com/news/2011/01/24/states_make_more_cuts_in_spending_on_higher_education.

Jehl, Douglas. 2002. "Atlanta's Growing Thirst Creates Water War." *New York Times*, May 27.

Jenkins-Smith, Hank C. 1990. *Democratic Politics and Policy Analysis*. Pacific Grove, Calif.: Brooks/Cole.

Jerald, Craig D. 2002. *All Talk, No Action: Putting an End to Out-of-Field Teaching*. Washington, D.C.: The Education Trust.

Jones, Charles O. 1975. *Clean Air: The Policies and Politics of Pollution Control*. Pittsburgh, Penn.: University of Pittsburgh Press.

_____. 1984. *An Introduction to the Study of Public Policy*. 3rd ed. Monterey, Calif.: Brooks/Cole.

_____. 1999. *Separate but Equal Branches: Congress and the Presidency*. 2nd ed. New York: Chatham House.

Jost, Kenneth. 2001. "Affirmative Action in Undergraduate Admissions." *CQ Researcher*, September 21, 737–760.

Kamarck, Elaine Ciulla, and Joseph S. Nye Jr., eds. 2002. *Governance.com: Democracy in the Information Age*. Washington, D.C.: Brookings Institution.

Kamieniecki, Sheldon, and Michael E. Kraft, eds. 2013. *The Oxford Handbook of U.S. Environmental Policy*. New York: Oxford University Press.

Karapin, Roger. 2016. *Political Opportunities for Climate Policy: California, New York, and the Federal Government*. New York: Cambridge University Press.

Kavanagh, Jennifer. 2011. "The Dynamics of Protracted Terror Campaigns: Domestic Politics, Terrorist Violence, and Counterterror Responses." Ph.D. diss., University of Michigan.

Kelman, Steven. 1980. "Occupational Safety and Health Administration." In *The Politics of Regulation*. Edited by James Q. Wilson. New York: Basic Books.

Kerwin, Cornelius M., and Scott R. Furlong. 2011. *Rulemaking: How Government Agencies Write Law and Make Policy*. 4th ed. Washington, D.C.: CQ Press.

Kingdon, John W. 1995. *Agendas, Alternatives, and Public Policies*. 2nd ed. New York: HarperCollins College.

Klyza, Christopher McGrory, and David Sousa. 2013. *American Environmental Policy: Beyond Gridlock*. Updated and expanded ed. Cambridge, Mass.: MIT Press.

Koch, Kathy. 2000. "Hunger in America." *CQ Researcher*, December 22, 1033–1056.

Kraft, Michael E. 1981. "Congress and National Energy Policy: Assessing the Policy Process." In *Environment, Energy, Public Policy: Toward a Rational Future*. Edited by Regina S. Axelrod. Lexington, Mass.: Lexington Books.

_____. 1992. "Technology, Analysis, and Policy Leadership: Congress and Radioactive Waste." In *Science,*

Technology, and Politics. Edited by Gary C. Bryner. Boulder, Colo.: Westview Press.

_____. 1994. "Population Policy." In *Encyclopedia of Policy Studies*. 2nd ed. Edited by Stuart S. Nagel. New York: Marcel Dekker.

_____. 2000. "Policy Design and the Acceptability of Environmental Risks: Nuclear Waste Disposal in Canada and the United States." *Policy Studies Journal* 28, no. 1: 206–218.

_____. 2013. "Nuclear Power and the Challenge of High-level Waste Disposal in the United States." *Polity* 45, no. 2: 265–280.

_____. 2016. "Environmental Policy in Congress." In *Environmental Policy*. 9th ed. Edited by Norman J. Vig and Michael E. Kraft. Thousand Oaks, Calif.: CQ Press.

_____. 2017. "Environmental Risk: New Approaches Needed to Address Twenty-first-Century Challenges." In *Conceptual Innovation in Environmental Policy*. Edited by James M. Meadowcroft and Daniel J. Fiorino. Cambridge, Mass.: MIT Press.

_____. 2018. *Environmental Policy and Politics*. 7th ed. New York: Routledge.

Kraft, Michael E., and Sheldon Kamieniecki, eds. 2007. *Business and Environmental Policy: Corporate Interests in the American Political System*. Cambridge, Mass.: MIT Press.

Kraft, Michael E., Mark Stephan, and Troy D. Abel. 2011. *Coming Clean: Information Disclosure and Environmental Performance*. Cambridge, Mass.: MIT Press.

Kriz, Margaret. 2001. "Hot Rod Targets." *National Journal*, December 15, 3838–3840.

Lasswell, Harold D. 1958. *Politics: Who Gets What, When, How*. New York: Meridian Books. Originally published in 1936 by McGraw-Hill.

Layzer, Judith A. 2008. *Natural Experiments: Ecosystem-based Management and the Environment*. Cambridge, Mass.: MIT Press.

Layzer, Judith A. 2013. "Ecosystem-Based Management and Restoration." In *The Oxford Handbook of U.S. Environmental Policy*. Edited by Sheldon Kamieniecki and Michael E. Kraft. New York: Oxford University Press.

Levi, Margaret, James Johnson, Jack Knight, and Susan Stokes, eds. 2008. *Designing Democratic Government: Making Institutions Work*. New York: Russell Sage Foundation.

Levine, Bertram J. 2009. *The Art of Lobbying: Building Trust and Selling Policy*. Washington, D.C.: CQ Press.

Lewis, Kristen, and Sarah Burd-Sharps. 2010. *The Measure of America 2010–2011: Mapping Risks and Resilience*. New York: NYU Press.

Lieske, Joel. 1993. "Regional Subcultures of the United States." *Journal of Politics* 55, no. 4: 888–913.

Light, Paul. 1995. *Still Artful Work*. 2nd ed. New York: McGraw-Hill.

Lindblom, Charles E. 1972. "Integration of Economics and the Other Social Sciences through Policy Analysis." In *Integration of the Social Sciences through Policy Analysis*. Edited by James C. Charlesworth. Philadelphia: American Academy of Political and Social Science.

Lindblom, Charles E., and David K. Cohen. 1979. *Usable Knowledge: Social Science and Social Problem Solving*. New Haven, Conn.: Yale University Press.

Lindblom, Charles E., and Edward J. Woodhouse. 1993. *The Policy-Making Process*. 3rd ed. Upper Saddle River, N.J.: Prentice Hall.

Looney, Adam, and Constantine Yannelis. 2015. "A Crisis in Student Loans? How Changes in the Characteristics of Borrowers and in the Institutions They Attended Contributed to Rising Loan Defaults." *Brookings Papers on Economic Activity*, September 10–11. Available at www.brooking s.edu/wp-content/uploads/2016/07/ConferenceDraft_ LooneyYannelis_StudentLoanDefaults.pdf.

Loprest, Pamela. 1999. "Long Ride from Welfare to Work." *Washington Post,* August 30.

Lowi, Theodore J. 1964. "American Business, Public Policy, Case Studies, and Political Theory." *World Politics* 16 (July): 667–715.

———. 1979. *The End of Liberalism*. 2nd ed. New York: Norton.

Lowry, William R. 2006. "A Return to Traditional Priorities in Natural Resource Policies." In *Environmental Policy*. 6th ed. Edited by Norman J. Vig and Michael E. Kraft. Washington, D.C.: CQ Press.

Lubchenco, Jane. 1998. "Entering the Century of the Environment: A New Social Contract for Science." *Science*, January 23, 491–497.

Lubell, Mark, and Brian Segee. 2013. "Conflict and Cooperation in Natural Resource Management." In *Environmental Policy*. 8th ed. Edited by Norman J. Vig and Michael E. Kraft. Thousand Oaks, Calif.: CQ Press.

Mackenzie, G. Calvin, and Judith M. Labiner. 2002. "Opportunity Lost: The Rise and Fall of Trust and Confidence in Government after September 11." Washington, D.C.: Brookings Institution, Center for Public Service. Available at www.brook.edu.

MacRae, Duncan, Jr., and Dale Whittington. 1997. *Expert Advice for Policy Choice: Analysis and Discourse*. Washington, D.C.: Georgetown University Press.

MacRae, Duncan, Jr., and James A. Wilde. 1979. *Policy Analysis for Public Decisions*. North Scituate, Mass.: Duxbury.

Mann, Thomas E., and Norman J. Ornstein. 2012. *It's Even Worse Than It Looks: How the American Constitutional System Collided with the New Politics of Extremism*. New York: Basic Books.

Manza, Jeff, Fay Lomax Cook, and Benjamin I. Page, eds. 2002. *Navigating Public Opinion: Polls, Policy, and the Future of American Democracy*. New York: Oxford University Press.

Marmor, Theodore R. 2000. *The Politics of Medicare*. 2nd ed. Hawthorne, N.Y.: Aldine de Gruyter.

Marmor, Theodore R., Jerry Mashaw, and John Pakutka. 2013. *Social Insurance: America's Neglected Heritage and Contested Future*. Thousand Oaks, Calif.: CQ Press.

May, Peter J., Ashley E. Jochim, and Joshua Sapotichne. 2011. "Constructing Homeland Security: An Anemic Policy Regime." *Policy Studies Journal* 39, no. 2: 285–307.

Mayer, Jane. 2016. *Dark Money: The Hidden History of the Billionaires behind the Rise of the Radical Right*. New York: Doubleday.

Mayhew, David R. 1974. *Congress: The Electoral Connection*. New Haven, Conn.: Yale University Press.

———. 1991. *Divided We Govern: Party Control, Lawmaking, and Investigations 1946–1990*. New Haven, Conn.: Yale University Press.

Mayo, Bernard, ed. 1942. *Jefferson Himself: The Personal Narrative of a Many-Sided American*. Charlottesville: University Press of Virginia.

Mazmanian, Daniel A., and Michael E. Kraft, eds. 2009. *Toward Sustainable Communities: Transition and Transformations in Environmental Policy*. 2nd ed. Cambridge, Mass.: MIT Press.

Mazmanian, Daniel A., and Paul A. Sabatier. 1983. *Implementation and Public Policy*. Glenview, Ill.: Scott Foresman.

McConnell, Grant. 1966. *Private Power and American Democracy*. New York: Random House.

McCool, Daniel C. 1990. "Subgovernments as Determinants of Political Viability." *Political Science Quarterly* 105: 269–293.

———, ed. 1995. *Public Policy Theories, Models, and Concepts: An Anthology*. Englewood Cliffs, N.J.: Prentice Hall.

McCormick, John. 1989. *Reclaiming Paradise: The Global Environmental Movement*. Bloomington: Indiana University Press.

McGann, James, and Richard Sabatini. 2011. *Global Think Tanks: Policy Networks and Governance*. Clifton, N.J.: Routledge.

McKenna, Elizabeth, and Hahrie Han. 2014. *Groundbreakers: How Obama's 2.2 Million Volunteers Transformed Campaigning in America*. New York: Oxford University Press.

McQueen, Anjetta. 2001. "Welfare Law's Big Question: Has Success Been Real?" *CQ Weekly*, March 30, 869–870.

Mead, Lawrence M. 1986. *Beyond Entitlement: The Social Obligations of Citizenship*. New York: Free Press.

———. 2007. "Why Welfare Reform Succeeded." *The Journal of Policy Analysis and Management* 26, no. 2: 370–374.

Meier, Kenneth J. 1993. *Politics and the Bureaucracy: Policymaking in the Fourth Branch of Government*. Pacific Grove, Calif.: Brooks/Cole.

Metcalf, Kim K. 1999. "Evaluation of the Cleveland Scholarship Program, 1996–1999." Bloomington: Indiana University, Indiana Center for Evaluation.

Metcalf, Kim, William J. Boone, Frances K. Stage, Todd L. Chilton, Patty Muller, and Polly Tai. 1998. *A Comparative Evaluation of the Cleveland Scholarship and Tutoring Program and Evaluation of the Cleveland Scholarship Program, Second Year Report, 1997–98*. Bloomington: Indiana University, Indiana Center for Evaluation.

Mettler, Suzanne. 2014. *Degrees of Inequality: How the Politics of Higher Education Sabotaged the American Dream*. New York: Basic Books.

Millikan, Max F. 1959. "Inquiry and Policy: The Relation of Knowledge to Action." In *The Human Meaning of the Social Sciences*. Edited by Daniel Lerner. New York: Meridian Books.

Miringoff, Marc, and Marque-Luisa Miringoff. 1999. *The Social Health of the Nation: How America Is Really Doing*. New York: Oxford University Press.

Mitchell, Alison. 2002. "Law's Sponsors Fault Draft of Campaign Finance Rules." *New York Times*, May A16.

Mortenson, Thomas G. 2011a. "State Fiscal Support for Higher Education FY1961–FY2011." *Postsecondary Education Opportunity*, February.

———. 2011b. "How to Limit Opportunity for Higher Education FY1980–FY2011." *Postsecondary Education Opportunity*, August.

Murray, Kasia O'Neill, and Wendell E. Primus. 2005. "Recent Data Trends Show Welfare Reform to Be a Mixed Success: Significant Policy Changes Should Accompany Reauthorization." *Review of Policy Research* 22: 301–324.

Murray, Mark. 2002. "Road Test." *National Journal*, May 25, 1548–1553.

National Academy of Medicine. 2002. *Care without Coverage: Too Little, Too Late*. Washington, D.C.: National Academy Press.

National Academy of Public Administration. 1995. *Setting Priorities, Getting Results: A New Direction for the Environmental Protection Agency*. Washington, D.C.: National Academy of Public Administration.

———. 2000. *Environment.gov: Transforming Environmental Protection for the 21st Century*. Washington, D.C.: National Academy of Public Administration.

National Center for Public Policy and Higher Education. 2008. *Measuring Up 2008: The National Report Card on Higher Education*. Available at http://measuringup2008.highereducation.org/print/NCPPHEMUNationalRpt.pdf.

National Commission on Retirement Policy. 1999. *The 21st Century Retirement Security Plan: Final Report of the National Commission on Retirement Policy*. Washington, D.C.: Center for Strategic and International Studies, CSIS Press.

National Conference of State Legislatures. 2005. *Task Force on No Child Left Behind Final Report*, February.

National Education Association. 2014. "Rankings of the States 2013 and Estimates of School Statistics 2014." Available at www.nea.org/home/rankings-and-estimates-2013–2014.html.

Nestle, Marion. 2002. *Food Politics: How the Food Industry Influences Nutrition and Health*. Berkeley: University of California Press.

———. 2015. *Soda Politics: Taking on Big Soda (and Winning)*. New York: Oxford University Press.

Nozick, Robert. 1974. *Anarchy, State, and Utopia*. New York: Basic Books.

Nye, Joseph S., Philip D. Zelikow, and David C. King, eds. 1997. *Why People Don't Trust Government*. Cambridge, Mass.: Harvard University Press.

O'Connor, Karen, and Larry J. Sabato. 2006. *American Government: Continuity and Change*. Boston: Allyn and Bacon.

Office of Personnel Management. 2004. *Federal Civilian Workforce Statistics: The Fact Book, 2004 Edition*. Available at www.opm.gov/feddata/factbook/2004/factbook.pdf.

O'Leary, Rosemary. 2016. "Environmental Policy in the Courts." In *Environmental Policy*. 9th ed. Edited by Norman J. Vig and Michael E. Kraft. Thousand Oaks, Calif.: CQ Press.

Olson, Mancur. 1971. *The Logic of Collective Action*. Cambridge, Mass.: Harvard University Press.

Ophuls, William, and A. Stephen Boyan Jr. 1992. *Ecology and the Politics of Scarcity Revisited: The Unraveling of the American Dream*. New York: Freeman.

Ostrom, Elinor. 1998. "A Behavioral Approach to the Rational Choice Theory of Collective Action." *American Political Science Review* 92, no. 1: 1–22.

_____. 2007. "Institutional Rational Choice: An Assessment of the Institutional Analysis and Development Framework." In *Theories of the Policy Process*. 2nd ed. Edited by Paul A. Sabatier. Boulder, Colo.: Westview Press.

Paehlke, Robert. 2013. "Sustainable Development and Urban Life in America." In *Environmental Policy*. 8th ed. Edited by Norman J. Vig and Michael E. Kraft. Thousand Oaks, Calif.: CQ Press.

Page, Benjamin I. 1992. *The Rational Public: Fifty Years of Trends in Americans' Policy Preferences*. Chicago: University of Chicago Press.

Parry, Ian W. H. 2002. "Is Gasoline Undertaxed in the United States?" *Resources* 148 (Summer): 28–33.

_____. 2005. "Should Fuel Economy Standards Be Raised?" *Resources* 159 (November): 15–19.

Patashnik, Eric M. 2008. *Reforms at Risk: What Happens after Major Policy Changes Are Enacted*. Princeton, N.J.: Princeton University Press.

Patel, Kant, and Mark E. Rushefsky. 2015. *Health Care Politics and Policy in America*. 4th ed. New York: Rutledge.

Patton, Carl V., and David S. Sawicki. 1993. *Basic Methods of Policy Analysis and Planning*. 2nd ed. Englewood Cliffs, N.J.: Prentice Hall.

Patton, Carl V., David S. Sawicki, and Jennifer J. Clark. 2016. *Basic Methods of Policy Analysis and Planning*. 3rd ed. New York: Routledge.

Pear, Robert. 2000. "A Million Parents Lost Medicaid, Study Says." *New York Times*, June 20.

_____. 2004. "Despite Sluggish Economy, Welfare Rolls Actually Fell." *New York Times*, March 22.

Perrow, Charles. 2007. *The Next Catastrophe: Reducing Our Vulnerabilities to Natural, Industrial, and Terrorist Disasters*. Princeton, N.J.: Princeton University Press.

Persily, Nathaniel, ed. 2015. *Solutions to Political Polarization in America*. New York: Cambridge University Press.

Peters, B. Guy. 2000. *American Public Policy: Promise and Performance*. 5th ed. New York: Chatham House.

_____. 2009. *American Public Policy: Promise and Performance*. 8th ed. Washington, D.C.: CQ Press.

Peterson, Paul E., William G. Howell, and Jay P. Green. 1999. "An Evaluation of the Cleveland Voucher Program after Two Years." Cambridge, Mass.: Harvard University, Program on Education Policy and Governance.

Peterson, Paul E., and Mark Rom. 1988. "Lower Taxes, More Spending, and Budget Deficits." In *The Reagan Legacy: Promise and Performance*. Edited by Charles O. Jones. Chatham, N.J.: Chatham House.

Portney, Kent E. 2013. *Taking Sustainable Cities Seriously: Economic Development, the Environment, and Quality of Life in American Cities*. 2nd ed. Cambridge, Mass.: MIT Press.

_____. 2016. "Taking Sustainable Cities Seriously: What Cities Are Doing." In *Environmental Policy*. 9th ed. Edited by Norman J. Vig and Michael E. Kraft. Thousand Oaks, Calif.: CQ Press.

Portney, Paul R., and Robert N. Stavins, eds. 2000. *Public Policies for Environmental Protection*. Washington, D.C.: Resources for the Future.

Presidential/Congressional Commission on Risk Assessment and Risk Management. 1997. *Risk Assessment and Risk Management in Regulatory Decision Making, Vol. 2: Final Report*. Available at www.riskworld.com.

President's Council on Sustainable Development. 1996. *Sustainable America: A New Consensus for Prosperity, Opportunity, and a Healthy Environment for the Future*. Washington, D.C.: Government Printing Office.

Price, Tom. 2016. "Student Debt." *CQ Researcher*, November 18.

Putnam, Robert D. 1995. "Tuning In, Tuning Out: The Strange Disappearance of Social Capital in America." *PS: Political Science and Politics* 28 (December): 664–683.

_____. 2000. *Bowling Alone: The Collapse and Revival of American Community*. New York: Simon and Schuster.

Quindlen, Anna. 2005. "Testing: One, Two, Three." *Newsweek*, June 12, 88.

Rabe, Barry G. 2004. *Statehouse and Greenhouse: The Emerging Politics of American Climate Change Policy*. Washington, D.C.: Brookings Institution.

_____. 2010. *Greenhouse Governance: Addressing Climate Change in America*. Washington, D.C.: Brookings Institution.

_____. 2016. "Racing to the Top, the Bottom, or the Middle of the Pack? The Evolving State Government Role in Environmental Protection." In *Environmental Policy*. 9th ed. Edited by Norman J. Vig and Michael E. Kraft. Thousand Oaks, Calif.: CQ Press.

_____. Forthcoming. *The Politics of Carbon Pricing*. Cambridge, Mass.: MIT Press.

Rabe, Barry G., and Philip A. Mundo. 2007. "Business Influence in State-Level Environmental Policy." In *Business and Environmental Policy*. Edited by Michael E. Kraft and Sheldon Kamieniecki. Cambridge, Mass.: MIT Press.

Radin, Beryl A. 2006. *Challenging the Performance Movement: Accountability, Complexity, and Democratic Values.* Washington, D.C.: Georgetown University Press.

Rawls, John. 1971. *A Theory of Justice.* Cambridge, Mass.: Harvard University Press.

Raymond, Leigh. 2016. *Reclaiming the Atmospheric Commons: The Regional Greenhouse Gas Initiative and a New Model of Emissions Trading.* Cambridge, Mass.: MIT Press.

Rein, Martin. 1976. *Social Science and Public Policy.* New York: Penguin Books.

Ricci, David M. 1993. *The Transformation of American Politics: The New Washington and the Rise of Think Tanks.* New Haven, Conn.: Yale University Press.

Rich, Andrew. 2004. *Think Tanks, Public Policy, and the Politics of Expertise.* New York: Cambridge University Press.

Rinfret, Sara R., and Scott R. Furlong. 2013. "Defining Environmental Rule Making." In *The Oxford Handbook of U.S. Environmental Policy.* Edited by Sheldon Kamieniecki and Michael E. Kraft. New York: Oxford University Press.

Ripley, Randall B., and Grace A. Franklin. 1986. *Policy Implementation and Bureaucracy.* 2nd ed. Chicago: Dorsey Press.

———. 1991. *Congress, the Bureaucracy, and Public Policy.* 5th ed. Pacific Grove, Calif.: Brooks/Cole.

Rochefort, David A., and Roger W. Cobb, eds. 1994. *The Politics of Problem Definition: Shaping the Policy Agenda.* Lawrence: University Press of Kansas.

Rodgers, Harrell. 2005. "Evaluating the Devolution Revolution." *Review of Policy Research* 22: 275–299.

Rosenbaum, Walter A. 2013. "Science, Politics, and Policy at the EPA." In *Environmental Policy.* 8th ed. Edited by Norman J. Vig and Michael E. Kraft. Thousand Oaks, Calif.: CQ Press.

———. 2015. *American Energy: The Politics of 21st Century Policy.* Thousand Oaks, Calif.: CQ Press.

Rossi, Peter H., Mark W. Lipsey, and Howard E. Freeman. 2004. *Evaluation: A Systematic Approach.* 7th ed. Thousand Oaks, Calif.: Sage.

Rouse, Cecilia E. 1997. *Private School Vouchers and Student Achievement: An Evaluation of the Milwaukee Parental Choice Program.* Princeton, N.J.: Princeton University Press.

———. 1998. "Private School Vouchers and Student Achievement: An Evaluation of the Milwaukee Parental Choice Program." *Quarterly Journal of Economics* 113 (May): 553–602.

Rouse, Cecilia E., and Lisa Barrow. 2009. "School Vouchers and Student Achievement: Recent Evidence, Remaining Questions." *Annual Review of Economics* 1: 17–42.

Rushefsky, Mark E., and Kant Patel. 1998. *Politics, Power, and Policy Making: The Case of Health Care Reform in the 1990s.* Armonk, N.Y.: M. E. Sharpe.

Russell, Milton. 1993. "NAPAP: A Lesson in Science, Policy." *Forum for Applied Research and Public Policy* 8: 55–60.

Sabatier, Paul A., Will Focht, Mark Lubell, Zev Trachtenberg, Arnold Vedlitz, and Marty Matlock, eds. 2005. *Swimming Upstream: Collaborative Approaches to Watershed Management.* Cambridge, Mass.: MIT Press.

Sabatier, Paul A., and Hank C. Jenkins-Smith, eds. 1993. *Policy Change and Learning: An Advocacy Coalition Approach.* Boulder, Colo.: Westview Press.

Sabatier, Paul A., and Christopher M. Weible, eds. 2014. *Theories of the Policy Process.* 3rd ed. Boulder, Colo.: Westview Press.

Sachs, Jeffrey D. 2005. *The End of Poverty: Economic Possibilities for Our Time.* New York: Penguin.

———. 2015. *The Age of Sustainable Development.* New York: Oxford University Press.

Sanger, David E. 2002. "Bush Was Warned Bin Laden Wanted to Hijack Planes." *New York Times,* May 16.

Savas, E. S. 2000. *Privatization and Public-Private Partnerships.* New York: Chatham House.

Schattschneider, E. E. 1960. *The Semisovereign People: A Realist's View of Democracy in America.* New York: Holt, Rinehart, and Winston Press.

Scheberle, Denise. 2004. *Federalism and Environmental Policy: Trust and the Politics of Implementation.* 2nd ed. Washington, D.C.: Georgetown University Press.

Schneider, Anne L., and Helen Ingram. 1997. *Policy Design for Democracy.* Lawrence: University Press of Kansas.

Schubert, Lewis, Thomas R. Dye, and L. Harmon Zeigler. 2014. *The Irony of Democracy: An Uncommon Introduction to American Politics.* 16th ed. Boston: Wadsworth.

Selin, Henrik, and Stacy D. VanDeveer. 2016. "Global Climate Change: Beyond Kyoto." In *Environmental Policy.* 9th ed. Edited by Norman J. Vig and Michael E. Kraft. Thousand Oaks, Calif.: CQ Press.

Shepsle, Kenneth A., and Mark S. Bonchek. 1997. *Analyzing Politics: Rationality, Behavior, and Institutions.* New York: Norton.

Shipan, Charles R., and William R. Lowry. 2001. "Environmental Policy and Party Divergence in Congress." *Political Research Quarterly* 54 (June): 245–263.

Shokraii Rees, Nina. 2000. "School Choice 2000: Annual Report." *Heritage Foundation Backgrounder*, March 30, 1354. Available at http://www.heritage.org/research/reports/2000/03/school-choice-2000-annual-report.

Shrader-Frechette, K. S. 1993. *Burying Uncertainty: Risk and the Case against Geological Disposal of Nuclear Waste.* Berkeley: University of California Press.

Sinclair, Barbara. 2012. *Unorthodox Lawmaking: New Legislative Processes in the U.S. Congress.* 4th ed. Thousand Oaks, Calif.: CQ Press.

Skocpol, Theda. 1995. *Social Policy in the United States: Future Possibilities in Historical Perspective.* Princeton, N.J.: Princeton University Press.

————. 2003. *Diminished Democracy: From Membership to Management in American Civic Life.* Norman: University of Oklahoma Press.

Skocpol, Theda, and Morris P. Fiorina, eds. 1999. *Civic Engagement in American Democracy.* Washington, D.C.: Brookings Institution.

Skocpol, Theda, and Vanessa Williamson. 2012. *The Tea Party and the Remaking of Republican Conservatism.* New York: Oxford University Press.

Skrzycki, Cindy. 2003. *The Regulators: Anonymous Power Brokers in American Politics.* Lanham, Md.: Rowman and Littlefield.

Slovic, Paul. 1987. "Perception of Risk." *Science* 236: 280–285.

Spinner, Jackie. 2002. "Don't Mess with Accountants." *Washington Post National Weekly Edition*, May, 20.

Starling, Grover. 1988. *Strategies for Policy Making.* Chicago: Dorsey Press.

State Higher Education Executive Officers (SHEEO). 2010. *State Higher Education Finance FY 2010.* Available at www.sheeo.org/finance/shef_fy10.pdf.

Steinberg, Paul F., and Stacy D. VanDeveer, eds. 2012. *Comparative Environmental Politics: Theory, Practice, and Prospects.* Cambridge, Mass.: MIT Press.

Stone, Deborah. 2012. *Policy Paradox: The Art of Political Decision Making.* 3rd ed. New York: Norton.

Switzer, Jacqueline Vaughn. 1997. *Green Backlash: The History and Politics of Environmental Opposition in the U.S.* Boulder, Colo.: Lynne Rienner.

Tauras, John A. 2005. "Can Public Policy Deter Smoking Escalation among Young Adults?" *Journal of Policy Analysis and Management* 24, no. 4: 771–784.

Teske, Paul. 2004. *Regulation in the States.* Washington, D.C.: Brookings Institution.

Texas Comptroller of Public Accounts. 2005. "The Impact of the State Higher Education System on the Texas Economy." Available at www.laits.utexas.edu/txp_media/html/pec/0503.html.

Thomas, Craig W. 2013. "Bureaucracy and Natural Resources Policy." In *The Oxford Handbook of U.S. Environmental Policy.* Edited by Sheldon Kamieniecki and Michael E. Kraft. New York: Oxford University Press.

Thomas, Norman C. 1975. *Educational Policy in National Politics.* New York: David McKay.

Thurber, James A. 1991. *Divided Democracy: Cooperation and Conflict between the President and Congress.* Washington, D.C.: CQ Press.

————, ed. 1996a. *Rivals for Power: Presidential-Congressional Relations.* Washington, D.C.: CQ Press.

————. 1996b. "Congressional-Presidential Battles to Balance the Budget." In *Rivals for Power: Presidential-Congressional Relations.* Edited by James A. Thurber. Washington, D.C.: CQ Press.

Thurber, James A., and Antoine Yoshinaka, eds. 2015. *American Gridlock: The Sources, Character, and Impact of Political Polarization.* New York: Cambridge University Press.

Tong, Rosemarie. 1986. *Ethics in Policy Analysis.* Englewood Cliffs, N.J.: Prentice Hall.

Toor, Will, and Spenser W. Havlick. 2004. *Transportation and Sustainable Campus Communities: Issues, Examples, Solutions.* Washington, D.C.: Island Press.

United Nations. 1993. *Agenda 21: The United Nations Programme of Action from Rio.* New York: United Nations.

U.S. Department of Agriculture. 2005. "National School Lunch Program." Available at www.fns.usda.gov/cnd/Lunch/AboutLunch/NSLPFactSheet.pdf.

U.S. Department of Education. 1999. "Annual Earnings of Young Adults, by Educational Attainment." Washington, D.C.: National Center for Education Statistics. Available at https://nces.ed.gov/pubs99/1999009.pdf.

————. 2001. "Digest of Education Statistics, 2001." Washington, D.C. Available at https://nces.ed.gov/PUBSEARCH/pubsinfo.asp?pubid=2002130.

————. 2005. "10 Facts about K–12 Education Funding." Washington, D.C. Available at www.ed.gov/about/overview/fed/10facts/index.html.

————. 2010. National Center for Education Statistics. *Civics 2010*, NCES-2011-466. Available at http://nces.ed.gov/nationsreportcard/pdf/main2010/2011466.pdf.

U.S. Department of Labor, Bureau of Labor Statistics. 2004. "Highlights of Women's Earnings in 2003." Available at www.bls.gov/opub/reports/womens-earnings/archive/womensearnings_2003.pdf.

U.S. Environmental Protection Agency. 1990. *Reducing Risk: Setting Priorities and Strategies for Environmental Protection*. Washington, D.C.: EPA, Science Advisory Board.

U.S. Government Accountability Office (formerly the General Accounting Office). 1998. *Welfare Reform: States Are Restructuring Programs to Reduce Welfare Dependence*. Washington, D.C.: U.S. Government Printing Office (June 17).

———. 1999. *Welfare Reform: Information on Former Recipients' Status*. Washington, D.C.: U.S. Government Printing Office (April 28).

———. 2004. *Informing Our Nation: Improving How to Understand and Assess the U.S.A.'s Position and Progress*. Washington, D.C.: U.S. Government Printing Office (November 10).

Van Natta, Don, Jr., and David Johnston. 2002. "Wary of Risk, Slow to Adapt, F.B.I. Stumbles in Terror War." *New York Times*, June 2, 24–25.

Vaughan, Shannon K., and Shelly Arsneault. 2013. *Managing Nonprofit Organizations in a Policy World*. Thousand Oaks, Calif.: CQ Press.

Vig, Norman J. 2016. "Presidential Powers and Environmental Policy." In *Environmental Policy*. 9th ed. Edited by Norman J. Vig and Michael E. Kraft. Thousand Oaks, Calif.: CQ Press.

Vig, Norman J., and Michael Faure, eds. 2004. *Green Giants? Environmental Policies of the United States and the European Union*. Cambridge, Mass.: MIT Press.

Vig, Norman J., and Michael E. Kraft, eds. 1984. *Environmental Policy in the 1980s: Reagan's New Agenda*. Washington, D.C.: CQ Press.

———. 2016. *Environmental Policy: New Directions for the Twenty-first Century*. 9th ed. Thousand Oaks, Calif.: CQ Press.

———. 2019. *Environmental Policy: New Directions for the Twenty-first Century*. 10th ed. Thousand Oaks, Calif.: CQ Press.

Wald, Matthew L. 2002. "Bury the Nation's Nuclear Waste in Nevada, Bush Says." *New York Times*, February 16.

Walker, Jack L. 1977. "Setting the Agenda in the U.S. Senate: A Theory of Problem Selection." *British Journal of Political Science* 7: 423–445.

Weaver, R. Kent. 2000. *Ending Welfare as We Know It*. Washington, D.C.: Brookings Institution.

Weber, Edward P. 2003. *Bringing Society Back In: Grassroots Ecosystem Management, Accountability, and Sustainable Communities*. Cambridge, Mass.: MIT Press.

Weimer, David L., and Aidan R. Vining. 2016. *Policy Analysis: Concepts and Practice*. 6th ed. New York: Routledge.

Weiss, Carol H. 1978. "Improving the Linkage between Social Research and Public Policy." In *Knowledge and Policy: The Uncertain Connection*. Edited by Laurence E. Lynn Jr. Washington, D.C.: National Academy of Sciences.

———, ed. 1992. *Organizations for Policy Analysis: Helping Government Think*. Newbury Park, Calif.: Sage.

———. 1997. *Evaluation: Methods for Studying Programs and Policies*. 2nd ed.: Upper Saddle River, NJ: Prentice Hall.

Weiss, Edith Brown. 1990. "In Fairness to Future Generations." *Environment* 32, no. 3: 7–11, 30–31.

West, Darrell M. 2005. *Digital Government: Technology and Public Sector Performance*. Princeton, N.J.: Princeton University Press.

Whiteman, David. 1995. *Communication in Congress: Members, Staff, and the Search for Information*. Lawrence: University Press of Kansas.

Wildavsky, Aaron. 1979. *Speaking Truth to Power: The Art and Craft of Policy Analysis*. Boston: Little, Brown.

———. 1988. *Searching for Safety*. New Brunswick, N.J.: Transaction Books.

Williams, Juan. 1987. *Eyes on the Prize: America's Civil Rights Years 1954–1965*. New York: Penguin Books.

Williamson, Vanessa, Theda Skocpol, and John Coggin. 2011. "The Tea Party and the Remaking of Republican Conservatism." *Perspectives on Politics* 9, no. 1: 25–43.

Wilson, Edward O. 1998. *Consilience: The Unity of Knowledge*. New York: Knopf.

Wilson, James Q. 1977. *Thinking about Crime*. New York: Vintage Books.

———, ed. 1980. *The Politics of Regulation*. New York: Basic Books.

Winerip, Michael. 2003. "Superior School Fails a Crucial Federal Test." *New York Times*, November 19.

Winter, Greg. 2005. "Study Finds Shortcoming in New Law on Education." *New York Times*, April 13.

Witte, John F. 1997. *Achievement Effects of the Milwaukee Voucher Program*. University of Wisconsin–Madison.

———. 2000. *The Market Approach to Education*. Princeton, N.J.: Princeton University Press.

Witte, John, Troy D. Sterr, and Christopher A. Thorn. 1995. *Fifth Year Report: Milwaukee Parental Choice Program*. University of Wisconsin–Madison.

Wolfensberger, Donald R. 2005. "Congress and Policymaking in an Age of Terrorism." *Congress Reconsidered*. 8th ed. Edited by Lawrence C. Dodd and Bruce I. Oppenheimer. Washington, D.C.: CQ Press.

Wolpe, Bruce E., and Bertram J. Levine. 1996. *Lobbying Congress: How the System Works*. Washington, D.C.: CQ Press.

Wondolleck, Julia M., and Steven L. Yaffee. 2000. *Making Collaboration Work: Lessons from Innovation in Natural Resource Management*. Washington, D.C.: Island Press.

World Commission on Environment and Development. 1987. *Our Common Future*. New York: Oxford University Press.

Worldwatch Institute. 2012. *State of the World 2012: New Approaches to Sustainable Prosperity*. Washington, D.C.: Island Press.

Index